Things Need to do: ① Lab s... in Lab
② Lab Exercise
③ Research Assignment only 1 per wk.



# Information Security Perspective on Intranets, Internets, and E-Commerce

Project 1 wk5
Project 2 wk7
→ 5-8 pages

Taken From:

*Protect Your Windows Network: From Perimeter to Data*
by Jesper M. Johansson and Steve Riley

*Apache Administrator's Handbook*
by Rich Bowen, Allan Liska, Daniel Lopez Ridreujo

*Windows Server 2003 Security: A Technical Reference*
by Roberta Bragg

*The Practice of Network Security: Deployment Strategies for Production Environments*
by Allan Liska

*Electronic Commerce: A Managerial Perspective 2006*
by Efraim Turban, David King, Dennis Viehland, and Jae Lee
with contributions by Rajiv Kohli, Christi Cheung, and Linda Lai

*Understanding PKI: Concepts, Standards, and Deployment Considerations*, Second Edition
by Carlisle Adams and Steve Lloyd

**Taken from:**

*Protect Your Windows Network: From Perimeter to Data*
by Jesper M. Johansson and Steve Riley
Copyright © 2005 Jesper M. Johansson and Steve Riley
Published by Addison-Wesley
A Pearson Education Company
Boston, Massachusetts 02116

*Apache Administrator's Handbook*
by Rich Bowen, Allan Liska, Daniel Lopez Ridreujo
Copyright © 2002 by Sams Publishing
A Pearson Education Company
Indianapolis, Indiana 46240

*Windows Server 2003 Security: A Technical Reference*
by Roberta Bragg
Copyright © 2005 Pearson Education, Inc.
Published by Addison-Wesley

*The Practice of Network Security: Deployment Strategies for Production Environments*
by Allan Liska
Copyright © 2003 Pearson Education, Inc.
Published by Prentice Hall PTR
Upper Saddle River, New Jersey 07458

*Electronic Commerce: A Managerial Perspective 2006*
by Efraim Turban, David King, Dennis Viehland, and Jae Lee
with contributions by Rajiv Kohli, Christi Cheung, and Linda Lai
Copyright © 2006, 2004, 2002, 1999 by Pearson Education, Inc.
Published by Prentice-Hall, Inc.

*Understanding PKI: Concepts, Standards, and Deployment Considerations,* Second Edition
by Carlisle Adams and Steve Lloyd
Copyright © 2003 Pearson Education, Inc.
Published by Addison-Wesley



This special edition is published in cooperation with Pearson Custom Publishing.



Printed in the United States of America

10 9 8 7 6 5

ISBN 0-536-20516-7

2006200071

EM

Please visit our web site at *www.pearsoncustom.com*

PEARSON CUSTOM PUBLISHING
75 Arlington Street, Suite 300, Boston, MA 02116
A Pearson Education Company

# CONTENTS

CHAPTER 1

# E-Commerce Security

## Learning Objectives

### Upon Completion of this Chapter, you will be able to:

1. Document the trends in computer and network security attacks.
2. Describe the common security practices of businesses of all sizes.
3. Understand the basic elements of EC security.
4. Explain the basic types of network security attacks.
5. Describe common mistakes that organizations make in managing security.
6. Discuss some of the major technologies for securing EC communications.
7. Detail some of the major technologies for securing EC networks components.

## Phishing

### The Problem

On November 17, 2003, a number of eBay customers were notified by e-mail that their accounts had been compromised and were being restricted. The message contained a hyperlink to an eBay Web page where they could reregister. All they had to do was enter their credit card information, Social Security number, date of birth, mother's maiden name, and ATM personal identification numbers. The only problem was that eBay had not sent the e-mail, and the Web page the account holders were directed to did not really belong to eBay. Although the page looked authentic, having eBay's logo and familiar look and feel, the page was actually part of a bogus site run by Internet scaay customemmers. Those eBay customers who reregistered were victims of a **phishing attack**.

---

**PHISHING ATTACK:** A high-tech scam that uses e-mail, pop-up messages, or Web pages to trick a user into disclosing sensitive information such as credit card numbers, bank account numbers, and passwords.

---

## THE SOLUTION

Phishing attacks are not new. What *is* new is the method. In the past, scam artists relied on the telephone. Today, they rely on spoofed e-mail (spam), fraudulent pop-up messages, or fake Web pages to fool victims into thinking they are dealing with a legitimate business. The message usually links unsuspecting recipients to a Web site where they are asked to update or validate their account information. Although the Web site appears to be legitimate, it is not. At the fake site, the victims are scammed into revealing their credit card numbers, account numbers, user names, passwords, Social Security numbers, or other sensitive information. The information is then used to perpetrate credit card fraud or identity theft.

The Anti-Phishing Working Group (APWG; *antiphishing.org*) is an industry association focused on eliminating identity theft and fraud resulting from phishing and e-mail spoofing. In July 2004, 1,974 unique phishing attacks were reported to the group, up 39 percent from June 2004. The most targeted industry sector was financial services (1,649 out of 1,974 reports). The most targeted brand names were Citibank, U.S. Bank, eBay, and PayPal (1,191 out of 1,974 reports). The United States hosts the largest percentage of phishing sites (35 percent), followed by South Korea, China, and Russia. To avoid detection, most of the phishing sites have a short life span, lasting on the average about 6 days.

Computer security companies such as VeriSign (*verisign.com*) and NameProtect (*nameprotect.com*) are working to stop phishing attacks. Both companies offer services that actively search the Web (domain name servers, pages, sites, news groups, chat rooms, etc.) for signs of phishing activity. These services are used by companies such as MasterCard and other financial and retail enterprises. Once found, information about the illegal activity is passed on to the customer paying for the service and to law enforcement officials.

Although such services assist companies whose brands are being exploited, they provide little direct help to the individuals being scammed. In that case, it is really up to the individuals to avoid being hooked. As the Federal Trade Commission (FTC) (2004) suggests, individuals should:

- Avoid replying to e-mail or pop-up messages that ask for personal information.
- Avoid sending personal or financial information.
- Review credit card and bank account statements.
- Use and keep antivirus software up-to-date.

- Be cautious about opening any attachment or downloading any files received via e-mail.
- Report suspicious activity to the FTC.

### THE RESULTS

The Anti-Phishing Working Group estimates that approximately 5 percent of recipients respond to phishing attacks. The overall economic impact of these attacks is uncertain. Even though there are laws on the books against e-mail spamming and identity theft, both activities are rampant. To date, there have been virtually no prosecutions against the perpetrators of phishing attacks.

**SOURCES:** APWG (2004), FTC (2004).

### WHAT WE CAN LEARN . . .

Any type of EC involves a number of players who use a variety of network and application services that provide access to a variety of data sources. The sheer numbers and interconnections are what make EC security so difficult. A perpetrator needs only a single weakness in order to attack a system. Some attacks require sophisticated techniques and technologies. Many, however, are like the scams perpetrated by phishing attacks—simple techniques preying on poor security practices and human weaknesses. Because most attacks are unsophisticated, standard security risk management procedures can be used to minimize their probability and impact.

This chapter focuses on the basic security issues in EC, the major types of attacks that are perpetrated against EC networks and transactions, and the procedures and technologies that can be used to address these attacks. Because security is a multifaceted and highly technical problem, the complexities cannot be addressed in a single chapter. Those readers interested in a more comprehensive discussion should see Panko (2003) or Thomas (2004).

## The Continuing Need For E-Commerce Security

Evidence from a variety of security surveys provides a mixed picture of the incidence of cyber attacks and cyber crimes in EC. The best known and most widely cited survey is the one conducted by the **Computer Security Institute (CSI)** and the San Francisco Federal Bureau of Investigation's (FBI) Computer Intrusion Squad. This survey has been conducted annually since 1999. The results from the 2004 survey were based on the responses of 494 computer security practitioners in U.S. corporations, government agencies, financial institutions, medical institutions, and universities. Their responses reinforced trends that began in 2001 (see Online File W11.1 for a discussion of the 2001 and 2002 trends). Some specific trends include the following (CSI and FBI 2004):

---

**COMPUTER SECURITY INSTITUTE (CSI):** Nonprofit organization located in San Francisco, California, that is dedicated to serving and training information, computer, and network security professionals.

---

1. For the fourth year in a row, the overall frequency of successful attacks on computer systems declined. In 2001, the percentage of respondents indicating that their organization's computer systems had experienced unauthorized use was approximately 65 percent. In 2004, the percentage was 53 percent. Among those organizations that experienced unauthorized use, the median number of incidents was between one and five incidents. Last year the median was 6 to 10 incidents.
2. The incidence of all types of attacks or misuse has declined. Of the 280 organizations that had been victimized, the percentage of companies who were successfully attacked by viruses was 78 percent. In the previous year, the percentage was 83 percent. The percentage of victimized organizations that experienced insider abuse of net access dropped from 80 percent in 2003 to 59 percent in 2004. Similarly, for these same organizations, the percentage that experienced denial-of-service attacks declined substantially, from 37 percent in 2003 to 17 percent in 2004.
3. As in the past, the majority of respondents were either unable or unwilling to estimate the dollar losses resulting from attacks or misuse. Among those who did report, there was a significant decline

in the total losses reported. In 2004, total losses were approximately $140 million, down from $202 million in 2003. Virus and denial-of-service attacks accounted for approximately $81 million of those losses. This was a significant change from previous years, where the primary losses resulted from theft of proprietary information.

4. Most of the organizations in the survey conduct security audits and employ a variety of technologies and procedures to defend against cyber attacks. Virtually all of the respondents indicated that they employed antivirus software and firewalls. Between 65 and 70 percent also use access control lists, intrusion detection, and data encryption.
5. Organizations still are reticent to report computer intrusions to legal authorities. Less than 50 percent of the respondents did so in 2004. Most of the organizations indicated that they did not report the intrusion because they feared negative publicity or were worried that their competitors would use it against them.

Contrary to the declines noted in the CSI/FBI survey, data and survey results from the **Computer Emergency Response Team (CERT)** (cert.org) at Carnegie Mellon University (CMU) indicate that cyber attacks are on the rise. CERT is a federally funded research and development center located at CMU's Software Engineering Institute. It was established in 1988 to deal with security issues on the Internet. Today, CERT works with the Department of Homeland security to coordinate responses to security compromises; identify trends in intruder activity; identify solutions to security problems; and disseminate information to the broader community.

**COMPUTER EMERGENCY RESPONSE TEAM (CERT):** Group of three teams at Carnegie Mellon University that monitor the incidence of cyber attacks, analyze vulnerabilities, and provide guidance on protecting against attacks.

Since its inception, CERT has received incident reports of cyber attacks from Internet sites. In 2003, the number of reported incidents was approximately 138,000, up substantially from the 82,000 incidents reported in 2002 (CERT/CC 2002). Indeed, the dramatic rise in incidents prompted CERT to discontinue collecting and reporting incident data. Instead, CERT now works with the U.S. Secret Service and *CSO Magazine* to conduct an e-crime watch survey. The 2004 survey (*CSO Magazine 2004*) was conducted in April 2004 and involved 500 security and law enforcement professionals. Seventy percent reported that their organizations experienced at least one e-crime or intrusion, and 43 percent reported that the number of incidents had increased over the previous year. The total cost of these incidents was approximately $666 million. Like the respondents in the CSI/FBI survey, the respondents to the e-crime watch survey indicated that they employed a variety of technologies to combat e-crimes, including firewalls (98 percent), physical security systems (94 percent), and manual patch management (91 percent). Firewalls were viewed by the majority of respondents as very effective, while patch management is seen as very ineffective.

Although the two surveys offer differing pictures about the trends in cyber crimes and intrusions, both provide ample evidence that e-commerce security is still a substantial problem that can result in significant financial losses for an organization. Organizations continue to take the problem seriously and exert considerable effort to thwart these unauthorized and illegal activities.

**Review Questions**

1. Are cyber crimes increasing or decreasing?
2. What types of technologies and procedures do organizations use to combat cyber attacks?
3. What is CERT?

## Security Is Everyone's Business

As the technology underlying e-commerce has become more complex and more intertwined, the opportunities for intrusion and attack have increased. Not only are the underlying components more vulnerable, they also are harder to administer. Teenage hackers, industrial spies, corporate insiders, agents of foreign governments, and criminal elements have all taken advantage of the situation. The variety of potential perpetrators makes it difficult to deter potential attacks and detect them once they have occurred.

According to International Data Corporation (IDC), worldwide spending on corporate digital security was over $70 billion in 2003, including costs associated with people, products, and services (Market Research Summaries 2003). IDC estimates that the figure will reach $116 billion by 2007. Although spending on security has increased significantly, the average company still spends very little of its IT budget on security and very little per employee (for a discussion of the basic security spending patterns by organizational size, see Online File W11.2).

Because the Internet now serves as the control system of many of our critical infrastructures—private and public, cyber and physical, local and global—computer security can no longer rest on the efforts of individual organizations. Instead, it must also be addressed from a national and international perspective. In the United States, the coordination of cyber security efforts falls to the Department of Homeland Security (DHS). Towards this end, the DHS formulated *The National Strategy to Secure Cyberspace* (Department of Homeland Security 2004). The DHS strategy includes five national priorities:

1. A national cyberspace security response system
2. A national cyberspace security threat and vulnerability reduction program
3. A national cyberspace security awareness and training program
4. Securing governments' cyberspace
5. National security and international security cooperation

Accomplishing these priorities requires concerted effort at five levels:

- **Level 1—The Home User/Small Business** Although not necessarily part of the critical infrastructure, unprotected home and small business computers can be used by hackers as a base of operation from which to attack key Internet nodes, important enterprises, or critical infrastructure.
- **Level 2—Large Enterprises** These are common targets for cyber attacks. Many of these enterprises are part of the critical infrastructure. As such, these enterprises are a key element in securing cyberspace. In the future, these enterprises will need to implement information security policies and programs that comply with cyber security best practices.
- **Level 3—Critical Sectors/Infrastructure** The security burden placed on individual enterprises can be reduced when organizations in the private sector unite with government and academic organizations to address common cyber security problems. As an example, several sectors have formed Information Sharing and Analysis

Centers (ISACs) to not only monitor cyber attacks, but also to share information about trends, vulnerabilities, and best practices.

- **Level 4—National Issues and Vulnerabilities** Some cyber security problems have national implications. Because all sectors share the Internet, any weaknesses in its underlying infrastructure (e.g., protocols) requires coordinated activities to address the problem. The same is true for weaknesses in widely used software and hardware products (e.g., the Microsoft Windows operating system).
- **Level 5—Global** The boundaries of the Internet are global. Cyber security problems affecting one part of the world can potentially impact another part. International cooperation to share information and to prosecute cyber criminals is needed to detect, deter, and minimize the impacts of cyber attacks.

In June 2003, the DHS created the **National Cyber Security Division (NCSD)** to implement U.S. cyberspace security strategy. More specifically, the NCSD was charged with identifying, analyzing, and reducing cyber threats and vulnerabilities; disseminating threat warning information; coordinating incident response; and providing technical assistance in continuity of operations and recovery planning.

---

**NATIONAL CYBER SECURITY DIVISION (NCSD):** A division of the Department of Homeland Security charged with implementing U.S. cyberspace security strategy.

---

**Review Questions**

1. What are the major priorities of the National Strategy to Secure Cyberspace?
2. What sectors does the National Strategy to Secure Cyberspace address?
3. What is the National Cyber Security Division (NCSD)?

## Basic Security Issues

EC security involves more than just preventing and responding to cyber attacks and intrusion. Consider, for example, the situation in which a user connects to a Web server at a marketing site to obtain some product literature. In return, the user is asked to fill out a Web form providing some demographic and other personal information in order to receive the literature. In this situation, what kinds of security questions arise?

From the user's perspective:

- How can the user be sure that the Web server is owned and operated by a legitimate company?
- How does the user know that the Web page and form do not contain some malicious or dangerous code or content?
- How does the user know that the owner of the Web site will not distribute the information the user provides to some other party?

From the company's perspective:

- How does the company know the user will not attempt to break into the Web server or alter the pages and content at the site?
- How does the company know that the user will not try to disrupt the server so that it is not available to others?

From both parties' perspectives:

- How do both parties know that the network connection is free from eavesdropping by a third party "listening" on the line?
- How do they know that the information sent back and forth between the server and the user's browser has not been altered?

These questions illustrate the types of security issues that can arise in an EC transaction. For transactions involving e-payments, additional types of security issues must be confronted. The following list summarizes some of the major security issues that can occur in EC:

- **Authentication** When users view a Web page from a Web site, how can they be sure that the site is not fraudulent? If a person files a tax return electronically, how does the taxpayer know that it has been sent to the taxing authority? If a person receives an e-mail, how can he or she be sure that the sender is who he or she claims to be? The process by which one entity verifies that another entity is who he, she, or it claims to be is called **authentication**.

Authentication requires evidence in the form of credentials, which can take a variety of forms, including something known (e.g., a password), something possessed (e.g., a smart card), or something unique (e.g., a signature).

---

**AUTHENTICATION:** The process by which one entity verifies that another entity is who he, she, or it claims to be.

---

- **Authorization** Once authenticated, does a person or program have the right to access particular data, programs, or system resources (e.g., files, registries, directories, etc.)? **Authorization** ensures that a person or program has the right to access certain resources. It usually is determined by comparing information about the person or program with access control information associated with the resource being accessed.

---

**AUTHORIZATION:** The process that ensures that a person has the right to access certain resources.

---

- **Auditing** If a person or program accesses a Web site, various pieces of information are noted in a log file. If a person or program queries a database, that action also is noted in a log file. The process of collecting information about accessing particular resources, using particular privileges, or performing other security actions (either successfully or unsuccessfully) is known as **auditing**. Audits provide the means to reconstruct the specific actions that were taken and often enable IT personnel to identify the person or program that performed the actions.

---

**AUDITING:** The process of collecting information about attempts to access particular resources, use particular privileges, or perform other security actions.

---

- **Confidentiality (Privacy)** The idea behind **confidentiality** is that information that is private or sensitive should not be disclosed to unauthorized individuals, entities, or computer software processes. It is intertwined with the notion of digital privacy, which is now a regulatory issue in many countries. Some examples of things that should be confidential are trade secrets, business plans, health records, credit card numbers, and even the fact that a person visited a particular Web site. Confidentiality requires that people and companies know what data or applications they want to protect and who should have access to them. Confidentiality is usually ensured by encryption.

---

**CONFIDENTIALITY:** Keeping private or sensitive information from being disclosed to unauthorized individuals, entities, or processes.

---

- **Integrity** Data can be altered or destroyed while it is in transit or after it is stored. The ability to protect data from being altered or destroyed in an unauthorized or accidental manner is called **integrity**. Financial transactions are one example of data whose integrity needs to be secured. Again, encryption is one way of ensuring integrity of data while it is in transit.

---

**INTEGRITY:** As applied to data, the ability to protect data from being altered or destroyed in an unauthorized or accidental manner.

---

- **Availability** If a person is trying to execute a stock trade through an online service, then the service needs to be available in near-real time. An online site is *available* if a person or program can gain access to the pages, data, or services provided by the site when they are needed. Technologies such as load-balancing hardware and software are aimed at ensuring availability.
- **Nonrepudiation** If a person orders an item through a mail-order catalog and pays by check, then it is difficult to dispute the veracity of the order. If the same item is ordered through the company's "1-800" number and the person pays by credit card, then there is always room for dispute. Similarly, if a person uses the company's Web site and pays by credit card, the person can always claim that he or she did not place the order. **Nonrepudiation** is the ability to limit parties from refuting that a legitimate transaction took place. One of the keys to nonrepudiation is a "signature" that makes it difficult for a person to dispute that they were involved in an exchange.

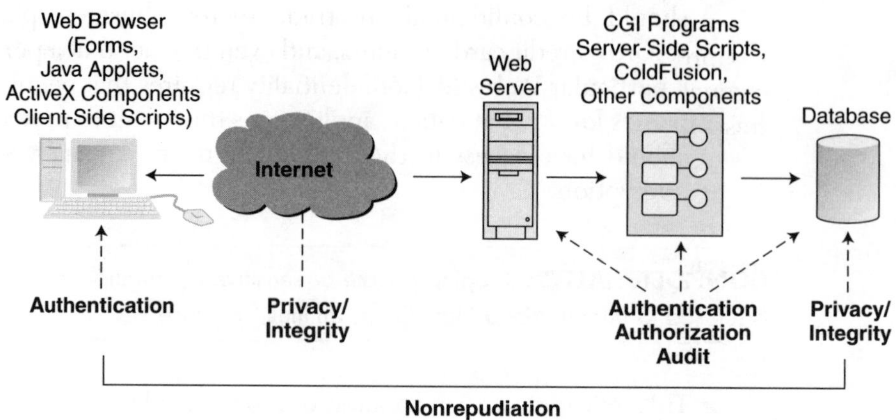


**Figure 1-1** General Security Issues at EC Sites.
**Source:** Scambray, J. et al. *Hacking Exposed*, 2d ed. New York: McGraw-Hill, 2000. Copyright © The McGraw-Hill Companies.

**NONREPUDIATION:** The ability to limit parties from refuting that a legitimate transaction took place, usually by means of a signature.

Figure 1-1 depicts some of the major components involved in most EC applications and indicates where the above security issues come into play. It is safe to say that virtually every component in an EC application is subject to some sort of security threat.

**Review Questions**

1. If a customer purchases an item from an online store, what are some of the security concerns that might arise?
2. What are the major security issues facing EC sites?

## Types of Threats and Attacks

Security experts distinguish between two types of attacks—nontechnical and technical. **Nontechnical attacks** are those in which a perpetrator uses chicanery or some other form of persuasion to trick people into revealing sensitive information or performing actions that can be used to compromise the security of a network. These attacks also are called *social engineering*. The phishing attacks described earlier are of this sort. In contrast, software and systems knowledge are used to perpetrate *technical attacks*. A computer virus is an example of a technical attack. Often, attacks involve a combination of the two types. For instance, an intruder may use an automated tool to post a message to an instant messaging service. The message may offer the opportunity to download software of interest to the reader (e.g., software for downloading music or videos). When an unsuspecting reader downloads the malicious software, it automatically runs on his or her computer, enabling the intruder to take control of the machine and use it to perpetrate a technical attack.

---

**NONTECHNICAL ATTACK:** An attack that uses chicanery to trick people into revealing sensitive information or performing actions that compromise the security of a network.

---

## Nontechnical Attacks: Social Engineering

IT staffs tend to concentrate on the technical side of network security—firewalls, encryption, digital signatures, and the like. However, the real Achilles' heel of most networks is the humans who use them. Tricking individual users into providing information or carrying out actions that seem innocuous but are not is known as social engineering. **Social engineering** preys on an individual's desire to help, an individual's fear of getting into trouble, or the general trust among individuals.

---

**SOCIAL ENGINEERING:** A type of nontechnical attack that uses social pressures to trick computer users into compromising computer networks to which those individuals have access.

---

Consider, for example, the following e-mail that was received by one of the authors at his place of work:

> *Dear user of xyz.com,*
>
> *We have detected that your e-mail account was used to send a large amount of spam during the recent week. Obviously, your computer had been compromised and now runs a trojan proxy server.*

*We recommend you to follow the instructions in the attachment (xyz.com.zip) in order to keep your computer safe.*
*Have a nice day,*
*xyz.com technical support team.*

The message was sent from the e-mail PostMaster@xyz.com and appears to be a legitimate request from the company's technical support team. The sender is using the authority of the technical support team and playing on the recipient's fear that he has done something wrong and needs to comply with the request to rectify the situation. However, opening the attached zip file will install the Trojan horse proxy server the recipient is being requested to remove. This is basically a social engineering attack because it is the recipient's decision to open the zip file that determines whether the attack is successful, not the technical skills of the sender.

There are two categories of social engineering—human based and computer based. Human-based social engineering relies on traditional methods of communication (in person or over the phone). For example, a hacker posing as IT support staff might call up an employee and simply ask the employee for his or her password under the guise that the IT staff needs to fix a problem with the system. Or, a hacker might turn the tables. The hacker, posing as an officer of a company, might call the IT support staff asking for a password that the hacker claims to have forgotten. Fearing that they may seem uncooperative to upper management, the IT support staff complies. Employees also are notorious for writing their passwords on sticky notes or desk pads that easily can be viewed by people walking by or that are discarded in the trash and later retrieved by a hacker.

With computer-based social engineering, various technical ploys are used to encourage individuals to provide sensitive information. For example, a hacker may simply send an e-mail requesting sensitive information or create a Web page that surfaces a form that looks like a legitimate network log-on request for user ID and password. Over the past couple of years, Internet chat rooms and instant messaging also have been used to perpetrate social engineering attacks.

Kevin Mitnick, who spent 5 years in prison for breaking and entering into computers, and whose exploits were documented in the bestselling book *Takedown* (Shimomura 1996), was quoted as saying that more than half of his successful attacks were carried out through social engineering. From Mitnick's perspective (Mitnick and Simon 2002), the key to successful social engineering is trust: "You try to make an emotional connection with the person on the other side to create a sense of trust. That's the whole idea: to create a sense of trust and then exploit it" (quoted in Lemos 2000).

Because the key to successful social engineering rests with the victims, the key to combating social engineering attacks also rests with the victims. Certain positions within an organization are clearly more vulnerable than others. These are the individuals who have access to private and confidential information and who interact with the public on a frequent basis. Some of the positions with this sort of access and contact are secretaries and executive assistants, database and network administrators, computer operators, call-center operators, and help-desk attendants.

A multiprong approach should be used to combat social engineering (Damle 2002):

- **Education and training** All staff, but especially those in vulnerable positions, need to be educated about the risks associated with social engineering, the social engineering techniques used by hackers, and ways and means to combat these attacks.
- **Policies and procedures** Specific policies and procedures need to be developed for securing confidential information, guiding employee behavior with respect to confidential information, and taking the steps needed to respond to and report any social engineering breaches.
- **Penetration testing** The policies, procedures, and responses of individual staff need to be tested on a regular basis by outside experts playing the role of a hacker. Because of the possibility of adverse effects on employee or staff morale, they should be debriefed after the penetration test, and any weaknesses should be corrected.

## Technical Attacks

In contrast with nontechnical attacks, software and systems knowledge are used to perpetrate **technical attacks**. In conducting a technical attack, an expert hacker often uses a methodical approach. Several software tools are readily and freely available over the Internet that enable a hacker to expose a system's vulnerabilities. Although many of these tools require expertise, novice hackers easily can use many of the existing tools.

---

**TECHNICAL ATTACK:** An attack perpetrated using software and systems knowledge or expertise.

---

In 1999, Mitre Corporation (**cve.mitre.org**) and 15 other security-related organizations began to enumerate all publicly known **common (security) vulnerabilities and exposures (CVEs)**. A *vulnerability* is a mistake in software that can be directly used by a hacker to gain access to a system or network; an *exposure* is a mistake in software that allows access to information or capabilities that can be used by a hacker as a stepping-stone into a system or network. One of the goals of the CVE list is to assign standard and unique names to each of the known security problems so that information can be collected and shared with the security community throughout the world. The number of known CVEs has grown from approximately 320 in 1999 to more than 3,000 in 2004. Additionally, there are almost 4,250 CVE *candidates*, which are those vulnerabilities or exposures under consideration for acceptance as CVEs (**cve.mitre.org** 1999–2005).

---

**COMMON (SECURITY) VULNERABILITIES AND EXPOSURES (CVES):** Publicly known computer security risks, which are collected, listed, and shared by a board of security-related organizations (`cve.mitre.org`).

---

Since 2000, the SANS Institute, in conjunction with the FBI's **National Infrastructure Protection Center (NIPC)**, has produced a document summarizing the "Top 20 Internet Security Vulnerabilities" (SANS 2004). This year's list is actually two top 10 lists: the 10 most commonly exploited vulnerabilities in Windows and the 10 most commonly exploited vulnerabilities in UNIX and Linux. Although there are thousands of security incidents each year, the vast majority of successful attacks focus on the top 20 vulnerabilities. This list is used by organizations to prioritize their security efforts, allowing them to address the most dangerous vulnerabilities first.

---

**NATIONAL INFRASTRUCTURE PROTECTION CENTER (NIPC):** A joint partnership under the auspices of the FBI between government and private industry; designed to prevent vulnerabilities and protect the nation's infrastructure.

---

Examining the list of the top 10 or 20 CVEs, one quickly realizes that all of the CVEs are very technical in nature. For this reason, we will confine our discussion to two types of attacks that are well known and that have affected the lives of millions—distributed denial-of-service (DDoS) attacks and malicious code attacks (viruses, worms, and Trojan horses).

### *Distributed Denial-of-Service Attacks*

At the beginning of 2004, the MyDoom.A e-mail viruses infected hundreds of thousands of PCs around the world (Fisher 2004). Like many other e-mail viruses, this virus was propagated by sending an official-looking e-mail message with a zip file attached. When the zip file was opened, the virus automatically found other e-mail addresses on the victim's computer and forwarded itself to those addresses. However, there was more to MyDoom.A than simple propagation. When the zip file was opened, the virus code also installed a program on the victim's machine that enabled the intruders to automatically launch what is known as a denial-of-service attack against a company called the SCO Group. The attack involved nothing more than having hundreds of thousands of infected machines send page requests to SCO's Web site. The site was brought to a standstill because it was overwhelmed by the large number of requests. It was first thought that SCO was a victim of irate Linux proponents who were angered by SCO's multimillion-dollar lawsuit against IBM for having allegedly included SCO's code in IBM's Linux software. Later, it was suggested that the attack was actually launched by spammers out of Russia. For another example of a brute force attack perpetrated by relatively simple means, see Online File W11.3.

In a **denial-of-service (DoS) attack**, an attacker uses specialized software to send a flood of data packets to the target computer, with the aim of overloading its resources. Many attackers rely on software that has been created by other hackers and made available over the Internet rather than developing it themselves.

---

**DENIAL-OF-SERVICE (DOS) ATTACK:** An attack on a Web site in which an attacker uses specialized software to send a flood of data packets to the target computer with the aim of overloading its resources.

---

With a **distributed denial-of-service (DDoS) attack**, the attacker gains illegal administrative access to as many computers on the Internet as possible. Once an attacker has access to a large number of computers, he or she loads the specialized DDoS software onto the computers. The software lays in wait, listening for a command to begin the attack. When the command is given, the distributed network of computers begins sending out requests to the target computer. The requests may be legitimate queries for information or very specialized computer commands designed to overwhelm specific computer resources. There are different types of

DDoS attacks. In the simplest case, like MyDoom.A, it is the magnitude of the requests that brings the target computer to a halt.

---

**DISTRIBUTED DENIAL-OF-SERVICE (DDOS) ATTACK:** A denial-of-service attack in which the attacker gains illegal administrative access to as many computers on the Internet as possible and uses the multiple computers to send a flood of data packets to the target computer.

---

The machines on which the DDoS software is loaded are known as *zombies.* Zombies are often located at university and government sites and, increasingly, on home computers that are connected to the Internet through cable modems or DSL modems (see Figure 1-2).

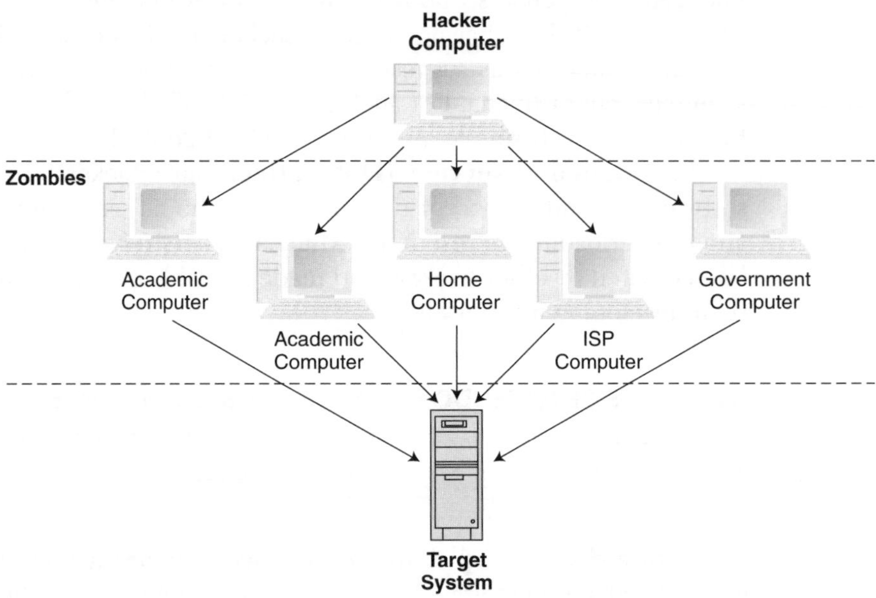


**Figure 1-2** Using Zombies in a Distributed Denial-of-Service Attack.

**Source:** Scambray, J. et al. *Hacking Exposed*, 2d ed. New York: McGraw-Hill, 2000. Copyright © The McGraw-Hill Companies.

Due to the widespread availability of free intrusion tools and scripts and the overall interconnectivity on the Internet, virtually anyone with minimal computer experience (often a teenager with time on his or her hands) can mount a DoS attack. EC Application Case 1-1 provides a description of one such attack.

DoS attacks can be difficult to stop. Fortunately (or unfortunately), they are so commonplace that over the past few years the security community has developed a series of steps for combating these costly attacks. In the case of SCO, the attacks were scheduled to run from February 1, 2004 to February 12, 2004. During that time, SCO shut off its original Web site **sco.com** and set up a new homepage at **thescogroup.com**. Microsoft, which was the target of MyDoom.B, redirected its Web to specialized security servers run by Akamai Technologies, Inc. **(akamai.com)**. Depending on the type of attack, a company can sometimes thwart a DoS attack by reconfiguring its network routers and firewalls.

### *Malicious Code: Viruses, Worms, and Trojan Horses*

Sometimes referred to as **malware** (for malicious software), malicious code is classified by the way in which it is propagated. Some malicious code is rather benign, but it all has the potential to do damage.

---

**MALWARE:** A generic term for malicious software.

---

New variants of malicious code appear quite frequently. In their ninth annual survey of virus prevalence, the Computer Security Association (ICSA 2004) found that almost 90 percent of the companies surveyed felt that the problem of malicious code was "worse or much worse" than the previous year. Virtually all the respondents had been the victims of malicious code. More importantly, the number who reported that they were victims of "virus disasters"—defined as more than 25 computers infected with the same virus and suffering substantial monetary damage—was 92 out of 300 respondents, up 15 percent from the previous year. The cost of disaster recovery was also up 23 percent, to $100,000 per organiza-tion per event.

## CASE 1-1
## EC Application
### ARE HACKERS USING YOUR PC?

For Christmas 2003, Betty Carty, a 54-year-old grandmother living in southern New Jersey, purchased a Dell computer. At home, the computer was connected to the Internet through a high-speed connection from Comcast. Within a short time, her connection began to slow and her machined crashed frequently. In June 2004, Comcast curtailed her e-mail privileges. They determined that her PC was a major source of e-mail spam. However, it was not her fault. A hacker had turned her PC into a zombie, distributing up to 70,000 pieces of e-mail spam per day.

Carty's PC could have been infected in a number of ways. She could have opened an infected e-mail, visited a Web page containing malicious code, or been the victim of a network worm that worked its way onto her machine through a security hole in her computer's operating system.

Carty's machine is not alone. According to an interview study by *USA TODAY* of tech-industry and security experts (Achohido and Swartz 2004), many top-tier hackers are now focused on creating malicious code aimed at amassing networks of zombies. Once assembled, they sell access to the zombies to spammers, blackmailers, and identity thieves. Supposedly, the number of zombies has reached the millions. There is no way to determine the exact number, but one measure of the rising tide of zombies is the amount of e-mail spam. In July 2004, 94 percent of e-mail traffic was estimated to be spam. This is more than double the estimated amount from the year before. Based on another estimate, 40 percent of spam comes from zombies.

Like Carty, most home users think their PCs are safe and, as a consequence, have done little to protect against viruses, spyware, hackers, or other online threats. In October 2004, America Online (AOL) and the National Cyber Security Alliance (NCSA) released the results of a comprehensive, nationwide, in-home study of computer security. The study involved interviews with 329 participants in 22 cities and towns across the United States. In addition to being questioned, the participants' computers were examined by technicians to examine their firewall settings, antivirus software, potential virus infections, and the like. Among the key findings of the study were:

- Eighty-four percent of the participants keep sensitive information (e.g., financial records) on their computers, and over 70 percent of the participants use the Internet for sensitive transactions (e.g., online banking).
- Over 75 percent of the participants said they think their computers were very or somewhat safe from online threats.

- Over 60 percent of the participants said they had been victimized by viruses; however, a scan of their computers indicated that less than 20 percent currently had viruses.
- Over 50 percent of the participants thought that their machines had been infected by spyware, but a scan of their machines indicated the actual percentage was 80, with an average of 93 spyware components per machine.
- Eighty-five percent of the participants had antivirus software on their machines, but only one-third of the machines had been updated in the past week.
- Thirty-three percent of the participants' machines had a firewall currently running, but over 70 percent of these machines did not have the firewall properly configured.
- The majority of users were confused by the difference between a firewall and antivirus software, and a majority indicated that they did not understand how a firewall works.

In general, most users think their computers are safe from online threats but lack basic protection against viruses, spyware, hackers, and other online threats.

**SOURCES:** Achohido and Swartz (2004) and AOL/NCSA (2004).

**QUESTIONS**

1. What sorts of precautions do most home users employ to secure their computers?
2. What are some of the major vulnerabilities on home users' computers?

A number of factors have contributed to the overall increase in malicious code. Among these factors, the following are paramount (Skoudis and Zeltser 2003):

- **Mixing data and executable instructions** In the past, data and executable instructions were separate. This is no longer the case. For example, all the major database programs, such as Oracle, IBM's DB2, and Microsoft's SQL Server, not only store data, but also execute database commands and have their own programming languages (e.g., PL/SQL for Oracle). Similarly, applications such as Microsoft Excel and Microsoft Word have their own scripting languages, which make it possible to embed programs in spreadsheets and Word documents. Likewise, Web pages combine HTML (which underlies the content and formatting of a page) with JavaScript,

VBScript, and other languages. All of these combinations provide easy entry points for intruders to embed and mask malicious code.

- **Increasingly homogenous computing environments** About 20 years ago we had minicomputers and mainframe computers, as well as PCs. They all had different kinds of computer chips and ran on a variety of operating systems and networks. Today, we are down to Windows and UNIX/Linux operating systems, Intel chips dominate the market, and virtually everything is connected via a TCP/IP network. This means that an attacker only has to develop a single piece of code in order to wreak havoc across the globe.
- **Unprecedented connectivity** In the past, networks were basically islands of connectivity. Today, everything is connected—government computers, emergency services, financial systems, home PCs, medical systems, retail operations, airline reservation systems, and the like. Most of it is connected by high-speed lines. This connectivity offers the opportunity for malicious code to spread at unprecedented rates.
- **Larger clueless user base** The average computer user has minimal understanding of the complexities of his or her computer, the networks with which the computer is connected, or the risks posed by malicious code. The implication is that few users have the skills or knowledge required to install and configure the security systems (e.g., personal firewalls) and patches needed to combat malicious code. This makes home PCs and small business systems fertile ground for hackers.

As the number of attacks increases, the following trends in malicious code are emerging (Symantec 2004; Slewe 2004):

- **Increased speed and volume of attacks** The Slammer worm exemplifies this trend. On January 25, 2003, the Slammer worm was released. The worm exploited a vulnerability in Microsoft's SQL Server database. Upon release, the worm doubled in size every 8.5 seconds, infecting approximately 75,000 machines within 10 minutes.
- **Reduced time between the discovery of a vulnerability and the release of an attack to exploit the vulnerability** In the first half of 2004, the average time between the discovery of a vulnerability and the appearance of code exploiting the vulnerability was 5.8 days. Once the exploitive code is made available, a new vulnerability can be widely scanned for and quickly attacked, especially if the vulnerability is in a widely deployed application.

- **Remotely controlled bot networks are growing** In the world of computer security, *bots* (short for "robots") are programs that are installed covertly on a targeted system. They allow an unauthorized user to remotely control the compromised computer for a wide variety of malicious purposes. Over the first 6 months of 2004, the number of monitored bots rose from well under 2,000 computers to more than 30,000. Bots can be upgraded easily and quickly to run malicious code designed to exploit recently discovered vulnerabilities.
- **E-commerce is the most frequently targeted industry** During the first 6 months of 2004, e-commerce received more targeted attacks than any other industry (16 percent in 2004 versus 4 percent in 2003). This rise may indicate that the motivation of attackers may be shifting from looking for notoriety to seeking illicit financial rewards.
- **Attacks against Web application technologies are increasing** Concomitant with the increase in e-commerce attacks is an increase in attacks on Web applications. In the first half of 2004, 39 percent of disclosed vulnerabilities were associated with Web application technologies. These attacks often provide access to confidential information without having to compromise any servers. They allow attackers to gain access to the target system simply by penetrating one end user's computer, bypassing traditional perimeter security measures.
- **A large percentage of *Fortune* 100 companies have been compromised by worms** Over the first 6 months of 2004, Symantec observed worm traffic originating from *Fortune* 100 corporations. This data was gathered by analyzing attack data that revealed the source network (IP) addresses of attack activity. The purpose of this analysis was to determine how many of these systems were infected by worms and actively being used to propagate worms. More than 40 percent of *Fortune* 100 companies controlled network (IP) addresses from which worm-related attacks propagated. This indicates that, despite the measures taken by organizations, their systems are still becoming infected. Continued worm traffic coming from these networks indicates to potential attackers that the network is still susceptible to exploitation.

Malicious code takes a variety of forms—both pure and hybrid. The names for such codes are taken from the real-world pathogens they resemble.

**Viruses** This is the best known of the malicious code categories. Although there are many definitions of a computer virus, the Request for Comment (RFC) 1135 definition is widely used: "A **virus** is a piece of code that inserts itself into a host, including the operating systems, to propagate. It cannot run independently. It requires that its host program be run to activate it." Although viruses are self-replicating, they cannot propagate automatically across a network; they require a human to move them from one computer to another.

---

**VIRUS:** A piece of software code that inserts itself into a host, including the operating systems, in order to propagate; it requires that its host program be run to activate it.

---

A virus has two components. First, it has a propagation mechanism by which it spreads. Second, it has a payload that refers to what the virus does once it is executed. Sometimes the execution is triggered by a particular event. The Michelangelo virus, for instance, was triggered by Michelangelo's birth date. Some viruses simply infect and spread. Others do substantial damage (e.g., deleting files or corrupting the hard drive).

A whole industry has grown up around combating computer viruses. Companies such as Network Associates (owner of McAfee products) and Symantec (owner of Norton products) exist for the sole purpose of fighting viruses—providing antivirus software and software updates to individuals and companies. McAfee's Anti-virus and Vulnerability Response Team (AVERT) has a virus information library (**vil.nai.com**) and keeps a running list of the 10 biggest malicious threats, including viruses, worms, Trojan horses, and the like. A sizeable percentage of those threats include "Potentially Unwanted Programs," which give recipients the option to decide whether they want to keep software.

**Worms** The major difference between a worm and a virus is that a worm propagates between systems (usually through a network), whereas a virus propagates locally. RFC 1135 defines a worm in this way: "A **worm** is a program that can run independently, will consume the resources of its host from within in order to maintain itself, and can propagate a complete working version of itself onto another machine." A worm attacks one computer, takes it over, and uses it as a staging area to scan for and attack other machines. No human intervention is required to spread a worm across a network. Code Red and SQL Slammer are examples of worms.

**WORM:** A software program that runs independently, consuming the resources of its host in order to maintain itself, that is capable of propagating a complete working version of itself onto another machine.

Worms consist of a set of common base elements: a warhead, a propagation engine, a payload, a target-selection algorithm, and a scanning engine. The warhead is the piece of code in a worm that exploits some known vulnerability. Once a worm exploits the vulnerability, its propagation engine is used to move the rest of the worm's code across the network. The move usually is accomplished with a file transfer program. Once the entire worm is moved across, it delivers its payload and then utilizes its target-selection algorithm to look for other potential victims to attack (e.g., e-mail addresses on the victimized machine). The scanning engine determines which of the other potential victims can be exploited. When a suitable target is found, the entire process is repeated. The entire process takes seconds or less, which is why a worm can spread to thousands of machines.

Antivirus software can be used to thwart viruses as well as other forms of malware, including worms. Because worms spread much more rapidly than viruses, organizations need to proactively track new vulnerabilities and apply system patches as a defense against their spread.

**Macro Viruses and Macro Worms** A **macro virus** or **macro worm** is usually executed when the application object (e.g., spreadsheet, word processing document, e-mail message) containing the macro is opened or a particular procedure is executed (e.g., a file is saved). Melissa and ILOVEYOU were both examples of macro worms that were propagated through Microsoft Outlook e-mail and whose payloads were delivered as Visual Basic for Application (VBA) programs attached to e-mail messages. When the unsuspecting recipient opened the e-mail, the VBA program looked up the entries in the recipient's Outlook address book and sent copies of itself to the contacts in the address book. If you think this is a difficult task, note that the ILOVEYOU macro was about 40 lines of code.

**MACRO VIRUS OR MACRO WORM:** A virus or worm that is executed when the application object that contains the macro is opened or a particular procedure is executed.

**Trojan Horses** A **Trojan horse** is a program that appears to have a useful function but contains a hidden function that presents a security risk. The name is derived from the Trojan horse in Greek mythology. Legend has it that during the Trojan War the city of Troy was presented with a large wooden horse as a gift to the goddess Athena. The Trojans hauled the horse into the city gates. During the night, Greek soldiers, who were hiding in the hollow horse, opened the gates of Troy and let in the Greek army. The army was able to take the city and win the war.

---

**TROJAN HORSE:** A program that appears to have a useful function but that contains a hidden function that presents a security risk.

---

There are many types of Trojan horse programs. The programs of interest are those that make it possible for someone else to access and control a person's computer over the Internet. This type of Trojan horse has two parts: a server and a client. The server is the program that runs on the computer under attack. The client program is the program used by the person perpetrating the attack. For example, the Girlfriend Trojan is a server program that arrives in the form of a file that looks like an interesting game or program. When the unsuspecting user runs the program, the Trojan program is installed. The installed program is executed every time the attacked computer is turned on. The server simply waits for the associated client program to send a command. This particular Trojan horse enables the perpetrator to capture user IDs and passwords, to display messages on the affected computer, to delete and upload files, and so on.

One key malware trend is the rise of code that exploits and alters the user's operating system down to the kernel level. The kernel controls things such as a computer's memory, file system, hardware, and other critical components that are crucial to the operation of the machine. **Rootkits** fall into this category of code. They are special Trojan horse programs that modify the existing operating system software so that an intruder can hide the presence of the Trojan program. For example, in the UNIX operating system the "–ls" command is used to list the files on the machine. Using a rootkit, an intruder could substitute his or her own "-ls" command that would hide the Trojan program's presence by failing to list it when the "-ls" command is issued.

---

**ROOTKIT:** A special Trojan horse program that modifies existing operating system software so that an intruder can hide the presence of the Trojan program.

---

The best way to defend against Trojan horses is to implement strict policies and procedures for installing new software. In an organization, end users should be forbidden from installing unauthorized programs. Administrators need to check the integrity of programs and patches that are installed. In the same vein, new programs and tools should be installed in a test environment before putting them into a production environment.

**Review Questions**

1. Describe the difference between a nontechnical and a technical cyber attack.
2. What is a CVE?
3. How are DDoS attacks perpetrated?
4. What are the major forms of malicious code?
5. What factors account for the increase in malicious code?
6. What are some of the major trends in malicious code?

## Managing EC Security

Although awareness of security issues has increased in recent years, organizations continue to make some fairly common mistakes in managing their security risks (McConnell 2002):

- **Undervalued information** Few organizations have a clear understanding of the value of specific information assets.
- **Narrowly defined security boundaries** Most organizations focus on securing their internal networks and fail to understand the security practices of their supply chain partners.
- **Reactive security management** Many organizations are reactive rather than proactive, focusing on security *after* an incident or problem occurs.
- **Dated security management processes** Organizations rarely update or change their security practices to meet changing needs. Similarly, they rarely update the knowledge and skills of their staff about best practices in information security.
- **Lack of communication about security responsibilities** Security often is viewed as an IT problem, not an organizational one.

Given these common mistakes, it is clear that a holistic approach is required to secure an EC site. Companies must constantly evaluate and address emerging vulnerabilities and threats to their Web sites. End users must recognize that IT security is as important as physical security and must adopt responsible behavior. Senior management must articulate the need for IT security, play a key role in formulating organizational security policies, and actively support those policies. Those organizations with sound security practices rely on comprehensive risk management to determine their security needs (Kay 2003; Microsoft 2004).

## Security Risk Management

Consider an online CRM database containing confidential information about a company's customer accounts. An information asset of this sort is extremely valuable to the company, to the customers, and potentially to the company's competitors. Imagine what it would cost the company if this database were unavailable, damaged or destroyed, or fell into the hands of another party. The risks and potential threats against this asset are both physical (e.g., the machine on which the database is housed could be destroyed) and nonphysical (e.g., the data could be compromised by an irate employee or attacked by a hacker). Obviously, the asset needs to be secured in a variety of ways, including physically securing the computer on which the database is run, backing up the database to another computer, password protecting the database, putting the database on a secure network behind a firewall, and so on. For this particular asset, the costs of reducing the risks far outweigh the potential costs associated with securing the asset. The systematic process of identifying key computer, network, and information assets; assessing the risks and threats against those assets; and actually reducing those security risks and threats is known as **security risk management**.

---

**SECURITY RISK MANAGEMENT:** A systematic process for determining the likelihood of various security attacks and for identifying the actions needed to prevent or mitigate those attacks.

---

Security risk management consists of three phases:

- **Asset identification** In this phase, an organization determines its key computer, network, and information assets and places a value on those assets. The valuation includes the costs of obtaining, maintaining, and replacing the asset, as well as the costs if it fell into the hands of another party. Once the assets are identified, the organization can assess the security threats, vulnerabilities, and risks against those assets.

- **Risk assessment** Once an organization's key assets have been identified, the next step is to perform an assessment of the risks against those assets. This involves identifying threats, vulnerabilities, and risks. *Threats* include things such as natural disasters, equipment malfunction, employees, intruders, hackers, terrorist attacks, and the like. *Vulnerabilities* are those aspects of the asset that can be compromised by the potential threats. *Risks* involve the probabilities of the vulnerabilities being compromised by various threats, as well as the potential financial losses resulting from the compromises. One way to evaluate the threats and vulnerabilities facing a specific organization is to rely on the knowledge of the organization's IT personnel or to use an outside consultant, such as Granite Systems (*granitesystems.net*), to conduct a security assessment. Another way is to utilize software that scans for vulnerabilities, does penetration testing, or enables a firm to safely view and study attacks as they occur.
- **Implementation** After the risks have been assessed, they need to be prioritized by probability and potential loss. A list of solutions and countermeasures should be proposed and reviewed for each of the high-priority risks. These solutions and countermeasures need to be evaluated in terms of their overall cost-benefits (e.g., a company would not spend $50,000 for a security measure when the asset is only worth $25,000) and the security measures that are currently in place. Once a set of security measures has been selected and implemented, not only does the organization need to monitor the performance and effectiveness of those measures, but it also needs to continually review its asset base and any new threats, vulnerabilities, and risks that may arise.

**Review Questions**

1. What are some common mistakes that EC sites make in managing their security?
2. Describe the basic steps in security risk management.

## Securing EC Communications

As indicated by the CSI/FBI and CERT surveys cited in Section 1.1, most organizations rely on multiple technologies to secure their networks. These technologies can be divided into two major groups: those designed to secure communications *across* the network and those designed to protect the servers and clients *on* the network. This section considers the first of these technologies.

### Access Control and Authentication

The simplest aspects of network security are access control and authentication. **Access control** determines who (person or machine) can legitimately use a network resource and which resources he, she, or it can use. A resource can be anything—Web pages, text files, databases, applications, servers, printers, or any other information source or network component. Typically, access control lists (ACL) define which users have access to which resources and what rights they have with respect to those resources (i.e., read, view, write, print, copy, delete, execute, modify, or move). By default, a user's rights often are set at full access or no access. This is fine as a starting point, but each resource needs to be considered separately, and the rights of particular users need to be established individually. This process of assigning rights often is simplified by creating various roles or groups (e.g., system administrators, northwest sales reps, product marketing department, trading partners, etc.), assigning rights to those groups, and then specifying the individuals within those groups. Users often are denoted by their network login IDs, which are usually checked when the user first accesses the system.

---

**ACCESS CONTROL:** Mechanism that determines who can legitimately use a network resource.

---

Once a user has been identified, the user must be authenticated. As noted earlier, authentication is the process of verifying that the user is who he or she claims to be. Verification usually is based on one or more characteristics that distinguish the individual from others. The distinguishing characteristics can be based on something one knows (e.g., passwords), something one has (e.g., a token), or something one is (e.g., fingerprint).

Traditionally, authentication has been based on passwords. Passwords are notoriously insecure because people have a habit of writing them down in easy-to-find places, choosing values that are guessed easily, and willingly telling people their passwords when asked.

Stronger security is achieved by combining something one knows with something one has, a technique known as *two-factor authentication*. Tokens qualify as something one has. Tokens come in various shapes, forms, and sizes. **Passive tokens** are storage devices that contain a secret code. The most common passive tokens are plastic cards with magnetic strips containing a hidden code. With passive tokens, the user swipes the token through a reader attached to a personal computer or workstation and then enters his or her password to gain access to the network.

---

**PASSIVE TOKENS:** Storage devices (e.g., magnetic strips) that contain a secret code used in a two-factor authentication system.

---

**Active tokens** usually are small stand-alone electronic devices (e.g., key chain tokens, smartcards, calculators, USB dongles) that generate one-time passwords. In this case, the user enters a PIN into the token, the token generates a password that is only good for a single log-on, and the user then logs on to the system using the one-time password. ActivCard (*activcard.com*) and CRYPTOcard (*cryptocard.com*) are companies that provide active token authentication devices.

---

**ACTIVE TOKENS:** Small, stand-alone electronic devices that generate one-time passwords used in a two-factor authentication system.

---

### *Biometric Systems*

Two-factor authentication also can be based on something one is. Fingerprint scanners, iris scanners, facial recognition systems, and voice recognition all are examples of **biometric systems** that recognize a person by a physical trait. Biometric systems can *identify* a person from a population of enrolled users by searching through a database for a match based on the person's biometric trait or the system can *verify* a person's claimed identity by matching the individual's biometric trait against a previously stored version. Biometric verification is much simpler than biometric identification, and it is the process used in two-factor authentication.

**BIOMETRIC SYSTEMS:** Authentication systems that identify a person by measurement of a biological characteristic, such as fingerprints, iris (eye) patterns, facial features, or voice.

To date, the uptake of biometric security has been slow. For instance, in the CSI/FBI survey cited earlier only 11 percent of the organizations indicated they were using biometric systems. A security technology adoption survey conducted by International Data Corporation showed that only 0.6 percent of North American companies use biometrics for Internet and network security (Shen 2003). In terms of overall market share, biometric security products account for around 5 percent of the security product market.

Interest in biometric security is increasing, spurred by declining prices in biometric systems, the worldwide focus on terrorism, and soaring fraud and identity theft. In a survey of 840 corporate IT directors in 21 countries conducted by Hitachi Data Systems, 65 percent said that they expected to be using biometrics sometime in the near future (Sherwood 2004). Many financial institutions, for instance, are interested in using a combination of smartcards and biometrics to authenticate customers and ensure nonrepudiation for online banking, trading, and purchasing transactions. Retail point-of-sale system vendors are looking to biometrics to supplement signature verification for credit card purchases. Biometrics also are being tested in various national security and governmental applications, including airport security, passport verification, and social service fraud prevention.

Fingerprint scanning is probably the best known and most widely used biometric. However, fingerprint scanning is only one of a number of possible biometrics that can be used to verify an individual's identity (authentication). Biometrics come in two "flavors"—physiological and behavioral. **Physiological biometrics** are based on measurements derived directly from different parts of the body. In contrast, **behavioral biometrics** are derived from various actions and indirectly from various body parts (e.g., voice scans or keystroke monitoring).

**PHYSIOLOGICAL BIOMETRICS:** Measurements derived directly from different parts of the body (e.g., fingerprint, iris, hand, facial characteristics).

**BEHAVIORAL BIOMETRICS:** Measurements derived from various actions and indirectly from various body parts (e.g., voice scans or keystroke monitoring).

In practice, physiological biometrics are used more often than behavioral biometrics. Among the physiological biometrics, the scans of fingerprints, irises, hands, and facial characteristics are the most popular.

To implement a biometric authentication system, the physiological or behavioral characteristics of a participant must be scanned repeatedly under different settings. The scans are then averaged to produce a biometric template, or identifier. The template is stored in a database as a series of numbers that can range from a few bytes for hand geometry to several thousand bytes for facial recognition. When a person uses a biometric system, a live scan is conducted, and the scan is converted to a series of numbers, which is then compared against the template stored in the database. Examples of various types of biometric templates are detailed in the following text.

**Fingerprint Scanning** Fingerprints can be distinguished by a variety of "discontinuities that interrupt the smooth flow of ridges" (Kroeker 2002) on the bottom tips of the fingers. Ridge endings, dots (small ridges), and ponds (spaces between ridges) are examples of such discontinuities. In **fingerprint scanning**, a special algorithm is used to convert the scanned discontinuities to a set of numbers stored as a template. The chance that any two people have the same template is one in a billion. Fingerprint recognition devices for desktop and laptop access are now available from a variety of vendors at low cost. Online File W11.4 describes the use of fingerprint scanning in a retail situation.

---

**FINGERPRINT SCANNING:** Measurement of the discontinuities of a person's fingerprint, which are then converted to a set of numbers that are stored as a template and used to authenticate identity.

---

**Iris Scanning** The iris is the colored part of the eye surrounding the pupil. The iris has a large number of unique spots that can be captured by a camera placed 3 to 10 inches from the eye. Within a second, a special algorithm can convert the iris scan to a set of numbers. The numbers can be used to construct an iris-scan template that can be used in **iris scanning**, in which a camera scans a person's iris, compares the scan to a template, and verifies the person's identity. The chance that any two people have identical iris templates is considerably smaller than the chance that they have the same fingerprint templates. EC Application Case 1–2 (page 35) describes the use of iris recognition for passport verification.

**IRIS SCANNING:** Measurement of the unique spots in the iris (colored part of the eye), which are then converted to a set of numbers that are stored as a template and used to authenticate identity.

**Voice Scanning** Differences in the physiology of speech production from one individual to the next produce different acoustical patterns that can be converted into a template that can be used in **voice scanning**. In most voice-scanning systems, the user talks into a microphone or telephone. The word that is spoken is usually the user's system ID or password. The next time a user wants to gain access to the system, the user simply repeats the spoken word. It takes about 4 to 6 seconds to verify a voice scan. Unlike fingerprint and iris scanning, the hardware needed to capture voice input (e.g., a microphone) is inexpensive and widely available.

**VOICE SCANNING:** Measurement of the acoustical patterns in speech production, which are then converted to a set of numbers that are stored as a template and used to authenticate identity.

**Keystroke Monitoring** This biometric is still under development. **Keystroke monitoring** is based on the assumption that the way in which users type words at a keyboard varies from one user to the next. The pressure, speed, and rhythm with which a word is entered are converted through a special algorithm to a set of numbers to form a keystroke template. Again, the word that is employed in most of these systems is the user's system ID or password. When a user wants to gain access to a system, the user simply types in his or her system ID or password. The system checks the pressure, speed, and rhythm with which the word is typed against the templates in the database. The main problem with these systems is that there is still too much variability in the way an individual types from one session to the next.

**KEYSTROKE MONITORING:** Measurement of the pressure, speed, and rhythm with which a word is typed, which is then converted to a set of numbers that are stored as a template and used to authenticate identity; this biometric is still under development.

**The Biometric Consortium** The Biometric Consortium (BC) is a focal point for research and evaluation on biometric systems and applications. The consortium has over 800 government, industry, and university members and is co-chaired by the National Institute of Standards and Technology (NIST) and the National Security Agency (NSA). The BC Web site (*biometrics.org*) contains a variety of information on biometric technology, research results, federal and state applications, and other topics.

### CASE 1-2
### EC APPLICATION
#### THE EYES HAVE IT

With increasing concerns over terrorism, air safety, and fraud, the UK has begun testing biometric identification and authentication for both security and commercial purposes. In one pilot project, British Airways and Virgin Atlantic tested an iris-scanning system from EyeTicket Corporation at Heathrow Airport in London, JFK Airport in New York City, and Dulles Airport outside Washington D.C. The 6-month pilot, which occurred in 2002, was arranged by the UK's Simplifying Passenger Travel Project (SPT) of the International Air Transport Association (IATA). The major goal of the project was to determine whether iris scanning could be used with passports to speed the authentication process for international travelers entering the UK.

The two airlines chose participants from among their frequent flyer programs, focusing on passengers who made frequent trips between the United States and the UK. Potential participants registered for the program via e-mail. They were interviewed by the UK Immigration Service to ensure that there were no security issues. Approximately 900 people registered for the program.

The actual tests involved iris-scanning enrollment stations at Heathrow, JFK, and Dulles, as well as video cameras and a recognition station located at Heathrow. Passengers who participated in the program enrolled only once. This was done at the enrollment stations by taking a close up digital image of the passenger's iris. The image was then stored as a template in a computer file. When a passenger landed at Heathrow, the passenger's iris was scanned at the recognition station and compared to the stored template. If a match occurred, the passenger was allowed to pass through immigration. On average, the scan and match took about 12 seconds. If the match failed, the passenger had to move to the regular immigration line. The failure rate was only 7 percent. Watery eyes and long eyelashes were some of the major sources of failure.

According to the IATA's SPT regional group in charge of the project, the initial findings of the pilot project were encouraging. Not only did the biometric system simplify and speed the arrival process, but the system also successfully verified passengers, maintained border integrity, and was well received by the participants.

Despite the success of the pilot project, there are barriers to using the system for larger populations of passengers. One of the major barriers is the initial registration. According to the Immigration Service, the most difficult and time-consuming aspect of the pilot program was working through the processes and procedures for registration and risk assessment. As noted, the pilot only involved around 900 passengers. Obviously, it would be much more difficult to register thousands or millions of passengers. Likewise, it would be a much slower process to compare a scanned iris against thousands or millions of iris templates.

Another barrier to wider deployment is the lack of technical and procedural standards. On the technical front, there are no standards for iris scanning. The EyeTicket system is based on an iris-scanning algorithm originally created by Jeffrey Daugman, a professor at Cambridge University. Other iris enrollment and scanning devices use other algorithms. This makes it difficult to share templates across systems and across borders. There is also a need for standard procedures. Without common enrollment, authentication, and identification procedures, there is little basis for trust among different government agencies or different governments.

Even with standards, the prospects for using iris scanning or any other biometric at airports for identification are poor. In 2003, face-recognition systems at Boston's Logan Airport failed to recognize volunteers posing as terrorists 96 times during a 3-month period and incorrectly identified the innocent an equal number of times. Similar results were obtained in an earlier trial at Palm Beach International Airport, with more than 50 percent of those who should have been identified going undetected and two to three innocent passengers being flagged every hour. Such results in a larger population would bring airport security to its knees.

**SOURCES:** Emigh (2004) and Venes (2004).

### Questions

1. What were the major components in the EyeTicket iris-scanning system?
2. What are some of the difficulties in using iris scanning to verify passengers for passport control?
3. Is it reasonable to use iris scanning or any other biometric to identify terrorists at airports?

## Public Key Infrastructure

The "state of the art" in authentication rests on the **public key infrastructure (PKI)**. In this case, the something one has is not a token, but a certificate. PKI has become the cornerstone for secure e-payments. It refers to the technical components, infrastructure, and practices needed to enable the use of public key encryption, digital signatures, and digital certificates with a network application. PKI also is the foundation of a number of network applications, including SCM, VPNs, secure e-mail, and intranet applications.

---

**PUBLIC KEY INFRASTRUCTURE (PKI):** A scheme for securing e-payments using public key encryption and various technical components.

---

### *Private and Public Key Encryption*

At the heart of PKI is **encryption**. Encryption is the process of transforming or scrambling (encrypting) data in such a way that it is difficult, expensive, or time-consuming for an unauthorized person to unscramble (decrypt) it. All encryption has four basic parts (shown in Figure 1-3): **plaintext**, **ciphertext**, an **encryption algorithm**, and the **key**. The simple example in the exhibit forms the basis of an actual encryption algorithm called the *Vigenère cipher*. Of course, simple algorithms and keys of this sort are useless in the networked world. More complex encryption algorithms and keys are required.

---

**ENCRYPTION:** The process of scrambling (encrypting) a message in such a way that it is difficult, expensive, or time-consuming for an unauthorized person to unscramble (decrypt) it.
**PLAINTEXT:** An unencrypted message in human-readable form.
**CIPHERTEXT:** A plaintext message after it has been encrypted into a machine-readable form.
**ENCRYPTION ALGORITHM:** The mathematical formula used to encrypt the plaintext into the ciphertext, and vice versa.
**KEY:** The secret code used to encrypt and decrypt a message.

---

The two major classes of encryption systems are *symmetric systems*, with one secret key, and *asymmetric systems*, with two keys.

| Component | Description | Example |
|---|---|---|
| Plaintext | Original message in human-readable form | Credit Card Number 5342 8765 3652 9982 |
| Encryption algorithm | Mathematical formula or process used to encrypt/decrypt the message | Add a number (the key) to each number in the card. If the number is greater than 9, wraparound the number to the beginning (i.e., modulus arithmetic). For example, add 4 to each number so that 1 becomes 5, 9 becomes 3, etc. |
| Key | A special number passed to the algorithm to transform the message | Number to be added to original number (e.g., 4). |
| Ciphertext | Plaintext message after it has been encrypted into unreadable form | The original 5342 8765 3652 9982 becomes 9786 2109 7096 3326. |

**Figure 1-3** Encryption Components.

### *Symmetric (Private) Key System*

In a **symmetric (private) key system**, the same key is used to encrypt and decrypt the plaintext (see Figure 1-4). The sender and receiver of the text must share the same key without revealing it to anyone else—thus making it a so-called *private* system.

---

**SYMMETRIC (PRIVATE) KEY SYSTEM:** An encryption system that uses the same key to encrypt and decrypt the message.

---

For years, the **Data Encryption Standard (DES)** (itl.nist.gov/fipspubs/fip46-2.htm) was the standard symmetric encryption algorithm supported by U.S. government agencies. On October 2, 2000, the National Institute of Standards and Technology (NIST) announced that DES was being replaced by **Rijndael**, the new Advanced Encryption Standard (**csrc.nist.gov/encryption/aes**) used to secure U.S. government communications.

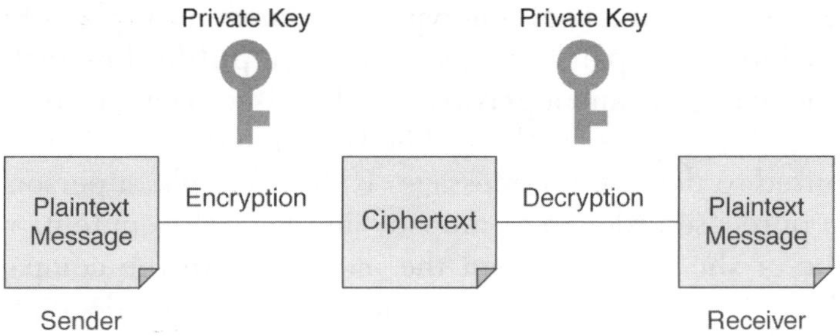


**Figure 1-4** Symmetric (Private) Key Encryption.

**DATA ENCRYPTION STANDARD (DES):** The standard symmetric encryption algorithm supported the NIST and used by U.S. government agencies until October 2, 2000.
**RIJNDAEL:** The new Advanced Encryption Standard used to secure U.S. government communications since October 2, 2000.

Because the algorithms used to encrypt a message are well known, the confidentiality of a message depends on the key. It is possible to guess a key simply by having a computer try all of the encryption combinations until the message is decrypted. High-speed and parallel-processing computers can try millions of guesses in a second. This is why the length of the key (in bits) is the main factor in securing a message. If a key were 4 bits long (e.g., 1011), there would be only 16 possible combinations (i.e., 2 raised to the 4th power). One would hardly need a computer to crack the key. Now, consider the time it would take to try all possible encryption keys. According to Howard (2000), there are over 1 trillion possible combinations in a 40-bit key—but even this number of combinations can be broken in 8 days (using a computer that can check 1.6 million keys per second) or in just 109 seconds (at 10 million keys per second). However, a 64-bit encryption key would take 58.5 years to be broken (at 10 million keys per second) (Howard 2000).

### *Public (Asymmetric) Key Encryption*

Imagine trying to use one-key encryption to buy something offered on a particular Web server. If the seller's key were distributed to thousands of buyers, then the key would not remain secret for long. This is where public key (asymmetric) encryption comes into play. **Public key encryption** uses a pair of matched keys—a **public key** that is publicly available to anyone and a **private key** that is known only to its owner. If a message is encrypted with a public key, then the associated private key is required to decrypt the message. If, for example, a person wanted to send a purchase order to a company and have the contents remain private, he or she would encrypt the message with the company's public key. When the company received the order, it would decrypt it with the associated private key.

---

**PUBLIC KEY ENCRYPTION:** Method of encryption that uses a pair of matched keys—a public key to encrypt a message and a private key to decrypt it, or vice versa.
**PUBLIC KEY:** Encryption code that is publicly available to anyone.
**PRIVATE KEY:** Encryption code that is known only to its owner.

---

The most common public key encryption algorithm is **RSA (rsa.com)**. RSA uses keys ranging in length from 512 bits to 1,024 bits. The main problem with public key encryption is speed. Symmetrical algorithms are significantly faster than asymmetric key algorithms. Therefore, public key encryption cannot be used effectively to encrypt and decrypt large amounts of data. In practice, a combination of symmetric and asymmetric encryption is used to encrypt messages.

---

**RSA:** The most common public key encryption algorithm; uses keys ranging in length from 512 bits to 1,024 bits.

---

### *Digital Signatures*

In the online world, how can one be sure that a message is actually coming from the person whom he or she thinks sent it? Similarly, how one be sure that a person cannot deny that he or she sent a particular message?

One part of the answer is a **digital signature**—the electronic equivalent of a personal signature that cannot be forged. Digital signatures are based on public keys. They can be used to authenticate the identity of the sender of a message or document. They also can be used to ensure that the original content of an electronic message or document is unchanged.

Digital signatures have additional benefits in the online world. They are portable, cannot be easily repudiated or imitated, and can be time-stamped.

---

**DIGITAL SIGNATURE:** An identifying code that can be used to authenticate the identity of the sender of a document.

---

Figure 1-5 shows how a digital signature works. Suppose a person wants to send the draft of a financial contract to a company with whom he or she plans to do business as an e-mail message. The sender wants to

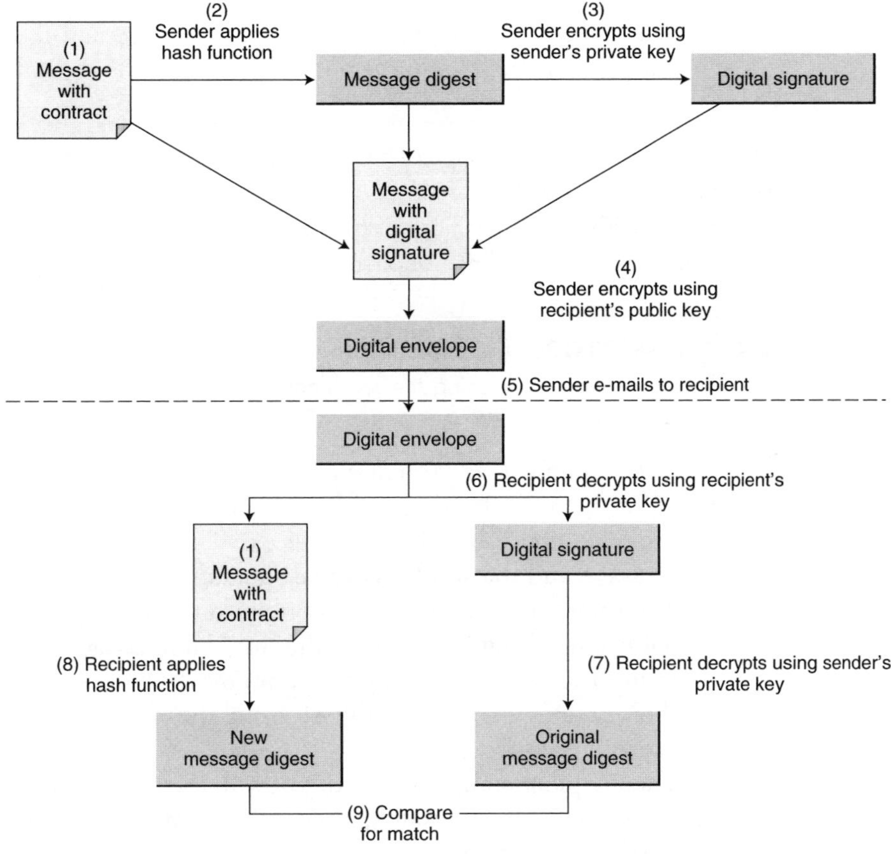


**Figure 1-5** Digital Signatures.

assure the company that the content of the draft has not been changed en route and that he or she really is the sender. To do so, the sender takes the following steps:

1. The sender creates the e-mail message with the contract in it.
2. Using special software, a mathematical computation called a **hash** function is applied to the message, which results in a special summary of the message, converted into a string of digits called a **message digest**.
3. The sender uses his or her private key to encrypt the hash. This is the sender's *digital signature*. No one else can replicate the sender's digital signature because it is based on the sender's private key.
4. The sender encrypts both the original message and the digital signature using the recipient's public key. This is the **digital envelope**.

---

**HASH:** A mathematical computation that is applied to a message, using a private key, to encrypt the message.
**MESSAGE DIGEST:** A summary of a message, converted into a string of digits, after the hash has been applied.

---

**DIGITAL ENVELOPE:** The combination of the encrypted original message and the digital signature, using the recipient's public key.

---

5. The sender e-mails the digital envelope to the receiver.
6. Upon receipt, the receiver uses his or her private key to decrypt the contents of the digital envelope. This produces a copy of the message and the sender's digital signature.
7. The receiver uses the sender's public key to decrypt the digital signature, resulting in a copy of the original message digest.
8. Using the same hash function employed in step 2, the recipient then creates a message digest from the decrypted message (as shown in Figure 1-5).
9. The recipient compares this digest with the original message digest.
10. If the two digests match, then the recipient concludes that the message is authentic.

In this scenario, the company has evidence that the sender sent the e-mail because (theoretically) the sender is the only one with access to the private key. The recipient knows that the message has not been tampered with, because if it had been the two hashes would not have matched.

According to the U.S. Federal Electronic Signatures in Global and National Commerce Act that went into effect in October 2000, digital signatures in the United States have the same legal standing as a signature written in ink on paper. Although PKI is the foundation of digital signatures, two-factor authentication is often employed to verify a person's legal identity. For example, PKI can be used with personal smart cards or biometric systems to corroborate an identity.

### *Digital Certificates and Certificate Authorities*

If one has to know someone's public key to send that person a message, where does the public key come from and how can one be sure of the person's actual identity? **Digital certificates** verify that the holder of a public and/or private key is who he or she claims to be. Third parties called **certificate authorities (CAs)** issue digital certificates. A certificate contains things such as the holder's name, validity period, public key information, and a signed hash of the certificate data (i.e., hashed contents of the certificate signed with the CA's private key). Certificates are used to authenticate Web sites (*site certificates*), individuals (*personal certificates*), and software companies (*software publisher certificates*).

---

**DIGITAL CERTIFICATE:** Verification that the holder of a public or private key is who he or she claims to be.

**CERTIFICATE AUTHORITIES (CAS):** Third parties that issue digital certificates.

---

There are a large number of third-party CAs. VeriSign (verisign.com) is the best known of the CAs. VeriSign issues three classes of certificates: Class 1 verifies that an e-mail actually comes from the user's address. Class 2 checks the user's identity against a commercial credit database. Class 3 requires notarized documents. Companies such as Microsoft offer systems that enable companies to issue their own private, in-house certificates.

### *Secure Socket Layer*

If the average user had to figure out how to use encryption, digital certificates, digital signatures, and the like, there would be few secure transactions on the Web. Fortunately, many of these issues are handled in a transparent fashion by Web browsers and Web servers. Given that different companies, financial institutions, and governments in many countries are involved in e-commerce, it is necessary to have generally accepted protocols for securing e-commerce. One of the major protocols in use today is Secure Socket Layer (SSL), also known as Transport Layer Security (TLS).

The **Secure Socket Layer (SSL)** was invented by Netscape to utilize standard certificates for authentication and data encryption to ensure privacy or confidentiality. SSL became a de facto standard adopted by the browsers and servers provided by Microsoft and Netscape. In 1996, SSL was renamed **Transport Layer Security (TLS)**, but many people still use the SSL name. It is the major standard used for online credit card payments.

---

**SECURE SOCKET LAYER (SSL):** Protocol that utilizes standard certificates for authentication and data encryption to ensure privacy or confidentiality.
**TRANSPORT LAYER SECURITY (TLS):** As of 1996, another name for the SSL protocol.

---

SSL makes it possible to encrypt credit card numbers and other transmissions between a Web server and a Web browser. In the case of credit card transactions, there is more to making a purchase on the Web than simply passing an encrypted credit card number to a merchant. The number must be checked for validity, the consumer's bank must authorize the card, and the purchase must be processed. SSL is not designed to handle any of the steps beyond the transmission of the card number.

**Review Questions**

1. What are the basic elements of an authentication system?
2. What is a passive token? An active token?
3. What are the differences between physiological and behavioral biometrics?
4. Describe some of the basic types of physiological biometrics.
5. Describe the basic components of encryption.
6. What are the key elements of PKI?
7. What are the basic differences between symmetric and asymmetric encryption?
8. Describe how a digital signature is created.
9. What is a digital certificate? What role does a certificate authority play?
10. What is the SSL protocol?

## Securing EC Networks

Several technologies exist that ensure that an organization's network boundaries are secure from cyber attack or intrusion and that if the organization's boundaries are compromised that the intrusion is detected. The selection and operation of these technologies should be based on certain design concepts, including (Thomas 2004):

- **Layered security** Relying on a single technology to thwart attacks is doomed to failure. A variety of technologies must be applied at key points in a network (see Figure 1-6). This is probably the most important concept in designing a secure system.

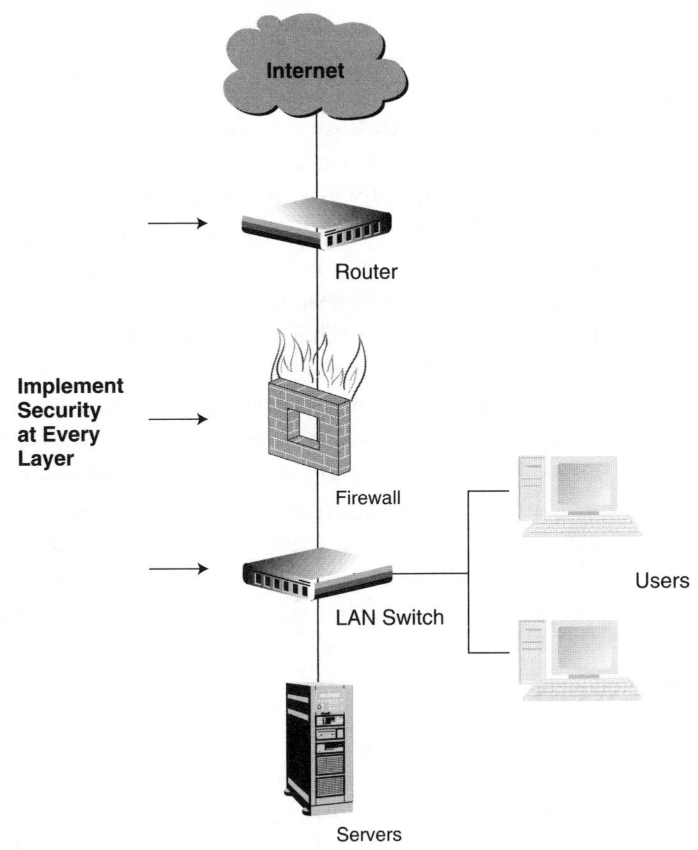


**Figure 1-6** Layered Security.

- **Controlling access** Access to a network ought to be based on the **policy of least privilege (POLP)**. By default, access to network resources should be blocked and permitted only when required to conduct business.

---

**POLICY OF LEAST PRIVILEGE (POLP):** Policy of blocking access to network resources unless access is required to conduct business.

---

- **Role-specific security** An access to particular network resources should be based on a user's role within an organization.
- **Monitoring** As a well-known infomercial says, many organizations simply "set it and forget it." More specifically, they go through the process of establishing security plans and policies, setting up security technologies, and then fail to monitor their networks to ensure that they remain secure.
- **Keep systems patched** Most large organizations are painfully aware that vendors (such as Microsoft) are continually patching or upgrading their software, applications, and systems to plug security holes. Obviously, the only way to take advantage of these fixes is to install the patches or upgrades. Newer versions of software (e.g., perating systems such as Windows XP) have automatic update functionality built in. This makes it easier for organizations and individuals to track fixes.
- **Response team** Regardless of the organization's size, there is a good chance that an organization whose networks are connected to the larger Internet will be victimized by a network security attack of some sort. For this reason, organizations need to have a team in place that can respond to these attacks. The team needs to have well-established plans, processes, and resources and should practice responding when the pressure is off rather than learning during a crisis.

## Firewalls

The term *firewall* came into use in the 1700s to describe the gaps cut into forests so that fires could be prevented from spreading to other parts of the forest (Garfinkel 2002). The term also describes a protective shield between a car engine and the interior of the car. In the world of networked computing, a **firewall** is a network node consisting of both hardware and software that isolates a private network from a public network. Hazari (2000) provides a simple analogy to understand the general operation of a firewall:

---

**FIREWALL:** A network node consisting of both hardware and software that isolates a private network from a public network.

---

> *We can think of firewalls as being similar to a bouncer in a nightclub. Like a bouncer in a nightclub, firewalls have a set of rules, similar to a guest list or a dress code, that determine if the data should be allowed entry. Just as the bouncer places himself at the door of the club, the firewall is located at the point of entry where data attempts to enter the computer from the Internet. But, just as different nightclubs might have different rules for entry, different firewalls have different methods of inspecting data for acceptance or rejection.*

Some firewalls filter data and requests moving from the public Internet to a private network based on the network addresses of the computer sending or receiving the request. These firewalls are called **packet-filtering routers**. On the Internet, the data and requests sent from one computer to another are broken into segments called **packets**. Each packet contains the Internet address of the computer sending the data, as well as the Internet address of the computer receiving the data. Packets also contain other identifying information that can be used to distinguish one packet from another. **Packet filters** are rules that can accept or reject incoming packets based on source and destination addresses and the other identifying information. Some simple examples of packet filters include the following:

---

**PACKET-FILTERING ROUTERS:** Firewalls that filter data and requests moving from the public Internet to a private network based on the network addresses of the computer sending or receiving the request.
**PACKETS:** Segments of data and requests sent from one computer to another on the Internet; consist of the Internet addresses of the computers sending and receiving the data, plus other identifying information that distinguish one packet from another.
**PACKET FILTERS:** Rules that can accept or reject incoming packets based on source and destination addresses and the other identifying information.

---

- **Block all packets sent from a given Internet address** Companies sometimes use this to block requests from computers owned by competitors.
- **Block any packet coming from the outside that has the address of a computer on the inside** Companies use this type of rule to block requests where an intruder is using his or her computer to impersonate a computer that belongs to the company.

However, packet filters do have their disadvantages. In setting up the rules, an administrator might miss some important rules or incorrectly specify a rule, thus leaving a hole in the firewall. Additionally, because the content of a packet is irrelevant to a packet filter, once a packet is let through the firewall, the inside network is open to data-driven attacks. That is, the data may contain hidden instructions that cause the receiving computer to modify access control or security-related files.

Packet-filtering routers often are used as the first layer of network defense. Other firewalls form the second layer. These later firewalls block data and requests depending on the type of application being accessed. For instance, a firewall may permit requests for Web pages to move from the public Internet to the private network. This type of firewall is called an **application-level proxy**. In an application-level proxy, there is often a special server called a **bastion gateway**. The bastion gateway server has two network cards so that data packets reaching one card are not relayed to the other card (see Figure 1-7). Instead, special software programs called **proxies** run on the bastion gateway server and pass repackaged packets from one network to the other. Each Internet service that an organization wishes to support has a proxy. For instance, there is a Web (i.e., HTTP) proxy, a file transfer (FTP) proxy, and so on. Special proxies also can be established to allow business partners, for example, to access particular applications running inside the firewall. If a request is made for an unsupported proxy service, then it is blocked by the firewall.

---

**APPLICATION-LEVEL PROXY:** A firewall that permits requests for Web pages to move from the public Internet to the private network.

**BASTION GATEWAY:** A special hardware server that utilizes application-level proxy software to limit the types of requests that can be passed to an organization's internal networks from the public Internet.

**PROXIES:** Special software programs that run on the gateway server and pass repackaged packets from one network to the other.

---

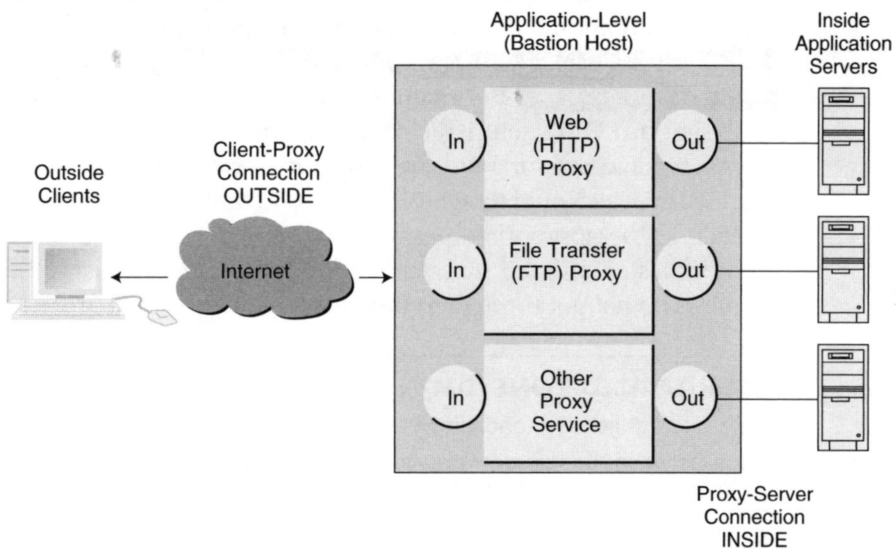


**Figure 1-7** Application-Level Proxy (Bastion Gateway Host).

In addition to controlling inbound traffic, the firewall and proxies control outbound traffic. All outbound traffic requests are first sent to the proxy server and then forwarded by the proxy on behalf of the computers behind the firewall. This makes all the requests look as if they were coming from a single computer rather than multiple computers. In this way, the Internet addresses of the internal computers are hidden to the outside.

One disadvantage of an application-level proxy firewall is performance degradation. It takes more processing time to tie particular packets to particular applications. Another disadvantage is that the users on the internal network must configure their machines or browsers to send their Internet requests via the proxy server.

Firewall systems can be created from scratch. However, most companies rely on commercial firewall systems. ConsumerSearch.com provides a review of a number of commercial firewall products (`consumersearch.com/www/index.html`).

## Demilitarized Zone

The term **demilitarized zone (DMZ)** often is used to describe a buffer area between two enemies, such as the DMZ between North Korea and South

Korea. In computer security terms, a DMZ is a network area that sits between an organization's internal network and an external network (Internet), providing physical isolation between the two networks that is controlled by rules enforced by a firewall. For example, suppose a company wants to run its own Web site. In a DMZ setup, the company would put the Web server on a publicly accessible network and the rest of its servers on a private internal network. A firewall would then be configured to direct requests coming from the outside to the appropriate network and servers. In most cases, the internal network also is fronted by a second firewall to doubly ensure that intrusive requests do not get through to the private network (see Figure 1-8).

**DEMILITARIZED ZONE (DMZ):** Network area that sits between an organization's internal network and an external network (Internet), providing physical isolation between the two networks that is controlled by rules enforced by a firewall.

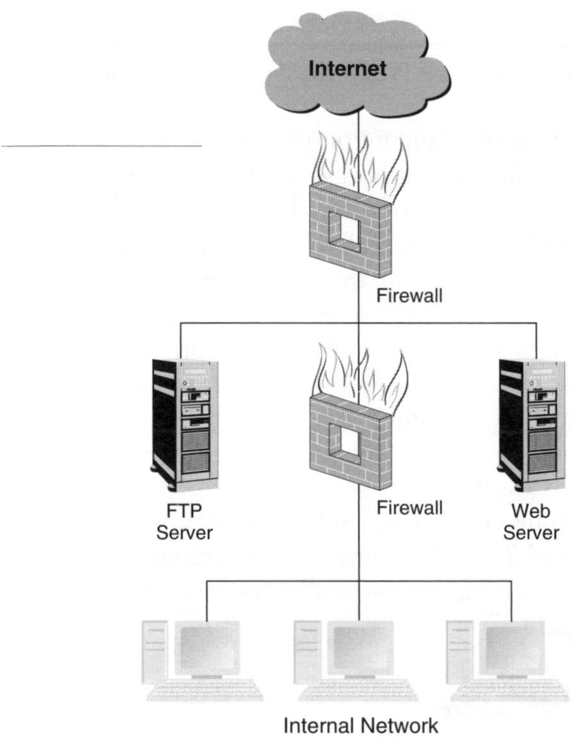


**Figure 1-8** Demilitarized Zone (DMZ).

## Personal Firewalls

In recent years, the number of individuals with high-speed broadband (cable modem or digital subscriber lines [DSL]) Internet connections to their homes or small businesses has increased. These "always-on" connections are much more vulnerable to attack than simple dial-up connections. With these connections, the homeowner or small business owner runs the risks of information being stolen or destroyed, of sensitive information (e.g., personal or business financial information) being accessed, and of the computer being used in a DoS attack on others.

**Personal firewalls** are designed to protect desktop systems by monitoring all the traffic that passes through the computer's network interface card. They operate in one of two ways. With the first method, the owner can create filtering rules (much like packet filtering) that are used by the firewall to permit or delete packets. With the other method, the firewall can learn, by asking the user questions, how particular traffic ought to be handled. A number of personal firewall products are on the market, including the highly rated Norton Personal Firewall from Symantec (`symantec.com`) and ZoneAlarm firewall from Check Point (`checkpoint.com`). For a detailed comparison of a number of these products, see `firewallguide.com/software.htm`.

---

**PERSONAL FIREWALL:** A network node designed to protect an individual user's desktop system from the public network by monitoring all the traffic that passes through the computer's network interface card.

---

## VPNs

Suppose a company wants to establish a B2B application, providing suppliers, partners, and others access not only to data residing on its internal Web site, but also to data contained in other files (e.g., Word documents) or in legacy systems (e.g., large relational databases). Traditionally, communications with the company would have taken place over a private leased line or through a dial-up line to a bank of modems or a remote access server (RAS) that provided direct connections to the company's LAN. With a private line, the chances of a hacker eavesdropping on the communications between the companies would be nil, but it is an expensive way to do business.

A less expensive alternative would be to use a **virtual private network (VPN)**. A VPN uses the public Internet to carry information but remains private by using a combination of encryption to scramble the communications, authentication to ensure that the information has not been tampered with and comes from a legitimate source, and access control to verify the identity of anyone using the network. In addition, a VPN can also be used to support site-to-site communications between branch offices and corporate headquarters and the communications between mobile workers and their workplace.

---

**VIRTUAL PRIVATE NETWORK (VPN):** A network that uses the public Internet to carry information but remains private by using encryption to scramble the communications, authentication to ensure that information has not been tampered with, and access control to verify the identity of anyone using the network.

---

VPNs can reduce communication costs dramatically. The reduced costs come about because VPN equipment is cheaper than other remote solutions, private leased lines are no longer needed to support remote access, remote users can place local calls or use cable or DSL lines rather than long distance or international calls to access an organization's private network, and a single access line can be used to support multiple purposes. The estimated cost savings for site-to-site networks is 20 to 40 percent for sites in the same country and 60 to 90 percent if they are in different countries (NetGear 2002). The savings for mobile and remote workers is estimated at 60 to 80 percent (Prometheum Technologies 2003).

The main technical challenge of a VPN is to ensure the confidentiality and integrity of the data transmitted over the Internet. This is where **protocol tunneling** comes into play. With protocol tunneling, data packets are first encrypted and then encapsulated into packets that can be transmitted across the Internet. The packets are decrypted at the destination address by a special host or router.

---

**PROTOCOL TUNNELING:** Method used to ensure confidentiality and integrity of data transmitted over the Internet, by encrypting data packets, sending them in packets across the Internet, and decrypting them at the destination address.

---

Three technologies can be used to create a VPN. First, many of the firewall packages—hardware and software—provide VPN functionality.

Second, routers (i.e., special network components for controlling communications) cannot only function as firewalls, but they also can function as VPN servers. Finally, software solutions are available that can be used to handle VPN connections. The VPN Consortium (`vpnc.org/vpnc-features-chart.html`) provides a comparison of a number of commercial VPN products.

Many telecommunications carriers and larger ISPs offer VPN services for Internet-based dial-up and site-to-site communications. These carriers use their own private network backbones to which they have added security features, intranet connectivity, and new dial-up capabilities for remote services. Two of the carriers providing these services are AT&T VPN Services (`att.com`) and Cable & Wireless IP-VPN Internet (`cw.com`).

## Intrusion Detection Systems

Even if an organization has a well-formulated security policy and a number of security technologies in place, it still is vulnerable to attack. For example, most organizations have antivirus software, yet most are subjected to virus attacks. This is why an organization must continually watch for attempted, as well as actual, security breaches.

In the past, *audit logs,* which are produced by a variety of system components and applications, were manually reviewed for excessive failed log-on attempts, failed file and database access attempts, and other application and system violations. Obviously, this manual procedure had its flaws. For example, if intrusion attempts were spread out over a long period of time, they could be easily missed. Today, a special category of software exists that can monitor activity across a network or on a host computer, watch for suspicious activity, and take automated action based on what it sees. This category of software is called **intrusion detection systems (IDSs)**.

---

**INTRUSION DETECTION SYSTEMS (IDSS):** A special category of software that can monitor activity across a network or on a host computer, watch for suspicious activity, and take automated action based on what it sees.

---

IDSs are either host based or network based. A *host-based IDS* resides on the server or other host system that is being monitored. Host-based systems are particularly good at detecting whether critical or security-related files have been tampered with or whether a user has attempted to access files that he or she is not authorized to use. The host-based system does this by computing a special signature or check-sum for each file. The IDS checks files on a regular basis to see if the current signatures match the previous signatures. If the signatures do not match, security personnel are notified immediately. Some examples of commercial host-based systems are Symantec's Intruder Alert (`symantec.com`), Tripwire Security's Tripwire (`tripwiresecurity.com`), and McAfee's Entercept Desktop and Server Agents (`mcafee.com`).

A *network-based IDS* uses rules to analyze suspicious activity at the perimeter of a network or at key locations in the network. It usually consists of a monitor—a software package that scans the network—and software agents that reside on various host computers and feed information back to the monitor. This type of IDS examines network traffic (i.e., packets) for known patterns of attack and automatically notifies security personnel when specific events or event thresholds occur. A network-based IDS also can perform certain actions when an attack occurs. For instance, it can terminate network connections or reconfigure network devices, such as firewalls and routers, based on security policies. Cisco Systems' NetRanger (`cisco.com`) and Computer Associates' eTrust Intrusion Detection (`www3.ca.com/solutions/product.asp?id=163`) both are examples of commercially available network-based IDSs.

## Honeynets and Honeypots

Honeynets are another technology that can be used to detect and analyze intrusions. A **honeynet** is a network of honeypots designed to attract hackers like honey attracts bees. In this case, the **honeypots** are information system resources—firewalls, routers, Web servers, database servers, files, and the like—that are made to look like production systems but do no real work. The main difference between a honeypot and the real thing is that the activities on a honeypot come from intruders attempting to compromise the system. In this way, researchers watching the honeynet can gather information about why hackers attack, when they attack, how they attack, what they do after the system is compromised, and how they communicate with one another during and after the attack.

---

**HONEYNET:** A way to evaluate vulnerabilities of an organization by studying the types of attacks to which a site is subjected using a network of systems called *honeypots*.

**HONEYPOTS:** Production systems (e.g., firewalls, routers, Web servers, database servers) designed to do real work but that are watched and studied as network intrusions occur.

Honeynets and honeypots originated in April 1999 with the Honeynet Project (Honeynet 2004). The Honeynet Project is a worldwide, not-for-profit research group of security professionals. The group focuses on raising awareness of security risks that confront any system connected to the Internet and teaching and informing the security community about better ways to secure and defend network resources. The project runs its own honeynets, but makes no attempt to attract hackers. They simply connect the honeypots to the Internet and wait for attacks to occur.

The Honeynet Project was divided into four phases. The first three are complete. The goal of the current phase, which runs from 2004 to 2005, is to create a centralized system that can collect and correlate data from distributed honeynets.

With the Honeynet Project, honeypots are used for research. Honeypots also can be used in production systems to mitigate security risks. An organization does this simply by adding a honeypot to its existing network. Although a honeypot cannot prevent an attack, it can simplify the detection and reaction to an attack. Because the only traffic on a honeypot comes from intruders, it is easier to analyze the data produced by a honeypot (e.g., log files of system activity) to determine what is happening and how to respond. Honeypots can be built from scratch or commercial or open source versions can be used. Back Officer Friendly (`nfr.com/resource/back officer.php`), Specter (`specter.com/default50.htm`), Honeyd (`honeyd.org`), and Decoy Server (`enterprisesecurity.symantec.com/products/products.cfm?productid=157`) are examples of commercial or open source systems.

Before a company deploys a honeynet, it needs to think about what it will do when it becomes the scene of a cyber crime or contains evidence of a crime and about the legal restrictions and ramifications of monitoring legal and illegal activity. These issues are discussed in EC Application Case 1-3.

**Review Questions**

1. List the basic types of firewalls and briefly describe each.
2. What is a personal firewall?
3. How does a VPN work?
4. Briefly describe the major types of IDSs.
5. What is a honeynet? What is a honeypot?

## CASE 1-3
## EC APPLICATION

### HONEYNETS AND THE LAW

Millions of networks and computers are on the Internet. Given this, what is the chance that a small collection of computers connected to the Internet will be victimized by an outside intruder? In the first phase of the Honeynet Project, which ran from 1999 to 2001, the honeynet consisted of eight honeypots that were designed to mimic a typical home computer setup. Within 15 minutes of being connected to the Internet, one of the honeypots was hit. Over the course of the next few days, all of the honeypots were compromised, and over the course of the next 2 years they were attacked repeatedly.

During the first phase, many of the attacks were crude and fairly innocuous. Today, the character of both the intrusions and the intruders has changed. The proportion of hackers involved in illegal activities of all sorts has risen dramatically. If a company deploys a honeynet, there is a good chance that it will be the scene of a cyber crime or contain evidence of a crime. Some intruders may be focused solely on attacking the honeynet itself. Others may want to use it as a zombie for launching attacks, as a place to store stolen credit cards, or as a server to distribute pirated software or child pornography. Regardless, companies need to understand the types of crimes that may occur and the legal issues that may ensue if they choose to either report or ignore these crimes. Just because the activities on a honeynet are perpetrated by intruders, it does not mean that the operator has unlimited rights to monitor the users of the network.

Although many crimes can be perpetrated against or with a honeynet, the most frequent and obvious crime is network intrusion. In the United States, the federal Computer Fraud and Abuse Act, passed in 1986 and later amended in 1996, covers most computer network crimes. In addition, a number of state laws outlaw unauthorized access and damage to computers or networks. The Computer Fraud and Abuse Act makes it a crime to attack "protected computers," including computers "used in interstate or foreign commerce or communication." If a computer is on the Internet, it is used in interstate communication. All government computers and those used by banks and financial institutions also are protected. This means that most honeynets are going to be protected by the Act.

The Act also defines the types of attacks that constitute a crime. It is a felony if an attacker "knowingly causes the transmission of a program, information, code, or command, and as a result of such conduct, intentionally causes damage without authorization, to a protected computer." Damage occurs when there is "any impairment to the integrity or availability of data, a program, a system or information." The limitations are that in order for an attack to be a felony, one or more of the following must result: aggregate damage of at least $5,000; modification or impairment to the medical examination, diagnosis, treatment, or care of one or more individuals; physical injury to a person; a threat to public health or safety; or damage to a government computer used for the administration of justice, national defense, or national security. Under these provisions, the Act covers a wide range of activities, including:

- Denial-of-service attacks, viruses, and worms
- Simple intrusions in which the attacker causes damage
- Unauthorized information gathering, especially if the information is used for commercial advantage, financial gain, in furtherance of another crime, or the information is worth more than $5,000
- Unauthorized access to nonpublic U.S. government computers
- Using computers to obtain classified information without authorization
- Computer-related espionage, which may also constitute terrorism
- Trafficking in passwords
- Threatening to damage a computer
- Attempting to commit a network crime, even though the crime was never consummated

In running a honeynet, a company needs to be careful to ensure that it is not facilitating or helping further a crime. Precautions and actions must be taken to prevent potential or actual criminal activity from harming others; to inform authorities when criminal activities or evidence comes to light; and to ensure that the data, code, programs, and systems running on the honeynet are legal (e.g., do not store contraband on the system in an effort to trap an intruder).

The primary purpose of a commercial honeynet is to monitor and analyze intrusion and attacks. Under certain circumstances, the monitoring of these activities may constitute a criminal or civil action. In the United States, the federal Wiretap Act and the Pen Register, Trap, and Trace Devices statute place legal limits on monitoring activity. The Wiretap Act makes it illegal to intercept the contents of a communication. If intruders cannot store (either directly or indirectly) data or information on a honeynet, then the Act does not apply. If they can, then there are exceptions to the rule. For instance, if the monitoring is done to prevent abuse or damage to the system, then monitoring it is not illegal. The implication is that certain honeynet purposes and configurations are illegal and others are not.

In contrast to the Wiretap Act, the federal Pen Register, Trap, and Trace Devices statute applies to the "noncontent" aspects of a communication. For example, with telephones, telephone numbers are "noncontent." Similarly, in a network communication, network addresses are "noncontent." This statute makes it illegal to capture the noncontent information of a communication, unless certain exceptions apply. The exceptions pertain primarily to actions that are taken by the communication provider (in this case the honeynet operator) to protect its rights or property. Again, certain honeynet purposes and configurations are legal and others are not.

When a company monitors the network activities of insiders and outsiders, a number of legal issues arise. Because monitoring is one of the primary activities of a honeynet, a company should consult legal counsel before a honeynet is deployed and become familiar with local law enforcement agencies that should be involved if illegal activities are observed.

**SOURCE:** Honeynet Project (2004).

**QUESTIONS**

1. What constitutes a crime under the Computer Fraud and Abuse Act?
2. What types of activities are prohibited by the Computer Fraud and Abuse Act?
3. What types of activities are illegal under the federal Wiretap Act? The Pen Register, Trap, and Trace Devices statute?

## MANAGERIAL ISSUES

Some managerial issues related to this chapter are as follows.

1. **Have we budgeted enough for security?** If one asked the senior management of the *Fortune* 500 corporations whether they take network security seriously, they would certainly answer with a resounding, "Yes." Yet, in spite of this answer, most of these organizations spend only a small percentage of their budgets on network security, have fairly small staffs working on network security issues, and generally relegate network security matters to personnel on lower rungs on the organizational ladder. Because the consequences of poor network security can be severe, it is imperative that senior management have a basic understanding of best practices in network risk management.
2. **What are the business consequences of poor security?** Ineffective security opens the door to computer and network attacks that can result in damage to technical and information assets; theft of information and information services; temporary

loss of a Web site and Internet access; loss of income; litigation brought on by dissatisfied organizational stakeholders; loss of customer confidence; and damaged reputation and credibility. In some cases, attacks literally can put a company out of business, especially if EC is its sole source of revenue.

3. **Which e-commerce sites are vulnerable to attack?** Suppose you decide to set up a B2B site in order to service your suppliers and partners. Because it is not a public site, the only ones who are likely to know of its existence are you, your suppliers, and your partners. You assume that there is no need to institute strong security measures. Wrong! Because of the prevalence of automated scanning tools, it will be only a matter of days before hackers discover your site. Once discovered, it will be only a matter of hours or minutes before the hackers have compromised your site and taken control if your system has known vulnerabilities. Regardless of how obscure, uninteresting, or unadvertised a site is, no EC site can afford to take security for granted. All sites should thoroughly review their security requirements and institute stringent measures to guard against high-priority threats.
4. **What is the key to establishing strong e-commerce security?** Most discussions about security focus on technology. One hears statements like "firewalls are mandatory" or "all transmissions should be encrypted." Although firewalls and encryption can be important technologies, no security solution is useful unless it solves a business problem. Determining your business requirements is the most important step in creating a security solution. Business requirements, in turn, determine your information requirements. Once your information requirements are known, you can begin to understand the value of those assets and the steps that should be taken to secure those that are most valuable and vulnerable.
5. **What steps should businesses follow in establishing a security plan?** Security risk management is an ongoing process involving three phases: asset identification, risk assessment, and implementation. By actively monitoring existing security policies and measures, companies can determine which are successful or unsuccessful and, in turn, which should be modified or eliminated. However, it also is important to monitor changes in business requirements, changes in technology and the way it is used, and changes in the way people can attack the systems and networks. In this way, an organization can evolve its security policies and measures, ensuring that they continue to support the critical needs of the business.
6. **Should organizations be concerned with internal security threats?** Except for viruses and worms, breaches perpetrated by insiders are much more frequent than those perpetrated by outsiders. This is true for both B2C and B2B sites. Security policies and measures for EC sites need to address these insider threats.

## RESEARCH TOPICS

Here are some suggested topics related to this chapter.

1. **Certification Programs**
   - Limitations on the use of digital certificates
   - Certification programs that ensure trust, privacy, and safety
   - Effectiveness of certification programs in enhancing security
   - Evaluation factors for certification
   - International certification programs for secure international trades
2. **Risk Perception and the Adoption of Security Measures**
   - Customers' perceptions of risk in e-commerce and e-payment
   - Impact of consumers' perceptions of risk in conducting EC transactions
   - Inhibitors of security measure adoption
   - Relationship between a corporation's risk management system and their overall values
   - Reducing operational risk to cope with the BASEL II Accord
3. **EC Security Technologies**
   - The application of biometric technologies to authentication
   - Customer preferences for authentication schemes
   - Intelligent detection of criminal patterns on the Internet
4. **Secure Electronic Payment Protocols**
   - Protocols that avoid the disclosure of customers' bank and credit account information to merchants
   - Comparative evaluation of protocols
   - Problems with adopting the Secure Electronic Transaction (SET) protocol
5. **Design of Secure E-Commerce Sites**
   - Framework for designing secure e-commerce sites
   - Risk assessment of e-commerce sites
   - Cost and benefit of security systems for e-commerce
6. **Study Security Violation Cases and Lessons to Avoid Mistakes**
   - Cases concerning disasters caused by violated security
   - Measurements taken and studied after the violation
   - Protection schemes before the crucial violation
   - Security ethics
   - Effect of codes of conduct and certificates

## Summary

In this chapter, you learned about the following EC issues as they relate to the learning objectives.

1. **Trends in computer attacks** Recent surveys of trends in computer and network attacks offer a mixed picture. Computer and network security attacks are on the rise. Data collected by the Computer Security Institute (CSI) and the FBI indicate that the number of security incidents has steadily declined over the past couple of years. In contrast, survey results from the Computer Emergency Response Team (CERT) and *CSO Magazine* indicate that there has been a substantial increase in the incidence of e-crime. Although the results of the two surveys differ substantially, both indicate that computer and network attacks are still a substantial problem that can result in sizeable economic losses.
2. **Security is everyone's business** Because the Internet serves as the control system for many of the critical infrastructures in the United States, the coordination of efforts to secure cyberspace now falls to the Department of Homeland Security (DHS). The DHS aims to build a security response system, reduce security threats and vulnerabilities, build awareness of security issues, secure government cyberspace, and encourage international cooperation on security issues. Accomplishing these diverse aims is a complex task requiring action at multiple levels, including home users and small businesses, large enterprises, critical sectors and infrastructure, and national and international agencies.
3. **Basic security issues** The owners of EC sites need to be concerned with a variety of security issues: authentication, verifying the identity of the participants in a transaction; authorization, ensuring that a person or process has access rights to particular systems or data; auditing, being able to determine whether particular actions have been taken and by whom; confidentiality, ensuring that information is not disclosed to unauthorized individuals, systems, or processes; integrity, protecting data from being altered or destroyed; availability, ensuring that data and services are available when needed; and nonrepudiation, the ability to limit parties from refuting that a legitimate transaction took place.

4. **Basic types of network security attacks** EC sites are exposed to a wide range of attacks. Attacks may be nontechnical (social engineering), in which a perpetrator tricks people into revealing information or performing actions that compromise network security. Or they may be technical, whereby software and systems expertise are used to attack the network. DoS and DDoS attacks bring operations to a halt by sending floods of data to target computers or to as many computers on the Internet as possible. Malicious code attacks include viruses, worms, Trojan horses, or some combination of these. Over the past couple of years, various trends in malicious code have emerged, including an increase in the speed and volume of attacks; reduced time between the discovery of a vulnerability and the release of an attack to exploit the vulnerability; the growing use of bots to launch attacks; an increase in attacks on Web applications; and a shift in motivation behind attacks toward illicit financial gain.
5. **Managing EC security** Even with increased awareness of security issues, organizations continue to be reactive in their security practices, with little understanding of their information assets or security needs. A systematic security risk management approach must be adopted to address these needs. This approach involves three phases: identification and valuation of key computer and network assets; assessment of the security threats, vulnerabilities and risks associated with those assets; and the selection, evaluation, and implementation of a set of security policies and measures to reduce high-priority threats, vulnerabilities, and risks.
6. **Securing EC communications** In EC, issues of trust are paramount. Trust starts with the authentication of the parties involved in a transaction; that is, identifying the parties in a transaction along with the actions they can perform. Authentication can be established with something one knows (e.g., a password), something one has (e.g., a token), or something one is (e.g., a fingerprint). Biometric systems can be used to confirm a person's identity. Fingerprint scanners, iris scanners, facial recognition, and voice recognition are examples of biometric systems. Public key infrastructure (PKI), which is the cornerstone of secure e-payments, also can be used to authenticate the parties in a transaction. PKI uses encryption (private and public) to ensure privacy and integrity and digital signatures to ensure authenticity and nonrepudiation. Digital signatures

are themselves authenticated through a system of digital certificates issued by certificate authorities (CAs). For the average consumer and merchant, PKI is simplified because it is built into Web browsers and services. Such tools are secure because security is based on SSL (TSL) communications.

7. **Technologies for securing networks** At EC sites, firewalls, VPNs, and IDSs have proven extremely useful. Honeynets and honeypots also are being employed to detect and analyze intrusions. A firewall is a combination of hardware and software that isolates a private network from a public network. Firewalls are of two general types—packet-filtering routers or application-level proxies. A packet-filtering router uses a set of rules to determine which communication packets can move from the outside network to the inside network. An application-level proxy is a firewall that accepts requests from the outside and repackages a request before sending it to the inside network, thus ensuring the security of the request. Personal firewalls are needed by individuals with broadband access. VPNs are generally used to support secure site-to-site transmissions across the Internet between B2B partners or communications between a mobile and remote worker and a LAN at a central office. IDSs are used to monitor activity across a network or on a host. The systems watch for suspicious activity and take automated actions whenever a security breach or attack occurs. In the same vein, honeynets and honeypots are being installed at some companies in an effort to gather information on intrusions and to analyze the types and methods of attacks being perpetrated.

## Key Terms

| Term | Page |
|---|---|
| Access control | 30 |
| Active tokens | 31 |
| Application-level proxy | 48 |
| Auditing | 10 |
| Authentication | 9 |
| Authorization | 10 |
| Bastion gateway | 48 |
| Behavioral biometrics | 33 |
| Biometric systems | 32 |
| Certificate authorities (CAs) | 43 |
| Ciphertext | 37 |
| Common (security) vulnerabilities and exposures (CVEs) | 16 |
| Computer Emergency Response Team (CERT) | 5 |
| Computer Security Institute (CSI) | 4 |
| Confidentiality | 11 |

## Questions For Discussion

1. Survey results on the incidence of cyber attacks paint a mixed picture; some surveys show increases, others show decreases. What factors could account for the differences in the results?
2. Pretend that you are a hacker who would like to trick people into giving you their user IDs and passwords to their Amazon.com accounts. What are some of the ways that this might be accomplished?

3. B2C EC sites continue to experience DDoS attacks. How are these attacks perpetrated? Why is it so difficult to safeguard against them? What are some of the things a site can do to mitigate such attacks?
4. All EC sites share common security threats and vulnerabilities. Discuss these threats and vulnerabilities and some of the security policies that can be implemented to mitigate them. Do you think that B2C Web sites face different threats and vulnerabilities than B2B sites? Explain.
5. Based on the results of the AOL/NCSA in-home study of computer security, what advice would you give to home owners about securing their computers?
6. A business wants to share its customer account database with its trading partners and customers, while at the same time providing prospective buyers with access to marketing materials on its Web site. Assuming that the business is responsible for running all of these network components, what types of security components (e.g., firewalls, VPNs, etc.) could be used to ensure that the partners and customers have access to the account information and others do not? What type of network configuration (e.g., bastion gateway server) will provide the appropriate security?
7. A company is having problems with its password security systems and decides to implement two-factor authentication. What biometric alternatives could the company employ? What are some of the factors it should consider when deciding among the alternatives?
8. A company has decided to set up a honeynet to monitor attacks against its networks and servers. To make the honeynet more attractive, the company decides to put a customer mailing list on a Web server located on the honeynet. By doing this, what legal issues will the company encounter? What if the company did not use the customer mailing list, would the honeynet still be legal? Explain.

## Internet Exercises

1. Dan Verton's book *Black Ice: The Invisible Threat of Cyber-Terrorism* argues that it is possible for terrorists to attack the U.S. infrastructure (e.g., power grid, banks, air traffic control, etc.) through the Internet. Using online reviews of Verton's book, determine the arguments for and against his claim.

2. The Computer Vulnerabilities and Exposures Board (`cve.mitre.org`) maintains a list of common network security vulnerabilities. Review the list. How many vulnerabilities are there? Based on the list, which system components appear to be most vulnerable to attack? What impact do these vulnerable components have on EC?
3. Your B2C site has just been hacked. You would like to report the incident to the Computer Emergency Response Team (`cert.org`) at Carnegie Mellon University so that they can alert other sites. How do you do this and what types of information do you have to provide?
4. McAfee's AVERT maintains a running list of the top malware threats on the Internet (`vil.nai.com`). Select one of the specific threats on the list. Using other online materials, describe the threat and the steps that can be and have been used to combat it.
5. ICSA Labs (`icsalabs.com/html/communities/firewalls/newsite/cert2.shtml`) provides a detailed list of firewall products for corporate, small business, and residential use. Select three corporate firewall products from the list. Using online materials, research and compare the benefits of each product. Based on the comparison, which product would you choose and why?
6. Select a single type of physiological biometric system. Using the Internet, identify at least two commercial vendors offering these systems. Based on the materials you have gathered, what are the major features of the systems. Which of the systems would you select and why?
7. *The National Strategy to Secure Cyberspace* provides a series of actions and recommendations for each of its five national priorities. Obtain a copy of the strategy online. Selecting one of the priorities, discuss in detail the actions and recommendations for that priority.
8. The AOL/NCSA survey (`staysafeonline.info/news/safety_study_v04.pdf`) of in-home computer security dealt with the presence and problems of spyware and file-sharing software. Obtain a copy of the survey. Summarize their key findings with respect to these two classes of software.
9. The *Symantec Internet Security Threat Report* provides details about the trends in attacks and vulnerabilities in Internet security. Obtain a copy of the report and summarize the major findings of the report for both attacks and vulnerabilities.

## Team Assignments and Role Playing

1. At least six motives have been identified that explain why hackers do what they do. These motives are money, entertainment, ego, cause, entrance to social groups, and status. Using the Web as your primary data source, have each team member explore one or more of these motives. Each member should describe the motive in detail, determine how widespread the motive is, the types of attacks that the motive encourages, and the types of actions that can be taken to combat the associated attacks.
2. Several personal firewall products are available. A list of these products can be found at `firewallguide.com/software.htm`. Assign each team three products from the list. Each team should prepare a detailed review and comparison of each of the products they have been assigned.
3. Assign each team member a different B2C or B2B Web site. Have each team prepare a report summarizing the site's security assets, threats, and vulnerabilities. Prepare a brief security-risk-management plan for the site.

### REAL-WORLD CASE
### DO I REALLY NEED THIS?

The Internet Security Alliance (ISAlliance; *isalliance.org*) was formed in April 2001. The ISAlliance is a collaborative endeavor of Carnegie Mellon CERT Coordination Center (CERT/CC); the Electronics Industries Alliance (EIA), a federation of trade groups; and other private and public member organizations and corporations. Its goal is to provide information sharing and leadership on information security and to represent its members and the larger security community before legislators and regulators. In the group's own words, it is not a policy shop. Instead, it is interested in practical methods to achieve pragmatic behavioral change resulting in improved security.

For the past few years, the focus of the ISAlliance has been on larger enterprises. Based on information gathered from the daily operations of CERT/CC, the ISAlliance prepared a best practices manual for top executives in July 2002—"A Common Sense Guide for Senior Managers." The advice provided in that manual is discussed in Online File W11.5. The manual became part of *The National Strategy to Secure Cyberspace* (2003), which was referenced in Section "Security is everyone's Bussiness". At the end of 2003, the ISAlliance was asked by the National Cyber Security Summit to produce a similar guide for small businesses.

The ISAlliance's security guide for small businesses (ISAlliance 2004) opens with the statement, "I'm very busy; do I really need this?" Although large businesses have more to lose in absolute terms, attacks on a small business are more likely and can be devastating. For example, a survey of the spread of the MyDoom virus noted that one in three small businesses was hit by the virus, which was twice the rate for large businesses. Although the dollar value of an attack on a large business can be huge, a major attack can potentially put a small firm out of business because of the smaller margins on which it operates. It is not the size of the business that makes one organization more vulnerable than another; it is the lack of protection that makes them a target. These days, larger businesses are likely to employ risk management and other best security practices. Because of costs, lack of expertise, time constraints, and other business factors, many small businesses have virtually ignored security altogether.

In constructing the best practices guide for small businesses, the ISAlliance felt that a different approach had to be taken. Small business owners are aware of the security threats that exist. Yet, they persist in doing nothing. Given this fact, the ISAlliance utilized input from 10 focus groups, involving 100 small business owners, to construct the guidelines. The focus groups revealed that small businesses:

- Were sympathetic to national security needs, but were not going to take the time and expense to improve their network security based on common appeals
- Were not intimately familiar with computer security technology
- Had unrealistic expectations that they would not be victimized because they were too small or because they had taken elementary steps to protect their systems
- Saw security materials as too technical and hard to follow, even if they were favorably disposed to institute stricter security measures
- Needed more than information for any program to have a lasting effect on behaviors

Based on the focus group input and revelations, the ISAlliance came up with a "12 Step Program" for improving and maintaining cyber security for small businesses. The steps include:

1. Use strong passwords and change them regularly.
2. Look out for e-mail attachments and Internet download modules.
3. Install, maintain, and apply antivirus programs.

4. Install and use a firewall.
5. Remove unused software and user accounts; clean out everything on replaced equipment.
6. Establish physical access controls for all computer equipment.
7. Create backups for important files, folders, and software.
8. Keep current with software updates.
9. Implement network security with access control.
10. Limit access to sensitive and confidential data.
11. Establish and follow a security financial risk management plan; maintain adequate insurance coverage.
12. Get technical expertise and outside help when you need it.

For each of these steps, the guidelines address not only the appropriate steps to be taken, but also the costs, participants, technical skills, and consequences. A case study also is provided for each guideline. For the most part, the costs and required technical skills are minimal. For the others, the costs and skills depend on the specific approach that is selected. For example, the cost of a firewall and the skills need to install and administer it depend on the particular firewall that is chosen.

In implementing the "12 Step Program," the ISAlliance suggests that a small business address them completely rather than using a staged approach. Because most small businesses will have implemented one or more of these steps, they need to concentrate on the gaps. Once the program has been implemented, the business needs to budget for these steps on an annual basis. Like all businesses, small businesses also need to stay current on emerging threats, vulnerabilities, and security practices. Toward that end, the ISAlliance provides updated information on key security issues.

**SOURCES:** Clinton (2004), ISAlliance (2002), and ISAlliance (2004).

**QUESTIONS**

1. Most of the ISAlliance's recommendations seem like common sense. Why do you think that commonsense advice is required in this case? Based on what you know about information security, what other recommendations would you make for small businesses?
2. For each step, the best practices guidelines for small businesses provide the consequences for adopting the practice. Using one of the steps, explain whether this is sufficient motivation for a small business to adopt the practice. Overall, do you think these guidelines will have much impact on the behavior of small businesses? What else could be done to encourage them to adopt the practices?

3. The ISAlliance's best practice guidelines are available on its Web site. Download the guidelines for large and small businesses. What are the major differences between the two sets of guidelines?
4. Given the breadth of known vulnerabilities, what sort of impact will any set of security standards have on the rise in cyber attacks?

## References

Achohido, B., and J. Swartz. "Are Hackers Using Your PC to Spew Spam and Steal?" *USA TODAY*, September 8, 2004. usatoday.com/tech/news/computersecurity/2004-09-08-zombieuser_x.htm (accessed October 2004).

Anti-Phishing Working Group (APWG). "Phishing Attack Trends Report." 2004. antiphishing.org/APWG_Phishing_Attack_Report-Jun2004.pdf(accessed March 2005).

AOL/NCSA. "AOL/NCSA Online Safety Study." October 2004. staysafeonline.info/news/safety_study_v04.pdf(accessed October 2004).

CERT/CC. "CERT/CC Statistics 1988–2002." 2002. cert.org/stats/cert_stats.html (accessed April 2003).

Clinton, L. "Hearing on Protecting Our Nation's Cyber Space: Educational Awareness for the Cyber Citizen." Internet Security Alliance, April 2004. isalliance.org/testimonyLarry416.doc (accessed October 2004).

CSI and FBI. "2004 CSI/FBI Computer Crime and Security Survey." 2004. gocsi.com (accessed October 2004).

CSO Magazine. "2004 E-Crime Watch Survey Shows Significant Increase in Electronic Crimes." *CSO Magazine*, May 25, 2004. cert.org/about/ecrime.html (accessed October 2004).

cve.mitre.org (accessed 1999–2005).

Damle, P. "Social Engineering: A Tip of the Iceberg." *Information Systems Control Journal* 2 (2002).

Department of Homeland Security. *The National Strategy to Secure Cyberspace*, 2004. whitehouse.gov/pcipb (accessed October 2004).

Emigh, J. "The Eyes Have It." *Security Solutions*, March 1, 2003. securitysolutions.com/mag/security_eyes/ (accessed October 2004).

Federal Trade Commission (FTC). "How Not to Get Hooked by a 'Phishing' Scam." FTC Consumer Alert, June 2004. ftc.gov/bcp/

conline/pubs/alerts/phishingalrt.htm (accessed October 2004).

Fisher, D. "MyDoom E-Mail Worm Spreading Quickly." *eWeek*, January 26, 2004. eweek.com/article2/0,1759,1460809,00.asp (accessed October 2004).

Garfinkel, S. *Web Security, Privacy and Commerce*. Sebastopol, CA: O'Reilly and Associates, 2002.

Hazari, S. "Firewalls for Beginners." *SecurityFocus.com*, November 6, 2000. securityfocus.com/infocus/1182 (accessed March 2005).

Honeynet Project. *Know Your Enemy: Learning about Security Threats*, 2d ed. Boston, MA: Addison-Wesley, 2004.

Howard, M. *Designing Secure Web-Based Applications for Microsoft Windows 2000*. Redmond, WA: Microsoft Press, 2000.

ICSA. "Malicious Code Problem Continues to Worsen, According to 9th Annual ICSA Labs Virus Prevalence Survey." TruSecure Corporation, 2004. trusecure.com/company/press/pr_20040322.shtml (accessed October 2004).

ISAlliance. "Common Sense Guide for Senior Managers." Internet Security Alliance, July 2002. isalliance.org/news/BestPractices.pdf (accessed October 2004).

ISAlliance. "Common Sense Guide to Cyber Security for Small Businesses." Internet Security Alliance, March 2004. /resources/papers/common_sense_sm_bus.pdf (accessed October 2004).

Kay, T. *Security+*. Berkeley, CA: McGraw-Hill/Osborne, 2003.

Kroeker, K. "Graphics and Security: Exploring Visual Biometrics." *IEEE Computer Society*, 2002. computer.org/cga/homepage/2002/n4/biometrics.htm (accessed April 2003).

Lemos, R. "Mitnick Teaches 'Social Engineering.'" *ZDNet News*, July 17, 2000. zdnet.com.com/2100-11-522261.html?legacy=zdnn (accessed November 2004).

Market Research Summaries. "Security, Continuity Top IT Spending Priorities." *Print on Demand.com*, September 25, 2003. printondemand.com/MT/archives/001335. html (accessed October 2004).

McConnell, M. "Information Assurance in the Twenty-First Century." *IEEE Security and Privacy*, 2002. computer.org/security/supplement1/mcc/?smsession=no (accessed November 2004).

Microsoft. "The Security Risk Management Guide," 2004. microsoft.com/technet/security/topics/policiesand procedures/secrisk/default.mspx (accessed October 2004).

Mitnick, K., and W. Simon. The *Art of Deception*. New York: Wiley, 2002.

NetGear. "Security and Savings with Virtual Private Networks." *ZDNet UK*, May 2002. whitepapers.zdnet.co. uk/0,39025945,60068895p-39000459q,00.htm (accessed October 2004).

Panko, R. *Corporate Computer and Network Security*. Upper Saddle River, NJ: Prentice Hall, 2003.

Prometheum Technologies. "How Does Virtual Private Network (VPN) Work?" April 2003. prometheum.com/ m_vpn.htm (accessed November 2004).

SANS. "The SANS Top 20 Internet Security Vulnerabilities." SANS Institute, 2004. *sans.org/top20/#threats* (accessed October 2004).

Scambray, J. et al. *Hacking Exposed*, 2nd ed. New York: McGraw-Hill, 2000. Copyright © McGraw-Hill Companies, Inc.

Shen, M. "Trends in Biometric Security (Part 3): Buyer Behavior Analysis." *BiometriTech*, March 2003. biometritech.com/features/shen031903.htm (accessed October 2004).

Sherwood, J. "IT Bosses Eye Up Biometric Security." *Vnunet.com*, September 2004. vnunet.com/news/1158422 (accessed October 2004).

Shimomura, T., et al. *Takedown: The Pursuit and Capture of Kevin Mitnick, America's Most Wanted Computer Outlaw, By the Man Who Did It*. New York: Warner Books, 1996.

Skoudis, E., and L. Zeltser. *Malware: Fighting Malicious Code*. Upper Saddle River, NJ: Prentice Hall, 2003.

Slewe, T., and M. Hoogenboom. "Who Will Rob You on the Digital Highway?" *Communications of the ACM* 47, no. 5 (2004): 56–60.

Symantec. "Symantec Internet Security Threat Report: Trends for January 1, 2004–June 30, 2004." Symantec, 2004. enterprisesecurity.symantec.com/content.cfm?articleid=1539 (accessed October 2004).

Thomas, T. *Network Security: First-Step*. Indianapolis, IN: Cisco Press, 2004.

Venes, R. "A Closer Look at Biometrics." *Computeractive*, June 24, 2004. infomaticsonline.co.uk/features/1156173 (accessed October 2004).

CHAPTER 2

# SERVER AND CLIENT HARDENING

Server and client protection is a fascinating area of security. When people think about protecting (or hardening) hosts, they are usually thinking about security configuration changes, or tweaks. On a Windows system, this typically involves applying some form of "security template" containing a number of security tweaks—primarily Registry changes. These templates can also contain access control lists (ACLs), service modifications, privilege settings, and so on. On a non-Windows system, a similar set of procedures is followed, albeit not with templates.

The problem is that security tweaks are not the be all and end all of security. Nor is security configuration going to be able to stop you from getting hacked. That does not make security tweaks meaningless and does not mean that you should avoid them. You should absolutely consider them, but only after you have performed a number of other steps that are required. To level the playing field a little, we do not devote this chapter to explaining all the security settings. Instead, we start out by trying to dispel some of the myths around security configuration. It is very important to understand what you gain, and do not gain, from security changes. Note that there is a lot of opinion belonging to the authors in here. Many of the issues we discuss are basically ongoing debates that have no right answer, although we are, of course, partial to our opinions!

After discussing the myths surrounding security configuration, we jump into a section discussing the top 10 client and server security tweaks. These are the 10 (more or less) things that we believe make a significant enough security difference to consider modifying. We discuss each in some level of detail as well as address where we know things break when using this setting (or settings—some consist of several settings). The list is, however, different from clients to servers, because the threats are different. Keep in mind too, while reading this list, that none of the changes make sense unless you have first established a threat model for your environment and know what you are trying to protect against.

There is also a section of changes you do *not* want to make. These are settings that degrade security, that degrade functionality (without a corresponding improvement in security), or that we just do not like for one reason or another.

That means that we will not discuss *how* to actually make security changes. This is discussed in great lengths in the various security guides. If you have not already done so, you should immediately go and download the guides. They are available in the Security Guidance Center at `http://www.microsoft.com/security/guidance`. We do, however, give some guidance to how to choose between the guides and a really interesting new tool called the Security Configuration Wizard (SCW).

Security tweaks usually fall into the following categories:

- Registry hacks
- Registry ACLs
- File system ACLs
- Service startup configuration
- Service ACLs
- User rights assignment
- Password policy
- Audit policies

Some of these, particularly the ACL settings, should be used with more caution than others. We cover that at some length in the sections on settings you should and should not make. Typically these guides implement the settings using security templates—an INF file that can be imported into either Group Policy or another tool for application on a system. Using the guides and the SCW to roll out security policy is considerably easier if you have Group Policy, but even without that, they are still highly useful.

## Security Configuration Myths

Security configuration changes and guides have been around for about 10 years in the Windows world, longer in other areas. The original Windows NT 4.0 guides published by the U.S. National Security Agency and SANS were basically just lists of changes, with a little bit of rationale behind each setting, but no overall cohesiveness. They were a response to a demand for what we call the "big blue 'secure-me-now' button." The problem is that such a button does not exist. If it did, the vendor would ship it.

There is a lot at stake in security configuration guidance. It is easy to understand why people are clamoring for it. Everyone can see the benefit in turning on some setting and blocking an attack. In some environments, doing so is not even an option. A system must be configured in accordance with some security configuration or hardening guide to be compliant with security policy. In other environments, security configuration guidance is strongly encouraged. We believe that it is very important before you start making security tweaks, however, that you understand some of the fundamental problems with security tweaks. These are what we call the myths.

Before we start sounding like we hate security guides (which we do not), let us point something out: the authors have taken part in authoring, co-authoring, or editing almost all the commonly available guides for Windows in the past 10 years. Guides are valuable, done right. To do them right, you must understand what they cannot do, however. That is why the myths are important.

---

**WARNING:** This section is somewhat (OK, very) cynical. Take it with a grain of salt and laugh at some of the examples we give. Do not lose sight, however, of the message we are trying to get across. These are myths, and you need to be careful of falling into the trap of believing them. If you can avoid that, you can focus your efforts on the things that make a real difference instead of being lured into staring at a single tree and failing to see the security forest, like so many others.

---

## Myth 1: Security Guides Make Your System Secure

Hang on, why is this a myth? Is not the basic purpose of a security guide to make you secure? Yes, that is the general idea. The term secure connotes an end state. We will never actually get there. Security is a process, to be evaluated on a constant basis. There is nothing that will put you into a "state of security." Unfortunately many people (surely none of you readers though) seem to believe that if you just apply some hardening guide your system will now be secure. This is a fallacy for several reasons.

First, consider any of the recent worms, Sasser, Slammer Blaster, Nimda, Code Red, ILOVEYOU, and friends, etc., ad infinitum ad nauseum. Not a single one of them would have been stopped by any security settings. That is because these worms all exploited unpatched vulnerabilities (for unpatched users). While most of the guides tell you that you need the patches applied, we have seen many systems that had the guides installed and whose owners therefore believed the patch was less important. If you are unsure of which patches to install, the proper answer is "all of them." Ideally, you should have more of a process around patch management, however. Few settings can prevent your network from getting attacked through unpatched vulnerabilities.

Security guides are meant to be simplistic, whereas sophisticated attacks are complex. Security guides provide a great starting point, but to really improve your security you need to do a lot more. Generally, you need to resort to complex measures to stop complex attacks, and complex measures do not package well in the form of a security template.

A security guide does not make your system secure. At best, it provides an additional bit of security over the other things you have already done, or will already do, to the system, as explained in other chapters. At worst, it compromises your security. For instance, a guide may very well compromise the availability portion of the Confidentiality-Integrity-Availability triad by destabilizing the system.

## Myth 2: If We Hide It, the Bad Guys Will Not Find It

If only we had a dime for every time we have seen someone try to hide their system ... Hiding the system so rarely helps. Some examples are in order. For instance, some people advocate turning off SSID broadcast in wireless networks. Not only does this mean you now have a network that is not compliant with the standard, your clients will also prefer a rogue network with the same name over the legitimate one. Oh, and it takes only a few minutes to actually find the network anyway, given the proper tools. Another example is changing the banners on your Web site so the bad guys will not know it is running IIS. First, it is relatively simple to figure out what the Web site is running anyway. Second, most of the bad guys are not smart enough to do that, so they just try all the exploits, including the IIS ones. Yet another one is renaming the Administrator account. It is a matter of a couple of API calls to find the real name. Our favorite is when administrators use Group Policy to rename the Administrator account. They now have an account called

Janitor3, with a comment of "Built-in account for administering the computer/domain." This is not really likely to fool anyone.

Renaming or hiding things is generally speaking much more likely to break applications than it is to actually stop an attack. Attackers know that administrators rename things, and go look for the real name first. Poorly written applications assume the Program Files directory is in a particular place, that the Administrator account has a particular name depending on region, and so on. Those applications will now break. Arguably, they were already broken, but the result is that they no longer function.

## Myth 3: The More Tweaks, the Better

Security guides contain a lot of settings, and why not, there are a lot to choose from. Windows Server 2003 contains 140 security settings in the Group Policy interface, and that does not count ACLs, service configuration, encrypting file system (EFS) policies, IPsec policies, and so on. The "best" configuration for these for every environment is nebulous at best. Therefore, a number of people take the approach that if you only make more changes you will be more secure. We distinctly remember a very memorable headline from late summer 2003 (in the northern hemisphere). It read "Dell Will Sell Systems That Are Secure by Default." Dell had just announced they would start selling Windows 2000 systems configured with the CIS Level 1 benchmark direct from the factory. The article went on to point out that this guide applies "over 50 security changes … significantly improving the default security of Windows 2000."

Well, there were a couple of problems with that statement. First, the benchmark only made 33 changes, not "over 50." Second, only three of them had any impact on security at all. And third, although Dell may have configured some security settings on the system, it was being sold without the latest service pack slipstreamed, which would seem, at least to us, to be a basic requirement for security. Do not get us wrong, it is encouraging to see vendors that step back and look at older operating systems and evaluate whether they can be made more secure than what was considered prudent several years ago when they were first released. The problem, however, is that first this was presented as a way to get a "secure" system, when there is obviously no such thing. Second, the vendor had missed many of the basic requirements for a protected system.

Many settings people make have no real impact on security. Consider, for instance, the "Restrict floppy access to locally logged on user only" setting. It ensures that remote users cannot access any floppy disks via the network. However, this setting works *if and only if* (IFF) a user is currently logged on to the system hosting the floppy (otherwise, the setting does not take effect), *and* a share has been created for the floppy disk (not done by default), *and* the ACL on the share specifies that the remote user can get to it, *and* the system has a floppy drive in the first place, *and* there is a disk in it. Most systems sold today do not even have a floppy disk drive, not to mention how unlikely the other requirements are to occur together. We are inclined to say that this setting has no impact on security whatsoever.

We are also very fond of the NetworkHideSharePasswords and NetworkNoDialIn settings that several of the guides have advocated for years. The former is designed to ensure that when you set a share password it is obscured in the user interface dialog; if you are running Windows 95. The setting has not worked since then. (Windows NT, including Windows 2000, Windows XP, and Windows Server 2003, has never supported share passwords.) Of course, even on Windows 95, the setting would have been much more effective had it been spelled correctly (network\hidesharepass-words). The latter setting, also misspelled, controlled modem dial-in permissions, also on Windows 95. In spite of the fact that these settings have never worked on any Windows NT-based operating system, there are still "security auditors" running around explaining to management that the security guys are not doing their job unless these two settings are configured—on Windows 2000 and even Windows XP. Far too often, the guides we see are taken directly from obsolete and technically inaccurate documents for other, obsolete, operating systems. Then they are made a requirement by people who do not understand security *or* the operating system they are trying to protect. Actually designing security to a threat model seems to be a luxury when it is so much easier to just charge exorbitant consulting fees for parroting back what someone else, who also did not understand the product, claimed was correct.

There are some basic ground rules:

- Requiring settings that are already set by default do not improve security.
- Settings that only modify behavior already blocked elsewhere do not improve security (although in some cases defense in depth is appropriate so long as you do not break required functionality in the process).

- Settings that destabilize the system do not improve security.
- Misspelled settings do not improve security.
- Settings that do not work on the relevant product do not improve security.

If you are one of the unfortunate people who get evaluated based on the number of settings you make, go ahead and make a bunch of these meaningless changes. Heck, invent a few of your own (everyone else seems to). Here are a few you could use without breaking anything:

- HKLM\Software\Microsoft\WindowsNT\CurrentVersion\DisableHackers=1 (REG_DWORD)
- HKLM\Wetware\Users\SocialEngineering\Enabled=no (REG_SZ)
- HKCU\Wetware\Users\CurrentUser\PickGoodPassword=1 (REG_BINARY)
- HKLM\Hardware\CurrentSystem\FullyPatched=yes (REG_SZ)
- HKLM\Software\AllowBufferOverflows=no (REG_SZ)

Make sure you set proper ACLs on them, too. This way you can show that you are actually doing much more than anyone else. If you also create a pie chart showing how much you are improving return on investment (ROI) with your careful management of security, your promotion into useless management overhead (UMO) is a virtual certainty!

Meanwhile, the rest of us will focus on actually improving security through designing security measures to a threat model.

## Myth 4: Tweaks Are Necessary

Some people consider tweaks a necessity, claiming that you cannot have a secure (read "protected") system without making a bunch of tweaks. This is an oversimplification. Tweaks block things you cannot block elsewhere. For instance, if you have two systems on a home network behind a firewall, or a corporate system that has IPsec policies that only allow it to request and receive information from a few well-managed servers, tweaks are mostly not necessary to improve security. Those systems will be perfectly fine without making any tweaks.

Even on highly exposed systems, most of the tweaks are not necessary. In eWeek's Open Hack IV competition in 2002 (see `http://msdn.microsoft.com/library/en-us/dnnetsec/html/`

openhack.asp), we built what was probably the most protected network we have ever built. In all, we made only four Registry tweaks, a couple of ACL changes, and set a password policy. The rest of the protection for those systems was based on proper network segmentation, a solid understanding of the threats, turning off unneeded services, hardening Web apps (see *Writing Secure Code*, 2nd Edition, by Howard and LeBlanc, MS Press, 2003), and properly protecting the SQL and Web servers (see Chapter 4, "Protecting Services and Server Applications"). Of course, this was a specialized system with very limited functionality, but it still shows that less is often more.

Proper understanding of the threats and realistic mitigation of those threats through a solid network architecture is much more important than most of the security tweaks we turn on in the name of security.

## Myth 5: All Environments Should At Least Use <Insert Favorite Guide Here>

One size does not fit all. Every environment has unique requirements and unique threats. If there truly was a guide for how to secure every single system out there, the settings in it would be the default. The problem is that when people start making these statements, they fail to take into account the complexity of security and system administration. Administrators usually get phone calls only when things break. Security breaks things; that is why some security-related settings are turned off by default. To be able to protect an environment, you have to understand what that environment looks like, who is using it and for what, and what the threats are that they have decided need mitigated. *Security is about risk management, and risk management is about understanding and managing risks, not about making a bunch of changes in the name of making changes solely to justify one's own existence and paycheck.*

At the very least, an advanced system administrator should evaluate the security guide or policy that will be used and ensure that it is appropriate for the environment. Certain tailoring to the environment is almost always necessary. These are not things that an entry-level administrator can do, however. Care is of the essence when authoring or tailoring security policies.

## Myth 6: "High Security" Is an End Goal for All Environments

High security, in the sense of the most restrictive security possible, is not for everyone. As we have said many times by now, security will break things. In some environments, you are willing to break things in the name of protection that you are not willing to break in others. Had someone told you on September 10, 2001 that you needed to arrive three hours ahead of your flight at the airport to basically be strip-searched and have your knitting needles confiscated, you would have told them they are insane. High security (to the extent that airport security is truly any security at all and not just security theater) is not for everyone, and in the world we lived in until the morning of September 11, 2001, it was not for us. After planes took to the skies again, few people questioned the need for more stringent airport security.

The same holds true of information security. Some systems are subjected to incredibly serious threats. If they get compromised, people will die, nations and large firms will go bankrupt, and society as we know it will collapse. Other systems are protecting my credit card numbers, for which I am liable up to $50 if they get compromised. The protective measures that are used on the former are entirely inappropriate for the latter; however, we keep hearing that "high security" is some sort of end goal toward which all environments should strive. These types of statements are an oversimplification that contributes to the general distrust and disarray in the field of information security today.

## Myth 7: Start Securing Your Environment by Applying a Security Guide

You cannot start securing anything by making changes to it. Once you start changing things the environment changes, and the assumptions you started with are no longer valid. We have said this many times, but to reiterate, security is about risk management; it is about understanding the risks and concrete threats to your environment and mitigating those. If the mitigation steps involve taking a security guide and applying it, so be it, but you do not know that until you analyze the threats and risks.

## Myth 8: Security Tweaks Can Fix Physical Security Problems

A fundamental concept in information security states that if bad guys have physical access to your computer, it is not your computer any longer! Physical access will *always* trump software security—eventually. We have to qualify the statement, however, because certain valid software security steps will prolong the time until physical access breaches all security.

Encryption of data, for instance, falls into that category. However, many other software security tweaks are meaningless. Our current favorite is the debate over USB thumb drives. In a nutshell, after the movie *The Recruit*, everyone woke up to the fact that someone can easily steal data on a USB thumb drive. Curiously, this only seems to apply to USB thumb drives, though. We have walked into military facilities where they confiscated our USB thumb drives, but let us in with 80 GB i1394 hard drives. Those are apparently not as bad.

One memorable late evening, one author's boss called him frantically asking what to do about this problem. The response: head on down to your local hardware store, pick up a tube of epoxy, and fill the USB ports with it. While you are at it, fill the i1394 (FireWire), serial, parallel, SD, MMC, memory stick, CD/DVD-burner, floppy drive, Ethernet jack, and any other orifices you see on the back, front, top, and sides of the computer, monitor, keyboard, and mouse with it, too. You will also need to make sure nobody can carry the monitor off and make a photocopy of it. You can steal data using all of those interfaces.

The crux of the issue is that as long as there are these types of interfaces on the system, and bad guys have access to them, all bets are off. There is nothing about USB that makes it any different. Sure, the OS manufacturer can put a switch in that prevents someone from writing to a USB thumb drive. That does not, however, prevent the bad guy from booting to a bootable USB thumb drive, loading an NTFS driver, and then stealing the data.

In short, any software security solution that purports to be a meaningful defense against physical breach must persist even if the bad guy has full access to the system and can boot in to an arbitrary operating system. Registry tweaks and file system ACLs do not provide that protection. Encryption does. Combined with proper physical security, all these measures are useful. As a substitute for physical security, they are usually not.

## Myth 9: Security Tweaks Will Stop Worms/Viruses

Worms and viruses (hereinafter collectively referred to as *malware*) are designed to cause the maximum amount of destruction possible. Therefore, they try to hit the largest numbers of vulnerable systems and, hence, they tend to spread through one of two mechanisms: unpatched/unmitigated vulnerabilities and unsophisticated users. Although there are some security tweaks that will stop malware (Code Red, for instance, could have been stopped by removing the indexing services extensions mappings in IIS), the vast majority of them cannot be stopped that way because they spread through the latter vector. Given the choice of dancing pigs and security, users will choose dancing pigs every single time. Given the choice between pictures of naked people frolicking on the beach and security, roughly half the population will choose naked people frolicking on the beach. Couple that with the fact that users do not understand our security dialogs and we have a disaster. *If a dialog asking the user to make a security decision is the only thing standing between the user and the naked people frolicking on the beach, security does not stand a chance.*

## Myth 10: An Expert Recommended This Tweak as Defense in Depth

This myth has two parts. Let us deal with the defense-in-depth aspect first. Defense-in-depth is a reasoned security strategy applying protective measures in multiple places to prevent unacceptable threats. Unfortunately, far too many people today use the term *defense in depth* to justify security measures that have no other realistic justification. Typically, this happens because of the general belief in myth 3 (more tweaks are better). By making more changes, we show the auditors that we are doing our job, and therefore they chalk us up as having done due diligence.

This shows an incredible immaturity in the field, much like what we saw in western "medicine" in the middle ages. Medics would apply cow dung, ash, honey, beer, and any number of other things, usually in rapid succession, to wounds to show that they were trying everything. Today, doctors (more typically nurses actually) clean the wound, apply a bandage and potentially an antibiotic of some kind, and then let it heal. Less is very often more, and using defense in depth as a way to justify unnecessary and potentially harmful actions is inappropriate.

The first part of this statement is one of our favorites. As a society, we love deferring judgment to experts, because, after all, they are experts and know more than we do. The problem is that the qualification process for becoming an expert is somewhat, shall we say, lacking. We usually point out that the working definition of a security expert is "someone who is quoted in the press." Based on the people we often see quoted, and our interaction with those people, that belief seems justified. It is no longer actions that define an expert, just reputation; and reputation can be assigned. Our friend Mark Minasi has a great statement that we have stolen for use in our own presentations. To be a security consultant, all you have to know is four words: the sky is falling. Having been security consultants and seen what has happened to the general competence level in the field, this statement certainly rings true. There are many, many good security consultants, but there are also many who do not know what they need to and, in some cases, fail to recognize that and then charge exorbitant amounts of money to impart their lack of knowledge and skills on unsuspecting customers.

## On to the Tweaks

Now that you have received the impression that we (or at least Jesper, who wrote most of this chapter) are the most cynical people on the planet (which, according to our respective lovely, talented, and beautiful wives, is probably true) is there really anything left to do? Yes, there is. There are certainly very useful tweaks that every environment should at least consider. However, it is important to understand the myths, and why they are myths, before we go on to the tweaks. Otherwise, it is really easy to fall into the traps represented by the myths.

This section is very simply structured. There are 10 or so server tweaks, 10 or so client tweaks, and a list of tweaks you should not make. For each, we describe the tweak, the threat it mitigates, and the side-effects (where known).

Throughout these tweaks, we refer to the various Windows security guides from Microsoft. Those guides are available for download as follows:

- Windows Server 2003 Security Guide
  `http://go.microsoft.com/fwlink/?LinkId=14845`
- Windows XP Security Guide
  `http://go.microsoft.com/fwlink/?LinkId=14840`
- Windows 2000 Security Hardening Guide
  `http://go.microsoft.com/fwlink/?LinkId=28591`
- Threats and Countermeasures: Security Settings in Windows Server 2003 and Windows XP
  `http://go.microsoft.com/fwlink/?LinkId=15159`

# Top 10 (or so) Server Security Tweaks

## IPsec filters

Our favorite "tweak" is not actually a tweak at all. It is a technology that you can use to prevent systems from talking to each other. IPsec is a layer 3 and 4 host-based security mechanism that enables you to configure authentication and/or encryption settings on a per-port basis. It is one of the most powerful and important security tools ever devised. It is what we use to ensure that hosts cannot send or receive traffic that is not essential for their functioning.

**CAUTION**

IPsec, incorrectly configured, can be hazardous to your network health; and your career.

IPsec is an absolutely marvelous technology for blocking traffic. In fact, even if you did not intend to block any traffic, that usually is the end result in the first few tries. Do not deploy an IPsec policy on a production network until you have thoroughly tested it and are sure it will work as intended.

## Software Restriction Policies

Our second favorite "tweak" is also not a tweak. It is technology used to prevent, or allow, software to execute on the system. Software restriction policies (SRPs) can be used, for example, to prevent any account from executing certain files even when those files cannot be removed. For instance, one might use the tftp.exe tool to upload the attack tools to a compromised server. You cannot delete tftp.exe unless you disable system file protection. However, you can set up an SRP that prevents attackers from executing tftp.exe. Software restriction policies can identify the file four different ways:

- By Internet Explorer security zone
- By full or relative path
- By a certificate used to sign the files
- By a hash

Figure 2-1 shows an SRP that is quite restrictive. It consists of the following rules:

- All files underneath the %systemroot% directory can execute (a path rule).
- All files underneath the %systemroot%\system32 directory can execute (a path rule).
- Certain chosen files underneath the %systemroot% directory are restricted (a path rule).
- Certain chosen files underneath the %systemroot% directory are restricted (a hash rule).

In addition, the default security level is set to Disallowed, meaning only those files explicitly listed can be executed. With this policy set, the system will boot and you can log on. However, many of the Start menu items are blocked because they are located under \Documents and Settings and that location is

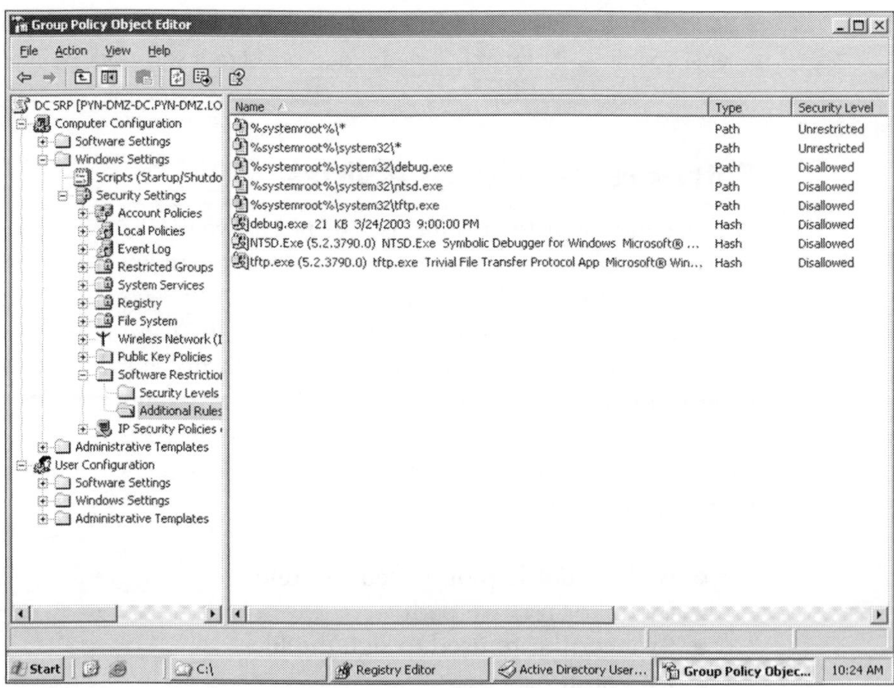


**Figure 2-1** Software restriction policies on a domain controller.

blocked. For instance, you cannot launch the command prompt from the Start menu, but you can do it from the Run dialog. Figure 2-1 shows the rules.

SRP applies in order of specificity. Because the %systemroot% rule is more specific than the blanket rule, it takes precedence. Because a hash rule is always more restrictive than a path rule, the hash rules take precedence. Note, however, that a hash rule is specific to a particular version of a file. If the file is updated to a newer version, the hash rule is no longer valid. Hence, we also have a path rule to restrict these files, just in case we forget to update the hash rule.

A full discussion of how to use these options is quite lengthy, and the interested reader is referred to the *Security Resource Kit*, by Smith and Komar, MS Press, 2002, which has a lengthy discussion on SRP. The Windows XP Security Guide also has a discussion on SRP.

Of course, ideally, you should set up an SRP that allows execution only of those files that are necessary for operating the server, but doing so is quite complicated. Windows binaries are not signed directly, and therefore a certificate rule would not be valid. (Windows binaries do have an associated digital signature, but it is not attached to the file; it is stored in the manifest, called nt5.cat.) Thus the simplest approach is the one we used above where everything is restricted and particular things are allowed using a combination of hash and path rules.

What breaks? The simple answer is potentially everything, but hopefully nothing. SRP, correctly used, will ensure that the system can perform its intended function and absolutely nothing else. SRP, incorrectly used, will turn your system into a boat anchor. SRP is another setting you should never roll out on a production network until you are 100 percent certain that the systems will not break. Virtual machines are absolutely wonderful for developing and troubleshooting software restriction policies because you just reboot and discard the undo file should the system not function properly.

## Do Not Store LAN Manager Hash Value

This is actually a tweak. NoLMHash is the name of the Registry value (on Windows XP and Server 2003) or key (Windows 2000) that you set to turn on this tweak. In Group Policy on Windows XP and higher, the setting is called "Network Security: Do not store LAN Manager hash value on next password change."

Using this setting, you can turn off creation of LM hashes across a domain or system. Ideally, this setting will never have any direct impact on security because if it does it means your domain controller has been hacked; but just in case, *we recommend disabling storage of LM hashes*. In most cases, the primary benefit of this setting is that it breaks compatibility with Windows 9x.

---

**NOTE:** If bad guys have access to your password hashes, you have already been hacked. Cracking hashes will not give them any additional access on the domain where they came from. Cracking hashes will only allow them to access other domains where the same users are using the same passwords. In addition, with the proper tools, attackers do not need to crack passwords at all; they can use the hashes directly. Therefore, the actual security benefit of turning off LM hash storage is realistically quite minimal.

---

## Anonymous Restrictions

Windows 2000 (and also XP), volunteers large volumes of information about itself to anonymous users. Turning on anonymous restrictions will block it from doing so. There are a number of settings involved here, such as RestrictAnonymous, EveryoneIncludesAnonymous, and so on. On Windows Server 2003, except for on domain controllers, most of these settings are on by default, eliminating the need to configure them.

The settings include the following:

- *Network access: Allow anonymous SID/Name translation*—Windows XP and Server 2003 only. This setting governs whether anonymous users can call the LookupAccountSid API (for more information on this and other APIs discussed here, refer to the MSDN library at `http://msdn.microsoft.com`) and other functions that resolve a security identifier (SID) to a username. Configuring this setting prevents anonymous users from "SIDwalking," which is the process of resolving each SID separately. The dumpinfo tool implements SIDwalking. Had this setting been made, that tool would not have returned any usernames or the administrator name. This setting will break certain interactions with Windows NT 4.0 and Windows 9x, as well as some poorly written software that requires anonymous enumeration. *We recommend that you disable anonymous SID/Name translation.*

- *Network access: Do not allow anonymous enumeration of SAM accounts*—The Registry key this setting configures is called RestrictAnonymousSAM on Windows XP and higher. On Windows 2000, this setting is equivalent to RestrictAnonymous at level 2. It does very little good actually. It only prevents calling the NetUserEnum API, but as long as LookupAccountSid is still allowed, getting a list of all users is trivial. On the other hand, this setting really does not break very much, so you may as well set it.
- *Network access: Do not allow anonymous enumeration of SAM accounts and shares*—This is the RestrictAnonymous setting on Windows XP and Server 2003. On Windows 2000, this is equivalent to setting RestrictAnonymous to 2. This setting breaks not only NetUserEnum but also the NetShareEnum API on all platforms and LookupAccountSid on Windows 2000 only. If this setting is configured, dumpinfo and similar tools would not return any information at all to anonymous users. However, configuring this setting has a significant adverse impact on compatibility with older software, as well as with Windows NT 4.0 and Windows 9x. *We recommend that you restrict anonymous enumeration.*
- *Network access: Let Everyone permissions apply to anonymous users*—This setting, available on Windows XP and Server 2003, controls the membership in the Everyone group. Up through Windows 2000, access tokens generated for the ANONYMOUS user included SID S-1-1-0, the Everyone SID. (See the sidebar on SIDs for more information.) Starting with Windows XP, the inclusion of SID S-1-1-0 in anonymous access tokens is controllable with this setting known technically as the EveryoneIncludesAnonymous after the Registry key that configures it. By default, the setting is turned off. This will break access from systems that cannot authenticate as anything other than ANONYMOUS, notably Windows NT 4.0. Of important note, however, is that resources available to the NETWORK identity (SID S-1-5-2) are still available to ANONYMOUS as the NETWORK SID is added to an ANONYMOUS access token. *We recommend that you ensure that the default setting of not including the Everyone SID is still in force.*
- *Network access: Named Pipes that can be accessed anonymously*—This setting controls which named pipes are available anonymously. Named pipes is a data-sharing mechanism that basically acts as a virtual file. By default on Windows XP and Server 2003, only those

named pipes listed in this setting, known as NullSessionPipes, are available anonymously. Many systems do not even need those. Things that will break if you remove them depend on what you are doing with the system. For instance, removing the Browser entry will break anonymous (Windows NT 4.0 and 9x) access to the browse list. Note also that although this setting is available on Windows 2000, it has no effect immediately. The reason is that by default on Windows 2000 all named pipes can receive remote requests. To restrict anonymous access to named pipes on that platform, you need to create the RestrictNullSessAccess value and set it to 1. This value is not exposed in the Group Policy editor UI by default, although the Windows 2000 Security Hardening Guide from Microsoft adds it. To manually add it, create a REG_DWORD value called RestrictNullSessAccess under HKEY_LOCAL_MACHINE\SYSTEM\CurrentControlSet\Services\LanmanServer\Parameters and set it to 1. Although you can configure RestrictNullSessAccess on Windows XP and Server 2003, as well, it is turned on by default even if the setting is missing from the Registry. Thus, you would only need to configure it if you want to enable anonymous access to all null session pipes. In Windows Server 2003 Group Policy, RestrictNullSessAccess is exposed as "Network access: Restrict anonymous access to Named Pipes and Shares." *We recommend you leave RestrictNullSessAccess turned on, or configure it if you are running Windows 2000.*

- *Network access: Shares that can be accessed anonymously*—This setting is analogous to the named pipes setting above, but it governs anonymous access to shares. Unless you are publishing DFS shares or hosting COM objects for down-level systems, you can probably get away with clearing out all values in this setting. The implications of RestrictNullSessAccess on this setting are identical to how it affects null session named pipes access. *We recommend that you investigate which values you can remove on each of your systems and present only those named pipes and shares that are necessary for operation.*
- *Network access: Remotely accessible registry paths*—Remote access to the Windows Registry is governed by the ACL on the HKEY_LOCAL_MACHINE\SYSTEM\CurrentControlSet\Control\SecurePipeServers\winreg registry key. However, underneath that key is another key called AllowedPaths. On Windows Server 2003, there is also a key called AllowedExactPaths. In Windows Server 2003,

AllowedPaths is exposed as "Network access: Remotely accessible registry paths and sub-paths," and AllowedExactPaths is exposed as "Network access: Remotely accessible registry paths." In Windows 2000 and XP, only AllowedPaths is available and it is exposed as "Network access: Remotely accessible registry paths." These keys govern exceptions to the ACL on the winreg key. Any Registry path listed in these keys is available anonymously over the network. In Windows XP and 2000, this includes the entire Registry tree underneath that key. In Windows Server 2003, AllowedExactPaths specifies that only that key is accessible. Its subkeys are not available. The default settings for these keys are mostly fine unless automatic administrative logon (autoadminlogon) is used on Windows 2000 primarily. Credentials for autoadminlogon (which is a bad idea all by itself) are stored in HKEY_LOCAL_MACHINE\Software\Microsoft\Windows NT\CurrentVersion\Winlogon. HKEY_LOCAL_MACHINE\Software\Microsoft\Windows NT\CurrentVersion is available remotely to anyone. When you remove paths from AllowedPaths or AllowedExactPaths, you will break things. For instance, if you remove the "printers" entry from a print server, users will no longer be able to print to it. Tread carefully here. The primary reason to worry about this key is to ensure that autoadminlogon credentials are not available remotely; however, the proper way to ensure that is to not allow autoadminlogon. *We recommend that autoadminlogon be disabled on all systems.*

- *Hide browsers*—By default, all Windows systems will announce themselves and all services they provide to others across the network, even if they do not provide any services at all! Not only does this create an awful lot of unnecessary network traffic, it also can be considered an information disclosure threat. However, the primary reason to turn this off is for pure performance reasons. To do so, set the hidden value under HKEY_LOCAL_MACHINE\SYSTEM\CurrentControlSet\Services\LanmanServer\parameters to 1. This setting is not exposed in Group Policy by default. The Windows 2000 Security Hardening Guide will install it in the Group Policy UI, and the Windows XP and Server 2003 security guides contain instructions for how to do the same on those platforms. *We recommend that all systems that should not act as general-purpose file or print servers have this value configured.*

### SECURITY IDENTIFIERS (SIDs)

Every user in Windows NT is represented by a unique security identifier (SID). SIDs for users always start with S-1-5-21 in Windows, denoting that they are issued by the NT identifying authority and that they may not be unique within the universe of SIDs. User SIDs are based on machine SIDs. For instance, S-1-5-21-1095672315-1787444531-3518664281 may be the SID of a machine. Users, in turns, will have SIDs based on the machine or domain SID, with a relative identifier (RID) appended. For example, the administrator on the machine will have a SID of S-1-5-21-1095672315-1787444531-3518664281-500.

For a more thorough discussion on SIDs, refer to the MSDN library.

## Password Policies

Everyone needs a password policy. The password policy settings in Group Policy help you enforce it, and the options in there are relatively self-explanatory. The exact options to configure vary by environment, but in virtually all enterprise environments you should enforce at least 7-character complex passwords that change no less often than 180 days. In many, if not most, environments, you probably want to go to 8-character complex passwords that change every 90 days.

You cannot enforce some things using the built-in policies, however. For example, in many environments, we make policies such that administrators cannot use the same password on two different systems. Since you cannot enforce that with built-in technical means, we need a different way to do so. One option that works is to use a logon script. For example, if you are not allowed to use the same password on system A as on system B, you put a logon script on system A that connects, without specifying credentials, to system B, and vice versa. If the connection succeeds, you have a violation of the policy. At this point, you can automatically generate a termination notice or take some other appropriate action.

## SMB Message Signing

SMB message signing is actually four different settings:

- Microsoft network client: Digitally sign communications (always)—Sets the Workstation service to require message signing on outbound requests to SMB servers. We recommend you turn this setting on for all systems making outbound Windows networking requests to other systems, including all systems that are used for browsing the Web.

- *Microsoft network client: Digitally sign communications (if server agrees)*—Sets the Workstation service to request message signing on outbound request to SMB servers. This is the only setting of the four that is on by default.
- *Microsoft network server: Digitally sign communications (always)*—Sets the Server service to require message signing on inbound requests from SMB clients. *We recommend you turn this setting on for all systems if possible.*
- *Microsoft network server: Digitally sign communications (if client agrees)*—Sets the Server service to request message signing on inbound requests from SMB clients. *We recommend that at a bare minimum this setting is configured on all systems acting as servers.*

Turning on SMB message signing is a tricky operation. The reason is that if you set it to require signing on the Workstation service, the system will fail to connect to any Windows system in a default configuration because message signing on the Server service is not enabled by default. The reason it is not on by default is that it generates a small overhead—up to about 5 percent—which was believed to be unacceptable on many systems.

We think, however, that this setting is incredibly valuable and should be required on all systems. The reason is that SMB message signing helps thwart entire classes of man-in-the-middle attacks known as the SMB reflection attack. These have been used in the wild since at least 2000. It also breaks other types of man-in-the-middle attacks that rely on forwarding SMB messages.

On Windows XP Service Pack 2 and higher, the SMB reflection attack is broken even if SMB message signing is not enabled. However, because there are other man-in-the-middle attacks that are not mitigated this way, it is still important to configure SMB message signing on Windows XP.

## LAN Manager Authentication Level

LMCompatibilityLevel, or "Network security: LAN Manager authentication level" as it is called in Group Policy on Windows XP and higher (it is called "LAN Manager authentication level" on Windows 2000), governs the authentication protocols a system is allowed to use and accept.

*We recommend that it be set to at least 4 or "Send NTLMv2 response only\refuse LM" on all systems.* When you do so, you will break access to and from Windows 9x systems as well as some versions of SAMBA.

It is important to recognize that even with LAN Manager authentication level configured to 4, the system will still emit LM and NTLM responses in certain cases; for instance, with programs that use the NTLM Security Support Provider (SSP) directly, such as RPC. To prevent this, you need to configure the "Network security: Minimum session security for NTLM SSP based (including secure RPC) clients/servers" settings. These settings govern the protocols used by the SSP. There are four combinations of settings.

1. Require message integrity
2. Require message confidentiality
3. Require NTLMv2 session security
4. Require 128-bit encryption

To use NTLMv2, you need to select at least option 3. In addition, if you turn off storage of LM hashes, you must select options 1, 2 and 3 to allow RPC authentication over UDP to function properly. Services that use such authentication include the Windows Clustering Service. If you simply disable LM hash storage, you may break your clusters unless you also configure the NTLM SSP client-side settings. *We recommend setting the NTLM SSP client to require message integrity, confidentiality, as well as NTLMv2.* Use 128-bit encryption at your discretion, but most applications will use that anyway. Configuring this setting will only break applications that are specifically coded not to allow use of NTLMv2.

## TCP Hardening

The TCP stack in Windows 2000 and higher is quite solid actually. However, you should consider making at least one tweak on servers. SynAttackProtect makes the system considerably more resilient to TCP SYN-flood attacks—an attack where the attacker simply attempts to make many concurrent connections to a system to exhaust its capability to service legitimate users. SynAttackProtect is a REG_DWORD under HKEY_LOCAL_MACHINE\System\CurrentControlSet\Services\Tcpip\Parameters. Note that it may not be there by default, in which case you have to add it. It can take three values: 0, 1, and 2. 0, the default, is appropriate for clients and servers on slow links. *We recommend that servers on the Internet or otherwise subject to*

*SYN-floods have SynAttackProtect set to 2.* Systems on slow links cannot have this value set because it would cause legitimate connections to be timed out. The Windows 2000 Hardening Guide will add this value to the Group Policy UI. The Windows Server 2003 guide contains information on how to manually add it.

There are several other TCP hardening settings, but the majority of them have a relatively low or specialized impact. For information about the remaining values, refer to the "Threats and Countermeasures" guide at `http://go.microsoft.com/fwlink/?LinkId=15159`.

## Restricted Groups

Restricted groups is a way to control group membership with Group Policy. A lot of administrators have tried to control groups by making wholesale ACL changes on the system. This typically has the result that the system ends up being less secure than it was before and that they still have not achieved complete control of the group they wanted to restrict.

Restricted groups provides a much better way to control certain groups, such as Power Users, Server Operators, and Backup Operators. For instance, if you do not want anyone who is a member of Server Operators to be able to access any files because of that membership, make Server Operators a restricted group and control who can be a member of it.

Restricted groups also provide a very strong way to control who is an administrator. For instance, at one point we had an administrator who was running a lab for one of the authors. That must have been a terrible job because he was charged with keeping us out of his lab. We, on the other hand, kept trying to hack him. To prevent us from becoming administrators, he made that group a restricted group using domain policy; and we were not in it. That means that we had only 15 minutes from the time we became administrators to turning off the policy. Some of the time, that actually worked. To stop this, he then set the Group Policy refresh interval to one minute, which pretty much stopped us cold. Although we cannot recommend refreshing Group Policy every minute, *we do recommend using restricted groups to manage group membership for certain sensitive groups.*

## Audit Settings

By and large, the default audit settings on Windows Server 2003 are fine. However, on Windows 2000, they could use a little adjusting. Well, actually, they are basically turned off on Windows 2000 by default.

We recommend that you tweak the audit policies as follows:

- *Account logon events*—Success and failure
- *Account management*—Success and failure
- *Logon events*—Success and failure
- *Object access*—Success and failure
- *Policy change*—Success
- *Privilege use*—Success and failure
- *System events*—Success

You should also adjust the log sizes; however, do not just increase sizes blindly. There are some practical limits on event log sizes. Event logs are loaded in services.exe, along with several other things. They are also memory-mapped files, and each process can only have 1 GB of those. That means that the log files have to share the 1 GB of available memory in the services.exe process with everything else in there. In addition, event logs cannot be fragmented in memory, so the system has to find sufficient contiguous memory. It is pretty likely that these issues will constrain you to about 300 MB as a practical limit on total event log size (not 300 MB each). Take that into account when setting log sizes. Of course, you must also analyze the logs, but that is a different topic.

## Top 10 (or so) Client Security Tweaks

### Limiting Malicious Code

We combine things a little differently for clients. The most important "tweak" to do on clients is to make malicious code less likely to run. Basically, there are three objectives, in decreasing order of desirability:

1. Prevent malicious code from getting onto the system.
2. Prevent malicious code from running.
3. Prevent malicious code from communicating.

Obviously, we would prefer to keep the malicious code off the system in the first place. However, if it gets on the system, we want to prevent it from running, and if it should happen to run, let us try to keep it from infecting anyone else. Four technologies (not necessarily tweaks) are critical here.

### *Firewalls*

Host-based firewalls are becoming all the rage. Windows XP includes a free host-based firewall, and Windows XP Service Pack 2 includes a very good, free host-based firewall, called Windows Firewall (WF). WF includes some very sophisticated management functionality that affords network administrators great control over the firewall. For instance, they can configure it to behave one way when on the internal network, another way when not. They can open up an authenticated IPsec bypass allowing all authenticated IPsec traffic to bypass the firewall, and they can set up program-based exceptions that allow certain firewall-unfriendly programs, such as instant messenger programs, to work properly. In all, the firewall has only one real or imagined shortcoming—it does not perform outbound filtering. There are three reasons why: (1) Users do not understand it and therefore it will not help. As we mentioned earlier, if a dialog asking the user to make a security decision is the only thing standing between them and dancing pigs, security does not stand a chance. (2) Given that outbound filtering is a delay feature for the vast majority of users, why expend the limited available resources on that instead of giving administrators a great centrally manageable firewall? (3) Outbound filtering is available in IPsec already.

This does not, of course, mean that outbound filtering is not a worthwhile feature, just that it is not worthwhile for all users. For those who do need it, outbound filtering can be had through third-party firewalls.

*We recommend using host-based firewalls on all your clients because they help stop malicious code from getting on the system in the first place.*

### *IPsec Filters*

IPsec filters can be used in many different ways on clients. As a general recommendation, *we recommend that you use IPsec filters to prevent your clients from talking to each other.*

### *Software Restriction Policies*

SRP is more difficult to use on clients than on servers, because clients are more general-purpose machines. Setting up SRP to allow a client to actually function is a significant upfront time investment. However, if you spend the time doing this, you will be rewarded with a much more secure machine. *We recommend that you use SRP as much as possible to protect clients from malicious code.*

### Anti-Malware

Antivirus software is the traditional malicious code prevention technology. The problem with antivirus software is that it is only signature based. It cannot prevent viruses that it does not know about, which SRP can by allowing only trusted code to run. As a defense-in-depth measure, antivirus is tremendously important, but it is important to understand its limitations.

Do not forget about other types of anti-malware programs either. Anti-spyware is rapidly becoming a requirement as well. Of course, if you run as LUA (see Chapter 3, "Protecting User Applications"), it is unlikely you will get much spyware on the system, but it is very useful if you have to run as an administrator.

There is also the problem that not all machines can use antivirus tools. For instance, we do penetration testing, and the antivirus products delete the tools we use in that job. Therefore, we cannot run them. As a general rule, however, *we recommend using antivirus products on most, if not all, clients.*

## SafeDllSearchMode

Remember the summer and fall of 2001? The world was changing, significantly. There were attacks from everywhere. On the Internet we had Code Red. When you finally had cleared that off all your systems, your boss came running into the office screaming that there was another worm on the loose. No worries, you responded; IIS was already patched. There was only one problem: This one spread other ways, too. The next thing you knew you had Nimda on your hands, and it spread through file shares.

Nimda searched all available file shares it could find for Microsoft Word documents. The reason was that one of those "security researchers" who believe the world is safer if he tells all the script kiddies how to exploit something without giving the vendor a chance to fix it first had posted a treatise on how to load and execute code when users double-clicked Word documents. The issue stems from how the operating system searches for dynamic link libraries (DLLs). DLLs are used to allow programs to share common functionality. Programs load them by calling LoadLibrary or LoadLibraryEx. When a program calls this function specifying just the name of the DLL, as opposed to a full path, the OS will search to find the right version in the following way:

1. *Memory*—If the program is already running and has the DLL loaded, it will not load it again.
2. *Application directory*—To allow programs to keep their own copies of DLLs so they can load specific versions, those have very high priority.
3. *Current working directory*—This allows programs to use SetCurrentDirectory to load a particular DLL.
4. *System directories*—These are the %systemroot%, %systemroot%\system, and %systemroot%\system32 directories.
5. *Path*—Some DLLs are found along the path.

This list can be modified by various technologies such as manifests and .local files, but that is beyond the scope of this book. This has been the way Windows has worked since the very first versions of the OS. What the "researcher" figured out was that Word will load certain DLLs at startup. If you dropped a copy of one of those, the one he used was riched20.dll, into a directory with documents, it would be loaded by Word when the user double-clicked one of the documents. Nimda used this exact issue as one of the ways to spread.

Several interesting observations can be made here. First, neither the person who discovered how to use this for malicious purposes nor the writers of Nimda (we are not aware of any connections between the two) understood nearly as much about the OS as they have been given credit for. Riched20.dll is the "rich text editor" DLL. It is used to provide bolds, italics, and so on. It is actually loaded by the OS automatically for an awful lot of programs. In other words, they could have looked for almost any file they wanted and dropped it there. At one point, we swear we saw WinZip load this DLL. Second, this is core operating system functionality. It has worked this way for years. The fact that no bad guys had made use of it until 2001 was astounding. Third, the basic functionality is really broken. If you go tell any decent UNIX administrator to put a period (.) as the first thing in his path, he will claim you are smoking some funny tobacco. They all know not to do that. Yet, that is how Windows was always designed to work.

This all changed with Windows XP Service Pack 1. Starting with that release, the SafeDllSearchMode setting switched items 3 and 4 in the load order, protecting system DLLs from spoofing. To understand how important this switch is, consider that it would have stopped Nimda in many cases!

The SafeDllSearchMode functionality is available and turned on by default in Windows XP Service Pack 1 and higher, and in Windows

Server 2003. It is available but turned *off* by default in Windows XP RTM and Windows 2000 Service Pack 3 and higher. *We highly recommend turning on SafeDllSearchMode in Windows 2000 as well. (Windows XP RTM should be upgraded to Service Pack 2 or higher.)* To turn it on, set a REG_DWORD called SafeDllSearchMode to 1 under HKLM\System\CurrentControlSet\Control\Session Manager. On Windows Server 2003, this value does not exist, but if it is absent the default value is 1.

When you make a fundamental change to how the operating system works, like this, there is always some breakage. In this particular case, surprisingly, the number of breaks was low. SQL 2000 includes a component known as the Starfighter Foundation Classes in SFC.DLL. Unfortunately, SQL Server instead loaded SFC.DLL—the system file checker—from the system directory. That was fixed in SQL Server 2000 Service Pack 3. The only other breakage we are aware of was with Outlook 2000 loading add-ins.

This setting protects against an extremely common scenario whereby an internal attacker drops binaries in file shares. The breakage caused by turning it on is minimal. *For these reasons, we believe SafeDllSearchMode is one of the most important settings to turn on to protect clients.*

### Local Administrator Account Control

We have a confession to make. Up until now, we have pretty much made an implicit assumption that we are dealing with clients in an enterprise. Although it has made no particular difference in how we configure the systems up until now, it changes how you deal with accounts. On a client in an enterprise, there is usually a domain controller, which means that clients really only have one account locally—the built-in Administrator account. This is important, because the policies we set from now on will be different in an enterprise versus a small business or a home office. For more specific details on how to run systems in small businesses, see Chapter 5, "Security for Small Businesses."

### Do Not Store LAN Manager Hash Value

The first thing to do to protect the local Administrator account is to keep the LM hash from being stored. In a home or small business, this may be harder to do using the NoLMHash switch if there are accounts defined on the system that have to be accessible by Windows 9x clients. However, if no accounts defined on the system are used by down-level clients, we recommend turning off storage of LM hashes.

**NOTE:** Although you can technically turn off LM hash storage even if you have Windows 9x machines in your environment, doing so requires installing and configuring the DSClient on your 9x machines. Frankly, we recommend you spend your time getting rid of 9x instead. Your time will have been better spent and your environment will be more secure if you do.

## Password Policies

Administrator accounts should have very strong passwords. *We recommend that they should be 10 to 14 characters long and appear essentially random.* You can configure the local password policy on all systems in a domain by setting a password policy on the Organizational Units that those systems are in. Password policy on an OU only applies to local accounts on the member systems of that OU. Therefore, it is ideal for controlling the local Administrator account. If there are user accounts on the clients, you may need to adjust the password policy to make it palatable to users.

## SMB Message Signing

We discussed SMB message signing at length above. Therefore, we do note reiterate that discussion here. *We do recommend turning on SMB message signing and setting it to required on both the Workstation and Server services on all clients.*

## LAN Manager Authentication Level

The LAN Manager authentication level issue has been discussed at length already. For clients, the main concern is emanating LM responses, which can be much more easily cracked. To prevent this, *we recommend configuring the "LAN Manager Authentication Level" to 4 or "Send NTLMv2 response only/refuse LM" as well as configuring security on the NTLM SSP, as mentioned previously in this chapter.*

## Limit Local Account Use of Blank Passwords to Console Logon Only

One of the coolest features with Windows XP is how it handles blank passwords. By default, if an account has a blank password it can only be used at the console, not over the network. This is designed as a home-user feature to allow them to have the same experience they would have with Windows 9x, where passwords provide no real value. The Group Policy setting is there only to enforce this functionality. It is important to ensure that it stays on.

For the record, you can use this functionality with Windows Server 2003 as well. We have recommended its use in cases where we have servers locked in physically secure racks. Setting a blank Administrator account password allows physically trusted personnel to access the systems in case of severe failure, but those Administrator accounts cannot be used across the network by an attacker.

## Anonymous Restrictions

Clients should look like black holes on the network to all systems other than management points. The authenticated IPsec bypass in the Windows XP Service Pack 2 firewall is a great way to make that happen, but the same lockdown should also be done with respect to anonymous restrictions. Pure clients have no business volunteering anything to anonymous users, and *we recommend configuring all the anonymous settings discussed above.*

We have even gone so far on some particularly threatened clients as turning off the Server service. This will, however, render the machine unmanageable since the Server service is used by virtually all remote management tools. On a system that is particularly threatened where remote management is not a requirement, however, this may be a reasonable course of action.

## Enable Auditing

How much auditing you really want to do on clients depends on a lot of factors, such as the threats, management processes in place for audit logs, the number of clients, etc. Generally speaking, however, you probably do not want to collect gigantic logs from clients. However, a few events can prove very useful in forensics.

### *Logon Events*

Logon events are recorded when someone logs on to the system, regardless of the account used. In other words, if you log on to a domain member using a domain account, you get a logon event recorded on the domain member. You would also get a logon event recorded if you log on with a local account.

### *Account Logon Events*

Account logon events are recorded when someone authenticates using an account defined on this system. In other words, if you log on to a domain member using a domain account, the account logon event gets recorded on the domain controller, not on the client. If you log on to the domain member using a local account, the account logon event gets recorded on the client.

One of the authors once was in a situation of doing forensics on a system that had been hacked by a student in his lab. The student had logged on to the machine, shut it down, set a boot and BIOS password, and changed the system clock. The student had then booted the system to ensure everything worked, logged on again, shut down the system, and then left. The logon events on the system itself were incorrectly ordered due to the system clock change. However, by correlating those events with the account logon events on the domain controller, we were able to determine conclusively both who had performed the attack and when. This information was enough to take action against the student. Thus, logon events can be very useful on clients. Other useful types of events include object access auditing. For any object access events to be recorded, however, you need to first configure system ACLs (SACLs) on objects, because none are configured by default.

*We recommend configuring audit settings that are consistent with your security policy and audit needs.*

## Allowed to Format and Eject Removable Media

The right to format and eject removable media hardly sounds like a security setting, does it? Besides, it is granted only to administrators by default, so why change it? This right allows a user to burn CDs and DVDs. Doing so is increasingly becoming a job requirement for many people. Without changing this setting, that means that all those people would need to be administrators on the system. By granting this permission (which is a security option, not a privilege, in Group Policy) to interactive users, you allow those users who need to burn CDs to do so without having to make them administrators. This improves the overall security posture of the system, which is why we include it as the last of the client security tweaks we recommend.

## The Caution List—Changes You Should Not Make

There are certain tweaks that you should not make. Nevertheless, you see them recommended in various sources. It is worth mentioning these and why you should not make them.

### Account Lockout

Account lockout will almost certainly increase your help desk cost significantly. In addition, it also only protects bad passwords. You would be better off getting rid of guessable passwords.

### Full Privilege Auditing

FullPrivilegeAuditing, or "Audit: Audit the use of Backup and Restore privilege" in Group Policy, configures the system to audit all file access even when they are performed by a backup program. This setting is one of several "blow up my event logs" settings that will simply fill your event logs with a large amount of mostly useless information that you probably do not care about anyway.

### Crash on Audit Failure

CrashOnAuditFail, or "Audit: Shut down system immediately if unable to log security audits" in Group Policy, causes your system to crash if it cannot log security events. This setting is designed for military intelligence environments and should not be used on the vast majority of systems. Use the feature built in to the OS to alert an administrator when the event logs reach a certain threshold and then go archive them instead. Better yet, get an event log collection system and use it to archive event logs. By the time you read this, Microsoft will hopefully have released its Audit Collection System (ACS), which provides this functionality.

### Disable Cached Credentials

Many of the security guides out there recommend disabling cached credentials on all machines. You should consider this carefully, especially on laptops. There is no real problem with disabling them on servers and desktops. However, if you disable them on laptops, you will break domain logon while disconnected from a domain. That means users will have to log on with a local account instead. Not only will this make them irate because their resources no longer show up, but in most cases we have seen they will use the Administrator account, which will (hopefully) degrade security since their domain account is not a local administrator. (It isn't, is it?) Even if they use a local non-admin account, the chances they will use the same password as on their domain account are significant, which means the password is much more exposed than through cached credentials. Be careful where you turn this setting on.

### Clear Virtual Memory Page File

Many administrators want to have the system clear the page file on shutdown to avoid attackers sniffing through it for interesting data in case the system is stolen. Although we have no problem in principle with this, you really have to ask yourself how likely it is that they will actually (a) steal the system, (b) find something interesting, and (c) actually be able to tell that it is interesting. OK, if you are up against a foreign intelligence service, the answers to these questions may dictate that you should clear the page file. If they do, you still need to consider shutdown times, however. It could take up to an additional 40 minutes to clear the page file at shutdown. Do you really want your laptop to take an additional 40 minutes to shut down after the flight attendants announce that "we have now reached an altitude where portable electronics devices may no longer be used?"

## Security Configuration Tools

In Windows NT 4.0 Service Pack 4, Microsoft first released the Security Configuration Editor (SCE). It was a revolutionary tool at its time, both because of its legendary user-unfriendliness, and because it presented most security-relevant settings in one place. However, although the tool shipped with several "security templates" containing specific settings you could apply to a system, use of at least one of those templates was likely to significantly impair the system's ability to function. Several third parties shortly published security guides describing their recommendations for settings to use, based most on the one template that would break everything. Testing of these guides on general purpose systems usually ranged from non-existent to poor, making them a prime call generator for Microsoft's product support services. Some exceptions are noted, but these were exceptions designed for very specific environments, such as military systems, and were completely unsuited for virtually all general purpose systems; as well as most military systems.

Several years ago, in an attempt to decrease the support costs associated with security configuration, as well as provide realistic and actionable guidance on hardening systems, Microsoft embarked on an effort to document security hardening of various products through security guides. The first of these guides was the Windows 2000 Security Hardening Guide (`http://go.microsoft.com/fwlink/?LinkId=28591`), followed shortly by the Windows Server 2003 Guide (`http://go.microsoft.com/fwlink/?LinkId=14845`), the Windows XP Guide (`http://go.microsoft.com/fwlink/?LinkId=14840`), their associated Threats and Countermeasures Guide (`http://go.microsoft.com/fwlink/?LinkId=15159`), and the Exchange Server 2003 Guide (`http://go.microsoft.com/fwlink/?LinkId=25210`). The purpose of the guides was to provide more information on security settings that can be configured in these products, as well as how to configure them to provide adequate protection for particular systems filling relatively generic roles. The guides have also been adopted as configuration standards by various organizations.

With Windows Server 2003 Service Pack 1, Microsoft released the Security Configuration Wizard (SCW). SCW is the first new security policy tool from Microsoft in six years. It is designed to assist in configuring security on a particular system, tailoring the security on that system to the specific needs of the organization. Although client systems generally need to be multipurpose systems and there consequently are few specific roles that apply to them, servers can, and in many cases should, be configured to very specific roles.

To assist with authoring security policies in such environments, SCW was designed for relatively advanced administrators who want to tailor the security of their servers to the specific roles those servers should perform. It can also be used by system architects to create new roles and new policies by combining roles. Finally, even relatively junior system administrators can use it to apply policies authored or tailored by others. Contrary to SCE, SCW includes significant intelligence on the needs of a system performing a particular role and allows an analyst to walk through each option for reducing the attack surface on that role.

One way to look at how these two resources relate is to view security configuration as an organizational chart where items get more specific the further down the chart you move, as shown in Figure 2-2.

The base operating system provides a default level of security, but because systems can be deployed in different roles, security can, and should, be tailored to that role to achieve a lower attack surface. A default installation cannot account for these roles since the security settings in a default installation must

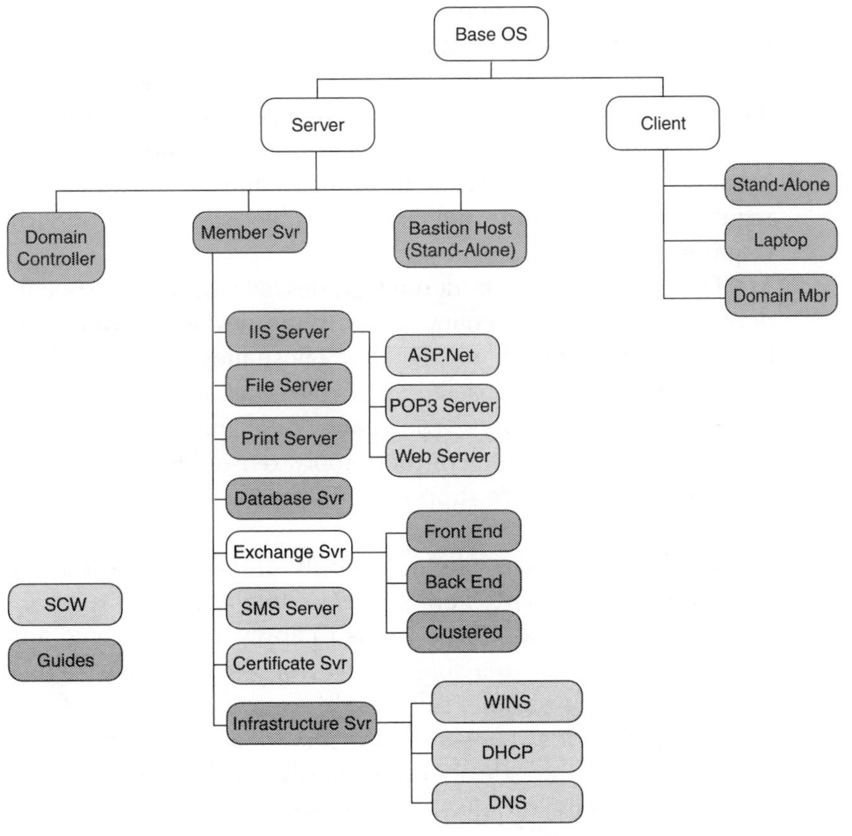


**Figure 2-2** Server roles can be viewed as an organizational chart.

allow for a greater range of use of the system. To that end, the guides, as well as SCW, provide security configuration for a wide range of roles, accounting for many, if not most, deployment scenarios for servers and clients. Note that the roles shown in Figure 2-2 are only a sampling and may not be available for all operating systems. The diagram is merely meant to show that the guides, in general, provide more generic configurations, with more specific configuration offered by a customized role designed using SCW.

The hardening guides include a relatively small set of roles. They also include settings for several levels of each role to tailor the role to a particular threat level in the environment. Those levels allow use of the guides in extremely hostile environments, such as military facilities, as well as in environments where interoperability with legacy systems is required, necessitating a decreased security posture. The guides should be used by administrators who need to configure security on more generic systems, by architects who simply want to learn more about the settings available on the operating systems and other products, and by administrators who are required to configure a system in accordance with an approved configuration based on the assurance level needed at their site. This latter category primarily applies to government agencies and facilities that are subject to regulatory requirements, such as those subject to HIPAA or Sarbanes-Oxley requirements.

The roles in the hardening guides are designed specifically to be deployed using Group Policy (GP). SCW does not produce GP configurations, but rather portable XML files. Those files cannot be directly used in a GP object (GPO). To use an SCW role in a GPO, it must be transformed into a GPO using the `scwcmd transform` command.

The decision of which of these tools to use depends on your objective. Although all options are supported, they serve different purposes:

- If you need to configure security on clients, use the guides. SCW does not support client security configuration.
- An administrator who wants to apply a relatively generic security configuration to a single server or a set of servers, to allow them to perform various roles at different times, should use the hardening guides. The "member server" and "standalone server" configurations are designed primarily for this purpose, although they will usually require that certain features be unlocked to work properly. They are essentially baseline policies that allow systems to function without providing specific services to users and clients.

- An architect who is designing generic security guidance for a specific environment should build upon either the configurations provided in the hardening guides or develop a new policy for use with SCW. The choice of route to take would depend primarily on personal preference.
- An advanced administrator or architect who is tailoring configurations for single- or multi-role servers in a specific environment may chose one of three options:

    1. Develop a new role for SCW.
    2. Use SCW to tailor a custom role based on one or more existing roles.
    3. Develop a custom configuration based on the hardening guides, resulting in a new security template.

  This new role can subsequently be deployed by administrators using either SCW or Group Policy. The latter option is preferred if the role will be deployed using Group Policy. The former two options are preferred if the configuration is deployed using SCW or if they can be transformed into a GPO later using the `scwcmd transform` command.
- An administrator, who needs to deploy a finished SCW policy on a single- or multi-role server, or set of identical servers, may use SCW to deploy this role.
- An administrator who needs to configure a single- or multi-role server for which neither the guides nor SCW has a tailored configuration should either use a generic role in the guides, or leave the system in a default configuration. Although the "member server baseline" and "standalone" roles in the guides are designed for generically described systems, it is likely that some function of the server will not operate properly after they are applied. Creation of a rollback template is highly encouraged in this situation. If a role exists in SCW that is close to the role performed by the system, the administrator may choose to customize and test this role for adequate functionality. SCW includes rollback functionality, making such testing simpler. Be extremely careful applying such a "near-match" role to a production system, however. Doing so is likely to result in an immediate need for an up-to-date resumé.
- An administrator or architect who is interested in learning about a specific product, about security settings used with that product, and about the threats they mitigate, should refer to the guides.

SCW provides the ability to operate in conjunction with the security guides by importing a template, such as provided with the guides. This functionality, however, should be used with great caution. It is possible, even likely, that the settings made by SCW are overridden by the guides, and vice versa, with the result that the system will not perform the functions intended by either.

## Summary

Hardening systems is not an easy task. You can find a plethora of information on the subject, but the vast majority of it seems to be geared toward military systems used in incredibly hostile environments. In addition, there is a definite belief that the more settings you make, the better off you are. In this chapter, we tried to dispel some of these myths and instead focus on the things that will significantly impact your security. If you have a home system behind a hardware firewall, you probably do not need to make any of these changes. If you are looking at configuring data center servers sitting behind firewalls with restrictions on who they can receive requests from, you may only need a few. The second-most important rule is to analyze the security needs of your system and then select a reasoned set of steps that mitigate threats you care about instead of making as many changes as you can just so you can say you have done something. The most important rule is to test, test, and re-test, before you roll things out. Most of the people recommending security tweaks have not tested them themselves to any great extent, much less understand what they would break in your environment.

## What You Should Do Today

- Look at your security practices and see whether you have implemented any of the myths.
- Evaluate all critical servers to ensure the critical settings are set on all systems where they can be set.
- Evaluate whether you have any of the troublesome settings set on any of your production systems and turn them off if possible.

CHAPTER 3

# Protecting User Applications

Protecting user applications is a complicated business. In contrast to server applications, which are relatively predictable—we have a reasonably good idea what functionality they need to provide—the exact usage scenario of user applications may not be so obvious. User applications, by and large, are information worker applications, and information workers are somewhat unpredictable. Sure, we can make assumptions about common functionality—everyone will read e-mail and use a word processor, they may need a presentation program, possibly a spreadsheet application, and, of course, they cannot do their job without that most insidious of applications: a Web browser! The problem is that it is much harder to tell what exactly they will do with those applications, and harder still to control them so they can do only that. Couple that with the fact that they are *user* applications and we have a security disaster waiting to happen. As mentioned in Chapter 2, "Server and Client Hardening," for most users given the choice of dancing pigs and security, security does not stand a chance.

In this chapter, we summarize some of the steps you can take to protect user applications. Although we cannot possibly cover all of the tweaks and other steps you can take to secure user applications, we will get you started by looking at the basics. In a sense, this is mostly about protecting your users from themselves and your networks from compromise through users.

## Patch Them!

Step one in securing anything is patching it. If you do not patch, you will get hacked; it is that simple. Unfortunately, patching users is nontrivial, so we largely have to resort to patching the applications they use. Applications, however, are not easy to patch either. First, you have to find out that they need patches. Doing so is not as straightforward as it should be either. Start out by taking an inventory of what is installed on your systems. If you have an enterprise management system, or better yet, a standard desktop environment, you are far ahead of the game at this point. Use those to generate a list of which applications you have and where. If you have some kind of centralized application distribution system, use it to generate a database of what is installed where. If you do not have any of these technologies, use some creative scripting to discover what people are using. When you install applications that are recognized by the operating system, they will create a Registry key underneath HKEY_LOCAL_MACHINE\SOFTWARE\Microsoft\Windows\CurrentVersion\Uninstall. Querying that key will give you some idea of what is available. Each uninstallable component listed there has a value called DisplayName listing the name of the application. There are usually many more items listed in that key than what shows up in Add/Remove Programs. This is normal because not everything should show up there. Some of these items are device drivers, others are merely components of a larger piece of software (or suite), and so on.

### PATCH SCANNING

Hopefully by the time you read this, Microsoft has released version 2.0 of MBSA, which includes much better patch scanning for user applications. However, the real killer app will be version 3.0; as of this writing, however, it does not even have a product name yet. Keep an eye on the MBSA Web site (`http://www.microsoft.com/mbsa`) for these new tools.

There are also third-party tools that do a reasonably good job of patch scanning. One of the most popular is Shavlik's HFNetChk, which uses the same engine as MBSA version 1.x.

Listing applications that can be uninstalled is not sufficient, however. Some older applications do not show up there, and ActiveX controls, which are basically applications that also need patched, do not get listed there either in general. ActiveX controls can be seen in the Manage Add-ons dialog in Internet Explorer (IE) starting with Windows XP Service Pack 2. Figure 3-1 shows this dialog.

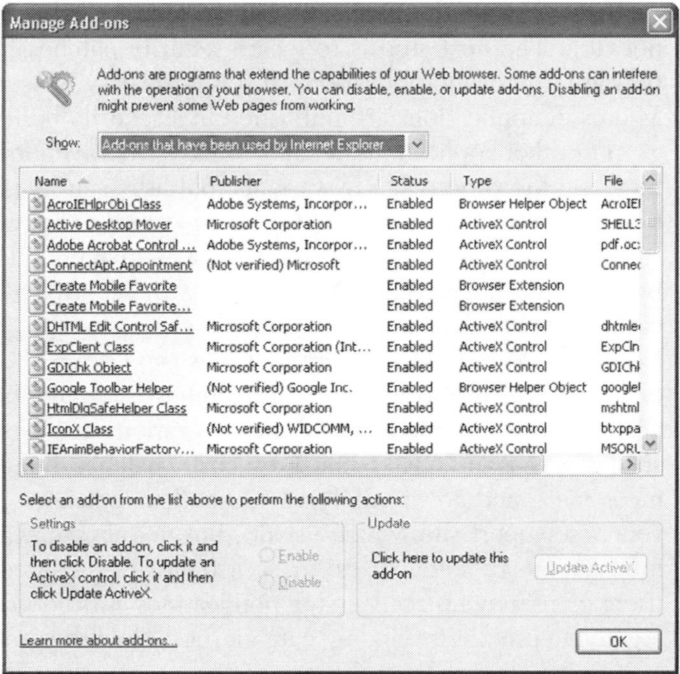


**Figure 3-1** The Manage Add-ons dialog in Internet Explorer 6.0 Service Pack 2.

The Manage Add-ons dialog is fine, but there is one problem with it: what good does a GUI do us? By the time we run around to every single machine to enumerate all the add-ons, we have probably been attacked already. To programmatically determine which add-ons are in use by IE requires evaluating each user's profile on each system. The class ID (CLSID) for each add-on is listed in HKEY_CURRENT_USER\Software\Microsoft\Windows\CurrentVersion\Ext. You would then have to resolve each of these key names under HKEY_CLASSES_ROOT\CLSID, where each CLSID has a key with information on the actual control involved. Typically, the default value of the key has a string that explains the control. If you have an enterprise management system, such as SMS, this may be feasible; without that, however, getting this information from every machine is almost not worth the effort. You may just want to consider the Group Policy option of only allowing authorized ActiveX controls to execute instead.

Let's assume that you now have a list of all the applications on your network. The next step is to locate security patches for each of them. If they are Microsoft applications, this is fairly easy. Most security patches for Microsoft applications are published in a security bulletin.

For other applications, it is not as easy. Many vendors, particularly those targeting the various UNIX variants, publish security patch notification on the BugTraq mailing list (`http://www.securityfocus.com`). Secunia (`http://www.secunia.com`) also has a relatively good list of security flaws, but flaws do not necessarily correlate with security patches, and in some cases Secunia's database is not completely up-to-date. Mitre maintains the Common Vulnerabilities and Exposures (`http://cve.mitre.org`) database, which also lists security patches for a number of products; but again, it is not complete. There are also various mailings from organizations such as SANS and CERT that list security patches, but they tend to be both incomplete and focus on flaws more than patches. Then there is each vendor's support site, which usually, but not always, will list security patch information. In some cases, these listings are provided only to registered users or users who register for notifications. In the end, you need to put together a process for finding patches for each of the products you are using. Use any or all of these resources as well as any others that you find helpful. There is no easy solution here, so feel free to innovate and come up with something that works for you. Also feel free to put pressure on vendors to put together a program to notify you of patches. If you spend money on their products, it is only right that they help you keep those products safe.

After you have the patches, how do you get them installed? Ultimately, you have to build a process around patching, as well as a process around mitigation.

## Make Them Run As a Nonadmin

After you have an inventory of the applications used on your network, you need to figure out how to run them using the least user access (LUA). Putting it another way, user applications should not require the user to be an administrator. Many applications will work just fine as non-administrator. For instance, if you only have the most recent version of Microsoft Office, maybe WinZip and Acrobat, you can almost certainly run those applications as a regular user. Throw older applications or more obscure ones into the mix and the answer is not so clear any more.

The need to run things as LUA is clear. If an exploit enters through an application, it has whatever access to the system that the user running the application has. As an example, take the case of spyware. While on one of our innumerable world speaking tours in 2004, one of the authors got a phone call from his wife complaining about a home computer acting up. The culprit seemed to be spyware installed on the computer. When we got home, both of us installed a couple of spyware detection tools and ran them to see how bad off we were. The following week, while on yet another continent, we compared notes. The one of us who got the call had found 162 separate pieces of spyware on the system. The other author? Zero. The difference? One of us gave in to domestic pressure and made the family (or at least some of it) administrators. The other is the bastard operator from hell (BOFH) and did not. (Of course, one of us was now able to act the hero while the other is still considered a mean bastard.) The lesson is clear, however: if software is not running as an admin, the damage it can do is significantly less.

Start out your quest for nonadmin with your inventory of software. Then designate a few guinea pigs to run them as LUA. These should probably be relatively technical people who can give good feedback on what breaks. Make them nonadmins and watch what happens. If things break, follow the procedure we lay out in Chapter 4, "Protecting Services and Server Applications," for how to unlock the system sufficiently to run these applications as nonadministrators. In many cases, you will find that with relatively few tweaks you can make the applications function perfectly fine without having to make users admins. Before you embark on this, however, you need to get manager approval and executive buyoff. Getting such buyoff is an entirely different story, however. Both of us went into IT primarily to avoid having to deal with people, so we are not experts at this by any stretch of the imagination.

## Turn Off Functionality

Far too often, applications come with all the bells and whistles turned on—everything including the kitchen sink is installed by default. Just take a look at the default toolbars in Microsoft Word. There are more than 50 icons on there! Having used Word for over 10 years, we still do not know what all of them do. Getting rid of functionality that you do not need is a good step toward securing applications.

## Unused Components

There have been many examples of problems with optional components of applications. For instance, in September 2003 Microsoft had to release a security update for a flaw in the WordPerfect converter in Office. If you did not need the WordPerfect converter, it should not have been installed. The key rule here is not to install anything you do not need. Creating a standard desktop environment that contains only the functionality your users can and should use is the general rule to follow. Many applications, the Microsoft Office suite included, come with administrative installation options that enable you to customize what is installed.

There are also opportunities to turn off functionality. Some applications allow central control over components of the application. For instance, the Office applications can be managed using IntelliMirror—the functionality within Active Directory that installs applications on systems. By creating a custom Windows Installer Transform file that includes a predefined Office profile, you can control the default behavior of your Office applications. These files can be deployed using IntelliMirror in Active Directory, ensuring that the Office applications are configured the way you want them from the start. Figure 3-2 shows the Office Profile Wizard from the Office Resource Kit (ORK).

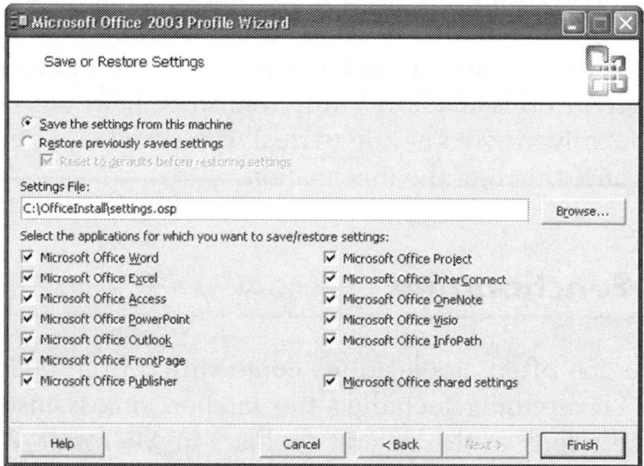


**Figure 3-2** The Office Profile Wizard in the Office 2003 Resource Kit.

To create transforms for Office, you need an Enterprise edition license for Office along with the ORK, which you can get at `http://office.microsoft.com/en-us/FX011417911033.aspx`. Although the ORK is free, the software license is obviously not. However, the additional control you can obtain this way may justify the cost of the license. It only takes five licenses to get the media. For more information on how to deploy Office, refer to the Solution Accelerator for Business Desktop Deployment at `http://www.microsoft.com/technet/desktopdeployment/bddoverview.mspx`.

## Macros

Of particular note when it comes to application security is macros. Many applications are themselves application platforms. It is quite common for word processors, for instance, to have some kind of automation functionality through macros. In the case of the Microsoft Office suite, this programmability has been taken to a level bordering absurdity. You could practically write an operating system in Microsoft Excel! Macro viruses were quick to take advantage not only of this incredible functionality but also of users' propensity to open documents from anyone (remember the dancing pigs?) and click Yes on dialogs. It was not until recent versions of Office that the default security settings on macros started approaching reasonable default levels. Of course, users can reconfigure these settings at will, even if they are LUA.

Fortunately, you can configure the macro-level settings using Group Policy. This is done using administrative templates. Administrative templates, or ADM templates, are basically text files that allow you to configure settings in the HKEY_CURRENT_USER Registry hive via Group Policy. If you used the Policy Editor tool in Windows NT 4.0, the format of ADM templates will be familiar to you; it is basically the same format. You can import ADM templates into a Group Policy by right-clicking Administrative Templates under either Computer Configuration or User Configuration and selecting Add/Remove Templates. Templates added under Computer Configuration are primarily designed to modify non-security-related settings under HKEY_LOCAL_MACHINE. The main templates of interest from a security perspective are those that you add under User Configuration because these are the ones that can modify settings under

HKEY_CURRENT_USER. This mechanism provides the only way in Group Policy to customize settings under that Registry hive in a centralized fashion.

You can write your own custom ADM templates. The file itself is just a text file formatted in a particular way. The syntax is described in the platform SDK under the topic Template File Format (Setup and System Administration | Policies and Profiles | System Policies | Using the System Policy Editor | Template File Format). You can also obtain templates from other sources. The Office Resource Kit as well as the Windows XP Security Guide (`http://www.microsoft.com/ security/ guidance`) both come with several templates for adding security settings.

We highly recommend that you configure the macro-level settings to High. This allows signed macros only to run. Of course, a macro virus author could probably sign the virus and get a user to click the "Trust this certificate" dialog, but that becomes a user configuration problem. At least by forcing only signed macros to run we have done the best we can.

## Restrict Browser Functionality

The ultimate application platform is Web browsers. Although you will find thousands of claims as to why one browser (not IE) is more secure than another (IE), these claims overlook one fundamental fact, namely that the entire purpose of Web browsers is to enable users to go to untrusted software publishers and download and run code from them. They are designed to enable a function that is fraught with security problems. To further exacerbate the problem, browser developers have kept adding cool functionality to entice more developers to develop for their platform, thereby making more users use their platform.

To deal with this problem, the principle is really simple. Web browsers should have three things:

1. A solid patch management model allowing timely and well-tested updates for security problems
2. A thought-out security architecture that allows granular control of functionality, ideally on a per-site basis, to control what can be done by which sites
3. Good central manageability tools to enable administrators to centrally control the functionality in requirement 2

To our knowledge, no Web browser today delivers on all these points. IE comes close on 3, has some of 2, but some would argue is deficient in area 1.

The types of functionality that should be restrictable include anything that gives the ability to run code other than display code on a user's machine. This includes add-ins, scripts, plug-ins, and so on. However, it also includes things such as IFRAMES—a way to allow Web pages to put seamless frames on the screen showing one page within another. IFRAMES are commonly used to fool users into believing they are on one site when in reality they are actually on another. Some of the newer Dynamic HTML (DHTML) functionality is also quite dangerous. The ability to position windows offscreen, make windows transparent, or make windows larger than the screen have all been used to fool users into thinking they are looking at something other than what is there. Then there is, of course, the most annoying feature ever invented by stupid programmers: pop-up windows! We have some good suggestions for what to do with the person who came up with the idea of being able to programmatically launch windows. Unfortunately, we cannot find anywhere where those actions would be legal.

Restricting IE functionality is possible using Group Policy. In fact, the amount of power Group Policy gives you over IE is quite significant, particularly under XP Service Pack 2 (SP2). Yes, that is correct: you can manage Group Policy under Windows XP. What we mean here is that you use an XP client to manage domain group policy on the server. The reason is that a lot of settings were added in the user interface on XP SP2, and you will not see those if you manage the policy on a server unless that server is running Windows Server 2003 Service Pack 1 or better.

To open a Group Policy object from a server, open a new MMC instance, add a new snap-in, and select Group Policy. When the dialog comes up that asks you which Group Policy object to select, click Browse and then type in the name of the server. You can also open the object from the command line with a command such as this:

```
gpedit.msc /gpobject:"LDAP://CN={31B2F340-016D-11D2-945F-
00C04FB984F9},CN=Policies,CN=System,DC=PYN-DMZ,DC=LOCAL"
```

The first `CN` entry is the CLSID for the policy, which you get by just looking at the properties of the policy. The first `DC` entry is the name of the domain, and the second is the domain suffix. There may be additional ones, depending on the domain name you are using. When you

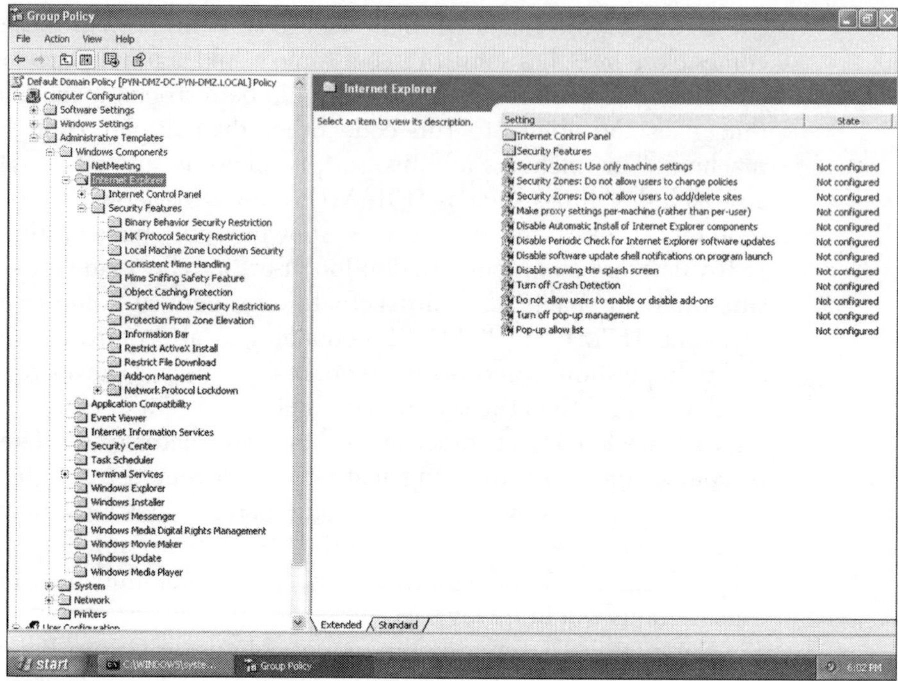


**Figure 3-3** Internet Explorer machine-based Group Policy configuration interface.

open this policy object, you have the full XP SP2 UI available. Even if the policy is applied from an older DC, it will make the changes you specify here.

You can lock down IE both by user and by machine. However, certain features can only be restricted by user. To control IE through Group Policy, go to either Computer Configuration or User Configuration, and then to Administrative Templates | Windows Components | Internet Explorer. Figure 3-3 shows the Computer Configuration display.

To configure allowed ActiveX controls, you have to go to the User Configuration display. This is shown in Figure 3-4.

We highly encourage you to test locking down the allowed controls in IE. Doing so will significantly limit your exposure to security issues in third-party ActiveX controls. As with all security measures, however, there is a drawback. In this case, it is that many Web sites will stop working. You

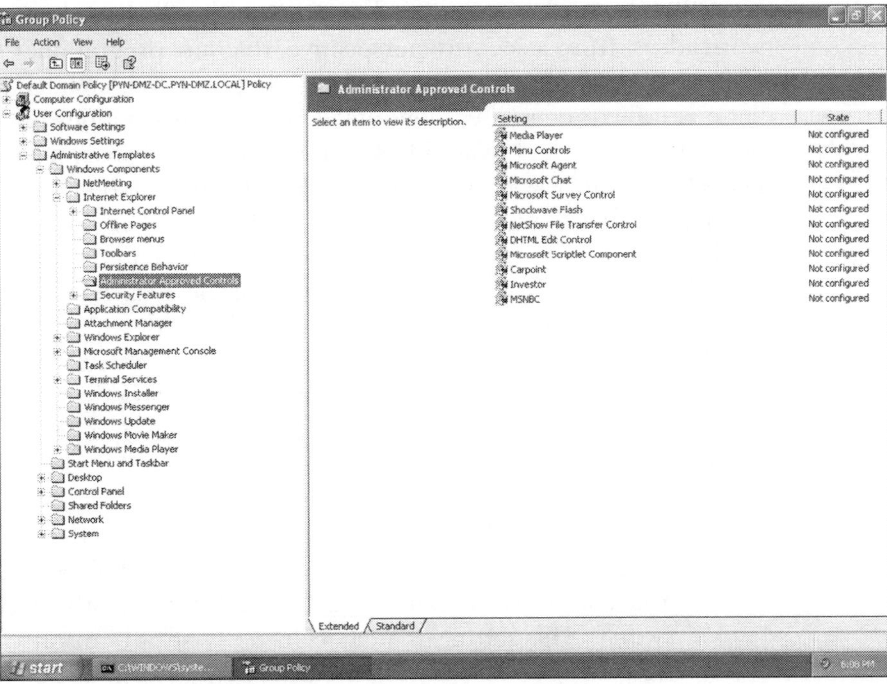


**Figure 3-4** Internet Explorer user-based Group Policy configuration interface.

may want to mitigate that problem by creating separate policies for particular types of users. Some types of users (for example, sys admins) may need significantly fewer restrictions than others (for example, managers).

## HTML E-Mail Security

For years, the Internet Explorer security philosophy was based on the premise that if users just would not go to hostile Web sites they would not have any security problems. This would work really well if Google could only get that "hostile Web site identification" feature working. Then all you would have to do is not click the sites with the skull and crossbones icon and you would be safe—except for one thing. Many years ago now, some genius came up with a way to allow hostile Web sites to come to you—HTML e-mail.

HTML e-mail in its original incarnation has to have been one of the worst ideas, from a security perspective, that any programmer could have ever devised. The entire concept of allowing code to be mailed around and automatically executed without any controls or restrictions on what it can do sounds like a bad joke out of a cheap novel. Yet that was exactly what HTML e-mail was. Eventually, but not nearly soon enough, some restrictions were put in place. For instance, Microsoft Outlook and Outlook Express both added the ability to read mail in the Restricted Sites zone. Of course, even the default settings in the Restricted Sites zone are not quite restrictive enough for our tastes. Font download, for example, should never be allowed via e-mail, and it was not until XP SP2 that we got restrictions in place for binary behaviors. (Ever wonder what a "binary behavior" was? Just think of it as an ActiveX component without any security controls.) The rule of thumb is that you need to do two things:

1. Ensure that all mail is read in the Restricted Sites zone. In Outlook, this can be controlled only via the Office Resource Kit. You could also create a custom ADM template to control this switch. The setting is in HKCU\Software\Microsoft\Office\<version>\Outlook\Options\General\Security Zone, and it needs to be set to 0x4 to be in the Restricted Sites zone. In Outlook Express, there is no way to control this centrally. The setting is made in HKCU\Identities\<profile GUID>\Software\Microsoft\Outlook Express\5.0\Email Security Zone. Because the profile GUID is dynamic and unknown, it cannot be controlled centrally—one of the major reasons not to use Outlook Express in an enterprise. If you use any other mail client that supports HTML mail, you need to ensure that it has equivalent functionality to control what can run. Unfortunately, many ISPs recommend Outlook Express, primarily because of its cost, even though until recently it has had much worse security controls than Outlook.
2. Block *everything* in the Restricted Sites zone. Use Group Policy to configure this. The basic rule of thumb is that everything should be set to "disabled" (or whatever the most restrictive setting is) except for the pop-up blocker setting, which is a double negative, and should be set to "enabled" to turn on the pop-up blocker. After you have done that, you end up with a somewhat confusing Group Policy list, shown in Figure 3-5, where everything lists as enabled. That is because "enabled" in Group Policy "enables" you to control the setting and disable it.

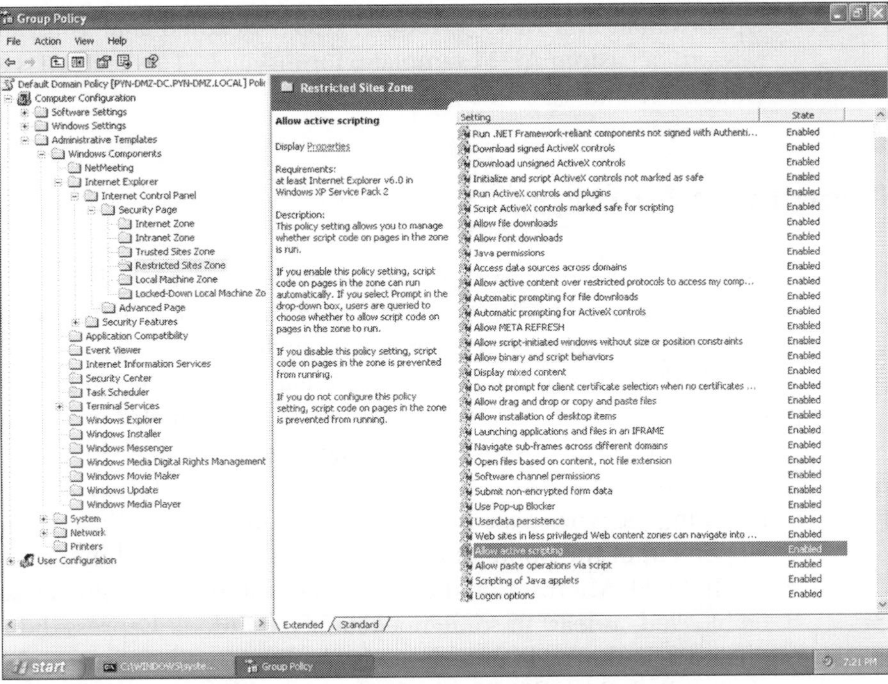


**Figure 3-5** Configure the Restricted Sites zone in Group Policy to ensure that it blocks everything.

As you may have been able to tell, we are not fans of HTML e-mail. It has gotten better in recent years, however, and one of the authors now uses it. The one advantage it has is the additional expressiveness it affords as well as the portability that you do not get with rich text. We do, however, use the Preview pane and Auto Preview features sparingly, and always ensure that they are turned off in the junk-mail folders.

One alternative to reading mail in HTML is to use the new features in some e-mail clients, including Microsoft Outlook, to enable you to read mail in plain text. Unfortunately, doing so has a great drawback: your users are not really likely to put up with it quietly for very long. HTML e-mail in plain text is an ugly thing. To see the effect for yourself, just turn on the feature (it is in Tools | Options | E-Mail Options), and then try to read your daily Dilbert mail. Reading mail in plain text would be a very useful mitigation to many HTML-borne attacks, however. We do highly recommend turning it on temporarily in the face of an outbreak. The setting is made in HKEY_CURRENT_USER\Software\Microsoft\Office\<version>\Outlook\

Options\Mail in a REG_DWORD called ReadAsPlain. You can configure this with a custom ADM template, for instance. This feature is available in Outlook 10 and 11 (Office XP and 2003).

## Attachment Manager

How is it that e-mail worms manage to spread so well? Typically it happens because, as we have said before, given the choice between security and dancing pigs, dancing pigs win every single time.

Fairly early on, some clever criminal realized this and started sending out e-mails like the one shown in Figure 3-6. Sometimes the message had a more suggestive subject line, such as ILOVEYOU, although strictly speaking, it does not seem necessary to be all that suggestive—just including the word *naked* in the e-mail seems to be sufficient to get at least 50 percent of the population to double-click the attachment.

In 2000, Microsoft and other vendors started enabling attachments to be blocked, at least in some mail clients. (Outlook Express did not receive effective and usable attachment blocking until Internet Explorer 6.0 Service Pack 2 in XP SP2.) In Outlook, the blocking consisted of a blacklist of file extensions and file type identifiers that were blocked from being

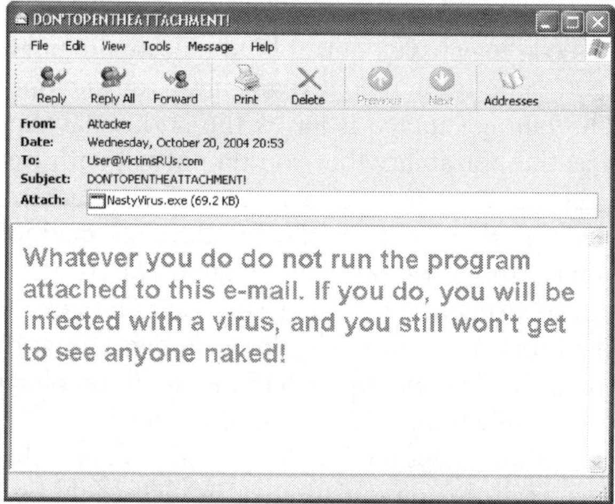


**Figure 3-6** Would your users open this attachment?

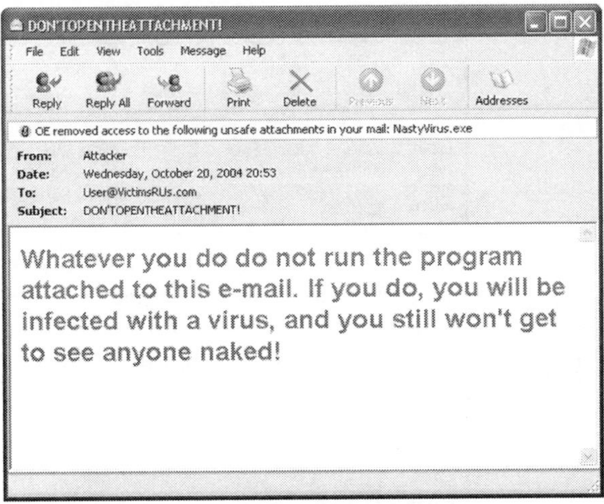


**Figure 3-7** Now users cannot open the attachment.

opened in the UI. The net result was that the e-mail the user saw looked like the one in Figure 3-7.

This worked well until the bad guys came up with a simple workaround. Just zip or rename the attachment and then include instructions for how to open it in the e-mail body. This worked reasonably well; the user population that was able to follow the instructions was slightly smaller than the number that would have opened the original attachment, but worms still spread nicely. Eventually, the antivirus vendors figured out how to identify some (but not all) of these attachments as evil anyway, and the ball was back in the bad guys' court. The workaround this time was to zip and encrypt the attachment. Now the e-mail looks like Figure 3-8.

At this point, we are somewhat stuck. We can hardly block zip files in e-mail. The productivity loss would be quite severe unless we provide alternate file transfer mechanisms, and it is likely they will be even less secure. Some anti-malware vendors have tried identifying the password in the e-mail, but this is too difficult to work most of the time. The basic problem here really is a Layer 8 problem—a political problem in the nine-layer OSI model. (Remember, there are at least nine layers in the OSI model: physical, data link, network, transport, session, presentation, application, political, and religious layers.) The unfortunate fact is that unless users will

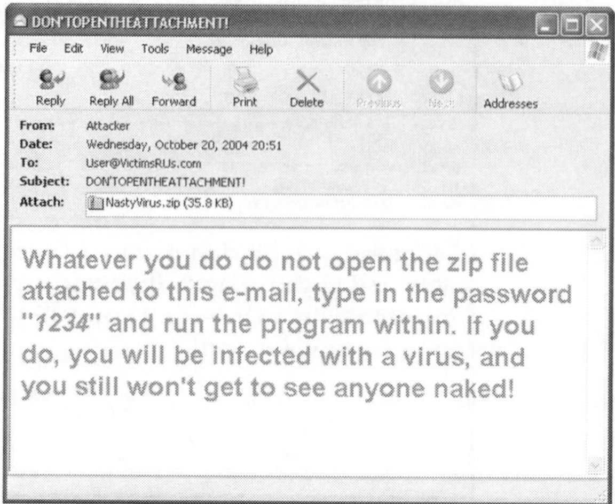


**Figure 3-8** Most users can figure out how to spread this worm.

stop double-clicking untrusted attachments, the only way to stop worms is to prevent them from doing so. We can easily do this with Group Policy now thanks to the new attachment manager in XP SP2.

The attachment manager is a way to control which attachment types are considered dangerous and generate a prompt. Prior to XP SP2, each application would need to maintain a list of these attachments. Starting with XP SP2, a centrally manageable list can be honored by all applications through the Attachment Execution Prevention (AEP) set of APIs. Figure 3-9 shows the settings you can control using the attachment manager.

After you configure the attachment manager in Group Policy, any application that calls the AEP to determine how to handle a particular file attachment or file download from the Internet will benefit from the central list. KB article 291369 lists the file types that should be considered unsafe as a baseline. You may freely add others, too. For users who consistently choose dancing pigs over security, we suggest creating a separate OU, and then giving them a policy that considers .* unsafe. This may sound drastic, but if it is the only way to protect them from themselves, you should at least be consider it (and of course, your policy should allow you to do so).

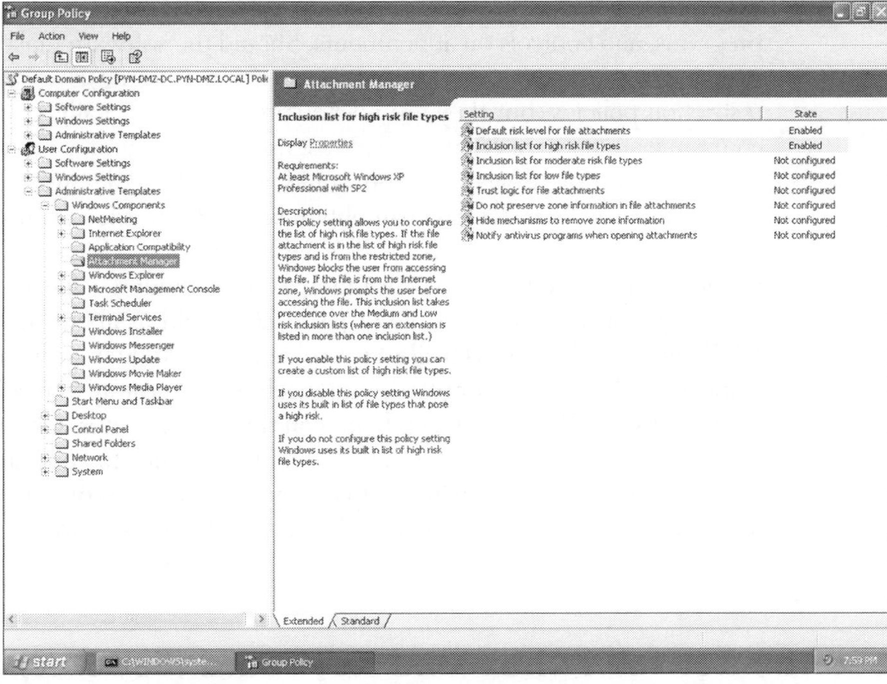


**Figure 3-9** The Windows XP SP2 attachment manager.

## Spyware

Spyware is a pretty ugly type of malware that spreads through browsers, e-mail, and pretty much any other mechanism users have for installing files. We mentioned earlier the primary way to stop spyware—do not let users run as admins. There are other supplemental measures, however. There are three principles behind spyware and malware protection:

1. Do not allow the malware to get onto the box.
2. If the malware should get onto the box, stop it from running.
3. Should the malware get onto the box and run, stop it from communicating.

The first objective is best served with defensive browsing, anti-malware programs, and controls on attachments. Should the software make it onto the machine anyway, the only way to stop it from running is to use software restriction policies, but they are not foolproof either. Finally, to stop it from communicating, we need firewalls. Most users will not understand host-based outbound filtering firewalls, so you would need to block known malware sites at the router or firewalls. You can obtain lists of these sites from some of the anti-spyware vendors, such as AdAware. Blocking at the firewall will not help traveling machines, however. For them, we recommend using a method that a colleague of ours by the name of Jason Zions told us about. Jason, being a UNIX guy, used a HOSTS file to resolve all the known spyware sites to a loopback address. In other words, the machine has no way to resolve them to the actual site; effectively black-holing all the spyware sites. Of course, if the spyware sites use IP addresses rather than host names to communicate, this method will not help, nor will it help if they change names or as new ones pop up. Nevertheless, it is a reasonable defense-in-depth measure.

## Security Between Chair and Keyboard (SeBCAK)

The final, and most important, piece in client application security, however, is security between chair and keyboard (SeBCAK). The fact of the matter is that as soon as you put a computer in the hands of a user, you lose a lot of control over that computer. In the end, the user has to make security decisions, which means the user must have an incentive to make the right security decisions and must have the knowledge, training, and skills to do so. A while ago, we spoke to a consultant friend of ours about a security breach on a sensitive network. When asked whether the network was air-gapped, he responded that the network was not, but the users were—between the ears. Although this is taking a bit of a glum outlook, particularly with respect to trying to blame users, the fact remains that users must take responsibility for security.

## Summary

In this chapter, we introduced some solutions to dealing with user application security. We have spent the past 30 combined working years trying to secure servers and networks, not necessarily user applications.

Therefore, our approach to user application security has often been to try to protect the servers from the user apps. This is not necessarily a bad idea, but it means that we have a lot more to say about server security than client security. It also means that we take the stance that user application security is a race between users' desire to see dancing pigs and your ability to stop them. Virtually all the things we have discussed in this chapter have been based on the principle of making the dancing pigs more difficult to access. In the end, however, we must say that there are two things more important to us than user application security. The first is user education—without educated users, nothing in this chapter will protect you. The second is server security—without server security, your servers are subject to whatever bad things can be done from the clients. You need to build a risk management plan that weighs and trades off between all those components.

## What You Should Do Today

- Start developing a process for keeping all your client applications patched.
- Start building a program to systematically evaluate applications to determine what it takes to run them with least privilege.
- Experiment with the tools available to secure client applications and to develop standardized client installations.

CHAPTER 4

# PROTECTING SERVICES AND SERVER APPLICATIONS

This chapter is about server applications and other services—or, more specifically, what you can do to protect them. Generally speaking, we are much more interested in protecting server applications than we are user-side applications. There is a really simple reason for this: most of the attacks against user-side applications are annoyance attacks, worms, e-mail viruses, and so on. These are mostly aimed at causing destruction and mayhem by disrupting large numbers of users and possibly stealing their personal information one at a time. However, if what you want is massive destruction, loads of personal information, and huge financial, political, or spiritual gain, there is nothing like taking over a few servers and stealing all the data that all the people who use them have stored there.

We said this before, but we are not all that interested in user-side attacks. Those are largely based on (a) unpatched vulnerabilities and (b) users who will do exactly as they are told, even if it is a criminal telling them to do it.

Rather, a typical problem that interests us is someone who breaks into your network and adds himself to your payroll, after making off with all the information on the patents you were about to file. Those types of attacks almost always start and end with servers. Therefore, you must learn how to protect services and server applications.

## You Need a Healthy Disrespect for Your Computer

The most important principle of protecting anything, and servers in particular, is to have a healthy disrespect for the rules. You will constantly run into statements like "that is not supported" and "we have never tested that." Those statements are very important, but they do not mean you cannot do something. They just mean you may be on your own doing it.

Certain things are known to be really bad for your career—such as wholesale replacement of Everyone access control lists (ACLs) with Authenticated Users—but there are a lot of others that simply have not been thoroughly tested but may be valuable nevertheless. You should feel free to experiment here. The fact remains that what is tested are things that will work in every, or almost every, environment. Your environment is unique and only you know how unique. If you want an optimally protected system for your environment, you need to analyze your environment, apply steps that are appropriate to mitigate the risks you find are important, and be willing to test some new things and break some rules in the process. This is not magic, just tedious. Nevertheless, some things simply do not make sense, such as the aforementioned replacement of Everyone with Authenticated Users. Since the two groups are functionally identical since Windows XP, the risk associated with doing so is considerably higher than the non-existent benefit. Also keep in mind one fundamental rule: *Do NOT test "hardening" steps on production systems, unless you feel your career has progressed as far as you are interested in going already.*

Turning on untested hardening tweaks on production systems is known as a CLM—a career-limiting move. We do not like those. Feel free to break things; experimentation is important. Just make sure you do it on test systems, such as virtual machines or lab machines.

## Hardening vs. Supportability

A note on hardening versus supportability is worthwhile here. As mentioned earlier, vendors often claim that some setting, tweak, or configuration is "unsupported." In some cases, as in the aforementioned ACL case, there is really good reason for this. Some tweaks simply put the system into an unstable or unreliable state. In other cases, the reason for a setting being unsupported is more likely that it has not been adequately tested. Supportability means that the vendor understands the configuration, can replicate it, and has tested it with a reasonable number of other applications and systems. Just because something is "unsupported" does not necessarily mean it will not work. What it does mean is that it may have interesting and exciting side-effects that you may not get vendor help in resolving, or that what you get is "best efforts" support, which might be limited to undoing your configuration. For this reason, it is critical that you maintain adequate documentation on what you did, understand the impact of the changes you are making on the functionality of the system, and understand how to undo the changes you make. ACL changes, for instance, cannot be undone in some cases—such as wholesale ACL changes on the root of the boot partition—whereas Registry changes are trivial to undo, as long as the system still boots. You also need to understand how to test things because the vendor has not always done it.

OK, enough warnings, on to some of the basics of hardening services and server apps.

## Rule 1: All Samples Are Evil

There is no other way to describe this: samples are evil! The simple fact is that sample applications shipped with other software are designed to demonstrate some cool functionality, not to be secure. The examples abound of sample problems:

- *MSADC Sample* `<http://www.securityfocus.com/bid/529/>`—This was probably the most famous vulnerability of 1999. In a nutshell, an attacker could pass commands to a Web server through sample databases installed with IIS 4.0 and execute commands on the server. In addition, a component called vbBusObj allowed the same thing, but using a slightly different method that was not fixed in the original patch. Both the sample database and the vbBusObj were samples installed with a default install of IIS 4.0.
- *Cold Fusion Expression Evaluator* `<http://www.securityfocus.com/bid/115>`—This is probably my favorite sample of all time, the expression evaluator from Cold Fusion 2.x through 4.0. In a nutshell, it allows an attacker to go to a Web form and send commands to the server which get executed there under the IIS service account (LocalSystem). It is a bit more involved than that but that is the gist of it.

What this really means is one thing, which is a fundamental piece of hardening any server app: *Samples do not belong anywhere near a production system!*

All samples should be considered evil and they should never be left, or installed, on a production system.

## Three Steps to Lowering the Attack Surface

Much of the hardening we can do on services and service accounts falls into three categories—all designed to reduce the attack surface of the host. *Attack surface* is a generic term that denotes anything that could potentially be attacked. Attack surface does not mean that a component has a vulnerability, nor that it could be exploited. Attack surface just means the host is presenting some interface that an attacker—should she be able to find a way to exploit it—can use. In essence, attack surface reduction (ASR) is about reducing the interfaces available to an attacker. There are three basic steps, which we review in the next few paragraphs.

### Uninstall Unnecessary Components

The first step in ASR is to uninstall unnecessary components where they can be uninstalled. You should always try to uninstall things because they can otherwise sometimes be turned on by an attacker. Some components also have multiple pieces, and not all of them can be turned off. Consider IPv6. It does provide some compelling functionality, but it also provides some new features that you should be careful with. For instance, `netsh interface portproxy` provides a port redirector, much like the ones attackers used to have to customize to perform tasks such as circumventing IPsec policies and tunnel Terminal Services through open firewall ports. If you do not need IPv6, turn it off.

Saying you should remove or turn things off is easy to say but not so easy to operationalize. First, some components cannot be easily uninstalled. We need to disable those instead. The harder part is to figure out what is unnecessary. For a year or so, we have lobbied to tag services, for instance, with better information on this. Consider, for instance, the Alerter service, the "porn advertisement service" as we like to call it from its most frequent use these days. If you go into the Services Control Manager (SCM), the description for the Alerter service is as follows:

> Notifies selected users and computers of administrative alerts. If the service is stopped, programs that use administrative alerts will not receive them. If this service is disabled, any services that explicitly depend on it will fail to start.

That sure helps you tell whether you can disable it doesn't it? We tried to get this changed to something more descriptive:

> Notifies selected users and computers of administrative alerts. This service is primarily used to advertise new porn sites, and is completely useless in just about every environment. You can freely turn it off without disrupting legitimate functionality.

The program manager in charge of the service was not all that amused, but we found this description to be a lot more useful. Unfortunately, this points to a frequent problem. How do you determine that something is unnecessary? The simple answer is that you turn it off. If everything still works, you did not need it. A lot of people will tell you that you should turn off everything and then turn stuff on again until everything works. The problem is figuring out what you can turn off and still boot the system. Either way works, but we find that starting with a system that boots gets us where we are going faster.

Things to uninstall include all optional services. For example, on Windows Server 2003, IIS is not installed by default, but on the Windows 2000 Server family, it is. The majority of Windows 2000 servers do not need IIS and should have it turned off and uninstalled. The Network Monitor tool is not needed on most systems. Remove it. Basically, if it is optional, turn it off and see whether everything still works. If it does, remove it if you can.

---

**TIP:** To determine whether a component is necessary, turn it off. If everything still works, you did not need it.

---

## Disable Unnecessary Features

For those things that can be uninstalled, do so. If they cannot be uninstalled, turn them off or disable them. For example, the aforementioned Alerter service is already disabled on Windows Server 2003 and Windows XP SP2. It can be freely disabled on most other systems as well, but it cannot be uninstalled. The Messenger service can go along with the Dodo bird and the Alerter service. The Workstation service is needed on most systems, but many systems can live without the Server service. For instance, laptops almost certainly do not need to be file servers, nor do many Web servers. Keep in mind, however, that if you turn off the Server service, you can no longer scan the machine for security patches remotely with MBSA. On the other hand, it is likely you need a lot fewer patches on that system.

## Block Access to Unnecessary Interfaces

If you cannot uninstall or disable a component, but you still do not need it, block access to it. How you do this depends on the component. For example, binaries that you do not need or want can sometimes not be removed because they are under Windows File Protection. If you try to delete them, they will be automatically restored by the OS. This applies, for instance, to tftp.exe. (Not that you could achieve the same effect with a different tool, but tftp.exe is just so darn convenient for attackers.) Not to worry, however; we can fix that problem a different way. Use software restriction policies (SRPs)—the second most powerful security feature in the OS (after IPsec)—to block execution of these files. Open up the Group Policy Editor, go to Software Restriction Policies, right-click it, and select Add Software Restriction Policies. Now right-click the Additional Rules node and add the rule you want. There are several types. One way is to add a hash rule, which will block execution of the file even if it is renamed. Another is to add a path rule, which will block execution of the file if it is replaced with a new version. We recommend adding both rules for each binary that you want to block, just to be on the safe side.

Software restriction polices can certainly be tremendously useful, but they are not bulletproof. Code that executes as an administrator or as local system can easily get around them, for example. Therefore, to get full effect of them, you must also make sure that your software runs with least privilege.

The astute reader might have wondered why we did not recommend just blocking everything and then unblocking specifically those things that were required for the system to function. That is the correct way to do things, but it is nontrivial to accomplish. Enumerating all the binaries used by a system simply is very hard, and SRP has the unfortunate side-effect that it is very easy to, and pretty likely that you will, end up with a system that does not boot. However, for the reader who puts in the time to figure out exactly what the minimum set is, the effort is well worthwhile.

There are a couple of shortcuts to help you determine exactly what needs to run. First, use System Internals' File Monitor (`http://www.systeminternals.com`) to log the system during startup. (Note that by the time you read this, File Monitor and Registry Monitor may have been replaced by Process Monitor, but that tool was not yet available at the time we wrote this.) That should give you a good idea of which files to unblock to make a system bootable. Second, *findstr* is your friend. Findstr is a built-in command-line tool that works much like grep on UNIX. Dump the File Monitor log to a text file, and then use findstr to find files that get executed. If you have a copy of the Interix tools (if you do not, why not? They are free!), use the `cut` command to parse the output and `sort` and `uniq` to remove duplicates.

By the way, SRP does not exist in Windows 2000 (or Windows XP Home Edition for that matter), so do not bother looking for it there. Yet another great reason to upgrade to Windows Server 2003.

## What About Service Accounts?

Service accounts are one of the simplest ways to turn a compromise of one system into a compromise of an entire network. Much of this stems from reuse of service accounts across systems, but we also find that most service accounts are granted privileges they do not need. It is extremely common to run services, just like all applications, as an administrator just because "everything works when we do that." To protect your network, you need to consider what privileges your services really need.

## Privileges Your Services Do Not Need

Many services are configured with privileges that they really do not need. Public enemy number one in this area is probably backup tools. Just about anyone who has installed a backup tool that has a client component for remote backups can testify to the fact that the client allegedly must run as an administrator. Therefore, the recommendation is invariably to configure the client component to run as a domain administrator. Enterprise management systems (EMSs) often suffer from the same problem.

**WARNING:** A process running on clients as a domain administrator are hazardous to your network health! It degrades the security of the entire domain to that of the least-secure machine in the domain.

Domain administrative accounts are for administering domain controllers. Period. Far too often, services such as backup and EMS require them because the developers would not take the time to figure out how to perform the same task with minimum privileges. If they just make them run as a domain admin, they can connect to the backup server and vice versa and everything will work. This is an extremely dangerous practice because it degrades the security of the entire domain to that of the least-secure machine in the domain. The probability of every system in a network being secure on any given day is virtually nil. You would do well to ensure that all systems in the environment are resilient to failure of other systems.

Some backup vendors configure their solutions to use the Backup Operators group. That is also undesirable. The Backup Operators group basically has two privileges: SeBackupPrivilege and SeRestorePrivilege. SeBackupPrivilege allows the user to bypass file system access control lists (ACL) and read all files on the hard drive. That privilege is required to back up files, but you need to make sure that the people that have it are actually allowed to read all files on the system. It takes only about four lines of code to bypass any ACL you want if you have this privilege.

SeRestorePrivilege is more interesting. It allows the user to bypass ACLs and *write* files to the file system. When you have that, you can *overwrite* operating system files and alter how the system functions. This creates a trivial path to take over the system—just overwrite a service binary that launches as LocalSystem and reboot. Given that restoring files is a rare operation (hopefully), the users with SeRestorePrivilege should be very limited.

There are other privileges that are just as bad. For instance, many services and some applications require the user who runs them to have SeDebugPrivilege. SeDebugPrivilege enables a user to debug a process that he does not own. More technically, it allows you to open a handle to the process which allows you to read and write into the processes address space and inject code into the process. SeDebugPrivilege is actually all that is required to run the pwdump and lsadump tools. Any user with that privilege can dump out password hashes and service account credentials.

---

**NOTE:** Sometimes the applications that require SeDebugPrivilege can take you by surprise. For instance, after removing that privilege from Administrators in the Windows Server 2003 Security Guide, we realized that we could no longer install security updates. A new version of the update.exe tool that installs Windows security updates by patching running binaries required SeDebugPrivilege.

---

SeTcbPrivilege, or the right to act as the operating system, is another extremely dangerous privilege. It allows a user to call certain APIs such as LogonUser. Using this privilege, a user can add arbitrary groups to its existing security token and essentially become a member of another group, thus obtaining additional permissions on-the-fly.

SeAssignPrimaryToken is a privilege that in-and-of-itself is pretty difficult to use for evil purposes. It allows a user to modify the process token on a process; however, it does not allow the user to create such a token. Thus, to misuse this privilege, some other mechanism for obtaining a privileged primary token must be used, and ordinary users do not have the ability to do that. However, in combination with SeTcbPrivilege or SeCreateToken, SeAssignPrimaryToken is deadly. The former allows the user to steal or create a primary token, and the latter allows him to stamp the token onto an existing process, thus elevating that process to run as any user on-the-fly. The net result looks something like this:

```
C:\warez>tlist
   0 System Process
   8 System
 152 SMSS.EXE
 200 CSRSS.EXE
 224 WINLOGON.EXE
 252 SERVICES.EXE
 264 LSASS.EXE
 372 termsrv.exe
 516 svchost.exe
 540 spoolsv.exe
 588 msdtc.exe
 720 svchost.exe
```

```
 744 LLSSRV.EXE
 820 sqlservr.exe
 856 regsvc.exe
 956 WinMgmt.exe
1004 svchost.exe
1024 dfssvc.exe
1052 mssearch.exe
1368 svchost.exe
1452 svchost.exe
1308 CMD.EXE
1472 tlist.exe


C:\warez>lsadump2
Failed to open lsass: 5.  Exiting.
C:\warez>whoami


PYN-SQL\_sql


C:\warez>ElevateProcess.exe 1308


C:\warez>whoami
NT AUTHORITY\SYSTEM


C:\warez>lsadump2
$MACHINE.ACC
 28 00 43 00 52 00 67 00 53 00 62 00 56 00 77 00  (.C.R.g.S.b.V.w.
 56 00 3E 00 4B 00 24 00 23 00 31 00 75 00 2B 00  V.>.K.$.#.1.u.+.
 73 00 43 00 4F 00 54 00 52 00 64 00 46 00 71 00  s.C.O.T.R.d.F.q.
...
```

This exploit works because Microsoft SQL Server 2000 gives these privileges to its service account automatically. According to the best practices (`http://www.microsoft.com/technet/prodtechnol/sql/2000/maintain/sp3sec00.mspx`) for SQL Server, the process should run as an ordinary user, not as LocalSystem. That part is great; it is what comes next that causes problems. The document recommends that you use Enterprise Manager to assign the account, as shown in Figure 4-1.

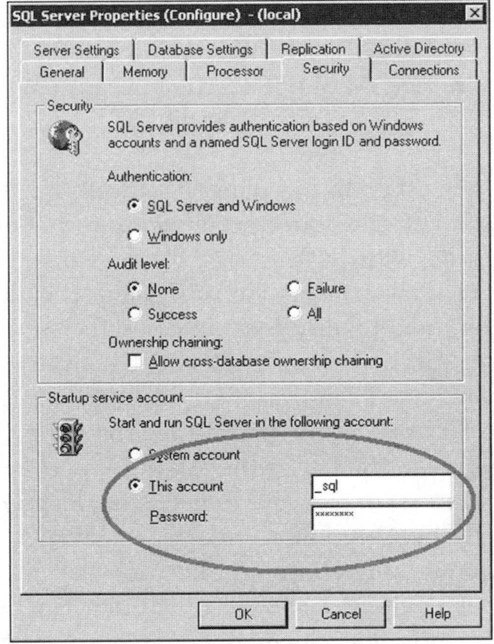


**Figure 4-1** Using SQL Enterprise Manager to change the SQL Server service account.

When you use SQL Enterprise Manager, the service account gets the following permissions and privileges:

- SeTcbPrivilege
- SeAssignPrimaryToken
- Full control over everything under
  - %ProgramFiles%\Microsoft SQL Server\<InstanceName> (or MSSQL for the default instance)
  - HKLM\SOFTWARE\Clients\Mail
  - HKLM\SOFTWARE\Microsoft\Microsoft SQL Server\80
  - HKLM\SOFTWARE\Microsoft\MSSQLServer\MSSQLServer
  - HKLM\SOFTWARE\Microsoft\MSSQLServer\<instancename>
  - HKLM\SOFTWARE\Microsoft\MSSQLServer\Providers
  - HKLM\SOFTWARE\Microsoft\MSSQLServer\Replication
  - HKLM\SOFTWARE\Microsoft\MSSQLServer\Setup

- HKLM\SOFTWARE\Microsoft\MSSQLServer\SQLServerAgent
- HKLM\SOFTWARE\Microsoft\MSSQLServer\Tracking
- HKLM\SOFTWARE\Microsoft\Windows NT\CurrentVersion\Perflib

A few other things happen as well, but these are the main ones of interest. With this set of permissions, just about anything you would ever want to do with SQL Server would work. Unfortunately, that includes taking over the entire system through a faulty application with an SQL injection vulnerability that accesses the SQL Server using a privileged account. After we have exploited the front-end application to give us a command shell on the SQL Server, we run an attack tool called ElevateProcess.exe and elevate an arbitrary process to run as LocalSystem. (The number 1308 after the ElevateProcess call is the process ID of the target process; in this case, our existing local command shell.)

In the next section, we show you how to stop this kind of attack. Doing so requires going above and beyond what the SQL Server Security Best Practices document shows you to do. This means that you have to be familiar with that document and have followed its recommendations already.

## Hardening SQL Server 2000

Before we continue, there is something you must know: If you follow the steps outlined in this section, your SQL Server is in an unsupported configuration. If you call Microsoft's support services, you will get only "best efforts" support. If you follow all the steps outlined below, your SQL Server will most certainly be incapable of performing certain tasks that you may or may not need.

It is *highly* advisable that you try these steps in a virtual machine before you start modifying a production server. It is quite possible that not all of these steps will work in your environment. Use caution when applying them.

This section covers how to lock down SQL Server in a "high-security" configuration, above and beyond the recommendations in the best practices paper. However, "high security" also means "limited functionality." There is a reason for most of the permissions and privileges granted to the SQL

Server service account. Without them, certain features will not work. Although we cannot predict all of the features that will break, we will do our best to outline which they are. Think of it this way: "High security" is a bit like the Berlin Wall. It does not stop all attacks, but it does stop many of them. It also gets in the way a lot, is very cumbersome to tear down or work around, and is surrounded by minefields. High security is the same. High security is for systems whose compromise would result in loss of life, state secrets, or significant amounts of money. High security is *not* for general-purpose use, which is why SQL Server does not come installed that way by default.

Now, after you have decided what you want to do with SQL Server, you should take a step that all installations should take, regardless of their security requirements: move the data and log files to a separate directory. As a general rule, data should reside where it can grow freely without disrupting operating system or application binaries and temp files. We will not tell you how to accomplish this. Think of it as a prerequisite. If you do not know how, the rest of these steps are probably too advanced for you! It is important that you are a relative expert at SQL Server before starting what comes next; otherwise, you will not be able to troubleshoot and undo the changes to solve any problems.

## Securing the Service Account

To secure the service account, we start the same way we did before, by creating a new user account; call it _sql for the sake of discussion. (For some reason, we got used to denoting service accounts with a leading underscore years ago.) Use a very strong pass phrase for the account. We also revoke all log on rights for the account, rendering it unusable locally as well as from the network. If you use the passgen tool to configure the password, it will actually revoke these logon rights for you. After you create the account, perform a couple of additional modifications:

- Set the "Password never expires" and "User cannot change password" options for the account. Service account passwords should always be managed manually.
- Remove the account from all default groups (including Users). This account is not for general use and does not need to be a member of any groups.

- On the Remote Control tab of the account properties, uncheck the "Require users permission" box. If this account should ever be used for a Terminal Services logon, we want to be able to monitor it.
- On the Terminal Services Profile tab, uncheck the "Allow logon to Terminal Server" check box. We do not want this account to be able to log on to Terminal Services.
- Use Group Policy (local or remote) to give the account the "Deny log on through Terminal Services," "Deny log on locally," and "Deny access to this computer from the network" rights. They are under User Rights Assignment.

We now have a completely worthless account. It really cannot do anything. Now open up the SCM and change the SQL Server logon account. *You must not do this in Enterprise Manager*; that is how we get all the permissions listed earlier. This is shown in Figure 4-2.

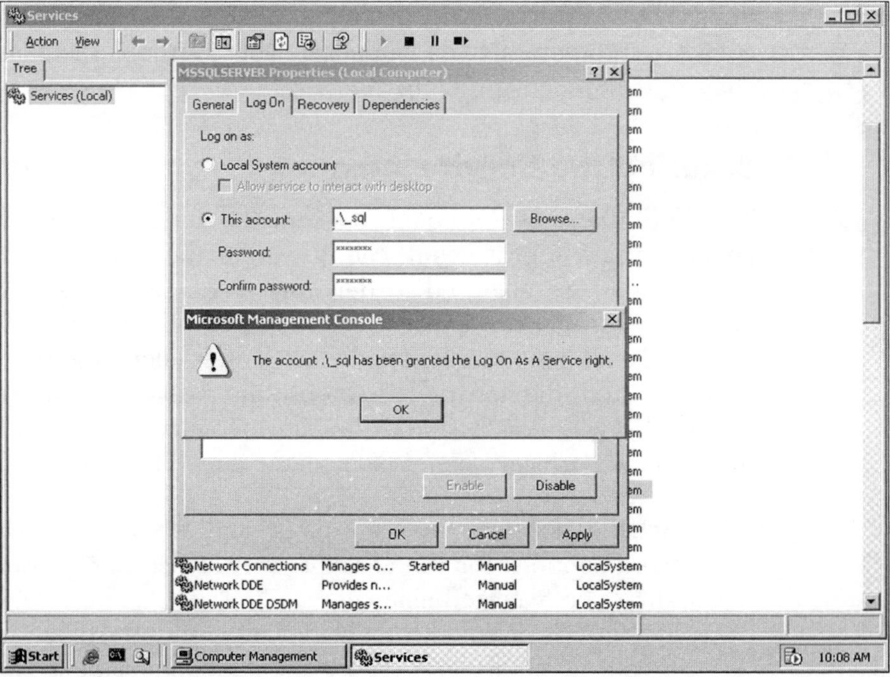


**Figure 4-2** Configure the new service account in SCM.

SCM will automatically grant the account the "Log on as a service" (SeServiceLogonRight) privilege. However, if you now try to stop and restart the service, you will get an error message that tells you "Access Denied." As descriptive as that error message is, it does not have much information to help resolve the problem. To do that, we turn to some third-party tools.

Now go to `http://www.systeminternals.com` and download File Monitor and Registry Monitor. These tools are your new best friend! They monitor all access to the file system and the Registry, respectively. That is a lot of accesses, however! To make the process more manageable, we set up some filters. Open each application, press Ctrl+L, and set up filters as shown in Figure 4-3. Note that although Registry Monitor enables us to monitor only errors, which is what we are looking for, File Monitor unfortunately does not have such an option yet.

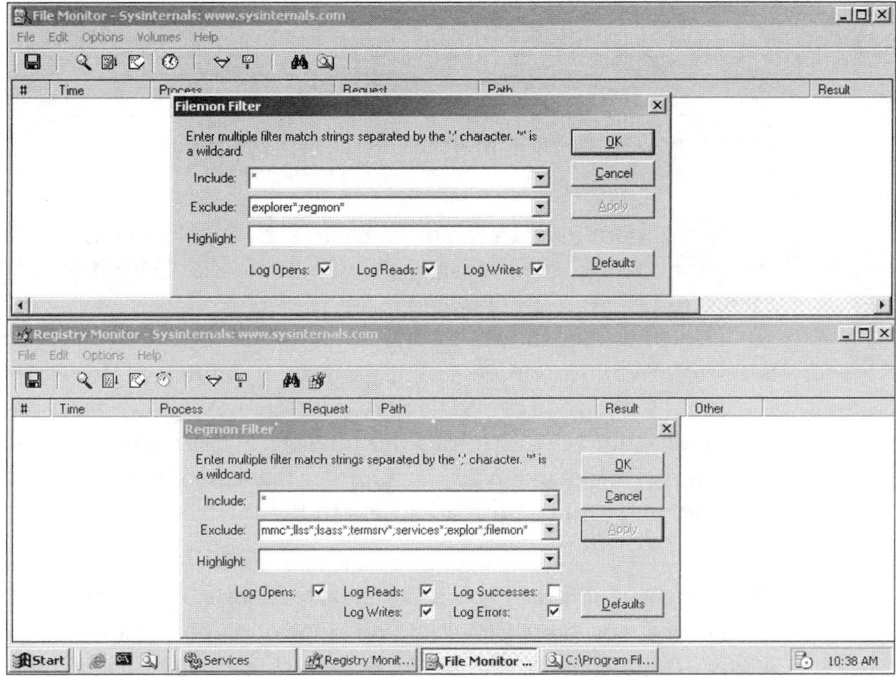


**Figure 4-3** File Monitor and Registry Monitor configuration settings.

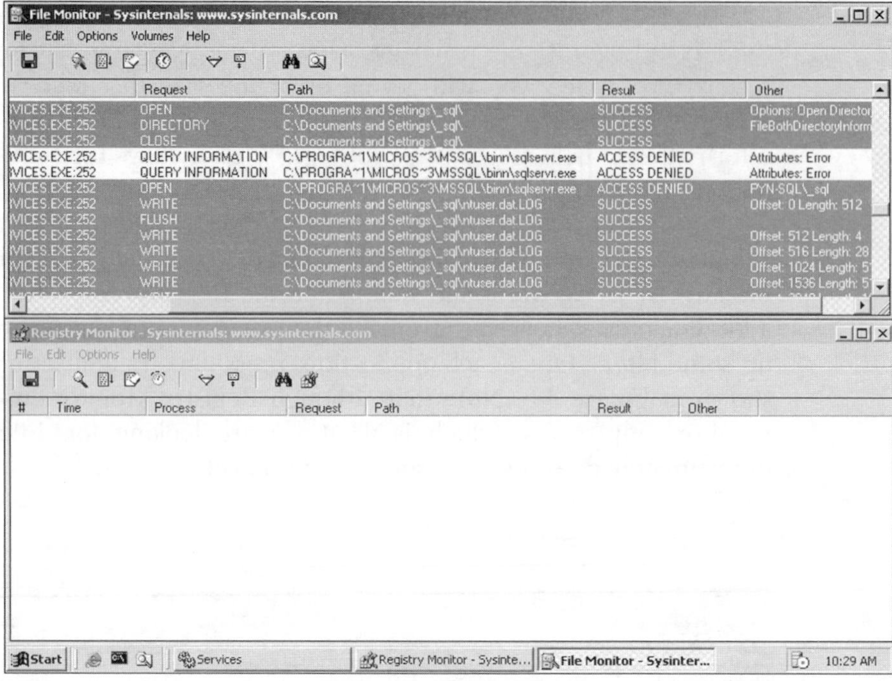


**Figure 4-4** File Monitor shows us our first problem.

At this point, we are ready to try to start the service again. The first of our monitors to give us any feedback is File Monitor, as shown in Figure 4-4.

The problem shown in Figure 4-4 has a very simple explanation. Services.exe, in the process of attempting to launch SQL Server, is impersonating _sql to read the SQL Server binaries. Well, we forgot to grant the service account permission to the binaries at %ProgramFiles%\Microsoft SQL Server\<InstanceName>. Oops. That is easily rectified. Go to that directory and grant _sql read access to the binaries.

**TIP:** Sometimes it is really hard to find the problems, particularly in File Monitor. To make it easier, press Ctrl+E (to stop logging) and then Ctrl+F to find. Type **Access Denied** in the Find dialog and press Enter. Just cycle through the output that way until you find something that appears to be a problem. Just do not forget to press Ctrl+E to start logging again when you have finished.

Having now given the service account the right to read its own binaries, we will try again. Press Ctrl+X in File Monitor to clear the log window and try starting SQL Server again.

This time you get a different error message: "The application failed to initialize properly (0xc0000022). Click on OK to terminate the application." Going back into File Monitor, we find that the problem is that sqlservr.exe is trying to open %ProgramFiles%\Microsoft SQL Server\<InstanceName>\binn\opends60.dll. What happened here is that during SQL Server installation, the installer removes the inheritance bit on all the SQL Server directories. Hence, no matter how we set permissions on %ProgramFiles%\Microsoft SQL Server\<InstanceName>, none of them have propagated below that point. To rectify the situation, go back into the permissions settings for %ProgramFiles%\Microsoft SQL Server\<InstanceName> and set up propagating permissions, as shown in Figure 4-5.

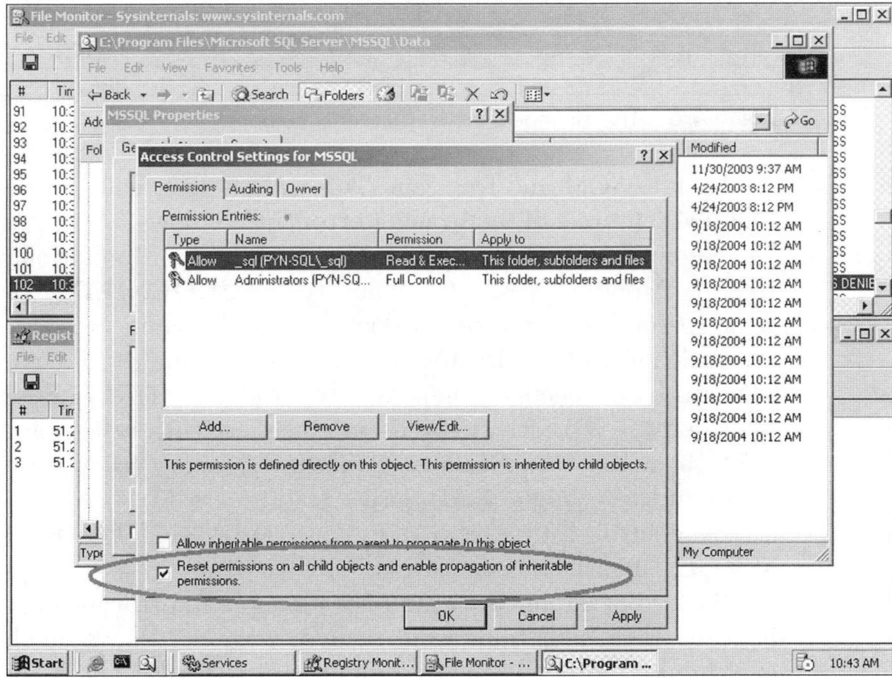


**Figure 4-5** The SQL Server installer resets all inheritable permissions.

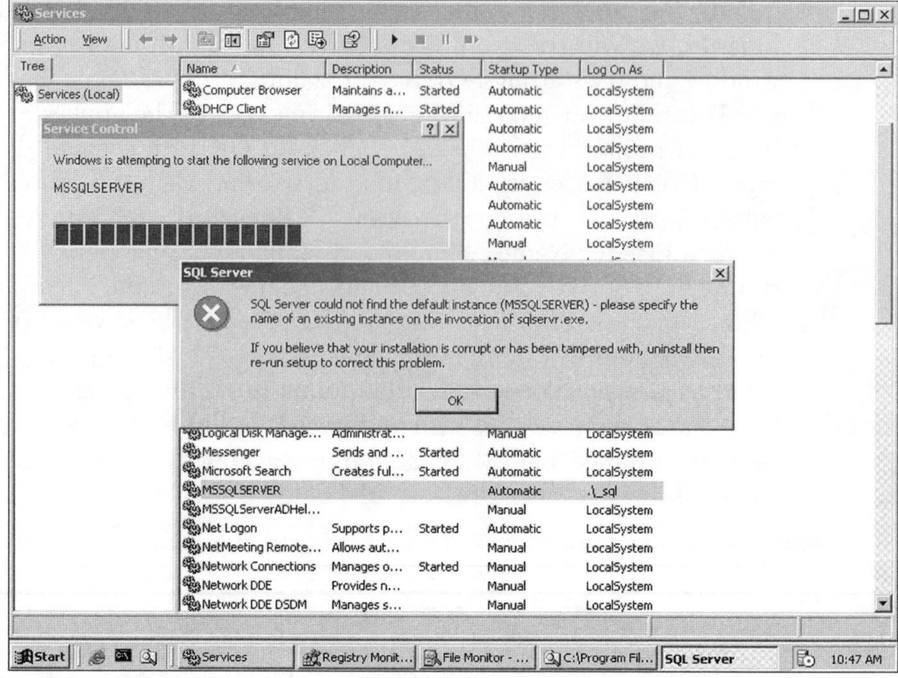


**Figure 4-6** The strangest error in recent memory.

Back to SCM and try again. This time it gets really interesting. See Figure 4-6 for one of the stranger errors in Windows.

The error is actually explained by the Registry Monitor output. Go to Registry Monitor, press Ctrl+F and type **ACCDENIED**. Note that for some reason Registry Monitor does not use the same string to denote an access denied as File Monitor (Mark, when are you ever going to fix that?). The problem occurs when we try to read HKLM\SOFTWARE\Microsoft\MSSQLSERVER\<instance name>\CurrentVersion. The code 0x20019 in the Other column denotes a request using a KEY_READ access mask; in other words, just a read access. We need to put a read access control list entry (ACE) on HKLM\SOFTWARE\Microsoft\MSSQLSERVER\<instance name>.

Back to SCM and try again. Now we get an error message that says basically, that "something went really wrong, but I have no clue what it is. Why don't you ask your system administrator for help?" Because we *are* the system administrator, we have pretty much exhausted the escalation chain at this point. Luckily, both Registry Monitor and File Monitor know what happened. The first problem is in Registry Monitor. We tried to access HKLM\SOFTWARE\Microsoft\MSSQLSERVER\Setup with 0x1 (KEY_QUERY_VALUE) access. We did not grant any permissions there, better do that. Grant it read permissions, that is all we need.

That is not the only error we have, however. For instance, we tried to access HKLM\SOFTWARE\Microsoft\MSSQLSERVER\<instance name> with 0x20006 access. That is KEY_WRITE access; in other words, we tried to write that key. Why is that? It turns out that key holds all kinds of volatile configuration information such as the network libraries that clients can use to access this server. You really do need write access to this key. Grant the service account KEY_CREATE_SUB_KEY and KEY_SET_VALUE—the difference between KEY_READ and KEY_WRITE.

After you have done that, notice that File Monitor is also throwing several errors. The problem there explains the strange (useless) error message. SQL Server is trying to write to its log file. This does not work because we did not give the account any write permissions. Although we add a "modify" ACE to the <instancename>\LOG directory (which should not be on the boot partition by the way), we would also do well to do so on the <instancename>\DATA directory. SQL Server tends to work much better if it is allowed to write to its databases.

If you now try to start SQL Server again, something astonishing will happen: it starts! Believe it or not, we have just created the minimum set of permissions to start SQL Server. Note that this does not mean that it will be able to do everything we expect. The fact that we can launch a process does not mean that the process will do anything useful. The only way to know for sure is to try. If we try the `www.victimsrus.com` site we find that it does actually still do something useful! We have finally arrived at the minimum set of permissions needed for our site. They are as follows:

- Read permissions to %ProgramFiles%\Microsoft SQL Server\<InstanceName> and everything below
- Modify permission on %ProgramFiles%\Microsoft SQL Server\<InstanceName>\LOG
- Modify permission on %ProgramFiles%\Microsoft SQL Server\<InstanceName>\Data
- Read and write permissions to HKLM\SOFTWARE\Microsoft\MSSQLSERVER\<instance name> and everything below it
- Read permissions to HKLM\SOFTWARE\Microsoft\MSSQLSERVER\Setup and everything below it

Note that these may not be sufficient minimum permissions for your installation and that you may still encounter problems with only these permissions set. For instance, in our tests, we were getting access-denied entries on the perflibs, both in the Registry and in the file system. If we do not care to performance monitor this SQL Server, we will leave those alone. If we care about performance monitoring, which many sites do, we must continue the above process until we have the permissions needed for that to work, too.

The set of permissions shown above has been used successfully on several nonclustered SQL Servers that feed data to a Web site over both trusted and untrusted connections. It will not work on servers that participate in SQL replication. In your installation, you may need to keep iterating through the tools to add additional permissions.

It is also worth pointing out here that you do not need Enterprise Manager on many production SQL Servers. Enterprise Manager is used only to administer the system. You can do that through isql.exe or osql.exe as well as through Enterprise Manager remotely. You may want to consider removing Enterprise Manager from the production servers, lest you accidentally change configuration on a production server—or someone else does.

This same process to discover the minimum set of permissions required to make an application work can be applied to almost any situation where you need to have an application run with reduced permissions. For instance, you may be able to use it to make your favorite game run as a nonadmin.

Getting a remote command shell on the SQL Server will still work even with these minimum permissions. However, after you have that shell, it will be very difficult to go any further since the account you are running as is extremely limited. The reason the shell still works is because we still have writable directories to upload the file into. We of course have write access to the SQL Server directories, but we also have write access to the C:\ since Everyone has been granted that. Even though our _sql user has been removed from the Users group, it is still granted all the permissions that Everyone has. Note that you should not try to go through the default ACLs and replace Everyone with something else, particularly not Authenticated Users, as many people attempt. First, _sql is an authenticated user; second, if you try to perform that kind of wholesale ACL change, you will almost certainly end up with a configuration with very strange problems. For instance, we have seen people destroying the recycle bin and making the administrator's profile world readable doing this. It is not really worth doing. There are other ways to block this attack that are more meaningful and less likely to cause strange side-effects.

## SQL Authentication Options

When users and applications connect to SQL Server, they authenticate to the database somehow. SQL Server supports two authentication options. One is Windows-only mode, meaning that all access is authenticated using Windows (domain or local) accounts. The other option is SQL Server and Windows mode. (These at one point were called "native" for Windows-only, SQL Server, and "mixed mode" for both.)

In mixed mode, SQL Server can use either Windows accounts or its own accounts, defined and usable only within the SQL Server. Using mixed mode, you lose the granular control you get with Windows accounts, and you lose much auditing capability and the stronger protocols used for authentication in Windows. Many developers write applications that use SQL Server login because they think they will be easier to use when there is a firewall between the SQL Server and the front-end application. However, because SQL Server can tunnel Windows authentication through its own protocols, that is not necessarily the case. On the other hand, it works properly with older applications written for SQL 6.x where SQL Server authentication was the default. Therefore, for application compatibility, SQL Server authentication may still be needed, but applications that require it should be rewritten with all possible speed to use "trusted connections," another name for native mode. After you have removed all those applications, or decided that you do not care about breaking the ones that are left, set the authentication to native mode.

In native mode, Windows accounts and groups are are mapped to SQL logins. This makes things much easier to manage. You do not need to maintain passwords within applications, and you can configure data access permissions to Windows users much more easily. In addition, you get the benefit of the reasonably strong authentication protocols used in Windows. Finally, some vulnerabilities have surfaced that apply only to mixed mode, such as accidentally getting the SA password stored in a log file.

## Securing Stored Procedures

One of the most powerful methods for securing SQL Server is to drop some of the built-in stored procedures. For instance, xp_cmdshell. Is it really necessary? If you are running replication, yes. If not, probably not. You can drop it easily enough using this command:

```
sp_dropextendedproc xp_cmdshell
```

However, to get the full effect out of this, you also need to drop the remaining procedures defined in the DLL that contains xp_cmdshell. The DLL involved is xplog70.dll. The following procedures are defined in that DLL:

- xp_cmdshell
- xp_enumgroups
- xp_logevent
- xp_loginconfig
- xp_msver
- xp_sprintf
- xp_sscanf

To drop all of them, run this command:

```
sp_dropextendedproc xp_cmdshell
sp_dropextendedproc xp_enumgroups
sp_dropextendedproc xp_logevent
sp_dropextendedproc xp_loginconfig
sp_dropextendedproc xp_msver
sp_dropextendedproc xp_sprintf
sp_dropextendedproc xp_sscanf
```

Removing all those will of course break things. For instance, Document Tracking and Administration (DTA) in Microsoft Biztalk uses these extended stored procedures as does the SQL Server Distributed Management Objects (DMO). If you are not using these features you may be able to drop all these extended stored procedures and in that case you can remove xplog70.dll. The reason you need to do that is because otherwise an attacker executing code as the sa or as a sysadmin (including the service account) can add the xprocs back. You want to ensure that you are not using any of them, however. This means you have to analyze the dependencies on them. For reference, the built-in dependencies on xp_cmdshell are listed in Table 4-1. You can get the dependencies on any stored procedure or extended stored procedure by right-clicking it in

Enterprise Manager, selecting All Tasks, and then selecting Display Dependencies. Of the extended stored procedures shown above, other than xp_cmdshell, only xp_msver has dependencies in a default install. Sp_addqueued_artinfo and sp_MSInstance_qv both depend on it.

You may want to think about whether you want to get rid of several other extended stored procedures, too. There are 170 extended stored procedures in all. Take a look at all of them. Should you decide later that

**Table 4-1** Dependencies on xp_cmdshell

| Object | Purpose |
| --- | --- |
| sp_ActiveDirectory_SCP | Add/change/delete AD objects |
| sp_adddistpublisher | Replication |
| sp_adddistributiondb | Replication |
| sp_attachsubscription | Replication |
| sp_changedistpublisher | Replication |
| sp_copysubscription | Replication |
| sp_MScopyscriptfile | Replication install |
| sp_MScopysnapshot | Replication |
| sp_MSget_file_existence | Replication install |
| sp_MSremove_userscript | Replication install |
| sp_replicationoption | Replication |
| sp_resolve_logins | Log shipping |
| sp_vupgrade_replication | Replication install |
| Sp_set_local_time | Changing the time |
| sp_msx_enlist | Multiserver operations to retrieve jobs from a central server. This stored procedure is used to enlist from such an environment. |
| sp_msx_defect | Multiserver operations to retrieve jobs from a central server. This stored procedure is used to defect from such an environment. |
| Sp_Msdeletefoldercontents | Replication |
| Sp_Msreplremoveuncdir | Replication |

you need them, you can use sp_addextendedproc to add them back in. In addition, the SQL Server Agent contains all the same functionality with different names. It is used to schedule jobs, such as maintenance operations. In environments that do not use this functionality, it can be disabled. Realize, however, that scheduled jobs will break if you do so.

The stored and extended stored procedures we just discussed do provide useful functionality, and, by default, they are available only to sysadmins. If you do need them, consider evaluating the permissions on them instead and seeing whether they should be tightened up. The defaults are not bad as long as no applications are accessing the database as a sysadmin, but you can consider changing them in your environment. If your applications are accessing the database as a sysadmin you should either modify the applications, or try to remove the functionality from SQL Server as a defense-in-depth measure.

Speaking of permissions, do you really need any for Public? Public is essentially equivalent to Authenticated Users in the operating system—it contains all users who have authenticated to the system. A user who does not have a login for a particular database would still be able to access a lot of resources that are available to Public. To be precise, such a user would be able to access 1,015 objects by default. If you want to allow access only to specifically defined objects, you should revoke these. On certain objects, you cannot revoke the permissions.

We are now left with an SQL Server installation that is very hard to exploit. Even if the bad guy should happen to get a command shell on the server, he will have one running as an extremely limited user that will be very hard to elevate to a higher context unless he can get additional tools on the system. We have seen attackers who add the stored procedures back in, for instance. To block that, you need to prevent them from getting their tools up onto the server and executing them there, Chapter 2, "Server and Client Hardening."

Before you leave your SQL Server, you should write some new stored procedures. Write one instead of each of the hard-coded queries in all the apps you have accessing the database. It is beyond the scope of this book to address this in detail; but in general, you should avoid ad-hoc queries at all cost. Stored procedures will not necessarily prevent problems such as SQL injection, but you will often have more control over what gets executed on the database server when you use a parameterized stored procedure. Howard and LeBlanc address this at length in Chapter 12 of *Writing Secure Code*, 2nd Edition. In the end, however, bad code is bad code, and it makes no difference whether it is in a stored procedure, C in a native application, or VBScript in a Web page. Everything we have discussed in this chapter so far is about making you more resilient to bad code, but nothing can make you immune to it.

The things we have talked about here are, as mentioned previously, not entirely supported. Microsoft has created Knowledge Base article 891984 to discuss these issues and the supportability surrounding them. Refer to that article for more information on exactly what support you can expect for which of these issues. It is available at `http://support.microsoft.com/?id=891984`.

## Hardening IIS 5.0 and 6.0

One of the most common services to be running is Web servers. Microsoft's built-in Web server, Internet Information Services (IIS), comprises a substantial portion of the Web servers on the Internet today. A few years ago, IIS garnered a not entirely undeserved reputation as being horribly insecure. Much of this was due to additional functionality and samples jammed into the Web server that were not directly relevant to the core function of serving Web pages. For instance, some rocket scientist actually thought it was a good idea to not only install IIS by default on Windows 2000, but also to include a component called the Internet Print Provider (IPP) that allows users on the Internet to print to internal printers, through IIS. Now, in spite of the fact that this is probably not functionality that 99 percent of Web servers ought to have, it probably would have gone relatively unnoticed had there not been a buffer overflow in the component that handled print requests. A few weeks later, a similar problem was discovered in the indexing services component, which was also installed by default in spite of the fact that the vast majority of Web servers do not need it. This problem overshadowed the complaints about the IPP, particularly a couple of weeks after it was discovered, once Code Red, which exploited the Index Server component flaw, came out.

Clearly, IIS 5.0 leaves a lot to be desired in the realm of security. Does that mean it is fundamentally unsafe? No. We have personally run Web servers on IIS 5.0 for many years without getting them hacked, because we took the pains to protect them. The most important step you can take is to run the IIS Lockdown Tool (`http://www.microsoft.com/technet/security/tools/locktool.mspx`). The Lockdown Tool is the single-most important thing you can do to protect IIS 5.0. Beyond that, we refer the interested reader to the white paper titled "From Blueprint to Fortress" (`http://www.microsoft.com/serviceproviders/security/iis_security_P73766.asp`).

IIS 6.0 is an entirely different story. The code base for IIS 6.0 is completely new. Basically, the product was rewritten from the ground up. To date, this has been very successful. As of this writing, there has not been a single security bulletin issued for IIS 6.0 itself. There have been several, however, that affect an IIS 6.0 Web server, but largely because it uses operating systems components that have problems. In the rest of this chapter, we cover how to protect an IIS 6.0 Web server.

## IIS Is an Application Platform

The first thing you have to realize is that IIS is much more than a Web server. It is an application platform. Therefore, the hardening you can do depends on what applications you are running. If all you are doing is serving plain Web pages, you can lock the system down pretty tight. However, if you are using more advanced application functionality, you must unlock some things. Yes, unlock. By default, IIS 6.0 installs only as a file server. All the functionality of the Lockdown Tool from IIS 5.0 is already built in. The key thing here is to only unlock exactly what you need. If you do not need the .NET Framework, do not install it. If you do not need Active Server Pages, do not enable them.

IIS uses application pools to execute Web applications. A Web application is basically a set of Web pages underneath one directory structure that are considered a single application. Whereas in IIS 5.0 Web apps by default executed within a single process, by default in IIS 6.0 you can much more easily manage each application, the account it executes under, and which process context it executes under. Although a complete discussion about how to run IIS 6.0 is the subject of several books, we will state that you should use this functionality to isolate applications from each other to make sure that if one gets compromised it happens in a low-privileged context, away from other applications.

## How to Make IIS Speak SQL

One of the most frequently asked questions about IIS is how to make it connect to a database server for processing requests from anonymous users on the Internet. One of the most common approaches is to create a text file defining the database connection and specified a set of SQL Server credentials in there. This approach is very flawed. First, it requires us to use SQL Server authentication, which is highly undesirable. Second, it requires us to maintain cleartext credentials as well as cleartext connection information somewhere in the Web application. A much better approach is to use Windows authentication and a Data Source Name (DSN). It is actually really easy to do this. First, create an account to use for the connection. We will call it Webuser, for simplicity. If both systems are in the same domain, use a domain account. Otherwise, create two identical accounts on the Web server and the SQL Server. Then, set IIS to use that account for authentication, as shown in Figure 4-7.

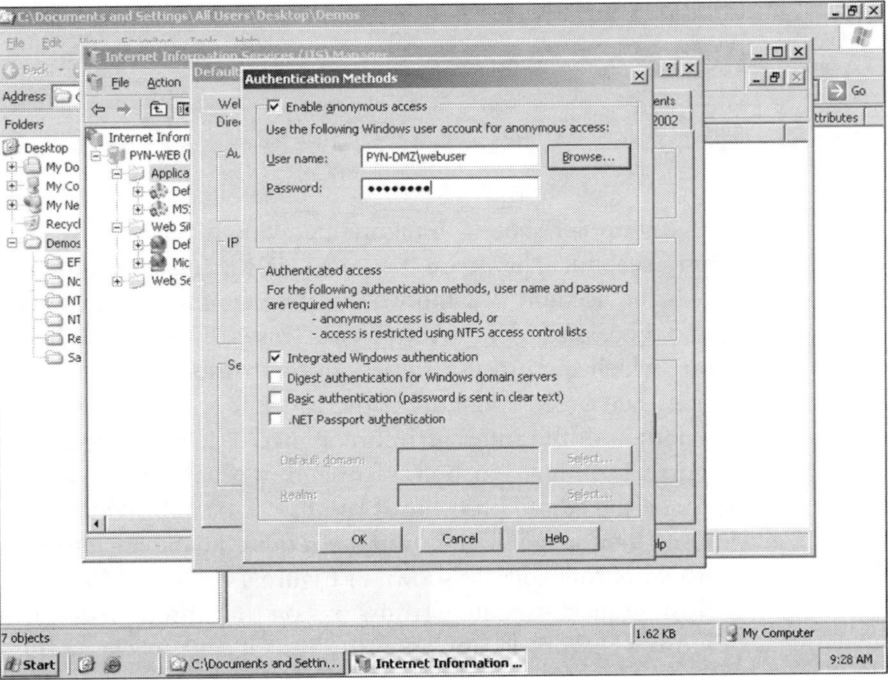


**Figure 4-7** Configuring the impersonation account.

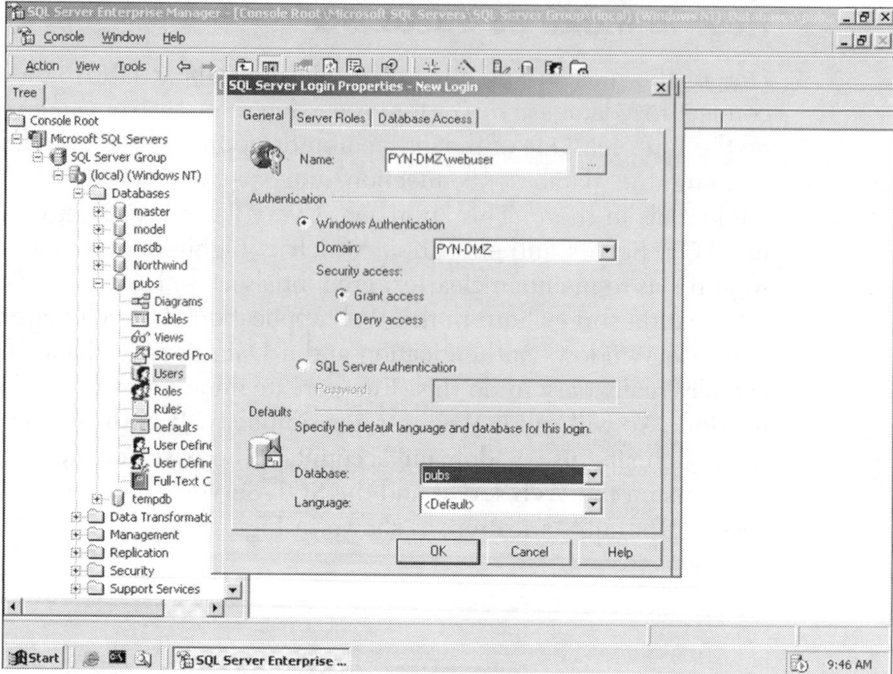


**Figure 4-8** Add Webuser as a database login.

As Figure 4-7 shows, configure anonymous access in IIS 6.0 to use the Webuser account. This account is known as the *impersonation* account in IIS 6.0. It is the account that the worker process impersonates when accessing files and processing identity those files. This is distinguished from the *process identity*, which the process identity of the worker process doing the impersonation. The process identity is the account configured in the Application Pools portion of the Internet Information Services Manager. After you have configured the impersonation, you need to grant this account execute permission on the stored procedures you use. First, add Webuser as a database login, and then map it as a user in the required database, ensuring that it has the proper permissions, as shown in Figure 4-8.

Next, grant it execute permissions on the stored procedures, as shown in Figure 4-9. You do not need to grant it any access to the underlying database.

All access in SQL Server happens inside the SQL Server process, which means that the actual access check happens only on the stored

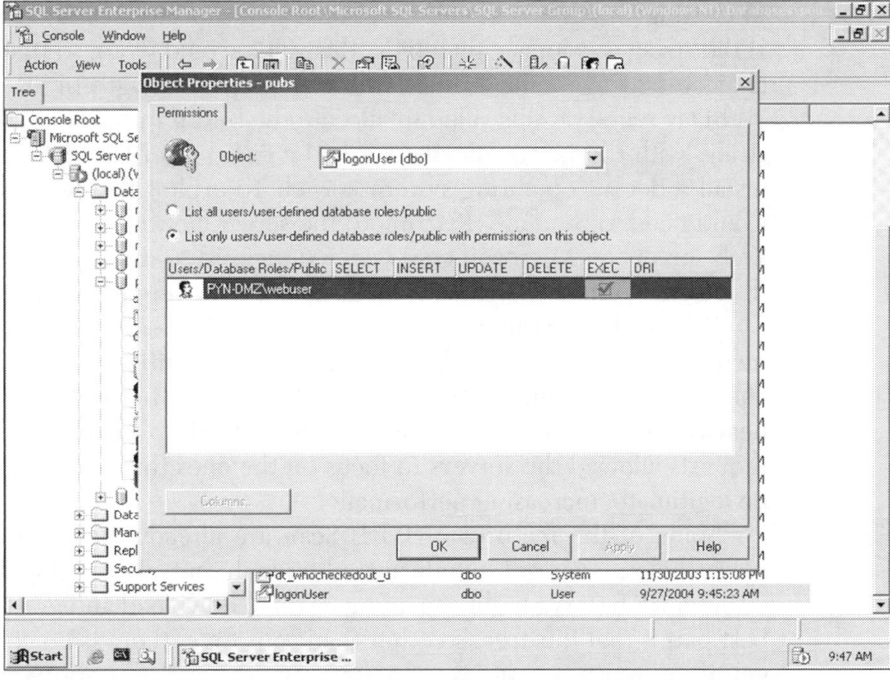


**Figure 4-9** Grant Webuser access to the required stored procedures.

procedure, as long as the same user owns both the stored procedure and the tables. In most Web applications, you probably have a finite set of stored procedures, making this a viable way to grant access to the application. Finally, make sure you have revoked Public access, as shown earlier. Otherwise, the Web user account has access to a large number of other objects that it does not need.

## URL Scan

We want to leave you with one of our favorite tools for protecting IIS: URL Scan. URL Scan enables you to scan requests before they are processed by IIS and throw away illegal ones before the server even processes them. It can control the verbs you permit, the lengths of requests, and many other things. To entice you to look further, we provide two examples here.

Microsoft Security Bulletin MS03-007 announced a vulnerability in WebDav. The problem was an integer overflow in a string-length variable.

The string length was stored in an unsigned short, which is a 16-bit value. If the string was longer than 64K, this value would wrap, so that a 64K+11 character string would actually show as having a length of 10 characters. WebDav relied on this value to allocate the buffer into which it copied the string, with the net result that we had a 64K buffer overflow—enough to install a decent operating system kernel. To exploit the issue, an attacker would need to send a 64K string to the server, however. URL Scan on the Web servers on Microsoft.com were configured to drop all requests larger than 16K. Without the patch even installed, they were immune to this issue.

When URL Scan was configured on Microsoft.com, performance increased significantly. This seems counterintuitive, because security checks usually reduce performance. However, Microsoft.com is a very heavily attacked site. Allowing URL Scan to drop obviously illegitimate requests allowed the servers to focus on the ones that were more likely to be legitimate, increasing performance.

Some of the features of URL Scan are already included in IIS 6.0. Nevertheless, you get significant additional control by using URL Scan even on IIS 6.0. We highly encourage you to download and evaluate it. The best part is that it is free, so other than your time, there is no cost. You can get it at `http://www.microsoft.com/technet/security/tools/urlscan.mspx`.

## Summary

If you take the time to implement the recommendations outlined in this chapter, you will probably find that it is not nearly as simple in practice as we have made it sound. This is fully expected. If you want a network that is secure and useful, we can give you that, but you have to put in some effort and spend some time at it. Security is not free. As vendors get more advanced, it will become less costly; right now, however, this takes time. Be sure to document every step you take painstakingly, and please, do not try these things on your production servers. Use virtual machines or a test lab to test all these steps out, unless you rather like searching for a job.

## What You Should Do Today

- Build a specification for a test bed where you can evaluate hardening for services.
- Get rid of all samples on all production servers.
- Ensure that production servers have no dependencies on test servers.
- Develop a list of all services in your environment that run with any kind of elevated privilege.
- Download URL Scan and learn how to use it.
- Download the System Internals tools and learn how to use those.

CHAPTER 5

# SECURITY FOR SMALL BUSINESSES

Most small businesses are not targets for direct attacks. Instead, they end up as collateral damage in larger attacks, such as mass worm outbreaks or efforts to harvest credit card numbers no matter where they come from. Nevertheless, a very significant cost is associated with this. Imagine if you couldn't use your computer systems for a week. Or if you lost all the data stored on all the computers in your company. Or that your worst competitor could obtain a list of all your customers, along with sales figures and sales notes for each customer. Or that someone added himself or herself to your payroll database and set up direct deposit to a bank account in the Bahamas. How long would it be before you noticed any of these?[1] What would these breaches cost your company? Can you afford these losses?

We understand that your business is your *business*—not the daily machinations of keeping computers and information secure. So, in this chapter, we describe a few critical steps that are important for any small business to understand. Follow these steps, and although we certainly can't *guarantee* that you'll never be attacked, we're pretty confident that the pointers here will help protect you from many attacks and even make you less interesting to someone looking to cause harm.

## Protect Your Desktops and Laptops

"Wait, I can't handle even a few steps!" some of you might be thinking. "All I want to do is run my business, and this computer and software can help me. Why do I have to worry about all this security stuff?"

We feel for you, we really do—although if it weren't for all the bad guys and girls, we'd have to find other jobs. But think for just a moment about

1. As an experiment, announce that next month you will do manual payroll. Print all checks, but don't distribute them—and don't do any direct deposits. Have employees appear in person—with company identification—to pick up their paychecks. Ideally, you should have none left over. If you do, it's time to consider improving the security of your payroll system.

all the security-related decisions you already make every day: you drive defensively, looking out for all the maniacs on the road; you rely on some hidden sense when walking around unfamiliar areas, staying away from places that give you the "willies"; you keep the contents of your office physically secure with a lock on the door. Every one of these security measures helps to mitigate some threat: unaware drivers, roving muggers, slippery thieves. Sure it's annoying to have to deal with these threats, but everyone does, every day.

It's the same with information security. There really are bad people afoot, people who want to cause you harm—or use you and your resources to harm another. It's imperative that you realize this and that you take appropriate actions. If you do nothing else after reading this chapter (or, we hope, the entire book), three tasks are absolutely essential for you to incorporate into your routine of managing your business: keep your software up-to-date, use antivirus and anti-spyware software, and set up firewalls. If you do these three things, you will thwart most attacks.

## Keep Your Software Up-to-Date

In the beginning, there was no testing: if the program compiled without errors, it went into immediate production. And, of course, bugs abounded. Then developers started testing their programs, using only valid and expected input. This process "improvement" helped ensure programs wouldn't barf during regular use, but didn't reveal any holes that might otherwise exist. Finally, most software houses now realize that testing is a specialized discipline and hire dedicated people for this purpose; these testers intentionally try to break programs by supplying unexpected input to make sure that the programs gracefully recover and don't fail in insecure ways. Good testers think like attackers.

Yet, software is imperfect: indeed, it can't be any different, because all software is written by fallible human beings. Software is *improving* because authors understand not everyone uses software as intended and because testers are starting to think like attackers, but patches and updates will be a fact of life for all time.

The best way to keep your software up-to-date is to rely on any automatic updating capabilities present in Windows and that might be present in whatever applications you're running. The Windows automatic update feature regularly checks with the Windows Update pages on Microsoft's

Web site and downloads and even installs all updates for your computer as they become available.

To enable automatic updates, click Start, right-click **My Computer**, choose **Properties**, and then choose **Automatic Updates**. Configure either automatic download or (better) automatic download and install; if you choose the latter, be sure that your computer is switched on during whatever time you enter in the dialog; if updates are downloaded but not installed, your computer will install them when you next switch it on.

## Updating Multiple Computers

If you have more than one computer in your organization, you can control automatic updating of all machines centrally, which helps you keep all of your configurations current. Two tools can help you here: software installation and maintenance and Windows Update Services (WUS). In Active Directory, which you have if you're using Small Business Server (SBS), you can configure software installation and maintenance for the computers in your domain. It's a fairly minimal tool, however; all it really does is provide you with a mechanism to require software to install itself on computers the next time they boot. You need to download and maintain all updates and services packs yourself and make them available someplace in your network for the feature to install from.

Because the software installation and maintenance feature can be pretty geeky,[2] a better approach is Windows Update Services.[3] Think of WUS as a version of Windows Update that works from inside your own network. The WUS server downloads all updates Microsoft publishes; you configure your computers (through Group Policy) to pull updates from your WUS server rather than directly from Microsoft.com. This gives you time to download, test, and approve patches, and then require their installation on your computers. WUS helps get you out of patch management hell by automating most of the work. A nice touch is that WUS is free and works with the auto-update clients already built in to Windows 2000 and Windows XP.

2. We won't cover this feature further here. Although it's already included in Active Directory, it's very difficult to configure, prone to mistakes, and requires a lot of testing. It really isn't intended for small businesses.

3. Visit `http://www.microsoft.com/windowsserversystem/wus/default.mspx` for more information and to download WUS, which is in beta as of this writing but should be available by the time you read this.

## Use Antivirus and Anti-Spyware Software

Malicious code manages to sneak into computers in so many ways. It's easy to trick people into installing something they really shouldn't, whether it's through some e-mail attachment with an alluring subject line or a script or control "required" by a Web site. We see over and over again that if people are given the choice between making a security decision and watching some cute dancing pigs, the cute dancing pigs win every time. Alas, often hidden within the cute dancing pigs is some very ugly malware that just might wreak havoc across your systems and the systems of anyone you might connect to.

Malware comes in many forms: viruses, worms, Trojan horses, spyware, adware, porn dialers, keyloggers. No single utility can detect and remove them all. Generally you need at least one antivirus program (to eliminate viruses, worms, and Trojans) and one anti-spyware program (to eliminate the rest). The antivirus industry is pretty mature,[4] and all the products generally find all the virus-type malware. The anti-spy industry is newer; not all products find everything, and many security experts recommend running more than one. To us, that approaches more work than typical small business people want to bother with, so choose one product from a reputable vendor and you'll be fine.

---

**WARNING:** Many products that claim to be spyware detection and removal tools are in fact monstrous spyware *installers*. Stay away from anything you see on Web sites with ridiculous URLs such as www.spyware-reviews-and-removal-utilities.com or similar. We've had excellent luck with AdAware (`http://www.lavasoft.nu`); with Computer Associates' PestPatrol (`http://www.ca.com/products/pestpatrol/`), especially its centralized management capabilities; and with Microsoft's new anti-spyware program acquired from GIANT (`http://www.microsoft.com/spyware`).

---

Don't forget that antivirus and anti-spyware programs are only as good as their scanning signature databases. Hundreds of new or variant pieces of malware materialize every month; you must keep your scanners up-to-date

4. It has been promulgated that the antivirus companies themselves are the purveyors of most viruses and worms running amok, that they do this to keep people afraid and to ensure a continual revenue stream. There is, however, no evidence to support such an assertion, and we do not believe the notion at all.

or they'll quickly become useless. Don't forget to tune the update engines of these programs. Many small business administrators we know have tuned the engines to update hourly.

If you have multiple computers in your organization, and you use Active Directory to centrally manage security settings and WUS to deploy updates, be sure that you follow the same thinking with your antivirus and anti-spyware programs. Select products that give you centralized control of installation and updating on all computers in your organization. The more you can rely on automation, the more secure you become: automation guarantees that all your computers are configured the way you want them to be and eliminates a lot of complexity from your environment (and from your life, too).

## Set Up Firewalls

You need firewalls in two locations: one between your network and the Internet, and one on every computer in your network. The network ("perimeter") firewall keeps much of the bad stuff from getting into computers that are attached to the network. But what about when mobile computers leave? You take your laptop home, right? Personal firewalls on individual computers serve two roles: they protect mobile computers when they're away from the network, and they protect computers on the network from *the rest of the network*. Even though you have up-to-date antivirus and anti-spyware programs on all your computers, there's a slim chance that some piece of malware might get onto one computer anyway, especially if it's mobile and enters the computer through, say, an e-mail attachment. When that infected computer returns to the network, the perimeter firewall is powerless to stop it. Personal firewalls on all the rest of the computers—laptops *and* desktops—just might be able to keep the malware from spreading.

Small Business Server Premium Edition includes an excellent firewall in the box: Microsoft Internet Security and Acceleration (ISA) Server. (SBS Standard Edition includes the RRAS firewall, which performs stateful packet filtering but not the more advanced application layer inspection of ISA Server.) Economic realities for many small businesses simply don't permit any other option: it's perfectly OK to run a firewall on the same computer that runs the rest of SBS. ISA Server inserts itself so low into the IP stack that it blocks exploit code before that code hits a running application. Installing ISA Server on a Windows

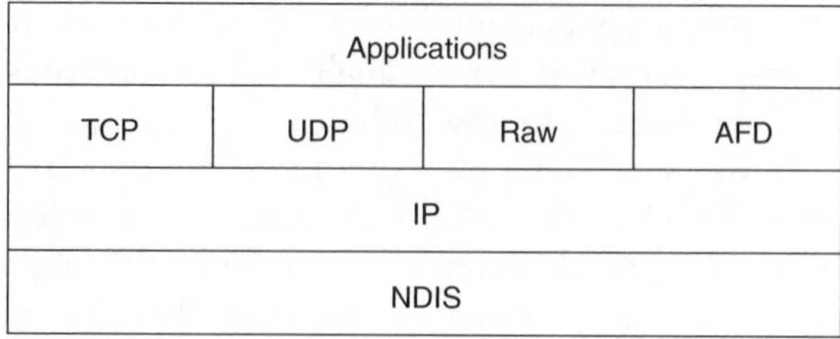


**Figure 5-1** Conceptual view of the Windows IP stack.

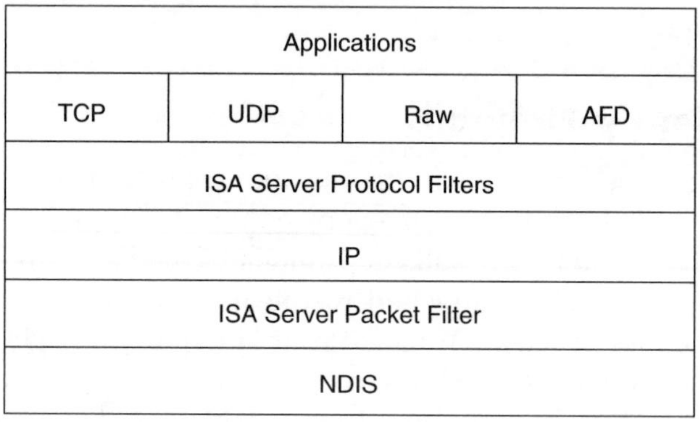

**Figure 5-2** The stack with ISA Server installed.

computer protects the computer itself from attack. Figure 5-1 shows a conceptual view of the IP stack in Windows.

Figure 5-2 shows the stack with ISA Server installed and running. Just like with RRAS, ISA Server's various inspection and filtering bits are so low in the IP stack that there's nothing for an attacker to exploit. Applications running on the computer are protected.

If you aren't running SBS, consider at a minimum a SOHO-type firewall like a SonicWall SOHO3 or WatchGuard Firebox SOHO 6. These are preferable to home routers because they give you more granular control over what individual users can do. Packet-filtering firewalls really aren't sufficient to protect against modern attacks. If your budget allows, deploy an application layer firewall like ISA Server that inspects *all* traffic entering and exiting your network. They cost more, but they offer significantly improved protection. Several vendors have released

ISA Server firewall "appliances" that are entirely appropriate for small businesses.[5]

Returning to personal firewalls, the question of which firewall to use arises. Windows XP includes a personal firewall; in Service Pack 2, it becomes something that you can manage better with its support for multiple profiles and group policy.[6] The firewall in Windows XP blocks only unsolicited *inbound* traffic; that is, it blocks stuff from trying to enter your computer unless it's a response to some outbound request your computer previously made. The firewall allows all outbound traffic (but it does block outbound traffic with spoofed source addresses).

This approach contrasts with that of many other personal firewall products on the market. Windows Firewall has been criticized for not offering "outbound protection." When the service pack was in development, Microsoft in fact considered outbound protection, but decided to eliminate it for some very sound reasons. In testing builds with outbound protection, Microsoft discovered that the constant dialogs from the firewall were confusing to most users and people quickly developed the habit of answering "yes" all the time or simply switched the firewall off completely to avoid the hassle. For the techies in the audience, such prompts are never a problem, but for ordinary users (which constitute the vast majority of people on the planet), a firewall that isn't so chatty and that blocks the greater source of danger (inbound traffic) is certainly better than a switched off firewall that serves no purpose at all. But more importantly, Microsoft's testers discovered that outbound protection is trivially easy to circumvent. It isn't all that difficult to create malware that simply hijacks or rides along with permitted outbound traffic; indeed, this is becoming the most popular way of bypassing many of the personal firewall products on the market. So Microsoft narrowed the focus of the firewall to do two things very well: to block the bad stuff from getting in and to give you a way to manage its configuration across your organization.

5. See `http://www.microsoft.com/isaserver/howtobuy/hardwaresolutions.asp`.

6. Susan Bradley, the SBS "Diva," writes an excellent blog about Windows XP Service Pack 2 that's imminently useful for all small business administrators. See `http://msmvps.com/bradley/archive/2004/10/14/15825.aspx`.

## Protect Your Servers

Protecting clients is important because attackers often use poorly secured clients to launch attacks against other devices. But your servers are even more important—this is, after all, where your data is, and where you and your customers and business partners intersect. If someone compromises your servers, your business pretty much just stops—and you can't do anything until you recover.

No matter what size of business you run, good physical security for servers is paramount. *Never* put any kind of server underneath someone's desk; no single location attracts more thieves and spilled coffee than this one popular office storage space. Servers belong in a locked room or cabinet—or at least shackled with a strong lock and cable to something large and immobile. Keep track of who has access to the room and change the key lock or combination every so often to (re-)ensure that only authorized people have access. Keep track of asset information such as model and serial numbers, which are often required if you need to make an insurance claim against damaged or stolen equipment.

Be sure your antivirus and anti-spyware programs are running on your servers, too. Worms, viruses, and Trojans don't know the difference between servers and clients—a computer is a computer is a computer. Unprotected servers often become the launching point for attacks against other computers; a server that's trying to infect the entire Internet isn't going to be too useful for anything else. (If you know that you'll never surf the Internet from your servers, you can safely omit the anti-spyware.) Likewise, keep your servers up-to-date with patches and service packs. Some people rely on automatic updates; others prefer to manually apply updates to servers. Regardless of your approach, do keep your servers updated; use the Microsoft Baseline Security Analyzer[7] (MBSA) to identify common misconfigurations and missing updates. To automate some of the steps for keeping an Exchange server current, download the Exchange Server Best Practices Analyzer Tool,[8] which compares your server's configuration to the best practices Microsoft recommends for Exchange Server 2000 and 2003.

7. `http://www.microsoft.com/technet/security/tools/mbsahome.mspx`.

8. `http://www.microsoft.com/exchange/downloads/2003/exbpa/default.mspx`.

Database servers deserve special attention. Many common business software products run in (at least) two tiers—a Web tier that handles all the presentation and business logic, and a database tier that stores all the information you interact with and store. All too often, people think only of securing the Web server and ignore the security on the database—but in most instances the attackers are interested in what's in the database and often just ignore the Web server if they can compromise the database server directly. So, it's critical that you keep your database server, whether it's just MSDE or the full Microsoft SQL Server, current with all service packs and updates. And if you have any influence with your application vendor, make sure that the application and database use Windows authentication and validate all input—SQL authentication is almost always passed in clear text with a blank password; unvalidated input leads to common SQL injection attacks that can give an attacker complete control of the database server.[9]

## Storing Client Information on Servers

Client computers often store mission-critical information: business plans, financial data, any kind of intellectual property the users are creating or updating. You can help protect this information by bringing it under the domain of your servers with a couple interesting technologies built in to Windows.

### *Roaming Profiles*

Windows keeps a lot of information about users in *profiles*—Registry keys, desktop icons, favorites, program files and links and settings, document folders, and so on. You can move a user's profile off the local computer and onto a server using *roaming profiles*. Now this information gets backed up according to whatever schedule you've implemented. It also allows users to move from computer to computer and have all their settings follow.

9. See also `http://msdn.microsoft.com/library/en-us/dnnetsec/html/openhack.asp` for a fascinating discussion of these attacks. There is, unfortunately, very little that you can do to fix broken third-party applications yourself, but you might enlist the aid of a techie friend to find a flaw or two and alert the vendor about the vulnerability.

To set up roaming profiles, first create a folder on your server to hold all the profiles. Share this folder to the network and give all users full control (the default NTFS permissions tighten down access appropriately). Then in Active Directory Users and Computers modify the profile location for each user (the Profile tab in Properties). Enter the folder for this specific user; `\\servername\profileshare\%USERNAME%` works in all cases. Windows creates subfolders and sets permissions appropriately; you don't need to manage that.

### *Redirecting Folders and Offline Storage*

As with user profiles, you can also configure clients to store documents and other content on network shares instead of on local hard drives. And just like with profiles, by moving documents to server storage they are better protected from loss because they get backed up.

Setting up folder redirection is similar to setting up roaming profiles. SBS 2003 includes a Configure My Documents redirection wizard that automates setting up folder redirection, but it redirects only the My Documents folder, which isn't enough to keep a client completely backed up. So instead, we recommend you configure folder redirection manually. Create a folder on your server to hold everyone's document subfolders. Share this folder to the network and give all users full control. Then in Active Directory Users and Computers, create a new Group Policy object in the domain (or organizational unit) containing your users. Edit this GPO and navigate to **User Configuration | Windows Settings | Folder Redirection**. Redirect **My Documents**, **My Pictures**, **Application Data**, and **Desktop**; don't redirect **Start Menu**. Configure basic redirection for each and use `\\servername\redirectshare\%USERNAME%` in all cases.

Sometimes administrators choose not to redirect **Application Data** and **Desktop** and instead allow them to roam with the profile. But by redirecting them, you can often reduce the amount of time it takes for a user to log on, which is especially important if mobile users are on slow links. A few applications behave improperly when **Application Data** is redirected; test this if you see erratic results.

A downside of moving personal storage to the server is that users must be connected to the network to work on their files. Windows has a feature that "mirrors" server content to local folders to alleviate this problem; the feature is especially useful for mobile computers. Windows XP automatically makes redirected folders available offline, so there's nothing you need to do here. The default setting is to automatically cache files so that the operation is transparent to the user. When users log off, any changes made to files are automatically synchronized so that the network and local versions are identical.

Various Group Policy settings enable you to change the synchronization behavior—you can schedule it to occur at certain times or to occur whenever the computer is idle. You can even choose to encrypt the offline files cache with EFS, which is a good idea for mobile computers.

## Extending Server Protection to Clients

An important tenet of information security is the *principle of least privilege*. Alas it's so easy (and too common) to give everyone administrator access to all resources—everything is guaranteed to work when you do this. Everything is also guaranteed to be compromised eventually, too, because malware runs in the same user context as whoever's logged on to the box. And users running as administrators will execute malware as administrators, which very likely can permit successful attack of your servers.

Throughout the book, we discuss technologies such as group policy and software restriction policies (SRPs), technologies you can use to manage all your clients from your servers and to help keep those servers protected. SBS includes Active Directory, which means that group policy and SRPs are already there, just waiting for you to use. Group policy can apply many security settings and permissions automatically, keeping you out of the business of manually configuring (and making mistakes on) the settings of each of your client computers. User-based roles, such as "sales rep" or "admin assistant," help you assign consistent privileges and permissions to users; each role's set of allowed behaviors should be consistent with whatever that role's job duties happen to be.[10] Create organizational units that reflect the roles of users and computers and apply settings to them. Then group those resources together into the appropriate organizational units, and all of the security settings you defined at the OU are automatically assigned to the resources.

10. Although not written with small businesses in mind, many of the principles described in the *Windows Server 2003 Security Guide* and the *Windows XP Security Guide* are very appropriate here, especially the use of AD group policy to grant privileges and assign permissions by role.

Add WUS for centralized updating and (after it gets released) Audit Collection Services (ACS)[11] for centralized monitoring and from a single location you can keep track of what your clients are doing and keep them updated. Finally, configure roaming user profiles and local folder redirection with offline files—now clients are disposable; a compromised client is something you can "nuke and pave" quickly without worrying about lost data or extended downtime.

Think about the roles of computers and people, and take advantage of these technologies to simplify your work. By automating these settings, which can prevent users from installing or running unapproved software and limiting which resources users can access, you can advance far along the path toward strong effective protection—and quite possibly ahead of your competitors, too.

## Protect Your Network

Even the smallest of businesses often see the value in wireless networks and remote access. But securing these technologies can appear difficult; how can any small business expect to enjoy the benefits while avoiding attacks? A few basic precautions are really all that are important.

We've already discussed firewalls. To simplify any remote access deployments, use a product that's not only a good firewall but also includes VPN functionality. Conveniently, ISA Server in SBS Premium Edition helps you configure Windows Routing and Remote Access Services (RRAS) for most popular client-to-server VPN scenarios. PPTP is more than adequate—it's easier to maintain than L2TP + IPsec since you don't need a certificate authority and it works over pretty much all network address translation devices without any configuration, which some of your employees probably have at home. So long as you use good passwords, PPTP as configured by the wizards (MS CHAPv2 authentication, 128-bit RC4 encryption) is safe from cryptographic attacks.

### Securing Your Wireless LAN

When we first started writing this book, we knew that in this chapter we'd stake the controversial position that plain old 128-bit WEP was good

11. Not released as of this writing.

enough. After all, using the tools available at the time (early 2004), an attacker needed to collect a few *gigabytes* of data from the air before WEP cracking tools could do their thing. Just changing your key once a month—say on the first Monday of each month as an easy-to-establish habit you can put in your calendar—was enough to foil an attacker. To brute force the key, an attacker needed far more data than what a small network usually generated in that time—meaning that an attacker was unable to get enough data to brute force the key before your key-change interval approached. All you needed was a good strong random key created by a key generator.[12]

Wow, how things change. The cracking tools have gotten so good[13] that now an attacker needs only about 500,000 frames, which is about 715 megabytes—easily generated in a matter of minutes if you're transferring large amounts of data over your wireless network. Therefore, we urge you to move beyond WEP as soon as you can. Take our advice in the previous paragraph to make your existing WEP better, but plan to move to WPA quickly.

Best for small businesses is WPA-PSK (preshared key). Regular WPA requires a RADIUS server, something generally beyond the needs of small businesses; WPA-PSK gives you all the benefits of WPA and allows you to get completely out of the key-management business without needing RADIUS. WPA uses a key-management mechanism called TKIP (Temporal Key Integrity Protocol). You program a preshared *authentication* key into each access point and client; WPA generates new *encryption* keys for every frame (packet) of data that passes between clients and access points. That's a lot of encryption, so it's better to use the AES encryption algorithm rather than WEP's RC-4 because AES is so much faster. Change your authentication key every six months. Note also that you need capable hardware. Devices manufactured after August 2003 are required to support WPA and WPA-PSK to receive the Wi-Fi Alliance logo. Older hardware might have firmware updates available; check the manufacturer's Web site.

Oh, and please change the default SSID name in your access point. We see far too many wireless networks called "default" and "linksys." This is nearly the equivalent of hanging out a sign that says "Hack me."

12. `http://www.warewolflabs.com/portfolio/programming/wlanskg/wlanskg.html` has one.

13. "WEP dead again, part 1" by Michael Ossman (`http://securityfocus.com/infocus/1814`). Part 2 wasn't published as of this writing.

## Choosing Good Passwords

Because of the intense debate swirling around passwords, we devoted an entire chapter to the topic earlier in the book. For small businesses, we have two easy recommendations: pass phrases or joined words. A pass phrase would be something like this:

*My dog and I went out.*

Pass phrases are easy to remember, simple to type quickly, and are complex: the example here has mixed case and a symbol. You can even vary the phrase so that you have a collection of easy-to-remember phrases that are unique for different locations you visit:

*My dog and I went to the auction.* (auction site)
*My dog and I bought some books.* (bookstore)
*My dog and I got the mail.* (Web mail)
*My dog and I went gambling.* (online casino)
*My dog and I admired some art.* (porn site)

Joined words also work very well as passwords, for example:

*stuck + suppose*[14]

Like pass phrases, joined words are easy to remember and simple to type. They also have a good amount of complexity because of the symbol.

No matter what you choose, the point is to select something that's both strong and easy to type and remember. Passwords such as dT54*x;j7\]2 are absolutely terrible: they have no associations with their uses, they take forever to type, and they are impossible to remember. Phrases and joined words satisfy all the requirements.

14. This is the very first CompuServe password one of us had, back in 1987. Ah, CompuServe … whatever happened to the good old days, eh?

## Keep Your Data Safe

Information is an important asset of yours—perhaps as important as the products you sell. If your information suddenly became unavailable, how would your business continue? How long would it take to recover, and what would that recovery cost? When many people consider necessary steps for protecting computers, they stop after considering ways to limit and control access. But that isn't enough, because access controls can be circumvented; data protection is equally as important.

In Chapter 7, "Data-Protection Mechanisms," we give data protection a full treatment, covering important techniques such as access control and rights management. Essentially the goal is, again, to achieve the notion of least privilege—give users access only to what they need and nothing more. Because most people are honest this notion helps protect against accidental "attacks," but it also limits what malicious users are capable of perpetrating.

Another critical procedure to develop is a regular backup process. Data storage hardware is not immune to failure, and some failures can destroy your data. Backups are your only insurance against data loss caused by failed hardware or by accidental or malicious data destruction. In SBS, it's easy to keep a system backed up using the Backup Configuration Wizard from the To Do List.[15] The utility uses the volume shadow copy service in Windows, which even backs up open files, so that users can continue to work while the backup is in progress. Note, however, that large backups over the network might affect the network's performance, so it's best to schedule backups to occur after normal work hours.

The backup utility can copy data to several locations: another hard drive, an optical device such as a CD or DVD recorder, and a tape drive. It's probably faster and cheaper these days to back up to USB drives—five-gigabyte drives are for sale in some places; DVD is probably okay, too, especially the new dual-layer drives and media now available. CD just doesn't have the necessary capacity and tape is prohibitively expensive. And if you've scheduled backups for after-hours, don't forget to load your removable media before you go home.

15. "Backing up and restoring Windows Small Business Server 2003" (`http://www.microsoft.com/smallbusiness/gtm/securityguidance/articles/backup_restore_sbs2003.mspx`).

If you should ever have to restore a server, you can choose an alternate location, which can be useful if you need to restore right away to some other computer to get back online right now. The alternate computer's hardware configuration must match the previous computer pretty closely: same hard drive controller, motherboard chip set, processor count, hard disk volume sizes, and boot partition drive letter.

Test your backups regularly! Backup media, like any other kind, can go bad. So many people have used the same media over and over again, only to discover during an actual disaster that the media is corrupt and the restores therefore fail. And when you do eventually have to replace the backup media, be sure to completely destroy the old tapes or discs: don't just toss them in the garbage, because someone *will* find them. Cut them into small ribbons with a band saw.

## Use the Internet Safely

Believe it: not all Web sites are safe! HTML is a powerful display language that can send all kinds of executable code to the browser that the computer then runs locally. Local code can create very compelling and interactive browsing experiences—and it can wreak security havoc on a machine. Remember one of the ten immutable laws:[16]

> If a bad guy can get code to run on your computer, it isn't your computer anymore.

Good antivirus and anti-spyware programs can help to keep a lot of the bad code off your computer—if the programs know how to find them (meaning that your signature files are always up-to-date). But you can't stop there because new malware materializes all the time. This is one of the reasons that Windows XP Service Pack 2 (and Windows Server 2003 Service Pack 1) include a number of Internet Explorer-related security changes to stop much of the bad code from getting onto the computer or executing.

Try to avoid surfing the Internet from your servers as much as you can. The main purpose of a server is to respond to requests from clients for

16. "10 immutable laws of security" (`http://www.microsoft.com/technet/archive/community/columns/security/essays/10imlaws.mspx`).

information. Don't use a server as a client. About the only time your SBS server should ever make connections to the Internet is when it needs to update patches for your WUS installation; earlier we already discussed the value of running WUS in your small business.[17] If you do have any requirements for surfing from your servers, we encourage you to install Virtual PC on the server, create a Windows XP virtual image, and surf from that. Configure the image to discard all changes; when you finish surfing, just shut down the image—anything some nefarious Web site drops on your computer (that is, on the image) simply gets discarded. *We must, however, again strongly recommend that you not surf from your servers.* Workstations are cheap; avoid creating situations where people have to surf from your servers.

## An Internet Use Policy

Yes, even for small businesses, a basic acceptable use policy is important. Policies help clear up confusion and provide guidance to help people make decisions. Good policies encourage compliance by helping people understand the value and don't get in the way of daily work.

Resist the urge to be heavy-handed in enumerating all of the things people *aren't* allowed to do. Work these days rarely happens within a defined eight-hour period: Blackberries and smartphones have extended work hours well into nearly the entire day, and you as the employer do benefit from this. It's only fair, then, to let people take care of a few personal needs during "normal" working hours because sometimes there's simply no other choice. What you need to explain in your policies—and monitor, too—is consequences for abuse.

Describe in your policy the behaviors that are and aren't acceptable; common sense should help you select the specifics.[18] (Porn and peer-to-peer file sharing are the usual culprits.) Make it clear in your policy

17. At the time of this writing, WUS was still in beta. SUS, the prior version, is still useful if WUS isn't yet out by the time you read this book. See "Updating a Windows Small Business Server 2003 Network using Software Update Services Server 1.0" (`http://www.microsoft.com/downloads/details.aspx?familyid=5f1cc6f0-79b7-4a95-bcab-49bee6d5df13&displaylang=en`). Look for a WUS version of the document when WUS becomes available.18. Visit the SANS Security Policy Project at `http://www.sans.org/resources/policies/` for some pointers.

18. Visit the SANS Security Policy Project at `http://www.sans.org/resources/policies` for some pointers.

whether you monitor individual actions—most people assume a certain amount of privacy exists unless you explicitly state otherwise. Have each employee sign a copy of the policy.

## Small Business Security Is No Different, Really

Regardless of size, all networks face pretty much the same threats. The difference with networks in small businesses is that they rarely have someone dedicated to their proper care and feeding. There's a difference between Windows Server 2003 and Small Business Server 2003: SBS includes a number of wizards that, if you follow them, automate much of the work needed to get and stay secure. Spend a little time learning about and configuring the security of your servers and your network can become largely self-maintaining, letting you spend time managing your business instead.

Small businesses aren't large enterprises; they don't have the luxury of enterprise consultants who can tweak every setting (and maybe that means small businesses are better off, because tweaking can be dangerous).[19] Yes, with SBS you're running all your roles on one box, but if you don't follow basic security practices then it really doesn't matter how many boxes you have! But with good security practices, such as we describe in this chapter, you can safely combine roles onto a single computer (or maybe two)—it's all about balancing cost, time, and security.

### More Small Business Resources

Microsoft has published several resources useful for security in small businesses. Please spend time with these to make sure you're as secure as you can be:

**Security Guidance Center for small businesses**

- `http://www.microsoft.com/smallbusiness/gtm/securityguidance/hub.mspx`

**Small business computer security checklist**

- `http://www.microsoft.com/smallbusiness/gtm/securityguidance/checklist/default.mspx`

19. For the enterprise folks reading this chapter, you can learn a lot about the special concerns of small businesses by checking out the thriving Windows Small Business Server Community at `http://www.microsoft.com/windowsserver2003/sbs/community/default.mspx`.

**The e-security guide for small businesses**

- http://www.microsoft.com/smallbusiness/desktopsecurity/pdf.mspx

**Securing Your Windows Small Business Server 2003 Network**

- http://www.microsoft.com/technet/security/secnews/articles/sec_sbs2003_network.mspx

**Securing Your Network: Identifying SMB Network Perimeters**

- http://www.microsoft.com/technet/security/secnews/articles/sec_net_smb_per_dev.mspx

**Securing Windows XP Professional Clients in a Windows Server Environment**

- http://www.microsoft.com/technet/security/secnews/articles/sec_winxp_pro_server_env.mspx

## What You Should Do Today

- Ensure the software on all your desktops and servers with the latest service packs and updates.
- Implement a plan for regular updates, and automate it as much as possible.
- Deploy antivirus and anti-spyware on all your computers. Enable host-based firewalls.
- Physically secure your servers. A locked room is best; heavy cables are better than nothing.
- Plan for rolling out roaming profiles and folder redirection (with offline folders) so that client computers can be rebuilt with ease.
- Upgrade your wireless networking to WPA.
- Change all your passwords to pass phrases.
- Implement a backup plan; don't forget to regularly test the media.
- Write an Internet acceptable use policy and have all your employees sign it.

CHAPTER 6

# EVALUATING APPLICATION SECURITY

So you just forked over half a boatload of your shareholders' hard-earned equity to a small Web shop for a nifty new storefront for your company. The new storefront will go on the company Web server, and you expect that it will generate huge sales. Then this creeping suspicion starts: is this thing really secure? After all, the company was recommended by your son, who is a high school senior, and it consists mostly of his snow-boarding buddies. What do they know about security?

Well, we cannot make an application hacker out of you in the span of a few pages. However, we can give you some tips for what to look for in new applications to determine whether they present any glaring vulnerabilities. We will not limit ourselves only to custom developed Web apps from small Web shops run by high school seniors. We also include some things to look for in server applications, a couple of client application hints, and even some things for general application security. Hopefully, there is something in here for everyone, although the largest piece will be on input validation in applications.

---

**WARNING:** Just because an application does not exhibit any of the flaws we discuss in this section does not mean it is safe! You can never prove safety. You can only prove lack thereof. Do not take this chapter as final advice as to whether to deploy a mission-critical application. Consider your security policy and get a comprehensive review by experts if the policy warrants it.

---

## Caution: More Software May Be Hazardous to Your Network Health

Far too often, we think all our problems can be solved by adding more software. Well, that is logical. After all, we are technologists. Technology is cool, and our technology of choice is software. After all, more toys must be a good thing, right? Not necessarily. There are many examples where software caused more problems than it solved.

For instance, it is not at all uncommon to deploy some sort of centralized logging solution or intrusion detection system (IDS) to detect attacks. A couple of years ago while doing a penetration assessment on a large network, one of the authors discovered a service account with the name PYN-DMZ_ids. It was the service account used to run the IDS service. The IDS service relied on an agent to collect the logs from all the protected machines. Since this is a privileged operation, the IDS service ran in the context of an administrator. Once we had compromised one of the systems running the IDS, it was a simple matter of dumping out the LSA Secrets to take over all the other systems with that service, which in this instance was the entire network, including domain controllers.

---

**WARNING:** Consider this when deploying domain-wide management software: A domain is only as secure as the least-secure system running a service under a domain admin account.

---

Any given system is only as secure as the least-secure system with which it shares administrative or service accounts.

## Baseline the System

The first step in evaluating application security is to baseline the system. The purpose is to evaluate what happens when you install the software. There are several interesting things you want to know:

- Any new users that were added
- Any new groups that were added
- Any new files, folders, and registry values that were added
- Any privileges granted to any users
- Any access control list (ACL) entries (ACEs) that were added
- Security settings that were changed

You need to use various tools to do this. One very useful one is InCtrl5, which does most of the work automatically for you. You can get it at `http://www.pcmag.com/article2/0,4149,9882,00.asp`. However, we have had problems running certain installers under tools like this, not to mention how slow the installer gets, so we usually prefer to baseline the system first and then create a second snapshot afterward, letting the installer work the way it should. InCtrl5 also does not track some of the things we list above because it is primarily written as a troubleshooting tool for advanced end users. To that end, we usually use a series of other tools that can track all this information.

Few tools in the operating system will help you here, but a couple are worth pointing out. The secedit.exe tool in Windows Server 2003 contains a `/generaterollback` switch. It is used to snapshot the security state of a system. Run secedit.exe with that switch prior to installing anything. Save the log file as baseline.log and copy it to a different system. It will contain a list of privileges and security settings currently set on the system.

To determine the ACLs, use the showaccs.exe tool from the Windows Server 2003 or Windows 2000 Support Tools. The syntax is relatively self-explanatory:

```
Showaccs V1.0
Copyright  1998 Microsoft Corporation
Usage: Showaccs <access profile file> [/f [<path>] /r /s /p /g /m <map file> /no
builtins]
<access profile file>  path of the .csv file to be generated
```

```
/f    [<path>]            for all NTFS files
/r                        for Registry
/s                        for file shares
/p                        for printer shares
/g                        for local groups
/m                        generate a map file
<map file>                map file path for /m option
/nobuiltins               for no built-in groups
```

Use the appropriate options to generate the right log files. For instance, to find out what happens to the ACLs in the Program Files directory, use this command:

```
showaccs c:\progfiles.csv /f "c:\program files"
```

A map file is very useful because it contains a mapping from SIDs to usernames that are used in the directory or Registry structure. Run this tool five times, once each for the file system, the Registry, the file shares, the printer shares, and, finally, once for a list of the local groups. Save each of the log files (which will usually be huge).

The last thing we need is the user list. A simple `net user` will give us that list, but keep in mind that it will not show any user that has a $ at the end of the name. You will only see those in the GUI users and groups management tools.

Now install the software. Then run the same tools again. At this point, you have a before and after snapshot. Use some file differencing tool to find out what the differences are. For instance, windiff.exe, also shipped with the support tools, will do this nicely. The Windows ports of the UNIX diff tools are more powerful, however, because they enable us to create a text file with just the differences. You can get those tools in several places, including the free Interix toolkit, part of the Service for UNIX, from Microsoft. You can get those at `http://www.microsoft.com/windows/sfu/productinfo/overview/default.asp`.

After you have a list of the changes, you are ready to analyze what was done by the software installer. Make a list of all the changes, and look for anything that seems suspicious, such as full control ACLs, new privileges added to users, new administrators, new services, new databases, and so on. In the following section, we examine a number of things that should be red flags.

# Things to Watch Out For

Applications can do a lot of things that will degrade your security. In the end, we will not be able to find all of them, but there are a number of them that should be a cause for concern. In most cases, to perform a complete review, you need to contract an expert, or set of experts; if you find anything that looks blatantly suspicious, however, contact the software vendor. If they cannot satisfactorily address your questions, take your business, and your money, and go elsewhere.

## Database Application Security Problems

Since we started the attack in Chapter 2 with a faulty database front-end application, let us take a look at one of those first. The main problem to afflict database front-end applications, is SQL injection.

### *SQL Injection*

An SQL injection bug can be devastating. The core problem with any SQL injection issue is poor input validation. Altogether too many programmers forget or ignore the first rule of security: All user input is evil until proven otherwise!

Trustworthy user input is user input that you have determined to be trustworthy. As any administrator knows, anything that comes from a user must be considered evil, and should be treated as such. Programmers often do this backward. They take the input and then try to prove that it is bad.

---

**NOTE:** You can never prove that something is bad. To do so you would have to enumerate all the possible ways something could be bad, and you will forget at least one.

---

In *Writing Secure Code*, 2nd Edition (Howard and LeBlanc, Microsoft Press, 2003), Michael Howard and David LeBlanc pointed out the Turkish I problem, which is worth repeating here.

Suppose that you have a Web application that takes URLs as input. You want to reject file URLs, so you write some code like this:

```
<%
  if(InStr(0,UCase(input),"FILE",VbTextCompare)) then
    'error condition, we are getting hacked
  else
    'do some sensitive operation
  end if
%>
```

The problem with this is that you may not find all the file URLs. Turkish, and allegedly also Azerbaijani, has four different letter I's: i, I, İ, and ı. When you do the comparison, it will only match the first two. Then you will drop into the else statement, and the OS will translate the latter two into the former two, and you have now circumvented the check. The proper thing to do in this case would have been to look for the URLs you want to accept, not the ones you do not want. If you only want HTTP URLs, which is probably the case here, then look for those and reject all else. That will probably mean that you will reject valid input that you had not thought of, but frankly, we would much rather take that problem than getting ourselves hacked. Should you accidentally reject valid input you will usually find out very quickly from your users and can add those to the allowed list.

### *Input Validation in SQL Server*

In database applications, poor input validations can be used in SQL injection attacks. Using an attack like this, an attacker can actually rewrite the queries that run on the database server. These are not unique to one type of database server or another. All database management systems are vulnerable to SQL injection attacks if the front-end applications are not properly written.

In a sample application, the code used to query for the username and password looks like this. (Do not worry if you do not understand the code completely. The implications of it will be clear imminently.)

```
//Three mistakes in this statement alone:
SqlConnection conn = new SqlConnection();
conn.ConnectionString =
```

```
"data source=PYN-SQL;" +
"initial catalog=pubs;" +
"user id=sa;" +
"password=password;" +
"persist security info=True;" +
"packet size=4096";
```

This statement just opens the connection to the database server. There are three bad mistakes here. The first is in the line that says "data source." It uses a data source specified in the code rather than a system Data Source Name (DSN). This means that the parameters for the connection are hard coded in the application. If the file that holds these parameters is not adequately protected, the attacker may get information on the database server, as we get here where we find out that the name of the server is PYN-SQL. The next two mistakes are in the "user id" and "password" lines. First, we are making a connection to the database as a very privileged user—the sa, or system administrator user. Second, that user has a really bad password of password.

### "SAFE" PROGRAMMING LANGUAGES

It may be worthwhile to point out here that most of the code we are demonstrating in this chapter is written in C# using ASP.NET. This is not the typical way to do things in ASP.NET. In fact, you have to try pretty hard to screw up this bad. If you just follow the standard wizards for creating database connections in ASP.NET, it will not hard code the connection information in this way, but rather use a DSN. Obviously, if the programmer chooses to do it in the unsafe way shown here, however, there is nothing ASP.NET can do to save you. For information about how to do this better, see Chapter 4, "Protecting Services and Server Applications." Keep in mind, however, that safer functions, or even safer languages, do not necessarily mean you will have safer programmers. It just means they will have to work a bit harder to screw things up.

Keep in mind where the database credentials should *not* be found. We mentioned that you should use a DSN. However, we have seen apps that put them in a text file. Worse still, we saw one once that put it in a text file underneath the Web root. That means that any user on the Internet can just request the text file and then receive the database credentials in clear text.

Now consider this code snippet. This is the code that actually processes the logon:

```
conn.Open();
//Don't do this at home folks: SQL Query Composition
string strQuery;
strQuery = "select * from Users where UserName = '" +
             username.Text +
            "' and Password ='" +
             password.Text + "';";
```

This code is even worse than the code that makes the connection. Username.Text and password.Text are the form fields holding the username and the password. This code simply passes those on to the database with no validation whatsoever! The attacker is free to send anything he wants to the database.

### *Finding SQL Injection Vulnerabilities*

Finding SQL injection problems is not always as straightforward. What if you do not want or cannot read the source code, or do not have access to it. In that case, you should get familiar with SQL Profiler, which comes with your SQL Server installation. SQL Profiler is a tool that lets you see *exactly* what SQL Server sees. If we do not have the source code, we fire up Profiler and start a new trace. You need to configure the trace to look for something, so go to the Events tab and select some things that make sense. If your application uses stored procedures, select SP:StmtStarting under the Stored Procedures node. If it uses T-SQL statements, select SQL:STMT Starting under the TSQL statements node. If you are unsure which it uses, select both of them. If you have no idea what T-SQL is, hire a consultant. You need to understand a little bit about SQL to do this.

It is not a bad idea to also audit logon events, so you may want to leave those in. When you are done, you will have a dialog similar to Figure 6-1.

Now go to the Data tab and select the columns you want in the output. If you are interested in which user context the queries execute select DBUsername and/or TargetUsername columns. Otherwise, the default settings are mostly fine for our purpose. When you are done, click Run.

Go to the Web app and start generating queries. For instance, you may want to start with a legitimate query, such as the one in Figure 6-2.

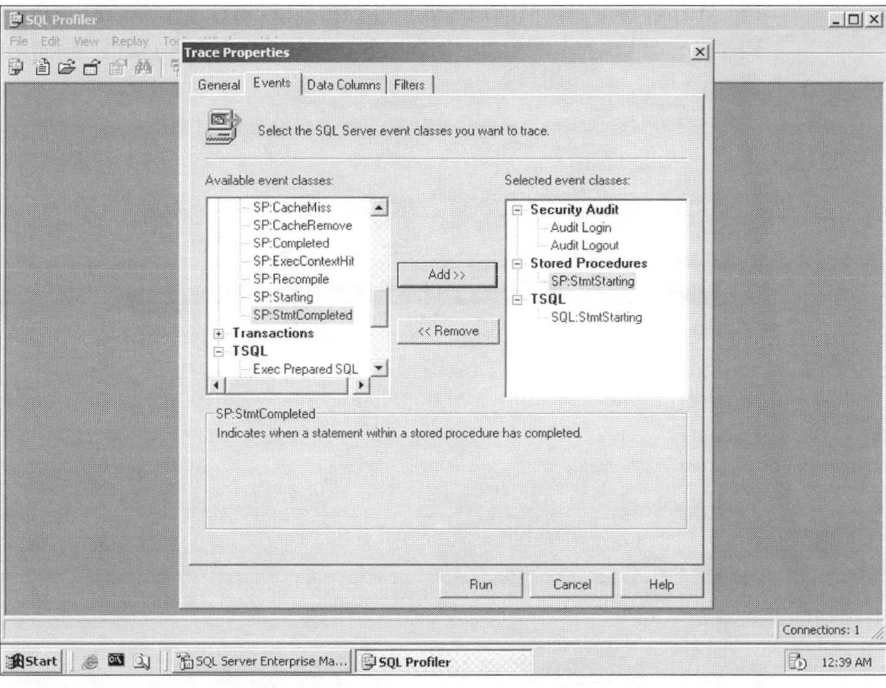


**Figure 6-1** Configure SQL Profiler to trace statements.

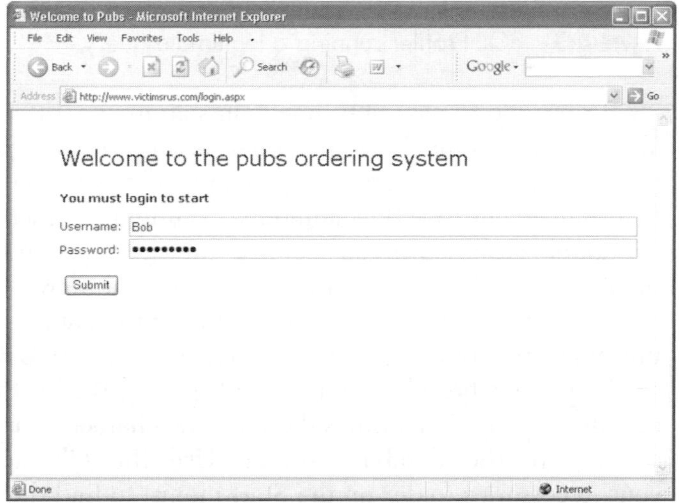


**Figure 6-2** Run a legitimate query to learn what the output looks like.

When you run this query, you should see some output happen in SQL Profiler. If you have done everything correctly, you will see something like Figure 6-3.

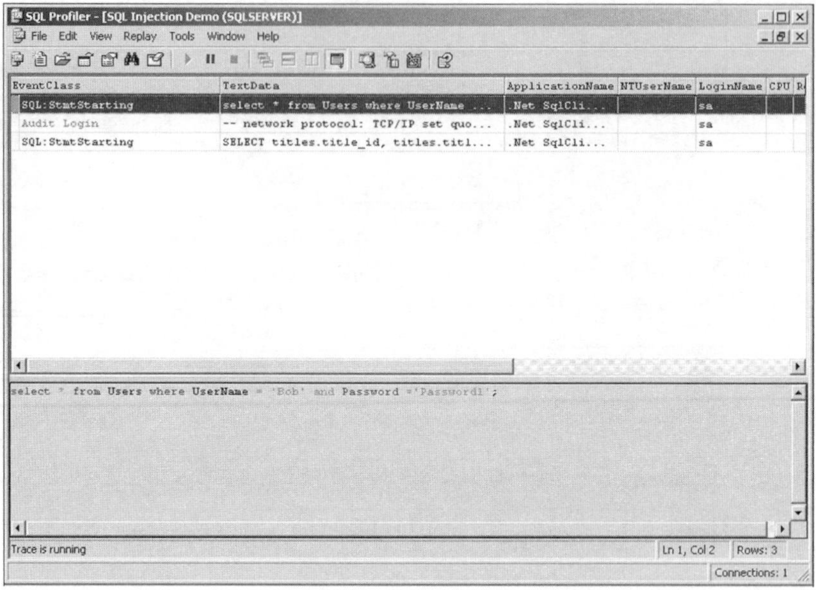

**Figure 6-3** SQL Profiler running a legitimate query.

To be able to pass SQL injection statements, the attacker needs to be able to pass certain characters. First, he may need to pass in single quotes to terminate a string statement. Second, he may need to pass in semicolons to terminate entire SQL statements. Comment characters, which in T-SQL are double dashes, are also useful, as are operators and SQL Server stored procedures such as xp_cmdshell. What you do now is to play a little with these parameters in the form and see what the database sees. The application may strip out single quotes, but what if you URL-escape them? A single quote is hex character 27, so try using %27 if the app throws away the single quote. Sometimes these escape characters are unescaped before sending to the database server. Use the Character Map tool (in your Accessories folder on the Start menu) to find the appropriate escape codes for things such as single quotes, double quotes, semicolons, dashes, and so on.

If the input handling is done properly, the illegal characters will be stripped out before Profiler sees them. For instance, try something like what you see in Figure 6-4.

The result is shown in Figure 6-5 and should be self-explanatory.

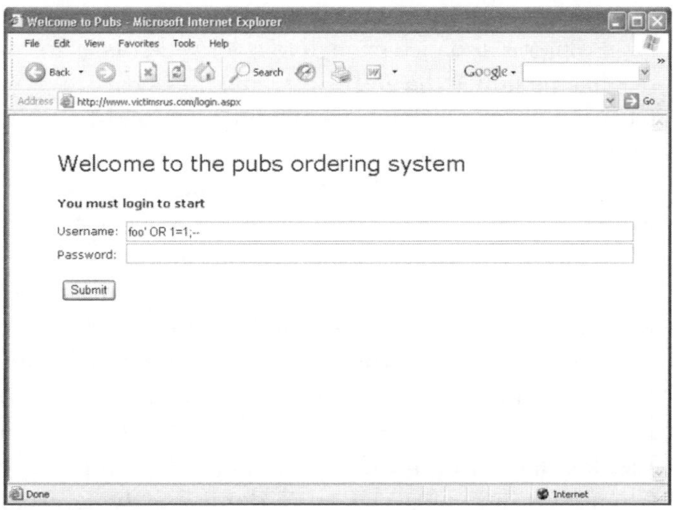


**Figure 6-4** Testing some bad input.

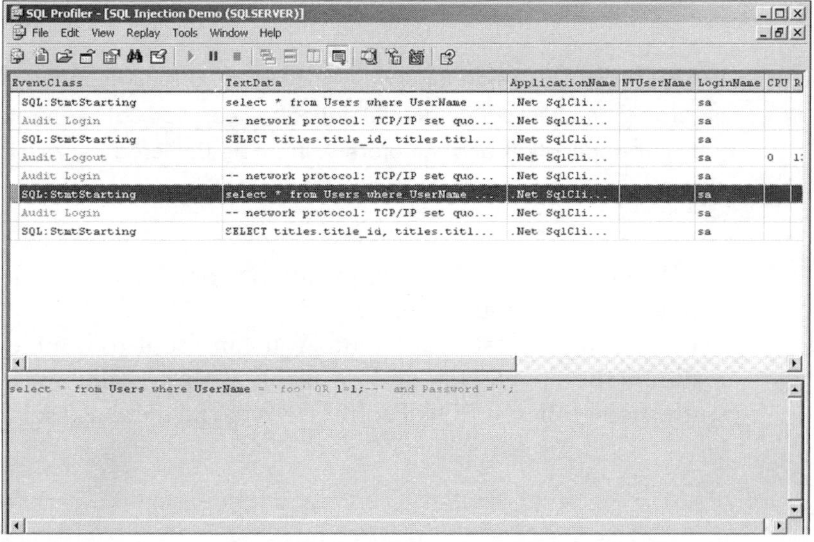


**Figure 6-5** SQL Profiler shows exactly what the database server sees.

As you can see in Figure 6-5, the database sees this query:

```
select * from Users where UserName = 'foo' OR 1=1;--' and
Password ='';
```

Profiler is also nice enough to color code things for you, so you can plainly see that the stuff at the end (`;--' and Password ='';`) is considered a comment. As we can see here, there is no input validation whatsoever. We can play with other characters as well, but in this case it is plain to see that the database will receive any query the attacker wants. This application is fundamentally flawed.

A note of caution is worthwhile here. We have seen Web applications that limit the amount of data a user can type in a form field. Input validation needs to happen on a system you control (the server), not one the attacker controls (the client). An attacker can, and will, trivially circumvent it by not using the Web application itself. Attackers frequently use a custom program to send any parameters they want. Field length limitations are client-side attempts at input validation. Client-side input validation is done mostly as a convenience to avoid having to round-trip data to the server to perform basic sanity checks. Client-side input validation does *not* obviate the need for server-side input validation.

---

**WARNING:** Client-side input validation is *not* a security feature. You must never rely on client-side input validation to keep you safe. An attacker will not use your application and therefore will not be bothered by your client-side input checks.

---

If you purchase Web applications, or if you are deploying Web applications from in-house developers, SQL Profiler may just have become your newest best friend. You can use it to double-check claims made by the developers and ensure that they really are telling you the truth. Remember, if SQL Profiler sees it, the database server sees it, and if the database server sees it and it is bad, you may have just been hacked.

For the interested reader, there is a wealth of information on SQL security on the Web. The OWASP project (`http://www.owasp.org`) is a project dedicated to Web application security and includes information on SQL injection and how to prevent it. SQL Security.com (`http://www.sqlsecurity.com`), run by Microsoft SQL Server MVP Chip Andrews, is a site dedicated to security in SQL Server.

One final word before we go on to the next topic; some developers will try to explain away SQL injection with claims such as "well, but we have secured the database." Any hardening of the database, including what we did in Chapter 4, is simply a band-aid on top of a known SQL injection problem. Although it is worthwhile as a defense-in-depth measure against the unknown, it should not be used as the primary defense strategy. If an app contains a SQL injection problem, it is unsafe. Period. It should not be used until it is fixed.

## Cross-Site Scripting

In a cross-site scripting attack, the Web server is not actually the victim. Rather, the victim is someone else. For instance, suppose that some bank has a cross-site scripting bug. An attacker can now lure a victim to click a link that goes to the bank, but that includes a script embedded in the link. When the victim clicks the link, the script executes as if it came from the bank, and has access to any data that the bank Web site would, such as cookies. The script could now take the content of the cookie and send it to the attacker.

Finding cross-site scripting problems is notoriously hard, particularly if you do not have access to the application source code. However, there are a couple of tell-tale signs. First, anytime you see anything that you entered in a form or in a link parameter echoed to the screen, you should be suspicious. In the Web application we showed earlier, we are clearly echoing the username to the screen. To see what else we echo, take the same approach we did for finding SQL injection problems. Send bad input. This is the second clue. To perform a cross-site scripting attack, we need to send < and > characters.

Will the app strip them out? Use something like what you see in figure 6-6 to find out.

Figure 6-7 shows the result. The angle bracket went through!

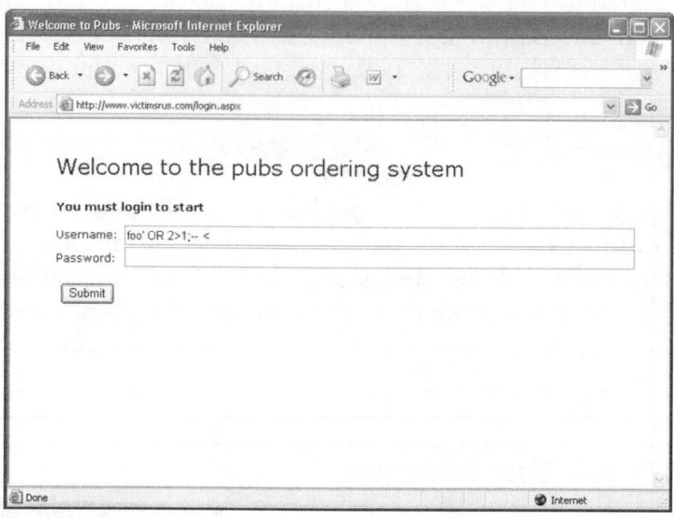


**Figure 6-6** Try sending angle brackets to search for cross-site scripting problems.

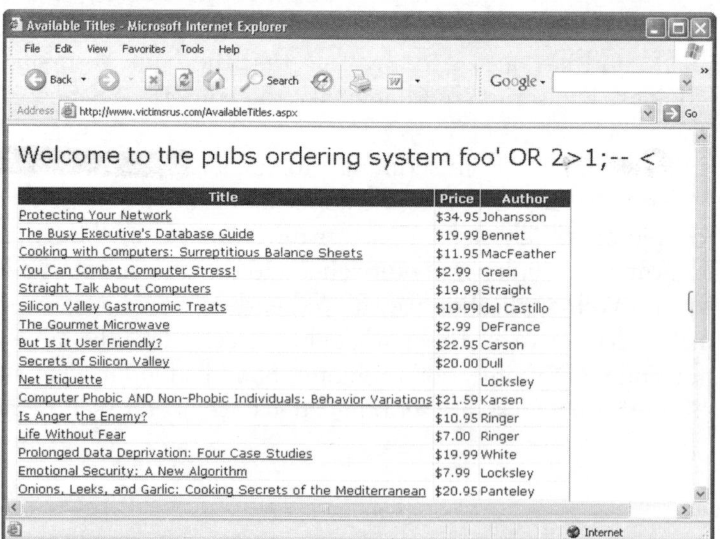


**Figure 6-7** The angle bracket was echoed to the screen successfully.

As it turns out, however, there may still be something there to protect you. Try using this as the username instead: `foo' OR 2>1;-- <script> alert(UROwn3d!)</script>`. If the cross-site scripting problem is unmitigated, we should now get an alert dialog when we open the page. However, in this particular case, we get what you see in Figure 6-8 instead.

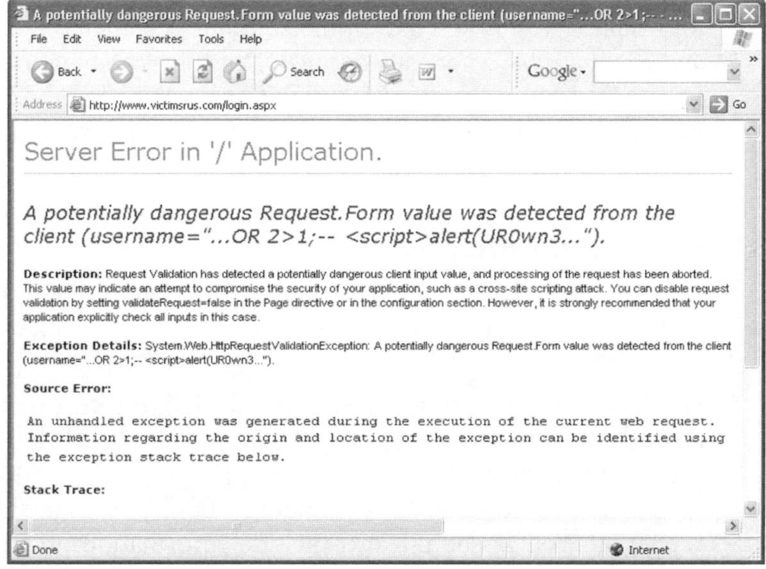


**Figure 6-8** The .NET Framework contains built-in code to capture cross-site scripting attacks.

This is really very cool! We did not implement any input validation. In fact, the cross-site scripting attack would have worked—had the code been written in Active Server Pages or Java Server Pages instead. However, the .NET Framework will automatically check for cross-site scripting attacks for us and throw an error if it thinks it has found one. Yet another good reason to use the Framework. For more information on how it protects you against cross-site scripting attacks, see the .NET Framework SDK at `http://www.microsoft.com/downloads/details.aspx?FamilyID=9b3a2ca6-3647-4070-9f41-a333c6b9181d`.

## Poor Database Security

Poor database security covers a number of different concepts. In Chapter 4, we talked about how to connect to the database server, how to harden it, and how to enumerate who has permissions. One issue we have not discussed, however, is encryption. Several people have recently asked us how to encrypt data in SQL Server. The answer is that you use the application to do that. SQL Server performs all data access in the context of the service account. That means that if you use the encrypting file system (EFS) on the database files, for instance, you would have to make them available to the service account, and you really have not gained much. Data encryption is an application function. SQL Server takes in a blob and stores it. Whether the blob is a plaintext password or a an encrypted one, for instance, is irrelevant to SQL Server. It will store it fine in either case.

## Poor Authentication

Authentication can be done in so many places. A full discussion of authentication can, and should, take up an entire book. However, the primary issues here are replay attacks and attacks against plaintext or poorly obfuscated credentials. Instead of trying to explain what all the possible ways to screw up are, it is easier to outline briefly what the right way to authenticate is.

First, an authentication sequence should be time-stamped to avoid replay attacks. It should also include information about the requested resource so that the sequence cannot be captured and used against a different resource. Both of these values need to be digitally signed, preferably using a public key from the authentication server, such as you may obtain through an SSL channel. Encryption of these values is not important.

Second, an authentication sequence should always use some form of challenge-response to prove the identity of the user as opposed to sending the actual credentials across the wire. Preferably, the credentials used to generate the response token should not be the same as those used to verify it. This protects against use of the hashed credentials should they be stolen off the authentication server.

In general, if an accepted authentication protocol, such as NTLMv2 or, better yet, Kerberos, can be used, it should be. These protocols were developed by experts on the matter and are probably better than anything we could custom make for an application.

This is an admittedly brief discussion of authentication. For more details, refer to Matt Bishop's *Computer Security: Art and Science* (Addison-Wesley, 2002), which contains an excellent discussion on authentication.

## Buffer Overflows

Buffer overflows are a huge security problem today. A buffer overflow is where an application tries to stuff more data into a buffer than what the buffer can hold. When this happens, the excess data goes somewhere on either the stack or the heap, depending on how the buffer was allocated. From there, an attacker can usually use the buffer overflow to execute arbitrary code.

A buffer overflow that involves user input is particularly worrisome. A buffer overflow in a user application, such as most of the command-line tools is not really a problem. For instance, we have received reports that if you pass a long server name to ftp.exe, it will overflow a buffer. Frankly, this is a code quality bug, not a security bug. If you manage to exploit that, you can only make it run code as yourself. A buffer overflow is only a security bug if it allows you to run code as someone else. Otherwise, it is merely a code quality bug.

If there were a foolproof way to find buffer overflows, we would tell you about it. However, there is not, and there are experts on the subject who are still learning. We refer the interested reader to that book rather than try to reiterate what they say here. They also cover other similar types of problems, such as integer overflows, format string bugs, and so on.

## Unsafe Security Settings

Some applications contain unsafe security settings. Particularly worrisome are those that are set in an unsafe state by default. Any time you deploy an application, you should ask for information on the available security settings, their default values, and what will break when you turn them on. Invariably, something will break; otherwise the settings will be on by default. You should hold vendors accountable for producing this type of information on demand.

An example of this is the authentication options in SQL Server. By default, SQL 2000 will not accept SQL authentication. However, because of that older applications that use it will break. Some products even have a security configuration guide that describes available security settings and how to use them. All current versions of Windows, as well as Exchange 2003, have one, for example.

## Cannot Run as a Nonadmin

Any application of a nonadministrative nature that cannot run as a nonadministrator should be considered broken. Administrative privileges are needed to reconfigure the OS, add users, load and unload device drivers, etc. It should not be needed to balance your checkbook. If the manufacturer claims that it is, return the application and ask for a full refund. That application is broken. Unfortunately, we will never get software that runs as a nonadministrator for nonadministrative operations unless the folks that pay money for those applications demand it.

A very large number of applications suffer from this problem. Many need to run as an administrator the first time they are executed but can run as a nonadmin after that. Although this will keep them from being Windows Logo certified, it is a more acceptable condition.

In Chapter 4, we showed a way to figure out whether an application that claims it needs admin privileges can actually run as a nonadmin. In many cases, it is possible and very worthwhile to do that. Keep in mind, however, that you may have to unlock too much. For instance, if the app needs write access to some binary, this could be used to compromise some other user. A rogue user could just replace the binary with a modified one to do his or her evil bidding.

## Cleartext Data

Does the application store cleartext sensitive data or, worse yet, send cleartext data over the Internet? If it does, you have a problem. In many jurisdictions, you are now required to adequately protect customers' confidential information, and an application that fails to do so would probably put you in breach of that requirement.

To discover how the data is stored is relatively easy: just look at the data store and see what is there. To see how it traverses the network is a bit harder. The best way to find out is to break out a network sniffer. Ethereal is very good but can sometimes be difficult to configure. Microsoft's Network Monitor is a cinch to use but not quite as good. In addition, the version of

Network Monitor that comes with Windows Server does not support promiscuous mode, so it will only log traffic to and from the machine where Network Monitor is running. To get promiscuous mode, you need the version that comes with Systems Management Server (SMS). If you do not have a copy of SMS, get a copy of Ethereal instead. It is free from `http://www.ethereal.com`.

Use the network sniffer to look at the data as it is going across the wire. If you can read it, you have a broken application. Keep in mind, however, that just because you cannot read it does not mean it is protected. Very often a programmer will obfuscate the data by running it through a base64 routine, or by XORing it with something. Neither of those is adequate protection. To protect the data, it must be encrypted, which brings us to the next topic.

## Home-Grown Crypto

If there is one thing that makes the little hairs on the back of our necks stand up, it is the statement "we do not trust any of the commercial crypto algorithms, so we invented our own." If you have a software vendor or programmer tell you that, run, do not walk, away from there. 99.9 times out of 100 they are using base64, XOR, ROT-13, or some other encoding mechanism. Collectively, these things fall under the term *encraption*. None of them provide sufficient protection. If an application needs to protect data under Windows, it should use the CryptoAPI with a strong protocol. AES is a good block cipher. RC4, properly used, is a reasonable stream cipher. For hashes, use nothing less than SHA-1 or SHA-256.

If the objective is to store passwords instead, the app may want to use the Credential Manager API. It is a set of APIs to store passwords for things such as Passport, other Windows systems, and so on. In actuality, it is just a thin wrapper on top of CryptoAPI, designed specifically for storing passwords.

Do not let programmers lure you into believing that they understand how to write cryptographic algorithms. The chances that they understand it better than the professionals are about the same as us winning the lottery, considering neither of us plays. Make them use proper existing algorithms, properly.

## Lack of SLA

One of the biggest problems with software is a lack of a service level agreement (SLA). For instance, several vendors of large business software refuse to certify their software to run on patched systems. This leaves you with three options: (1) run it on unpatched systems and get yourself hacked, (2) patch the boxes anyway and risk breaking them and losing your expensive support contract, (3) get your money back and go buy from a vendor that cares about your security.

For a critical security vulnerability, a vendor must certify their software on a patched system within hours, or a few days at most. For an important security vulnerability, certification must take no more than two weeks. If a vendor cannot live up to that kind of SLA, they are not taking your security seriously. If they will not take due diligence to protect your systems, they probably have not taken due diligence to protect their own software either and you should reevaluate whether there are other vendors who perform better.

Note here that we have heard stories of fingerpointing at government agencies, stating that they are the ones responsible for certification of patches that are supported or required for special-purpose systems, such as medical systems. The government barely knows its own operations. It is totally unreasonable to expect it to test all special-purpose systems on every patch. It must be the vendor's responsibility to test its software on patched platforms.

## Unbelievable Claims

The last warning flag is an unbelievable claim. Many software vendors will claim things such as "our software makes your network secure," or "our software is secure," or "our software is unbreakable." In the Old West, they called such claims "snake oil." They are untrue. There are several facts you need to consider about such claims.

- No software is secure. To realize why, remember the unicorns.
- No software can make a network secure. Again, the unicorns are important. However, also keep in mind what we said earlier about the IDS service. Sometimes software intended to secure the network makes it less secure instead.

- No software can stop physical attacks. Software can make physical attacks more difficult, but the only way to stop physical attacks is to use physical security
- No software is unbreakable. See the first item in this list.

Although software may stop "all known attacks," is that really interesting? In most cases, patching your systems will accomplish the same thing. It is the unknown attacks that we have to worry about.

Software that uses "the strongest possible cryptography" usually does not. Make sure you understand not only what crypto it is using, but also for what and how.

Software written by "security experts" is usually not. Recall the basic definition of a security expert: someone who gets quoted in the press. If a company needs to advertise that it uses security experts to write its software, there is a really good chance that it would not recognize a real security expert should it happen to run across one.

## Summary

This chapter is not intended to make you safe. It is intended to help you find easy exploits to prove that something is unsafe. It is very important to realize, however, that even if you do not find anything that looks suspicious when you perform your investigation, the software may still be flawed. Software security is an extremely complicated and large field, and experts spend years becoming adept at evaluating software security. In other words, this is truly the unicorn chapter. You can use the techniques to prove that something is unsafe, but not that it is safe. If you want to become an expert in that field, read *How to Break Software Security* (Addison-Wesley, 2003), *How to Break Software: A Practical Guide to Testing* (Addison-Wesley, 2002), or *Exploiting Software: How to Break Code* (Addison-Wesley, 2004).

## What You Should Do Today

- Create an inventory of applications.
- Determine which applications have the most exposure to untrusted users.
- Build a schedule to start evaluating each application, in priority order, for glaring security problems.
- If you write any programs at all, get a copy of *Writing Secure Code*.

CHAPTER 7

# DATA-PROTECTION MECHANISMS

We sincerely hope that what you have learned so far from this book will benefit you as you build (or rebuild) your network's security infrastructure. It is now time to explore securing the data itself. Data is why you have networks and computers; data is what makes all modern organizations tick. And for some attackers, it is also the most enticing target. Attackers know they can cause you lots of grief if they simply prevent you from getting to your data, whether through a denial-of-service attack or through active data destruction. And because data is becoming increasingly mobile, it is becoming increasingly more important that organizations invest in sound data-protection mechanisms, because there are times where you cannot rely on any of the other layers to provide sufficient protection.

In this chapter, we investigate technologies that can protect data at rest:[1] access control lists, rights management, and a bit on encryption. We also cover a little on auditing. And although it might make sense to have included EFS in this chapter, we put it in the physical security chapter instead because we believe that EFS's principal role is to protect the data on stolen laptops.

Access control is part of the authorization (sometimes referred to as authz) function of a computer system. Authorization is part of the three A's that a secure product must be able to perform: authentication, authorization, and auditing. A brief discussion of authentication before we move on to the other two is appropriate.

Authentication is the process of identifying a user and binding that user to an identity within the computer system. In Windows, the user identities are held within the Security Accounts Manager (SAM) database or in Active Directory (AD). Although it is possible to have authentication without identification, normally the two are so intertwined that we consider them part of the same functionality. (An example of authentication *without* identification is where multiple users could use the same computer system identifier [shared accounts, for instance]. You only know which computer system identifier was used, not which actual person performed the operation.)

1. Protecting data in flight is mostly the job of IPsec and SSL.

Authorization is the process of asserting whether a computer system identity (hereinafter referred to as a user) has the right to perform some task or another. Typically, the functionality of authorization is implemented through an access control list (ACL), but there are other mechanisms as well. For instance, Windows has the concept of account rights and privileges. An account right is the right to log on or not log on through a particular mechanism, such as logging on locally (SeInteractiveLogonRight internally). A privilege is the right to perform certain system-related operations, such as replacing a security token on a process (SeAssignPrimaryTokenPrivilege). Although account rights and privileges are different constructs and are even defined in different header files (for the programming-inclined account rights are defined in NTSecAPI.h, while privileges are defined in WinNT.h), they are usually considered together under the common moniker "privileges."

As often as possible, it is better to assign rights to groups than to individual users. Because users can belong to many groups, create groups that represent the various rights you will use throughout your network and add or remove members as appropriate.[2]

Auditing is the ability to hold users accountable for their actions. The system should have the ability to create an audit trail of accesses to the objects the system protects. This is typically also implemented through ACLs, but a different kind of ACL.

## Security Group Review

We discuss security groups a lot in this chapter, so just to be sure there is no confusion, we review them here. Security groups are classified according to *scope*—the extent that a group applies in the domain or forest. There are four types: local, domain local, global, and universal. Some important points to remember:

- Members of universal groups can include other groups and accounts from any domain in the domain tree or forest and can be assigned permissions in any domain in the domain tree or forest.

2. See "Client, service, and program incompatibilities that may occur when you modify security settings and user rights assignments" (`http://support.microsoft.com/default.aspx?kbid=823659`) for an excellent discussion of how modifying user rights and security settings can affect applications and various parts of the operating system.

- Members of global groups can include other groups and accounts only from the domain in which the group is defined and can be assigned permissions in any domain in the forest.
- Members of domain local groups can include other groups and accounts from Windows Server 2003, Windows 2000, or Windows NT domains and can be assigned permissions only within a domain.
- Members of local groups can include local accounts, domain accounts, and domain local groups and can be assigned permissions on local resources.

For a detailed discussion of groups, see `http://www.microsoft.com/resources/documentation/WindowsServ/2003/all/deployguide/en-us/dsscd_grp_gdjg.asp`.

## Access Control Lists

For most of the history of computing, ACLs have been the principal means of verifying and enforcing authorization to resources and data. After you have identified and authenticated yourself, some mechanism (tokens, tickets, or similar) authorizes you against an ACL and either permits or denies access. And for the most part, ACLs have worked well—at least until the advent of portable computing.

### Types of Access Control Lists

There are three types of ACLs:

- Mandatory ACLs (MACLs)
- Discretionary ACLs (DACLs)
- System ACLs (SACLs)

An MACL is a system-enforced ACL that even the administrator cannot modify. It is not used in most general-purpose operating systems. Rather, it is a core component of a multilevel security (MLS) operating system. MLS systems are not in common use today, although there have been many variants produced in the past. They might use an MACL, for instance, to enforce data classifications, such as Top Secret, Confidential, and so on. The administrator cannot modify this ACL.

As soon as something is classified, the system automatically enforces access from users based on their classification rating and the operation they are performing. Since Windows does not support this type of ACL, we do not consider it in the rest of this chapter. If you want to learn more about them, pick up just about any textbook on security or take a Certified Information Systems Security Professional (CISSP) review seminar. In spite of the fact that no off-the-shelf systems today provide this functionality, both devote significant amount of time to the topic.

A DACL is what we typically mean when we refer to an ACL. It is an ACL that is at the discretion of the data owner, the administrator, or both. A DACL is composed of access control list entries (ACEs). Each ACE defines some permission that is allowed or not allowed to some user or group. For instance, some object may have an ACE that defines that administrators have full control and another that defines that Everyone has read access.

An SACL is identical in structure to a DACL, but it defines not what access is allowed but what access is audited. If the ACEs in an SACL defined Administrators:Full Control and Everyone:Read, as we showed earlier, it would instead mean that any access by administrators is audited but that only read access is audited for Everyone.

Because DACLs are identical in structure to SACLs, we use the term *ACL* collectively to refer to both of them. If we specify either DACL or SACL, we refer only to that specific form of ACL.

## Security Descriptors and Access Control List Entries

*Permissions* defined on objects are granted to security principals; they define who can do what to those objects. Objects always have an owner, and the owner can always alter an object's permissions. Remember that permissions are hierarchical throughout much of Windows—in the file system, in the Registry, in the directory—so keep this in mind as you develop your ACL'ing scheme. There are times when rights will override permissions—the classic example is file backups. Even if the owner of a file sets a permission that denies Everyone access, those who have the right to back up files will still be able to read the file.

The implementation of the permission is in the form of a security descriptor (SD). When a program tries to access a securable object on behalf of some user, the program presents an access token which contains information about the user, membership in groups, privileges, and so on. The program also presents an access mask containing the desired access. The OS compares the information in the security descriptor with the information in the access token and the requested access methods. As long as the user, or some group or set of groups the user is a member of, has all the requested access methods listed in an allow ACE in the DACL, the access is permitted. If any single requested access method listed in a deny ACE is encountered before collecting all the access methods from allow ACEs, the entire access is disallowed.

The SD on an object contains both the DACL and the SACL (if one is defined). All objects have an SD, but they may have an empty, or null, DACL or SACL field in them. If an SD has a null SACL, it simply means that there will not be any auditing done on that object. However, a null DACL is much more problematic. It means that there are no restrictions on access to that object. In other words, a null DACL means that all users, including anonymous users, get full control over the object. Null DACLs are rare on the file system and Registry, but there have been multiple security bulletins issued to correct null DACLs on other objects, such as services and various other system objects.

SDs are typically represented in string format in the Security Descriptor Definition Language (SDDL). Since this is the way they are represented in the security templates we use to harden systems, it is worth reviewing the format here.

An SD contains information on the owner of the object, the primary group (not used in Windows but included for compatibility with other operating systems), the DACL, and the SACL. The format is as follows:

```
O:owner_sid
G:group_sid
D:dacl_flags(string_ace1)(string_ace2)...  (string_acen)
S:sacl_flags(string_ace1)(string_ace2)...  (string_acen)
```

The security identifier (SID) was explained in Chapter 2, "Server and Client Hardening," so we do not repeat that description here.

The line that starts with `D:` represents the DACL, and the line that starts with `S:` represents the SACL. They are formatted identically, containing a set of flags and zero or more ACEs. The flags define the inheritance behavior of the ACL. There are three possible flags. (These show the DACL names for the flags. The SACL names are identical, except they have SACL instead of DACL.)

- *SE_DACL_PROTECTED*—The ACL is protected and cannot be modified by inherited ACEs from parent objects. In SDDL, this flag is represented by the letter *P*.
- *SE_DACL_AUTO_INHERITED*—The ACL is inherited by child objects that have been configured to inherit their ACL from parent objects. This flag would be set by the system on both of the child objects, indicating that the ACL is inherited, and on parent objects, indicating that the ACL should be inherited by child objects. In SDDL, this flag is represented by the letters *AI*.
- *SE_DACL_AUTO_INHERIT_REQ*—The ACL is automatically propagated to child objects and the SE_DACL_AUTO_INHERITED flag is set on the ACL of those child objects. This flag, set by the programmer and represented in SDDL by the letters *AR*, is used to ensure that all child objects get their ACLs propagated from their parent. It should be used with great caution because it could potentially overwrite a carefully crafted set of ACLs on child objects. For instance, one of the authors once was managing a large lab with student shares. The student shares had very finely crafted ACLs allowing only each student modify access. When the inheritance of ACLs was first rolled out in Service Pack 4 for Windows NT 4.0, he tried to use it to control the ACLs on that hierarchy. Unfortunately, he set the SE_DACL_AUTO_INHERITED_REQ flag on the DACL for the parent directory with the result that all the student directories were now readable by all the other students and not modifiable by anyone.

A string ACE is a string representation of the ACE. The string representation has the following fields, separated by semicolons:

- *ace_type*—A one- or two-letter code defining the type of ACE this is. The values possible are as follows:
  - A—Access allowed ACE, used to apply an ACE to a container like an allowed ACE.
  - D—Access denied ACE. This is simply the corollary to the access-specific objects, for instance. Typically, this ACE type is used with an object GUID, defining the object that the ACE applies to.

- OA—Object access allowed. Object ACEs are used in Active Directory to apply ACLs to a domain or OU, but so that they only apply to specific objects, for instance. Typically, this ACE type is used with an object GUID, defining the object that the ACE applies to.
- OD—Object access denied. The corollary to the object allowed ACE.
- AU—Audit ACE. This type denotes a standard audit ACE and is used where you would find the A flag.
- AL—Alarm ACE. Alarm ACEs are not used in Windows today. They are included for future use, for instance, to throw an administrative alert when some object is touched.
- OU—Object audit ACE. The audit ACE on an object.
- OL—Object alarm ACE. Alarm ACE on some object.

- *ace_flags*—A two-letter code denoting how the ACE should be processed, as follows:
  - CI—Container inherit flag. Child objects that are containers, such as directories and Registry keys, inherit the ACE as an effective ACE. This inherited ACE is inheritable by children of the container if the NP flag is not set.
  - OI—Object inherit flag. Noncontainer child objects, such as files, Registry values, etc. inherit this ACE as an effective ACE. For container child objects the ACE is inherited as an inherit-only ACE unless the NP flag is set, in which case the ACE is not inherited at all.
  - NP—No Propagate flag. The ACE is not inherited by any further child objects. If this flag is used together with the CI or OI flags, the ACE is inherited by the first generation of children, but the CI and OI flags are then cleared to prevent it from being inherited further. This flag is represented by the "Apply these permissions to objects and/or containers within this container only" check box in the GUI ACL editor. This is shown in Figure 7-1.
  - IO—Inherit only. This flag indicates that the ACE does not control access to the object it is applied to but rather is only used for inheritance. This flag is for example used in the default ACL on the C: drive in Windows XP. As shown in Figure 7-2, it is used on the Creator Owner ACE as well as one of the Built-in Users ACEs.

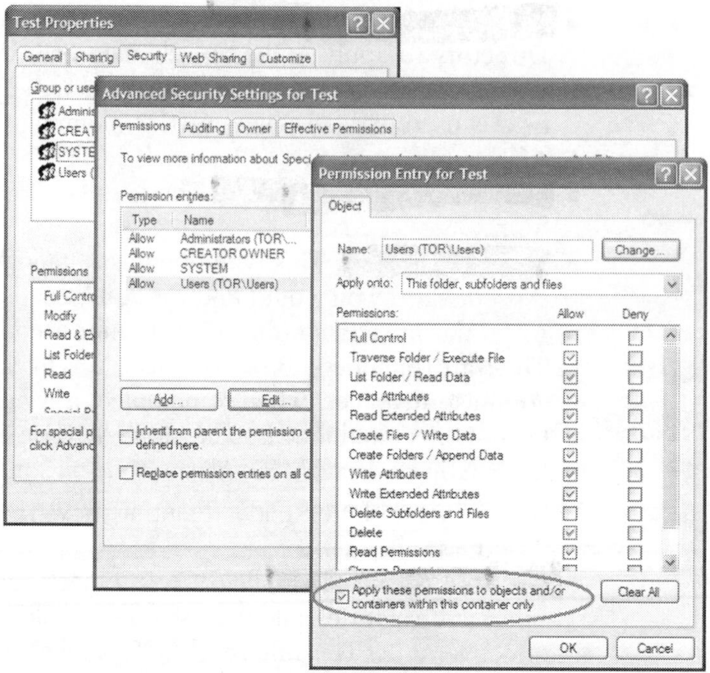


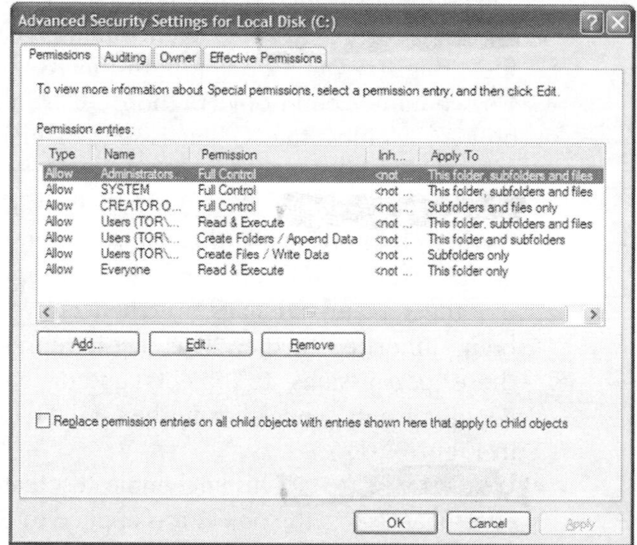


**Figure 7-1** The NP flag as it shows up in the GUI.

**Figure 7-2** The default DACL on the C: drive in Windows XP.

    - ID—Inherited ACE. This flag is set when an ACE is inherited from another object. It is typically not used in security templates. Ordinarily, you will only see this if you write programs that parse security descriptors on existing objects.
    - SA—Successful audit ACE. Used in SACLs to generate audit messages for successful access attempts.
    - FA—Failed audit ACE. Used in SACLs to generate audit messages for failed access attempts.
- Rights—This is the string that specifies the rights the subject (the group or user that the ACE applies to) has to the object under control. The rights expression can take two forms. One is the use of a two-letter code indicating one of the generic, standard, or object-specific rights. The other is a hexadecimal string representing a bitmask of the access rights. For instance, the generic access rights are the following:
    - GA—Generic all. Indicates full control to the subject
    - GX—Generic execute
    - GR—Generic read
    - GW—Generic write

  The generic access rights are mapped to a combination of standard and object specific access rights, as appropriate for the object. The standard access rights are a bit more granular than the generic ones and provide additional control over the actual settings. They include the following:
    - RC—Read control. Denotes the ability to read the SD (excluding the SACL) for the object
    - SD—Standard delete. The ability to delete the object
    - WD—Write DAC(L). Defines the ability to modify the DACL on the object
    - WO—Write owner. The ability to change the owner of the object

  Finally, there are object-specific rights that define the meaning of particular rights for an object. For instance, for a file or a directory, they are as follows:
    - FA—File all. Full control on a file or directory. Specifying GA and FA in an SD has the same effect.
    - FR—File read. Read access to the file or directory. Identical effect to GR.
    - FX—File execute. The right to execute the file or traverse into the directory. The effect is identical to GX.

**Table 7-1** The Actual Meaning of the Generic Rights on a File

| Generic Right | File-Specific Rights |
|---|---|
| Generic execute | The ability to read the attributes of the file.<br>The ability to read the SD of the file. This is defined as the STANDARD_RIGHTS_EXECUTE and is what gives the subject the ability to execute the file.<br>The ability to use the file handle in a wait object. This right, known as SYNCHRONIZE, is typically used in multithreaded programming to be alerted to when a file changes. It is not particularly important for administrators. |
| Generic read | The ability to read the attributes of the file.<br>The ability to read the data in the file. Note that if you have only execute permission on a file but not read you cannot actually read the data in the file.<br>The right to read the extended attributes for the file.<br>The ability to read the SD of a file. This is defined as STANDARD_RIGHTS_READ and is identical currently to STANDARD_RIGHTS_EXECUTE because they are both defined as READ_CONTROL.<br>The ability to use the file handle in a wait object. This right, known as SYNCHRONIZE, is typically used in multithreaded programming to be alerted to when a file changes. It is not particularly important for administrators. |
| Generic write | The right to append data to an existing file, or to add subdirectories to a directory.<br>The right to change the attributes of a file.<br>The right to add data to a file or add files to a directory.<br>The ability to modify the extended attributes of a file.<br>The ability to read the SD of a file. This is defined as STANDARD_RIGHTS_WRITE and is identical currently to STANDARD_RIGHTS_EXECUTE since they are both defined as READ_CONTROL.<br>The ability to use the file handle in a wait object. This right, known as SYNCHRONIZE, is typically used in multithreaded programming to be alerted to when a file changes. It is not particularly important for administrators. |

- FW—File write. The right to write data to the file or create new files in the director. The effect is identical to GW.

The generic and standard rights on a file or directory define a set of file and directory-specific rights. Table 7-1 shows the actual meaning of these rights.

Although Table 7-1 only shows the meaning of the generic rights on a file, the same exercise can be undertaken for any securable object. The exact meaning is defined in the Windows Platform Software Developers Kit (SDK). If you want to learn more, start with the definition of an SDDL string at `http://msdn.microsoft.com/library/en-us/security/security/security_descriptor_string_format.asp`.

- *object_guid*—Used to represent some object in AD. This field is not typically used on other containers.
- *inherit_object_guid*—Used to represent the inherited object type in an inherited ACE structure for a particular object. Again, this field is not typically used outside of AD.
- *account_sid*—The SID of the account that this ACE applies to. This can be either a SID like the ones we saw in Chapter 2, or a SID string that defines a well-known SID. For instance, the SID string BA denotes Built-in Administrators. For more information, refer to the platform SDK: `http://msdn.microsoft.com/library/en-us/secauthz/security/sid_strings.asp`.

Now that you understand the structure of an SDDL string, we can work through an example to drive home how these are used. Consider the default ACL on the C: drive in Windows XP and Server 2003. It is shown in Figure 7-2.

The SDDL representation of this DACL is as follows:

```
D:(A;OICI;FA;;;BA)(A;OICI;FA;;;SY)(A;OICIIO;GA;;;CO)(A;OICI;0x1
200a9;;;BU)(A;CI;LC;;;BU)(A;CIIO;DC;;;BU)(A;;0x1200a9;;;WD)
```

There are seven separate ACEs in this DACL. The first is (A;OICI;FA;;;BA). The ACE type A denotes that this is an access allowed ACE. The OI and CI ACE flags indicate that it should be inherited by both directories and files. The right FA indicates that the ACE gives the subject full control. The object GUIDs are empty, because this is a file. Finally, we see that the SID is the SID string for built-in administrators (i.e., the local Administrators group). The GUI shows this ACE as the first line.

The next ACE, (A;OICI;FA;;;SY), is identical to the first, except that the SID string specifies SA, for Local System, i.e. the operating system itself.

The third ACE, (A;OICIIO;GA;;;CO), is very much like the first two, with a few distinct differences. First, the flag IO is also specified, indicating that ACE is only used for inheritance. This ACE, specified for the user CO, or Creator/Owner, is what gives users access to directories they create underneath the C: drive. The right they get is GA (in other words, generic all, or full control).

The next three ACEs apply to BU, or the built-in Users group. The first one, (A;OICI;0x1200a9;;;BU), specifies access on C: as well as is inherited by subdirectories and files. The right is specified by a hexadecimal bitmask, in this case 0x1200a9. This indicates the bits that are used in the access mask. An access mask is a 32-bit construct that is shown in Table 7-2.

Using Table 7-2, it is simple to interpret the bitmask. 0x1200a9 is specified in binary as follows:

```
100100000000010101001
```

In Table 7-3, we have pasted in this bitmask as the second row and added a row below showing how each of these bits is interpreted for files.

As we can see from Table 7-3, the rights granted to users by specifying 0x1200a9 are as follows:

- SYNCHRONIZE
- READ_CONTROL
- FILE_READ_ATTRIBUTES
- FILE_EXECUTE
- FILE_READ_EA
- FILE_READ_DATA

**Table 7-2** The Access Mask in Windows Specifies Granular Object Rights

| 31 | 30 | 29 | 28 | 27 | 26 | 25 | 24 | 23 | 22 | 21 | 20 | 19 | 18 | 17 | 16 | 15 | 14 | 13 | 12 | 11 | 10 | 9 | 8 | 7 | 6 | 5 | 4 | 3 | 2 | 1 | 0 |
|---|---|---|---|---|---|---|---|---|---|---|---|---|---|---|---|---|---|---|---|---|---|---|---|---|---|---|---|---|---|---|---|
| GR | GW | GE | GA | Reserved | | MA | AS | Standard access rights | | | | | | | | Object-specific access rights | | | | | | | | | | | | | | | |

**Table 7-3** Evaluating an Access Mask

| 31 | 30 | 29 | 28 | 27 | 26 | 25 | 24 | 23 | 22 | 21 | 20 | 19 | 18 | 17 | 16 | 15 | 14 | 13 | 12 | 11 | 10 | 9 | 8 | 7 | 6 | 5 | 4 | 3 | 2 | 1 | 0 |
|---|---|---|---|---|---|---|---|---|---|---|---|---|---|---|---|---|---|---|---|---|---|---|---|---|---|---|---|---|---|---|---|
| 0 | 0 | 0 | 0 | 0 | 0 | 0 | 0 | 0 | 0 | 0 | 1 | 0 | 0 | 1 | 0 | 0 | 0 | 0 | 0 | 0 | 0 | 0 | 0 | 1 | 0 | 1 | 0 | 1 | 0 | 0 | 1 |
| | | | | | | | READ SETSACL | | | | SYNCHRONIZE | WRITE_OWNER | WRITE_DAC | READ_CONTROL | DELETE | | | | | | | | FILE_WRITE_ATTRIBUTES | FILE_READ_ATTRIBUTES | FILE_DELETE_CHILD | FILE_EXECUTE | FILE_WRITE_EA | FILE_READ_EA | FILE_APPEND_DATA | FILE_WRITE_DATA | FFILE_READ_DATA |
| GR | GW | GE | GA | Reserved | | MA | AS | Standard access rights | | | | | | | | Object-specific access rights | | | | | | | | | | | | | | | |

The file-specific access right FR includes READ_CONTROL, SYNCHRONIZE, FILE_READ_DATA, FILE_READ_ATTRIBUTES, and FILE_READ_EA. The file-specific right FX includes READ_CONTROL, FILE_READ_ATTRIBUTES, FILE_EXECUTE, and SYNCHRONIZE. In other words, 0x1200a9 is equivalent to granting both FR, read, and FX, execute to Users. If you go back to Figure 7-2, you will find that there is an ACE shown in there for Read and Execute on this folder, subfolders, and files. That is the ACE we just found.

The next ACE, (A;CI;LC;;;BU), is also for Users. It specifies the right LC. LC is actually a directory service-specific access right. It is not normally used on files. On an Active Directory object, it specifies the right to list child objects. It corresponds to 0x4 in hex, in other words, bit 3 in the access mask. Bit 3 is FILE_APPEND_DATA. In other words, even though LC is not a valid object-specific access right on a file or directory object, it just represents a bitmask that can be interpreted on a file or directory object.

The result is the ACE that gives Users the right to create folders in the C: directory. It is inherited by subdirectories, as we see by the CI flag.

The following ACE, (A;CIIO;DC;;;BU) is also defined for Users. This one is also inherited by containers, but in this case it specifies the IO, or inherit only, flag. That means it does not define any ACE on the C: directory itself. The right, DC in this case, is another directory service-specific right that would govern whether the subject can delete child objects were it applied to an AD object. It evaluates to 0x2, or bit 1 in the access mask. Applied to a directory, bit 1 means FILE_ADD_FILE, or the ability to create files. This is the ACE we see in Figure 7-2 that allows users to create files and write data in subfolders.

### THE "TROUBLESOME" EVERYONE GROUP

We hear far too often from various people who think they understand security that the Everyone group is extremely troublesome and needs to be removed at all cost. Typically, that means they replace it with the Authenticated Users group instead. This is completely counterproductive. The reason is that Everyone is *identical* to Authenticated Users in Windows XP and Server 2003. Unless the security policy has been changed from the default, the Everyone group no longer includes the anonymous user, which was the only difference between Everyone and Authenticated Users in Windows 2000. Thus, performing wholesale ACL replacements to replace Everyone with Authenticated Users does absolutely nothing to secure the system. And, if you have actually set the switch to include anonymous in Everyone, chances are it was done for a reason. In this case, replacing Everyone with Authenticated Users breaks that change, calling into question why it was done in the first place.

To make things worse, these types of changes are typically made by people who do not fully understand SDDL strings and treat them very casually. The last time we dealt with a network where the administrators had attempted to replace Everyone with Authenticated Users, we found that the Administrator's profile was now world readable and that the recycle bin no longer worked. This happened because they had propagated the new ACL down the tree, blowing away the built-in ACLs on those directories. Because there were user directories already defined on the system it was impossible to automatically return the ACLs to the defaults. The net result was that they needed to rebuild several thousand machines that had these new ACLs defined.

The final ACE on the C: directory, (A;;0x1200a9;;;WD), applies to the SID string WD, or World (in other words, Everyone). No inheritance bits are specified, and hence this ACE is not inherited. The right is 0x1200a9, which we now know means read and execute. In other words, this ACE gives Everyone the right to read and execute everything in the C: directory.

Using the same method, you can analyze any SDDL string. For example, as an exercise we leave you to analyze the SDDL representation of the ACL on the %systemroot% directory, which is

```
D:P(A;CIOI;GRGX;;;BU)(A;CIOI;GRGWGXSD;;;PU)(A;CIOI;GA;;;BA)(A;C
IOI;GA;;;SY)(A;CIOI;GA;;;CO)
```

You do not need to understand SDDL strings to set ACLs on files and directories that you create yourself, but an intricate knowledge of them will help impress people at cocktail parties. In addition, you absolutely must understand them forward and backward if you are going to modify the built-in ACLs. You must also understand the concept of Creator Owner. There are, as you have seen, a lot of ACEs for Creator Owner. When a user creates a directory, or the system creates a directory on behalf of the user, that ACE is replaced with one containing the user's SID on the new directory. This happens, for instance, on all the subdirectories under Documents and Settings. Now, if you go through and propagate an ACL through that hierarchy, you would reset not only the Creator Owner ACL on the Documents and Settings directory, you would also reset the ACL on the subdirectories owned by particular users. To restore those, you would have to manually re-create all the ACLs on those directories. It was by propagating ACLs through the Documents and Settings directory that the administrators mentioned in the sidebar "The 'Troublesome' Everyone Group" managed to make the Administrator's profile world readable. We ask you to make life easier on yourself by leaving system-defined ACLs alone and focusing on setting appropriate ACLs on objects you create yourself. The system-defined ACLs are perfectly adequate in Windows XP and higher. In Windows 2000, you need to set one ACL, on the root of the C: drive. However, do not do this yourself. Use the Windows 2000 Hardening Guide to do it for you. It took us the better part of a day to ensure we got exactly the right effect on the ACL in that guide. The guide is available at `http://go.microsoft.com/fwlink/?LinkId=28591`.

**WARNING:** Do not try to modify the default ACLs on files installed by the operating system. There is nothing wrong with them in Windows XP and higher, and the risk is much greater that you will put the system into an unrecoverable state than the chance that you will actually provide any additional security.

Typically, we see administrators trying to change these ACLs to remove the Everyone group, or to destroy the Power Users group. Neither of these is a worthwhile thing to do. As described in the sidebar "The 'Troublesome' Everyone Group," there is nothing wrong with the Everyone group any longer. The Power Users group should not be used at all. Power Users are basically administrators who have not made themselves administrators yet. It provides no meaningful separation from administrators other than to make it take one additional API call to shoot yourself in the foot. Instead of trying to destroy that group, use security policy to make it a restricted group and ensure there is nobody in it. That way it does not matter what permissions and rights it has.

## Layers of Access Control

Access control is a layered process. Think of it as a funnel, where you have to be able to pass through the smallest tightest part of the funnel to get through. Suppose you want to do something with an object—a file, a Registry key, a directory element, whatever—on a network resource. Your authorization to access that object passes through a series of access control checks; if your authorization fails at any point, you do not get access. Let us examine the layering present in file access controls:

1. *Can you access the resource over the network?*
   This is controlled through the logon right "Access this computer from network" (SeNetworkLogonRight) in security policy. If you want to get to some object on a network resource, you need this right. And, hopefully, you do not also have the "Deny access to this computer from network" because that right supersedes the former.
2. *Can you map a drive letter?*
   This is controlled through share-level permissions and can be one of three types: read, change, or full control.

3. *Can you get to the folder containing the file?*
   The file might live deep within some folder structure with tightly controlled access throughout. Although you might not have access to any of the parent folders, you do need at least to pass through, or traverse, them. This is controlled through the privilege "Bypass traverse checking" (SeChangeNotifyPrivilege). By default, Everyone has this right, so it is probably not something you need to worry about.
4. *Do you have access to the folder containing the file?*
   You will need access to the folder containing the file you are after, and this is controlled by permissions on the folder.
5. *Finally, do you have access to the file itself?*
   You will need the correct permission on the file to do whatever your task requires—execute, read, write, append, delete, or others.

Besides the file system, you can assign permissions to other objects, such as Registry keys, services, printers, Terminal Server connections, WMI objects, and Active Directory objects. Just about anything in Windows that can be considered an object can have an ACL.

On services, you can assign permissions that govern who can modify the service, start it, read its configuration, and so on. In addition to the ability to read the service configuration and start the service, the service account also needs the "Log on as a service" (SeServiceLogonRight) right. As we discussed in Chapter 4, "Protecting Services and Server Applications," also make sure that you either configure the service account so that the password never expires or remember to change the password before the expiration date—otherwise, the service will not start. And speaking of service accounts, here is another good reason for eliminating account lockouts from your security policies. A simple denial-of-service attack against an IIS server is to lock out its IUSR and IWAM accounts, which is trivial for an attacker who knows the name of your Web server.

Terminal Services security can be configured either on the whole computer or on individual connections. Default computer-wide control grants the Remote Desktop Users group the RemoteInteractiveLogon right. For more fine-grained control—say you want to prevent users from ending sessions—you can modify individual user and group permissions on the Properties tab of the connections in the Terminal Server UI.

## Access Control Best Practices

Obviously you should assign ACLs such that users only have access to the minimum number of things they need to perform their tasks. Doing so is a bit trickier, however, and requires some planning. Also keep in mind that it is not just permissions on files and Registry keys that matter. You must also take into account permissions on shares, permissions within applications (such as a database management system), and so on. Particularly, share permissions seem to engender some debate. Our opinion is that there is usually nothing wrong with a share permission of Everyone full control. All that means is that the user will be allowed whatever access permissions are specified on the files and directories underneath the share. In other words, what it really means is "I do not want to manage permissions here." This was the default share permission until Windows Server 2003, where the default permission changed to read for Everyone. That means that unless you actually modify the permissions on a share, users cannot modify data on shares on Windows Server 2003. This has generated countless support calls, and we generally consider it a bad idea. It is confusing enough to manage permissions as it is without having to add the additional complexity of share permissions interacting with file system permissions into it. We recommend leaving the share permissions at Everyone full control. The only time we would not do that is if there is some reason a user should have fewer permissions on a file if he or she is accessing it remotely than the same user would have on that same file if he or she accessed it locally.

Whenever possible, assign permission for a resource to a group rather than individual users. Although there are many kinds of groups in Active Directory, for ACLs it is best to limit your choices to only a few. Use global groups to reflect roles or create membership based on business function or department location. This keeps replication traffic to a minimum[3] as you go through your daily tasks of modifying the members of these groups. Then on individual resources, use local groups to control access and add the appropriate global groups into the various local groups.

Be careful with "deny" ACEs. These override all other permissions, and it can be pretty easy to lock even an enterprise administrator out of a resource by, say, creating a "deny" ACE with Everyone as its member.

3. Global groups do not replicate outside their own domain, and global catalogs list only the groups, not the members. Universal groups replicate everywhere in the forest, and global catalogs list all members.

### THE BUILT-IN SHARES

Windows includes a number of built-in shares. For instance, all fixed drives in the systems have a share denoted by the driver letter with a $ sign appended. For instance, there is a C$ share by default. There is also a share called Admin$, which maps to the %systemroot% directory (C:\Windows on most systems), as well as an IPC$ share used for interprocess communication, possibly a print$ share for printing, a netlogon share on domain controllers, and a few others depending on your system.

We have seen guidelines on securing the system that recommend changing the permissions on these shares. *You cannot change the permissions on these shares.* All except the IPC$ share are accessible only by administrators by default. The IPC$ share is accessible by anyone, but what you can do after you map it depends on what permissions you have to the objects it exposes, such as the Registry.

There are guidelines that recommend removing these shares. We do not like that idea much either. They are there for administration purposes. If you remove them, remote administration breaks. In addition, an attacker can easily add those shares back in should he need them, so removing them does not stop a competent attacker. Because only administrators can get to them by default, they are already pretty well locked down. If you want to protect them further, turn on the firewall and then set up an authenticated IPsec bypass, allowing only administrators to get to them. This is a much more usable and more secure option.

Deny ACEs can prove useful, however, when you want to exclude a subset of a group that has permissions you do not want that subset to have or when you want to exclude a certain permission from groups you have granted full control to. However, use deny ACEs sparingly. Generally it is simpler to create a new group that contains the subset you want to give access to instead, for example. Deny ACEs confuse the security model and generally make the system more difficult to manage. Most people who have administered systems for awhile have funny stories about deny ACEs.

Once upon a time, when one of the authors still allowed his users to have local administrative privileges on their workstations, he received a phone call from one of them. The woman on the other end stated that her machine just suddenly decided to log her out and that it now will not allow her to log in any longer. When asked what she was doing at the time this happened, she replied, "Nothing, no, nothing, nothing at all." (That is known as a "hint" by the way.) I then asked what exactly it was she was not doing when the system logged her out. She said she was not changing any permissions. Exactly what permissions was she not changing? Well, she had discovered that Everyone had full control over her C: (which was the default up through Windows 2000). To rectify this situation, she changed that to deny Everyone full control instead. I asked whether she read the dialog box that popped up when she did so that states that deny ACEs take precedence over allow ACEs. She had clicked OK there. She also clicked OK on the following dialog box that said, in effect, "I do not think you heard me the first time. This is a bad idea." She clicked yes on that, too. She even clicked yes on the third dialog box that said, in effect, "OK, I will give you one more chance before you destroy your system. This is a really stupid thing to do, and you should click Cancel." After the propagation had proceeded far enough that she no longer had read access to any of the system binaries, the system decided to log her out. Fortunately, she did not reboot; had she done so, the system would not have booted. Since this was Windows NT 4.0, and before the "recovery console," that would most likely have meant flattening and rebuilding the box (because I felt no particular desire to take it apart and put the drive in another machine). As it were, the problem was resolved by mounting the C$ share from another system, taking ownership of the files in it, and then getting rid of the deny ACE. Of course, at this point, all the system-defined ACLs were lost, but at least she could now log on to the machine.

Inheritance, as we saw earlier, can be a tricky concept, but it is very useful. You should rely on inheritance to take care of most of your permission assignments. Whenever possible, assign permissions as high in the object tree as you can and configure branches and subtrees to use inheritance. Then, as necessary, add additional ACLs to fine-tune access control if the inherited ACL is too permissive or too restrictive.

Sometimes, however, a change or two makes some sense. For instance, Everyone has read access to the Domain Administrators group on a domain controller. There is usually no need for ordinary users to see this information, so consider removing access from everyone except members of the Domain Administrators. We have actually seen this done on production domains, and it makes things a bit more difficult for attackers if they cannot determine who the administrators are.

## Analyzing Existing Systems

The effective permissions tool,[4] shown in Figure 7-3, in Windows XP and Windows Server 2003 can show you all the permissions that a certain user has on a particular object. To use it, open the properties on the object as if you were going to set permissions on it. Click the Security tab, and then click the Advanced button. Then click the Effective Permissions tab. Once there, click the Select button and pick a user. When you do, you get a dialog similar to what you see in Figure 7-3.

Often, it is very handy to list *all* the files (and Registry keys) that a user has access to. A product called SecurityExpressions from Pedestal Software[5] can help you learn a lot about who can do what with the resources across your network. The auditing capabilities of Security-Expressions can check the current state of a machine and compare it against typical recommended configurations. SecurityExpressions includes

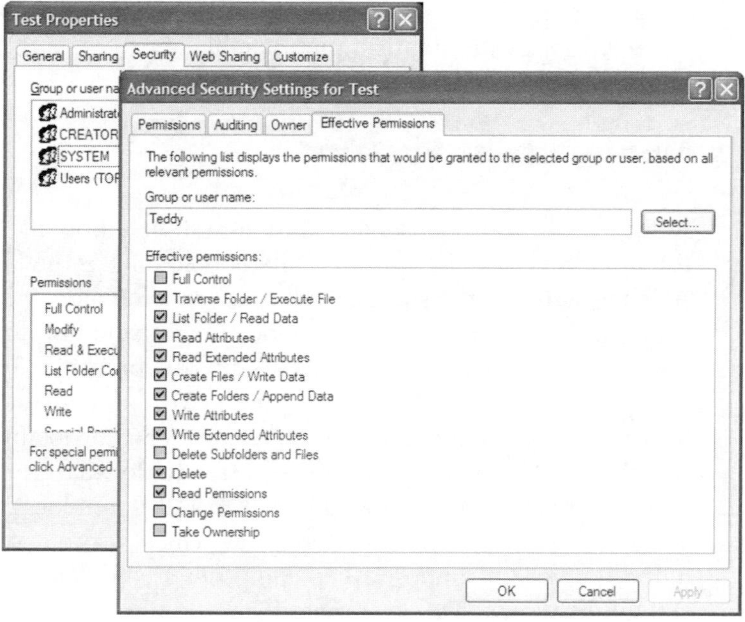


**Figure 7-3** The effective permissions tool in Windows XP and Server 2003.

4. http://www.microsoft.com/resources/documentation/WindowsServ/2003/standard/proddocs/en-us/acl_effective_perm.asp.

a querying engine that can help you learn a number of things about the permissions and activities of your users:

- Files or Registry keys that a particular user owns
- Files or Registry keys created or modified during some time interval
- All files or Registry keys a particular user can access
- Files or Registry keys with unknown or deleted users in the ACL
- Users with blank or expired passwords
- Users who have not changed their passwords or are inactive
- Users who have not logged in over some time period (or who never have)
- Users who directly or indirectly belong to the Administrators group
- Users with local log on rights to a server
- Users with dial-in privileges
- Groups with a specific, administrative, guest, or disabled member
- Groups with identical memberships

## Rights Management Systems

ACLs usually rely on some external system enforcing the control. For example, NTFS ACLs apply to a file only so long as the file lives within the ACL'ing system—the share on a file server. When an otherwise-authorized user moves or copies the file to a location outside the ACL'ing system, for instance to a USB drive, the ACLs no longer apply. Suppose Alice has read-only access to a share containing a Word document. When she loads Word and opens the document, a copy of the document lives in the memory on Alice's computer. Alice is free to do whatever she wants to this copy—perhaps modify it—and save it to a different location where she has write access. Now how will Bob know which version of the document is authoritative? Or suppose Alice composes a confidential e-mail and in big red letters writes "Do not forward!" at the top. At this point there are no technical controls to prevent Bob from forwarding it to his friends at a competing company. Would you like a way to control this? Mobility demands new forms of controlling access, forms that work regardless of where the data might live.

5. http://www.pedestalsoftware.com/products/se/.

Windows Rights Management Services[6] (RMS, no W) is an alternative form of access control; that is all. RMS enables creators ("producers") of content to project a usage policy onto the information they compose, and the policy persists with the information regardless of where it lives: on network shares, on local hard drives, on CD-ROMs, in e-mail attachments, anyplace. A policy describes what other users ("consumers") are allowed to do: view, modify, copy, print, save, forward. Policies can also be time based, prohibiting all access after a certain date and time. RMS does not rely on any external system to impose and maintain rights.

Unlike other forms of access control, RMS truly helps you keep internal information internal. Recall our discussion in Chapter 2, about USB drives and how trying to disable them is really a fruitless effort. If there is a risk of people exporting information from your organization, RMS gives you some level of control because the rights are persisted onto the objects themselves—the information now takes part in its own protection.

RMS sounds similar to but is not the same thing as digital rights management (DRM), a form of copy protection popular in the entertainment industry. RMS really is not designed for protecting music and video files. RMS gives you a powerful tool for expressing policies on information, but, like all security tools, cannot guarantee unbreakable, attacker-proof security. For instance, RMS cannot protect against analog attacks. An example of such an attack would be someone taking a photocopy of the monitor. Other examples include taking a photograph of the monitor with a digital camera and e-mailing the image, dictating the contents over a telephone, or smuggling away a printout. Of course, ordinary ACLs cannot stop these kinds of attacks, either.

Think of RMS as an ACL'ing system that does not require network administrator involvement, thus allowing producers to set their own levels of access that are followed no matter where users happen to be.[7] We like RMS because it moves the access decision away from the network guys, who are usually disinterested, and puts it directly in the hands of those who care: the creators of the content. Of course, without a security policy in place to assist the creators in selecting the proper level of protection for their information, RMS will not be particularly helpful. You must have guidance on how to classify information in your policy for the technology to reach its full potential.

6. This section is only an introduction to RMS, how it works, and why we like it so much. For more detailed information, including planning and deployment guidance, see `http://www.microsoft.com/rms/`.

**WARNING:** Do Not Use RMS for State Secrets

RMS is designed to protect run-of-the-mill corporate information from casual thieves. It is still basically just a software secret. Software secrets are composed of smoke and mirrors and they can be difficult to break, but they are all breakable by a determined attacker with unlimited resources. RMS is no different. It does not provide unbreakable, attacker-proof security. It simply aids in keeping honest people honest and in keeping some of the less-competent and -resourced attackers at bay.

## RMS Workflow

RMS works together with Active Directory to identify users. A user's RMS identity is his or her e-mail address; when producers grant permissions to people for documents, those permissions are granted to an identity represented by a canonical name, typically an e-mail address. The RMS server generates and keeps copies of all encryption keys—key archival is not a separate process you need to worry about. The server also audits all activities of both producers and consumers, so you can know when people create and access protected information and what they have done with it.

The RMS workflow is a five-step process:

1. A producer receives a client licensor certificate (CLC) the first time he or she protects information. This happens only once and allows this producer to create protected documents.
2. The producer defines a set of usage rights and rules (who can do what) for the file. The application first creates a publishing license that includes a symmetric encryption key (currently DES and AES are supported), and then encrypts the document with that key and encrypts the document key with the RMS server's public key. The application embeds the publishing license into the file.
3. The producer distributes the file.
4. When the consumer opens the file, again using the correct rights-aware application, the application verifies the identity of the user who opened the document against the RMS server and issues a use

7. And no, RMS is most certainly not the mark of any beast, contrary to the silly bombast in "Office 2003: The mark of the beast?" by Russ McGuire (`http://www.businessreform.com/article.php?articleID=10425`). Anyone using the correct rights-enabled application and possesses the necessary permissions can read protected documents.

license. To create a use license, the RMS server first uses its own private key to decrypt the document key, and then it uses the consumer's public key to encrypt both the document key and the details about this consumer's particular rights and restrictions and delivers this encrypted blob to the application.

5. The application uses the consumer's private key to decrypt the blob, thus obtaining information about the consumer's rights and the document key. The application uses the document key to decrypt the file, renders it in the application's window, and enforces the rights. Finally, the application appends the use license to the file and writes it back to its location.

Note the implication: RMS files will grow as authorized consumers access them. This allows consumers to access documents again without having to go through the complete authorization process. Rights-protected information, then, will need to live in storage where all authorized users have write access, even if their RMS-granted permission is view only.

## RMS Components

RMS is a system composed of an identity and authentication mechanism (Active Directory), an xRML certificate server (the RMS server), a client component and key "lockbox," and applications that are rights-aware. This last component is important: to produce and consume protected information, you must use an application that knows how to participate in the RMS system. At rest, protected information is encrypted; applications that are not rights-aware have no idea how to participate in the system and decrypt the information.

Microsoft Office 2003 includes a technology called "information rights management" (IRM). IRM is Office 2003's interface into RMS. Office 2003 Professional can both produce and consume rights-protected content; Office 2003 Standard can only consume. There is also a rights management client for Internet Explorer that can consume rights-protected content delivered by rights-aware Web applications. When you protect information in Office 2003 Professional, the protection process embeds an HTML version of the content in the encrypted document; for users who do not have either version of Office 2003, they can use the IE RMS client to render the HTML version of protected content. Office 2003 uses 128-bit AES encryption to protect the information.

Third-party software developers can use the Rights Management SDK[8] to develop their own rights management-aware applications. We have a customer who is developing a rights-aware version of a bill-of-lading system used to track contents and locations of shipping containers. By protecting this information with RMS, they can implement the important principle of least privilege—because most people involved in the movement of shipping containers need nothing more than view access to bills of lading, this customer is eliminating situations in which someone might be tempted to alter bills of lading for individual personal gain.

## Incorporating Data Protection into Your Applications

Often in your own applications, there is the need to securely store information—passwords, database connection strings, credit card numbers. For some time now, versions of Windows have included the protected storage system (PStore), a system service that includes several APIs for generating and storing keys. Most applications used PStore to store passwords—older versions of Internet Explorer, Outlook, and Outlook Express stored their passwords in the PStore. Microsoft has deprecated the PStore; indeed, there is no guarantee that it will continue to exist after Windows XP and Windows Server 2003.[9] It is also not secure and should not be used any longer for that reason alone.

Beginning with Windows 2000, the Data Protection API[10] (DPAPI) is the preferred method for applications that need to store secrets. DPAPI is much easier to use than PStore: there are only two calls, `CryptProtectData()` and `CryptUnprotectData()`. With DPAPI, there is no need for you to manage keys in your applications because this is all handled by the operating system. For every user on a computer, DPAPI generates a strong master key. To protect this key, DPAPI uses PKCS #5 to generate a key from the user's password and encrypts the master key with this password-derived key. DPAPI then stores the encrypted master key in the user's profile. When an application calls `CryptProtectData()`, DPAPI generates a session key based on the master key and some random bits. DPAPI uses this session key to encrypt

8. `http://msdn.microsoft.com/library/en-us/drmclsdk/drmclsdk/rights_management_client_sdk.asp`

9. `http://msdn.microsoft.com//library/en-us/devnotes/winprog/pstore.asp.`

10. See `http://msdn.microsoft.com/library/en-us/dnsecure/html/windataprotection-dpapi.asp` and `http://msdn.microsoft.com/msdnmag/issues/03/11/ProtectYourData/default.aspx` for good discussions.

the data passed to the function. It also stores the random bits in the encrypted blob so that it can regenerate the key when the application calls `CryptUnprotectData()`. The full session key is never stored anywhere.

Should you want to verify whether an application uses these APIs you can, but you need a development environment to do so. Microsoft's Visual Studio comes with a tool called `dumpbin`. If you run it with the `/imports` switch, it will tell you which libraries a particular binary imports, and which functions within that library it uses. If you find **crypt32.dll** being imported, it means that the application is at least using properly tested cryptographic functions. Whether it uses them properly itself is a different matter. However, seeing that library should make you feel better than if you see the function "MySuperSecretCrypto" being called.

## Protected Data: Our Real Goal

Why do we all go through so much trouble to keep our information assets protected? Earlier in the book, we emphasized the principal role of information security: to ensure availability. If information is not available to employees, to partners, to customers, who cares about the rest of the security?

As important as availability is, keeping your data protected is a similarly-important goal. Availability presents risks: people can access your data. Alas, not everyone with access necessarily shares our goal. And as access becomes more pervasive, with varying levels and multiple methods from disparate locations, protecting the actual data itself becomes increasingly important. Consider processes and technologies that can help you improve the security of the information you generate, gather, process, and store in the routine of your business.

## What You Should Do Today

- Put a plan in action to implement some of the techniques you have learned in this book.
- Ensure that your security policy addresses data protection.
- Evaluate a few critical data stores and ensure the ACLs are appropriate on them. For instance, ensure that you have proper ACLs on any stores for network installations of software.

CHAPTER 8

# RESTRICTING ACCESS TO SOFTWARE; RESTRICTING SOFTWARE'S ACCESS TO RESOURCES

Many of today's successful attacks are application layer attacks, which are the result of an exploit based on vulnerabilities in applications other than the operating system. While these attacks do cause enormous problems, many other problems are caused by accidental user actions such as clicking on email attachments, downloading software from the Internet, and misusing applications. These actions can result in accidental deletions, loss of data integrity, and loss of access to encrypted data. While we must strengthen defenses to protect applications from malicious attack, write applications that do not include vulnerabilities, and train users to make better decisions, we must also consider if we can design and manage applications better.

Perhaps the answer is blocking the use of specific software, or perhaps we should configure systems so that only approved software will run. Doing either may help. After all, if malware cannot run, it cannot cause harm. In addition to securely coding applications, perhaps we can do a better job of embedding control within the application to manage user rights and access to resources at the application level. We can accomplish these things by using the following components in a Windows Server 2003 network:

- **File, registry, printer and Active Directory access control lists (ACLs)**—Setting appropriate file ACLs on an executable program prevents unauthorized individuals from running it. Setting file, Active Directory, and registry ACLs can prevent unauthorized individuals from performing specific tasks with the software and can prevent them from copying files to areas of the hard drive. File and registry ACLs are explored in depth in Chapter 9, "Controlling Access to Data."

- **Authorization Manager Framework**—New in Windows Server 2003, Authorization Manager allows developers to build role-based security into their applications. Administrators manage the use of this software by adding users into Windows groups, Application Groups, Application Basic Groups, and LDAP Groups. Authorization Manager also permits control over who can run specific parts of software running on a system.
- **Software Restriction Policies**—New in Windows XP Professional and new to the server in Windows Server 2003, Software Restriction Policies can be used either to selectively prevent software from running or to only allow identified software to run on a computer.
- **Component Services: Permissions and Roles for COM+**—Applications can be managed using the Component Services tool. To be fully effective, COM+ applications must be developed with defined roles. Otherwise, the administrator is restricted to making changes in launching permissions and authentication levels. New in Windows Server 2003, you can set the Software Restriction security level directly in the COM+ properties pages of the application.
- **Group Policy**—Many applications can also be managed through Group Policy. Specific controls for managing system applets are contained in the Administrative Templates section of Group Policy. Special Administrative Templates are available for products such as Microsoft Office.
- **EFS**—Appl.ication files can be encrypted using the Encrypting File System (EFS).

Three major software management tools are available in Windows Server 2003: Authorization Manager, Software Restriction Policies, and the Component Services console. This chapter will describe them and how they can be used.

## Authorization Manager Framework

The Authorization Manager Framework enables the development and administration of Role-Based Access Control (RBAC) programs. Developers use the Authorization Manager Framework's Authorization Manager RBAC application programming interface (API) to develop the application, including the definition of user roles. Administrators use the Authorization Manager Microsoft Management Console snap-in to manage the applications by assigning user groups to role definitions.

Before you can administer these applications, you must understand how they are developed and how they work. The secret to understanding and championing Authorization Manager is to understand that it moves the responsibility for partitioning access to information resources from the administrator to the application.

The Authorization Manager application is pre-programmed to respond to the role of the user interacting with the program. The role, defined as part of the application, is explicitly designed to provide rights and permissions that allow the role holder to do her job and no more. The role might be allowed, for example, to run only certain parts of the program and only read some data while having permission to write, delete, or otherwise manipulate other data. At first glance, this may appear to provide control over computer system resources to the developer. However, in a properly managed development environment, developers work from and are held accountable to specifications developed by the data owners. An application developed to print payroll checks, for example, might have roles such as payroll clerk and payroll manager. Payroll department staff must develop the specifications that define what each role is allowed to do within the program and what files and printers role users may access. Payroll management approves the design and tells IT which employees should be assigned which roll. The system administrator maintains application control by assigning the correct users to the application roles.

The ordinary application, by comparison, does a poor job of granting and denying access to resources. The ordinary application sees data storage as a gray landscape of objects that it can or cannot manipulate depending primarily on the security context of the user. If it needs to interact with the internal processes of the computer, the ordinary application switches context and operates as programmed in ignorance of the security context of the user. Thus, management of the ordinary application is fractured. Authorization to run the application is separate from the right to access resources.

To manage ordinary applications, the system administrator must only decide who is authorized to run the application. She manages resources that the application might use separately. The administrator protects resources by determining what rights a user should be granted or denied and which objects a user should have permission to access. Application authorization and resource authorization are disconnected. In addition, while the administrator may grant a user permission to execute a specific program, she may not grant the user the right to run some part of the application while denying the user access to other parts of the application. There are exceptions to this. Both database applications and COM+ applications may have roles defined within their structure. Database administrators assign users to database roles.

In a well-defined and relatively static environment, the system administrator can manage the ordinary application and the burden of assigning rights and permissions. In the well-managed environment, data owners define who should do what with their data, and the administrator can mold the operating system authorization design to fit these requirements. In a relatively static environment, change is slow, so there is time to make these decisions for new applications and weigh the impact on older ones. Many organizations do not provide a well-defined or relatively static environment, though. Change often occurs rapidly, data owners and administrators sometimes don't communicate well, and applications are often adopted that require elevated privileges to run, not because of the way they must function, but because they were poorly written.

The secret to successfully adopting Authorization Manager is to realize that it will not solve the problems created by the past. It cannot be put to use to manage wayward applications or magically relieve the administrator of the burden of assigning rights and permissions. What Authorization Manager can do is provide the infrastructure for which applications can be developed to change the paradigm for the system administrator. For all Authorization Manager applications, the administrator does not need to assign individual users or groups access to objects; she merely has to respond to application owners' identification of which users should play what role in the application.

If this concept appeals to you, you will need to work with data owners and application developers to produce applications that can be managed by Authorization Manager. Writing applications that support RBAC is not within the scope of this book; however, managing such applications with Authorization Manager is. You may be asked to administer such an application, or you may be key in recommending that applications be written that are Authorization Manager-enabled and thus can provide RBAC.

---

**NOTE: Authorization Manager On Other Platforms**
The Authorization Manager RBAC API can be obtained for Windows 2000 from http://www.microsoft.com/downloads/details.aspx?FamilyID= 7edde11f-bcea-4773-a292-84525f23baf7&displaylang=en and can be used to develop Authorization Manager applications. Authorization Manager applications can only be administered using the Authorization Manager snap-in from a Windows Server 2003 server or a Windows XP Professional computer on which the Windows Server 2003 Administration Pack for XP has been installed. However, to create Authorization Manager stores in the Active Directory, the domain must be in Windows Server 2003 functional mode.

---

The following information can help you understand the basics of Authorization Manager and the steps that will need to be taken to use it.

### ROLE-BASED ACCESS CONTROL IN WINDOWS

Role-based access control is available without Authorization Manager for Windows systems based on NT technologies. Implementing RBAC in previous versions of Windows required administrators to develop roles by doing the following:

- Creating Windows groups.
- Assigning appropriate user rights to these groups.
- ACLing resources such as files, folders, registry keys, and Active Directory objects.
- Adding Windows accounts into and removing them from these Windows groups as individuals joined or left the company or changed roles within the company.
- Working with developers to introduce custom roles into applications. This includes working with .NET applications, COM+ applications, and applications based on prior programming paradigms.

There is nothing wrong with this model. However, much of its success relied upon the administration of permissions on a large number of objects. Get it right, and people can do their jobs, nothing more. Get it wrong, and the wrong people often have access they shouldn't, and those who officially require rights and permissions may be blocked from doing their work. Frustration becomes part of every administrator's and user's day. Eventually, wide holes in security may be created just so that users can do their jobs. It's especially difficult to scale this model when there is high turnover in personnel and rapidly changing job functions. In addition, although the model is highly flexible and offers granular control when it comes to object permissions, it cannot manage the use of software at a granular level.

The issue has not been that a way was needed to do RBAC control, but rather how the following details should be handled:

- Defining the roles. Who does what on which computer systems with what applications? What do people do?
- Translating the job into a set of object permissions. For each role, what programs do they need access to? Which files? Printers? Registry keys?
- Assigning the responsibility for creating the job/rights/permissions mapping. Who should be figuring all this out?
- Determining responsibility for implementation, maintenance, and audit of roles and role assignment. Who should actually configure the computer, make sure it's working the way it's supposed to, and audit the role and role assignments? Are the right people in the right roles? Are the roles defined correctly?

Authorization Manager removes the granular details of role development from the system administrator. Developers create the applications that define the roles based on specifications provided by those who know how the new applications should run. Developers assign object permissions and rights of code execution within the role definition in their application. Once a role is defined, it can be assigned to a group. Administrators simply add Windows users or groups to these groups to allow users or group members to perform the role. Administrators and data owners can participate in the design of the application and its roles. Data owners determine which individuals within the organization should play which role.

By comparison, ACLs attempt to manage software restrictions by setting permissions such as "execute" or "deny execute," and software restriction policies are based on the use of special designations that prevent or allow software to run. Authorization Manager-enabled applications define roles, which are then limited to certain operations within the application. With authorization, you define not only who can run an application, but also what role they can play within that software. This means that users are not only restricted to using only specific applications, but also to only executing some of the code within an application. Roles can also be confined to the use of a subset of the resources used by the application and limited with permissions as to what they can do with the resource. Authorization Manager is the administrative tool used to expose the underlying application, role, and resource partitions, and to assign users to roles. The use of well-defined roles to control system access is known as role-based security.

## Authorization Manager Basics

Authorization Manager provides a single interface that administrators can use to manage multiple applications. Authorization Manager-enabled applications, however, must be written to contain the necessary components to provide a deeper level of access control.

Application developers define the components that define the roles within the application. The application installation program populates the authorization policy, a set of rules that define the application roles. The authorization policy is stored in the authorization store and exposed in the Authorization Manager snap-in for use by the administrator. If the installation program does not deliver the authorization policy, components can be created directly in the Authorization Manager.

**NOTE: Administrator's Role**
The administrator's main responsibility is to assign Application Groups, Windows Groups, and Users to roles and to add users to groups, thus conferring upon them the appropriate role. However, administrators should understand how the process works so that they may understand the rights and permissions granted on their systems when a user is given a role.

To aid your understanding of how Authorization Manager applications work, the sections that follow both define the components and provide instructions on how they can be created in Authorization Manager. To perform many of these operations, you will need to change the operation mode of the Authorization Store from Administrator mode to Developer mode. Administrators cannot create applications, authorization stores, or operations and cannot change application names or version numbers. To change to Developer mode, add the Authorization Manager to an MMC console, and then do this:

1. Right-click on the Authorization Manager node and select `Options`.

2. Select `Developer mode`, as shown in Figure 8-1.
3. Click `OK`.

A complete Authorization Manager application requires the development of the following components:

- **Authorization Store**—The repository for the security policy.
- **Groups**—Entities that can be assigned roles.
- **Application**—Defines the relationship between the applications written to be managed by Authorization Manager and the authorization store.
- **Scope**—A file folder or other resource used by an application.
- **Roles**—A collection of related tasks that must be accomplished.
- **Tasks**—A collection of operations.
- **Authorization Scripts**—Scripts that check a user's authorization to perform a task.
- **Operations**—Lower-level operating system.

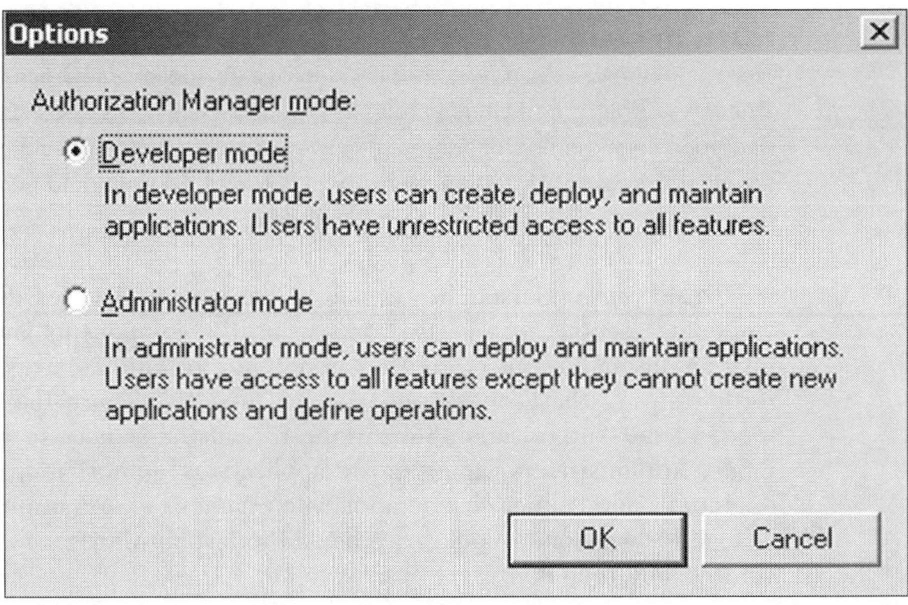


**Figure 8-1** The operations available in Authorization Manager depend on the mode that is set.

### *Authorization Store*

An Authorization Manager-based application reads its security policy from its Authorization Store during startup. The security policy consists of rules that indicate what a specific role can do. There is no default Authorization Store; instead, an Authorization Store is created for a specific purpose. Authorization Stores can reside in the Active Directory or in the NTFS file system (local or remote) in an XML file. Secure the file using ACLs. Table 8-1 illustrates the differences between the two types of stores.

**Table 8-1** Authorization Store Definition

| | Active Directory | XML |
|---|---|---|
| Delegation support | At the Authorization Store, application, and scope level | Not supported. Secured by its ACEs. |
| Authorization specification | URL with the prefix MMSLDAP:// or LDAP distinguished name (DN) like CN=store, CN=data, DN=mycompany, or DN=com | URL with the prefix MSXML:// or path such as C:\stores\thisstore.xml or \\servera\sharea\thisstore.xml |
| Windows Support | Windows Server 2003 domain functional level only | NTFS partition (including one on Windows 2000 servers) |
| Audit Support for Runtime auditing | Authorization Store level and application level | Authorization Store level and application level |
| Audit Support for Authorization Store change auditing | Authorization Store, application, and scope | Authorization Store level only |

An Authorization Store can be created programmatically, or manually in the Authorization Manager. When items such as groups, roles, operations tasks, and so forth are created in the Authorization Manager console, their information is added to the Authorization Store. To create a store, follow these steps:

1. Open Authorization Manager.
2. Right-click on the computer container and select `Create New Authorization Store.`
3. Select XML or Active Directory for the store location and enter the name and location of the store.

4. Enter a description, as shown in Figure 8-2.
5. Click OK to add the store. Figure 8-3. shows the store added to the Authorization Manager console.

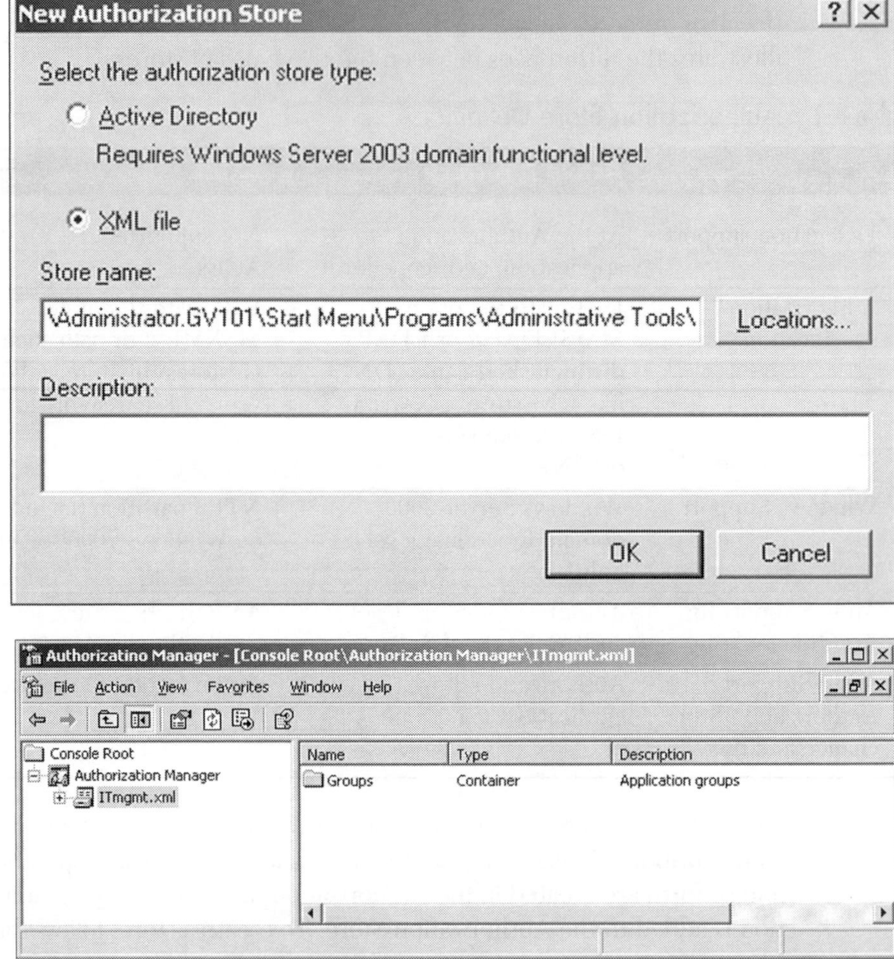


**Figure 8-2** The Authorization Store is created by specifying a name and location for its storage.

**Figure 8-3** After creation, the store is displayed in the Authorization Manager console.

**NOTE: Delegation**

Delegation in the Active Directory is a way of assigning administrative responsibility to users who are not members of the Administrators group. Delegation is accomplished by assigning user group permissions on Active Directory objects. Because an Authorization Store that is stored in the Active Directory is an object, you can delegate authority over the store and the objects within it. XML-based Authorization Stores are not in the Active Directory and do not support delegation.

### *Groups*

Groups are used to assign roles to users. Roles are assigned to groups, and administrators place user accounts in groups. Special groups can be created in Authorization Manager, or Windows groups can be used. If Authorization Manager groups are used, they can be created just for use by an application or even a scope within the application. The group nomenclature is as follows:

- **Application Groups**—A group of users in an Authorization Manager application. They can be created at all three levels in the console: Authorization Store, Application, and Scope. A group created in an upper level can be used at a lower level, but a group created at a lower level cannot be used at an upper level. Application groups are either Application Basic Groups or LDAP Query Groups.
- **Application Basic Group**—Includes a list of members and a list of non-members. A list of non-members is used to deny access to some subset of the larger, allowed access group. A group, therefore, might be provided access to the application but denied access to some subset of the application. Non-membership takes precedence over membership. Basic groups can be Windows Users and Groups or LDAP Query Groups.
- **Lightweight Directory Access Protocol (LDAP) Query Groups**—This is a dynamic group defined by an LDAP query. Any user attribute can be part of the LDAP query. For example, a query group could consist of all those users who live within the city limits of Chicago. Over time, this group might change. Other groups may be more volatile. An example would be all those users who had a birthday during the current month.

- **Windows Users and Groups**—These are standard user accounts and groups, either default or custom. When a role is assigned to a group, you can choose Windows Users and Groups or an Application Group.

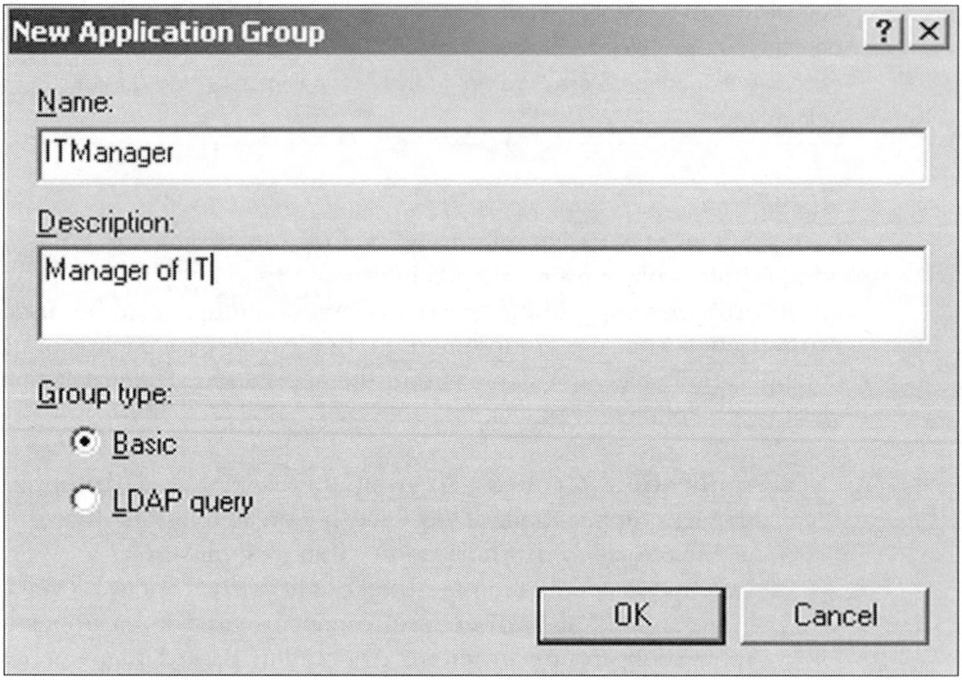

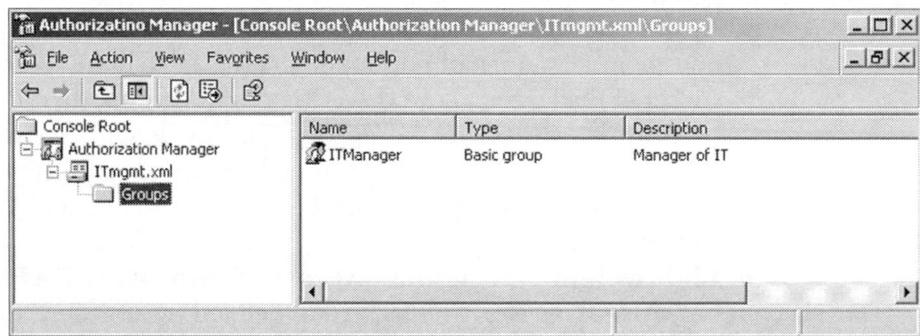


**Figure 8-4** The group type is selected during group creation.

**Figure 8-5** Groups live within the Groups container.

To add a group:

1. Right-click the `Groups` node of the Authorization Store, Application, or Scope and select `New Application Group.`
2. Enter a name and description for the Application Group.
3. Select either `LDAP query or Basic` group type, as shown in Figure 8-4.
4. Click `OK` and view the created group, as shown in Figure 8-5.

### *Application*

The development of each Authorization Manager-based application determines how roles will function within the application. The assignment of roles and users to groups defines who can perform which roles. The application object in Authorization Manager is created within its Authorization Store and contains the objects that define the RBAC present in the application. An application can exist in only one Authorization Store, but an Authorization Store can contain multiple applications. Table 8-2 lists common tasks the Authorization Manager application supports and compares them to the processing within an ordinary application.

**Table 8-2** Application Tasks Comparison

| | Authorization Management | Ordinary Application |
|---|---|---|
| 1 | During application development: define roles, implement operations, and roll operations into tasks. | May define roles, but typically does not. Role definition may mean that administrators can run some applications or operations while both users and administrators can run others. |
| 2 | The installation process creates the Authorization Store, operations, tasks, and application-based roles, in addition to defining files or databases used for application data. | The installation process defines files or databases to hold application data and places configuration data in the registry or in a file. |

**Table 8-2** *Continued*

| | Authorization Management | Ordinary Application |
|---|---|---|
| 3 | At runtime, the application uses the Authorization Manager to connect to the Authorization Store and read the security policy. | At runtime, the application may check configuration information in files or registry hives. During processing, authorization for access to objects is determined by user rights and permissions assigned by administrators. |
| 4 | When clients connect to an application, an application context is created. | When a user starts an application, the application runs in the user's security context. |
| 5 | Before a client uses an application, custom application behavior is developed based on roles. During operation, each user role may present a different UI based on his role. | Before a client can use the application, custom behavior is defined primarily by the user's rights and permissions on objects. The user interface may show error messages if a user's rights and permissions do not match those required to run the application. |
| 6 | When a client attempts to perform an operation, an access check is performed to see if the user's role includes the right to perform the operation. | When the application attempts to perform an operation, an access check is performed to see if the user has the right or permission needed to perform the operation. |

When you manage or participate in the development of an Authorization Manager application, you can manage roles in a different and very natural way. To create an Application object in the Authorization Manager, follow these steps:

1. Right-click on the `Authorization Store` node and select `Create New Application.`
2. Enter a name, description, and version number for the application, as shown in Figure 8-6.
3. Click `OK` and view the application in Authorization Manager, as shown in Figure 8-7.

New Application

Name:

EmployeeProvisioning

Description:

Manages IT resource assignment for employees

Version information (optional):

1.0

Note: The application name specified here must be the name that the managed application uses when initializing the Authorization Manager.

OK Cancel

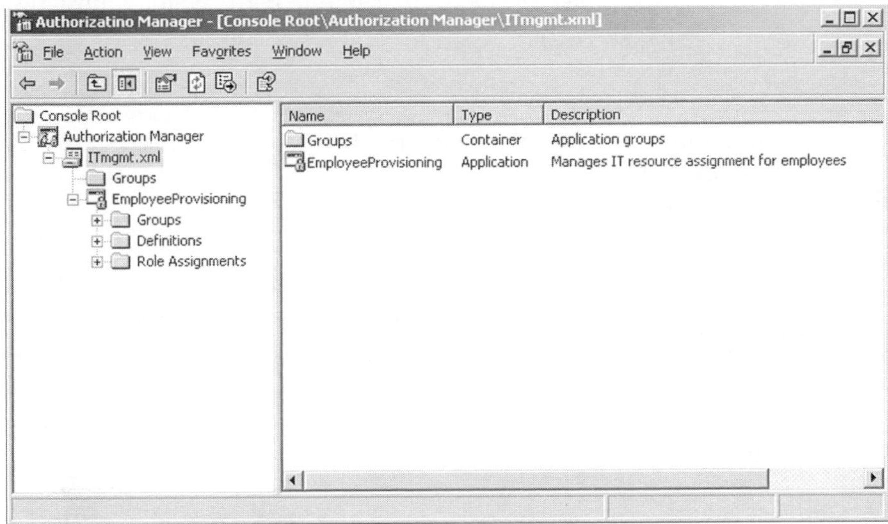


**Figure 8-6** Applications are containers created to hold the security policy as defined in roles, groups, operations, and tasks.

**Figure 8-7** Applications are created within their Authorization Store.

### *Scope*

Scopes are created within each application to restrict access to resources. A scope specifies resources such as file system folders, Active Directory containers, types of files (such as all *.doc files), URLs, and registry hives. You create Authorization Manager groups, role assignments, role definitions, or task definitions and assign them to the application scope rather than the application. (Operations, however, cannot be defined at the scope level.)

The groups created within the scope have access to the resources they define, while groups created in the application can be assigned access to resources in the entire application including the scope. Using scopes is a good way to restrict the access of some users while empowering others.

A scope can be an NTFS folder, an Active Directory container, a collection of files identified by a mask such as *.doc (a file-masked collection), a URL, and so on. These containers are identified in the Authorization Manager within the Application container.

To create a scope:

1. Right-click on the `Application` node and select `New Scope`.
2. Enter a name and description for the scope, as shown in Figure 8-8. Note that the name is a folder path. Names must represent real locations.
3. Click `OK`.

You must be careful when creating scopes to make sure they identify resources in a manner that the application can understand. Two things are important here. First, the resource should be identified by location, such as by using file paths, registry hives, or complete URLs, or by identifying existing Active Directory Organizational Units. Second, the application itself must be able to understand the resource. Web-based applications might have URLs as scope identifiers, while file-based applications might use file paths.

To effectively limit access to resources by using their location, follow these steps:

1. Create scopes for resources that need more granular protection.
2. Create application groups in these scopes. Figure 8-9 shows the C:\IT Files scope created within the Itmgmt application. Note how group containers are created at the Authorization Store, Application, and

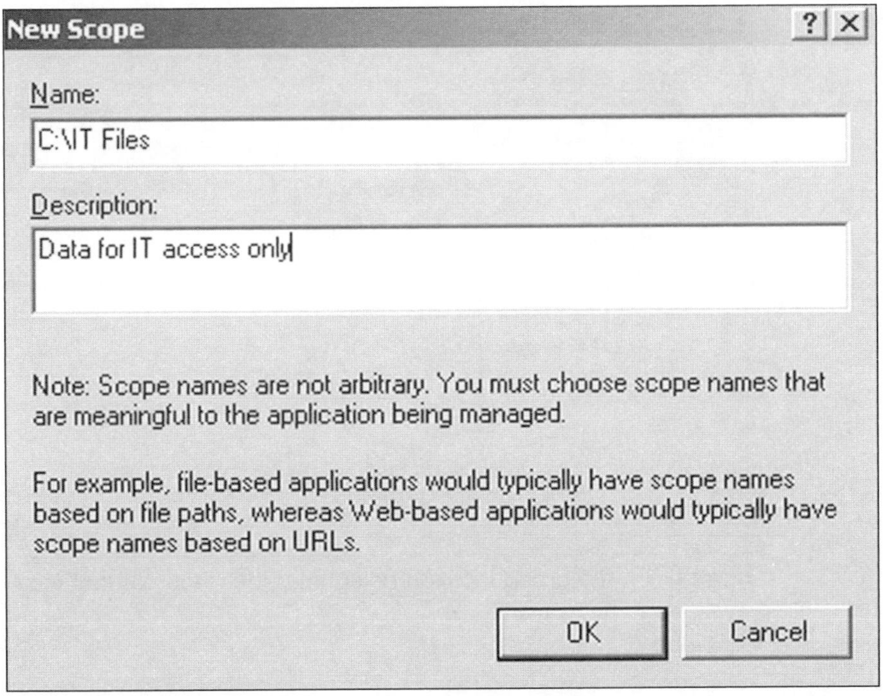

New Scope

Name:

C:\IT Files

Description:

Data for IT access only

Note: Scope names are not arbitrary. You must choose scope names that are meaningful to the application being managed.

For example, file-based applications would typically have scope names based on file paths, whereas Web-based applications would typically have scope names based on URLs.

OK Cancel

**Figure 8-8** Scope names must represent real locations.

Scope level and how definitions and role assignments are created at both the Scope and Application level. In the figure, any groups created in the Groups container of the C:\IT Files scope can only be granted access to files at that level. Groups created at the Application level may be granted access to all resources in the application, and groups created in the Authorization Store can be granted access to resources in all applications defined in the Authorization Store.

3. Assign users to these groups who should have access to these resources.
4. Create groups at the Application level.
5. Assign users to Application-level groups that should have access to all resources in the application.
6. Create groups at the Authorization Store level. Assign users to these groups who need access to all applications in the Authorization Store.

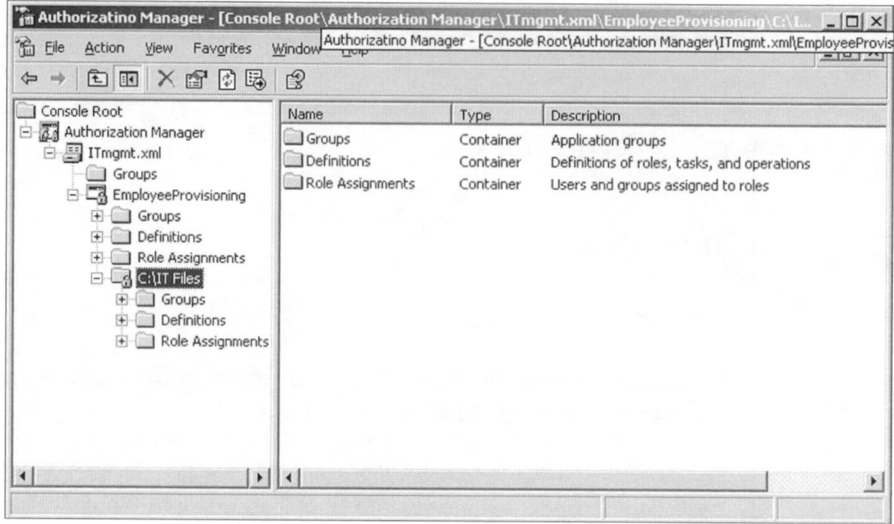


**Figure 8-9** The group location determines the resources that may be accessed by its members.

**NOTE: Reasons to Use Authorization Manager Groups**

You should use Authorization Manager groups for two reasons. First, using these groups provides more control over object access. Second, when Authorization Manager groups are used, the application may be more easily used in both workgroup and domain situations. This is because workgroup machines have different Windows groups from those that are available in the Active Directory. An application designed using Active Directory-based groups could not be used in a workgroup. Note, however, that an application developed specifically for an Active Directory environment may have no useful purpose in a workgroup. You should make your decisions on the types of groups to use based on the application requirements.

### *Roles, Tasks, Authorization Scripts, and Operations*

In an Authorization Manager application, tasks, operations, and authorization scripts define roles. Tasks are composed of lower-level tasks, operations, and authorization scripts. Operations are single units of lower-level operating system functionality. For example, a Help Desk task might be "reset password" for users within a specific organizational unit (OU). A task created within the application might be named ResetPassword. An operation, also created in the application, includes a reference to a number identifying the actual code within the application that allows the user to reset passwords for users within his assigned OU. The operation is assigned to the task, and the task is assigned to the help desk role. Finally, when the role definition is complete, it is assigned to the group created to identify users who will be assigned the help desk role.

When the application is written, operations are programmed. During the development of an Authorization Manager application, the elements for each role are written. During the application's installation, the tasks and operations that define the role populate the Authorization Manager, along with the groups and other application components.

You may have to manually add roles, authorization scripts, tasks, and operations to the Authorization Manager. Just remember that they must correspond to the programmed application, and the numbers defined in the operations forge the links between the Authorization Manager and the application code.

### Roles

Before you can control authorization by using roles, the roles must be defined. You do this by adding defined tasks and operations to the roles. Roles can be defined across multiple applications but managed from a single location. Roles can also be confined to specific applications and even to limited resources within the application.

The first step is to identify the roles required. To define roles, think of each one as an abstraction that corresponds to real-world operations and tasks. Help desk operator and systems administrator are roles that might be defined if the application were built to control systems operations. Payroll clerk, accountant, and accounting manager are roles that might be defined for an accounting application. During the development process, a specification based on the real-world tasks of each type of employee is identified. Each task is further broken down into smaller steps or operations.

A well-designed role is one that maps to a job category or responsibility. You can easily find loose role definitions in job titles, but you will need to search beyond the title to determine what it is that the individual actually does. Remember that many employees participate in discrete business functions, and job titles do not always map to specific roles within an application. The process of building a role within an application consists of the following tasks:

- Selecting a name
- Providing a definition

- Specifying lower-level tasks, roles, and operations that are part of the new role. Authorization rules may be written in scripts such as VBScript. Tasks become part of a role definition and can be added or viewed in the Role Definition container.

While the approval for membership in a specific application role is not an administrative task, the actual assignment of a user account to a role is. As usual, understanding what access and rights you are conferring with this assignment is critical. You need to know when a user's access or activity is normal and approved, and when it might represent a breach of conduct, such as an attack upon the system.

---

**NOTE: There's More Than One Way to Create the Role**
You can, of course, create all operations first, and then create each task and assign operations to the tasks as you create them. You'd follow this operation by creating roles and adding tasks to them as you create them.

---

To create and define a role in Authorization Manager, you must create tasks and operations and assign them appropriately. The first step in creating a role in the Authorization Manager is to create the role definition. To do so, follow these steps:

1. Expand the `Application` container, and then expand the `Definitions` container.
2. Right-click `Role Definitions` and select `New Role Definition.`
3. Enter a `name` and `description` for the role, as displayed in Figure 8-10.
4. If lower-level roles, tasks, or authorization scripts have been defined for this role, add them to the role definitions using the `Add` button.
5. Click `OK.`

### Tasks

Roles are composed of tasks. Tasks are collections of operations, authorization scripts, and possible other tasks. Tasks must be well defined and must be associated with roles. Well-designed tasks represent recognizable work items. Examples of well-defined tasks are as follows:

- Change password
- Enable an account

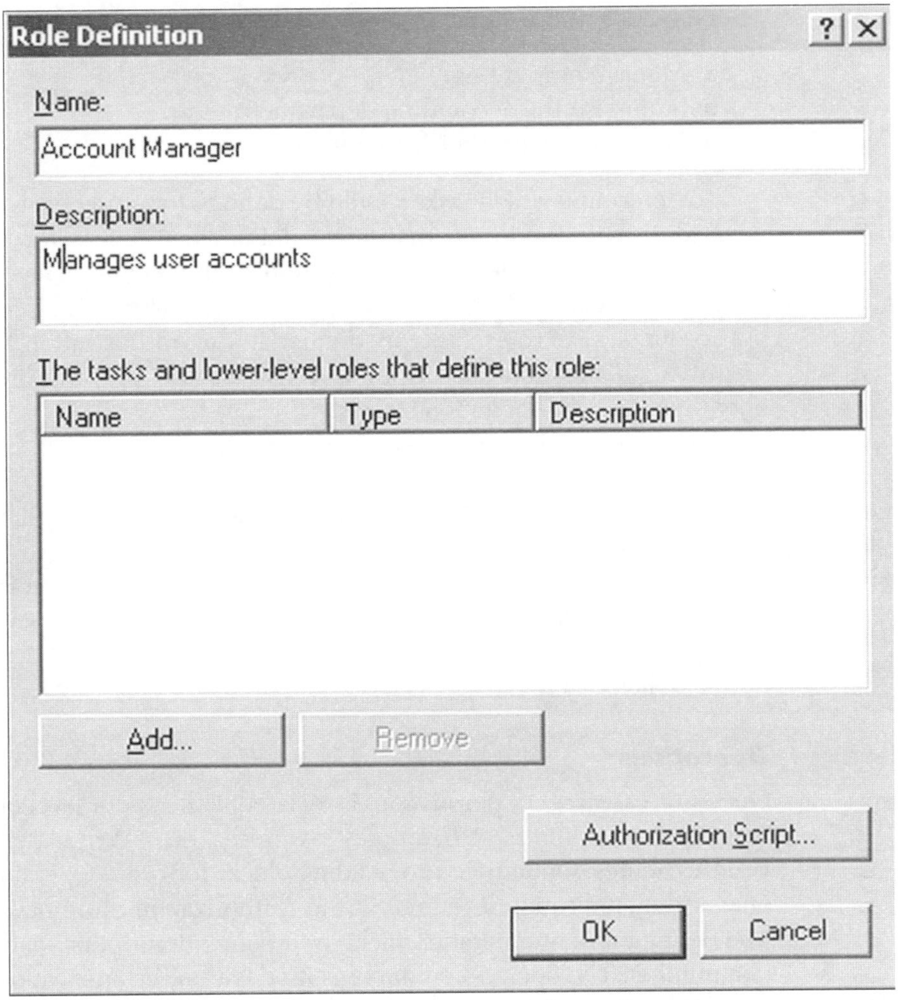

Role Definition

Name:
Account Manager

Description:
Manages user accounts

The tasks and lower-level roles that define this role:

| Name | Type | Description |
| --- | --- | --- |

Add... Remove

Authorization Script...

OK Cancel

**Figure 8-10** Roles are defined by the tasks defined for them and the authorization scripts written for them.

- Create a user
- Submit an expense
- Approve an expense
- Sign a check

Examples of tasks that are not well defined are:

- Manage employees
- Supervise the accounting department
- Help users with their computers

To determine which tasks should be defined for a specific role, you will need to identify the things that might define what a person performing a role does. For example, a network administrator might change the ACLs on a router. A help desk person might change passwords or reset locked out accounts. Like roles, tasks are defined in the Authorization Manager by identifying a name and description. A task consists of lower-level tasks or operations and authorization scripts.

To create a task, perform the following steps:

1. Right-click the `Task Definitions` container and select `New Task Definition.`
2. Enter a name and description for the task, as displayed in Figure 8-11.
3. If lower-level tasks, operations, or authorization scripts have been built for this role, then they can be added using the `Add button.`
4. Click `OK.`

### *Operations*

Operations are a set of permissions associated with system-level or API-level security procedures. Examples would be WriteAttributes or ReadAttributes. Operations are building blocks for tasks. Operations are set only at the application level, not at the Authorization Store or scope level. The definition of an operation includes a name, description, and an operation number. The operation number is used within the application to identify the operation. The operation number is critical because it ties all actions between the Authorization Manager and the application. Because tasks include operations, roles specify the tasks that can be accomplished, and groups are assigned roles, when you add a user to a group, you are giving the user whatever low-level operations make up the tasks assigned to the role.

---

**WARNING: Prevent Operations Number Errors**

The number must be an integer from zero to 2147483647. If you must manually enter the number, be sure that it is correct; an incorrect number will cause a bug in the application.

---

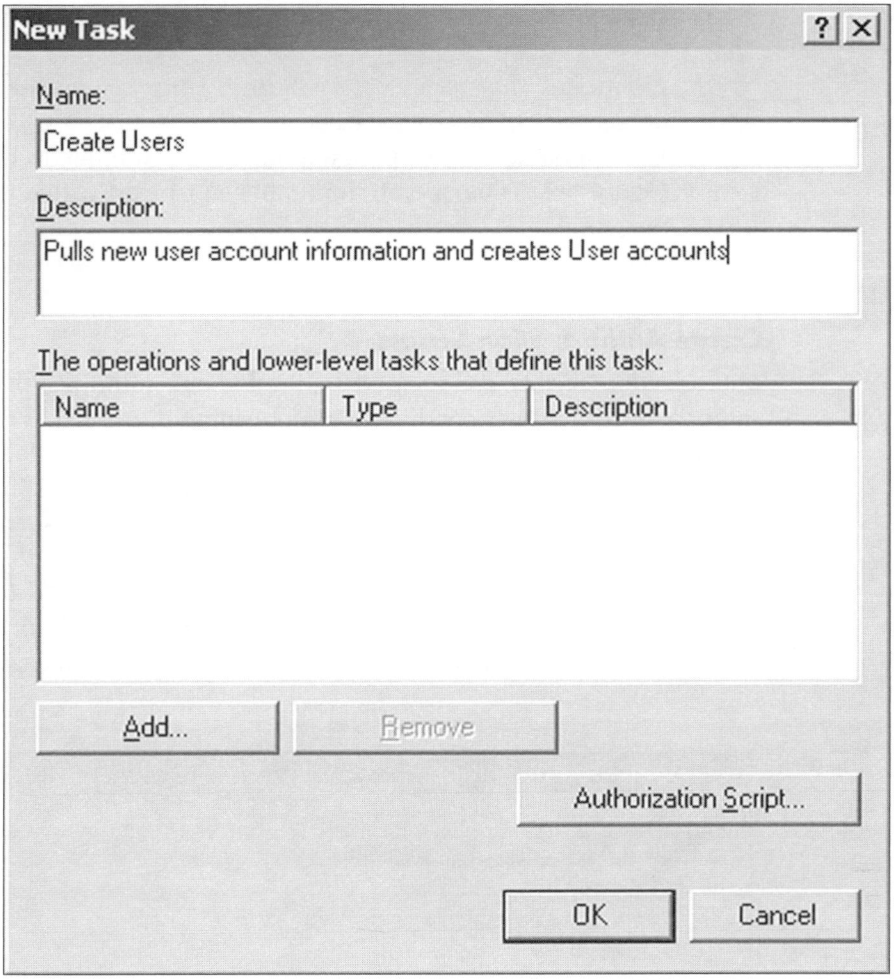

**Figure 8-11** Tasks are defined by operations and authorization scripts.

For example, if a number of operations defines the lower-level actions necessary to format the hard drive, and the operations make up the "format disk" task, which in turn is assigned to the Server Manager role, which is assigned to the Application Group ServerManager, then by putting a user in the ServerManager Application Group, you have given her the right to format the hard drive.

To create an operation, do the following:

1. Right-click the `Operation Definitions` container and select `New Operation Definition.`
2. Enter a name, description, and operation number, as displayed in Figure 8-12. The operation number must exist within the application code.
3. Click `OK.`

### *Create Authorization Scripts*

Authorization scripts are created to implement authorization rules. An authorization rule tests conditions to determine if a user has the right or permission required to perform a specific task. For example, users may belong to a group that has been assigned a role. The role is defined by tasks that empower a role member to complete some task, such as reading a file. An authorization rule can be used to take into consideration the operating systems rights and object permissions assigned to the user. If the file permissions do not allow the user to read the file, then he will not be allowed to, even though the members of his Application Manager Application

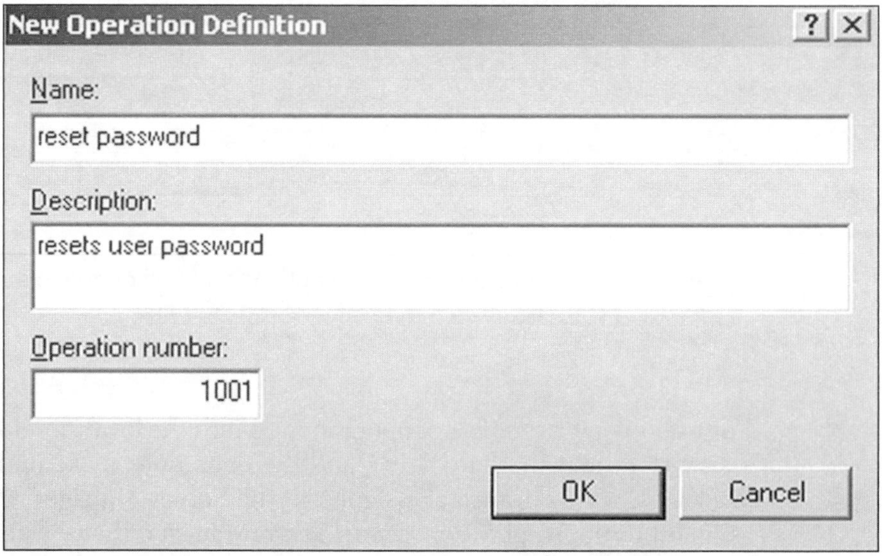

New Operation Definition

Name:
reset password

Description:
resets user password

Operation number:
1001

OK Cancel

**Figure 8-12** Operations are defined by an operation number.

group may normally do so. Scripts can be written in VBScript or Jscript and are usually written by programmers.

### *Define Tasks*

Define the task by assigning operations:

1. Double-click the task you want to define.
2. Select the `Operations` tab.
3. Click to select the operations necessary to define this task, as shown in Figure 8-13.
4. Click `OK`.

### *Define Roles*

Finally, you must define the role by assigning it a list of tasks it may perform:

1. Double-click on the role you want to define.
2. Click on the `Definitions` page.

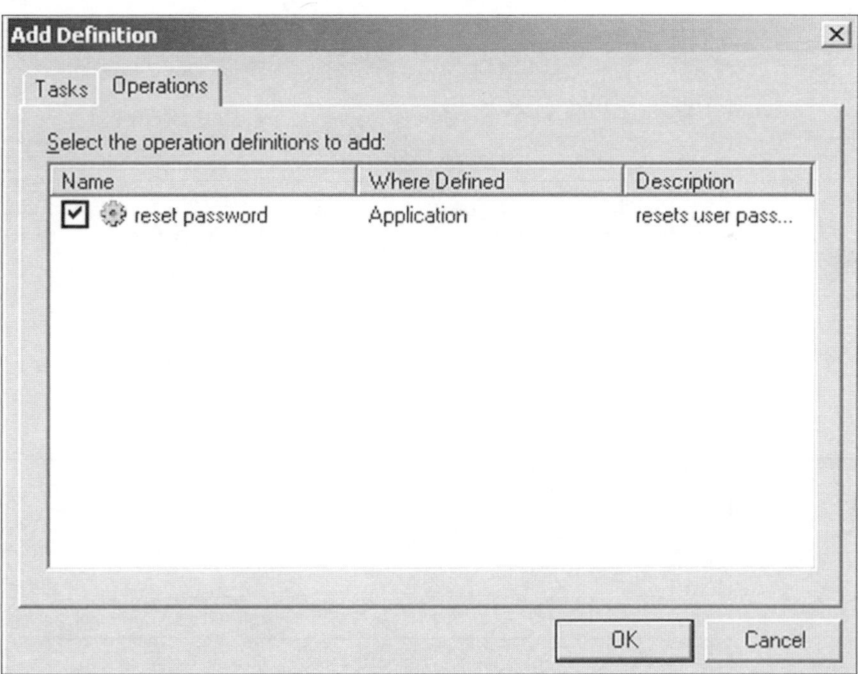


**Figure 8-13** Operations are added to tasks.

3. Select the tasks that define the role, as shown in Figure 8-14.
4. If there are authorization scripts that should be added, click the `Authorization Scripts` button. Enter the script or a path to its location and then click `OK`.
5. Click `OK`.

### *Assign Roles to Groups*

Finally, assign roles to groups:

1. Right-click the `Role Assignments` container and select `Assign Roles.`
2. Select `roles` from the Add Role dialogbox, as shown in Figure 8-15, and then click OK.
3. The role(s) will be added to the `Role Assignments` container. Right-click on the role you wish to assign and select `Assign Groups or Assign Windows Users and Groups.`
4. If `Assign Groups` is selected, select the application group, as shown in Figure 8-16.

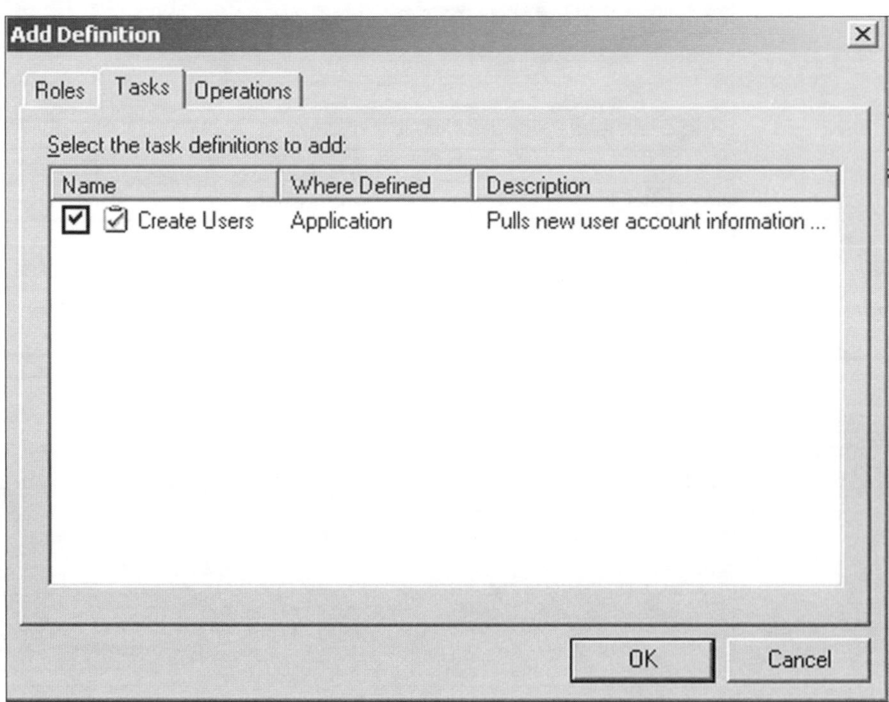


**Figure 8-14** Tasks are added to roles.

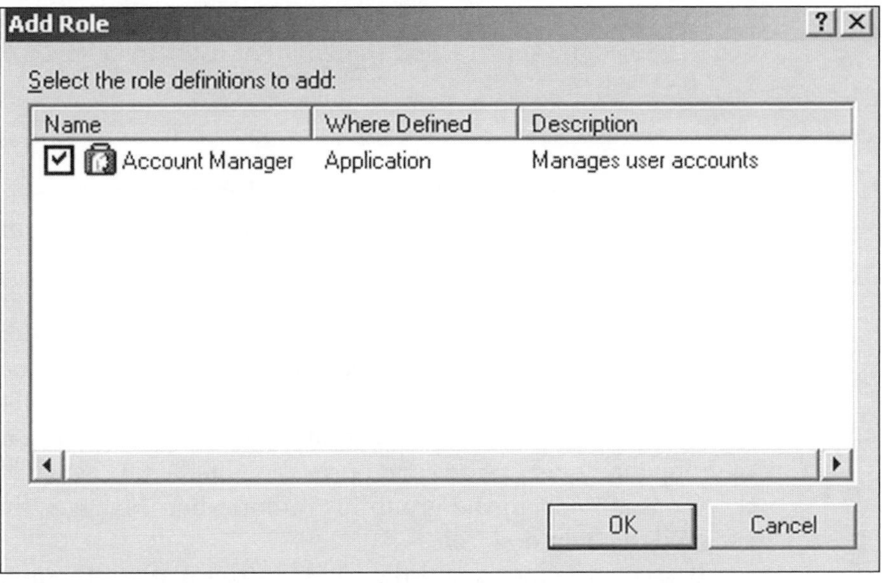


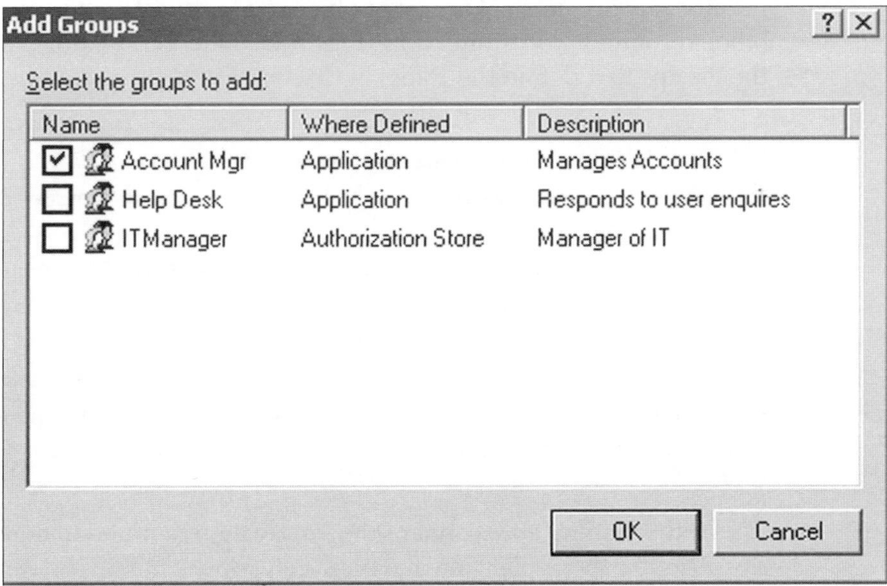


**Figure 8-15** Add defined roles to the Roles Assignment container.

**Figure 8-16** Assign the appropriate groups to each role.

5. If `Assign Windows Users and Groups` is selected, use the object picker to select the group or users to be given this role.
6. Click `OK`.

### *Authorization Manager Basics Summary*

Within Authorization Manager and within specific applications, each role is assigned the right to exercise tasks and operations. The role is assigned to a group, and the group becomes the interface that you, as administrator, will use to assign Windows accounts or groups authorization to use an application and work with resources. Instead of managing resources for the application, you will manage actions and workflow. For example, instead of using the Delegation of Control wizard or directly assigning a user account or group the `reset password` permission on the OU, you will simply add the user's account to the group in Authorization Manager that has been assigned the help desk role.

If access to objects and the rights to run parts of the application are defined, then the administrative role is simple. Instead of hundreds of discrete actions in which you create Windows groups and assign them rights, permissions on Active Directory objects, file objects, registry hives, and other resources, you simply place user accounts or Windows groups into the groups that define the roles.

---

**NOTE: Administrators Need to Know**

Administrators are not responsible for building Authorization Manager applications, defining roles, scripting tasks, or authorizing operations. These are developer functions and can be carried out programmatically or by using the Authorization Manager in Developer mode. The administrator's main responsibility is to assign Application groups and Windows groups and users to roles and to add users to groups, thus conferring upon them the appropriate role. However, administrators should understand how the process works so that they may understand the rights and permissions granted on their systems when a user is given a role.

---

The Authorization Store contains the information required to build the security policy for the application and physically represent it in the Authorization Manager. When the Authorization Store is located in the NTFS file system, it is represented in an XML file. Figure 8-17 is the XML file created by adding the objects defined in the exercises in this section.

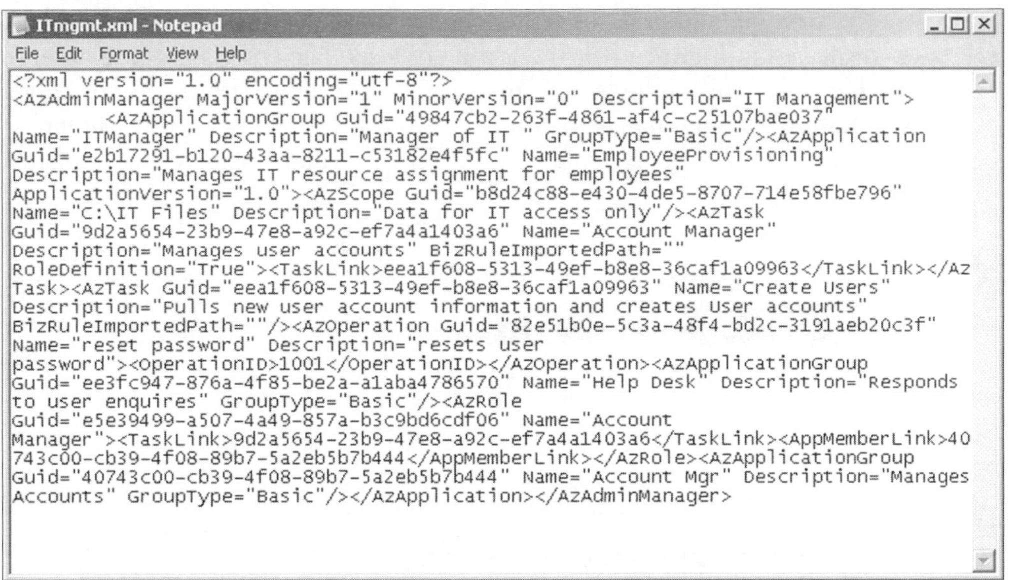


```
<?xml version="1.0" encoding="utf-8"?>
<AzAdminManager MajorVersion="1" MinorVersion="0" Description="IT Management">
	<AzApplicationGroup Guid="49847cb2-263f-4861-af4c-c25107bae037"
Name="ITManager" Description="Manager of IT " GroupType="Basic"/><AzApplication
Guid="e2b17291-b120-43aa-8211-c53182e4f5fc" Name="EmployeeProvisioning"
Description="Manages IT resource assignment for employees"
ApplicationVersion="1.0"><AzScope Guid="b8d24c88-e430-4de5-8707-714e58fbe796"
Name="C:\IT Files" Description="Data for IT access only"/><AzTask
Guid="9d2a5654-23b9-47e8-a92c-ef7a4a1403a6" Name="Account Manager"
Description="Manages user accounts" BizRuleImportedPath=""
RoleDefinition="True"><TaskLink>eea1f608-5313-49ef-b8e8-36caf1a09963</TaskLink></Az
Task><AzTask Guid="eea1f608-5313-49ef-b8e8-36caf1a09963" Name="Create Users"
Description="Pulls new user account information and creates User accounts"
BizRuleImportedPath=""/><AzOperation Guid="82e51b0e-5c3a-48f4-bd2c-3191aeb20c3f"
Name="reset password" Description="resets user
password"><OperationID>1001</OperationID></AzOperation><AzApplicationGroup
Guid="ee3fc947-876a-4f85-be2a-a1aba4786570" Name="Help Desk" Description="Responds
to user enquires" GroupType="Basic"/><AzRole
Guid="e5e39499-a507-4a49-857a-b3c9bd6cdf06" Name="Account
Manager"><TaskLink>9d2a5654-23b9-47e8-a92c-ef7a4a1403a6</TaskLink><AppMemberLink>40
743c00-cb39-4f08-89b7-5a2eb5b7b444</AppMemberLink></AzRole><AzApplicationGroup
Guid="40743c00-cb39-4f08-89b7-5a2eb5b7b444" Name="Account Mgr" Description="Manages
Accounts" GroupType="Basic"/></AzApplication></AzAdminManager>
```

**Figure 8-17** The Authorization Store XML file holds the security policy for the application.

## Auditing Authorization Manager

Event auditing for Authorization Manager Applications can be configured and events will be recorded in the Security event log. Two types of auditing of Authorization Manager are possible:

- **Runtime Auditing**—Audits are generated when policy defined in the Authorization Store is used. Auditing can report success, failure, or both. Client context and access checks are audited. Runtime auditing can be defined for the Authorization Store and the application. It cannot be defined at the scope level.
- **Authorization Store change auditing**—Audit records are generated when the Authorization Store is modified, regardless of location. Active Directory-based Authorization Store change auditing can be defined for Authorization Store, application, and scope. XML Authorization Store change auditing can only be defined at the Authorization Store level.

To turn on auditing, use the check boxes on the `Auditing` tab, as displayed in Figure 8-18. If auditing of a specific type is not available, the check box will not appear. If the success and failure boxes do not appear, auditing is being managed at a higher level. To change it, you will have to find where it is being managed (locally or Group Policy at the domain or

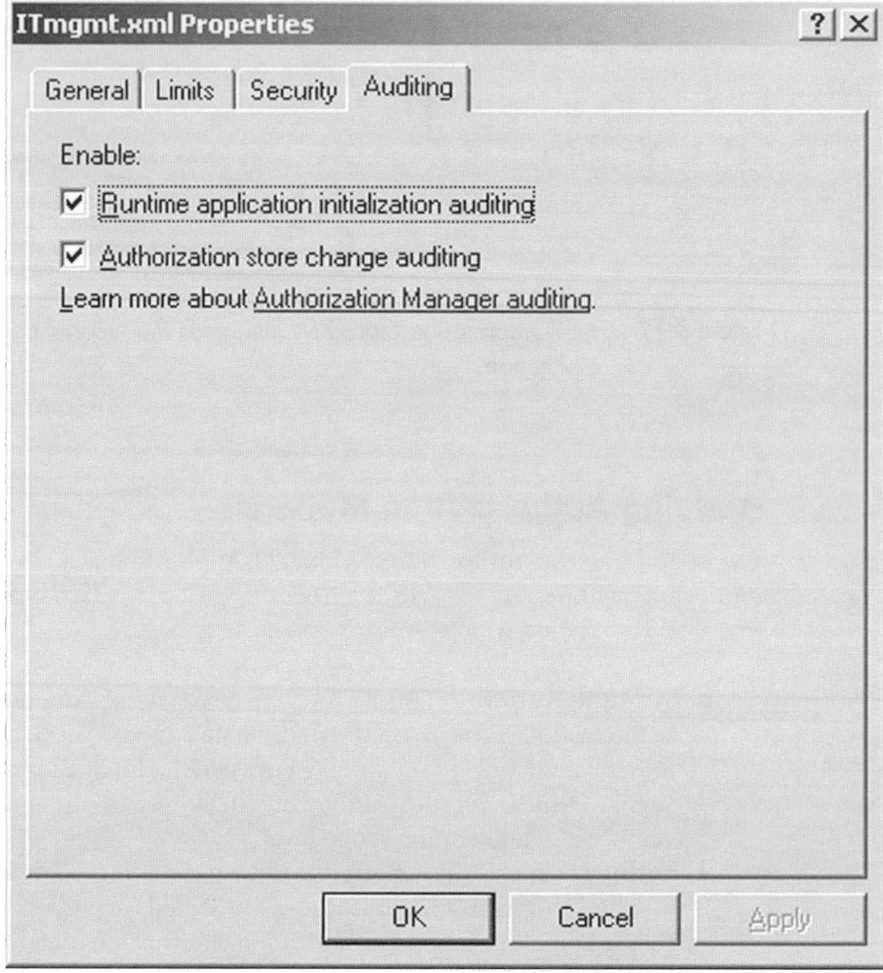


**Figure 8-18** Auditing is defined in the properties of the Authorization Store and the application.

OU level) and modify it there first. All applicable object auditing will be inherited. For example, object access auditing specified on a file in the file system that is a resource in an Authorization Store is inherited. To define auditing the following must apply:

- You must have the `Generate security audits` privilege.
- You must have the `Manage auditing and security log` privilege.
- Object access auditing must be turned on either using Group Policy or Local Security Policy as appropriate.

### Authorization Manager Administration

The administration of Authorization Manager-enabled applications is an easy task if administrators understand how it works and how Authorization Manager applications work. The primary task is to assign users to the groups used in the roles. The administrator may have to participate in the assignment of groups to roles and other tasks if the applications do not programmatically do so. However, like most administrative tasks, simple actions disguise complex operations. The knowledgeable administrator will understand these consequences, audit the activity, and restrain from duplicating or obviating the results by using her power to distribute access to resources and rights that should be left managed by the application.

It may be prudent to limit the number of administrators who can work with Authorization Manager. You can do so by defining the groups and users that may have Administrative access to Authorization Manager. Add or remove groups and users from the `Security` tab of the Authorization Store properties, as shown in Figure 8-19.

## Software Restriction Policies

Imagine if you could prevent a new virus from running on your systems even before your anti-virus vendor had prepared and made public a signature. Imagine if you could prevent well-known but forbidden software such as games or administrative tools from being run by anyone on your system.

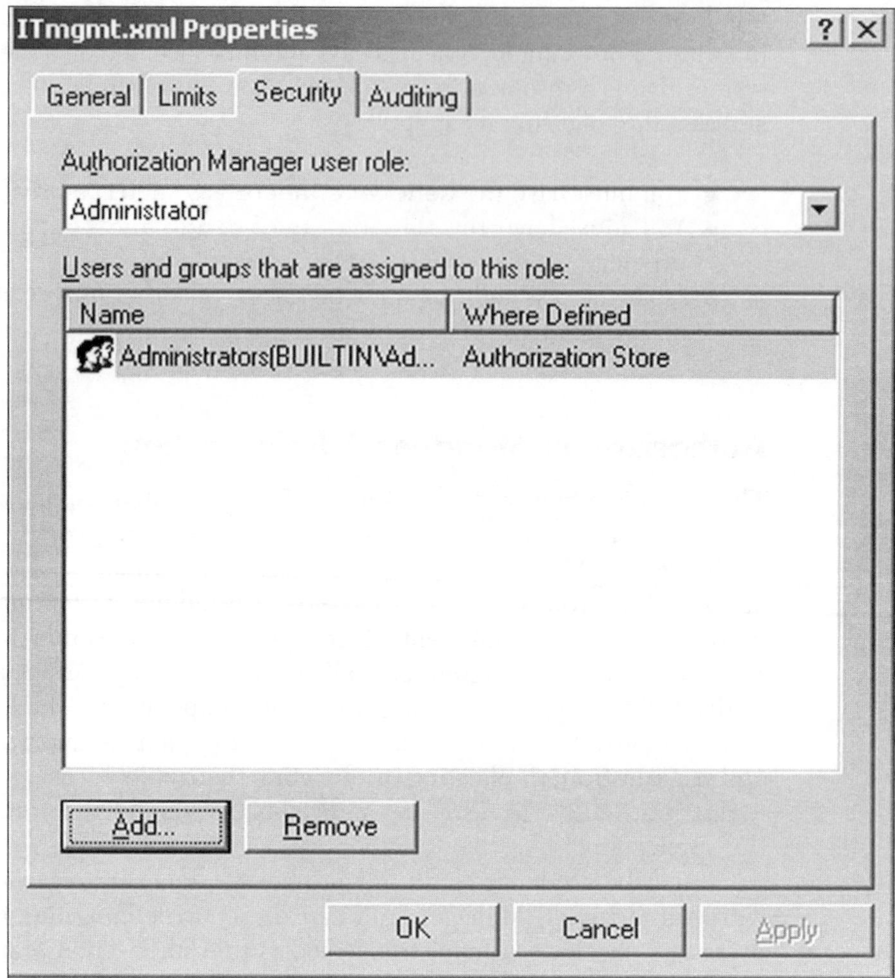


**Figure 8-19** Adjust the number of administrators who can administer Authorization Manager applications.

Imagine if you could prevent as-yet-unknown malicious software from running at all. Would you buy the product that allowed you to do so?

You don't have to. If you have Windows Server 2003 or Windows XP Professional, you already have such a product. Software Restriction Policies is a component that was introduced with Windows XP Professional for the management of a single computer. You can use

Windows Server 2003 to write group policies that impact a single server or desktop or thousands of XP Professional and Windows Server 2003 computers. Here's how.

## Software Restriction Policy Limitations

If you do not fully understand Software Restriction Policy scope—that is, what it can and cannot do to various things—you may either configure it incorrectly or rely on it for a level of security that it cannot provide. In either case, policies may not work the way you think they do, or worse, you may develop a false sense of security—you may believe you have protected computers from malicious software or prevented anything but authorized programs from running only to find out that this is not so. Properly designed Software Restriction Policies can provide improved security if you understand and work with Software Restriction Policy limitations. The following limitations should be understood.

### *Software Restriction Policies Have No Effect in Safe Mode*

When a computer is booted in Safe Mode, Software Restriction Policies have no effect.

---

**WARNING: Safe Mode**

Software Restriction Policies have no effect in Safe Mode. If the user can boot to Safe Mode, she can get around any Software Restriction Policies.

---

### *Local Security Policy Affects Every User of the Computer*

Software Restriction Policy created in the Local Security Policy will only affect that computer. Because it is a computer-wide policy, it affects every user unless its properties are set to exclude members of the Administrators group. If, however, you use a Group Policy-based Software Restriction Policy, you can create Software Restriction Policies in either the Computer or User Security settings of the GPO. You can determine whom the policy will impact by only applying it to OUs within which specific user or computer accounts lie, or you can filter the GPO's application by removing the Apply Group Policy permission for the desired user groups.

### *Some Software Is Not Affected by Software Restriction Policies*

Software Restriction Policies do not apply to the following:

- Drivers or other kernel mode software
- Programs run by the SYSTEM account
- Macros in Microsoft Office 2000 or Office XP documents (manage macros in Office with the Office Macro security settings)
- Programs written for the common language runtime (these programs use Code Access Security Policy)

### *There Are Ways to Get Around Rules*

Software restriction policies include individual rules that prohibit or allow the use of specific software. However, there are limitations to the effectiveness of each rule. This does not mean that you cannot create effective rules that prohibit use of software; it just means that you must understand each rule's limitations and use it appropriately. Examples of rule limitations are as follows:

- If the code of an application changes, a hash rule no longer applies.
- If the path of an application changes, a path rule no longer applies.
- Internet zone rules apply only to applications created with the Windows Installer.
- Certificate rules rely on the trust you place in the certificate.

For information about these rules, see the section "Creating and Using Software Restriction Policies."

## Software Restriction Policy Basics

Restricting access to software doesn't seem like a difficult task. All you have to do is not install it and not allow others to do so either. The problem is that you may lack the ability to control exactly what software should be installed, to control who can install it, and to control who can run software that is already installed on the computer. Some Windows default rights assignments help. A user needs administrative rights to install software that installs a service. But many applications do not do this and therefore do not require administrative rights to be installed. If a user has the right to copy a file to the disk, that simple process may be all the application requires to be installed. Finally, many applications such as Administrative Tools must be present on systems, yet we should deny ordinary users the right to use them. Access to these programs is controlled by user rights assignments and permissions and those you impose. Ordinary users, for example, cannot create or edit Group Policy Objects (GPOs). Other system applications and their associated registry values are protected by default from some types of users. Group Policy, object ACLs, careful control over user rights—all these things can be used to control access to objects. However, because of poorly coded applications, you may have had to give users administrative rights on their computers.

If you limit user access to resources such as files and registry settings, you may be able to mitigate the harm that might be done by running unauthorized applications. If you provide users awareness training and strictly enforce security policies, you may also prevent applications from being installed. However, none of these techniques will totally prevent the installation and use of rogue or malicious software.

---

**NOTE: Software Restriction Policy Design**

An excellent paper that includes information on designing software restriction policies is "Using Software Restriction Policies to Protect Against Unauthorized Software," available at http://www.microsoft.com/technet/prodtechnol/winxppro/maintain/rstrplcy.mspx. The paper includes design scenarios for Terminal services, line-of-business PC, and the use of different policies for different users.

---

When you use Software Restriction policies, however, you supplement default settings and hardening steps and provide a solution for controlling things that defaults and other operations cannot control. With Software Restriction Policies, you can do the following:

- Prevent any software from running and then authorize each piece of necessary software individually.
- Allow all software to run and then restrict specific software from running.

These basic security levels determine initially whether software will run or not. After a security level has been chosen, software restriction policies can identify software via hash, path, URL, or code signing certificate and prevent or allow the software to run based on its identification. The software does not have to exist on the system before a policy can be written to prevent or allow its use.

---

**WARNING: Automatic Path Rules**

Automatic path rules are created as a protection against locking all users out of the system. These path rules are always visible in the Additional Rules folder and are as follows:

```
%HKEY_LOCAL_MACHINE\SOFTWARE\Microsoft\Windows
NT\CurrentVersion\SystemRoot%
%HKEY_LOCAL_MACHINE\SOFTWARE\Microsoft\Windows
NT\CurrentVersion\SystemRoot%\*.exe
%HKEY_LOCAL_MACHINE\SOFTWARE\Microsoft\Windows
NT\CurrentVersion\SystemRoot%\System32\*.exe
%HKEY_LOCAL_MACHINE\SOFTWARE\Microsoft\Windows\Current
Version\ProgramFilesDir%
```

As a general rule, you should not modify these rules unless you are very knowledgeable about the registry and the access that the System requires to itself.

---

## Creating and Using Software Restriction Policies

To establish a Software Restriction Policy, you must first create the basic policy and then write rules. To establish the policy follow these steps:

1. Create a Software Restriction Policy.
2. Set the security level.
3. Determine enforcement.
4. Establish file types that define what an executable file is.

### *Create a Software Restriction Policy*

A Software Restriction Policy is created in the `Software Restriction Policy` container of a local policy or Group Policy Object (GPO) in the

Active Directory. Local policies only affect the machine that they are developed on, while Active Directory-based policies can be linked to domains and organizational units and can impact a multitude of systems and users in a uniform manner. Deciding where to link a GPO requires much thought and will depend on your Active Directory design. Regardless of where a policy is created, you should test its implementation on a single test computer that is configured in the manner typical for its use. If the policy is to be deployed on many machines in a domain, careful testing in a test domain or OU is required. Remember: Software Restriction Policies are powerful. It is possible to develop a policy that prohibits the use of software on a computer. Imagine what that would do if introduced into thousands of computers in your organization. As usual, deployment issues are the most complicated ones of this task; creating a policy for a single machine is simple. To create a Software Restriction Policy in the Local policy:

1. Click `Start`, `Run`, and in the `Run` box, type `secpol.msc`
   OR
   Click `Start`, `Programs`, `Administrative Tools`, `Local Security Policy`.
2. Select the `Software Restriction Policies` container.
3. If no policy exists, as shown in Figure 8-20, `right-click the Software Restrictions Policy` container and select `New Software Restriction Policy`.

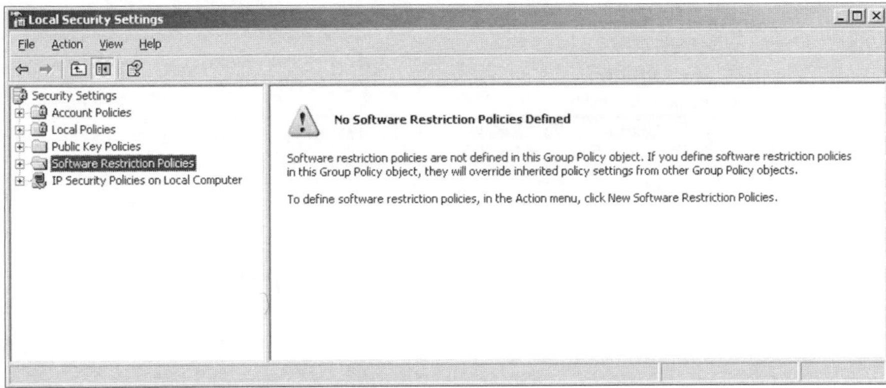


**Figure 8-20** By default, no Software Restriction Policy exists.

4. The default containers and objects will be created, as shown in Figure 8-21.

### Set the Security Level

The security level determines whether all software is allowed to run unfettered (in which case some software will be identified as not allowed) or no software is allowed to run (in which case some software will be identified as allowed). Sounds simple, doesn't it? It will take a bit of work, regardless of your decision. The interface may also be a bit confusing.

To allow all software to run and restrict some, the security level is "Unrestricted." Not "allowed," or "ok," or "let all software run unless otherwise identified"—nope, the security level you must choose (it happens to be the default, so we're okay at first) is "Unrestricted." Well, you might say, perhaps that makes sense; after all, the policies are called "Software Restriction Policies," so we want to indicate that unless software is restricted, it's unrestricted. However, the alternative security level is not "restricted," it's "disallowed." If all software is restricted, then it's "disallowed."

You'll find this funkiness repeated when you build the rules. Each rule has its own security level—it's either disallowed or unrestricted. We'll talk more about this use when we discuss each rule type; just keep this official naming convention straight at the policy level so you don't freeze

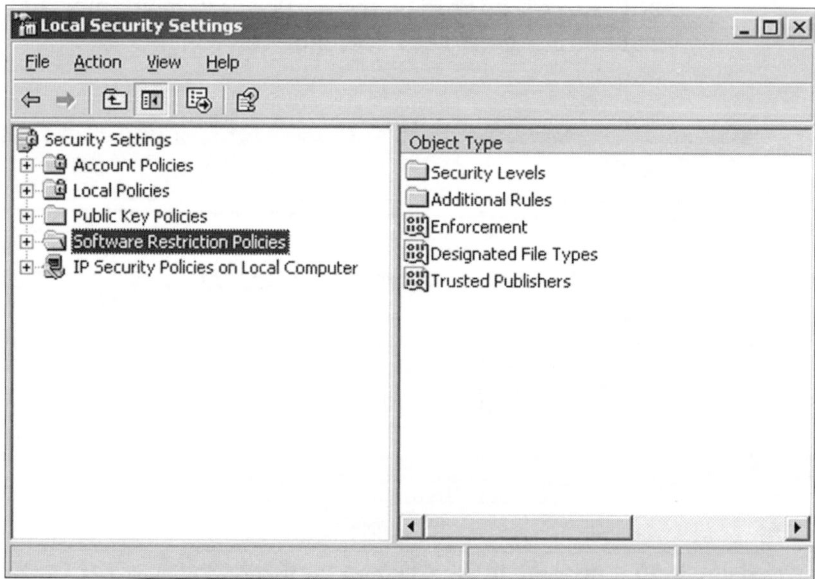


**Figure 8-21** Creating a policy populates the node.

thousands of user machines, okay? Remember: *Unrestricted* means anything can run unless you somehow restrict it. *Disallowed* means nothing can run unless it's allowed. A good rule of thumb is that you should set the security level to "disallow" only if you know all of the applications that must be run. Otherwise, set the security level to "unrestricted" (the default). Paradoxically, setting the level to "disallow" and then only unrestricting the software that is allowed to run can create the more secure environment. This, however, is more difficult than it might sound at first.

To set the security level for the policy, do the following:

1. Expand the Software Restriction Policy.
2. Double-click on the Security Levels Folder.
3. The detail pane shows both possibilities. The current default is marked with a check. If this is not what you want, double-click on the security level you desire: either `Disallowed` or `Unrestricted`.
4. Use the `Set as Default` button to set your choice to the default security level, as shown in Figure 8-22.
5. Click `OK`.

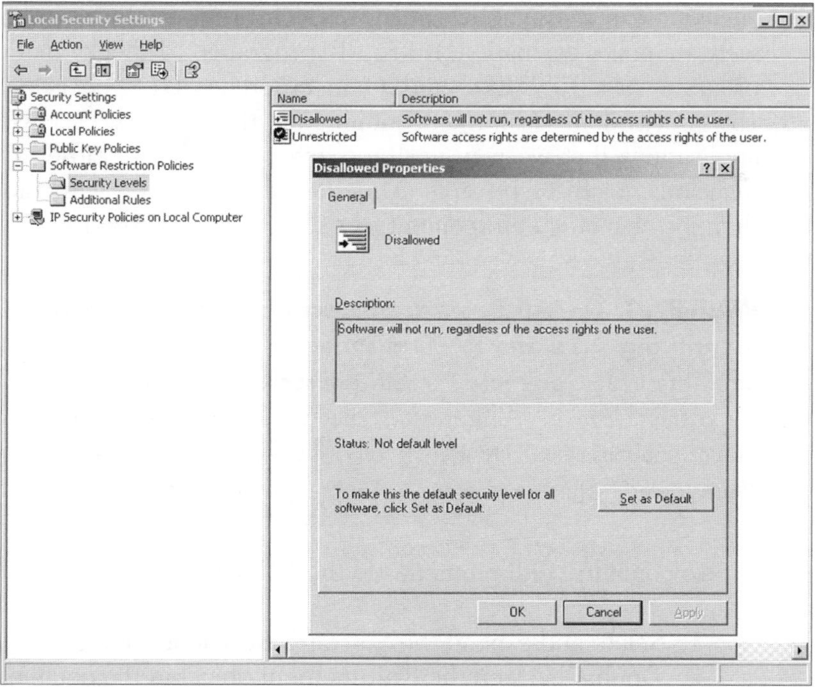


**Figure 8-22** The security level can be changed.

### *Determine Enforcement*

Local Software Restriction Policies are computer-based, while Group Policy-based Software Restriction Policies can be computer- or user-based. You can prevent administrators from being affected by policies by using the `All users except local administrators` enforcement rule. Alternatively, select `All users` to make sure the policy applies to all users—including members of the Administrators group. If users must be members of the local Administrators group on their own machine, be sure *not* to set enforcement for `All users except local administrators.`

A second enforcement choice determines if software libraries are restricted. Software libraries are code files that are not executable but are used by executable files. In most cases, this means a file type of DLL. Set either `All software files except libraries (such as DLLs)` or `All software files.` Choosing `All software files except libraries` simplifies policy writing and prevents performance degradation. It assumes that if you want to allow software to execute, you want its libraries to be accessible. It also assumes that if you want to disallow software, its DLLs won't be executed. It doesn't manage the libraries. However, you may want or need tighter control. Remember, however, that DLL checking can reduce performance. Each program the user runs causes a software policy evaluation. If I run 10 programs, 10 checks are done. If each program uses 15 DLLs, and I am enforcing DLL checking, there are 160 checks done. Libraries contain code that could be accessed by other applications that we may not be managing. If harm, either accidental or malicious, might be possible using these libraries, you may want to control them by changing enforcement to `All software files.`

---

**WARNING: The All Software Selection Means Extra Work Identifying DLLs and Writing Rules**

Be aware that if you chose the software security level of "disallowed" and an enforcement level of "All software," then to allow a specific software application to run, you must explicitly identify all of its libraries and give them the level of "unrestricted." This could prove to be an onerous task.

---

To configure enforcement, do the following:

1. Select and expand the Software Restriction Policy.
2. Double-click on the Enforcement object in the detail pane to open its properties, as shown in Figure 8-23.

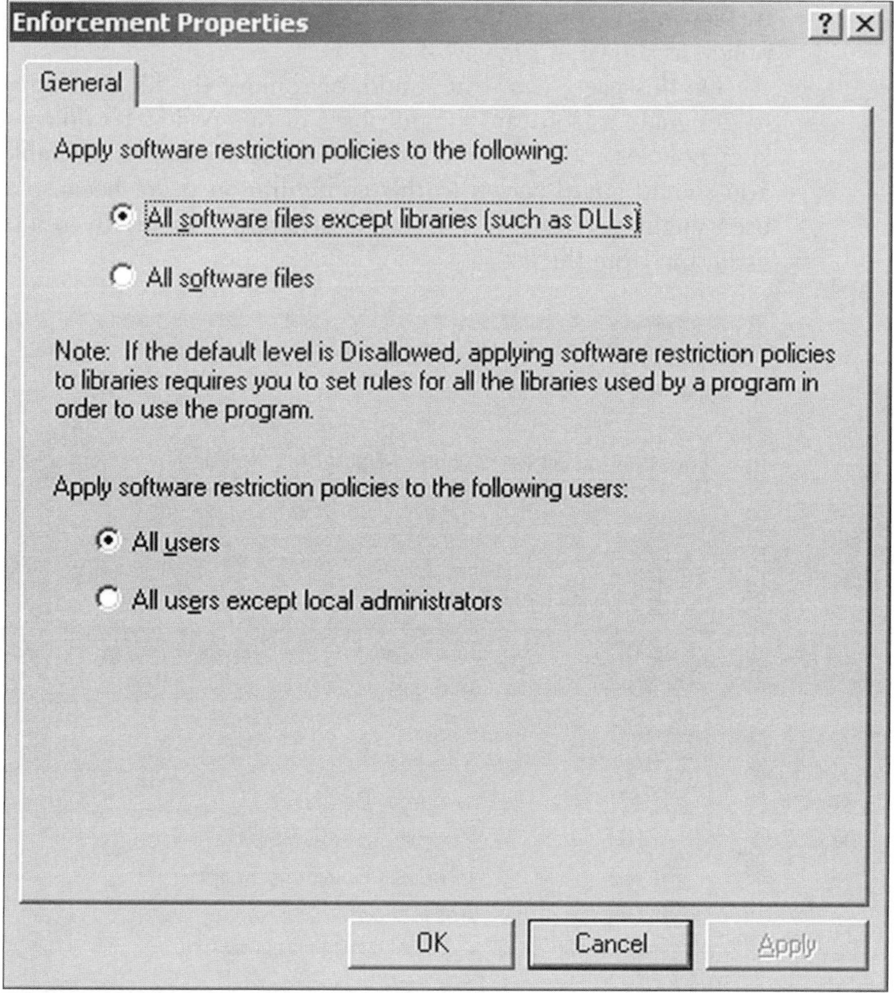


**Figure 8-23** Set enforcement rules for the policy.

3. Select the software enforcement level.
4. Select the user enforcement level.
5. Click OK to close the enforcement object.

### *Establish Designated File Types*

What constitutes an executable? What types of files will be restricted if you set the Security Level to "disallowed?" These questions can be answered by viewing the properties of the Designated File Types object within the policy, as shown in Figure 8-24.

On this page, you review, add, or remove the file types that you want to designate as software for purposes of this policy. By doing so, you can keep policies updated if new software introduces new executable file types. You should guard access to this configuration page, because a malicious user might get around software restriction policies by removing a file extension from the list.

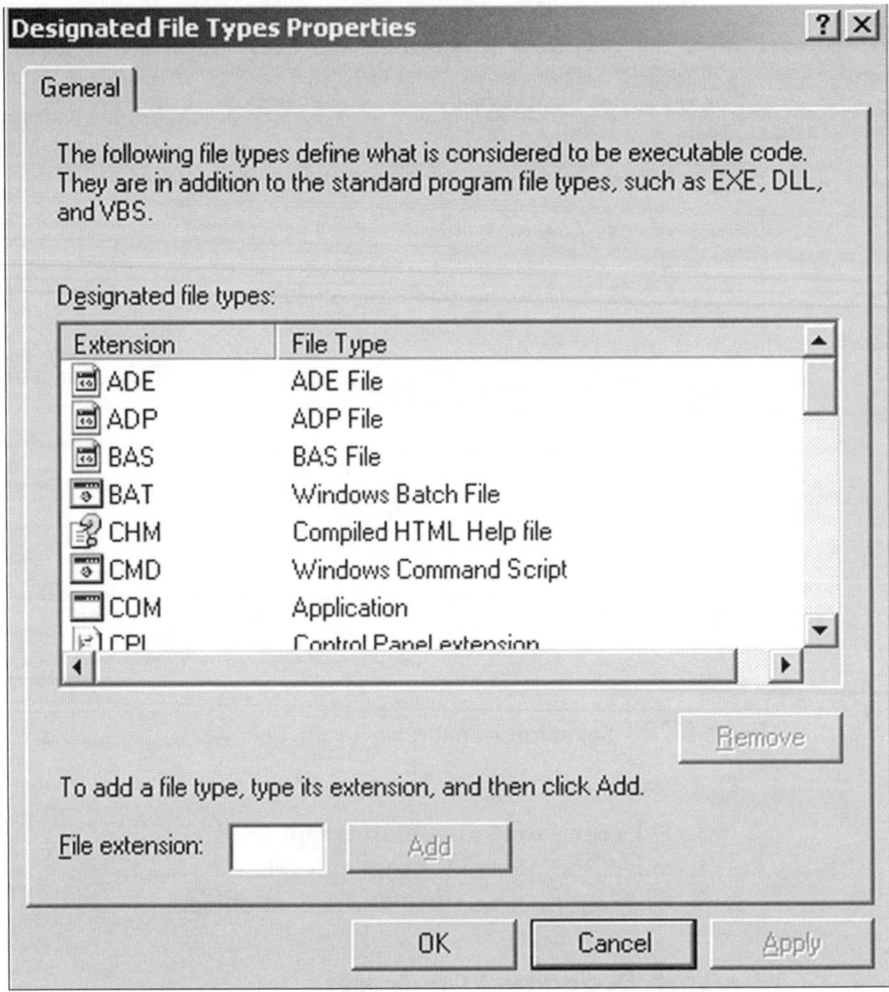


**Figure 8-24** Designated file types define "software" to the policy.

To inspect or modify designated file types, follow these steps:

1. Select the `Software Restriction Policies` container.
2. Double-click the `File Types` object in the details pane of the `Software Restriction Policy` container.
3. Scroll through the window, as shown in Figure 8-24, to see which file types are identified as being software.
4. To remove a file type, select it and click the `Delete` button. Click `OK` to dismiss the warning.
5. To add a file type, enter its extension in the `Extension` box and click the `Add` button.
6. Click `OK` to close the window.

### *Set Trusted Publishers Options*

Trusted publishers are those organizations that you trust to publish safe code. This option affects only ActiveX controls and other signed content. Trusted applications are identified to the system by their certificate, and they use their private key to sign code that they produce. By selecting approved, trusted publishers, you can control whether or not signed software can execute on the computer. Add trusted publishers by importing their certificate into the Trusted Publishers container of the computer certificate store.

You can use the Trusted Publisher options, as shown in Figure 8-25, to manage who can accept publisher certificates and what things should be checked before a certificate is considered valid.

You can select `End users`, `Local administrators`, or `Enterprise administrators` as authorized Trusted Publisher selectors. By default, only domain and enterprise administrators can determine Trusted Publishers for entire domains or groups of computers. However, local users and administrators can accept offered certificates as trusted certificates on local systems if policy is not controlled at a higher level. The value of restricting certificate acceptance to administrators is that users cannot simply click `OK` when offered a certificate while downloading or installing software. By setting this level, you prevent them, for example, from making decisions about trusting ActiveX controls that they may download from the Internet or receive as attachments in email. After all, no one has to pass an ethics test to purchase or obtain a code-signing certificate. The only thing the certificate can do is to authenticate the signer in some fashion. You can further extend the concept of using certificates to control software by writing certificate rules.

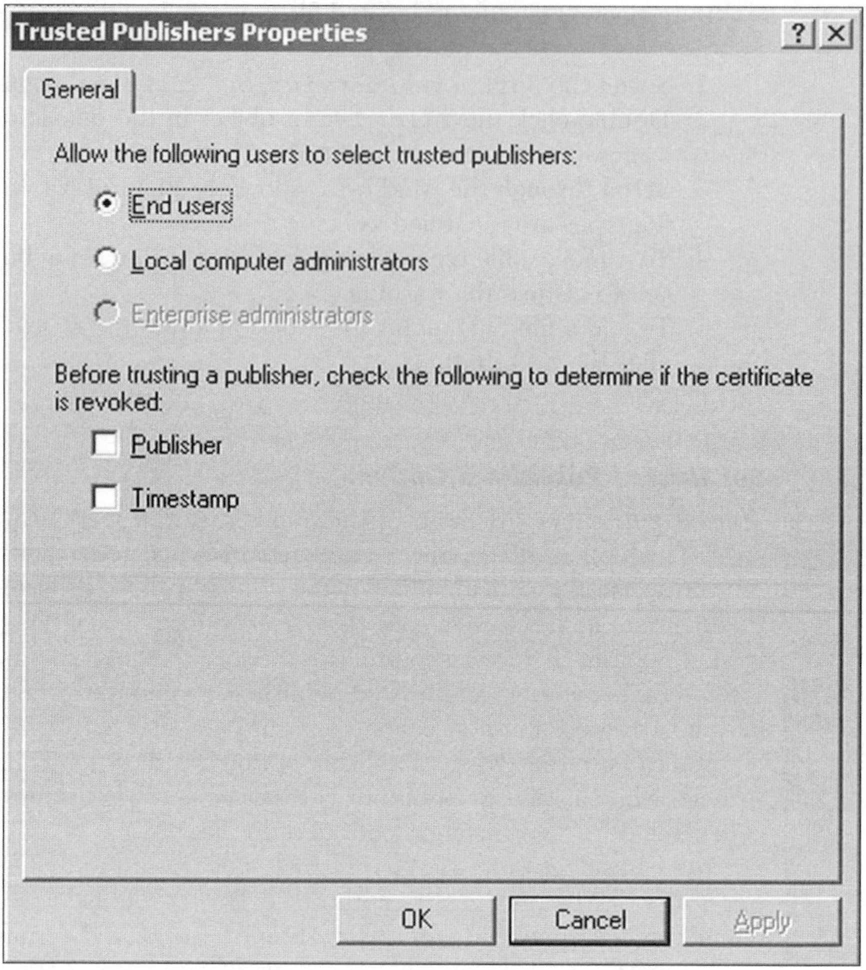

**Figure 8-25** Trusted Publisher options allow you to determine who can accept the publishers that will be trusted.

You can require that Publisher, Timestamp, or both characteristics be used to determine the validity of a certificate. Selecting Publisher requires that the certificate be checked for revocation. Checking the Timestamp requires that the certificate be checked for expiration.

### *Creating Software Restriction Policy Rules*

Software restriction policy rules are applied to specific software (using hash rules, certificate rules, computer path, and URL rules), to its location (using path rules and URL rules), and by referring to a registry path that controls it. Each type of rule has its own advantages and disadvantages. Path rules, for example, can unrestrict or disallow a large group of software in one simple rule. However, if a user can copy the file(s) to another path, she can execute the code. Hash rules can be applied only to a single executable per rule but will prevent a user from running that software, no matter its source, path, or name. However, if the software changes (the virus mutates or a new version of the game is produced), then you must write another rule. The best approach is not to rely on one type of rule, and especially not to set rules and then believe you will never have to set them again. The best approach even includes using file ACLs to further control a user's access to the executable objects.

### SOFTWARE RESTRICTION EXAMPLE

At a company I worked with, Sally was used to controlling her own computer. She downloaded cool tools and drivers from the Internet, brought software from home, and whiled away the hours playing Solitaire and FreeCell. She'd even convinced the powers that be that she needed to have local administrator group membership on her Windows XP Professional system. Then her organization implemented Software Restriction Policies. The first thing Sally noticed was that she couldn't play Solitaire. She'd double-click on the sol.exe shortcut on her desktop and get the warning message in Figure 8-26. So she copied the sol.exe program to another folder to play it. Next, that stopped working, too. Sally was getting mad. She found that many of her other pastimes were disappearing. She could no longer download just any software, and she no longer seemed to have full administrative privileges on her computer. She was losing control. Finally, frustrated and unable to find a way around the restrictions, Sally discovered that the reason for her troubles was the new administrator who'd convinced management to use Software Restriction Policies. Sally tried to sabotage the policies and the new administrator. She began to delete the program files of applications she was supposed to run and moved the location of others to paths that were restricted. When her programs would not run, she reported this and any error message she was able to trigger about policies.

The new administrator almost lost his job, and Software Restriction Policies were blamed for the trouble. Fortunately, the administrator was able to turn on auditing for Sally's computer and figure out what she was doing. With this proof, it was Sally who had to leave.

Since then, all Software Restriction Policies have been backed up by appropriate file ACLs, which prevent harmful action, support the restriction (deny execute), and track user attempts at access and possible attacks.

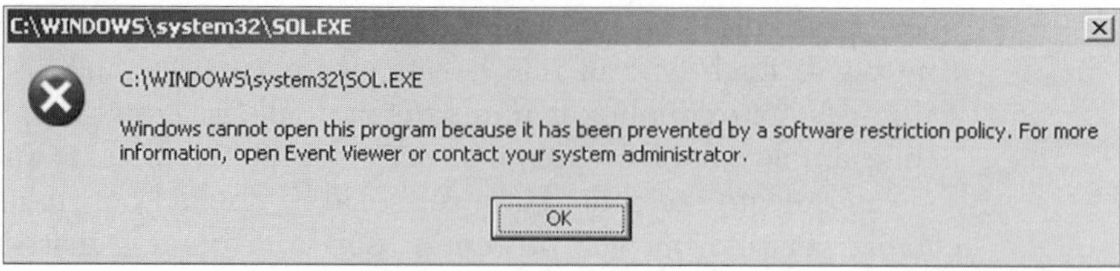


**Figure 8-26** When a user attempts to execute restricted software, a warning message is displayed.

Four types of rules can be created:

- Hash rules
- Certificate rules
- Path rules, including file path rules and registry path rules
- Internet zone rules

To complete your Software Restriction Policy, you must create rules. To begin, determine which software must run and which must not. Next, determine the type of rule to use, and finally, write the rules. The task of determining which software should run and which shouldn't is not easy. You will need to review your security policy and the jobs held by users of the computers, and you will need to consult with management. The suggestions in Table 8-3 may help you decide which type of rule to use.

When multiple rules affect the same software file, the precedence rule determines which rule will win by examining the rules against the precedence order. The order of precedence from top to bottom is as follows:

- Hash
- Certificate
- Path
- Internet zone

For example, if the security level of the policy is unrestricted, and a path rule disallows (prevents from running) the software, but a hash rule allows it, the hash rule wins, and the software can run. In the case of multiple path rules, the most restrictive rule will take precedence. For example, if a path rule is set on the C:\mysoftware folder that prevents software from running (the security level of the path rule is "disallowed"), but another path rule

**Table 8-3** Best Practices for Selecting Rule Types

| Rule | Purpose |
|---|---|
| Hash | Allow or disallow a specific version of a program |
| Zone | Allow software to be installed from Trusted Internet zone sites |
| Path | Allow or disallow a program that is always installed to the same location |
| Certificate | Identify a set of scripts that can be run |
| Registry path | Allow or disallow a program whose path is stored in the registry |
| Path using UNC format share (\\SERVER\share) | Allow or disallow a set of scripts located on a server |
| Two path rules *.vbs set to disallowed, and \\LOGIN-XRV\share*.vbs set to unrestricted | Disallow all VBS files except those in a login script—use two path rules |
| An flcss.exe path rule set to disallowed | Disallow a new virus that is always named flcss.exe |

names the C:\mysoftware\approved folder and sets the security level to "unrestricted," then software in the C:\mysoftware\approved folder can run.

**NOTE: Virus Rules**

Software Restriction Policies are not meant to take the place of anti-virus products. Remember that hash rules don't work when files change (and viruses often mutate). Recall that virus names also can change. Anti-virus programs work to recognize patterns or signatures that the viruses have and are more effective in preventing infection. However, a software restriction policy could be written that could add some protection when a new virus is identified but a signature pattern is not yet available from your anti-virus product vendor.

You should test each rule on test systems before putting them on production systems. After configuring rules but before testing, reboot the system to ensure the rule is in effect.

### *Hash Rules*

Hash rules work by creating a hash of the executable file. A hash can take a variable amount of information and reduce it to a unique digest of a standard size. Ideally, no two software files hashed by the same algorithm will ever produce the same hash. Signed and unsigned programs can be restricted with hash rules. The signed program may have a hash produced by either the MD5 or SHA-1 algorithm. When a hash rule is created, it will use whichever hash is present. If a file is not signed, the MD5 hashing algorithm will be used. The hash rule contains the hash, the file length, and an ID that identifies the hash algorithm.

---

**NOTE: Always Choose Collision-Resistant Hashing Algorithms**

While the possibility of collision (the production of the same hash from different data) is always present, it is unlikely to occur. When choosing hashing algorithms, developers should choose those currently considered to be less prone to collision. When considering choices between applications, administrators also should consider this. For more information, read http://www.rsasecurity.com/rsalabs/node.asp?id=2738, in which the 2004 results of research on collisions in MD5 are examined.

---

When a user attempts to run a program and there is a policy in place, a new hash is made and compared with the hash available in the hash rules. If there is a match, and the related hash rule specifies "disallowed," then the software will not run, no matter where the attempt to execute it is made. For example, if a hash rule is made for the sol.exe program, then it will apply to the program, no matter where the executable is stored or run from, even if it has been renamed. Users cannot get around the rule by copying the file to another folder. However, if the executable file changes, the hash made at attempted execution will not match any stored in the rules, and the software will run. To create a hash rule, follow these steps:

1. Open the Software Restriction Policy.
2. Right-click on the `Additional Rules` folder and select `Create New hash rule.`
3. In the New Hash Rule dialog box, click `Browse.`
4. Browse to and select the file you want to create a hash rule for.
5. Click `Open` to confirm this file and return to the dialog box.
6. The file hash is created and placed in the `hash` text box, and the information windows are automatically filled, as shown in Figure 8-27.
7. Select "disallowed" or "unrestricted." If the Security Level is unrestricted, to disallow this particular program, select "disallowed."

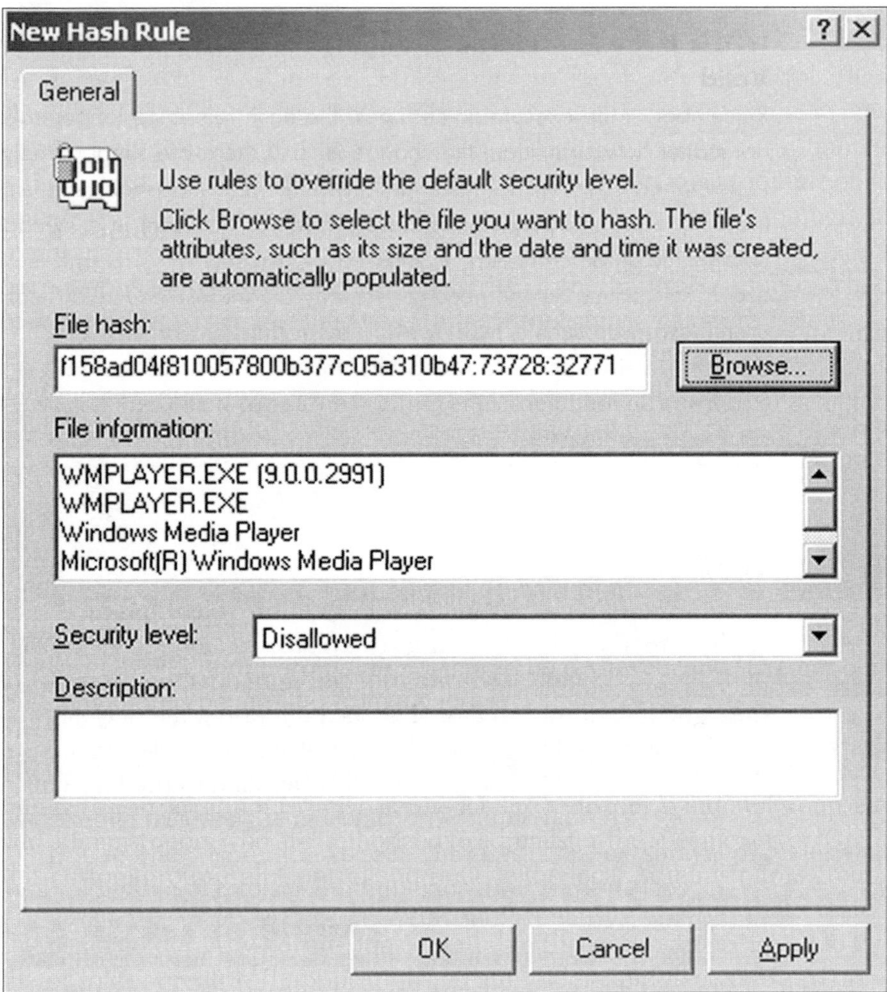


**Figure 8-27** After you browse to a file, the hash is copied from the digital signature of the file or is created for you.

If the Security Level is disallowed, then select "unrestricted" to allow the program to run. Remember: "Disallowed" will prevent the program from running, and "unrestricted" will permit the program to run.

8. Enter a description for the rule.
9. Click the OK button to finish the rule and return to the policy.

**NOTE: If the Executable Changes, the Hash Rule Is No Longer Valid**

Remember: If the executable changes, the hash rule is no longer valid. It does not matter how significant the change is, and there are simple, freely available tools that can be used to make minor modifications. Reshack.exe is such a tool. It is often used to modify the resources (such as the icon) in a Windows executable file. A determined user may easily discover this tool and learn how to use it. This points out the need for security awareness education, not to teach users how to do such a modification, but rather for administrators to recognize that it is possible and to develop alternatives to technical controls. It also makes a better case for establishing the use of "disallow all" and then only allowing approved executables.

### *Certificate Rules*

Certificate rules can restrict or allow software based on the digital signature applied to the file. A certificate rule specifies a code-signing software publisher certificate. The rule uses the signed hashes from the signature of the signed file to match files. The location of the file does not matter. If the software is signed by one of the certificates identified in a certificate rule, then the security level specified will be applied to the file. This type of rule might be used if a company's policy is to require that all ActiveX scripts are signed by a specific digital signature.

Certificate rules apply only to the file types identified in the Designated Files types folder. To write a certificate rule, you must have a copy of the certificate associated with the signed files. The use of certificate rules must also be enabled using Group Policy. For example, to use a certificate rule to allow only those VB scripts that are signed by your organization's code-signing certificate, you must do the following:

- Enable Certificate Rules in Group Policy.
- Sign your VB scripts.
- Extract a copy of the certificate to an accessible file location.
- Add a path rule that disallows all scripts of this type, such as *.VBS.
- Create a certificate rule that identifies your certificate and set the security policy to "unrestricted."

To enable the use of certificates rules, do this:

1. Open the Group Policy that affects this machine (Group Policy Object in Active Directory or Local Security Policy).
2. Navigate to `Local Security Policy, Security Options.`
3. Double-click on the option `System Settings: Use certificate rules on Windows executables for Software Restriction Policies.`
4. Select `Enabled.`
5. Click `OK` to close and assign the new security settings.

To create a certificate rule, follow these steps:

1. Open the Software Restriction Policy.
2. Right-click on the `Additional Rules` folder and select `Create New certificate rule.`
3. Browse to select a certificate.
4. Select a security level.
5. Click `OK` to complete the rule.

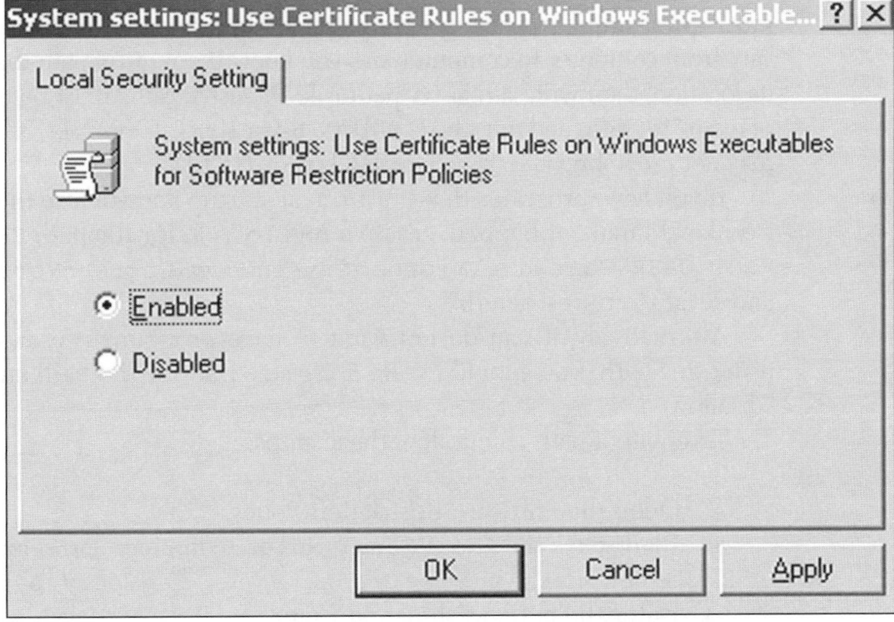


**Figure 8-28** To enable certificate rules, you must enable a Security Option.

### *Internet Zone Rules*

Internet zone rules only apply to applications that use the Windows Installer packages to install. Internet zone rules determine if an application from a site in that zone can be installed. All zones can be selected, including Local Computer, Internet, Local Intranet, Restricted Sites, and Trusted Sites.

To create an Internet zone rule, do the following:

1. Open the Software Restriction Policy.
2. Right-click on the `Additional Rules` folder and select `Create New Internet Zone rule.`
3. Select the zone to control.
4. Select a security level for the rule, as shown in Figure 8-29.
5. Click `OK` to complete the rule.

### *Path Rules and Registry Path Rules*

Path rules set restriction policies for software that is stored in or below that path. There are file path rules and registry path rules. You may use wildcards, such as * and ?, and environmental variables, such as %program files% or %system root%, in defining your file system path. If the location in the file system may vary from computer to computer and you know the registry path that specifies its location, then write a registry path rule. Registry paths must be enclosed in percent "%" signs and must be of a REG_SZ or REG_EXPAND_SZ value. You may not use abbreviations such as HKLM or HKLU.

If you have programs that must run at startup and you use the Run registry key to make it happen, create a registry rule for the path `HKEY_CURRENT_USER\Software\Microsoft\Windows\CurrentVersion\Run` and set it to "unrestricted."

Alternatively, if you do not want to have programs run at startup by using this path, you should create a registry rule for the path and set it to "disallowed."

To create a path rule follow these steps:

1. Open the Software Restriction Policy.
2. Right-click the `Additional Rules` container and select `Create a new path rule` or `Create a new registry path rule.`
3. Enter the path, as shown in Figure 8-30.
4. Click `OK` to close the windows and create the policy.

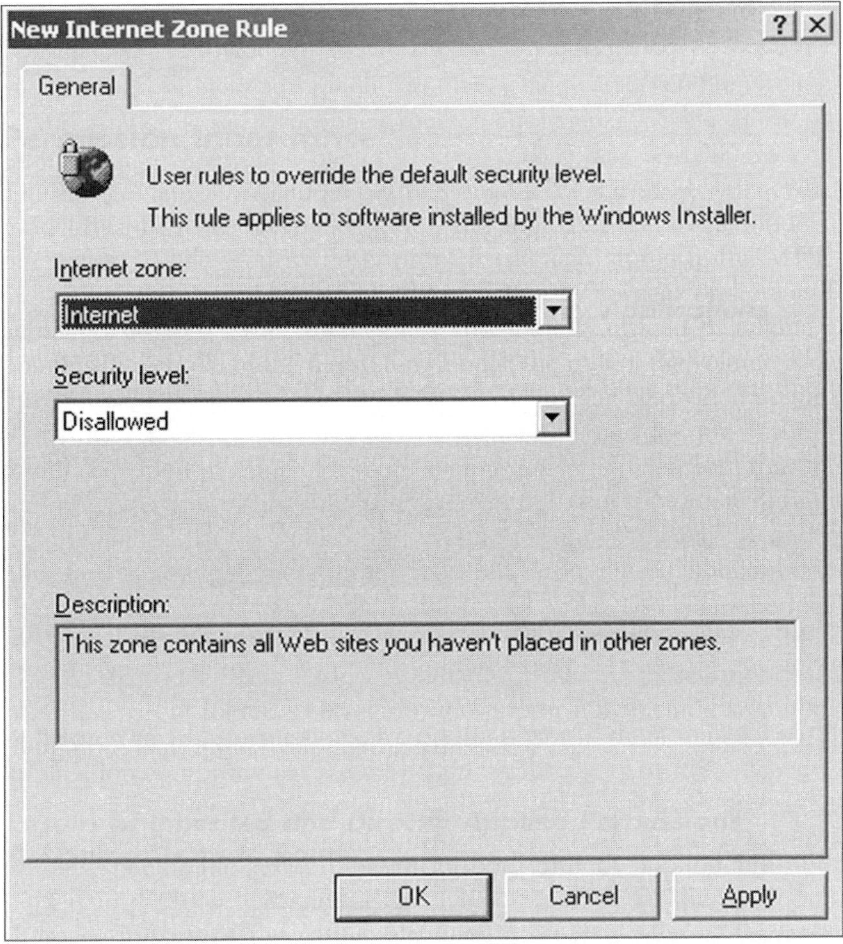


**Figure 8-29** Zone rules determine if software can be installed from sites in these zones.

### HACKING SOFTWARE RESTRICTION POLICY SECURITY LEVELS

As administrators, we are often gently suckered into reliance on the visible administrative controls presented in the GUI and in public documentation for command-line tools and registry modification. We often forget that acres of code lie underneath the public presentation provided to us, acres of code that might be used just as much for good as for evil. Don't let my use of the word "hacking" in the title here make you think of illegal activities or wanton disregard for proper testing and planning. Instead, think of it as a warning. I am not suggesting that you attempt to illegally obtain Windows source code or

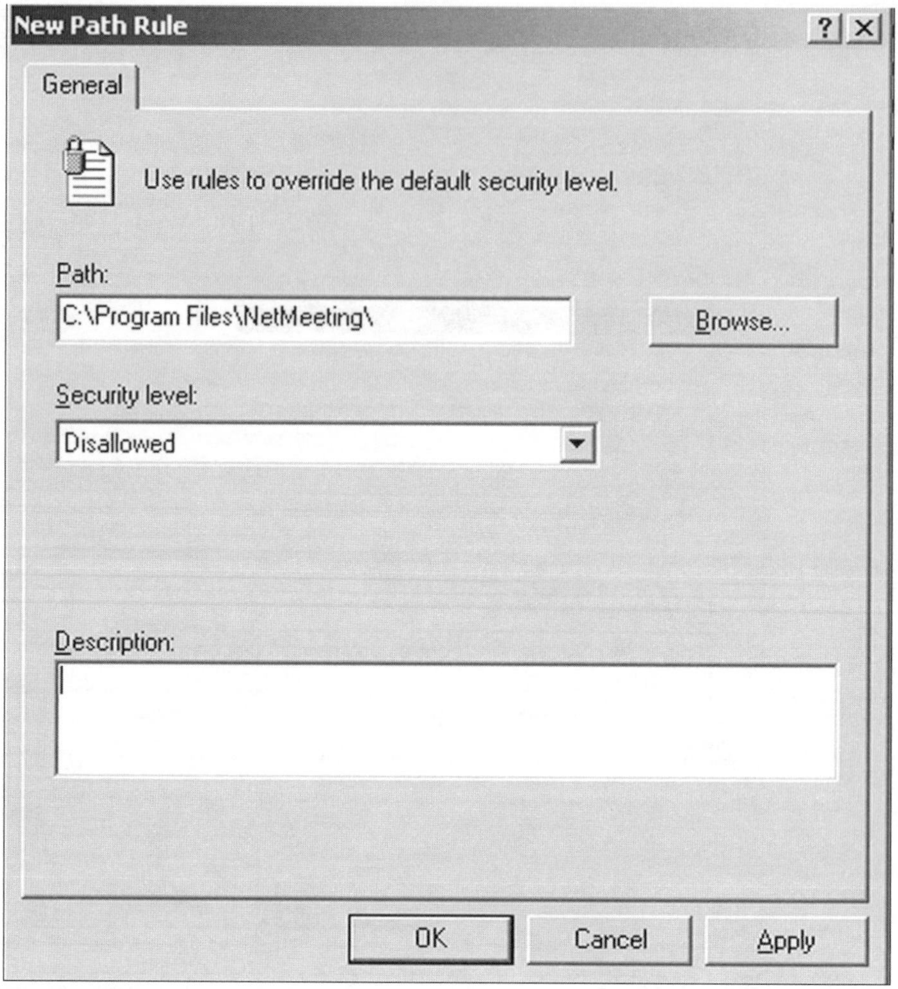

**Figure 8-30** Registry and file paths define locations where software is disallowed or unrestricted.

reverse engineer Windows to secure it. Like any good hack, this suggestion is not for use by every Windows administrator or in all circumstances, and it requires extensive testing in your environment to determine if it's suitable. Be forewarned: This hack may break applications. I suggest you thoroughly read documentation http://msdn.microsoft.com/library/default.asp?url=/library/ en-us/dncode/html/secure11152004.asp and continued at http://msdn. microsoft.com/library/default.asp?url=/library/en-us/dncode/html/secure 01182005.asp. The documentation discusses other ways to reduce user rights without using a separate user identity and includes the warning that this technology may change in future versions of Windows.

The hack consists of modifying the registry so that three new security levels are available in Software Restriction policies. The new levels are as follows:

- **Normal User (or Basic User)**—User does not have Administrator or Power user rights.
- **Constrained (Restricted User)**—HKEY_CURRENT_USER is read-only. %USRPROFILE% is inaccessible. Some crypto operations such as SSL negotiation do not work.
- **Untrusted**—Further constraints beyond Constrained but not documented.

Each level allows the execution of software identified as unrestricted but restricts what the user can do by successively reducing the privileges the user has. This is important because users may need some rights for some applications but may be able to run others successfully without them. It is always considered a good security practice to run any application with the least amount of privileges. For example, running Internet Explorer as an administrator while browsing the Internet is not a good idea. Use Software Restriction Policies and the Normal User Security level to restrict use of IE.

To make the new Basic User Security level available in Software Restriction Policies, you must edit the registry. Open the Registry Editor and navigate to `HKEY_LOCAL_MACHINE\SOFTWARE\Policies\Microsoft\WIndows\Safer\CodeIdentifiers`. Then add a DWORD value named Levels and set it to 0x20000.

## Troubleshooting Software Restriction Policies

Many problems with Software Restriction Policies are the result of administrators or users not understanding how and why policies are created. A number of common issues may occur, such as these:

- Users complain they received the message `Windows cannot open this program because it has been prevented by a software restriction policy.` This may be the expected result, because they are not supposed to run the program. Before changing the policy, ask the question, "Why is there a software restriction policy in place?" If the user should be able to run the application, look for possible conflicts between policies (inspect the precedence rule) and identify whether the policy is being applied to the correct Organizational Unit or domain in Active Directory or to the correct computer if Local Security Policy is being used.

- A user complains that he cannot run an application that he has permission to run, and has correct. There are numerous software restriction policies in the domain that may affect the user. You can find the policy that is the problem by inspecting the GUID assigned to the policy rule that is causing the problem. Each software restriction rule is assigned a unique GUID. An event in the user's log will contain the GUID. Running gpresult, a Windows resource kit tool, or Resultant Set of Policy (RSOP) identifies the GPO policy that contains this GUID, and thus this rule. Inspecting the Software Inspection Policy may reveal a mistake, which can then be corrected.
- Administrators complain that when running a utility from the command line, they get the message, "The system cannot execute the specified program." This may be a software restriction policy, because this is the message given if a policy prevents a program from running, and it is executed from the command line. Determine the administrator's right to run the utility, and look for possible conflicts. If the administrator should be able to run the program, but users should not, you may be able to set enforcement on that machine to "All users but Administrators."
- A Local Security Policy Software Restriction Policy is not taking effect. Software Restriction Policies created in Active Directory will take precedence over those created locally. Check to see if a policy exists in the AD.
- A Local Security Policy is taking effect, even though a domain policy exists. Check to ensure that the AD policy has refreshed. Check to ensure that the local computer is downloading the policy from the domain controller.
- A change to Software Restriction Policies is now preventing anyone from logging on at the computer. It is possible to create a rule that prevents some software necessary for successful boot, including logon. You can recover by booting in Safe Mode, logging on as the local administrator, and fixing the policy. Software Restriction Policies do not take effect in Safe Mode.
- A rule created to restrict a specific application is not taking effect. It is possible that the file type for the application is not included in the

`Designated File Types` container for Software Restriction Policies. You can add the file type to this list.

You will often be able to determine why a Software Restriction Policy is having a problem by exercising common sense, reviewing settings, and referring to the common problems listed previously. However, when these options do not help, enabling advanced logging will allow you to record every software restriction policy evaluation. Advanced logging is enabled by doing the following:

1. Create the registry key:
   `HKLM\SOFTWARE\Policies\Microsoft\Windows\Safer\Codeidentifiers`
2. Add the string value LogFileName.
3. Give the string value the path to a log file.

To disable logging, delete the key.

## Best Practices for Software Restriction Policies

When developing Software Restriction Policies, you will want to ensure that you get the best result. These policies can be a powerful agent in controlling what software can run on a computer, or they can hinder productivity and prevent work from getting done. Microsoft recommends the following best practices for software restriction policies.

- If used in a domain, never set software restriction policies in the domain policy. Always create a separate GPO for software restriction policies. Because no software restriction policies are set by default, you have the option of recovering from an incorrect software restriction policy by removing or disabling a created software restriction policy and allowing the domain policy to be reapplied.
- Never link to a software restriction policy in another domain, because it will result in poor performance.
- Use WMI filtering. You can create a filter that restricts the application of a GPO to, say, computers with a specific service pack. WMI filters are set in the property pages of the GPO.
- Use Security Filtering. You can filter which groups of users the policy will apply to. This is done by adding the group to the `Security` tab of the GPO property pages and (if you want the

group to be exempt from the Software Policy) making sure they do not have the "apply group policy" permissions. You can also improve performance by making sure they do not have the `read policy` permission. If they do not have the `read policy` policy permission, the GPO will not be downloaded to their computer.

- If you have problems with software restriction policies, reboot into Safe Mode. Software restriction policies have no effect in Safe Mode, so you can log on as administrator, change the policy, refresh the policy using gpupdate, and reboot.
- If you are going to change the default security level setting to "disallowed," change the Enforcement setting to "All users except administrators" at least until you can troubleshoot the system. Setting the security level setting to "disallowed" will mean you must write a policy to allow each bit of software to run.
- Use access controls (file and registry access control lists) in concert with software restriction policies. Users will attempt to go around policies by moving files, overwriting files, or adding other copies to other locations. You can deny them the ability to do so.
- Before implementing policies, test them in a test network. If policies are to be used in a domain, test them in a test domain.
- Do not guess about the effects of setting restrictions on files. Disallowing some files to run can prevent the system from running or can make it unstable.
- Filter software restriction policy application when applied in a domain policy by denying read and apply policy permissions on the GPO.
- Manage the designate file types container. This defines what file types besides EXE and DLL are considered to be programs. If you use "disallow" rules, which disallow all programs, and the file type is not defined here, the software will run. Path rules are also affected by this policy.
- Change the default on the trusted publishers from "user" to local computer administrators for standalone servers and either the local administrator or enterprise administrators if the server is in a domain.
- Ensure that users must periodically log off and log back on to systems. (When a new software restriction policy is implemented or there are changes to an existing software restriction policy, the user must log off and log back on again before the policy will take effect.)

- If users are members of the local administrator group on their computer, change enforcement settings so that the policy applies to administrators.
- Write a path rule for the attachment folder of email programs (the folder where attachments are temporarily placed and from which they can be run). If the path is disallowed, attachments cannot accidentally be run, and perhaps you will avoid the next attachment virus. If the attachment is a program that is okay and desired by the recipient, he must save it to another folder, one from which software is allowed to run.

## Securing COM, COM+, and DCOM Applications Using Component Services

Component Object Model (COM), COM+, and Distributed COM (DCOM) applications are managed from the Component Services console, as displayed in Figure 8-31. You can manage security for these applications in as much as the application provides interfaces for doing so. COM+ applications, for example, may define roles that have specific privileges and permissions within the application. You can manage roles using the console if roles have been defined in the application.

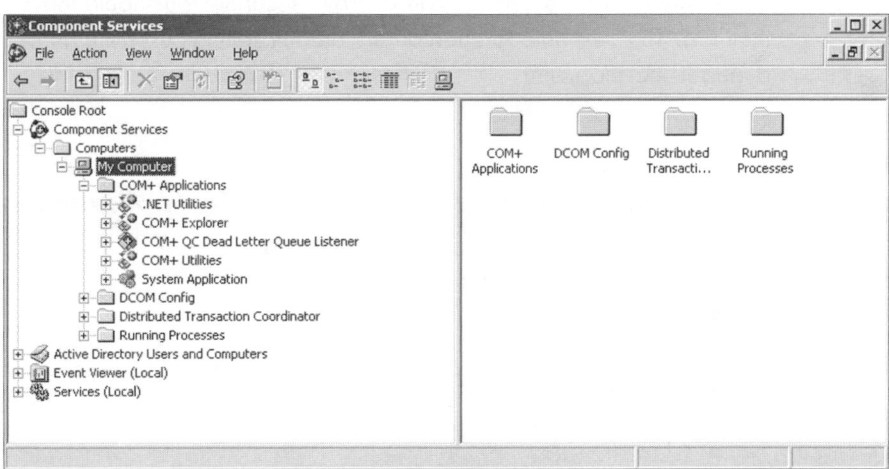


**Figure 8-31** The Component Services console is used to manage security for COM+ and COM applications.

Security for all COM, COM+, and DCOM applications consists of the following:

- Setting user rights, audit, and resources permissions such as those set on NTFS folders and files.
- Setting system-wide properties that will be used by all applications that you do not manage explicitly.
- Setting Application properties for each application that you want to manage explicitly.
- Adding users and groups to roles in role-enabled COM+ applications.
- Ensuring only administrators can modify application settings and add users to roles.
- Limiting the number of administrators who can modify COM+ security.

---

**WARNING: Don't Adjust Existing COM+ Application Properties**

It is not recommended that you adjust application properties because applications may contain code that requires the default settings to be in place. Modifying settings may cause an application to fail, become unstable, or behave less securely. Unless you thoroughly understand the application and know why modifying settings can improve security, you should leave settings as they are. The best time to question the default settings used on an application is during its development.

---

### *Configuring Security for COM and COM+ Application Interaction*

A number of properties can be configured:

- Authentication level for calls
- Authorization
- Security Level
- Impersonation
- Identification
- Launch Permissions
- Access Permissions

### *Authentication Level for Calls*

An identity is a characteristic such as a user ID or computer name. Authentication is the process by which an identity proves it is who it claims to be. Calls to COM+ components may be restricted to users with a specific role, in which case authentication is used to determine if the user is who they say they are, and then their membership is checked.

---

**NOTE: Resource**

You can learn more about managing COM+ applications from the platform Software Development KIT (SDK). You can locate a copy online at the MSDN site, http://msdn.microsoft.com.

---

Authentication level is specified in the Component Services tool, or it can be managed programmatically using Administrative SDK functions. COM+ server and client applications can require authentication. Authentication can be set to a range of degrees, from none to encryption of every packet and all method call parameters. The following list is ordered from no authentication to the highest level. Authentication is negotiated between the client and the server, and the more secure setting of the two is used. You can control authentication from the server side by setting authentication to the highest level you desire. Machine-wide settings (the default is connect) are used if the authentication level is not set for an application. Authentication levels are as follows:

- **None**—No authentication occurs.
- **Connect**—Credentials are checked only when a connection is made.
- **Call**—Credentials are checked at the beginning of each call.
- **Packet**—Credentials are checked, and verification that all called data is received takes place.
- **Packet integrity**—Credentials are checked, and verification that call data has not changed in transit takes place.
- **Packet privacy**—Credentials are checked, and verification that all information in the packet, including sender's identity and signature, are encrypted

To set machine-wide authentication level, follow these steps:

1. Open the Component Services administrative tool.
2. Right-click on the `Computer` container and click `Properties`.
3. Select the `Default Properties` tab, as shown in Figure 8-32.

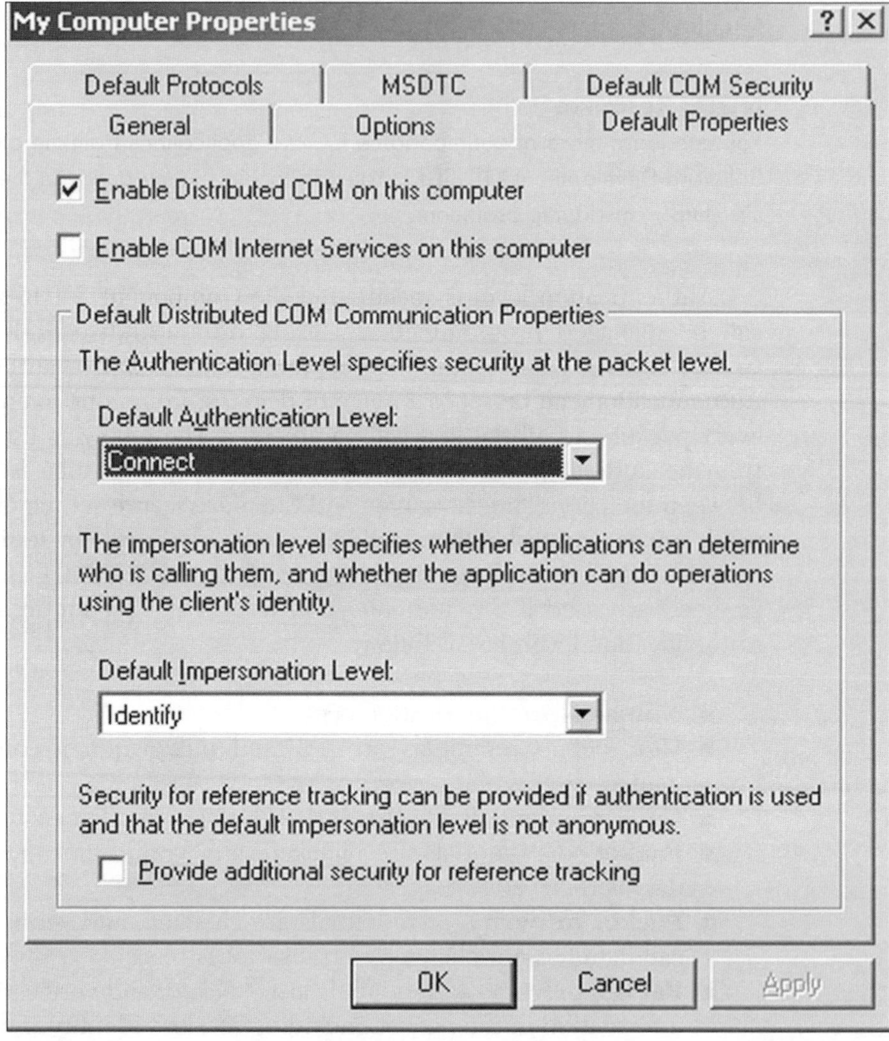


**Figure 8-32** The default properties of the application can enable the use of application-defined roles.

4. Ensure that the `Enable Distributed COM on this computer` option is checked.
5. Use the `Default Authentication Level` box to select a value.
6. Click `OK`.

### *Authorization*

If role-based security is available in the COM+ application, enable authorization checking. Users who access the application are checked for role membership before being authorized to do anything in the application. To enable authorization checking, follow these these steps:

1. Open the Component Services console.
2. Right-click on the `COM+ application,` and then click `Properties.`
3. Select the `Security` tab.
4. In the `Authorization` box, select the `Enforce access checks for this application` check box, as shown in Figure 8-33.
5. Click `OK`.

### *Security Level*

The security level sets the level at which access level checks are performed in role-enabled COM+ applications. Access checks can be set at the component level or at the process level. Setting access checks at the component level enables roles. Roles can be assigned to components, interfaces, and methods within the COM+ application. Process-level access checks apply only to application boundaries.

To set a security level, follow these steps:

1. Open the Component Services console.
2. Right-click the application and click `Properties.`
3. Select the `Security` tab.
4. Under Security level, as shown in Figure 8-33, select either
   `Perform access checks only at the process level`
   or
   `Perform access checks at the process and component level`
5. Click `OK`.
6. Restart the application for the checks to take place.

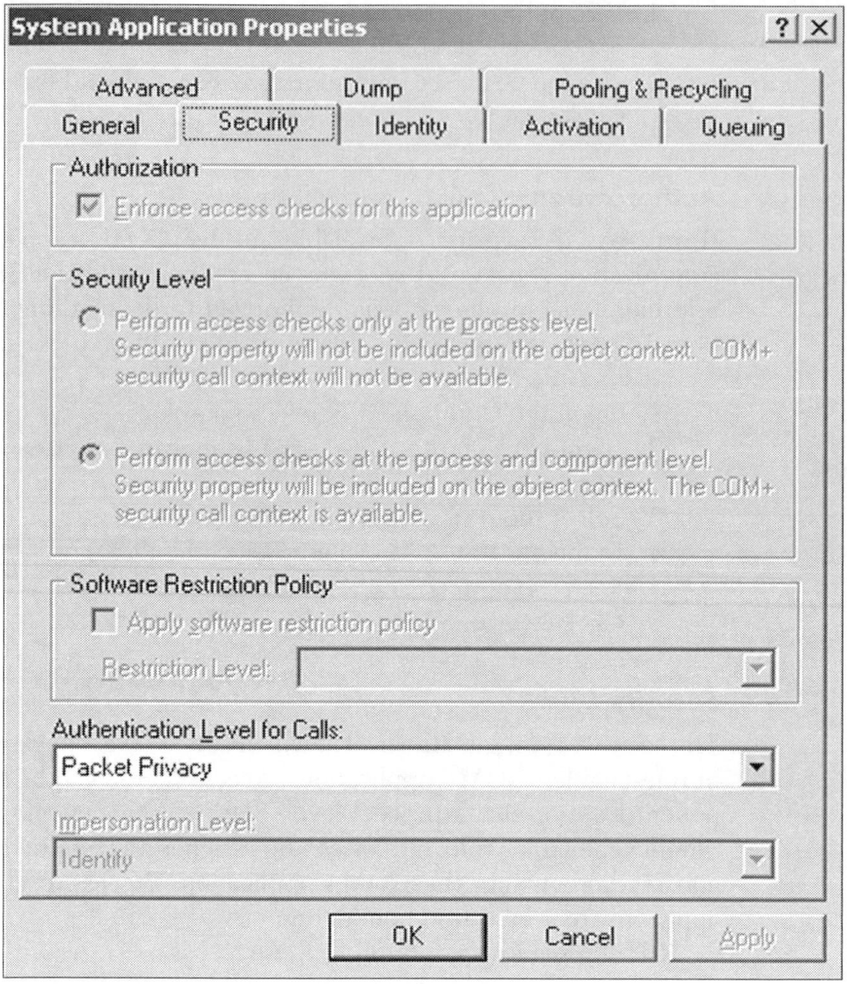

**Figure 8-33** Use the Security tab to set authorization level, security level, and impersonation level.

### *Impersonation and Delegation*

When a server makes a call on behalf of a client and uses the client's credentials instead of its own, it is performing impersonation. Resource access is thus expanded, or restricted, depending on what the user can do. For example, you may need the server application to access data in a database, in which case you would want it to be able to get any data that the client has permission to access.

Impersonation levels are as follows:

- **Anonymous**—Client is anonymous as far as the server is concerned. The server can impersonate the client, but no information about the client is in the impersonation token.
- **Identify**—The default; the server can obtain the client's identity and can impersonate. Used for determining access-checking levels.
- **Impersonate**—Default for COM+ server apps. The server can impersonate the client but is restricted. The server can access resources on the same computer as the client. If the server is on the same computer as the client, it can access network resources on the client's behalf. If it is not, it can only access resources on the computer it resides on.
- **Delegate**—The server can impersonate the client, whether or not it is on the same computer as the client. Client credentials can be passed to any number of machines.

To set the impersonation level, follow these steps:

1. Open the Component Services console.
2. Right-click the application and click `Properties`.
3. Select the `Security` tab.
4. Use the `Impersonation Level` box, as shown previously in Figure 8-32, to set the impersonation level.
5. Click `OK`.
6. Restart the application for the checks to take place.

Delegation is a special type of impersonation used over the network. The server and client applications do not reside on the same computer, and yet the server uses the client's identity to access resources on a third remote machine. Delegation is controlled with the Active Directory Service. Two requirements must be met:

- The identity the server is running under (the account it uses to run its service) must be marked "Trusted for delegation."

- The client application must be running under an identity that is not marked as "Account is sensitive and cannot be delegated."

### *Identification*

COM and COM+ applications may run as a service. When they do, they run within the security context of an account or the Local System. If they are not implemented as a service, they may impersonate or act on the authority of the user account used to run them.

Application identity is set during application installation and is only relevant for server applications. Identity is the user account that the application runs under and uses when it calls other applications and resources. Library identity is not set. Library COM+ applications use the identity of the host. Using a specific account, either Local service or an assigned user account is more secure than allowing the identity to be interactive. Interactive means that the COM+ application runs with the authority of the logged on user. If, for example, the local administrator is logged on, COM+ applications could be running with his authority and could be used to make calls and access resources, even for clients. If no one is logged on, then the application cannot be run. Identity can be set to this:

- **Interactive**—The user who is logged on
- **Local service user**—An account with minimal permissions to run a locally accessible service
- A specific valid user account

---

**WARNING: Password Storage for COM+ Identity**

COM+ stores passwords in LSA secrets, and thus an administrator can obtain them. Be sure to use an account created just for the COM+ application and deny the account the right to log on locally.

---

### *Launch Permissions*

Launch permissions specify a list of users who can be granted or denied permission to run or launch component model applications. When set in the properties of the computer, permission to launch is conferred for all applications that do not set their own launch permissions list. The default list is INTERACTIVE (anyone logged on locally), SYSTEM, and Administrators.

To set launch permissions:

1. Open the Component Services console.
2. Right-click the computer you want to set system-wide launch permissions for and click `Properties`.
3. Select the `Default COM Security` tab.
4. In the `Launch Permissions` box, select `Edit Default`, as shown in Figure 8-34.
5. Add user groups and assign them the launch permissions, either Allow or Deny.

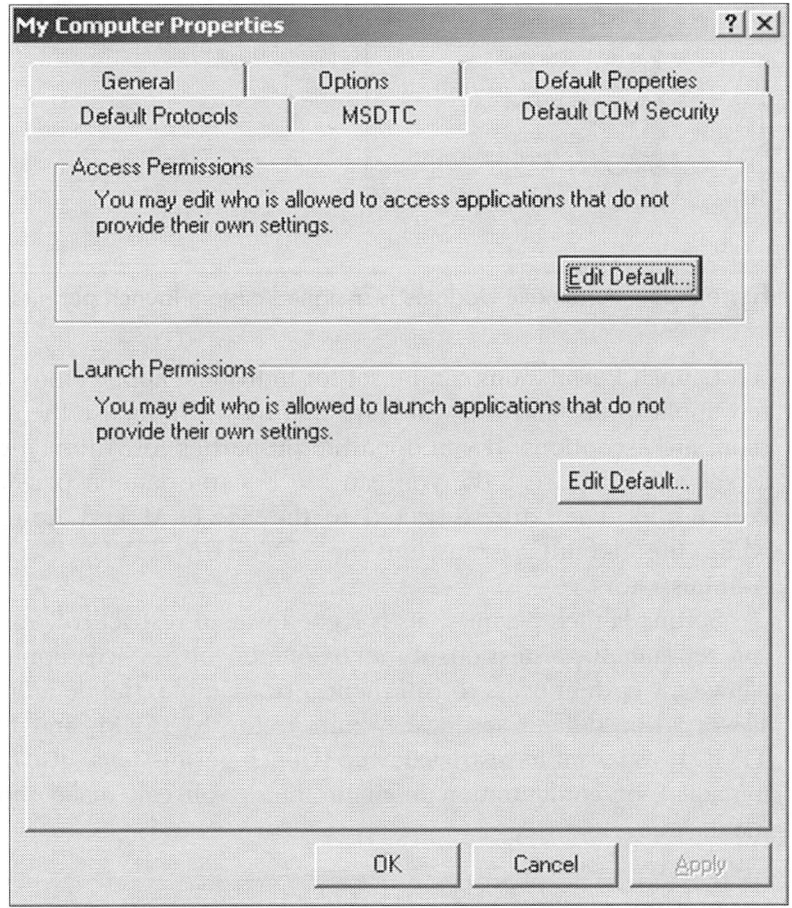


**Figure 8-34** Launch Permissions are set from the Default COM Security tab.

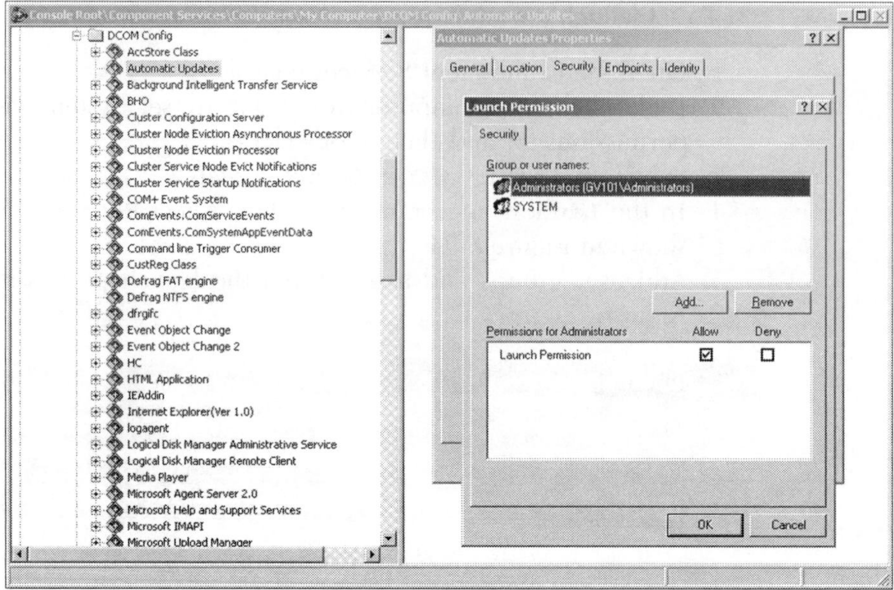


**Figure 8-35** Automatic Updates is assigned custom launch permissions.

Launch Permissions can be set for individual applications. Examine a few applications, and you will learn that most simply use the default, but there are exceptions. If you open the properties for Automatic Updates, as shown in Figure 8-35, you can see that the launch permissions are customized. They are restricted to the SYSTEM and Administrators, while the default permissions are INTERACTIVE, SYSTEM, and Administrators.

Setting launch permissions is a good way to restrict software use. You can set launch permissions on any Component Services application and allow only certain users to run them. For example, the default for Media Player is the default settings: Administrator, SYSTEM, and INTERACTIVE. If you want to restrict startup (launch permissions), use (access permissions), or configuration (configuration), you can make those adjustments here.

**WARNING: Modifying Settings**

Before you jump in and modify settings, you need to understand the impact of your actions. If you don't know what an application is doing, don't change its settings. If you do know, consider where you might want to restrict the application's use. If you feel no need to manage Media Player so closely, well then, how about NetMeeting? Should NetMeeting sessions be run from a server? Any desktop? By anyone? You can easily make locking down Component Services applications a part of a comprehensive security policy strategy. Just make sure it does not become part of a strategy that makes systems unusable.

### *Limiting Application Privilege with Library Applications*

There are two types of COM+ applications: applications and libraries. Libraries are hosted by another process, which means they run under the host security rather than their own user's identity. Their privilege is only that assigned to the host. Library applications may participate in authentication by default, but they can be configured not to use authentication by disabling it. (This is not a good idea.) A COM+ application can be deliberately limited by developing it as a library application. It can only access the resources that its client, the host process, can access. When calls are made outside of the application, or access to resources such as files depends on a security descriptor, they appear to be the client. If you are developing an application that performs sensitive work, and you want to limit its use to only those with permissions to do that work, then make it a library application.

### *Assigning Users to Roles*

Roles are user categories defined within an application by the developer. Like Authorization Manager-enabled applications, COM+ applications may define roles that dictate what a user can do when running the application. The roles enforce an access control policy specific to the application and are built into the application by the developers. Administrators assign Windows users and groups to application roles. An example of COM+ application roles can be viewed in the Component Services console. Open the console and expand My Computer, COM+ Applications, System Application, and then Roles. Expand each role and the `Users` container underneath it. The results are illustrated in Figure 8-36.

Each role also has a description that explains what the user who is assigned that role can do. For the System application, the roles, descriptions, and user groups are defined in Table 8-4.

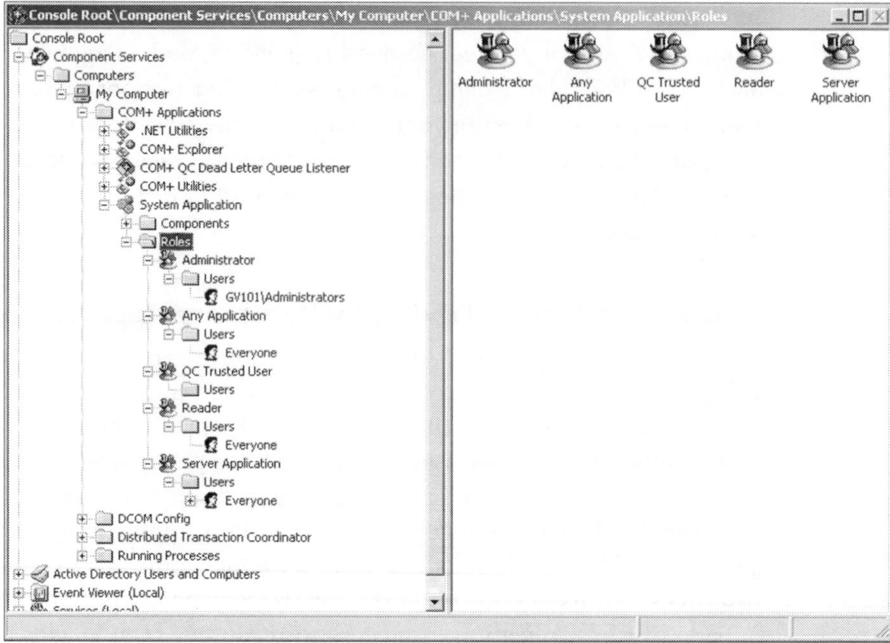


**Figure 8-36** The System Application has roles defined, and in many cases, Windows groups are assigned.

**Table 8-4** System Application Roles

| Role | Description | Default Users |
|---|---|---|
| Administrator | Can configure this COM+ application on this system. | Local Administrators |
| Any Application | Identities under which any application on this system may run. | Everyone |
| QC Trusted User | Trusted to transmit messages for queued components on behalf of other users. | No users are assigned to this role |
| Reader | Examine configuration of items and view performance information on running applications. | Everyone |
| Server Application | Identities under which COM+ Server applications run on this system. | Everyone |

An application that uses role-based security checks the role membership of a user every time he uses any part of the application. If he doesn't belong to the role that is authorized to access the resource or make the call, the call fails. You must carefully assign users to the roles that match their real-world roles. Application documentation should clearly state what each role means and what rights and permissions within the application it has. Administrators need to know which users' business needs map to the defined role. A breakdown in communications here can mean that a user who needs to do her job can't do it or that some unauthorized individual might gain access he shouldn't.

### CAN APPLICATION ROLE CONFUSION CAUSE DOS?

At the Advanced Services Corporation, a small Midwestern consulting firm, Donna Advertius was tasked with modifying the PBX system. This system had just been upgraded to Windows Server 2003 and used Microsoft SQL Server for its database of users, messages properties, rules, and restrictions. An advertised benefit of the system is the ability to record incoming calls and mail them to Microsoft Exchange so that mailbox owners can listen to their voice messages from their PCs. The company decided that this feature would be especially helpful to traveling consultants because they could check their voice mail at the same time they checked their email. The feature would also give all users more flexible access to messages. Another advantage would be that immediate callbacks could be made without entering a phone number.

Documentation was sparse, but Donna had studied the PBX systems and was very comfortable with Windows Server 2003, Exchange, and SQL Server. It looked like all she needed to do was set up SQL Mail and make a few other minor changes. Setting up SQL Mail is not difficult, but it requires a number of steps, one of which is to set up an account for the service to use and to create a profile for the account. SQL Mail then uses that account to send messages to any user account. A few quick adjustments, and SQL Mail was working.

Next, one line in the PBX documentation indicated changing the service account for the PBX system to the same account used for SQL Mail. Do you get the picture now? The PBX system would record the message and use SQL Mail to deliver it to the user's mailbox. Donna easily changed the account, and the PBX service started right back up. Good, she thought as she looked at the clock. A quick test of the system, and I'll be home by midnight.

To test the system, she decided to call her own number from the phone in the server room and then visit her PC to listen to the message. She couldn't make the call. There was no dial tone. Nothing. She checked at least a dozen phones—nada, no dial tone. She'd killed the phones. Was it some new problem with Windows Server 2003? Was the documentation missing steps? Had she done something wrong?

Then it hit her. COM+ roles? She fired up the Component Services console, and sure enough, the PBX application was listed there. A role called Administrator was present, but only the SYSTEM was assigned. She checked Launch Permissions and found that they, too were limited to SYSTEM. Because the initial PBX setting assigned the Local System as its service account, the system had worked fine. When she changed the account, PBX no longer had permission to access its own components. End of phone service. Changing the Administrator role assignment and giving Launch Permissions to the new service account was all that was needed to get the phones running again.

Even if you do not want to configure COM+ application security or don't have applications that have built-in roles for you to administer, you should manage roles on the System Application. These roles determine who can install COM+ applications and who can administer COM+ applications and the COM+ application environment. By default, the local Administrators group is a role member. While only members of the Administrators group can administer COM+ security, you may want to restrict administration further. To do so, follow these steps:

1. Open the Component Services Console (`Start, Programs, Administrative Tools`).
2. Expand the `System Application` node and then expand the `Roles` icon.
3. Expand the `Role` node.
4. Right-click the `Users` folder under the role, select `New,` and then click `User.`
5. Enter the username in the `Select Users or Groups` windows or use the `Advanced` button and then the `Find now` button to select a user or group from a list of users and groups on this computer.
6. Restart the computer for the changes to take effect.

### *Setting Software Restriction Policies for a COM+ Application*

A Software Restriction Policy can be set directly in COM+ Application properties on a Windows Server 2003 server. By default, the system-level Software Restriction Policy security level is set the same for all server applications because they all run in the same file, dllhost.exe. If you need to change the policy for specific COM+ applications, you do so by setting Software Restriction

Policies directly in the properties of a COM+ application. Software Restriction Policies set here take precedence over system-wide policy settings.

To set COM+ application Software Restriction Policy, do this:

1. Open `Administrative Tools, Component Services Tool.`
2. Right-click the COM+ application you want to manage.
3. Select the `Security` tab.
4. Select the `Apply software restriction policy` check box under `Software Restriction Policy` to enable setting the security level, as shown in Figure 8-37. (If the check box is clear, the system-wide Software Restriction Policy is in effect.)

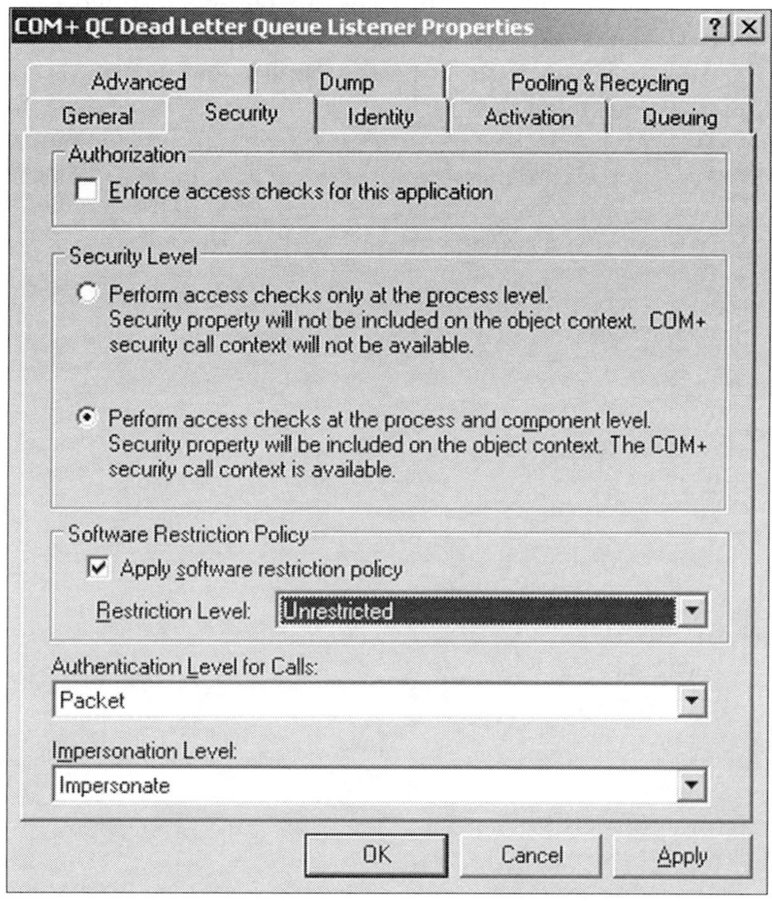


**Figure 8-37** Software Restriction Policy for a COM+ application can be set in its property pages.

5. Set the restriction level, either `Disallowed` (the application can load untrusted and trusted components but cannot use the full privileges of the user) or `Unrestricted` (the application has unrestricted access to the user's privileges; only components with an `Unrestricted` trust level can be loaded into it).

## Summary

The methods that can be used to restrict application execution are many, but for restriction to be granular, security must be built into the application in the form of roles. To be effective and easy to administer, roles should map to actual user job functions.

Even if sophisticated application security is in place, it is wise to remember that the first level of defense may be file, folder, and registry key ACLs. ACLs can prevent someone from running an application at all. If that is your purpose, even if you have more sophisticated tools to configure security, you would be wise to set file ACLs, too. The next chapter will discuss ACLs on files, folder, and registry keys.

CHAPTER 9

# CONTROLLING ACCESS TO DATA

Controlling access to data is the reason for information security. Let's not forget that. The reason for protecting servers or the network is to protect the data that resides on them. The best approach to controlling access to data is to use defense in depth. This can be accomplished by using perimeter controls such as firewalls, by monitoring the internal network using intrusion detection, by insisting on the use of VPNs and other types of encrypted data transport, and by properly managing authentication and the rest of the principles and practices that are explained elsewhere in this book. Ultimately, however, when all is done, if these other systems fail, it's the controls that are closest to the data that protect them, becoming their last bastion of defense.

Two kinds of data access controls exist—technical and cultural. Technical data controls are the permissions set on files, folders, shares, web folders, registry keys, and other objects. You should know them well; apply, maintain, and audit them. Cultural controls are the security orientation of the IT administrators, software developers, and data owners. This not only means they support, they are eager for the necessary technical controls to be properly in place, but also that they have an understanding of data security that allows them to evaluate new technologies with an eye to preventing users from getting around the technical controls used with older technologies. This chapter will provide information primarily to assist you with technical controls, first by reviewing the traditional technical controls for file systems and registry data, and then by examining new and improved data management technologies in Windows Server 2003 with an eye to securely implementing them.

## Controlling Access to Files and Folders Using NTFS Permissions

You do not have to use the Windows NTFS file system, but you should. If you do, different permissions can be applied to every file and folder. This is not usually necessary or practical. Instead, if data files are organized in folders according to data sensitivity and by ownership, permissions can be set at the folder level and applied carte blanche to all subfolders and files. If there is a need to modify permission settings within this hierarchy, it can easily be done. The hierarchical nature of the file system allows file permissions set on a top-level folder to be inherited by the files and folders below it. Permission inheritance reduces the burden on the administrator.

NTFS was introduced with Windows NT and modified for Windows 2000. Windows 2000 and Windows Server 2003 use a new model of inheritance, which changes the way permissions are applied and evaluated.

New in Windows Server 2003 are more secure volume root permissions, more secure default share permissions, and a change in the location of security descriptors.

### File and Folder Permissions

Configuring file permissions for files and folders is easy; determining the appropriate permissions you should set is not. Two problems exist: understanding the large number of permissions that can be set, and deciding which Windows groups should have which permissions. The latter must be determined in concert with the data owners. Administrators should not be deciding who should have access to specific folders, documents, and databases. Each department should inform IT of its needs. However, once an administrator understands the requirements, she can implement them within the framework of the permissions available. File and folder permissions are composed of generic permission sets, as shown in Figure 9-1 and defined in Table 9-1. Each generic permission is actually a permission set. Several special permissions are included in the permission set. Each special permission can be assigned individually. Figure 9-2 displays the special permissions that make up Full Control. These permissions are defined in Table 9-2. A permission can be set to either `Allow` or `Deny`. Some permissions are only used for files, and others are only used on folders (as indicated in the table).

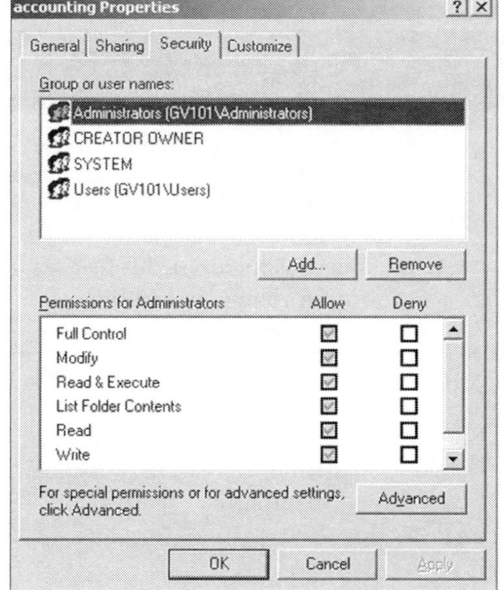


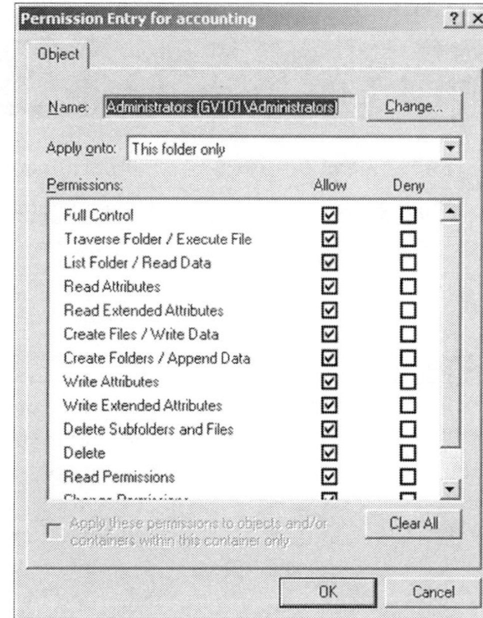


**Figure 9-1** Generic permissions sets.

**Figure 9-2** Special permissions that make up Full Control.

**Table 9-1** Generic File/Folder Permissions

| Permission | Description | Composed of Special Permissions |
|---|---|---|
| Full Control | All permissions | All permissions |
| Modify | Change data | Cannot delete subfolders and files (can delete the files in this folder or this file) Can change permissions, take ownership |
| File: Read & Execute Folder: List Folder Contents | Read files, execute programs and scripts, see folder contents.Both permission sets are visible at the folder level, but the `List Folder` permission setis only inherited by subfolders, `not` files. You will never see the `List Folder Contents` permission applied to files. | Traverse folder/execute files, list folder and read data, read attributes and extended attributes, read permissions, synchronize |
| Read | Read files | List folder/read data, read attributes and extended attributes, read permissions, synchronize |
| Write | Write files, add files to folder | Create files and write data, create folders, append data, Write attributes and extended attributes, read permissions |

**Table 9-2** Special File/Folder Permissions

| Permissions | Description | Folder/File |
|---|---|---|
| Traverse Folder/ Execute File | If the Bypass traverse checking user right is not granted, this permission can be granted to allow programmatic traversal of a directory tree to get to files and folders. | Setting Traverse Folder permission on a folder does not set the Execute File permission on the files in that folder. |

*(Continued)*

## Default Permissions

By default, Windows Server 2003 applies stronger access controls than Windows 2000. During installation, Windows 2000 applies granular permission sets to its system files. However, the group `Everyone` is granted `Full Control` at the root of the system drive. One concern at the time of its release was that changing permissions on the root drive during an upgrade might interfere with currently installed applications. Weak root file system permissions, however, weaken the security of the entire computer. When new applications are installed, they inherit the same weak permissions.

Windows Server 2003 applies stronger root file system permissions. The installation process sets access control lists on the root of the system volume that are more secure.

- **Administrators and SYSTEM**—Full Control
- **CREATOR OWNER**—Full Control on subfolders and files
- **Users**—Create folders, append data on folders and subfolders
- **Users**—Create files and subfolders only

However, the default permission set should be reviewed, and stronger permissions should be applied in many cases.

First, for some servers, it may be best to limit administrative access. An Exchange server or database server may be a good candidate for this treatment. To restrict administrative access, create a custom Windows group and add administrators who are authorized to administer the specific server. Grant this custom group Full Control and remove the local Administrators group.

The CREATOR OWNER group represents the account that created the file or folder. Any permissions granted to this group are assigned to the file or folder creator. If applications create folders and files, these permissions will be granted to the account that provides the security context for the application. That account may be an account assigned to the service or a user running the program. The CREATOR OWNER permission is often used to ensure that the appropriate permissions are applied. For example, when an application creates a file, the permissions applied to the file might be less than Full Control, thereby denying the person running the application ownership of the file. This is important because only the owner of a file can change its permissions to provide himself more access; therefore, if as the creator of the file, the user is not given ownership, he will be restricted to the access assigned. (Administrators and those assigned the user right Take Ownership can always take ownership and assign themselves any permissions on the file, but ordinary users do not have this right by default.) The specific requirements of applications and security policies of the organization may be different from those granted by the default permissions. Therefore, adjusting the default CREATOR OWNER permissions may be necessary. Default user permissions may also grant excessive permission on the files and folders they are authorized to create and should be reviewed to determine if they are appropriate. To determine the permission sets required for users, determine if users should be able to create files and folders on the server and determine where this may be necessary. It's not typically a requirement for the root of the drive. In many cases, a preferred arrangement is to provide users no access at the root and assign custom permissions to server folders where user access is required.

In all cases, permission inheritance should be reviewed. Unless a subfolder is marked to prevent inheritance, subfolders will inherit the permissions set on the root.

### WATCH OUT FOR SPECIAL PERMISSIONS

The CREATOR OWNER assignment at the root demonstrates an issue with the way that NTFS permissions are reported. When the CREATOR OWNER group is highlighted in the `Security` page of the root properties, as shown in Figure 9-3, it looks as if the group has no permissions assigned. However, when the `Advanced` button is used and the group permissions are opened in the editor, as shown in Figure 9-4, the special permissions are revealed. This combination of special permissions does not map to a task set and therefore is not displayed in the `Security` page. Take care to review special permissions on all groups and users assigned on the `Security` page.

Instead of granting the Everyone group Full Control, creating a new file share grants the Everyone group Full Control. In addition to strengthening default access to shares, Windows Server 2003 does not include the anonymous SID in the Everyone group. Therefore, even if an anonymous connection can be made to the server, the anonymous user has no default permissions via the shares.

## Permission Interpretation

Permission interpretation explains how permissions are evaluated. In its simplest form, the permissions that a user or group has on a file or folder

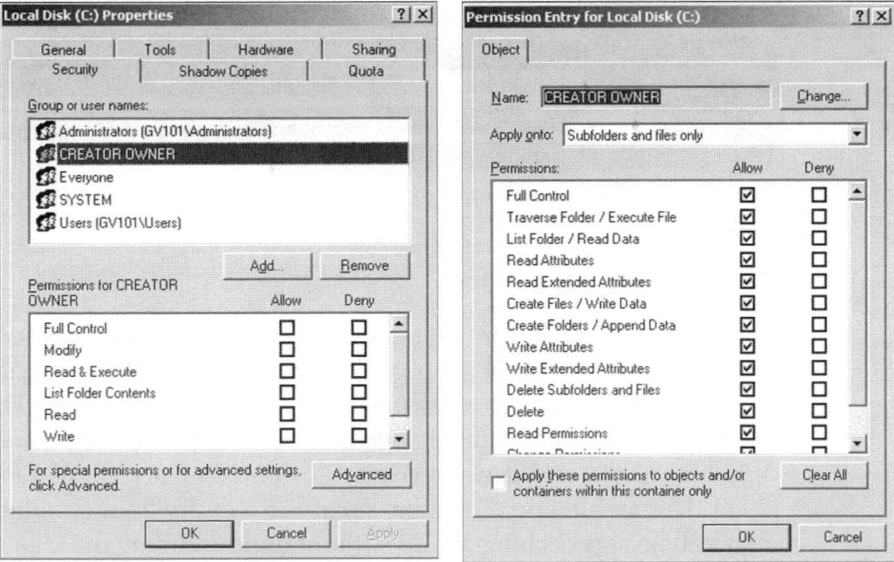


**Figure 9-3** CREATOR OWNER does not appear to have permissions applied.

**Figure 9-4** Check for special permissions by editing the CREATOR OWNER assignment from the Advanced page.

are the combination of the permissions assigned. Realistically, however, the ability of a user to do something with a file or folder depends on a number of factors. Basically, the user requests some form of access, and the operating system walks the access control list (ACL) assigned to the file or folder looking for a match. Both the user's account SID and his group membership SIDs are reviewed. If access is explicitly denied, then the processing stops, and access is denied. If access is not explicitly granted, then it is denied. This is the same algorithm used to determine access since Windows NT. However, there is one difference between the old algorithm and Windows 2000/Server 2003: Inheritance may break the old NT rule that any Deny would automatically override any Allows and stop processing of the ACLs. To understand this difference, you must learn more about the NTFS disk structure and the location of ACLs.

**WARNING: Deny Does Not Always Override Allow**

A different inheritance mode for NTFS means that old rules about access control permission may not be valid. This is true because of a change in ACL location and therefore in the manner in which permissions are evaluated. It is possible that a Deny permission may not be interpreted before the required Allow permission is processed. This is because permissions applied directly on the object are applied first, and the inherited permissions are not considered if the directly applied permissions grant the required access. More information is in the section "Permission Inheritance," later in this chapter.

---

## NTFS Disk Structure

Knowledge of file system architecture is useful should you need to forensically examine a disk, but more importantly, it can help you understand much about how NTFS works and the relationship between DACLs and performance. A significant change in the NTFS file structure was made for Windows 2000, and it was tweaked for performance in Windows Server 2003. This architectural change can affect security because administrators may still be approaching NTFS without understanding the change. Worse, trainers and experienced Windows administrators may communicate misinformation and perpetuate the problem. The change in the file structure itself is not a plus or a minus security-wise, unless you are forensically examining a disk, but it is important to understand. The primary change involves the location of the security descriptors.

Windows NT, Windows Server 2003, and Windows 2000 NTFS file volumes use a small database, the Master File Table (MFT), to assist in the location of files. MFT includes file and directory records that store and index filenames and other attributes, such as reparse points (mounts points for additional disks), link tracking information (to help in the location of files when locations are moved), and security descriptors. This is different than it was in Windows NT 4.0, where security descriptors (the attributes of files and folders that contain access control lists) were stored as attributes of the file objects they protected. Instead, a pointer in the file's attributes points back to the location in the MFT where the file's security descriptor can be found. Within the MFT, each file and folder has a record. The MFT metadata includes the $Secure record, which contains security descriptors for all MFT records. This does not mean that the MFT is bloated with double the data of earlier versions of NTFS. Instead, it only contains one copy of each unique security descriptor, which, of course, means that instead of one security descriptor for each file and folder on the entire disk, only a few security descriptors are stored. This arrangement also means that if a file has a large security descriptor (if many groups or users are given specific

Allows or Denies), the security descriptor will not be fragmented and won't cause excessive disk activity when the file is accessed.

## Permission Inheritance

The easiest way to think about permission inheritance is to construct a logical model that aligns with the file, folder, and subfolder hierarchal model of the file system. While security descriptors are actually stored in the MFT, they are applied to physical files and folders, so it's okay to speak of them as if they actually were properties of the files and folders, instead of talking about pointers to records. In the file system model, the root of the volume is divided into multiple volume-level folders, each of which can be divided up into subfolders, and on and on. Files can be located at the root and within every folder. The identification of a specific file is presented in a path that starts at the root and then may be followed by any number of subfolders until the file itself is named. In the NTFS file system, not only can each file and folder have files directly assigned permissions, but through permission inheritance, permissions assigned to a folder in the hierarchy can also be applied to every subfolder and file in the path. Inheritance can also be blocked or limited. If a new file is added to a folder, by default, it inherits its security descriptor from the parent folder. The security descriptor may include a combination of inherited and directly applied permissions.

### *Results of Inherited and Directly Applied Permissions*

On any specific file, a combination of both directly applied and inherited permissions may be assigned. Effective permissions are the resultant set of these permissions—the actual result of interpreting them. To determine what the effective permissions will be, use the following formula:

1. List the Deny permissions that are explicitly applied to the file.
2. List the Allow permissions that are explicitly applied to the file.
3. List the Deny permissions that are inherited.
4. List the Allow permissions that are inherited.
5. Review the requested access against each permission set in the order expressed above. Ask the following questions:
   If the request is denied by an explicitly applied permission, then the access is denied, and processing stops.
   If it is not denied, is it explicitly allowed by the set of explicitly applied permissions? If so, then it is allowed, and processing stops.

Is it denied explicitly by inherited permissions? Then access is denied, and processing stops.
Is it explicitly allowed by inherited permissions? Then access is granted, and processing stops.
Have all permissions been evaluated and access is not allowed? Then Access is denied and processing stops.

Windows Server 2003 also provides a report mechanism to evaluate permission combinations. To determine the effective permissions:

1. Open the `Properties` page of the file or folder.
2. Click the `Advanced` button.
3. Select the `Effective Permissions` page.
4. Click the `Select` button.
5. Enter the user or group name desired, or use the object picker to select the user or group.
6. Click `OK` and review the `Effective permissions`, as shown in Figure 9-5.

### *Impact of Copying and Moving NTFS Files and Folders*

Copying and moving files or folders may change the permissions applied to them. The resulting permission set applied to either object is dependent on on the following:

- The change is from and to folders on the same volume or to different volumes.
- The object is copied or moved.
- The object is marked to prevent inheritance.
- Permissions on parent folders or the root are modified.
- The inheritance mode of the objects is overridden.

The examples in this section can be reproduced on any Windows Server 2003 computer using the NTFS file system on which there are at least two volumes. The instructions listed were used to produce the results shown. Before proceeding, three top-level folders—test1, test2, and test3—were created on drive C:\. Each folder inherits permissions from the root, as shown in Figure 9-6. In addition, two new Windows groups—the Accountants group and the Sales group—were created.

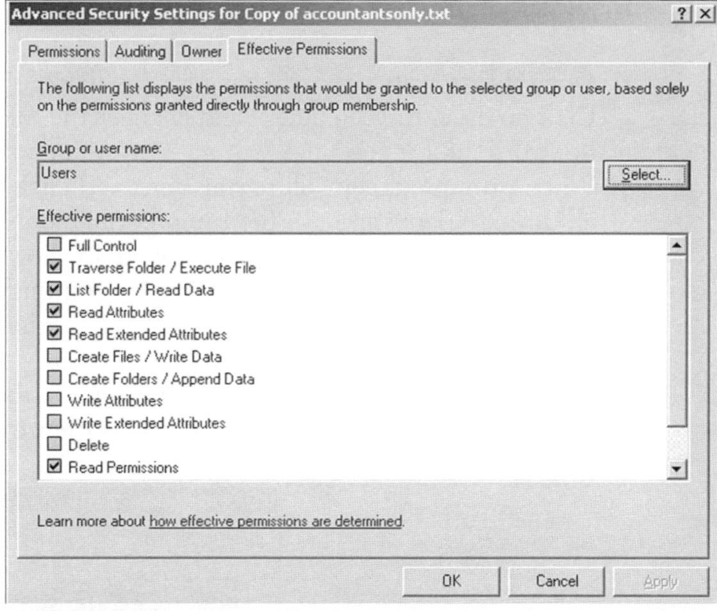


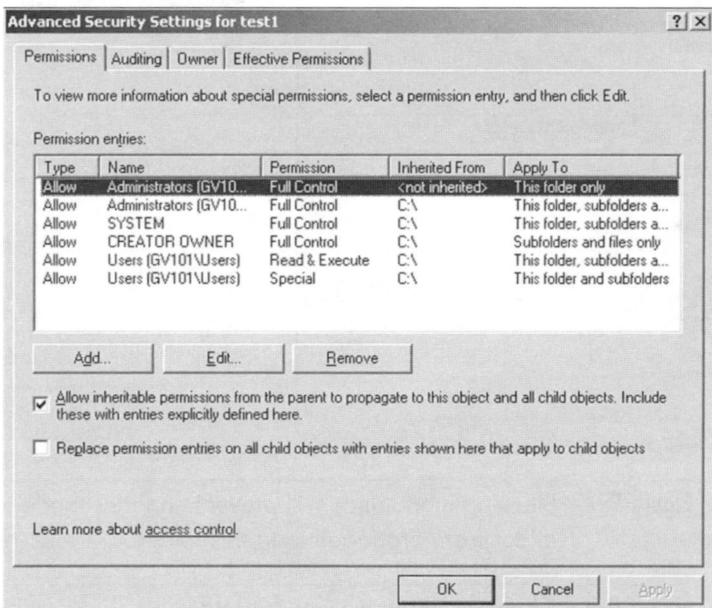


**Figure 9-5** The effective permissions are those actually available for a user or group on the selected object.

**Figure 9-6** New top-level folders inherit permissions from the root.

To prepare folders for testing, make the following changes:

1. Open the security property page for the test2 folder.
2. Click on the Advanced button and uncheck the Allow `Inheritable Permissions from the Parent to Propagate` check box.
3. When prompted, copy all permissions and click `OK`. At this point, all three folders still have the same permission sets, but the test2 folder's permissions are directly applied, as shown in Figure 9-7.
4. Change the permission set of test2 by granting the Accountants group the Modify permission, and remove the Users group, as shown in Figure 9-8.
5. Change to the second volume and change its root permissions to `Everyone Full Control`, as shown in Figure 9-9.

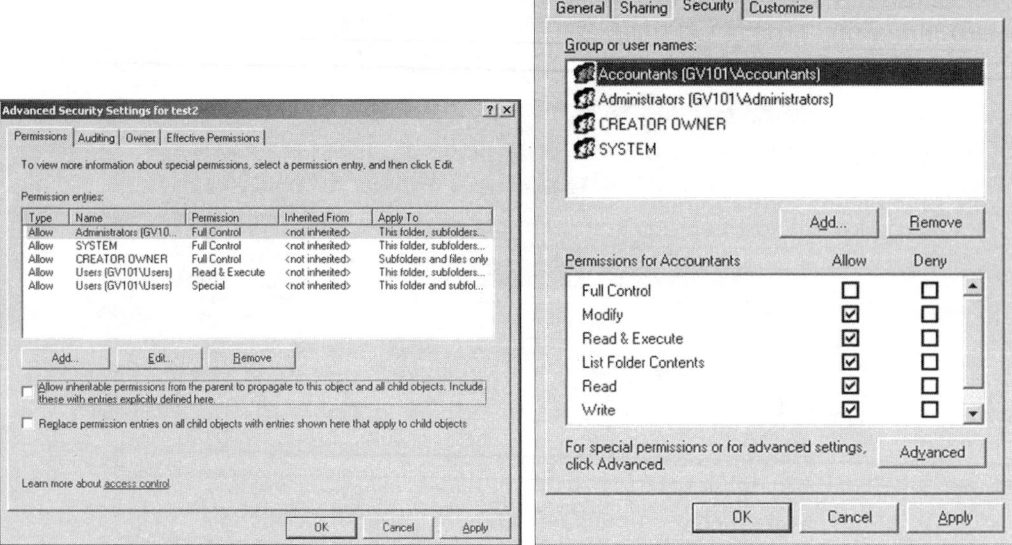


**Figure 9-7** Blocking inheritance will prevent changes made to the parent folder from propagating to this folder.

**Figure 9-8** Change permissions on the folder.

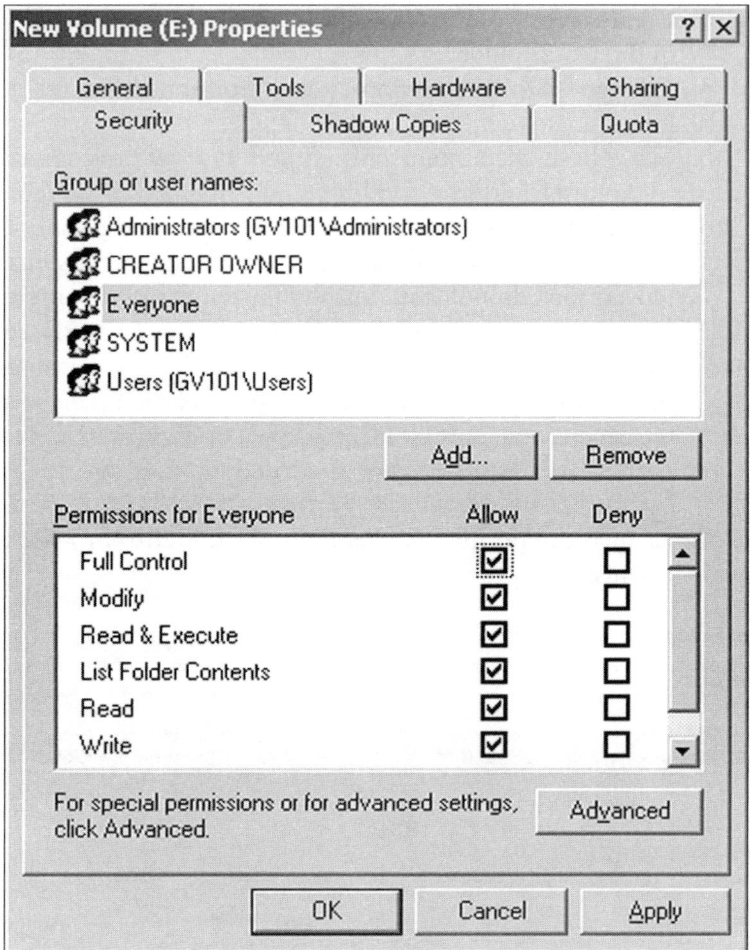


**Figure 9-9** The second volume is set to different permissions to show inheritance issues in later examples.

#### Moving Files from Folder to Folder on the Same Volume

When existing files and folders are moved to a new location on the same volume, they do not immediately lose their current permissions.

1. Create a file in the test2 folder called accountantsonly.txt.
2. Create a copy of the accountantsonly.txt file and save it in the test2 folder.

3. Create a copy of the copy of the accountantsonly.txt file and save it in the test2 folder.
4. Change the permissions on accountantsonly.txt to prevent inheritance.
5. Move both accountantsonly.txt and its copy of accountantsonly.txt to the test1 folder.
6. The test1 folder inherits its permissions from the root of C:\. When new files are added, they will inherit these permissions. However, moved files do not immediately inherit their new folder's permissions. View the copy of the accountantsonly.txt file permissions, as shown in Figure 9-10. The permissions will show that they have retained the permissions that were set earlier. This is also true of the accountantsonly.txt file, as shown in Figure 9-11. (Note that the permissions here are not inherited as they are in Figure 9-10 because of step 4.)
7. Change the permissions on the test1 folder to provide the Modify permission to the Sales group.

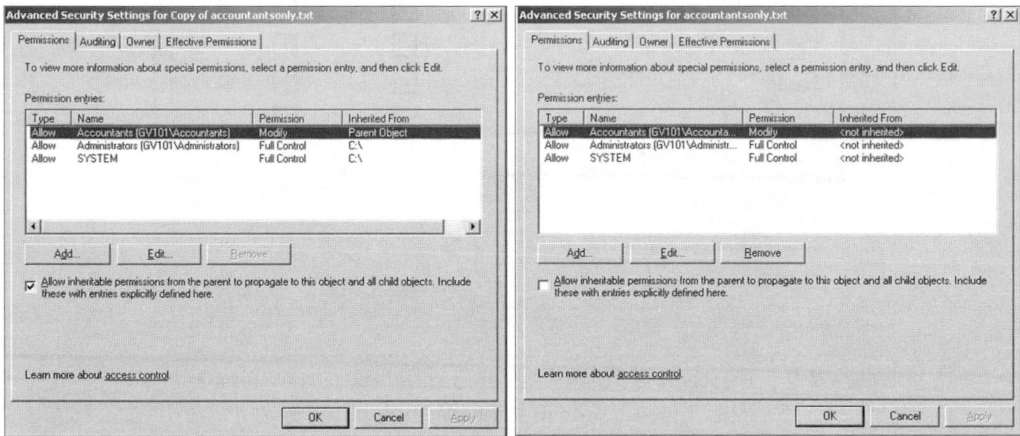


**Figure 9-10** Permissions are retained when a file is first moved from one folder to the next.

**Figure 9-11** When inheritance is blocked, permissions remain the same when a file is moved.

8. View the permissions on each file. The copy of the accountantsonly.txt file will have been modified via inheritance to provide access to the Sales group and to remove access from the Accountants group, as shown in Figure 9-12. This is because files moved from one folder on a drive to another will inherit the permissions of the new folder if and when the permission set is modified. This is not true of the accountantsonly.txt file because inheritance was blocked, so the permission set remains the same.

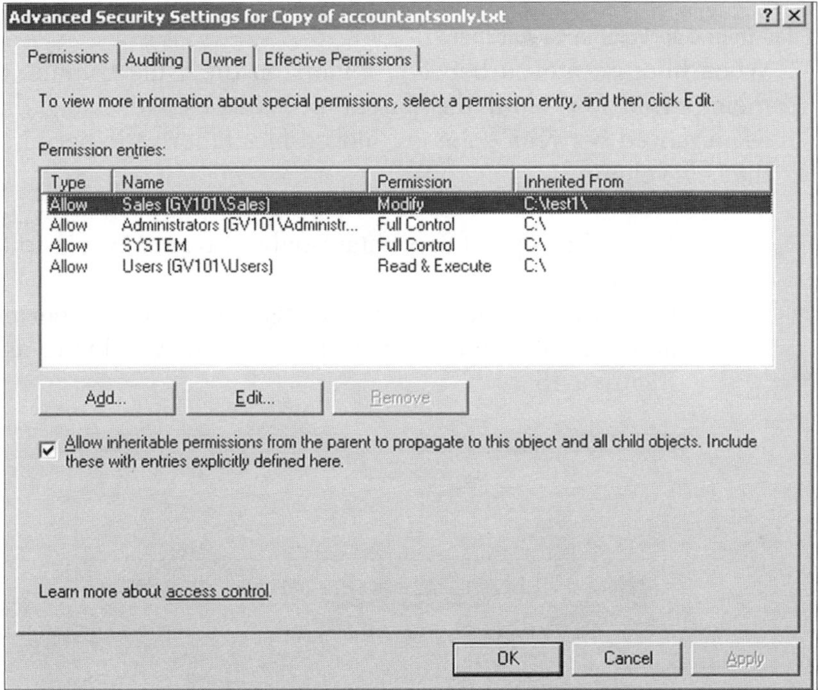


**Figure 9-12** When permissions on the parent object are changed, the moved file will inherit its permissions unless inheritance is blocked.

### Copying Files from Folder to Folder on the Same Volume

1. Create a text file in the test3 folder called forall.txt.
2. Open the forall.txt security properties page and note the permission inheritance, as shown in Figure 9-13.
3. Copy the forall.txt file to the test1 folder.
4. Open the security properties page of the forall.txt file and note that the file has inherited new permissions from the test1 folder, as shown in Figure 9-14.

### Moving Files from One Volume to Another

When files are moved between folders on the same volume, they retain their permissions until the parent permissions are changed. However, when moved between volumes, moved files inherit the permissions set in the new volume.

1. Move the copy of accountantsonly.txt from C:\test1 to the second volume.
2. Open the security properties page and note that permissions are now inherited immediately from the new volume, as shown in Figure 9-15.

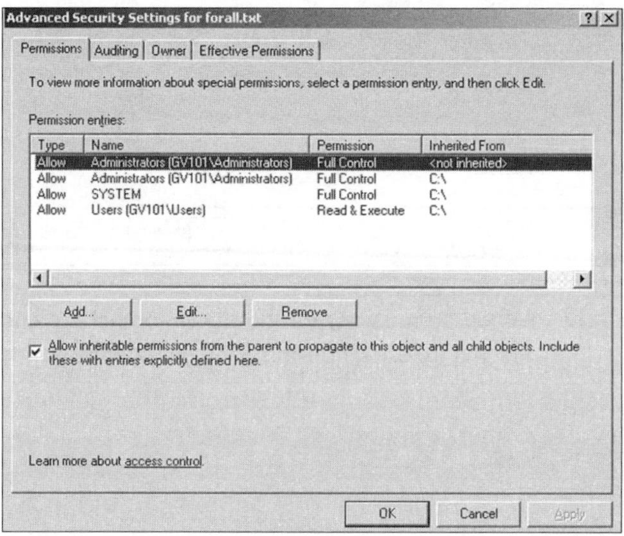


**Figure 9-13** The Forall.txt file inherits its permissions from the folder it is created in.

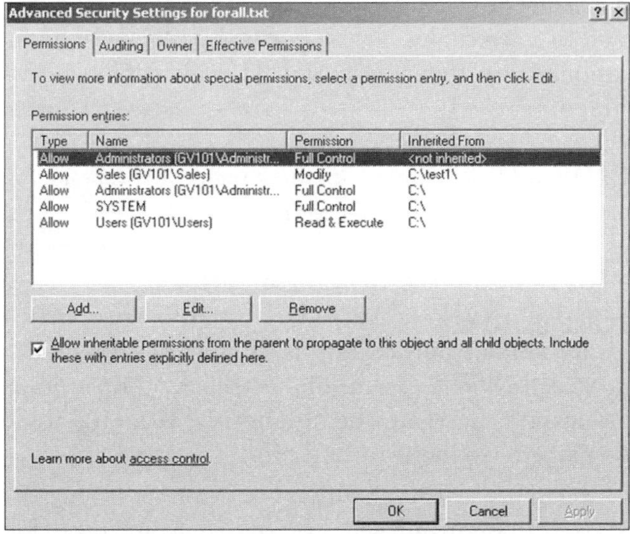


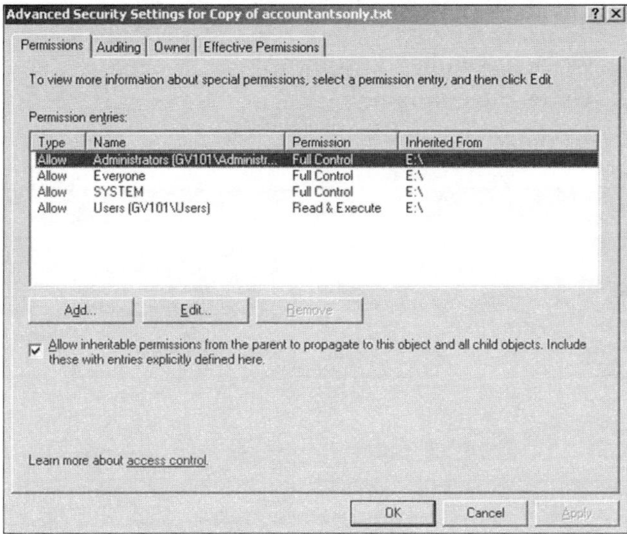


**Figure 9-15** Files moved between volumes immediately inherit the permissions from the new volume.

**Figure 9-14** Files copied from folder to folder inherit the permissions of the new folder.

#### Overriding Blocked Inheritance

If copied or moved files have inheritance blocked, the files will not inherit permissions from the new folder. However, blocked inheritance can be overridden.

1. Open the advanced security page of the test1 folder.
2. Check the box `Replace permission entries on all child objects with entries shown here that apply to all objects`, as shown in Figure 9-16.
3. Open the advanced security property page of the accountantsonly.txt file, as shown in Figure 9-17. You should recall that this file had inheritance blocking turn on. Note that the permissions have now been inherited from the folder, and the inheritance blocking is turned off.

#### Copying DACLs with Xcopy

If the `xcopy` command and its `/O` switch are used for copying, existing permissions are retained, and permissions are inherited from the new location.

1. Open a command prompt.
2. Enter the command:

```
xcopy /O C:\test1 E:\test1
```

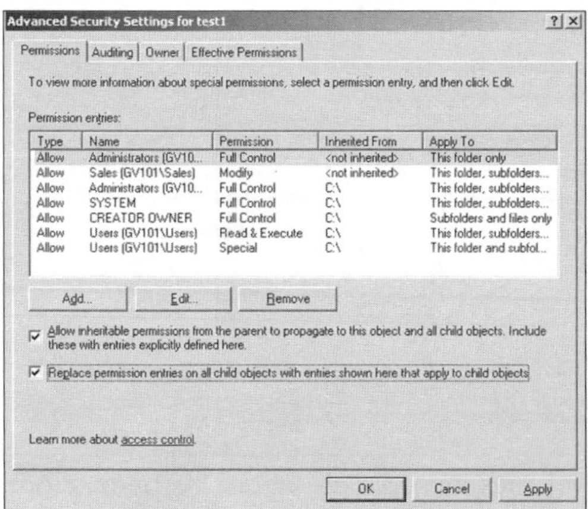


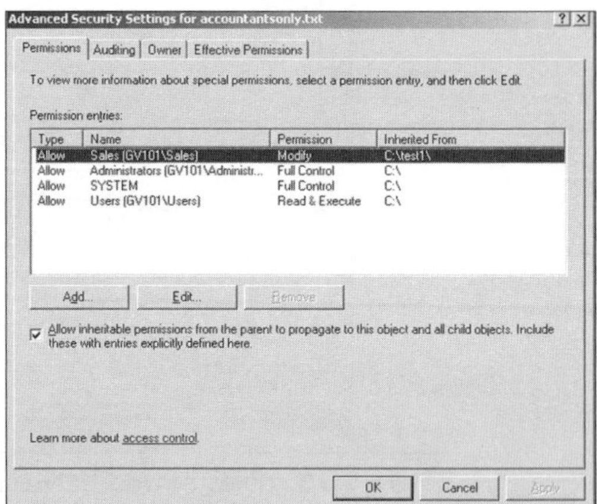


**Figure 9-16** Inheritance blocking can be overridden.

**Figure 9-17** When inheritance blocking is overridden, permissions will be inherited, and inheritance blocking will be turned off.

3. When prompted, enter a `D` to indicate that the `test1` name represents a folder name.
4. Open the advanced security property page, as shown in Figure 9-18, and note that the Sales group still retains its permission and is not inherited. Other permissions are inherited from E:\.

### *Permission Summary*

Be sure to determine if moving and copying files will have the correct effect on file access. As demonstrated previously, permissions may change. Prevent unexpected improper access control settings by keeping in mind that the permissions that are applied to moved or copied files and folders may change depending on these factors:

- Where they were created
- Whether they were moved or copied to a new location
- Whether xcopy or Windows Explorer was used

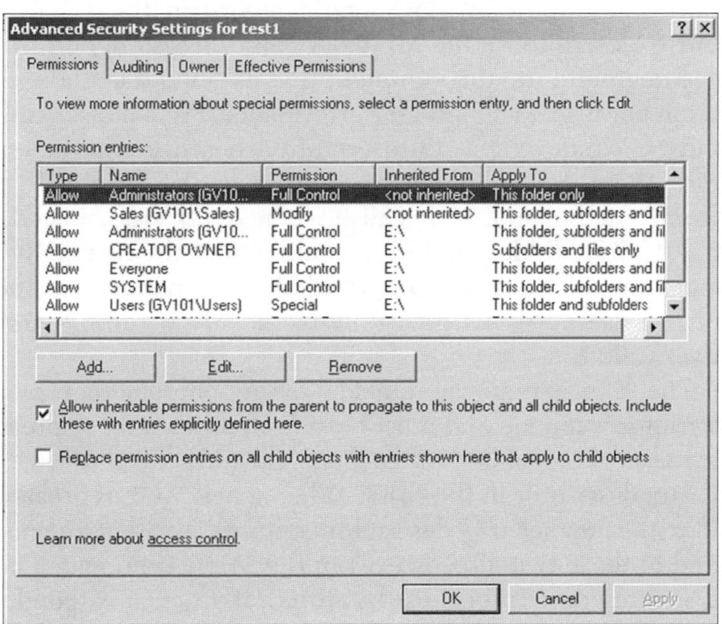


**Figure 9-18** Xcopy can be used to copy ACLs.

- Whether the new location was on the same volume or a different one
- Whether they had their own security descriptor or an inherited one
- Whether inheritance was blocked
- What the inheritance settings were on the folder moved or copied to

## NTFS Attributes and Performance Versus Security

Using a more complex file system and adding security may impact performance. The benefits of granular security must be weighed against any performance losses. Before making any configuration choices intended to improve performance, the new features and the security implications of making changes should be evaluated.

### *NTFS Performance Improvement—Location of File Descriptors*

Each file and directory contains a number of attributes. The file property $Standard_Information contains the regular file attributes, such as Read-Only, Hidden, System, Archive, Timestamps, and a pointer to the security descriptor in the $Secure record in the MFT. Locating the security descriptor in the MFT does aid file system performance and to some degree refute the argument that we should not add security information because it will hinder performance. (When discussing file system security, Windows NT 4.0 users often heard the argument that many large ACLs would reduce performance because the ACLs might become fragmented, or because when ACLs are changed in Windows NT 4.0, all subfolders and files would inherit the new ACL. Because the assignment of ACLs is now handled using pointers to the new ACL, and because all ACLs exist only in the MFT, the old argument is no longer valid.)

The file system can quickly figure out whether a new security descriptor is unique and must be stored, or whether it already exists and just needs to be pointed to. To do so, the file system stores a hash of each security descriptor in the MFT. When a new ACL is created on a file or folder, the new security descriptor is hashed by the system and then compared to those that already exist in the MFT. If no match is found, then the security descriptor must be stored; if a match is found, then it does not need to be stored. As you may already know, many hash algorithms exist for which it is statistically infeasible that two different pieces of data can produce the same result when hashed. This is why a match with an existing hash means no new security descriptor needs to be stored.

### *Timestamp Performance Issues*

Another potential performance issue concerns timestamps. Timestamps stored in file attributes indicate record creation, attribute modification, and data or index modification in addition to the time of last access. Updating timestamps does require disk activity. On a large disk with a large number of files that are frequently accessed, this could be significant enough that reducing the timestamp activity might provide some small gain in performance. However, be wary of advice that calls for eliminating the "update to last access" timestamp. The last access timestamp, of course, indicates when a file was last changed and can be useful forensics information, as a simple indication of possible tampering, or as proof that a file has not been affected by an attempted attack.

Administrators may eliminate last access update timestamps in an attempt to improve performance, but they should not. Accurate timestamps are necessary to obtain accurate audit and forensic information and to comply with policies that require it. You can determine if last access update has been modified by inspecting the `REG_DWORD` value `NtfsDisableLastAccessUpdate` at `HKEY_LOCAL_MACHINE\SYSTEM\Current Control Set\Control\filesystem`. Protect this value from change by using registry permissions, and turn on auditing to capture any change that might be performed by administrators.

## Controlling Access to Shares

Shares are connection points that provide access to data stored on Windows computers. Shares can be created at the root of a drive or on any folder or subfolder on the drive. Once a connection is established to the share, access may be provided to the contents of the drive that exist within the underlying folders, files, and subfolders. The ability to connect to the share is managed by access controls set on the share; access to data is managed by permissions set on folders and files in combination with the share permissions. While shares are created to provide authorized access, they must be protected to prevent unauthorized access and to manage authorized access.

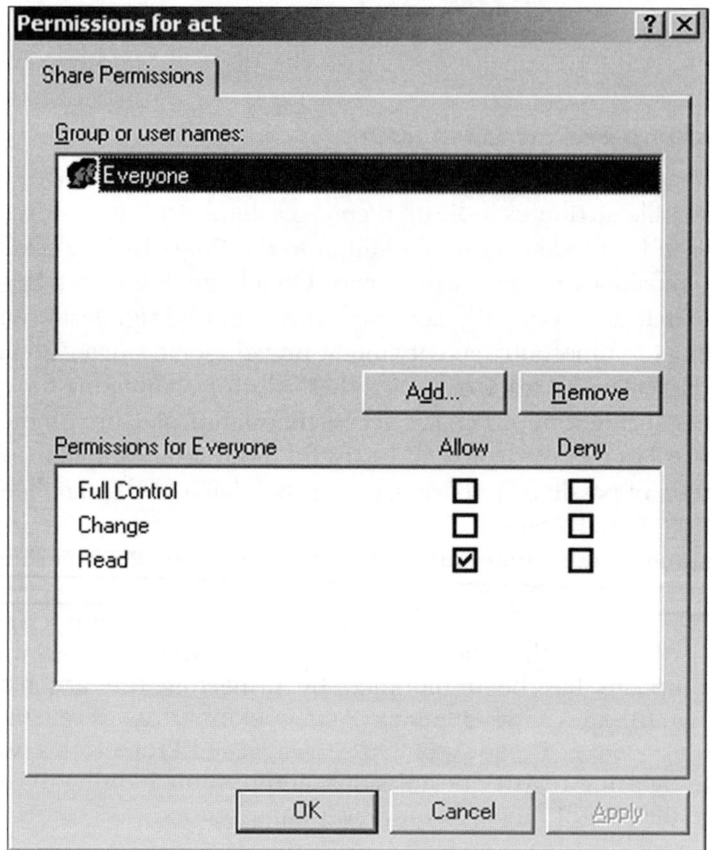


**Figure 9-19** Default share permissions may not be correct for all situations.

The default permission, `Everyone Read`, as shown in Figure 9-19 and described in Table 9-3, may not be appropriate. It may be necessary to lock it down further by applying specific permissions to the share for unique Windows groups, or it may be necessary to modify the `Everyone` permission.

Manage access control of shares according to the following:

- Shares should not be set at the root of drives or volumes.
- Permissions should be set on shares to prevent unauthorized access and manage authorized access to the computer.
- Permissions should be set on the underlying shared folder or drive to prevent unauthorized access and manage authorized access to the data.

**NOTE: Historical Hysteria**

Prior to Windows NT, access to Windows shares was limited by placing a password on the share. Knowledge of the password was the only barrier to connecting to the computer and accessing data. The FAT file systems used on these early Windows computers could not be permissioned; therefore the simple connection to the share provided carte blanche access to all of the data. Many of these early systems are still in use, and many of them have open shares. Open shares are shares with no passwords at all. All NT-based systems, when the NTFS file system is properly used, can provide solid security for files and folders and the ability to use this same user-based approach to shares.

Develop a strategy for share management of Windows Server 2003 networks by considering the available share permissions, the File and Printer sharing mode, default shares, simple file sharing for Windows XP, and the impact of combining share and folder permissions.

## Share Permissions

**Table 9-3** Share Permissions

| Permission | Description |
|---|---|
| Full Control | All access is granted or denied. |
| Change | Grants or denies the ability to read, write, and delete files; list folders and files. |
| Read | Only grants or denies read and list permissions. |

## File and Printer Sharing Mode

The default installation of Windows Server 2003 automatically enables File and Printer Sharing. Unless the server will be a domain controller, print server, or file server, this capability should either be disabled immediately after installation, or where possible, a custom installation script should ensure that File and Printer Sharing is *not* enabled during installation.

To disable File and Printer Sharing after installation:

1. Open the Control Panel and double-click `Network Connections`.
2. Click the `Properties` button.

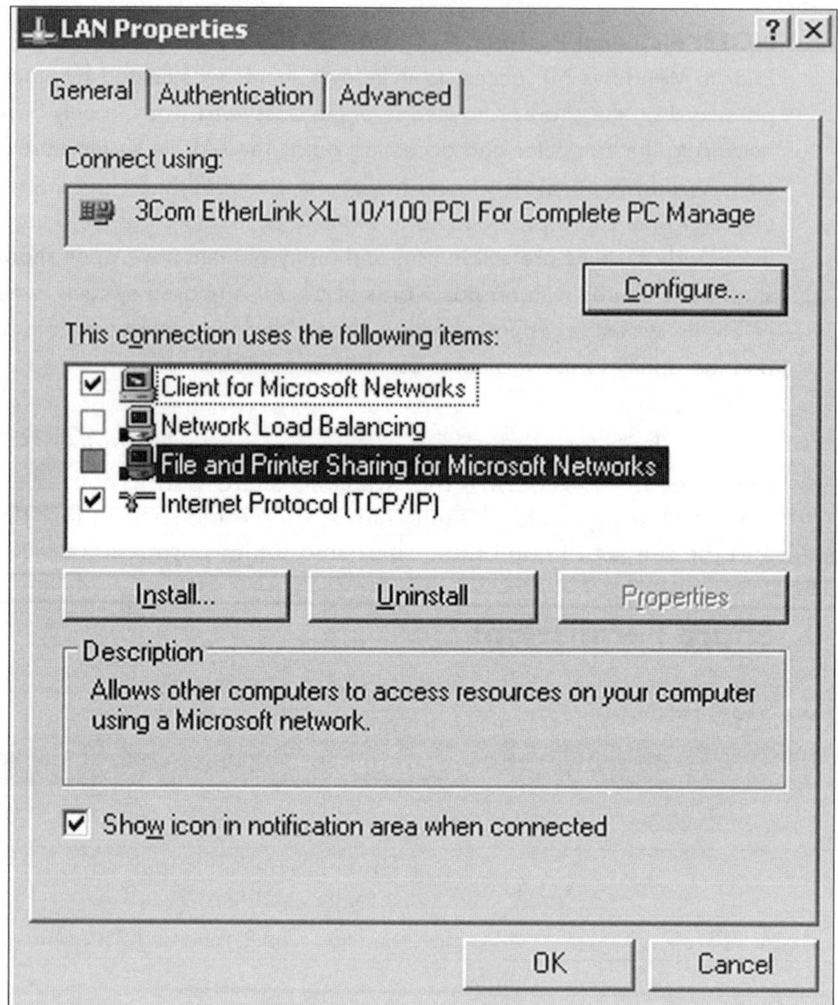


**Figure 9-20** Disable File and Printer Sharing.

3. Click to deselect the `File and Printer Sharing for Microsoft Networks` check box, as shown in Figure 9-20.
4. Click `OK`.

## Default Shares

Default shares are created during the installation of Windows Server 2003 systems and may also be created when server applications are installed. If File and Printer sharing is left enabled, access to the server via these shares is enabled by default. Access to these shares may be restricted to members of the local Administrators group, and the shares are not browsable—that is, they cannot be viewed when using Windows network browsing tools. Nevertheless, the share names are well known. Access to these shares should be curtailed by disabling the shares unless there is a reason for their existence on the specific computer. Determine the need for each share based on the security policy, risk picture, and access needs for computer roles. Weigh the risk of the shares' presence against their benefit; for example, many default shares are used for many remote administration tasks, are required on domain controllers, and are necessary when scanning for patching requirements with tools such as Microsoft Baseline Security Analyzer. The shares on the computer can be viewed by opening the Computer Management console, expanding the `Shared Folders` container, and then selecting `Shares`, as shown in Figure 9-21. Table 9-4 lists and describes the default shares.

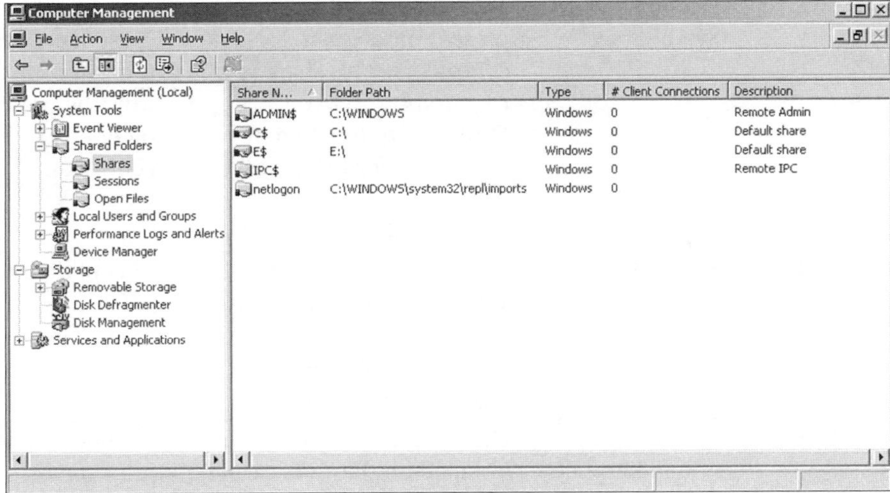


**Figure 9-21** Default shares can be viewed in the Computer Management, Shared Folders, Shares container.

**Table 9-4** Default Windows Server 2003 Shares

| Share Name | Location | Description | When to Enable/Disable |
|---|---|---|---|
| ADMIN$ | | The system folder. Used during remote administration of the computer. | Disable if using other methods for remote administration or if remote administration is not required. |
| IPC$ | | Interprocess Communication. Supports Remote Procedure Call (RPC) connections between Windows computers. The Named pipes necessary for many communications between programs are shared here. This share cannot be disabled. | Cannot be disabled. Is required for normal communications. |
| Sysvol | Windows\Sysvol\Sysvol | This share should only be present on domain controllers. This share is required for Active Directory to function, for logon, and for the distribution of Group Policies and logon scripts. | Should not be present on non-domain controllers. Must be present on domain controllers. |
| Netlogon | windows\sysvol\Sysvol\scripts | This share is the authentication share and is the classic systems policies and downlevel logon scripts location. | Do not disable. |
| Print$ | windows\system32\spool\drivers | Drivers for each printer installed on the server can be downloaded from this share. | Do not disable on print servers. |
| FxsSrvCp$ | Documents and Settings\All Users\Application Data\Microsoft Windows NT\MsFax\Common Coverpages | Enabled when the fax service is installed and is the location of fax cover pages. | |

| Share Name | Location | Description | When to Enable/Disable |
|---|---|---|---|
| RemInstall | | If the Remote Installation Service (RIS) is installed on the server, this share gives PXE (Preboot Execution Environment) clients access to installation files. | Remove if the server will not be used as an RIS server. |
| Driveletter$ (C$, D$, etc) | | Each local root partition and volume is shared but hidden from view and only accessible to members of the local Administrators group. | Disable. |

## Simple File and Printer Sharing: A New Model for Windows XP

This book is about securing Windows Server 2003. However, Windows Server 2003 security may be impacted by the security status of clients on its network. Therefore, to manage security, the security policies of Windows XP clients must also be considered. The file sharing models available for XP Professional may surprise uninformed administrators. Standalone XP desktops do not have network sharing enabled by default; instead, they use the Simple File Sharing model. It is the only option on Windows XP Home, but it may be modified on Windows XP Professional standalone systems. If the Windows XP Professional computer is joined to a domain, the model is changed to network shares.

To determine or modify file sharing on Windows XP Professional, open the Windows Explorer, `Tools, Folder Options, View tab` to display the `Simple File Sharing` check box. Alternatively, examine the registry value `ForceGuest` at

```
HKEY-LOCAL_MACHINE\SYSTEM\CurrentControlSet\Control\Lsa\
```

When `ForceGuest` is set to 1 (the `Simple File Sharing` check box is checked), Simple File Sharing is used, and when it is set to 0 (the box is unchecked), the normal Windows NT model is used. When Simple File Sharing is set the following applies:

- All access to the file share is through the Guest account. Every user who connects will only receive the permissions granted to the Guest account. Because the Guest account is disabled by default, there should be no accidental access to a shared folder.

- The MyDocuments folder can be made completely private if NTFS is the file system. A "private" setting means NTFS permissions for each user's MyDocuments folder are set to the user and SYSTEM Full Control. Another alternative is Private with access by local Administrators, which adds the local Administrators group. The All Users Documents folder is shared, giving all users access.
- Shares can be made available on the network by using the Sharing tab in folder properties and selecting Share this folder on the network. Checking or unchecking the Allow users to change my files option manages access to the share. If the setting is checked, permissions are set to Everyone Change, and if unchecked, permissions are set to Everyone Read.

## Creating Shares

When a share is needed, it must be created using appropriate permissions. Both share permissions and underlying folder permissions should be carefully determined and applied. Share permissions are set to manage access to the computers. However, previous versions of Windows NT-based systems set the default share permission to Everyone Full Control, and this is the way most administrators left it. In doing so, they missed a valuable ally in controlling access. Windows Server 2003 shares are created with the default access permission Everyone Read to prevent accidental privileged access to the computer. A default access permission of Everyone Read can have the following impact:

- Prevent accidental full access to data on the networked server. While access can be curtailed by setting permissions on underlying folders and files, if these permissions are not set correctly, unexpected access might be available.
- Require administrators to think through the permission sets on shared folders. In the past, many administrators left the Full Control permission in place and controlled access to folders via NTFS permissions.
- Create unnecessary troubleshooting efforts as administrators unfamiliar with the new permission settings attempt to determine why authorized users cannot manipulate data.

While many administrators will change the setting back to `Everyone Full Control` and only manage access via the underlying folder permissions, this is not a good practice. They do so to avoid the confusion that is sometimes caused by attempting to understand how share and folder permissions combine to restrict access to data. However, they miss an important tool for defense: if an intruder cannot gain access to the computer, the intruder cannot directly attack specific files and other resources. If there is no barrier to his access, the intruder's job is easier.

To create a share, follow these steps:

1. Right-click the folder in Windows Explorer and select `Sharing and Security` or `Properties`, as shown in Figure 9-22.
2. If necessary, select the `Sharing` tab.

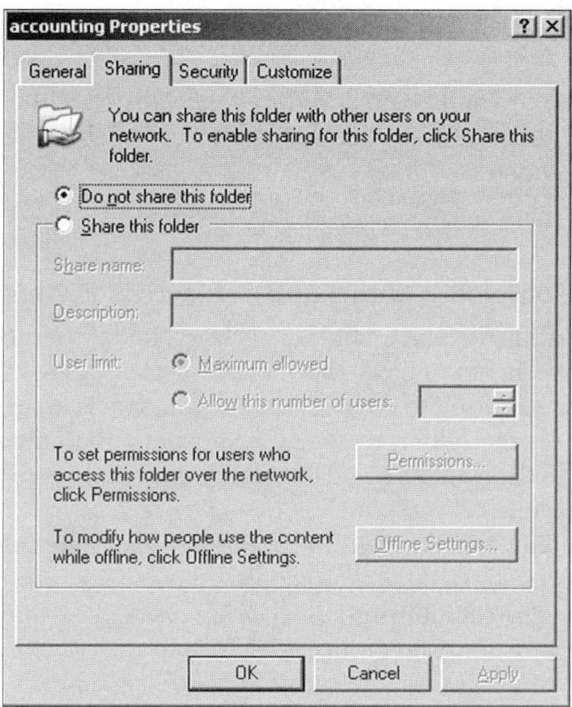


**Figure 9-22** The Sharing property page is configured to create a share.

3. Click the `Share this folder` radio button. This shares the folder with the share name equivalent of the folder name and the default permissions of `Everyone Read.`
4. Click the `Permissions` button to set the correct share permissions for the share.
5. Click to change the share name. A share name cannot be longer than 255 characters.
6. Click the radio button `Allow this number of users` and set the number in the adjacent text box to limit the number of simultaneous users who can connect to this share.
7. Click OK.

Alternative methods for creating shares are as follows:

- A share can be created on a remote computer using the Computer Management console's `Shared Folders, Shares` container.
- Shares can also be created at the command line.

The `net share` command is used to create shares at the command line. For example, to grant `Everyone Read` on a new share named "test," use the following command line:

```
Net share F:\test /grant:Everyone,Read
```

### *Impact of Combining Share and Folder/File Permissions*

The combination of share and underlying folder permissions controls access to data. In every case, the most restrictive access will be allowed. For example, because the default share permission is `Read,` even if NTFS permissions on the folder are `Full Control,` the only network access allowed to the data will be `Read.` (Console-based access is not affected by share permissions.)

Determining actual access by examining share and folder access permissions can become difficult, though, when many permissions are set. However, the correct interpretation can always be determined by using the following process for each group or user:

- Determine the permission granted on the share.
- Determine the permission granted on the folder.
- Select, from the two, the most restrictive permission, and that will be the access granted.

Table 9-5 describes permissions on a sample folder and its share.

**Table 9-5** Folder and Share Permissions for the Folder Test

| Folder Permissions | Share Permissions |
|---|---|
| John—Change, Read and Execute, List Folder contents, Read, Write | John—Full Control |
| Accountants—Full Control | Accountants—Change |
| Users—Read | Users—Read |

A quick scan of the table shows that the most restrictive permission for John is `Read`. This permission is granted to him directly, and via his membership in the Users group. However, relying on this evaluation to determine John's access to the data in the test folder is incorrect. John actually has `Read and Execute, List Folder Contents`, and `Read and Write` permissions. This is because access is determined by looking at the share and folder permission sets separately to determine what access each would grant and then selecting the most restrictive of the two access options. If only the share permissions are considered, John has `Full Control`. If only the folder permissions are considered, John has `Change, Read and Execute, List Folder Contents`, and `Read and Write`. Of the two options, the folder permission set is more restrictive and thus is the access that John is granted.

## Remote Administration of Shares

Remote administration of share permissions via Windows Explorer is not a good idea. When remote permissions are examined, only the permissions set on the folder is visible, not the permissions set for the share. Changing the folder permissions may or may not have the desired effect because changing folder permissions does not change share permissions, and users may not be given the correct access. Furthermore, when you change permissions this way, you remove the inherited permissions from the folder and by extension its subfolders. Manage shared folder permissions from the console. (Remotely changing the permissions of a subfolder of a shared folder will not affect inherited permissions.)

## Best Practices for File and Printer Sharing

File and Printer Sharing is on by default; when should it be disabled or enabled, and how should shares be protected?

- File and Printer Sharing is required on a domain controller. If you are going to use the server as a domain controller, do not turn off File and Printer Sharing.
- File and Printer Sharing is not required on a server unless the following applies:
  - The server will be a file server.
  - A remote management or vulnerability scanning tool requires it.
- Turn off File and Printer Sharing if you do not need it.
- If remote management tools are used, a server that contains sensitive information or performs a critical service may be too important to risk leaving File and Printer Sharing enabled. You can monitor, manage, and scan this server at the console or use management tools that do not require File and Print services.
- Bastion servers (servers with one network interface on an untrusted network, such as the Internet, and one network interface on a trusted network) should not have File and Print Services on the untrusted network interface.
- Remove, disable, or replace shares that are not required.
- Do not use Windows Explorer to delete default installation shares because they will reshared when the server service is stopped and then restarted. Instead, configure the `AutoShareServer` value at `HKEY_LOCAL_MACHINE\SYSTEM\CurrentControlSet\Services\LanmanServer\Parameters`. To permanently delete a default share, delete its value or set the value to 0 to remove the share, or 1 to replace shares, and then stop and restart the server service. This registry key has no effect on the IPC$ share.
- Shares for CD-ROM, CD-R/RWS, DVD-ROM, and DVD-RAM drives are not created by default; however, if you change system-assigned drive letters for them, they are shared. Configure security options to prevent network sharing of these devices when an administrator is logged on, and remove shares created when drive letters are changed.

## Controlling Access to Web Folders Using WebDAV

Web-based Distributing Authoring and Versioning (WebDAV) is an extension to the HTTP/1.1 standard, which allows clients to remotely publish, lock, and manage resources on the web. Before you discount this technique as just another way to update websites, and thus an area of concern only for those responsible for website security, think again.

- WebDAV can be used to transfer data to and from a web folder for which the user is given permissions. The data does not have to be HTML files or web-executable scripts and programs. It can be Word files, text files, or any kind of file.
- WebDAV folders allow properly permissioned users to copy and move files around in the WebDAV directory.
- If permissioned, users can retrieve and modify file properties.
- Multiple users can read a file concurrently, but only one user can modify a file at a time. (Files can be locked and unlocked.)
- Web folders can easily be created on any IIS server. The permissions assigned to these folders determine who can transfer data files to them.

Since these are the very things that server message block (SMB) shares allow users to do on a remote server, WebDAV should loom as large on your security horizon as SMB-based shares. (And perhaps it should be considered as a valid substitute for SMB-based shares, if properly secured.) Table 9-6 presents the similarities and differences between WebDAV publishing and SMB-based sharing.

**Table 9-6** WebDAV Versus SMB Shares

| Item | WebDAV | SMB Shares |
|---|---|---|
| Service | Requires IIS. | Requires File and Printer Sharing enabled, Server service. |
| Who can access data and what they can do | Depends on permission assigned. | Depends on permissions assigned. |
| Default permissions | `Read`. | `Everyone Read`. |
| Effect of underlying NTFS permissions | Most restrictive wins. | Most restrictive wins. |
| Created | A virtual directory must be created on a website. | A folder on the file server must be shared. |

| Item | WebDAV | SMB Shares |
|---|---|---|
| Authentication | Anonymous and Windows Integrated available on website by default. | Windows authentication required. |
| Authentication | Available at folder level settings. | Available at computer and domain level. |
| Clients | Windows 2000 and Windows XP; Internet Explorer 5.0 and 6.0; Microsoft Office 2000, 2003, and Office XP. | All Windows and DOS clients with networking. |
| Connection | Windows XP and 2000: Add directory to list of network places or command line. Internet Explorer 5.0 and 6.0. Open target directory as web folder. | Map drives, browse to drives, `net share` command. |
| Drag and drop? | Drag and drop file publishing. | Drag and drop file copies. |
| Command line | Set up connection using `net use` and UNC-formatted location. Uses WebDAV redirector. | Set up connection using `net use` and UNC-formatted location. Uses SMB. |

WebDAV is not new to Windows Server 2003, but in Windows Server 2003, implementation changes mean that from Windows XP or Windows Server 2003, a user can use simple UNC-based connections to copy files to WebDAV folders and use browser-based publication. For example, connecting to a WebDAV folder is now similar to connecting to a share. If the name of a WebDAV folder is `HR Feedback` and it resides on the server IAM, a user can connect using the `net use` command. Windows will also look for the virtual directory `HR Feedback` using HTTP and make a new network connection:

```
net use \\iam\HR Feedback
net use * http://IAM/HR Feedback
```

WebDAV cannot be used by default to provide access to data on Windows Server 2003 because IIS is not installed by default. Even if IIS is installed, WebDAV is not enabled by default. To use WebDAV, IIS must be installed, and WebDAV must be enabled. However, once enabled, clients can connect to and use WebDAV folders across a firewall if port 80 is open to the server. Unlike SMB ports, there is no special WebDAV port, so you cannot provide access to a website and block access to WebDAV shared data by setting firewall ports. Since port 80 is often open to allow access to a web server, and WebDAV uses HTTP, clients can connect to and publish and manipulate files on servers where connections to SMB shares are blocked. This is important to remember. For years, the security community has advised against allowing access to SMB shares over the Internet (and has not been successful in convincing companies and individuals to do so). Now, if WebDAV publishing is enabled, and access to the website is allowed, a connection is possible via the Internet right through the firewall. It is for this reason that you must develop a policy concerning when WebDAV is allowed, if it is allowed on Internet-accessible web servers, and how permissions and web server authentication will be configured to ensure the least risk of intrusion.

WebDAV permissions are not meant to replace NTFS permissions; they are meant to be used with NTFS permissions. Like share permission, WebDAV permissions combine with underlying NTFS permissions, and the most restrictive permission is the one that will be used. However, unlike share permissions, WebDAV permissions affect every user. You cannot give `Read` permission to one group of users and not to another. However, you can use the underlying NTFS permissions to implicitly or explicitly deny groups of users that you don't wish to read the files. Table 9-7 lists and describes the WebDAV permissions.

**Table 9-7** WebDAV Permissions Are Virtual Directory Permissions

| Permissions | Description |
|---|---|
| Read | View directory and file content and properties. |
| Write | Change directory and file content and properties. Modify files, change properties, publish files to folder. |
| Directory Browsing (called Browse in the wizard) | View a list of the contents. |
| Script Source Access | If enabled, users can read source code for scripts. If disabled, they cannot. |
| Execute: None, Scripts Only: Scripts and Executables | None—no scripts or executables can be run. Scripts Only—run only scripts on the server. Scripts and Executables—both scripts and executables can be run. (Only one execute permission can be assigned.) |

Enabling `Script Source Access` is a bad idea because users can read and possibly modify scripts. (If `Script Source Access` is enabled and either `Write` or `Read` is also assigned, users can access source files. If `Write` is assigned, then users can modify scripts.) It is always a good practice to place scripts and executable files in a separate folder on a website, and then set appropriate permissions. For example, set `Execute` permission in a folder that contains scripts and executable that users should be allowed to run, set `Read` permissions on folders used to make stored files available for reading, and set `Write` permission on folders used for file publishing. Never set both `Execute` and `Write` permissions on the same folder, because a malicious user could then publish a script to the folder and run it. Scripts may also contain sensitive information such as passwords and therefore should not be readable by all users.

Appropriate file and WebDav combinations are as follows:

- `Read, Write,` **and** `Directory Browsing` **enabled**—Clients can see a list of resources, modify them, publish their own resources, and manipulate files.
- `Write` **enabled and** `Read` **and** `Directory Browsing` **disabled**—Clients can publish information but cannot list or read anything published.
- `Read` **and** `Write` **enabled and** `Directory Browsing` **disabled**—Clients can open and read the files they know the names of, and publish files to the folder, but they cannot list the contents of the folder.

The `Write` access permission does not provide clients with the ability to modify script-mapped files. Script-mapped files are Active Server Pages (ASP) and others. To modify these files, both the `Write` and `Script` source access must be assigned.

To create a publishing directory, enable WebDAV, create a directory to share and assign NTFS permissions, create a virtual directory on IIS, and configure virtual directory permissions.

## Enable WebDAV

When IIS is installed, WebDAV is not enabled. To enable WebDAV, do the following:

1. Open the Internet Information Services (IIS) Manager and note that WebDAV is not enabled, as shown in Figure 9-23.

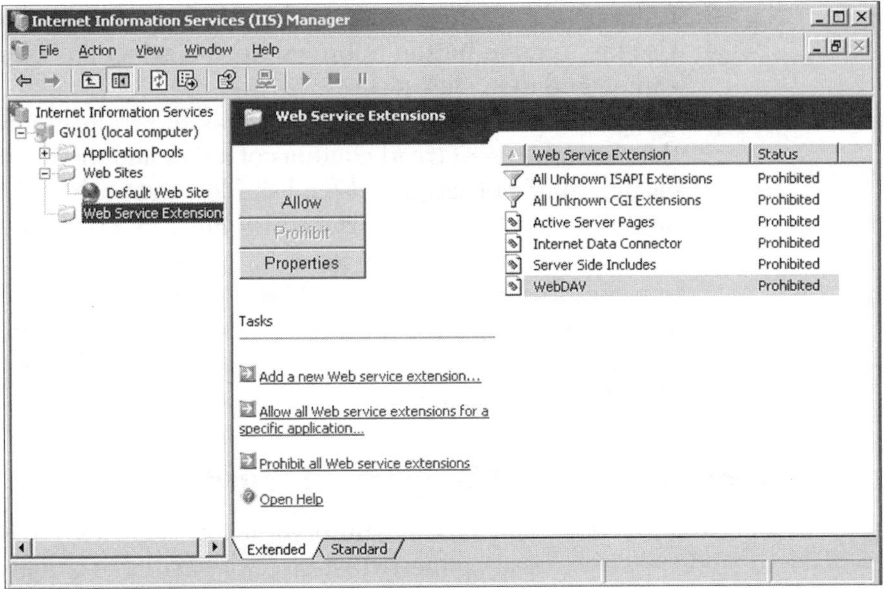


**Figure 9-23** WebDAV is not enabled by default.

2. Select the task `Allow all Web service extensions for a specific application` and then select WebDAV from the drop-down box.
3. Click OK to enable WebDAV.

## Create a Folder to Share and Set NTFS Permissions

Create a file system folder where files to be shared will be placed. Set appropriate NTFS permissions on the folder. For example, if the folder will be a repository where accountants may store and modify files, NTFS permissions should give the Accountants group `Modify` permission. `Full Control` would not be required.

## Create a Virtual Directory

The next step is to create a virtual directory on the web server that points to the created folder:

1. Open the Internet Information Services (IIS) Manager.
2. Right-click on the website and select `New, Virtual Directory`, and then click `Next`.

3. Enter an alias (name for the WebDav folder) for the directory.
4. Use the `Browse` button to browse to and select the folder created earlier, and then click `Next`.
5. Assign virtual directory permissions, as shown in Figure 9-24. In this example, `Read` (read contents of a file) and `Write` (access and change source of script and publish files) were selected. (If scripts or Common Gateway Interface files must be executed, the `Read` and `Execute` permissions need to be applied. In this case, the stated purpose is to store and access files. It is always a poor practice to allow `Write` and `Execute` permissions on web folders because a malicious script might be written to the folder and then executed.)
6. Click `Next` and then click `Finish`.

## Configure Virtual Directory Security

The wizard does not allow completion of security configuration. Immediately after creating the virtual directory and before allowing client access, care should be taken to apply further security:

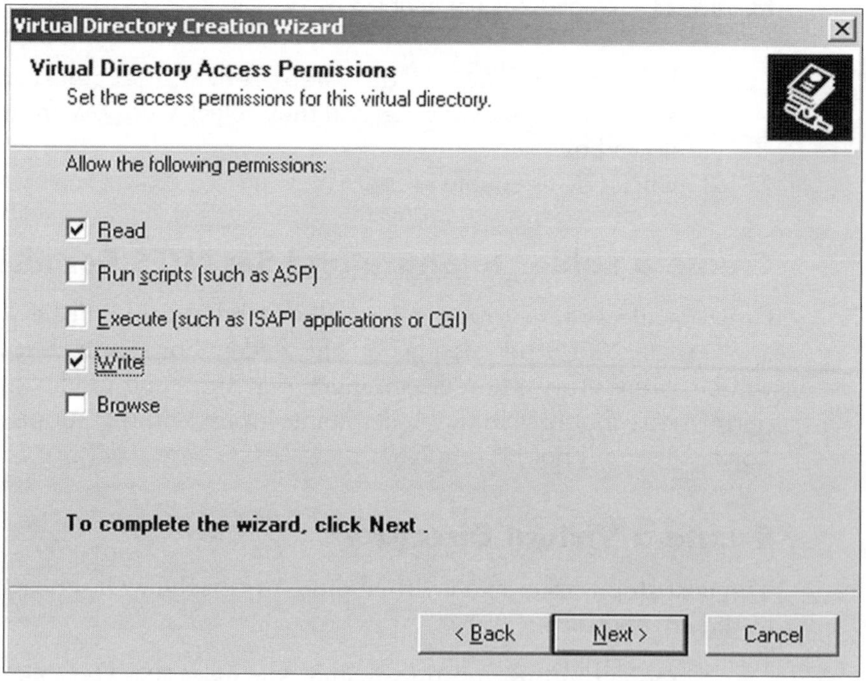

**Figure 9-24** Assign virtual directory permissions.

1. Right-click on the new virtual directory and select `Properties`.
2. On the `Virtual Directory` page, as shown in Figure 9-25, note that indexing and log visits are selected by default. Confirm that permission settings here match what is required on the site. If searching is required, make sure that the indexing service is running.
3. Select the `Directory Security` page, and then click the `Edit` button to edit `Authentication and access control.`
4. Select to disable the `Enable Anonymous Access` feature. Ensure that `Integrated Windows authentication` is checked, as shown in Figure 9-26, or that the appropriate authentication mechanism for your organization is selected.

## Client Side Configuration

Once WebDAV has been configured, enable and start the Web Client service on the client to take full advantage of the benefits. The Web Client service is disabled by default.

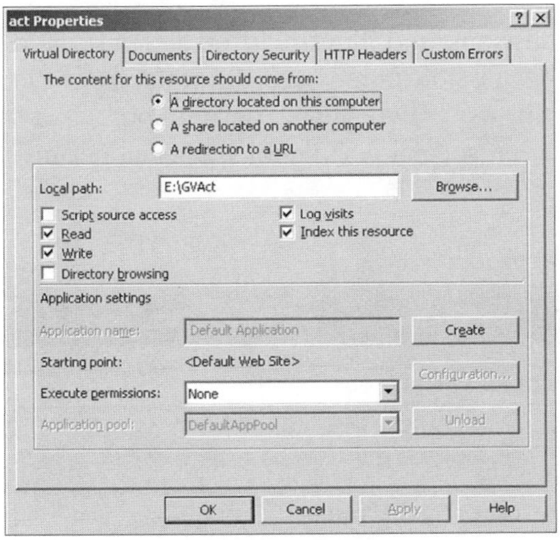

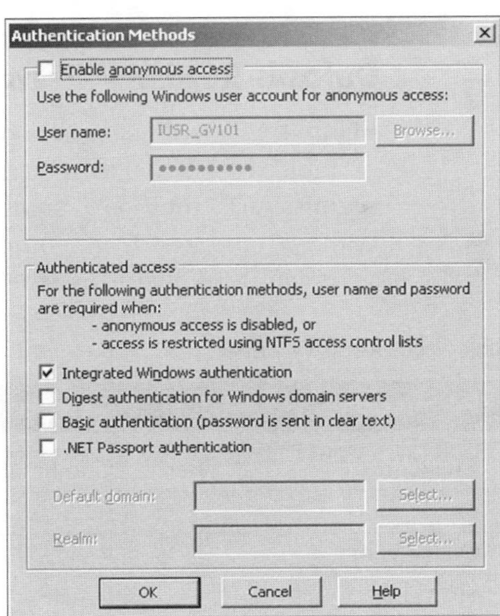


**Figure 9-25** Confirm permission settings on the virtual directory.

**Figure 9-26** Disable anonymous access to WebDAV folders.

WebDAV may already be in use in your organization. To make sure it doesn't become part of the data misuse in your organization, follow these best practices:

- Ensure WebDAV directories reside on NTFS-formatted volumes.
- Assign NTFS permissions on files and folders in the WebDAV directory.
- Use web folder permissions.
- Insist on Windows Authentication on intranet.
- Use but protect basic authentication on the Internet with SSL.

## Controlling Access to Registry Keys

Registry keys are permissioned by default and should not be modified without a thorough understanding of the impact of the modification. Registry keys are also added by applications and via configuration settings. Changing permissions on these keys may prevent applications from running.

### Default Registry Permissions

Figure 9-27 displays registry permissions, and they are listed and described in Table 9-8. Alhough registry permission names are different from file permissions, they are similar in use. Two main permissions, `Full Control` and `Read`, are composed of special permissions. Special permissions can be explicitly assigned.

**Table 9-8** Registry Permissions

| Permission | Description |
|---|---|
| Full Control | Combination of all permissions |
| Read Query | Includes enumerate, notify, read control |
| Query Value | Read value of a key |
| Set Value | Create, delete a set registry value |
| Create Subkey | Add a key |
| Enumerate Subkeys | List subkeys |

| Permission | Description |
|---|---|
| Notify | If present, can request change notifications for a registry key or its subkeys. This is useful, for example, in auditing. |
| Create Link | Used by the system to create links between registry paths |
| Delete | Delete key |
| Write DAC | Modify DACL, security permissions |
| Write Owner | Rights write, set value, create subkey |
| Read Control | Read permissions |

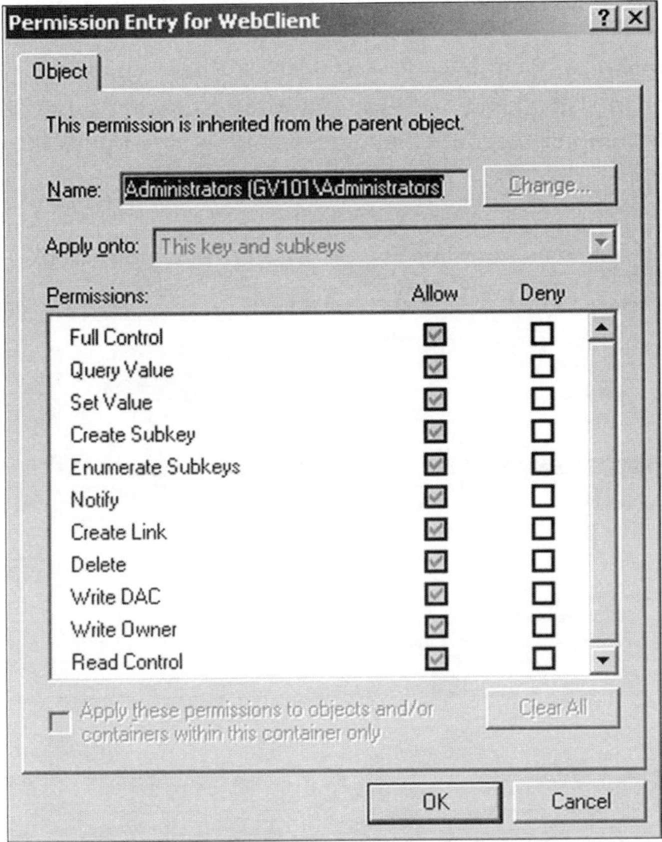


**Figure 9-27** Registry permissions work similarly to file permissions but consist of a different permission set.

Registry key permissions inheritance is similar to that described in the file system and can be blocked to protect permissions on sensitive subkeys, as shown in Figure 9-28.

## Applying Registry Permissions

Registry permissions, like object permissions for files and folders, may be applied directly using the object picker within the Registry Editor, by application through security templates, and by using Group Policy,

The regedt32.exe program is not part of Windows XP or Windows Server 2003. However, the features that differentiate it from regedit.exe, such as the ability to set security permissions, set audit permissions, and assign ownership of a key, have been added to regedit. An additional feature of regedit in Windows Server 2003 is the Favorites feature. As you work with registry keys, you can put your frequently used keys on the Favorites menu in regedit. Clicking the menu entry opens the stored subkey record.

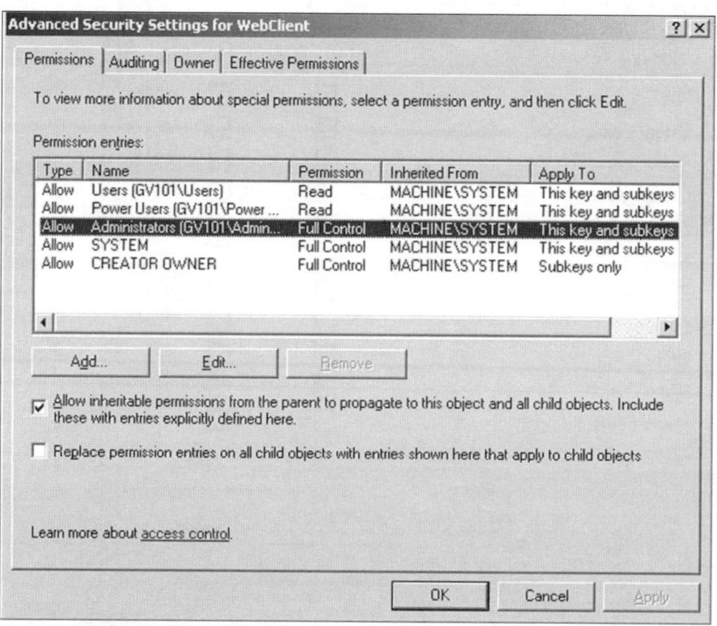


**Figure 9-28** Registry keys can also inherit or block inheritance of permissions.

To modify registry key permissions, follow these steps:

1. Select the key.
2. From the `Edit` menu, select `Permissions,` and then click `Add.`
3. Use the `Locations` box of the Select Users, Computers or Groups dialog box to select the computer or domain of the users and groups to give permission to.
4. Enter the group name and click `Check Users` to verify, or click the `Advanced` button and then the `Find Now` button to obtain a list of the users and groups. Then select the user or group to give permissions to.
5. In the Permissions dialog box, assign the type of access to the selected user or group, or click the `Advanced` button, select the `User`, and click the `Edit` button to select special permissions.

Changing ownership of a registry key is a two-part process: First, an administrator or other user with ownership permission must assign ownership to a new user, and then the designated user must take ownership. The exception to this rule is that users with the `Take Ownership` permission may change ownership to their own account. To change ownership of a registry key, do the following:

1. Select the key to change ownership for.
2. Select `Permissions` from the `Edit` menu.
3. Select `Advanced`, and then select the `Owner` tab.
4. Select `Change Owner` to select the new owner.

The new owner completes the owner change process by using `Take Ownership` of the key to complete the process. This two-part process serves a distinct security role. It separates the process of giving ownership permission from the process of taking ownership. This is important because it prevents a malicious person with the Take Ownership right from taking ownership, giving themselves permissions, changing, viewing, or deleting data, and then giving ownership back to the original owner in an attempt to avoid detection or to avoid being held accountable for his act. Because the duties are separated, the attacker retains ownership of the object and cannot deny that he had the opportunity to use this capability to obtain information or to do some task that he is not authorized to do.

## Practical Deployment Issues

Setting object permissions using the object picker is not the only way to secure objects. A sound understanding of object permissions and inheritance is critical; however, there are a number of processes that also affect data security and tools that can be used to further secure data. Object permissions cannot always be locked down to the requirements defined by data owners, and the operating system cannot be hardened as well as could be. These processes and tools are issues having to do with the following:

- Legacy applications
- Data streams
- Recovery and fault tolerance
- Native tools for permission application
- Clustering
- Distributed File System (DFS)
- Data security options in Group Policy and security templates
- Event log access security

### Legacy Application Permission Issues

Each new Windows version has made improvements in security and stability. However, these changes have often meant application compatibility issues. Applications designed to run on less secure versions of Windows may not be able to run on newer versions without significantly weakening security settings. Unfortunately, these issues are most frequently resolved by giving users administrative rights on their own desktop systems. This is not a good solution to the problem, though. It does work, however, because many of the compatibility issues have to do with file system and registry permissions. Older versions of Windows had little or no restrictions on file access. Newer versions of the operating system often give users little or no permissions to sensitive folders, files, and registry keys. The Administrators group, however, is given full access. By giving users Administrative group membership, the applications then work as expected. An alternative approach would be to determine exactly which files and folders the applications require access to and to provide users access to those files. This would allow the applications to run but would not provide users with elevated privileges on their systems. Many attacks attempted by viruses and worms will not work if the user running the infected file does not have administrative privileges. If applications disregard the permission requirements of newer operating system versions, and administrators cannot or do not want to create workarounds and thus provide users with administrative privileges, this weakens security.

To determine exact permission requirements, other options are as follows:

- Replacing older applications with applications that are built to conform to the new operating system.
- Using the pre-Windows 2000 compatible access group. This group can be used to provide backward compatibility access to domain resources for computers running Windows NT 4.0 or earlier that must be part of a Windows Server 2003 domain. For example, a Windows NT 4.0-based RRAS server that is a member of a Windows Server 2003-based domain must be able to access the remote access credentials of domain accounts. Adding the Everyone group to the pre-Windows compatible access group permits the RAS caller to be authenticated by the Windows NT 4.0 server.
- Determining the required permissions and replacing default permissions with these permissions.

### LEGACY APPLICATION PERMISSION EXAMPLE

Permissions on system files, folders, and registry keys are based on the needs of the operating system. Where users only need `Read`, they are only granted `Read` permissions, not `Change`. Administrators have broader permissions and use them to install programs that must change data in protected areas of the system and its registry. Unfortunately, applications are often written without careful regard to default permissions. Instead of only requesting `Read` access, they often request `Change` or `Full Control`. Often, the application does not need this permission; it was just easier for the developer to write it this way. It is also possible that the application does need elevated permissions at a location now protected from such activity. And sometimes an application places its own information in an area of the file system or registry where it does not need to be when it should have defined its own folder or key. When these applications are installed, they may work just fine for administrators but not for users. To compensate, the organization may believe it must give users `Administrator` rights on their systems.

Examples of applications that have caused problems in the past are RealPlayer Version 7 and Acrobat Reader 4.0. In both cases, the applications attempt to write to registry keys that by default only grant `Read` permission to ordinary users. RealPlayer attempts to write to the `HKEY_CLASSES_ROOT\Software\RealNetworks` key, while Acrobat Reader attempts to write to the `HKEY_CLASSES_ROOT\\AcroExch.Document` and the `HKEY_CLASSES_ROOT\CLSID\{B801CA65-A1FC-11D0-85AD-444553540000}` keys.

Fortunately, the problem can be fixed by giving the Users group the "Set Value" permission on the keys. Administrative group membership is not required.

These permissions should not be changed on servers, but these applications should not be run on servers either.

To determine which file, folder, or registry key permissions must be changed to allow legacy or poorly designed applications to run, two free tools can be downloaded from sysinternals.com: Filemon and Regmon. Running these tools while running the suspect application will provide a list of files and registry keys accessed. If users are denied access to any of these objects, or if the access granted them does not provide the application the access it needs, this is probably why the application doesn't work. Another way to determine problems with object access is to set system access control lists (SACLs) and record an audit of access failure. After compiling the list of objects where access is denied, grant users the access required instead of granting them administrative rights on the computer.

Providing users with elevated access permissions to some files or registry keys is a far more secure option than giving users administrative privileges.

## Alternative Data Streams

Data streams are locations assigned to files created in the NTFS file system. NTFS allows multiple data streams for each file. The first data stream is visible in Windows Explorer and is accessed by using the filename. Additional file streams can be created under the same filename but are not visible in Explorer. These alternative data streams (ADSs) are used for many things, including accommodation of dual-forked Macintosh files (which can be stored on Windows NT-based systems when Services for Macintosh (SFM) is installed), the `Summary` information property tab of a text file as displayed in Figure 9-29, and the web sharing property page of IIS folders. More information can be found in the Microsoft document "Multiple Data Streams" at http://www.microsoft.com/resources/documentation/Windows/XP/all/reskit/en-us/Default.asp?url=/resources/documentation/Windows/XP/all/reskit/en-us/prkc_fil_ xurt.asp.

Although ADSs perform useful functions, they are hard to detect without specialized non-native software and may be difficult to remove. Furthermore, an ADSs could pack a malicious payload. A proof-of-concept virus, the W32.stream virus, developed in 2000, attached itself to a harmless file as an ADSs.

### *Creating and Manipulating ADS*

Alternative data files can easily be created at the command prompt. An ADSs can be created using the following commands:

1. From a command prompt, enter the command below to create the file test.txt:

```
Echo "this is a text file" >C:\test.txt
```

2. Create an ADSs for this file:

```
Echo "stuff in a data stream" >
   C:test.txt:mydatastream.txt
```

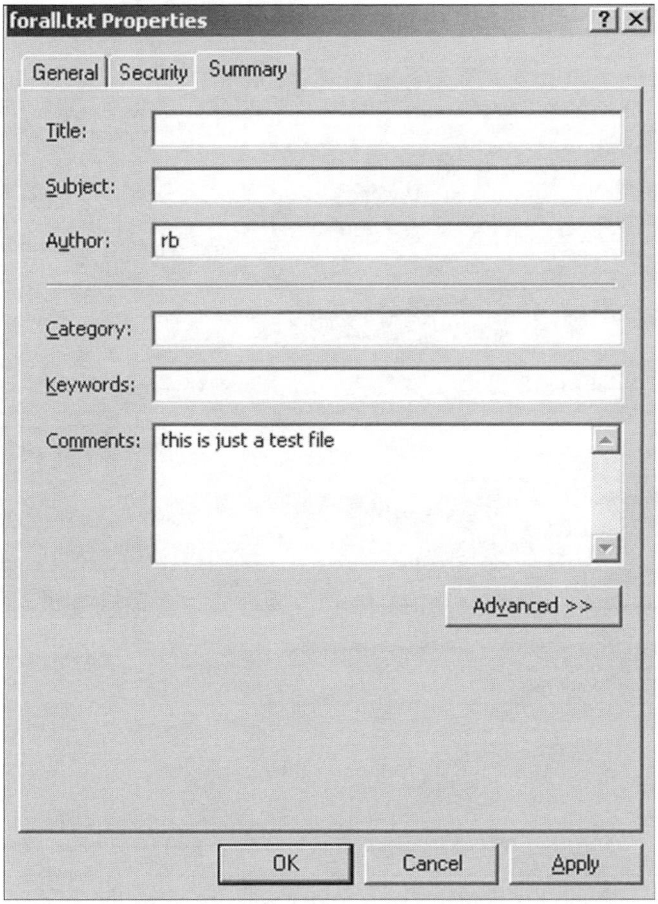

**Figure 9-29** The Summary page information in a text file is stored in a data stream.

The ADS is not displayed in Explorer or by using the `dir` command, as shown in Figure 9-30.

To read the ADSs, use Notepad with the following command:

```
Notepad file.txt:mydatastream.txt
```

The file contents will be displayed in Notepad, as shown in Figure 9-31. Reading a single data stream when you know it's there is not hard, but how do you discover the data streams that you don't know about? Data streams used by legitimate Windows systems are of little interest, but rogue data streams that contain malicious or undesirable data might be stored on a computer's hard drive. ADSs have been found on computer disks that contain pornographic material. At the least, unauthorized data streams use disk

```
C:\WINDOWS\system32\cmd.exe

C:\test2>echo "this is a text file" >c:\test2\test.txt

C:\test2>dir
 Volume in drive C has no label.
 Volume Serial Number is 34AB-AF3B

 Directory of C:\test2

08/07/2004  09:47 AM    <DIR>          .
08/07/2004  09:47 AM    <DIR>          ..
08/06/2004  05:36 PM                 0 Copy of Copy of accountantsonly.txt
08/07/2004  09:47 AM                24 test.txt
08/06/2004  06:10 PM                 0 xcopythis.txt
               3 File(s)             24 bytes
               2 Dir(s)  10,273,906,688 bytes free

C:\test2>edit test.txt

C:\test2>echo "stuff in a data stream" >c:\test2\test.txt:mydatastream

C:\test2>dir
 Volume in drive C has no label.
 Volume Serial Number is 34AB-AF3B

 Directory of C:\test2

08/07/2004  09:47 AM    <DIR>          .
08/07/2004  09:47 AM    <DIR>          ..
08/06/2004  05:36 PM                 0 Copy of Copy of accountantsonly.txt
08/07/2004  09:47 AM                24 test.txt
08/06/2004  06:10 PM                 0 xcopythis.txt
               3 File(s)             24 bytes
               2 Dir(s)  10,273,906,688 bytes free
```

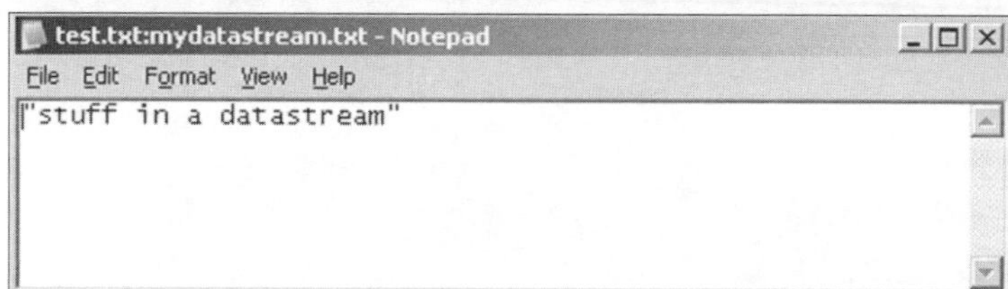


**Figure 9-30** Listing the contents of a folder will not show the ADSs.

**Figure 9-31** The content of an altered datastream can be read in Notepad.

resources. If you don't know if any are present, how can you determine if any of them hide malicious code or data that should not be on the computer? This is one of several security issues engendered by ADSs. Issue include these:

- Few administrators or security officers understand them; therefore, few administrators or security officers look for them. Data streams that harbor malicious code might be saved as the data stream of an innocent file. Two known viruses, Dumaru.y and W2K.Stream, take advantage of ADSs.
- Some anti-virus products may not scan data streams.
- Products that wipe disks (that replace data on the disk with zeros to ensure that no one can obtain the data that was once resident on the disk) may not replace the content of ADSs.

#### *Tools That Make Detection Easier*

There are third-party tools that check for ADSs. A few of the available tools are as follows:

- LADS (list alternative data streams) scan through directories and find ADS files. Available from http://www.heysoft.de/nt/ep-lads.htm.
- Streams is freeware available from Sysinternals (http://www.sysinternals.com/ntw2k/source/misc.shtml#streams).
- Crucial ADS is available from http://www.crucialsecurity.com/downloads.html.
- TDS-3 commercial can scan specific directories. A demo copy is available for download at http://tds.diamondcs.com.au/.

Deleting ADSs is difficult. To delete an ADS, you must either delete the file it is linked to, or delete the folder it resides in. You can also copy the file to a FAT file system (data streams cannot be preserved) and then copy the file back to the NTFS location. You cannot delete ADSs attached to the root directory. If the ADS is large, you can, however, create small ADSs and use them to overwrite the ADSs attached to the root.

Executable files can be attached as ADSs. Running them requires use of the `Start` command.

At one time, anti-virus programs and disk-wiping programs had problems processing ADSs, but today most products are ADS-aware.

## Setting Permissions Using Security Templates

File, folder, and registry permissions can be set in Security Templates and then applied to a single system or imported into a Group Policy. Permission settings can also be made directly in the GPO. The default security template, defltsv.inf, is used during Windows Server 2003 installation to set system, volume root, and registry permissions. If and when the server is dcpromoed (made into a domain controller), defltdc.inf is used to apply additional domain controller-specific permission sets. If you have additional security permissions for files, folders, and registry keys that are placed on every server, you can create your own default templates, save them using these names, and use them during your installs instead of using the ones provided on the installation CD-ROM. (You can find a copy of these templates in the <system root>\inf folder). Security templates can also be used to set permissions, test that permissions have not been altered, and reapply permissions as necessary.

---

**WARNING: Beware of Using Group Policy to Set Permissions**

The Security Setting portion of Group Policy is refreshed every 16 hours, even if nothing has changed. If a large number of permissions is changed via Group Policy, this can become a performance issue, as can replication of large GPOs.

---

## Recovery and Fault Tolerance

Several services that impact data security are as follows:

- The Windows File Protection (WFP) service protects the integrity of system files by preventing their replacement. WFP can help protect against accidental deletion or replacement and can prevent malicious replacement of system files.
- The System File Checker application can be used to check the status of system files on a specific computer.
- Volume Shadow Copy allows end users to recover previous versions of their files. This helps reduce help desk efforts required to recover files from backup when the user accidentally deletes them.

## Clustering

Clustering technology in Windows Server 2003 consists of two distinct technologies:

- Network load-balancing balances the network load between multiple (up to 32) identical computers. NLB is available on Windows Server 2003 Standard Edition and Web Edition. An example of such a cluster would be a group of ISA Server firewalls or a group of IIS web servers.
- Server clusters provide up to 8-way failover for network resources. Server clusters are available on Windows Server 2003 Enterprise and Datacenter Editions. This may be used to provide redundancy and fault tolerance for databases and other large collections of files.

Clusters present a challenging data security issue. They are often used to ensure data availability, which is usually considered to be part of security. However, they can cause a security issue. Permission sets must be kept consistent across multiple computers in the cluster. The following are best practices for permissions on clusters:

- Configure file share access by using permissions on the `Parameter` tab in Cluster Administrator, not the local computer file system share security. If permissions are changed using Windows Explorer instead, permission settings are lost when the resource is taken offline.
- Do not give permissions to local groups and user accounts, with the exception of the local Administrators group. All other local groups and user accounts only have meaning on the local system, not on other nodes in the cluster. In the case of node failure, any permission set for local groups or users is meaningless; it will have no impact on the other node.
- Set auditing for files and folders based on local user and group accounts using Windows Explorer. Audit events are by nature recorded only on the computer where they occur. If, however, you want to monitor usage by auditing, you will have to set consistent audit settings on resources of all nodes in the cluster.
- Protect the folder on the quorum disk that stores the quorum log. This log stores all the changes to the cluster state and configuration changes that cannot be committed to other nodes.

Because clustering hardware can be more proprietary than the average server, it is important to pay close attention to the manufacturer's recommendations. You'll find that many of the security issues pertaining to clusters will be unique to that manufacturer.

## DFS

To the ordinary computer user, file location on the network is a mystery. In fact, many users do not even recognize that the files they access every day are not stored on their local disks. If users are allowed to make their own connections to file shares to access network resources, it may be a daunting task for them. Even administrators, who must set up drive mappings for users, can have difficulty locating just the right mapping when there are many and the organization of shares is volatile or non-existent. Browsing, the de facto way of locating resources, does not work well in large distributed environments. The distributed file system (Dfs) was created to alleviate this situation. Dfs enables an organized architecture to be created. Once connected to the appropriate Dfs root, the user can expand the root to reveal resources named for their content. Just as resource location is unimportant to users, resource location is not important to Dfs, and multiple locations for the same resource can be listed. The selection of which specific resource to visit is made by the system, and if a server that maintains a copy of the resource is not available, another may be.

Dfs network resources do not have to be located on Windows systems. Dfs can be configured to point to targets on Novell servers and Unix systems in addition to Windows systems.

This great network resource management system does introduce new security issues. First, Dfs adds no additional security. Security must be configured at the network resource location. Second, although data can be in diverse locations, when planning the location of network file resources, consider how they will be secured. It is not a good idea, for example, to place network resources where no file permissions can be applied, or where the ability to set file permissions may weaken access controls. Finally, if multiple copies of the same data exist, care must be taken to ensure that the security permissions are consistently kept.

## Effective Security Options and User Rights Management

In addition to explicit permissions on file, share, and registry objects, the Security Options and user rights portions of Group Policy affect data security. The following elements should be considered when creating a secure data access architecture.

### *Restriction on Anonymous Access*

If anonymous access is granted to shares, the permissions created for shares will only restrict authorized users.

### *Do Not Make Anonymous Members of the Everyone Group*

Some anonymous access may be required. For example, users must be able to connect to domain controllers to authenticate. Nonetheless, take care to restrict anonymous access to data. In addition to preventing direct application of permissions for the Anonymous group, the Anonymous group should not be added back into the Everyone group. The Everyone group is granted broad access to files, folders, and registry keys.

### *The Bypass Traverse Checking User Right*

This user right allows the user to programmatically access files he has permission to access, even if he does not have access permission to the parent folders.

### *Format and Eject Removable Media*

The Security Option `Devices: Allowed to format and eject removable media` controls permission to format removable disks and remove them. Although most removable disks, such as USB and Firewire-based drives, can simply be unplugged, there is some danger that data will be damaged. Managing the ability to format may be more important because accidental or malicious formatting of these drives could be a problem.

### *Restricting Remote Access to CD-ROMs and Floppies*

If a user is logged on, the Security Option `Devices: Restrict CD-ROM Access to Locally Logged on User` prevents remote access to the

CD-ROM. However, if no user is logged on locally, this setting will not prevent remote access to the CD-ROM drive.

- `Devices: Restrict floppy Access to Locally Logged on User`—If a user is logged on, this setting prevents remote access to the floppy. However, if no user is logged on locally, this setting will not prevent remote access to the floppy drive.
- `Network Access: Remotely Accessible Registry Paths`—Allows controlled access to registry paths.
- `Network Access: Remotely Accessible Registry Paths and Subpaths`—Allows controlled access to registry paths and their subpaths.
- `Network Access: Shares that can be accessed anonymously`—Only these shares allow anonymous access if other anonymous restrictions are set.
- `Shutdown: Clear Virtual Memory Pagefile`—On shutdown, clears the pagefile. Any type of data may be paged to the pagefile while the system is running. The pagefile is protected while the system is operational; however, when the system is shut down, it is just an ordinary file and might be accessed from a boot to another OS. To ensure that sensitive data cannot be accessed in this manner, use this setting.

## Controlling Access to Event Logs

The operating system, services, and some applications automatically record information in the Windows event logs. Additional events are recorded when applications are configured to do so. These events may include useful information for troubleshooting, warnings that something needs attention, alerts of potential attacks, and historical documentation that may be necessary to compose an audit trail for criminal prosecution.

Processes within applications can be coded to post records, to read records, and to archive or clear the event logs. To perform these actions, the application must be running in the security context of an account with the privileges to do so, either because an individual with those privileges runs the application, or because the service account used to run the application is given those privileges. For example, Microsoft Exchange Server posts records to the logs under the authority of its services accounts. Logon audit records are posed by the SYSTEM account. On the other

**Table 9-9** Permission on the Event Logs

| Log | Local System | Local Administrators, Domain Admins | Ordinary Users |
|---|---|---|---|
| Application Log | Full access | `Read`, `Write`, and `Clear`. | `Read` and `Write` |
| System log | Full access | Local `administrators` have `Read`, `Write` and `Clear` permissions. Domain Administrators have `Read` and `Clear`. | `Read` |
| Security | Full access | Administrators by default are assigned the `Managing Auditing and Security` Log user right (the SE_SECURITY_NAME privilege), which gives them `Read` and `Clear` permissions. | Users can be assigned the `Managing Auditing and Security Log` user right. |

hand, only an administrator can use the Event Viewer application to delete the content of an event log.

By default, each log has its own permission settings. Default permissions on Windows Server 2003 event logs are displayed in Table 9-9.

Prior to Windows Server 2003, event log access could be granted to members of the Guest account by modifying the registry key `RestrictGuestAccess` at `HKEY_LOCAL_MACHINE\SYSTEM\CurrentControlSet\Services\EventLog\Application`. In Windows Server 2003, `RestrictGuestAccess` is ignored, and two new registry values can be used to determine access: one for access to the Application log and the other for the System log. Both values are part of subkeys of the EventLog key above. To manage access to the Application log, use the `CustomSD` key under the `EventLog\Application` key; to manage access to the System log, use the `CustomSD` key under the `EventLog\System` key. Acceptable values are as follows:

- 0x0001—Permission to read the log file.
- 0x0002—Permission to write to the log file.
- 0x0004—Permission to clear the log file.

These permissions have no value for the security log file. Regardless, only the Local Security Authority has write permission for the security log files. Likewise, if a user has the SE_Security privilege, he can read and clear the security log regardless of how `CustomSD` keys are configured.

---

**WARNING: Do Not Weaken Security on the Security Event Log**
Access to the security log is limited to prevent tampering with audit records. Rather than broadening access to this log, consider restricting it to a subset of administrators. The integrity of the records in this log is critical to proving an audit trail of activity on the system. This may be important for discovering security breaches and holding accountable system users and attackers.

---

## Summary

Many things contribute to data security. Of prime importance, though, are file, folder, and registry permissions. These form the foundation upon which other defenses can rely. Should all else fail, these need to be strong. This chapter explained these permissions and how they can work with other items to protect data. It also introduced interesting developments such as WebDAV, which can change the way data is remotely accessed and thus the way it must be secured.

Add SALT

CHAPTER 10

# DEPLOYING PKI

The purpose of this chapter is to consider some of the benefits realized through the deployment of a PKI. It also briefly discusses cost considerations (from a generic rather than monetary perspective).

Ultimately, it should be recognized that a sound and justifiable business case must drive the deployment of any technology. This applies equally to PKI technology. The key is to focus on business drivers, not technology.

It is not the intent of this chapter to provide a boilerplate for the development of a business case, but the chapter does identify many of the factors that should be taken into consideration when developing such a business case.

## Business Case Considerations

A PKI is a comprehensive security infrastructure, not myriad point solutions. A PKI offers a single security infrastructure that can be used across multiple applications in the most heterogeneous of environments. Specifically, a PKI can be used to enable confidentiality, integrity, authentication, and non-repudiation services in numerous contexts, including one or more of the following:

- Secure e-mail
- Secure Electronic Data Interchange (EDI)
- Secure electronic forms
- Secure desktop (for example, encryption of sensitive information on a laptop or PC)
- Secure intranets
- Secure extranets
- End-entity access control
- Secure remote access (for example, in support of mobile users or work-at-home)

- Secure Web applications
- Object signing
- Reduced logon

The benefits realized from offering these services are extensive, albeit in many cases hard to quantify. Benefits that can be realized through the judicious deployment of a PKI include the following:

- **Improvements in workflow efficiency** Significant timesavings can be realized (for example, letters, memos, and contracts can be handled electronically rather than through physical correspondence).
- **Work-force optimization** End users can spend more time on the job at hand rather than spending time dealing with details associated with the security infrastructure itself.
- **Work-force reduction** The deployment and operation of a single, unifying architecture rather than multiple point solutions should require fewer administrative resources.
- **Paper reduction** Savings can be realized in a number of ways, including lower material costs, less storage space, waste reduction, and less environmental intrusion.
- **Less administrative overhead** End users are less likely to require as much ongoing administrative assistance (for example, help desk support).
- **Reduced losses due to electronic theft** Corporate data is protected, which significantly decreases the risk of unauthorized disclosure.
- **Telecommunications cost savings** The ability to create a Virtual Private Network (VPN) over a public network such as the Internet can result in significant cost savings over leasing private lines.
- **Revenue generation** A PKI can be used not only to save money but also, in some cases, as the basis for offering for-fee services (for example, a financial institution may offer transaction validation services based on digital signatures and public-key certificates).

Electronic theft and fraud are clearly on the rise, and we can only assume that this trend will continue. A good source of information that helps illustrate this trend can be found in the Computer Security Institute's 2002 "Computer Crime and Security Survey" [CSI]. The tragic events of

September 11, 2001, have also had a side effect of increasing security awareness as a whole, and this heightend awareness seems to be filtering into the technology area. Statistics aside, the very fact that security is perceived to be a problem makes it something to be addressed.

It is important to recognize that security threats originate from both external and internal sources. Therefore, any comprehensive security solution must be able to secure both internal and external communications and corporate resources.

To help put things into perspective, consider what would happen if the CEO of your company had his or her laptop stolen. Is the sensitive information on that laptop encrypted? If not, try to imagine how much damage would be done if that sensitive corporate data fell into the wrong hands. A PKI offers the foundation for providing confidentiality services that can be used to protect against threats like this.

Although it is recognized that the CEO's laptop could have been secured without the use of a PKI, these solutions do not offer the comprehensive set of services that a PKI can offer. To illustrate this point, consider the case in which the laptop was not stolen but that the CEO was rendered incapacitated for some reason. How would the encrypted corporate data on that laptop be recovered? Intuitively, the value of a PKI that helps protect *and* recover mission-critical data is extremely high, even if its quantitative benefits can be almost impossible to measure precisely.

## Cost Considerations

Unfortunately, to determine the cost of deploying a PKI, no single formula can be applied to all organizations, and very few sources in the public domain provide a comprehensive, vendor-neutral appraisal.

Many organizations can leverage their existing IT (Information Technology) investments to help offset the cost of deploying the PKI. This applies both to personnel and to facilities. For example, Certification Authorities (CAs) need to be housed in protected facilities so that access by unauthorized personnel can be prevented and accountability can be maintained. Some organizations, especially large organizations, may have these types of facilities already available. Further, existing IT personnel can be utilized to help deploy and operate the components that comprise the PKI. Clearly, the degree of this leverage will tend to vary with each organization.

A ubiquitous repository service is also an important part of a large-scale enterprise PKI. Exploiting existing directory services is also possible in many organizations. This allows the PKI to consume directory services that are already part of the existing corporate IT infrastructure, thereby reducing procurement costs and distributing operational costs across multiple directory uses.

In any case, a number of considerations must be evaluated to help determine the *Total Cost of Ownership (TCO)* within a given organization, including the following:

- How many hardware components—that is, Registration Authorities (RAs), CAs, directory servers, and so on—are required to meet the demands of the target community? The number of components may depend on a variety of factors including the scale of the target community, geographic considerations, and the amount of autonomy afforded to the various departments or communities of interest.
- What is the cost of the necessary software and support tools? Both initial software procurement and ongoing software maintenance costs should be considered.
- How much of the existing corporate IT infrastructure can be exploited to support the target community? For example, is a separate directory product required, or can an existing corporate directory service be utilized?
- What are the resource requirements associated with the planning, deployment, operation, and ongoing maintenance of the infrastructure?
- What are the resource requirements associated with defining the policies and procedures necessary to support external users and/or external organizations?
- Are the necessary facilities available to house the infrastructure components; if not, what is required, and how much will it cost?
- What are the component availability requirements? Is full redundancy of any of the components (for example, the CAs) necessary?
- What are the training costs? This applies to administrators/operational personnel as well as end users.
- What level of administrative support is required (for example, help desk support, end-entity registration procedures, and so on)?

- Will the deployed PKI interoperate with other PKIs that may be based on technology provided by different vendors? Adopting standards-based technology is essential.
- What is required in terms of law- or policy-related doctrine? Liability protection is essential in many cases, especially when interoperability is required with external users or other PKI domains.

Ultimately, the key to success is to plan ahead; understanding as many of the issues as possible will help lead to the development of a solid business strategy.

## Deployment: Now or Later?

The perception of PKI has changed dramatically in the past few years. It seems like just yesterday that a number of trade journal articles and conference presentations were suggesting that PKI is still "in its infancy" and caution should be exercised when making a deployment decision. This seemed to stem from a reasonable concern that the technology was still fairly new and that the necessary standards and interoperability testing facilities necessary to guarantee multivendor interoperability were only beginning to mature. However, at the same time, these articles suggested that PKI is inevitably a "must have" technology.

More recently, however, we are hearing a different perspective from some individuals. Some argue that PKI has been overhyped and that it is both too complicated and too expensive to be viable. It is only natural that this might weigh on the minds of the corporate decision makers. However, we are certainly not ready to suggest that PKI is dead. We would argue that PKI is still maturing as a technology, and it continues to evolve in order to meet real-world business requirements. In fact, we are beginning to see a trend where PKI is becoming an essential building block that can be exploited by other security services such as privilege management. We believe that this trend will continue, and we will eventually see products where PKI is simply embedded, or integrated, within the overall security solution, rather than called out as a separate product.

Having said all that, we understand that a degree of uncertainty is still associated with PKI technology. The trend for the past few years has been to launch small-scale PKI pilots, and we would expect this trend to continue. These pilots typically focus on a single application (for example, secure e-mail), and they limit the size of the end-user community (typically no more than a few hundred end users). The main purpose of these pilots is to

- Educate administrators and operations personnel through controlled, hands-on experience
- Establish a small core of educated end users—including key players within the organization—to help promote corporate-level acceptance
- Allow a graceful rollout of new services over time
- Protect the initial PKI investment as new services are offered
- Demonstrate that the PKI technology is viable and that it will offer significant cost savings
- Allow additional time to achieve corporate-level "buy-in" (occasionally, even the most skeptical can be swayed through actual demonstration)

Although no one of course knows what the future will hold, we would expect that most enterprises will continue to proceed with caution. We also believe that it is up to the PKI vendors to work more diligently in the deployment area in order to help these small-scale pilots evolve into a more comprehensive, enterprise-wide security solution. To put it bluntly, there is no substitute for success.

To this point, we have focused on the benefits of a PKI and briefly discussed some of the cost considerations that should be evaluated as part of the business-case-development process. It is clear that the promise of ubiquitous security is seldom a sufficient business driver in itself. Ultimately, the business drivers and associated cost justification should dictate whether a given technology is appropriate.

Besides understanding the benefits and associated costs of a PKI, realizing that corporate-level buy-in is instrumental in achieving a successful deployment is also important. Approval from all major departments will greatly increase the chances that the PKI's deployment will be both graceful and successful. Further, if a given security solution is too intrusive and/or too expensive, it is usually dismissed as nonpractical.

For many environments, a properly deployed PKI offers a nonobtrusive, cost-effective solution that can be used to secure multiple applications across multiple domains.

See the next portions of this Chapter for additional information related to PKI deployment.

## Deployment Issues and Decisions

Now we will briefly discuss many of the issues an organization needs to consider before launching a PKI deployment. Most of these issues will also help an organization determine the best technology vendor (or service organization) available to meet its needs. The primary focus is on the enterprise PKI. Some enterprise issues to consider include

- Trust models
- In-sourcing versus out-sourcing
- Build versus buy
- Closed environment versus open environment
- X.509 versus alternative certificate formats
- Targeted applications versus comprehensive solutions
- Standard versus proprietary solutions
- Interoperability considerations
- On-line versus off-line operation
- Peripheral support
- Facility requirements
- Personnel requirements
- Certificate revocation requirements
- End-entity roaming requirements
- Key recovery requirements
- Repository requirements
- Disaster planning and recovery
- Security assurance
- Risk mitigation

## Trust Models: Hierarchical versus Distributed

PKI deployments might be based on any trust model. In practice, some of the more visible large-scale enterprise deployments are based on hierarchies (for example, Identrus), whereas others are based on the distributed trust model (for example, the GOC PKI).

The GOC (Government of Canada) PKI model is an example in which policy enforcement is from the top down, but the relationships between CAs (Certification Authorities) is bilateral rather than unilateral. The "top-level" node in the GOC PKI architecture is a logical root, but a bridge CA actually links the participating governmental departments together via bilateral cross-certification. This "top-level" node is also responsible for establishing cross-certification agreements with other PKIs (for example, the U.S. Federal PKI).

In the enterprise context, it can be argued that the distributed model is more flexible because it allows CAs to come and go with minimal disruption to the other interconnected CA domains. This is true in both an intra- and interorganizational context. In the case of a strict hierarchy, the disruption caused by the failure (for example, due to a compromise of the CA's signing private key) of a particular CA depends on the location (in terms of level) within the hierarchy. The closer to the top of the hierarchy the CA is, the more disruptive the failure of that CA will be to the enterprise as a whole. Of course, it is reasonable to expect that additional safeguards would be implemented for the higher levels—especially at the root level. The additional safeguards might include a longer key size (for example, a 2,048-bit RSA signing key rather than a 1,024-bit RSA signing key), and/or it may include a hardware module where the private-keying material can be stored more securely.

The hierarchical model is currently the rule in the Web environment, and some enterprise domains are also adopting it. A hierarchical model is often perceived to be a good mechanism for maintaining policy-related controls on subordinate CAs.[1] However, this is mainly a perception issue because similar controls can be levied on cross-certified CAs as well (for example, the GOC PKI).

## In-sourcing versus Out-sourcing

*In-sourcing* is when an enterprise decides to deploy its own internal PKI—utilizing its own resources (including personnel, hardware, and so on) and/or hiring external resources to help with any or all of the PKI's internal operation. The key here is that the PKI is under the control of the enterprise. *Out-sourcing* is when an organization allows an external party to supply and operate some aspects—perhaps even all aspects-of its PKI. In this case, at least some—perhaps all—of the PKI operation is not under the direct control of the enterprise.

1. We recommend that each organization examine the pros and cons of various trust models in light of their specific requirements.

Sometimes the decision of whether to in-source or out-source is based purely on economic considerations.[2] However, it is usually much more complicated than that. Not all organizations perceive things the same way, and many factors can affect this decision. For example, some organizations insist on maintaining total control over all aspects of the enterprise, especially anything to do with security and the source of trust associated with offering a particular service. These organizations are usually unwilling to depend on a third-party service provider. On the other hand, some organizations do not consider these factors to be as important with respect to their particular needs. Further, smaller organizations are much more likely to opt for an out-sourcing arrangement due to economic and resource constraints.

Hype and marketing propaganda, rather than the organization's real requirements, can sometimes decide the question of in-sourcing versus out-sourcing. To ensure that the right choice is made, the organization should exercise caution when making this decision. In the end, the basis of this decision should be a cost-benefit tradeoff analysis that takes into consideration as many relevant factors as possible. These factors include the following:

- Total cost of in-sourcing versus out-sourcing (including all related software, hardware, maintenance, personnel, facilities, training, legal fees, and so on)
- Degree of control that the organization feels must be maintained over the operation of the PKI
- The perceived source of trust that will be translated to the consumers of the PKI services (although ensuring that the issued certificates are appropriately branded may help control this)
- Response time associated with PKI-related service requests and information dissemination (for example, for end-entity and CA certificate requests, revocation information dissemination, key recovery requests, and so on)
- Level and availability of help desk support
- Flexibility and scalability considerations

2. There are various degrees of in-sourcing and out-sourcing. For example, an organization may decide to outsource the services of a CA from a third party, but the *Registration Authority (RA)* function would be retained in-house. As another example, an organization may want total control of the PKI, but it requires external resources to help deploy and operate the PKI. Sometimes done as a transitional step, this enables the organization's internal resources to develop—the goal being to take over complete operation of the PKI at some later time.

- Ability (and willingness) of the vendor to evolve to meet the future needs of the organization
- Disaster planning and recovery

## Build versus Buy

A *build* option implies that an organization is willing to invest in the development of PKI technology (for example, in CA and/or RA technology). A *buy* option simply means that an organization will purchase PKI products or services, either through in-sourcing or out-sourcing.

Some evidence shows that a few organizations are willing to pursue a build option, but most organizations are not. A number of obstacles make the buy option (whether it be in-source or out-source) more attractive:

1. PKI technology is relatively complex to implement. Most vendors that offer PKI software have invested substantially in the technology, and a return on investment can be realized only through sales to multiple organizations. It is difficult to see how costs would be recovered in an organization that elected to build its own PKI.
2. Given the complexity of the software, it is unlikely that most organizations would have sufficient (and proper) resources in place to even begin such a venture.
3. Existing technology patents might impact the development of such a product. Either royalties would have to be paid or workarounds (which are not always possible) to the patents would be required. A number of patents exist in the areas of revocation technology, time stamping (which is necessary to help support non-repudiation), and privilege management, to name a few. Additional patents related to PKI technology are likely to be introduced in the future.

Given these difficulties, it is fair to say that most organizations do not even consider the option of building their own PKI.

## Closed versus Open Environment

For the purposes of this book, a *closed environment* is an environment where only intradomain communications are of concern. The domain can be a single enterprise, or it can be a collection of enterprises all operating under identical technical and operational procedures and constraints. An *open environment* is an environment where interdomain communications will be required and supported. In this case, multiple technical and operating procedures are likely to be encountered.

Although multivendor interoperability may seem to be a relatively minor concern in a closed environment, multiple sources could conceivably supply technology in such an environment. Therefore, avoiding proprietary solutions that would hinder interoperability is important-especially as the needs of the closed community grow over time.

Multivendor interoperability is clearly a concern in the case of the open environment. The technology selected should be based on industry-accepted standards, and the technology vendor should demonstrate a commitment to achieving multivendor interoperability.

## X.509 versus Alternative Certificate Formats

Alternative certificate formats to the X.509 Version 3 public-key certificate exist. Not surprisingly, there are proponents of each format. For example, proponents of the *Simple Public Key Infrastructure (SPKI)* would suggest that the SPKI certificates are attractive because they focus on the notion of roles and authorizations rather than identity. Further, a *Pretty Good Privacy (PGP)* or OpenPGP advocate might claim that PGP certificates are more flexible than X.509 Version 3 public-key certificates and that they are more suitable for establishing trust relationships among individuals.

Although some of these alternative points of view may have merit in certain contexts, much of this debate is moot when it comes to meeting the needs of an enterprise. To date, corporate demand has overwhelmingly been in favor of X.509 Version 3 public-key certificates. If the market evolves in such a way that these environments require support for alternative certificate formats, these requirements will filter back to the technology vendors, and the products will evolve accordingly. At the moment, however, the vast majority PKI vendors support only X.509-based certificates.

In the future, certificate formats based on XML (eXtensive Markup Language)—such as the *assertions* defined by the OASIS Security Services Technical Committee in their Security Assertion Markup Language (SAML) specification—may take on prominence within the XML-based business application developer community. Such formats may replace X.509 certificates at the XML application level but are likely to coexist with X.509 certificates at another level in order to interconnect with other deployed infrastructures. The medium for such interconnection may be based upon the XML Key Management Specification, as defined in the W3C (World Wide Web Consortium), in order to hide the details of the underlying X.509-based PKI from the XML-based application.

## Targeted Applications versus Comprehensive Solution

It is possible to implement many security services without the benefit of a PKI. These are typically point solutions, and the specific security features are usually embedded within each application. This may be an option in a limited number of environments, but most mid- to large-scale domains cannot afford to deploy multiple point solutions—especially when a single security infrastructure can meet the needs of multiple applications, thereby leading to a much more cost-effective solution.

However, in small, closed-enterprise domains, point solutions may still turn out to be the most cost-effective way of meeting specific security requirements.

## Standard versus Proprietary Solutions

A solution is said to be based on *standards* when (1) it is based on industry-accepted standards and (2) no unique implementation details pose a threat to interoperability with another technology vendor that is also based on the same standards. A solution is said to be *proprietary* when it is based on unique implementation details that will, by definition, prevent interoperability with other technology vendors.

Given the current interest in and the level of activity with respect to standards and multivendor cooperation, it is difficult to see a business case for adopting proprietary solutions. However, there still may be a small number of environments in which this might be the best choice. Again, this is all part of the cost-benefit tradeoff analysis. However, if interdomain interoperability is even the slightest concern (and in most cases it will be), only standards-based solutions should be considered.

As pointed out earlier, when adopting proprietary solutions—even in an intradomain context—being careful is important because adopting standards-based solutions will help decrease the danger of being locked-in to a single vendor.

## Interoperability Considerations

A number of interoperability issues go beyond the standards themselves. Vendors can legitimately claim standards compliance, but multivendor interoperability still might not be possible for a variety of reasons. Understanding these reasons and ensuring that the vendor community cooperates to provide acceptable and interoperable solutions are essential.

### Certificate and CRL Profiles

Even when standards-based techniques are adopted, dictating implementation specifics that can vary from one domain to another is still possible. This is the case with the X.509 certificates and CRLs. Specifically, different certificate and CRL profiles are being defined to meet a variety of needs. As a deployment consideration, it is important to select technology vendors that offer flexible certificate and CRL generation so that meeting the requirements associated with multiple certificate and CRL profiles is easy to do.

### Multiple Industry-Accepted Standards

It is not sufficient to simply adopt a technology that is "standards based," especially when multiple standards and protocols are available. For example, end-entity certificates can be initialized through different mechanisms, cross-certification can be facilitated in both on-line and off-line operations, and revocation information can be disseminated in a variety of ways. From a requirement perspective, making sure that the technology meets the needs of the organization is important. The more flexible a vendor product is, the more likely it is that the vendor will be able to meet the needs of the organization—both now and in the future. Thus, vendors should offer multiple solutions based on standards and practices that are in widespread use throughout the industry.

### PKI-Enabled Applications

For a given application to consume the services of a PKI, it must be "PKI enabled." This lets the application invoke the necessary security services and key/certificate life-cycle management functions. Technology vendors should offer standard PKI-enabled applications (for example, secure e-mail via S/MIME) as well as generic toolkits that can be used to integrate other applications into the PKI as necessary.

### Policy/Business Control Issues

Certificate Policies must also be addressed to facilitate interdomain interoperability. Specifically, formal agreements need to be established between enterprise domains that want to communicate under one or more interdomain policies.

From a technology perspective, the established business controls must be enforced by the appropriate PKI components. This means that capabilities to populate the public-key certificates with the appropriate extensions must be supported and the appropriate business control settings must be initialized at the client system. It also means that clients must be capable of understanding and properly processing these business controls during certificate path processing.

Making sure that the PKI vendor is capable of supporting the organization's requirements in this area can be extremely important, especially in the interdomain context.

## On-line versus Off-line Operations

*On-line operation* is the situation in which end entities are directly connected to the network. Typically, end entities are capable of consuming all PKI-related services. *Off-line operation* enables end entities to consume at least a subset of the PKI services, even though they are not directly connected to the network.

Some techniques (for example, revocation information dissemination using the On-line Certificate Status Protocol) may require end entities to be on-line in order to perform particular PKI-related operations. These techniques are not suitable for off-line operation (for example, verifying signed e-mail on a laptop during circumstances in which access to the organization's PKI is not possible). To facilitate off-line operation, recent revocation information could have been cached that would enable the revocation status to be verified (within a certain window of time).

Alternatively, the revocation information could have been supplied along with the e-mail in this example. Off-line operation would also require that the necessary certificates and certification paths are available, which can be facilitated through caching or by including the necessary certificates with the e-mail.

Whether off-line operation should be permitted within a particular environment is a policy decision. After the policy is determined, a technology commensurate with the policy can be selected.

## Peripheral Support

Besides any hardware normally associated with the infrastructure components (for example, CA, RA, repository, and client systems), it should be determined if a cryptographic hardware module is required in association with the operation of the CA. This would enable the CA's keying material to be generated and stored on a hardware crypto-module rather than in software, which provides additional protection of the keying material.

Further, end-user hardware tokens or smart cards may also be required. For example, some environments may require multifactor authentication and they may levy a requirement to store private-keying material on a peripheral module rather than on the end user's personal computer. Biometric devices also may be required—either in lieu of or in addition to the hardware tokens or smart cards.

Not all technology vendors support these peripheral devices to the same degree. However, standard *Application Programming Interfaces (APIs)* have been defined, and vendors should adhere to these if they do offer support for peripheral devices. Once the policy decisions surrounding the requirement for these devices have been made, identifying a technology vendor that meets organizational needs will be easier.

## Facility Requirements

All sensitive PKI components must be adequately protected. Because CAs are the most sensitive component within the PKI, appropriately protected facilities must house them. Appropriate physical and procedural safeguards must also be established. Essentially, unauthorized access must be prevented, and individual accountability should be maintained at all times.

Although the physical and procedural security associated with the RA components is typically not as stringent as that for a CA, it may be necessary to protect these components to some degree as well.

Each organization should determine where these components will be placed and how they will be attended. If the organization does not already have adequate facilities in place, this will clearly have an impact on total cost of ownership, and an organization may determine (along with other factors) that it is more cost effective to use a trusted third-party service provider than to deploy their own PKI.

## Personnel Requirements

As alluded to earlier in this chapter, qualified personnel are required to maintain and operate the aspects of the PKI that fall under the direct control of the enterprise. The enterprise should determine the number and skill level of the appropriate personnel, which will depend on the scale of the PKI, as well as how much of the PKI is in-sourced. The types of personnel that may be required include

- *Security officers* responsible for enforcing the security policies dictated by the enterprise
- *Operators* to perform system installs, backups, reboots, and so on
- *Administrators* to perform day-to-day operations such as end-user registration

Also, it may be necessary to enlist the services of skilled consultants and legal counsel to develop and/or analyze Certificate Policies and/or Certification Practice Statements (CPSs).

This too may have a substantial impact on total cost of ownership.

## Certificate Revocation

Implementing a number of different certificate revocation mechanisms is possible. Variables associated with the dissemination of revocation information include protocols, timeliness, size, performance, scalability, and so on.

It is up to each organization to determine its revocation requirements, and it is up to the technology vendor to meet those requirements. PKI technology vendors will likely offer multiple solutions to maximize the chances of capably meeting the various needs of an extremely diverse market. In any case, ensuring that the technology vendor meets the organization's requirements (both now and in the future) is essential.

## End-Entity Roaming

Many organizations have a requirement to support personnel while traveling on business or personnel who are always moving from one place to another as part of their everyday job (for example, in association with parcel delivery companies). This is sometimes referred to as roaming.

The requirements associated with roaming can vary substantially. On the one hand, the roaming user may carry a laptop at all times and therefore have the necessary credentials and client software to engage in PKI-related operations whenever required. In other cases, the roaming user may move from computer to computer, and the software may or may not be the same at each desktop or kiosk. The roaming user may also be unable to personally carry the necessary credentials (for example, a signing private key stored on a hardware token).

If it is determined that roaming is a requirement for a given organization, it is important to ensure that the technology vendor can support this capability in a secure and robust manner.

## Key Recovery

Key recovery deals with the secure storage and distribution of encryption keys to recover corporate data that would otherwise be rendered unrecoverable. A given organization must assess the need for this functionality and determine the requirements associated with its implementation if required.[3]

It is possible to implement a key recovery facility as part of a CA or to implement a separate key recovery component. If an organization

3. Legal restrictions or legal mandates associated with key recovery may exist in some countries. Although not devoted solely to the topic of key recovery, "The Limits of Trust: Cryptography, Governments, and Electronic Commerce" [LOT] identifies existing legislation pertaining to confidentiality and digital signatures on a country-by-country basis.

determines that key recovery is essential to respond to their legitimate business needs, the implementation alternatives should be weighed carefully. Note that some vendors already support this capability, but they may offer only one option for achieving key recovery (for example, it may be supported only as a CA function, and a third-party key recovery center may not be available). Although several years old, information related to key recovery requirements (including a draft U.S. Federal Information Processing Standard (FIPS) on "requirements for key recovery products") can be found at `http://csrc.nist.gov/keyrecovery/`.

## Repository Issues

A number of options can be implemented to disseminate end-entity certificates, revocation information, and other PKI-related information such as policy information. A number of technology vendors that support one or more of these services also exist. It is important for each organization to understand these requirements and to select a technology vendor that can best suit the needs as identified.

As in the case of PKI technology vendors, it is also important to ensure that the repository vendor offers flexible functionality and that the vendor is committed to multivendor interoperability. This is important because interrepository communication and information exchange may be required in support of the certificate and revocation information dissemination requirement.

## Disaster Planning and Recovery

Although careful planning and the implementation of redundant components can minimize the risk associated with many sources of disaster, considering worst-case scenarios and ensuring that the best possible contingency plans are in place is important. This will expedite the recovery of the PKI in the event that a serious disaster does occur.

Perhaps one of the most serious disasters that can occur with respect to the PKI is when a CA's key is compromised (or even suspected to have been compromised). An organization should ensure that the appropriate safeguards are in place to minimize the risk of this event and that the technology vendor understands the problem and can provide recommendations and tools to help expedite recovery if such an event were to occur.

## Security Assurance

Security assurance has to do with how much confidence an organization can place in the proper and secure operation of the PKI components. A number of criteria can be used to gauge the level of confidence that should be associated with a given product, and specific certification or accreditation programs can help determine this confidence level in a formal manner. For example, the "Federal Information Processing Standards Publication 140-1" [FIPS140] establishes criteria for evaluating cryptographic modules, and there are independent laboratories approved to perform FIPS 140-1 evaluations. Other criteria and evaluation procedures are available, including government-sponsored endorsement programs that are based on common evaluation criteria. (See `http://www.cse-cst.gc.ca/en/services/common_criteria/documentation.html` for example.) There are also industry-sponsored testing laboratories that certify products against industry-specific criteria—see, for example, the BITS Financial Services Security Lab: `http://www.bitsinfo.org/overview.html`.

PKI products that are known to meet specific criteria may be much more attractive to an enterprise than products that do not. In fact, it is reasonable for an enterprise to specify minimum criteria that must be demonstrably met by a PKI product before that product will be considered.

## Mitigating Risk

In all cases, it is simply in the best interest of an organization to mitigate risk as much as possible. Understanding the organization's needs and requirements, both now and in the future, partially accomplishes this.

When it comes to selecting a specific technology vendor(s), a number of things should be considered to help ensure that the selection is as sound as possible, including

- **Reputation:** What do their existing customers have to say about the vendor?
- **Market penetration:** How pervasive is the vendor, and what is the estimated market share?
- **Longevity:** Is the vendor viable from a long-term perspective?
- **Cooperation:** Is the vendor willing and able to cooperate with the customer, especially if the vendor knows in advance that some customization will be required to more fully meet the needs of the organization?
- **Support:** What is the level of support (for example, help desk and software upgrades) offered by the vendor?
- **Standards compliance:** Is the vendor standards compliant, and does the vendor offer multiple alternatives?
- **Security:** Does the vendor offer products that have been formally endorsed by independent evaluation labs with respect to industry-established criteria (for example, FIPS 140-1)?
- **Multivendor interoperability:** Is the vendor committed to multivendor interoperability (as demonstrated, for example, through public, formally organized interoperability trials)?
- **Cost:** Is the vendor cost effective, and will the organization realize cost savings?

We have focused on many of the deployment issues to consider before an organization selects one or more technology vendors and launches its initial PKI deployment. The key is to understand the issues to the maximum extent possible and to make educated decisions based on facts and requirements rather than on marketing hype. If necessary, it is highly recommended that an experienced, vendor-independent consultant be hired to help the organization work through these issues.

## Barriers to Deployment

The purpose of this portion of the chapter is to briefly discuss some of the issues that can impede the successful deployment of a PKI within a given organization. Although solutions are being found to reduce or eliminate some of these potential obstacles, it is important to be aware of some of the difficulties that can be encountered.

## Repository Issues

Many enterprise domains utilize a ubiquitous on-line repository to allow for the timely and robust dissemination of certificates, certificate revocation information (for example, *Certificate Revocation Lists, or CRLs*) and any other PKI-related information (for example, policy information). Early PKI deployment experience has demonstrated that this is not without its problems-although these issues are expected to be corrected as the products offered by the vendor community continue to evolve. Our purpose in this section is to discuss some of these issues.

### Lack of Industry-Accepted Standard

One concern with a ubiquitous directory service is that there is no single accepted industry standard for offering these services. Some market segments have adopted the X.500 Directory standards [X500], but numerous (and usually competing) repository-related standards are also already developed or in the process of being developed. For example, the *Lightweight Directory Access Protocol (LDAP)*, which was developed under auspices of the *Internet Engineering Task Force (IETF)*, defines an access protocol between a client and a remote repository. From a technical perspective, LDAP is in direct competition to the X.500-based *Directory Access Protocol (DAP)*.[4]

There are still a number of open issues when it comes to other functions associated with both client-to-server and server-to-server interaction and information exchange. For example, the IETF LDAPext Working Group is developing a number of additional proposed standards, such as access control mechanisms and access control models. Further, the IETF *LDAP Duplication/Replication/Update Protocol (LDUP)* is also under development, which may compete with the X.500 counterpart, the *Directory Information Shadowing Protocol (DISP)*. There are also proprietary solutions, as well as solutions based on standard remote database access. Certificates and CRLs can also be distributed as part of a *Domain Name System (DNS)* function [RFC2538].

Although any one of these solutions may be well suited for a given organization's needs, the breadth of choices can lead to interoperability

4. It appears that LDAP has won the battle in terms of an access mechanism between a client and a remote repository. In fact, most X.500 vendors recognize this and now offer LDAP support in addition to DAP.

difficulties when it comes to interorganizational communication. Selecting standards-based solutions may help reduce some of these problems.

### Multivendor Interoperability

In addition to the standards issue, there is also the issue surrounding multivendor interoperability. Not all directory products are "created equal," and experience has demonstrated that all vendors do not implement some functions; or, if they are implemented, they are not necessarily implemented in a consistent manner from one vendor to another-even if these solutions are based on the same standards. However, this is clearly an issue that will improve with experience, and the directory vendors appear eager to eliminate these types of issues by cooperating with their technology partners, customers, and even their competitors.

### Scalability and Performance

Finally, potential scalability and performance issues are associated with the deployment of a ubiquitous repository service. Given the limited number of large-scale PKI deployments, there is little implementation experience with respect to how many repository servers are required to effectively service a given organization. Clearly, this will be a function of the number of end users, but the validity period of the CRLs (assuming caching is allowed) and other implementation variables (for example, whether Delta CRLs are supported) will have an impact as well. Also, the repository is unlikely to be devoted solely to the operation of the PKI; additional load is likely to be introduced by other uses (for example, a generic "white pages" service also may be supported).

## Knowledgeable Personnel

Even though public-key cryptography was introduced over two decades ago [DiHe76], the widespread availability of the technology itself has come to fruition only in recent years. Because this technology is still fairly new from an implementation and deployment perspective, the number of knowledgeable personnel in this particular field is rather limited. Evidence shows that the number of PKI-knowledgeable personnel is growing, but these resources may be difficult to hire and retain.

From a resource perspective, it is important to recognize that personnel requirements are not simply limited to one or two administrative personnel. Not only are PKI-knowledgeable administrators needed, but also fairly senior-level personnel are required to help develop policy-related documents and agreements. For example, Certificate Policies and interdomain interoperability agreements (for example, cross-certification agreements) may be required in many enterprise environments. Further, the PKI deployment strategy itself needs to be well thought-out and documented appropriately. This also requires fairly knowledgeable senior-level personnel. Of course, it is possible to out-source some or all of these positions, depending on the specific needs of the organization. If internal resources are to be used, were commend that they be formally trained in their particular area of responsibility.

## PKI-Enabled Applications

For a PKI to be useful, the software operating on behalf of end users, processes, or devices must be able to consume the services that the PKI has enabled. Specifically, encryption/decryption and digital signature generation and verification must be supported. In addition, the software must be able to access the key/certificate life-cycle management functions.

When the software is able to "tap into the PKI," it is often said to be *PKI enabled* or *PKI aware*. The list of PKI-aware software is growing, and this trend is expected to continue. For example, many of the more popular e-mail and electronic forms packages are now PKI-aware. This trend is also evident in the *Virtual Private Network (VPN)* market where multiple vendors implement public-key techniques (for example, those based on the proposed *Internet Key Exchange (IKE)* standard [RFC2409]).

In addition, Web browser and server technology may be viewed as "partially" PKI enabled. However, even though the Secure Sockets Layer (SSL) or the Transport Layer Security (TLS) [RFC2246] protocols (which base authentication between a client and a server on public-key techniques) are typically supported, the browser/server technology that is currently available clearly requires significant improvements before the Web environment will support full certificate-based services and key/certificate life-cycle management. However, this sitiuation has been improving and will continue to improve in the future.

Numerous applications (for example, legacy applications) will likely remain outside the PKI-enabled list, however. This is due to a variety of factors, including the inability to modify these applications so that they are capable of consuming the services offered by the PKI (because of a lack of available resources and/or the exorbitant cost associated with the necessary software modifications).

## Corporate-Level Acceptance

We cannot overemphasize the need for corporate-level "buy-in." Without the appropriate champions in place to usher in the deployment of the new technology, overcoming many of the hurdles likely to stand in the way of a successful deployment will be extremely difficult. If nothing else, resistance to change is commonly encountered in organizations, regardless of what that change might be. It is therefore necessary to build a solid business case and to "sell" that business case to the critical decision makers within a given organization.

This section briefly presented some issues that might impede the deployment of a PKI within a given organization. In many cases, however, significant improvements are helping reduce these issues. Eventually, most, if not all, of these issues will be effectively reduced to only minor considerations within many organizations.

## Typical Business Models

In this portion of the chapter, we discuss several different business models that might drive the deployment of a PKI. Although this may not be an exhaustive list, we do concentrate on some of today's more prevalent business models, as evidenced by many of the PKI deployments around the globe.

Several initiatives are also designed to offer scalable interdomain trust paths between organizations. Because these initiatives may have an influence on the external communications business model described here, we also give a brief discussion regarding these initiatives.

## Internal Communications Business Model

From a corporate-security perspective, the overall goal in any organization is to provide cost-effective, usable security that is commensurate with the perceived level of risk. If the cost of providing the security is too great or if the deployed security services are too difficult to use or administer, the business case for deploying that solution cannot be justified.

Justifying anything of this nature is extremely difficult without considering the true benefits that will be realized through the judicious deployment of a comprehensive security infrastructure. For example, significant cost savings can be realized by reducing the amount of time that individuals spend logging-in to multiple applications each day. Further, the proper protection of corporate information can help reduce significant financial losses that can result from the theft of unprotected electronic information (either in storage or in transit). Of course, cost considerations are not the only benefits realized from providing comprehensive security services. Improvements in workflow efficiency, reduction in administrative overhead, and even revenue generation are all factors that may contribute to the business case. (These considerations are discussed earlier in this chapter.)

Generally, the business drivers for deploying a particular security solution center on several specific areas, such as the following:

- Enhanced authentication and accountability
- Secure e-mail
- Desktop security (for example, encryption of sensitive files stored on a disk drive)
- Secure remote access
- Secure internal communications (for example, secure intranet)
- Secure external communications (for example, secure extranet)
- Reduced sign-on
- Paper reduction through adoption of secure electronic forms
- Secure (and robust) audit trails

In many cases, a single application is selected to help launch the initial PKI deployment, which is then used as a vehicle to prove the utility and necessity of the PKI itself. As discussed earlier in this chapter, launching a small-scale pilot that focuses on a single application enables an ordered and controlled PKI deployment. Over time, additional applications are folded in, which eventually leads to a single infrastructure that is capable of supporting a variety of applications in a number of different contexts.

Thus, the prominent intra-organizational business model is to enhance overall security in a number of areas but in a cost-effective, structured, and user-friendly manner. Ultimately, the benefit of a PKI-based solution is to provide a single infrastructure that can support myriad security services in a complex, heterogeneous, multiapplication, large-scale business environment.

## External Communications Business Models

Our purpose in this section is to briefly discuss some of the business models currently being adopted for external corporate communications. These will be addressed from two perspectives: business-to-business and business-to-consumer.

### Business-to-Business Communication

The main business driver for business-to-business communications is to provide secure and cost-effective interorganizational communications. Although this may seem to be a rather obvious statement, ubiquitous business-to-business interaction is not guaranteed. Solid business drivers must be in place to motivate corporations (or governments) to interconnect their PKI domains. To many, this falls under the general umbrella of secure electronic commerce (e-commerce).

A given business may want to communicate with a variety of external sources that have deployed or out-sourced their own PKI, including partners, separately incorporated subsidiaries, suppliers, and peers.

Further, a given business may want to communicate with these external sources for a variety of reasons, including

- Purchase-order exchange
- Collaborative research
- Preauthorization of financial transactions
- Payment transfers
- Interorganizational correspondence
- Supply chain management
- Secure document exchange

Not surprisingly, many of the applications listed in the Internal Communications Business Model section of this chapter can be used to accommodate the secure communications between two or more businesses. For example, secure e-mail might be suitable for collaborative research and interorganizational correspondence. On the other hand, some sort of automated payment-transfer protocol would be more appropriate to facilitate payment transfers between financial institutions.

In any case, an agreed-on set of common security capabilities is required to realize effective business-to-business communications.[5] Many view PKI technology as the very foundation to achieve these capabilities.

## Business-to-Consumer Communication

Much of today's business-to-consumer e-commerce would not be possible without the Internet or the World Wide Web (WWW). However, it is important to distinguish between two prevalent business models when it comes to providing business-to-consumer electronic commerce.

The first model is *user centric*. Individuals obtain their own certificates from a third-party service provider, or they generate their own certificates. In many cases, the individuals use standard "Web technology" to conduct their business. This is largely an unstructured and uncontrolled model, in which even the most basic certificate/key life-cycle management is simply unavailable (although we have seen recent improvements in this area).

In this model, e-commerce is typically based on the *Secure Sockets Layer (SSL)* protocol or *Transport Layer Security (TLS)* [RFC2246] protocol, which provides a confidentiality pipe between a browser and a server. Server-only or mutual client-server authentication can also be supported. However, the use of SSL/TLS has been criticized because client authentication is generally considered optional and is rarely used in today's Web environment. It has also been criticized due to a lack of "persistent" confidentiality. That is, once the server receives data, it is decrypted. If the server does nothing more to protect that data, it is vulnerable to attack.

In addition, SSL/TLS does not support digital signatures over the data, so there is no way to preserve a persistent digital signature in association with

5. Each organization can run the PKI services independently. In this case, *cross-certification* can be used to establish the necessary trust relationship(s) between the two organizations. Alternatively, a parent organization may offer PKI services to one or more of its subsidiaries, especially if the subsidiary is a relatively small organization that does not have the business need to run an internal PKI.

a given transaction, which is a serious limitation in many transaction-based applications. Nonetheless, many of the merchants on the Web rely on SSL/TLS for the protection of the transactions (for example, to protect credit card numbers while in transit between the client and the server).

The second model is more "organization centric." This second model, which has been adopted by a number of organizations, is arguably more controlled and more secure than the first. An example of this model is an organization (a bank, for example) that operates as a Certification Authority (CA); certificates are issued to that organization's constituents for the specific purpose of conducting business between the individual and that organization. This model may also include the use of special-purpose software, typically issued from the organization to the individual, to offer more comprehensive certificate/key life-cycle management and more secure communications than would normally be available. It also enables the organization to more easily control the purpose and scope of the certificates it issues.

## Internal/External Business Model Hybrids

Of course, it is natural for many organizations to offer both internal and external security services based on PKI technology. These two models must *not* be viewed as being mutually exclusive. In fact, many of today's PKI deployments begin with a modest-scale internal pilot (for example, deployment of a single PKI-enabled application with a community of users on the order of tens or hundreds). This is followed by larger-scale initiatives (for example, incorporating additional applications and increasing the number of users), including external business-to-business and business-to-consumer deployments.

## Business Model Influences

Besides internal business requirements, external events sometimes significantly influence the business model. For example, the U.S. health-care industry has witnessed the introduction of legislation that is likely to cast an unprecedented focus on the protection of electronic health-care information. Specifically, the Medical Records Confidentiality Act of 1995 levies severe penalties associated with the unauthorized disclosure of medical information. In addition, the Health Information Portability and Accountability Act of 1996 (HIPAA, also known as the Kennedy-Kassebaum Bill) mandates that the U.S. Congress enact federal laws for the protection of patient information. Clearly, this will have a profound impact on the business model of any health-care organization.

As more and more of the paper-based medical records are replaced with *Electronic Medical Records (EMRs)*, care must be taken to ensure that those records are accessed and updated in accordance with sound business (and ethical) practices *and* all applicable legislation. For example, the technology used to access EMRs can vary significantly, and the individuals that access EMRs also vary. Specifically, access to the EMR can be local or remote (including remote access over the Internet), and personnel accessing the EMR can be a primary care or consulting physician, a nurse, or even the patient him- or herself.

This brief example helps illustrate how secure electronic forms, secure remote access, and individual access control and accountability are required in a business model that must address the proper protection of EMRs.

[NAS] summarizes many of the issues associated with the protection of health-care information.

## Government-Sponsored Initiatives

A number of government-sponsored initiatives—for example, the Government of Canada Public Key Infrastructure (GOC PKI) and the U.S. Federal PKI (FPKI)—can be modeled in the same way as the internal, business-to-business and business-to-consumer models described in the preceding sections. In this case, the internal business model is driven by a need to facilitate interdepartmental communications among civil servants. The business-to-business model represents the need for peer-to-peer communications between governments on a national, regional, or local basis. The business-to-consumer model reflects the need for a government to offer services to its citizens—although the specific applications may vary substantially due to the nature of services traditionally offered by a government (as compared to a private organization).

The deployment strategy of the known governmental deployments also reflects that of an internal/external business model hybrid discussed previously in this chapter. Specifically, the government-based PKIs tend to begin with modest internal deployments (on the order of tens or perhaps hundreds of users), with the plan to expand and extend the reach of the PKI to offer external services to the citizen and to provide for intergovernmental communications.

## Interdomain Trust

Although it is possible for individual businesses to forge their own interorganizational trust relationships on a bilateral basis, a number of initiatives are designed to establish business-to-business trust relationships on behalf of these organizations. The purpose of this section is to briefly discuss a few of these initiatives.

### Identrus

*Identrus* is an organization that is designed to help establish business-to-business trust relationships for the purpose of conducting global e-commerce among financial institutions. Eight major financial institutions founded Identrus, and its membership has grown substantially over the past few years.

The Identrus infrastructure is based on a rooted hierarchy. Thus, each participating financial institution will "fall under" a common root. However, ultimately the basis of trust rests with the participating financial institutions.

Technology to support the Identrus infrastructure can be supplied by multiple vendors, as long as the vendors are capable of offering products that conform to the Identrus infrastructure guidelines.

Additional information regarding Identrus can be found at `www.identrus.com`.

### Bridge CA

The bridge capability is extremely powerful because it substantially reduces the number of bilateral cross-certifications and it preserves the autonomy of the individual CA domains (for example, governmental departments that have deployed their own CAs under the umbrella of the larger government-wide PKI domain). This model also allows individual departments to deploy without waiting on external events such as the deployment of a common root CA.

We believe that this model may very well become standard practice in a number of industry segments.

## VeriSignF Trust Network

The *VeriSign Trust Network (VTN)* exists because VeriSign has several root keys embedded in the Web browsers, and both individual and server certificates issued by VeriSign "fall under" one of those root keys. Thus, VTN is based on a rooted hierarchy trust model. This model can be extended to encompass interorganizational trust, as long as the certificates issued by each organization fall under a common VeriSign root.

## GTE CyberTrust/Baltimore Technologies OmniRoot

In May 1999, GTE CyberTrust announced a new service offering that is referred to as *OmniRoot*. From a "trust network" perspective, the GTE CyberTrust OmniRoot is analogous to the VTN. Specifically, GTE CyberTrust has several root keys embedded within the popular Web browsers available from Microsoft and Netscape. If an organization chooses to operate CAs that are subordinate to the GTE CyberTrust root CA, browsers will recognize certificates issued by those CAs.

Early in 2000, Baltimore Technologies acquired GTE CyberTrust, and the OmniRoot "trust network" is now part of their product portfolio.

## Other Trust Networks

It reasonable to suggest that any organization that issues certificates under the authority of a CA—whose root key is embedded in the browser and/or that issues organizational certificates under a common root—is in a position to claim that it, too, offers a "trust network" (as long as the individuals and the organizations are confident that the CA itself provides a solid foundation to enable those trust relationships). However, it may be important to appropriately constrain these CAs in the future perhaps through the use of the Name Constraints and/or Policy Constraints certificate extensions.

We have addressed some of the more common business models that may drive PKI deployment. In particular, this chapter presented the following business models:

- Business models related to internal communications requirements
- Business models related to external communications requirements

These models are not mutually exclusive (that is, an organization may implement both business models).

The goal of a PKI is to establish a single infrastructure that is capable of supporting multiple applications across multiple domains. This infrastructure must be cost effective, capable of evolving over time, and based on industry-accepted standards to help ensure interoperability with other domains.

Although the initial PKI deployments may be modest internal efforts, the objective for many organizations (and governments) is to extend the "reach" of interoperability across multiple CA and PKI boundaries. In other words, internal corporate communications is only the first step. Secure communications with external trading partners, subsidiaries, communities of interest (for example, collaborative research among many universities), or even peer organizations within a given industry (for example, the financial sector or the automotive industry) is also a highly desirable goal.

A number of national and regional government initiatives reflect the business models discussed here. For example, the GOC PKI is designed to facilitate secure interdepartmental communications for many of the applications that might be associated with the internal operations of a large corporation. The government of Canada is also working to provide governmental services to Canadian citizens through their Government On-Line (GOL) initiative.

Finally, we briefly discussed a few interdomain trust initiatives.

CHAPTER 11

# SERVER SECURITY

Servers are the last layer of defense against attackers. If an attacker does manage to bypass the security restrictions in place on the routers and firewalls, the servers have to be hardened enough to keep the attacker from gaining unauthorized access to information on the network.

The server security problem is complicated by the fact that some servers are, by nature, public servers, so everyone—even people outside the organization—has to be allowed access. Even if all the servers on your network are private, security measures still need to be put in place to prevent unauthorized users from gaining access. This includes access from unauthorized employees.

A server is any machine to which multiple network users must connect in order to perform their jobs. Generally these machines have more memory, storage capacity, and faster processors (or multiple processors) than end user machines, also called workstations. Servers usually run different operating systems than workstations, though not always. Microsoft, for example, has created Windows 2000 Professional and Windows XP Professional for workstations and Windows 2000 Server, Windows 2000 Advanced Server, and Windows 2000 Datacenter Server for servers. In a similar manner Red Hat Linux 8.0 Professional is designed for workstations, while Red Hat Linux Advanced Server is designed for servers. On the other hand, Sun Solaris and FreeBSD use the same operating system for both servers and workstations.

That is not to say that all these server operating systems should be in use on the network, simultaneously. Running several different operating systems within the network can actually be detrimental to network security. Chances are the company's server administrative staff has a core expertise with one or two operating systems. If a third or fourth server operating system is added to the network—for whatever reason—there may not be enough staff members who have the knowledge to secure it properly.

For this reason, many security experts recommend using no more than two server operating systems on a network. There are, of course, exceptions to this guideline. If an organization has separate administrative staff for different servers, then the staff will presumably have expertise in the server operating system. For example, if the administrators for the web farm have experience with FreeBSD then running FreeBSD poses no security problems, even if it is not in use anywhere else in the network. This guideline applies primarily to organizations where server management is centralized in one group.

There is a lot of debate about operating system security within organizations, and over the Internet.[1] The truth is that all server operating systems can be properly secured when managed by an administrator who understands the operating system and how to secure it. No server operating system is inherently more secure than any other, but some are more secure out of the box, making the security process easier.

If an administrator does not know what he or she is doing, it is very easy to weaken the security of a server, especially a public server. That's why it is so important to ensure that all members of the server administration staff within an organization are properly trained on good server operating system security procedures. These procedures should be operating system specific, and organization specific. General guidelines, such as those present in this book, are a good start for forming internal best practices for server security, but each organization has specific needs, and the internal documents should reflect them.

Remember, too, open source does not automatically equate to less secure. There is a lot of misinformation about the security of open-source projects, but it basically boils down to same mantra: Because everyone has access to the source code, anyone can find security holes and exploit them.

The people who point this out usually forget to mention the opposite: Because everyone has access to the source code, anyone can find security holes and fix them. The vast majority of developers fall into the latter category. Open-source projects like Apache, Sendmail, BIND, and Linux have been tested, reviewed, picked over, and beaten on by so many developers that they are both stable and secure. Do security holes still arise? Absolutely, but those holes are quickly patched and the code updated. More importantly, long-standing open-source projects, like the ones mentioned, do not report security incidents more frequently than their closed-source counterparts.

This is not to suggest that an enterprise network should dump all closed-source products in favor of open-source solutions. There are

1. Debate is the nice way of saying "flame war."

open-source products that have abysmal security records. Instead, organizations should not be afraid to evaluate open-source products alongside closed-source products for use in the network. If an open-source product can meet the security requirements of an organization there is no reason not to use it. If the product cannot meet the security requirements, let the developers know about the problems experienced, and maybe the next time an evaluation is performed, it will be able to meet the requirements.

The first section of this chapter covers general guidelines for server security, including some operating-system-specific guidelines. The other sections focus on different types of servers. Web, mail, file, and other servers are all discussed in general and specific terms.

## General Server Security Guidelines

There are two goals in the security process of any server: Allow authorized users to access the information they need, while preventing unauthorized users from gaining information they should not have. These goals seem to be almost polar opposites; an administrator has to let a user access his or her files, at the same time an attacker has to be prevented from accessing them. Considering that an attacker may be another employee who does have legitimate access to the server, it is easy to understand why server administrators are sometimes grumpy.

### Server Construction

The first place to start with server security is the server itself. Remember, redundancy, scalability, and availability are critical components of security. A server should be constructed with these features in mind.

Most large organizations do not build their own servers, relying instead on servers from companies such as Dell, IBM or Hewlett-Packard. Fortunately, these companies will allow organizations to configure servers to fit their needs. Take advantage of this by selecting equipment that is designed for availability, and configuring as much redundancy into the system as practical.

Server components most likely to fail are those that have moving parts: power supplies, hard drives, fans, CD-ROMs, and floppy drives. Power supplies, hard drives, and fans are crucial to a functioning server; CD-ROMs and floppy drives are not as critical as the server can generally run without a working CD-ROM or floppy drive until it can be replaced.

To ensure continual performance, all servers on the network should be equipped with dual power supplies. Both power supplies should be plugged in. The server will only use the primary power supply, switching to the secondary if the primary fails (the reason for keeping both power supplies plugged in).

Power failures are especially dangerous, not only because they take the server offline, but also some server operating systems are particularly sensitive to data corruption that can be caused by incorrectly shutting down the server. Databases and other applications that are continuously writing to the disk are also sensitive to corruption by incorrectly shutting down the server.

Failover from one power supply to another should be instantaneous, meaning there is no interruption in service if the power supply fails. One thing to bear in mind is that it is not enough just to have the dual power supplies. The server has to have a way of notifying administrators when the power supply fails. If there is no notification, then there is no way to know that the power supply needs to be replaced. Server vendors should provide information about the notification process; if not, ask.

---

**NOTE:** Many servers do not have power buttons. This is to prevent an unknowing administrator from inadvertently destroying a server by using the power button to turn the server off. Unfortunately, this does not stop the same novice administrator from pulling the power cord—yet another reason for dual power supplies.

---

Hard drives are equally important to component availability. After all, the reason for the server's existence is the information located on the server. The information on the server is crucial to the existence of an organization, and should be protected as such. Hardware experts recommend Small Computer System Interface (SCSI) hard drives over Integrated Device Electronics (IDE) hard drives. SCSI drives are faster, at 10,000 to 15,000 revolutions per minute, than IDE drives, at 7,200 to 10,000 revolutions per minute, and SCSI drives are designed to last longer, with a longer mean time between failures (MTBF). Some SCSI manufacturers claim up to 1.2 million hours MTBF for their drives, while IDE drives generally have claims in the 100,000 hours MTBF range.

In addition to a quality hard drive, drives should be deployed in a redundant fashion. This is accomplished using a redundant array of independent disks (RAID). The most common RAID configuration is to deploy the drives in a redundant fashion. All data written to Disk 1 is also written to Disk 2, also known as a RAID 1. A second type of RAID configuration is RAID 0, which treats the string of disks as a single large disk. This increases the amount of storage available, but does not provide data redundancy.

The third type of RAID configuration is RAID 5. In this configuration, data is striped across multiple disks in a redundant fashion, giving the best of both worlds: It allows an administrator to create a single large storage area from several smaller disks, and it still allows for redundant data.

SCSI drives arranged in a RAID configuration often run very hot, so they require additional cooling, and sometimes even a separate case for the drives. Server cooling is usually handled through small fans placed throughout the case to optimize the cooling effect. Server fans have small motors, which can fail. Server cases usually have four or more fans placed in the server; if one fails, the others will continue to cool the inside of the case.

Unfortunately because the motors in the fans are so small, they do not usually have a way of alerting the system if there is a failure. Instead many server motherboards now include thermostats. If the temperature inside the case starts to rise an alert is generated, and the administrator of the server can take a look during the next maintenance window (unless the temperature gets too high, in which case the server may shut down).

## Server Placement

Where the server is placed is just as important as its components. Two aspects of server placement have to be considered:

1. Physical location
2. Network placement

With regard to physical placement, the ideal location would be in a data center environment. Servers should be in a separate room, which is locked at all times, and to which only certain employees have access. Servers should be rack mountable, and they should be fully mounted. That sounds obvious, but many times rack mountable servers are simply stacked on top of each other within the rack. This makes it very easy for anyone who has access to the server room to walk off with a server.[2] In addition to physical security, rack mounting servers does increase availability. Computer racks are generally designed with air circulation in mind. If the servers are properly mounted, it will be easier for air to circulate through the rack, and assist in keeping the server temperature cooler.

The room should have a separate cooling and filtering unit. The HVAC unit should recycle the air at least every five minutes to keep dust and other contaminants out of the room. Dust is the biggest small-scale natural threat to computers. If dust begins to collect in the servers it can degrade the performance and decrease the life expectancy. The temperature of the data center should hover around 70 degrees Fahrenheit, or 21 degrees Celsius.

The room should also be equipped with FM200 fire suppression conduits, rather than traditional sprinkler systems. FM200, chemically known as heptafluoropropane, is a foam-like fire suppressant that can, unlike water, douse fires that occur in the data center without necessarily destroying the servers, or the data on the servers. Fires that occur as a result of overheated computers are extremely rare, but still possible, so good fire suppression is necessary for a data center environment.

Finally, the data center should have some form of backup power. The most common form of backup power used is an uninterruptible power supply. APC and Liebert are two manufacturers most often associated with data-center-wide UPS.

The two most important considerations when deciding on a backup power supply are the amount of power needed and the length of time the data center needs to stay up. The amount of power needed is based on the number of network devices in the data center and the amount of power they consume. The length of time that the data center needs to remain online will depend on what types of servers are housed there, and who needs to access them.

If the data center is used primarily for on-site employees to access information, then the backup power supply should need to provide power for only an hour or two. This should be ample time to contact the power company and determine when the power will be restored. A one- or two-hour window also gives the administrative staff time to shut down the servers.

On the other hand if there are public servers, or servers that employees from other locations need to access, located within the data center,

2. If you doubt this try unmounting a server that is fully mounted in less than 10 minutes.

then additional backup power requirements may needed. Generally, a UPS should not be used to provide more than six hours of backup power. If more time is required a generator should be used. Generators require special wiring to ensure that power will flip over to the generator in the event of a power failure. Before installing one check with building management to ensure that there are no restrictions against generators.

---

**NOTE:** If power outages are common in your area, make sure there is gas in the generator. Many companies have procedures in place to deal with power outages, but nothing in the procedures addresses what to do when the power returns. Either make refueling the generator part of the power outage procedure, or make it standard to check the generator once a month to make sure it has fuel.

---

Physically securing servers is not enough; servers have to be placed on the network in a manner that will ensure their security and availability.

Network administrators will often segment servers into a separate VLAN, as shown in Figure 11-1. This makes sense at one level because it makes the management and monitoring of the servers simpler. It can also make network security easier by isolating the servers and creating more restrictive security policies for those switches.

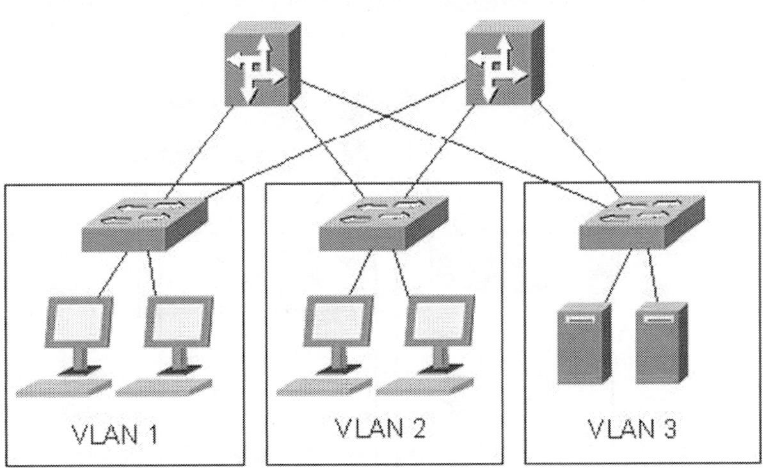


**Figure 11-1** A traditional network design. Each switch block is segmented into different VLANs, creating an unnecessary load on the network.

The downside is it increases network traffic. Requests from the workstations have to be routed to the servers and back. A better solution for servers that are workgroup specific is to include the server as part of the workgroup VLAN.

This network design does not work for all servers, only servers that need to be accessed by a specific workgroup. For example department-specific file servers, DHCP servers, or domain controllers can be isolated in this manner.

As Figure 11-2 shows, a server that is used by the workgroup associated with VLAN 1 is also placed in VLAN 1. Traffic going from the workstations to the server, and vice versa, needs only to be switched, not routed. This decreases the load on the core switches or routers, and makes more efficient use of bandwidth within the network.

Of course this won't work for all servers. web, mail, and DNS servers—among others—need to be accessed by all employees, as well as users outside the network. Public servers should be placed on a switch that is only used for public servers.

Having each server in a separate VLAN might seem like it would make it more difficult to effectively manage and monitor those servers. It will not if a separate network, a management network, is created.

A management network, sometimes referred to as a backnet, is an isolated network that can be used to manage the servers. This management network is designed to facilitate server upgrades, backups, configuration,

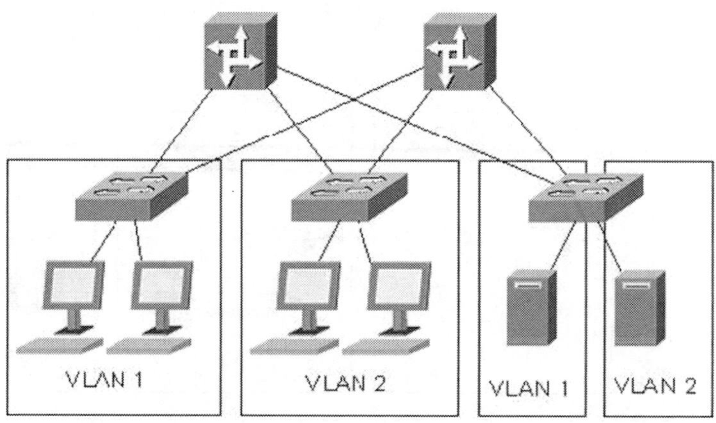


**Figure 11-2** Segmenting servers into VLANs associated with different networks can decrease the load on routers.

and monitoring. The most important aspect of a management network is that it has to be isolated. There should be no traffic, aside from management traffic, that traverses the backnet.

Figure 11-3 illustrates the typical setup of a management network. Each server on the backnet has a primary IP address in a separate VLAN. The back-net interfaces are all part of the same VLAN, and they are part of a separate network. A separate network infrastructure is in place to support the management network. Again, this is to keep management traffic apart from the rest of the network traffic.

There are two advantages to installing a management network in this manner:

- It isolates management traffic which improves overall network performance.
- It keeps management passwords, monitoring information, and other tools used to keep tabs on the network isolated from attackers and prying eyes.

In fact, many organizations with a management network in place will only allow human connections to be made through a VPN, further enhancing the security of the information shared across this network.

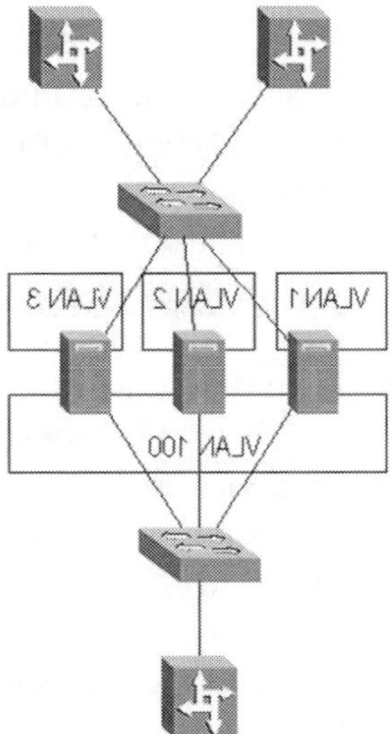


**Figure 11-3** Using a management network to control the type of traffic that is sent to the main server IP address and to better manage network traffic.

A backnet will not work well in all network environments, but it does make a great additional layer of security when it can be used.

## Server Security

The servers have now been physically secured and isolated on the network. The next step is to secure access to the servers. Because the most damaging network attacks require gaining access to a server, it is important to restrict access as much as possible to all servers.

Start by limiting servers to single-use machines. The web server should be used only to serve websites, the mail server should only be used for mail, and so on. It is easier to manage security on individual servers if an administrator can limit the number of services running on them.

A good example of this is the X-Windows management system that is installed on many Unix systems by default. Because Unix servers are generally managed through the command line, keeping the X-Windows system installed only leaves unnecessary accounts installed and potential security holes open.

Of course in order for this strategy to work, it is also important to follow through and disable any services that are unused. Not only should unnecessary services be disabled, but whenever possible they should be removed, or not installed in the first place.

Services should never be run as the administrative user. It may be necessary to start the service using the administrative user account to bind it to the port, but the service should continue to run as a nonprivileged user. If the service is run as a nonprivileged user then if the service is compromised it is less likely that an attacker will be able to cause any further damage to the network.

In addition to running services as nonprivileged users, unnecessary accounts should be removed from servers, or at a minimum, renamed. The Windows guest account is an example of an unnecessary account that should be deleted. The same goes for the Unix games, bin, and sys accounts as well as other well-known accounts. If the accounts cannot be removed entirely they should be configured with no login capabilities and a very restrictive password. All accounts on all network devices, but especially on servers, should have passwords.

Accounts created on the server should be subject to the same password policy as the rest of the network. This means that the passwords should be changed at regular intervals, and they should be sufficiently difficult to crack using password cracking tools.

Whenever possible information about user accounts should be stored in a centralized database. This helps decrease the likelihood that a wayward account will be created on a server. It also makes it easier for employees to hop from server to server, as long as they have permission to access the server. In cases where a centralized user database is in use, the authentication from the servers to the user database should use some sort of encryption. Kerberos is the type of authentication most often associated with this type of server management. Kerberos is also nice, because Unix operating systems, and Windows 2000, support it, making it possible for a user to authenticate against both types of servers, if necessary.

This does not mean that users should have the run of the network; servers should be configured so that only specific groups have access to specific servers. Users in the accounting group should not need access to the sales server, and so on. Again, limiting who has access to a server will limit the amount of damage an attacker who gains access to one of the servers can do.

Files on the system should be restricted as well. A common way of enforcing file security is to create separate partitions on the server. One partition should be used for system files, while a separate partition can be used for user files. This is a common practice on Unix servers, which are generally broken into /, /usr, /etc, /opt, and others, depending on the needs of the server administrator. This is a less common practice on Windows-based servers, but one that should be followed, even if it is as simple as putting the system files on a C:\ and user files on an F:\ partition.

Partitioning servers has two effects:

1. It separates system information in a logical manner. If something happens to one of the partitions, data on the second partition is usually safe.
2. It creates a separate root directory for users. Users on the F:\ partition, or in the /usr partition see F:\ and /usr, respectively, as their root directories, and are unable to access the system files on the other partitions. While this is not perfect security, it does make the job of an attacker more difficult.

Cording off partitions is not enough; servers should have file systems that are as restrictive as possible. No users should have executable access on file servers, and, ideally, the user should only be able to access files in his or her own directory. In other words, the user should not be able to browse the directories or files of other users. This is done by giving the user's directory read and write permissions, but no other user—except the administrative user—should have access to the user's directory. Figures 11-4 and 11-5 show the best practices file permissions for Unix and Windows 2000 servers. These permissions assume the server will be used solely for storing data, and no programs will need to be run directly on the server.

System files should always be owned by the administrative user, and should be viewable or executable only by the administrator. This may mean tightening default permissions on some operating systems. This change is necessary especially when dealing with configuration files. Configuration files are often plain text, so if one has weak permissions, it can be used by an attacker to gather more information about a server and increase the amount of damage an attacker is capable of inflicting on the server.

On Windows servers, the group "Everyone" should be removed from the server, or used sparingly. The "Everyone" group allows all users on a server to have access to a file or directory, including the guest user. Since the "Everyone" group defeats the purpose of restricting file systems, there is no point in using it on the server. Instead only groups that need access to the server should be installed on it.

If each department has its own dedicated server, the task of restricting access is a lot simpler. It is easier to restrict access to a group and then assign permission to individual folders. In some environments, especially within workgroups that are more collaborative in nature, it is acceptable to restrict individual folder access to the group, instead of the individual user.

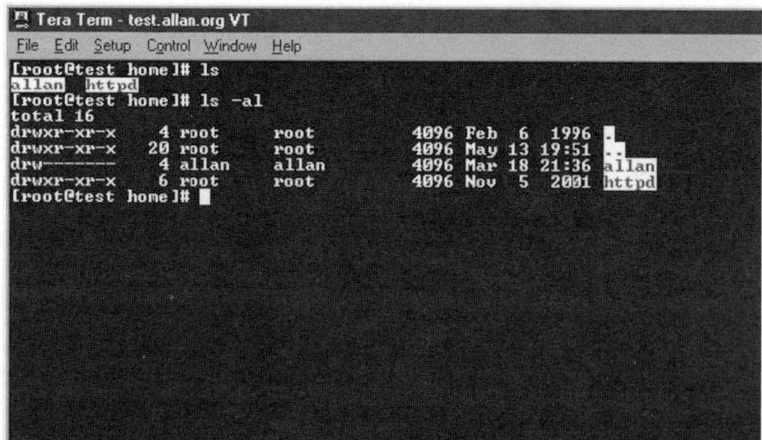


**Figure 11-4** Unix system file permissions. User Allan has read and write access to the directory allan; no other groups have read or write access.

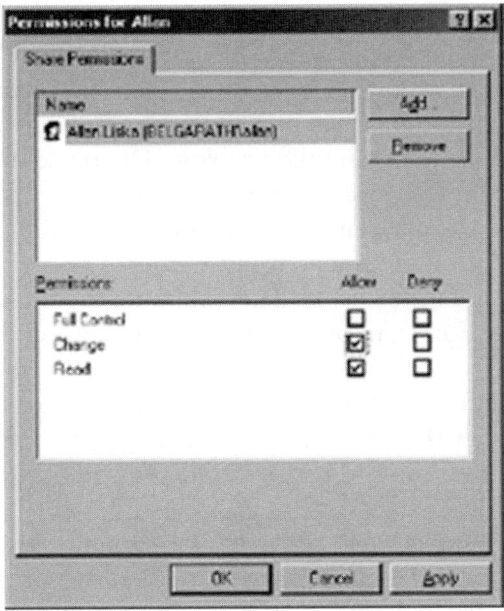

**Figure 11-5** Windows 2000 file permissions. The user Allan is the only person, aside from the Administrator, who has access to the folder allan.

This will allow group members to access files in each other's folders, share information, and still keep the data protected from outside users. Group permission is 660 (rw-rw----) on a Unix system and Read and Change on a Windows server.

Giving group access to an individual's folder can have negative consequences. If an employee's password is compromised the attacker will now have access to all files on the server, and can delete the files, make changes, or even copy them and use them against an organization. Many organizations have opted to use intranets to facilitate group collaboration. With an intranet, files that need to be shared with group members can be posted publicly, while files that are private, or still in development, can be left in the user's directory, keeping them segregated from other members in the group.

---

**NOTE:** Because servers, especially web servers, are susceptible to attacks, Unix administrators often install chkrootkit (*www.chkrootkit.org/*), or a similar program. These programs look for signs of known rootkits on the server and report any suspicious findings.

---

Another good practice is to monitor file permissions on the server. A task that looks for inappropriate file permissions can be scheduled to run nightly. Usually a report is generated, then permissions can be automatically changed, or e-mail can be sent to the offending users, explaining what needs to be done to correct the problem. Of course, this process should be monitored closely to ensure the users are actually making the permission changes.

On Unix systems, another method of file system security is to create a special environment using chroot. Chroot is a way to create a jailed environment for users. The jail limits the directories to which a user has access. For example, a typical Unix user's home directory might be /home/users/allan/. The directory /home is already a partition; however, an administrator may want to create an environment in which the user Allan sees the root directory as being /allan. This forces the user to stay within the home directory, and prevents users from searching through other files.

An environment protected by chroot is still vulnerable to attacks, so it should not be used as a single solution for securing file systems. However, when used in conjunction with other security precautions, chroot can add an extra level of security to a server.

## The Administrative User

The administrative user is the one user who can cause the most damage on a server. The administrator has access to the entire server and is able manipulate any file on the server. Limiting the capabilities of the administrative user is not a good idea; instead, it is better to restrict server access, making it difficult to become the administrative user.

Windows and Unix operating systems approach the administrative user in two distinct fashions, although the user performs the same tasks. The administrative user is known as administrator, which on a Windows server is a username that can be changed. In fact, many Windows security experts recommend changing administrator to an account name that is less obvious. This is another example of security through obscurity, which is not the recommended approach to securing a server, but it is a good idea when used in conjunction with other security measures.

Windows servers require that many services run as administrator, opening the possibility for root exploits. If an attacker is able to compromise one of these services remotely, the username is known, so it is just a matter of determining the password. If the attacker has to determine the username and password, breaking into the server is that much more difficult.

For the name change to be effective, the administrator account should be renamed to something non-obvious. Renaming it to root, or another common name, is very ineffective, and still leaves the server easily exploitable.

Different users can have administrative access to a server, and a user can be made the administrator of a single server, but not necessarily an entire server farm. However, if a user is logged in as a non-administrative user, that person has to log out and login as an administrator to gain server control.

This contrasts greatly with Unix, which allows users to login as one user and switch to the administrative user, known as root, using the substitute user (`su`) command. The obvious downside to `su` is that, in its most basic implementation, it allows any user to become root. To limit the security risks posed by allowing any user to become root, most administrators create a wheel group. The wheel group is a special Unix group which allows an administrator to control the users that have access to becoming root.

Unix, like Windows, allows users to belong to multiple groups, making it possible to give different users root access to different servers. For example, if the company webmaster needs root access on the web server, but no other servers, then the webmaster's account can be added to the wheel group on the web server, but not on any other servers. An administrator has the ability to add individual users to the wheel group, while leaving other users in the same group unaffected. Using the example of a web server, it is common to have a group of users maintain a website. These users are most likely part of the same group; the webmaster will also be part of this group. An administrator can give the web-master the capability of becoming root, without giving the other users in the group root access.

Unlike Windows-based servers, it is not recommended that administrators change the root user to a different name. There are too many services that rely on having access to the root user in order to start. In addition, Unix has built-in tools that allow administrators to limit how root is accessed.

One recommendation commonly made by security experts is to limit console and TTY access, so only the root user can login from the console. Within the server, limit the range of IP addresses that are able to access the server remotely, and log all connection attempts, as well as any attempts to change to the root user. Some security experts also recommend disabling remote root access. This forces administrators to log into the server, then su to root, in order to become the administrative user. The argument for this security step is that it forces a potential attacker to try to crack two passwords instead of one.

Finally, on Unix systems it is possible to give certain users permission to execute commands as the root user. The most common way to do this is using the superuser do (`sudo`) suite of commands.

Sudo has become a very popular method of delegating security on Unix servers. Using sudo allows the administrator to tightly restrict who has root access, while still giving users the ability to run commands necessary to perform their jobs. Sudo also has several security enhancements, including extensive logging facilities, creating a detailed trail whenever a command is executed through sudo.

The way sudo works is that a server administrator can assign permissions so that a process is owned by root, but a user, or group, is able to run it as well. The user or group runs the process without having to actually su to the root user, and the administrator can still restrict permissions on the file so that it is owned by root. Referring to the webmaster example, a webmaster should not need access to most system files; however, it is not uncommon for a webmaster to have to restart web services. Rather than make the webmaster part of the wheel group for this one task, an administrator can delegate the web server processes to the webmaster allowing him or her to start and stop web services as needed, but with no other administrative rights on the server.

Taking proper precautions to restrict access to the administrative access to the server can increase server security exponentially and can help protect against the most common system attacks.

## Backups

A common mistake made by administrators is to assume that installing RAID controllers on a server is the same as backing up data. It is not. The purpose of RAID is to provide failover in the event of a hard drive failure. Backing up data involves making a copy of existing information on a separate device. Backups are especially important in a server environment, as the purpose of a server is to store information.

Data backups are an inherent part of good network security. If a server, or another network device, is compromised, restoring proper data quickly is just as important as responding to an attack.

There are three different types of backups:

1. Full
2. Partial
3. Image

Full and partial backup combinations are the most popular. Initially a full backup of a system is created. Subsequent backups only copy files that have changed. If there is no change, the file does not need to be copied. Periodically, usually once every week or two weeks, a full backup is again completed, and the cycle restarts. A disk image is a sector-by-sector duplication of a disk that is stored as an image. The image can then be transferred to other media, or restored at a later date.

Backed-up data can be stored in several different ways. It can be stored to tape, or on multiple tapes using a tape jukebox, or data can be stored within a Storage Area Network (SAN). The two methods of storage are not mutually exclusive; tape servers can be included as part of a SAN, and, in fact, this is very common.

Using a SAN is the recommended method of performing backups. A SAN is a network of mass-storage devices that is isolated on a private network, segmenting SAN traffic from the rest of the network. Because SANs involve a lot of data, high-speed connections are used to connect devices on the network. Usually, this involves fiber optic connections between the devices.

The private network, combined with the fast connectivity between devices, has quickly catapulted SAN as the preferred backup technology, which makes sense, because backups are useless if they have been corrupted. So, it is important to secure backup data, just as you would any other communication.

Obviously, backup security would be enhanced if the data were encrypted, but the load on the network and the servers would be too great for a midsized network. Instead, by isolating the traffic, at least some level of security is achieved.

The backup process starts with the frequency and times of backup. Server backups should be performed on a daily basis, unless the information on the server does not change often, in which case every few days may be acceptable. No server should go more than a week without being backed up. Router, switch, and firewall configurations should also be backed up on a daily basis, or at least several times a week.

If an organization is run in a traditional manner, where employees access servers between 9:00 A.M. and 5:00 P.M., then anytime overnight is fine to perform backups. As more organizations more toward a 24x7 operation, it becomes increasingly difficult to set a time to do backups. In cases like this, it is important to monitor server and network traffic to determine the best time to perform backups. There is no rule that says all backups have to be performed at the same time; in fact, in many cases it helps to spread out the backups throughout the day.

Backups to a tape, or writable CD-ROM, are preferred as it is more difficult to write over, or corrupt, those mediums than it is a hard drive sitting on a server. In addition, whenever possible, backups should be encrypted. The backup process does not have to be carried out over an encrypted connection. Once the data is backed up it should be encrypted; this helps to prevent an attacker from tampering with data that should be safe.

Backups should be tested on a regular basis. Not only should they be tested to ensure that the data was successfully backed up, but restores should be tested as well. Backup software will sometimes report corrupted data as a successful backup, so everything looks fine in the log file, but the data is actually worthless. This is especially common when a bad tape or CD-ROM is used. Taking a few minutes a week to spot check backups by attempting to restore a file, or directory, is a good practice and may provide warning signs that a failure is about to occur.

Test restores of data can also help server administrators determine how long a restore will take. The most commonly asked question when a server fails is when it will be back online. The better answer administrators can provide to that question the happier network users will be. Practicing helps to ensure that the data will be restored in a timely manner.

Backup mediums should also be rotated to offsite facilities. Companies such as Archive Away, StorNet, and Storage Networks offer organizations ways to store backups in a separate facility, away from the corporate network. Data can either be transferred to these facilities across the WAN, using a private VPN, or even physically sent to the location.

A good rule of thumb is to keep two weeks of backup on site, and at least two or three months of backups at a remote location. In some instances, especially where financial or legal records are involved, this length of time may not be adequate. If this is the case, local or federal laws may govern the length of time the backups have to be stored.

## Disaster Recovery

Offsite backups are a critical part of a disaster recovery plan. Disaster recovery is the ability of an organization to recover and continue doing business, with minimal interruption, in the face of a catastrophic disaster.

As awareness of security network problems has increased so has the interest in disaster recovery. To address the problems associated with a catastrophic failure, a disaster recovery plan should be developed within an organization.

Such a plan outlines the steps necessary to bring an organization to a fully operational status in the event a disaster occurs. Disasters generally fall into one of four categories:

1. Accidental
2. Internal
3. Natural
4. Terrorism/Civil unrest

These categories are intentionally broad. Similar to a security plan, it is up to each individual organization to determine what constitutes a disaster (what would cause a business interruption) and what steps need to be taken to restore business operations.

While the categories have some leeway in terms of interpretation, there are guidelines as to what makes up each. An accidental disaster is a complete loss of power, a train derailment or other transportation accident, or an employee who accidentally destroys valuable corporate data.

Internal disasters include things like employee sabotage, theft, or even workplace violence. The difference between accidental disasters that involve employees and internal disasters is that with an internal disaster the action is intentional. Natural disasters include floods, hurricanes, heavy rain, blizzards, and other catastrophes initiated without human intervention.

Many offsite storage organizations also offer disaster recovery solutions. These solutions are mirrors of existing data that are activated in the event of a complete network failure at the primary location. If that is not an option, then determining the fastest way to recover data from an offsite location should be considered as part of a disaster recovery plan.

Disaster recovery is not inexpensive. In fact it can often seem to be excessively priced. However, the cost pales in comparison to the cost of hours, or days, of downtime, which is why many organizations opt to participate in some form of disaster recovery.

## Web Server Security

An organization's web server is an attacker's most common point of entry into the network. A web server is, almost by definition, a public server, so it makes an attractive target to attackers. In addition, depending on the nature of the web-site, breaking into the web server may give an attacker access to valuable customer information. Because web servers are such attractive targets, special steps need to be taken to secure the web server against attackers.

The web server should be a single-use server, and should have a very restricted access policy; only personnel who absolutely need access should have it. In fact, a staging server is commonly used as a means of further restricting access to the actual web server.

A staging server is a replica of the web server. It should have the same operating system, same patches, same file structure, and all of the same software as the web server. Content destined for the web server is loaded to the staging server and the pushed to the web server using software like RedDot Solution's Content Management Server (CMS). Different users, or departments, are given accounts on the staging server; the accounts are used to upload content to the staging server. The content is pushed from the staging server to the actual web server using a separate account to which the users do not have access. The web server is configured to only allow the staging account access from the IP address of the staging server.

As shown in Figure 11-6, the staging server should be placed on a separate VLAN than the web server. The staging server should be part of

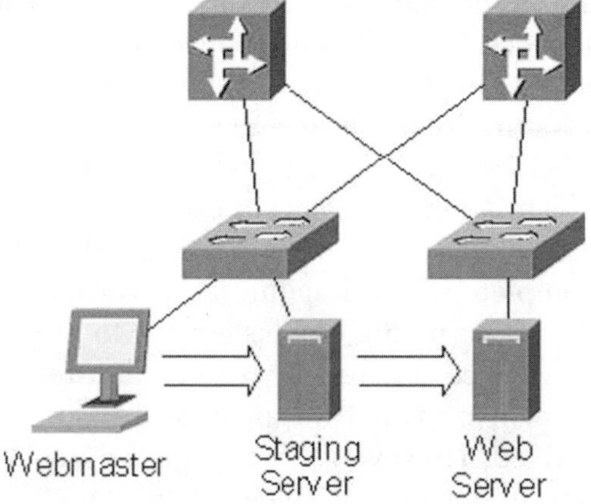


**Figure 11-6** A staging server is used as an added measure of web server security. Content is uploaded to the staging server then pushed to the web server.

a private VLAN that is not accessible through the firewall. This will prevent an attacker who does gain access to the web server from getting to the staging server and using it to launch additional attacks.

Because the staging server is the only machine that will send content to the web server, an administrator can restrict the ways of accessing the server. Depending on the type of server, content can be uploaded using either Secure Copy (SCP) or Secure FTP (SFTP), and standard FTP ports can be disabled on the server. If other forms of access are required, they should only be allowed from the staging server, and those ports should be blocked to the server through the firewall.

**NOTE:** If FTP is required to run on the server, it is critical that anonymous FTP be disabled on all servers—except servers that have files available for general download. An increasingly common attack is to scan for servers that have anonymous FTP enabled, with very loose file permissions. These servers are then used to store pirated software, and other files, leaving a company open to lawsuits and increasing the amount of bandwidth used exponentially.

Content on the web server should be stored on a separate partition from the operating system files. Programs installed to assist in serving web pages, such as Apache, Internet Information Server, and ColdFusion should have any sample files included as part of the default install deleted.

**NOTE:** A common practice among attackers is to look for sample files that programs like ColdFusion install by default, and exploit weaknesses in those default installs.

Within the content partition, file permissions should be as restrictive as possible. This probably sounds like an oxymoron; files on a web server have to be world-readable because anyone can visit a website. The difficulty is finding a balance between making the website user experience enjoyable and keeping the web server secure.

If the content of a website is largely static, consider using strict HTML pages, and setting the file permissions so they are world-readable but not writable, and certainly not executable. On the other hand, if website content is dynamic and database driven, the files will have to be world-readable and executable, but they should not be writable. Windows-based web servers have a special scripting permission separate from executable permissions; that permission should be used for dynamic content.

In cases where executable permissions are required, security precautions should be taken to secure the scripting software. Whether the site uses Perl, PHP, Java, VBScript, or ColdFusion, there are vendor-recommended practices that a server administrator can follow, like running PHP in safe mode, to increase the security of scripts on the server.

Outlining security steps for all of the commonly used scripting languages is beyond the scope of this book. There is plenty of excellent information available for locking down each language.

There are three general guidelines that all scripts in use on a website should follow to ensure security:

1. A script should never accept unchecked data.
2. All input should be validated.
3. Scripts should not rely on path information gleaned from the server.

Whether it is a form, database query, or some other type of user input, any data that is processed by a script should be validated. The data has to be checked to ensure it is not passing malicious information to the script.

All input being passed to another program on the server should be validated. While Rule 2 sounds similar to the first rule, the implications are different. In the first instance, the script is checking for potentially damaging input before processing it. This applies to information that is generally damaging to the server. For example, an attacker loads the command:

```
ls -al
```

into a feedback form, and is able to get a directory listing of the root web directory. In this case, information that is being passed to a specific program has to be validated to ensure it interacts properly with the program. Using the feedback form as an example, an attacker may be able to manipulate it so that the web server can be used to send unsolicited mail.

---

**NOTE:** Matt's Formmail is one of the most popular scripts in use on the Internet. Older versions of the script contained a security hole similar to the one described. Attackers were able to exploit that hole to send unsolicited commercial mail to millions of people. The hole has been patched for more than a year, but there are still older versions of the script in use on thousands of websites.

---

The problem becomes even more insidious when attackers use the same type of attack to submit queries to databases on the server. An attacker can use this type of attack to find out usernames, phone numbers, and even credit card information. Restricting the type of information that can be submitted to a web server helps to reduce the chances that this type of attack will occur.

The third rule is that scripts should not rely on path information gleaned from the server. The Common Gateway Interface (CGI) specification has a variable called PATH, which can prepend the server-supplied path to any files or directories used in a script. So, if a script needs to access a file called sample.exe, the file can be called like this:

```
$PATH/sample.exe
```

Unfortunately, the PATH variable can be manipulated allowing an attacker to view the directory contents of the server. Rather than rely on information gathered from the PATH variable, programmers should hard code data paths directly into the scripts. Hard coding path information into a script prevents an attacker from manipulating the PATH variable to display files on the web server.

New security holes are constantly being discovered in web applications. It is important that web server administrators stay abreast of current security problems that are introduced and update software as quickly as possible.

Attackers are especially quick to take advantage of security holes in web server software, so quickly patching security holes is critical. Web server attacks are successful because most of the time they resemble a standard HTTP connection attempt. Rather than using malformed packets or spoofing addresses, an attacker makes a standard HTTP GET request, but is sending bad information to the server.

In August 2001 hundreds of thousands of web servers started receiving quests like this:

```
"GET/
default.ida?NNNNNNNNNNNNNNNNNNNNNNNNNNNNNNNNNNNNNNNNNNNN
NNNNNNNNNNNNNNNNNNNNNNNNNNNNNNNNNNNNNNNNNNNNNNNNNNNNNNNN
NNNNNNNNNNNNNNNNNNNNNNNNNNNNNNNNNNNNNNNNNNNNNNNNNNNNNNNN
NNNNNNNNNNNNNNNNNNNNNNNNNNNNNNNNNNNNNNNNNNNNNNNNNNNNNNNN
NNNNNNNNNN%u9090%u6858"
```

These requests were part of the Code Red worm. The Code Red worm took advantage of a security hole in Microsoft Index Server, which was susceptible to buffer overflows.[3] The security patch had been available for months, but most administrators had not patched their systems, leaving them vulnerable. The Code Red worm spread across several continents in a few hours. While the damage that was done by this worm was relatively mild, it could have been much worse.

The Code Red worm made administrators painfully aware of the inadequate steps that are often taken to secure web servers. The impact of Code Red would have been a lot less severe if companies that were not using Microsoft Index Server (installed by default with an installation of Internet Information Server) had disabled the service and deleted files related to Index Server.

Just as a good administrator would not dream of leaving unnecessary services running on a server, unused web services should be disabled. The most popular web servers, Apache, Microsoft Internet Information Server, and Sun iPlanet, bundle additional services that not all websites will use. It is important to review configuration information when this software is installed to ensure there are no unnecessary web services running. Every unused web service presents a potential security hole, so leaving the service disabled will improve security, simply by not having it active.

Another common mistake made by web server administrators is to store customer information on the web server. No matter what precautions an administrator has taken it is still possible, if not likely, that the web server will be compromised. If this occurs, having a database filled with customer information is the worst thing that can happen. Customers are usually understanding about website defacements, but they are understandably less forgiving if an attacker gains access to confidential information.

To avoid this problem, website databases should be stored on a separate server. The web server can send database queries to the database server and pull the necessary information, on an as-needed basis. Queries between the web server and the database server should be encrypted, and the database username and password should also be secured.

The database server itself should be configured to not allow any logins using the public network address. All administration of the database server should be handled through the management network on the private network interface.

To provide an additional layer of protection, the database that is queried by the web server should be a scaled-down version of the real customer database. The web database can contain some customer contact

3. This is the reason why scripts should never accept unchecked data.

information, but it should not contain all customer information. If possible, the database should not contain billing information. Unfortunately, it is sometimes necessary to make billing information available, especially for sites that are e-commerce oriented. In cases like this, the website database should only contain partial information, such as the last 4 numbers of a credit card. Now, even if an attacker is able to bypass the database server defenses, the information gained will be significantly less valuable than if all the billing information had been available.

Protecting customer information has to be a top priority for a web server administrator. Taking the proper steps to secure a database, and a database server, goes a long way to protect that information. It also ensures that customer's faith in an organization remains strong.

## SSL Encryption

A common way to enhance the security of transactions conducted through a website is to use Secure Sockets Layer (SSL) encryption. Netscape developed SSL as a means of securing web-based transactions. The IETF has recently adopted most of the SSL specification to create a new protocol, designed to secure more than web-based transactions, called Transport Layer Security (TLS).

SSL uses public key cryptography developed by RSA Data Security, Inc., to secure transactions. Public key cryptography uses a public/private key pair to validate the information being sent between parties.

The default SSL port is 443 TCP; however, SSL can run over other ports, and many administrative applications now require SSL connections over different ports. Traditionally, to make an SSL connection to a web server to Port 443, a user simply typed in https://www.example.com; if the connection were to be made on a different port, the user would type https://www.example.com:[port number]. The effect is the same: The transactions between the user and the web server will be encrypted.

The process of setting up an SSL on a web server varies depending on the type of web server being used, but the backend functionality is the same across all web servers. The public/private key pair is generated on the web server. The private key is stored separately from the public key which is sent to a Certificate Authority (CA), such as VeriSign or Thawte. The CA verifies the identity of the organization that sent the key and issues an x.509v3 certificate. The x.509v3 certificate contains the organization's public key and is signed by the CA. The newly generated certificate is installed on the web server, and SSL sessions can begin.

**NOTE:** SSL sessions will actually run without a certificate generated by a CA. The web browser will generate an error window when a user visits an SSL-encrypted website that does not have a CA-signed certificate. The error will indicate that a trusted authority has not signed the certificate, and therefore the information is suspect. The data sent between the user and the server is still encrypted, but there is no third-party verification that the website is owned by the organization that claims to own it.

When a user attempts to connect to a web server using SSL, several things happen. The first is that the user initiates an SSL connection with the web server, and tells the web server the minimum SSL version it will accept (Version 3.0 is the current standard). The web server responds with a copy of the x.509v3 key. The web browser chooses a random symmetric key, encrypts it with the server's x.509v3 key, and sends it back to the web server. The web server decrypts the symmetric key using the server's private key.

The web server and the client use this symmetric key to encrypt traffic during the SSL session. The web server also assigns a unique ID to each encrypted session, called an SSL Session ID. The SSL Session ID is unencrypted and sent between the user and the server with each request.

SSL is a great tool for encrypting data between users and a web server. It should not be thought of as a tool for securing a web server. SSL does not assist with securing data once it is on a server. This is an important point: Many administrators feel that if they have SSL encryption their web server is automatically secure. That is not the case. SSL encryption should be used with other security measures as part of an overall web server security solution.

## Load Balancing

So far in this section, the discussion has revolved around attackers attempting to deface a website, and attempting to get customer information. Those attacks are common, but another common attack faced by web server administrators is a DoS attack.

DoS attacks are different in that they often serve no other purpose than to see if the attacker can take a website offline. The attacker may have a grudge against an organization, or may have been frustrated in attempts to attack a server in other ways. Whatever the reason, a DoS attack against a web server is often difficult to defend against, especially if it is a DDoS attack.

A typical website consists of a single server, with a database server sitting behind it. Even if a DoS attack does not saturate an Internet connection, it is not difficult to generate enough requests to knock a server offline.

Firewalls can stop many, but not all, DoS attacks, especially if the attacks appear to be a great number of legitimate requests—which they often are.

A common method used to protect a website against DoS, and other types of attacks, is to load balance the site across multiple servers. Load balancing has traditionally been used to distribute traffic across multiple servers as a means of improving performance and customer experience. As some websites increased in popularity, a single server was not enough to handle the number of requests received.

The solution was to set up multiple servers. At first these multi-server solutions were primitive. A company would create multiple records in their zone file pointing to the IP addresses of different servers, as shown in Figure 11-7.

From a security perspective, there are two problems with this approach. (1) It does not take into account availability. If a web server is unavailable, the DNS server will still direct people to it, because the DNS server does not have any way of knowing the server has failed. (2) DNS information is publicly available, so an attacker can find all of the servers associated with a website and attempt to break into sites.

Two other forms of load balancing have become popular for use with web servers: clustering and network load balancing. Clustering has been used with other types of servers for many years, but it has only recently

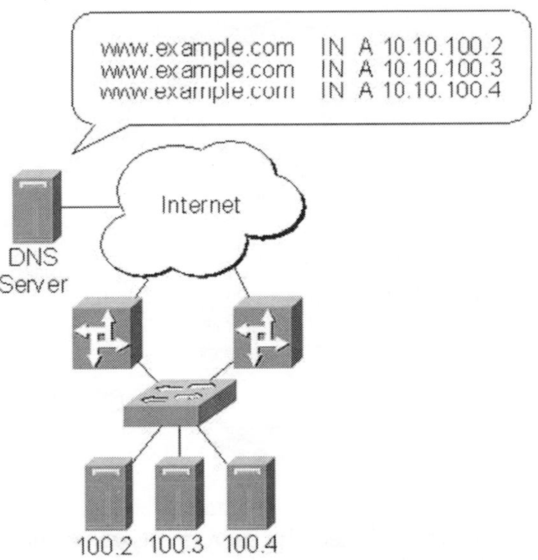


**Figure 11-7** Increase availability by having multiple DNS entries for the same domain pointing to different servers.

become commonplace for web servers. A cluster is a series of servers that act as a single server (Figure 11-8). The servers either communicate with each other or with a cluster controller to process requests as they are made. The cluster is assigned an IP address, and each individual server can learn that IP via ARP to requests for that IP address. The individual servers are also assigned unique IP addresses, which allow for server management and communication between the servers.

When a request to the web server is made, the clustered servers determine which is going to accept it based on a preprogrammed set of rules, known as metrics. Depending on the metrics used, a single server may handle all requests from one source IP address, or the requests may be distributed between the servers. If one of the servers fails, the other servers in the cluster pick up its requests and service goes uninterrupted.

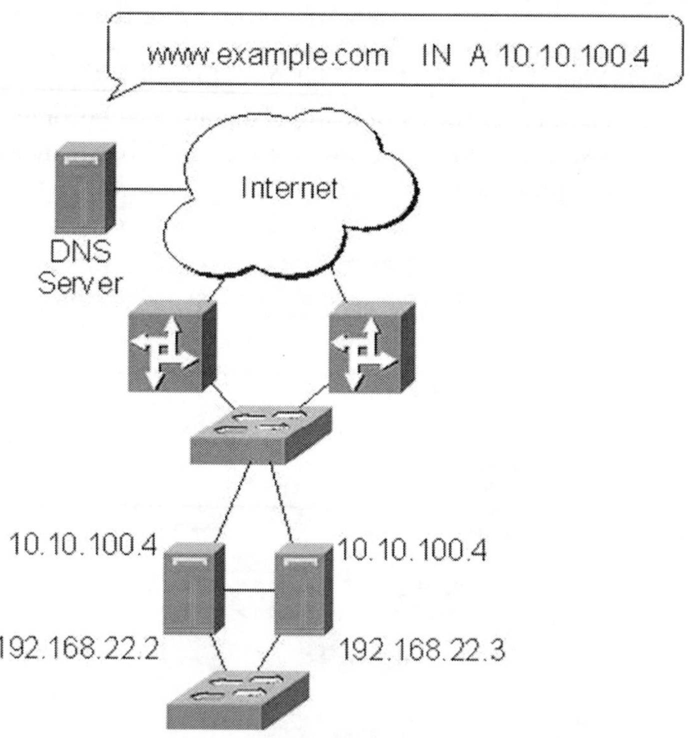


**Figure 11-8** A server cluster. The servers answer to the same IP address on the public side but have unique, private IP addresses for management and intraserver communications.

Clusters add to the security of a web server not simply because they increase availability, but also because they make it more difficult to launch an attack against a server. Each time a request to the website is made a different server may respond to the request. An attacker engaged in a complicated break-in attempt will need to restart the process each time a request is made because there is no way to guess which server will respond. In addition, if a private network is used to maintain the servers, then there is not a public address to which an attacker can latch on in order to complete an attack. Even within a small cluster, this advantage can give an administrator additional time to catch the alarm, track down the attacker, and stop the attack before it is successful.

One area in which clustering generally cannot assist is with DoS attacks. A well-executed DoS attack can still overpower several servers, rendering them unavailable to legitimate requests. For administrators concerned about DoS and DDoS attacks, network load balancing may be a better solution.

Network load balancing uses a switched device, such Cisco CSS11500, Nortel Network Alteon 184, Extreme Network SummitPx1, or F5 Network BIG-IP 5000, to direct traffic between multiple servers. The load balancer, or balancers, if deployed in pairs for redundancy, assumes the IP address of the website, as shown in Figure 11-9. Website requests reach

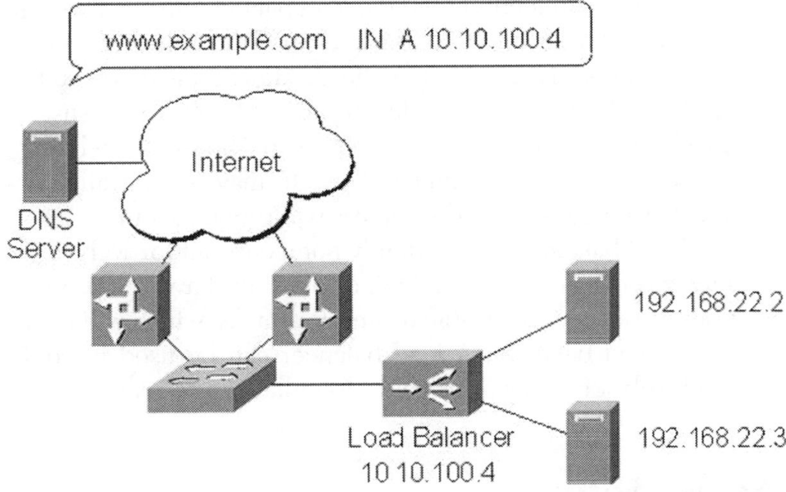


**Figure 11-9** Network load balancing. A switched device sits on the network in front of the servers and distributes traffic between the devices. The load balancer assumes the IP address of the website, and the servers are privately addressed.

the load balancer and are forwarded to the appropriate server, depending on the set metrics. Each server is configured with a private IP address that is used for management purposes.

If a server fails, it is taken out of rotation by the load balancer and an alert is generated. No traffic is lost as the load balancer simply redirects requests to another server. As with clustering, load balancing provides additional protection from attackers. Because there are multiple servers, each with a private IP address, an attacker may to have to continually restart an attack.

In addition, because most network load balancers are, essentially, switches, they are designed to handle large amounts of traffic. Many load balancers include DoS and DDoS detection utilities. These utilities can be used to drop bad requests before they reach the servers. The load balancer is able to pass legitimate traffic to the server and deny bad traffic without any performance degradation. Load balancers are usually deployed in pairs, so if an attacker is able to launch enough traffic to overwhelm one, and it becomes unreachable, the second load balancer will take over and continue to forward traffic.

Keep in mind that these devices are able to process several gigabits of information at any one time, so a DoS attack is more likely to overwhelm an Internet connection than the load balancer itself. The ability of load balancers to stave off a DoS attack, even if the Internet connection has been overwhelmed, is actually beneficial. Many attackers count on DoS attacks crashing the web servers, leaving the servers more susceptible to other attacks. If the load balancers can prevent the site from being overwhelmed, the server will remain intact. The site may be unavailable while the DoS attack is going on, but the servers will remain secure.

Load balancers are certainly not a cure-all for web server security. If a server is not properly patched, or does not have the proper access restrictions, it will be susceptible to simple attacks, which will fall below the radar of the load balancer. A load balancer can be used in conjunction with a solid web server security policy to enhance the security of a web server.

## Mail Server Security

There are two types of mail server security that need to be considered: the message transfer agent (MTA) and the user mailboxes. Most security resources are focused on the MTA, because that is the program responsible for routing mail to and from network users. It has also, traditionally, been one of the weakest security points on the network. Weak MTA security cannot only lead to attacks on a network, it can also result in mail from an organization being blacklisted. An organization that winds up on an MTA blacklist will be unable to send mail to sites that subscribe to the blacklist.

Before reading any further, conduct an experiment to gauge how secure your organization's MTA is. Visit the following website in your favorite browser: *www.abuse.net/relay.html.* Where it asks you to enter the address to test, put the address of your MTA (your outgoing mail server), and select test for relay.

The site performs a series of tests to determine how secure an MTA is against relaying. The results of your test should be similar to Figure 11-10. If not, there may be some serious mail server security work ahead.

This test, sponsored by the Network Abuse Clearinghouse, is one of many open relay testers on the Internet. The purpose of these tests is to help mail administrators determine the security of their mail relays.

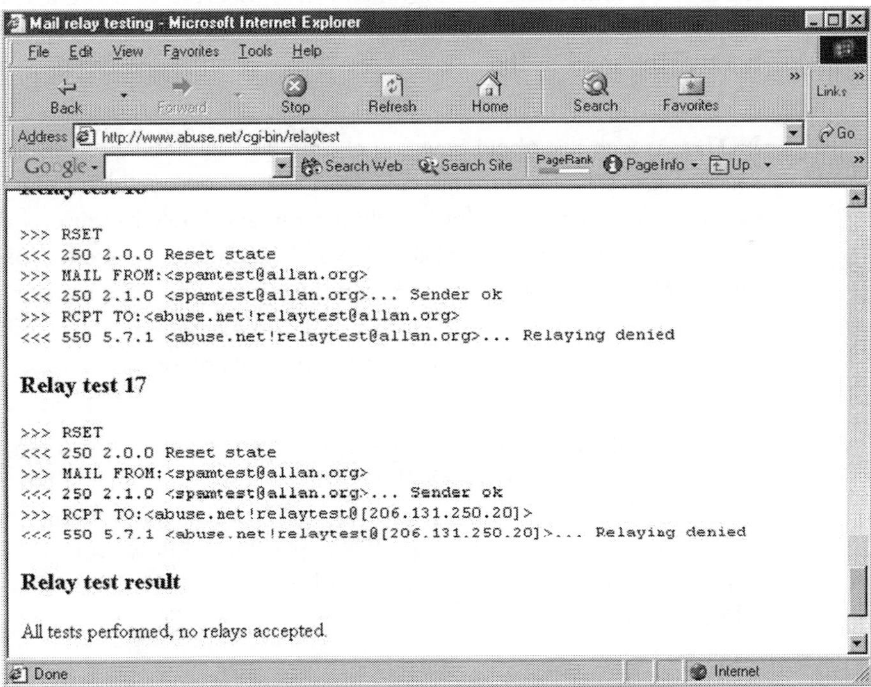


**Figure 11-10** Results of the Network Abuse Clearinghouse mail relay test.

The purpose of an MTA is to route mail traffic from one server to another, or from a server to the desired mailboxes. E-mail is, by far, the most used application on the Internet; more than 1 billion e-mails are exchanged everyday, and e-mail is generally considered crucial to large and small organizations.

Because e-mail is so ubiquitous, it is also a prime target for attackers. Until recently it was also an easy target. The most common method of attacking an MTA is to use it to send unsolicited bulk e-mail (UBE), commonly known as spam, to other organizations. As recently as a few years ago, it was not uncommon for an MTA to be left open, so anyone could send mail through the server.

As UBE has become more prevalent, organizations began closing their mail servers. Organizations that did not close their mail servers found that they were added to one or more of the many blacklists that have been created, and were unable to send mail to large portions of the Internet. Blacklists are generally maintained by a group of volunteers. The volunteers add IP addresses of machines that are either open relays or that allow UBE to be relayed. Other organizations subscribe to these lists and will not accept mail that originates from these mail servers,[4] effectively "black holing" the mail traffic.

---

**NOTE:** As with just about anything else on the Internet, these lists have stirred some controversy. Because the volunteers are not accountable to anyone, some lists have come under fire for blacklisting servers simply because of a grudge against the organization. Blacklists have also come under fire for failing to remove MTAs that have been changed to be compliant with the standards of the list owners. Most of these lists are run in a professional and responsible manner, but it is important to know that there is the potential for problems.

---

Fortunately, as awareness of the problems with open relays has increased, the security of the three most popular MTAs, Sendmail, Microsoft Exchange Server, and Lotus Domino Server, has increased as well. Out of the box, none of these products allows any relaying, so an administrator has to add the IP addresses or domains that should be allowed to relay.

4. In other words, you do not want to get listed on one of these lists.

One of the simplest and most effective ways to enhance the security of an MTA is to limit the range of IP addresses that can use it as a mail relay. An MTA cannot be closed off to all outside connections, because it has to be reachable by other servers that are sending legitimate mail to users on the network. But only users within the network of an organization should be able to send mail to remote mail servers using the MTA. Some administrators use the domain name as the determining factor, allowing users to relay mail through the mail server if the from address matches the organization's domain name. Unfortunately, it is too easy to bypass this security measure by forging the originating address in the mail program.

Another method of MTA security being used by many administrators is called POP-before-relay. Before a user can connect to send mail, he or she must first connect to the POP mail server and authenticate against it. If authentication is successful, that user's IP address will be allowed to relay for a set period of time, usually 5–15 minutes. This method of security is especially common when an MTA has users on diverse networks, or using dynamically assigned IP addresses (such as a dial-up ISP connection).

The other side of the mail server security problem is the user mailboxes. When the MTA delivers mail into the user's mailboxes, there are two protocols that can be used to retrieve it: the POP or Internet Message Access Protocol (IMAP). Of the two protocols, POP is more widely deployed, though both have similar security problems.

One of the primary problems associated with POP and IMAP is that users have to have an account on the MTA in order to receive their mail. In every other security situation, the rule of thumb is to remove any unnecessary accounts, and to restrict the number of accounts created on the server. In this case every user on the network needs to have an account on the mail server. To solve this dilemma, most administrators create a group on the mail server that is reserved for mail users. The group should have no access privileges to the server, only the ability to check e-mail. If the mail group is tightly controlled, with very restricted access, then none of the users should be able to cause any damage to the server, especially if their password falls into the wrong hands.

A second problem, but one that is equally important, is that both POP and IMAP transactions are conducted in clear text. The username and password, as well as all data, are transmitted so that anyone on the network with a packet sniffer can read them. In general this is a problem because it means anyone can find another user's login and password and check their mail. The problem is even more pronounced in networks that have centralized the login process. A username and password that may be used in multiple locations on the network will be exposed when the user logs into the mail server, thus jeopardizing the security for the entire network.

A mail server administrator can increase mail security by forcing users to use a different method of mail authentication. One way to increase security is to switch mail authentication to Authenticated Post Office Protocol (APOP). APOP functions in the same manner as POP mail, but it encrypts the user's password using the MD5 one-way hash algorithm. APOP also requires a separate authentication database, so that even if a user's password is compromised, an attacker will not be able to gain access to the rest of the network.

A more secure solution for POP or IMAP sessions is to connect over a TLS session. TLS is a form of encryption, based on Netscape's SSL. SSL is commonly used to encrypt web sessions, but the underlying technology is being used to encrypt other types of traffic.

TLS-encrypted POP and IMAP sessions function in the same manner that HTTPS-based encryption does. A certificate is generated and submitted to a CA, then the certificate is installed on the mail server. The mail clients are configured to use TLS (or SSL, depending on the client) encryption when connecting to the mail server.

Using this method, not only is the password encrypted, but the entire session is encrypted as well. This provides the greatest level of security, but it has a downside: Continuously encrypting and decrypting POP or IMAP sessions can create an extreme load on the server. This load is compounded by the fact that many users set their clients to check for mail every minute. On networks with a large number of mail users, this type of encryption should probably be used in conjunction with an SSL-accelerator. SSL accelerators, from companies like Intel, Nortel, and Cisco, offload the encryption-decryption process from the server, therefore decreasing the load. Using an SSL-accelerator in conjunction with TLS authentication of POP or IMAP sessions will increase security without negatively impacting the server's performance.

## Mail Scanning

Mail scanning is a common practice on enterprise networks. E-mail messages should be scanned for three things: viruses, UBE, and employee theft or violation of e-mail policy. As with any other security policy, when an e-mail security policy is implemented it should be clearly explained to network users. The explanation of the security policy should detail what is being scanned for, as well as why it is being implemented.

E-mail scanning is sometimes controversial because users think of their e-mail account as a private communication tool as opposed to a communication tool owned by the company. A detailed explanation, coupled with a gentle reminder that the mail server and its contents are property of the organization can help ease any tension a new policy may cause.

Prior to presenting the scanning policy to employees it should be reviewed by an organization's legal counsel. Privacy laws can vary from area to area. It is important that the policy be presented in such a way that an organization cannot be sued for scanning activities, or worse, sued because something was missed by the scanning.

Virus scanning is the most common form of mail server scanning and is something that should be implemented on every enterprise network. No matter how careful network users are when it comes to viruses, worms, and opening of attachments, users from remote networks may not show the same level of care. A virus or worm that is introduced into a network can cause tremendous damage before it is stopped.

Incoming and outgoing mail messages should all be scanned for viruses and worms. Many companies, like Trend Micro and Sophos, make virus scanners designed specifically for mail gateways. The products are fast and able to keep up with even a heavily loaded mail server.

Virus scanning on the mail server does not mean that virus scanning software should not be used on end user workstations. Instead, the two should be used in tandem, preferably running software from different vendors on the server and the workstations. Running two different virus detection software products decreases the chances that a new virus will slip through an organization's defenses.

Virus definitions on the mail server should be updated frequently, preferably daily. The mail server is the first line of defense against viruses and should have the most up-to-date information to prevent the viruses from spreading.

In addition to virus scanning, many companies have begun scanning mail messages for UBE. UBE has proliferated to such a point that some organizations have found that 20 percent or more of their incoming mail is UBE. There are many programs on the market that can help an organization eliminate UBE at the mail server. Messages are automatically deleted or filed away for review. These programs help shift the burden of deleting unwanted messages from employees to the server, where the process is automated.

Most UBE scanning programs will allow a mail administrator to mark the messages as UBE before delivering them to the end user mailbox. Before implementing a new UBE scanner, it is probably a good idea to do a test run for a couple of weeks in tagging mode to see if any false positives—messages tagged as UBE, but which are not—appear. If there are a lot of false positives, the server administrator will have to adjust the sensitivity level of the software.

In addition to scanning for UBE, the blacklists mentioned earlier are a common tool used by administrators to avoid being burdened by UBE. Before using one of these lists it is important to understand what the criteria are for getting listed, and the process for being removed from the list—information that should be publicly available. If the criteria seem excessive or harsh, do not subscribe to the list, especially if it might alienate existing customers.

The final, and often most controversial, form of scanning is content scanning of e-mail. Content scanning is used to ensure that no information that is not approved by an organization is transmitted through that organization's e-mail server. This can include scanning for inappropriate language, jokes, images, sound files, and video files. Content scanning can also be used to examine files to make sure that confidential information is not being sent to the wrong people, or at all.

Products from MessageLabs, Sandstorm, and Sophos will scan incoming and outgoing messages and flag those with the key words or phrases that need to be monitored. The messages can either be rerouted to an administrator's mailbox or a report can be generated and presented to the security administrator.

Once again, this type of monitoring should be done in consultation with the legal department to ensure that the organization is not doing anything that could run afoul of the law.

## Outsourcing

Mail servers and web servers are unique in that they are intended to be public. People from all over the world have to be able to reach an organization's web and mail servers to find out information and communicate. The uniqueness of these servers requires special security consideration, and the security monitoring and maintenance takes up an inordinate amount of time, compared to other servers.

Many organizations may choose to outsource the management of mail and web services to an ISP or Application Service Provider (ASP). Outsourcing mail and web service needs has several advantages, the primary one being that it can increase the security of the corporate network. Web server attacks are the most common type of external network attack. If the web server is removed to a remote location, even if it is successfully compromised, the rest of the network will most likely remain intact. In addition, outsourcing allows security administrators to tighten network security and further restrict the type of access allowed into the network, increasing overall network security.

Managed hosting and mail providers also usually have staff onsite 24x7 monitoring for network anomalies and looking for security breaches. Nontechnical organizations may not have the staff, or the resources, to monitor systems around the clock in this manner.

Some companies specialize in secure web and mail server hosting. These companies generally use secured versions of operating systems and provide very restrictive access to servers.

Setting up these services can be outsourced as well. A Managed Service Provider (MSP) will help an organization create secure web and mail solutions, either at the customer site or in a remote data center. These MSPs build the web infrastructure and handle the day-to-day maintenance of the servers. Some will also handle any security monitoring needs for an organization.

An organization that does not have a lot of experience with mail and web server maintenance should consider the possibility of outsourcing. The monthly costs involved are minimal compared to the costs of hiring competent staff, and certainly are nothing compared to the potential damage that can be caused if a web server is compromised.

## Summary

Server security is important because servers are the last line of defense against an attacker. While router and firewall security breaches are on the rise, servers are still the number-one target of attackers, and all servers should be configured to be as secure as possible.

The best way to ensure server security is to limit who has access to the server, limit which interface the server can be accessed on, and enforce a strong password policy. If these steps are combined with regular software patch updates, most servers will be relatively secure.

Public servers, such as web and mail servers, are a different story and these servers have special security considerations. These servers have to allow access to anyone, but they can be configured to restrict direct access, except through the required ports, and they can be made to be more secure.

Web and mail server services can also be outsourced to one of many companies that provide this type of service. If an organization does not have the in-house expertise to manage these servers in a secure manner, outsourcing may be a viable option.

Because servers may provide an attacker access to proprietary company data, it is important to take server security very seriously and monitor the server farm closely for break-ins and attempted break-ins. The sooner an attack is stopped, the less damage the attacker will do.

CHAPTER 12

# DNS SECURITY

DNS is complex, and can be difficult to understand. This complexity is compounded by often conflicting advice on how DNS should be managed. Most of this advice is accurate, depending on your needs, but it is important to understand that not all advice applies equally to all situations.

As with any other part of the network, there are several aspects of DNS security that need to be addressed:

- The domain name
- The authoritative DNS server
- Individual zone files
- The caching DNS server

Before understanding the idea behind DNS security strategies, it is important to know a little of the history of DNS. When the Internet was still a project, called ARPANET, run by DARPA, administrators realized they needed an easy way for machines to communicate with each other. To resolve this problem a file called hosts.txt was created and stored on a server run by the InterNIC. The purpose of the hosts.txt file was to map a host name to an address allowing servers connected to the DARPA network to talk to each other. Administrators would download the hosts.txt file from the InterNIC machines every night and have the latest information.

**NOTE:** The hosts.txt file obviously did not scale well, but it became an ingrained part of most operating systems. Chances are if you do a search for the file hosts.txt on your machine, you will find a remnant of that file.

In the 1980s ARPANET adopted TCP as the official protocol, and in 1983 Jon Postel released RFC 880, containing a proposed plan for developing DNS. Paul Mockapetris also introduced RFCs 882 and 883 outlining a domain name infrastructure. The ISI, a department of the University of Southern California was tapped in RFC 990 to manage the root name servers and SRI International was tapped to manage the first top-level domains (TLDs), which included: .arpa, .com, .edu, .org, .mil, and .gov.

---

**NOTE:** The first .com domain ever registered was symbolics.com on March 15, 1985.

---

In 1992 the Defense Information Systems Agency (DISA) transferred control of the .com, .org, .edu, .gov, and the .net domains to the National Science Foundation (NSF). In 1993 the NSF outsourced control of these domains to Network Solutions, a division of SAIC. Network Solutions began charging for domain names in 1995. When the contract between the NSF and Network Solutions expired in 1998, a new organization was formed. The Internet Corporation for Assigned Names and Numbers (ICANN) was created to open up the registration for TLDs. ICANN also coordinates the generic top-level domain (gTLD) and the country code top-level domain (ccTLD) system, and is responsible for ensuring the root name servers function properly.

The DNS architecture is often compared to a tree. While that analogy is not too far off it does not go far enough. To get a better idea of how DNS works think of the ugliest tree on the face of the earth. The tree has hundreds of limbs that grow off the trunk, each spreading out in a different direction. The branches are often ensnarled, and each limb appears to have a different type of leaf. Some branches have maple leaves, while others have oak leaves, still others look like they belong to weeping willows. Every sort of leaf, flower, or fruit imaginable hangs off this tree. If you have no trouble picturing this tree, then DNS should be a snap.

The DNS tree starts with the root domain, which is ".". All other domains stem from there, so the gTLD .com, is really .com. The same applies to .edu, .net, and so on. From the TLDs spring domain names, such as example.com, and a fully qualified domain name (FQDN), www.example.com for example, stems from the domain names.

Information about domain names is stored on domain name servers. There are different name servers assigned for each branch of a domain name. The root domains are hosted on the root name servers. There are currently 13 root name servers spread throughout the world; their names, IP addresses, and location are mapped out in Table 12-1.

The root name servers maintain information about all the ICANN-approved gTLDs and ccTLDs. The information they have is collected

**Table 12-1** The Root Name Servers

| FQDN | IP ADDRESS | LOCATION | OWNER |
|---|---|---|---|
| A.ROOT-SERVERS.NET | 198.41.0.4 | Herndon, VA | Network Solutions |
| B.ROOT-SERVERS.NET | 128.9.0.107 | Marina del Rey, CA | USC, ISI |
| C.ROOT-SERVERS.NET | 192.33.4.12 | Herndon, VA | PSINet (Cogent Communications) |
| D.ROOT-SERVERS.NET | 128.8.10.90 | College Park, MD | University of Maryland |
| E.ROOT-SERVERS.NET | 192.203.230.10 | Mountain View, CA | NASA |
| F.ROOT-SERVERS.NET | 192.5.5.241 | Palo Alto, CA | ISC |
| G.ROOT-SERVERS.NET | 192.112.36.4 | Vienna, VA | DISA |
| H.ROOT-SERVERS.NET | 128.63.2.53 | Aberdeen, MD | Army Research Laboratory |
| I.ROOT-SERVERS.NET | 192.36.148.17 | Stockholm, Sweden | NORDUnet |
| J.ROOT-SERVERS.NET | 198.41.0.10 | Herndon, VA | Network Solutions |
| K.ROOT SERVERS.NET | 193.0.14.129 | London, England | RIPE |
| L.ROOT-SERVERS.NET | 198.32.64.12 | Marina del Rey, CA | ICANN |
| M.ROOT-SERVERS.NET | 202.12.27.33 | Tokyo, Japan | WIDE |

from a master database maintained by the authority for the particular TLD. For example, the .com gTLD is maintained by VeriSign Global Registry Services (GRS). Veri-Sign GRS has a database of information that has to be retrieved by the root name servers periodically, so that information about the .com gTLD is available to everyone. The root name servers receive similar periodic updates from the authoritative registry servers for all the ICANN-approved TLDs.

The ICANN-approved label is important, because there is nothing preventing anyone else from starting a registry that competes with the ICANN-approved registry. In fact, every couple of years a new one, New.net is the current example, seems to surface. These competing registries generally allow individuals, or companies, to register domains with different TLDs, such as .tech, or .kids. The problem with a registry service not associated with ICANN is that the vast majority of the people on the Internet will not be able to access the domain names, because most people query the root name servers for information. These domains are not ICANN-approved, so they are not part of the data that is stored on the root name servers. A name server administrator can adjust their name servers to query the servers maintained by the alternate registry, but most won't.

How does the whole process work? When a user wants to visit a domain name, for example, types *www.example.com* into a web browser, the request is first sent to a caching name server. The caching name server has a list of the root name servers, usually in a file called named.root, root.hints, or db.cache, with information similar to what is in Table 12-1. The caching name server queries one of the root name servers for information about the domain example.com. The root name server answers the caching name servers with information about example.com; specifically, it tells the caching name server what the authoritative name servers for example.com are.

Authoritative name servers are generally either run by an ISP or are located within a company premises, and they provide information about a domain name. Each domain should have at least two authoritative name servers, in two different locations. The two authoritative name servers will have the same information about a domain name. The information is stored in a zone file.

The caching name server, having gotten the authoritative name servers from the root name servers, sends a query to the authoritative name server for information about *www.example.com.* Assuming the authoritative name servers are configured correctly, the IP address for *www.example.com* will be sent to the caching name server, which passes it to the user who made the original query. This process is illustrated in Figures 12-1 and 12-2.

The distributed, tree-like, nature of DNS is its greatest asset. Information is stored in a redundant manner: There are 13 root name servers, with identical information; there are at least two authoritative name servers for each domain, and most companies have at least two

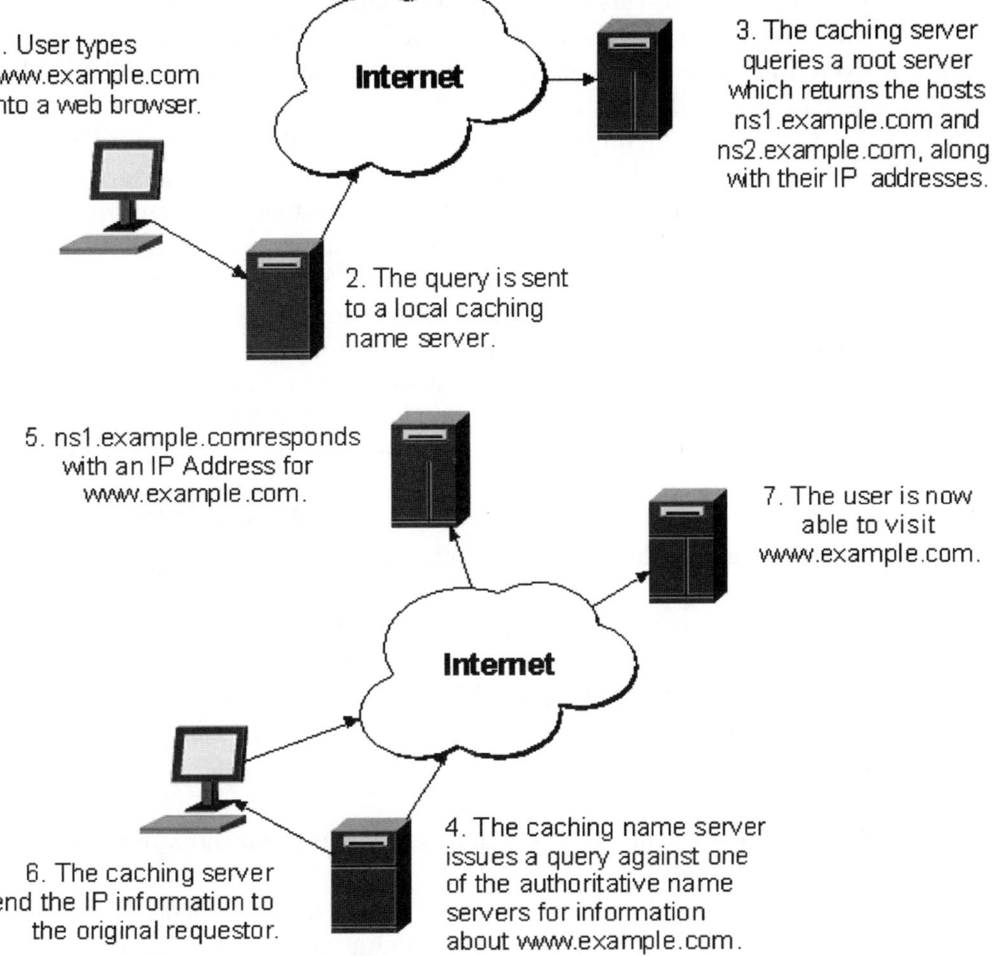


**Figure 12-1** The first part of the DNS process: a network user queries a caching name server, which queries a root name server.

**Figure 12-2** The caching name server uses the host information from the root name servers to query ns1.example.com, which returns an IP address for *www.example.com*. This address is passed onto the original user, which queries the name server.

caching name servers. This type of data replication provides a robust infrastructure, giving DNS a high level of availability. For the most part, even if multiple servers in the DNS process fail, a user will still be able to reach the intended destination.

It is extremely important to remember that distribution is crucial to the security of DNS. It is essential that authoritative name servers reside on two different networks, preferably in two different geographic locations (i.e., not the same office). This is known as the two-network rule. Many companies have fallen victim to DNS attacks because their DNS servers were sitting on the same network segment. If an attacker cannot exploit a security hole within the DNS server, then he or she only needs to launch a DoS attack against that network segment. It is significantly more difficult to launch a DoS attack against DNS servers in different locations, especially if one of those servers is located within your ISP's data center.

In addition to following the two-network rule, many DNS experts recommend running different operating systems on each server. The strategy is the same as the two-network rule: If an attacker is able to exploit a security weakness in one DNS server, the same weakness may not exist on the second server.

The distributed nature of DNS is also its greatest liability. With so many servers involved in the DNS process, there are many potential areas for security breaches:

- How does the caching name server know that the root name server has the right information?
- If it does get the right information, how does the caching name server know that the information from the authoritative name servers is accurate?
- How does the user know that the information coming from the caching DNS server is the right information?

These liabilities, part of the challenge of securing DNS, exist in part because DNS, as a protocol, has been around for so long. DNS is 20 years old and was not originally designed with security in mind. Obviously, things have changed, and there are ways to secure DNS, but not all of these methods are in widespread use. Because DNS is crucial to the infrastructure of the Internet, it is important to ensure that all aspects of your DNS process are secure.

## Securing Your Domain Name

When ICANN opened the registration process so multiple registrars were allowed to register domains, two things happened: Prices for domain names dropped and the number of new domains registered took off.

Millions of new domains are registered every month. As of this writing, there are 150 ICANN-accredited registrars, and countless resellers. All of these options mean that you have to be as concerned with the security of your registrar as you do with the security of your web host.

When ICANN created the rules for becoming a registrar, security was not included as a consideration, so there is no minimal level of information protection that a registrar has to provide. In fact it was not until March 2002 that a security committee was appointed by ICANN. While the committee will undoubtedly set minimum security standards that registrars must follow, it may take years before registrars are forced to comply.

Given the importance of a company's domain name, this is a scary thought. Knowing that there is no minimum security required by registrars is a red flag that a set of security questions needs to be posed to any prospective registrar. This is especially true if your company maintains a lot of domain names.

The primary question a company should ask of their registrar is how the registrar handles domain name updates. Each .com, .net, and .org domain name has five pieces of information that can be updated by the domain owner:

1. Company information
2. Administrative contact
3. Billing contact
4. Technical contact
5. Name server information

All registrars have to supply this information to the gTLD database for a domain to be activated. When Network Solutions controlled all domains, the contacts were three different accounts—as long as three unique contacts were listed. Some registrars still follow that model, but others have opted for a different approach: A single account is created, even though three separate contacts may exist.

A single account for a domain can create several problems. Generally one person maintains this account. If that person leaves the company, especially under less-than-pleasant circumstances, this person may or may not share that account information. If the circumstances are extremely unpleasant, that person may decide to make changes to the domain prior to departure.

If this does happen, most registrars have alternate ways of updating information, but those methods can take significantly longer, and the domain will be unavailable while the information is being changed.

Many companies opt to give multiple users access to the account provided by the registrar. Unfortunately, most registrars use a web-based interface to manage domain names, so there is no way to track which user logged in and made changes. There is also no fail-safe way to prevent a disgruntled employee from making changes to the domain before quitting or being asked to leave.

The best way to avoid problems associated with a single account is to avoid a single account. Some registrars specialize in working with enterprise organizations and understand the unique requirements of a midsize to large company. Consider using a registrar—such as Network Solutions, Domain Bank, or Alldo-mains.com—that has special corporate programs. These programs may be more expensive, but the cost is nothing compared to the amount of money that can be lost by having a domain disabled, or worse, redirected to another location.

Another security precaution is to store current domain name information in a file. This will make it easier to get the information restored, should a problem arise.

Most UNIX systems have a program called whois, which allows users to look up domain information. There are also Windows and MacOS whois clients available for download. The output of a whois query will look something like this:

```
whois example.com
[whois.crsnic.net]

Whois Server Version 1.3


Domain names in the .com, .net, and .org domains can now be
registered with many different competing registrars. Go to
http:// www.internic.net for detailed information.

Domain Name: EXAMPLE.COM
Registrar: NETWORK SOLUTIONS, INC.
Whois Server: whois.networksolutions.com
```

```
Referral URL: http://www.networksolutions.com
Name Server: A.IANA-SERVERS.NET
Name Server: B.IANA-SERVERS.NET
Updated Date: 07-jan-2002
```

The registrar for this domain is Network Solutions. Registrars have their own whois server, which can be queried for more information:

```
whois -h whois.networksolutions.com example.com
[whois.networksolutions.com]

Registrant:

Internet Assigned Numbers Authority (EXAMPLE-DOM)
  4676 Admiralty Way, Suite 330
  Marina del Rey, CA 90292
  US

Domain Name: EXAMPLE.COM

Administrative Contact, Technical Contact, Billing Contact:
  Internet Assigned Numbers Authority (IANA) iana@IANA.ORG
  4676 Admiralty Way, Suite 330
  Marina del Rey, CA 90292
  US
  310-823-9358
  Fax- 310-823-8649

Record last updated on 07-Jan-2002.
Record expires on 15-Aug-2010.
Record created on 14-Aug-1995.
Database last updated on 20-Apr-2002 14:07:00 EDT.

Domain servers in listed order:

A.IANA-SERVERS.NET     192.0.34.43
B.IANA-SERVERS.NET     193.0.0.236
```

The administrative, technical, and billing contact are all the same, so there is only one contact listing. This is another common mistake made by companies: not using three separate contacts. For something as important as a domain name, a company should not have a single contact. Whenever possible have three different contacts, and make sure those people are aware that they are the contacts for the domain. Also, make sure the people who are contacts are aware of the update procedures for the domain.

The three contacts are important not just for security reasons, but also for domain availability. If a company has a single domain contact, and that person leaves, even if it is on good terms, there is a good chance no one will know when the domain is up for renewal (most registrars send e-mail notification for domains that are about to expire). One of the most common forms of DNS failure is simply an expired domain. This is especially true now that registrars are allowing companies to register domains for up to 10 years. It may not occur to anyone to check the expiration date until e-mail and everything else stop working.

To this point, the focus has been on internal security breaches related to domains. The focus on internal security issues is because most security incidents concerning the domain name occur internally. While external security incidents related to domain names are less frequent—attackers tend to hit DNS servers rather than the domain name itself—they are not unheard of, and proper precautions should be taken.

If your registrar uses a web-based interface, make sure any changes are made over an SSL-encrypted connection. As with other services, make sure the password you choose for your account, or accounts, is secure. In addition to being secure, the password should be changed frequently.

Keep in mind that most companies will not use their registrar password very often. Most companies can go for years without making changes to their domain name (this is not the same as DNS changes, which happen more frequently). Regular password changes help keep a company protected in the event that a registrar's database is compromised.

If possible, request a method for domain name updates that is more secure than an SSL connection. An encrypted e-mail message, or at least one that is signed, would be preferable, although most registrars will not support methods other than web access for making domain changes. In that case, find out what security precautions are taken to protect both the web servers and the database. If a satisfactory answer cannot be given, transfer registrars.

Today a domain name is a crucial part of any company's business. Considering how important the domain name is, the cost, often less than $30 a year, to maintain it is insignificant. Unfortunately, because the cost is so low, some registrars do not take adequate security precautions. As with any other vendor a company has a relationship with, a registrar has to be able to show that it has adequately secured its data.

## A Secure BIND Installation

The discussion of DNS has largely focused on theoretical information to this point. It is time to shift to more practical aspects of DNS security; in particular, the focus will be on securing a BIND installation.

BIND is the software that allows DNS to function for most of the Internet; in fact, BIND servers handle more than 90 percent of all DNS queries on the Internet. BIND is incredibly robust. Many of the root name servers use BIND, and they are answering more than 200 million queries a day.

BIND was first developed in 1983 at the University of California-Berkeley as a way to handle DNS queries. Over the years the ownership of BIND has moved from organization to organization. Currently, the Internet Software Consortium maintains BIND. Like the DNS protocol itself, BIND was not originally designed with security in mind, and over the years BIND security exploits have given system administrators a fair share of headaches. Between 1998 and 2001, BugTraq reported 14 exploits found in various versions of BIND,[1] compared to five exploits found in Sendmail during the same time period.

BIND exploits often have a significant business impact because they can cause e-mail and websites to become unavailable, or, worse, directed somewhere else at the whim of an attacker.

BIND vulnerabilities first came into the public light in 1997 when Eugene Kashpureff, who operated a now-defunct alternative registry called AlterNIC, used a common BIND exploit to direct traffic away from the Network Solutions website and to the AlterNIC website. Mr. Kashpureff used a well-known exploit that would allow additional information to be sent to a caching name server when a request was made. More about this exploit will be explained shortly.

Two steps can be taken to immediately increase the security of a BIND installation:

1. Upgrade to the latest version.
2. Separate caching and authoritative functions.

The current version of BIND is Version 9.2.x; no known security holes have been exploited to date for this version of BIND. That does not mean

1. As of this writing no bugs had been reported for 2002.

they don't exist, but it does mean that upgrading to BIND Version 9.2 is one of the best ways to secure your BIND installation. It is also a good idea to subscribe to the ISC mailing list bind-announce, a low volume list that sends out announcements about new versions of BIND, security fixes, and patches. This allows administrators to stay current about the latest BIND information.

In addition to having the latest version of BIND, it is a good idea to separate caching from authoritative functions whenever possible. BIND is designed to handle both services. Because the two perform such different functions, there are usually different security policies associated with each function. By separating them it is easier to apply more stringent security restrictions to the servers.

Not only is it a good idea to separate the services, but also it is critical to ensure that BIND is not running on any machines that are not acting as DNS servers. Because BIND is an open-source software project, it is often distributed by default with operating systems, including Solaris and most versions of Linux. Whenever an audit is performed on a server, BIND should be one of the packages that is watched for and removed.

The separation of caching services gives an administrator a couple of benefits. First, it makes the firewall rule very easy: Block all traffic on Port 53 (the DNS port), but allow UDP and TCP traffic from any source IP address on any port destined for the authoritative server on Port 53.

Typical DNS traffic uses UDP to send and receive queries, but if a zone file is larger than 512 KB (the largest allowed UDP packet), a DNS server will return the information in one or more TCP packets.

Second, the separation allows administrators to apply different security policies to the different name servers. Machines from all over the world query an authoritative name server. On the other hand, a caching name server should only be queried by local users on your network—or possibly remote offices if they are connected to the network. Either way, an administrator should have control over who accesses a caching name server, and can limit to whom the caching name server will issue responses.

---

**NOTE:** In addition to standard server security precautions, it is usually a good idea to install software-based firewalls, such as IPFilter, on a DNS server.

---

## BIND Security

Before different types of BIND servers can be secured, a better understanding of how to secure a BIND installation is needed. BIND can be unwieldy to manage without a basic understanding of how the program works.

When BIND is first started it has to bind itself to Port 53. On most systems a program cannot bind itself to a port unless the system administrator runs it. This was one of the biggest security holes within BIND. Having the BIND daemon owned by the administrative user meant that it was susceptible to root exploits. A root exploit is carried out when an attacker is able to successfully gain administrative access to a system through a program that is owned by the administrative user.

Current versions of BIND do not have this problem. BIND is still started by the administrative user, but ownership of the BIND daemon is transferred to an nonprivileged user, in most cases a user created specifically for the purpose of running BIND. The conventional name for the BIND user is `named` because named is the program that actually handled DNS queries. : The process status command is great for determining the owner of a process, in this case the owner of named:

```
[root@nsl root]# ps -aux | grep named
named 4764 0.0 0.8 12276 4260 ? S 18:38 0:00 named -u named
named 4765 0.0 0.8 12276 4260 ? S 18:38 0:00 named -u named
named 4766 0.0 0.8 12276 4260 ? S 18:38 0:00 named -u named
named 4767 0.0 0.8 12276 4260 ? R 18:38 0:00 named -u named
named 4768 0.0 0.8 12276 4260 ? S 18:38 0:00 named -u named
```

In addition to running BIND as a nonprivileged user, many people recommend running BIND in a chrooted environment, on UNIX servers. Chroot creates a sandbox that can help limit the damage an attacker can cause should an application be exploited. A sandbox is a restricted shell that is used to limit the access a user has to a system, by essentially making that directory the root directory and keeping the user trapped.

As with any other security measure, it is important not to rely too heavily on chroot to protect a server. While it is a powerful tool, there are ways out of a chroot environment. That's why it is better to run BIND as an unprivileged user in a chrooted environment, rather than running BIND as the administrative user.

Running BIND in a chrooted environment is simply a matter of starting it with the -t flag:

```
[root@ns1 root]# /usr/sbin/named -u named -t /var/named/
```

This command will start BIND as root, but have it run as the user named. It also creates a chrooted environment with /var/named/ as the root directory. The only caveat to using this type of security is that the value of some of the variables in the named.conf file will need to be changed so that they are within this new root directory.

### Named.conf

The heart of any BIND installation is the named.conf file. Usually located in the /etc directory on a UNIX system, and dns\etc\ on a Windows system, this file is what allows an administrator to change the security and configuration settings of the DNS server. The owner of the named process should own the named.conf file. Permissions should be set so that only the named process owner has read access; other system users should have no access to the file (chmod 600 on a UNIX server). The named.conf file has several sections, and looks like this:

```
options {
directory "/var/named";
// query-source address * port 53;
};

zone "." IN {
type hint;
file "named.ca";
};

zone "example.com" {
type master;
file "example.com.hosts";
};

zone "example2.com" {
type master;
file "example2.com.hosts";
};
```

This is a simple version of the named.conf file. The first section, labeled options, defines information that will be universal to all of the zone files. The next section is a list of the actual zones that the name server has information about. The server is acting as an authoritative and caching name server. The first zone in the list ".", with the type hints, indicates that this server can be queried for information about domain names not located on the server.

If this were a caching-only name server this would be the only entry in the named.conf file. The next two zone entries, example.com and example2.com, are domains for which the name server thinks it is master. The actual zone is stored in the file listed in the file entry (i.e., example.com.hosts and example2.com.hosts).

The named.conf file allows an administrator to add directives, called statements, to modify the configuration of a zone file. A complete explanation of the various statements is beyond the scope of this book. For more information refer to the BIND documentation available online.

By default BIND logs all queries to syslog (generally /var/log/messages). Using the `logging` statement an administrator can direct logs to a separate file and monitor the BIND logs individually. This may not be an ideal solution for all companies. If syslog information is being sent to a separate server and monitored by third-party software, as is often the case with large companies, separate BIND logging may not provide any benefit.

However, the `logging` statement does allow an administrator to split logs depending on the channel, severity, or category. This is particularly useful if one person, or a group, is dedicated to managing the DNS infrastructure. It is possible to use the logging directive to send warning, and more severe, messages to the syslog daemon, while notice, and less severe, messages are send to a separate log file. A basic `logging` statement will look like this:

```
logging {
channel default_syslog {
syslog daemon;
  severity info;

};
channel default_debug {
file "named.debug";

};
};
```

This logging statement sends errors that are informational, and above, to the syslog daemon. All debug errors are sent to a file called named.debug. It is a relatively simple configuration, and will not meet the needs of a complex DNS solution. However, it makes a good starting point from which to grow.

Another commonly used practice to secure a name server is to hide the version information. Ordinarily, an attacker can use the dig command (installed by default with BIND) to determine the version of BIND a remote name server is running:

```
[root@nsl root]# dig .example.com version.bind chaos txt

;; QUESTION SECTION:
;version.bind.          CH    TXT

;; ANSWER SECTION:
version.bind.     0     CH    TXT   "9.1.3"

;; Query time: 2 msec
;; SERVER: 192.168.0.40#53(ns1.example.com)
;; WHEN: Sun Apr 21 18:31:06 2002
;; MSG SIZE rcvd: 48
```

Now an attacker can look for exploits to which Version 9.1.3 of BIND is susceptible and act accordingly. While version.bind is a BIND convention, it has been incorporated into other DNS servers, so this command is a common way of finding exploitable systems. You can change the information that is output by making the following adjustment under the options statement:

```
version "DNS, we aint got no stinkin DNS";
```

Now, if the same command is issued, the following will appear:

```
[root@nsl root]# dig @nsl.example.com version.bind chaos
txt
;; QUESTION SECTION:
;version.bind.          CH    TXT

;; ANSWER SECTION:
version.bind.     0     CH    TXT   "DNS, we aint got no
stinkin
DNS"
```

```
;; Query time: 2 msec
;; SERVER: 192.168.0.40#53(ns1.example.com)
;; WHEN: Sun Apr 21 18:38:33 2002
;; MSG SIZE rcvd: 74
```

As you can see this prints out the message "DNS, we aint got no stinkin DNS," instead of the version of BIND. The merits of this form of security are somewhat debatable. The wrong message may simply serve as an enticement for an attacker to try to break into your system. By changing the version information you are attempting to understand the psyche of an attacker, and that may or may not be a good idea. Some administrators prefer not to change the version, but simply leave it blank so that no information is provided to a potential attacker.

Other named.conf security considerations will be discussed in the next section.

## Limit Access to Domain Information

Generally there are two goals when trying to secure a DNS server: Limit information access to authorized users and limit the information authorized users can access. Of course, how DNS information is secured depends on the type of server that is being secured.

Regardless of whether you are trying to secure a caching or authoritative name server, a tool that can help this process is an ACL. ACLs are a statement within the named.conf file. An ACL can be applied universally, or to specific domains, depending on the administrator's needs.

Securing BIND using ACLs is very similar to using ACLs to protect routers, with the difference being that with BIND there is no need for an implied allow statement at the end of an ACL. BIND assumes that anything that is not implicitly denied is allowed. A common DNS security practice is to blackhole all requests that originate from RFC 1918 addresses:

```
acl badaddresses { 10.0.0.0/8; 172.16.0.0/12; \
192.168.0.0/16; };
```

In the `options` statement, include the following line:

```
options {
..
blackhole { badaddresses; };
..
};
```

Placing the ACL in the `options` statement blackholes all requests to the name server from addresses in the RFC 1918 space. An ACL can also be applied to only a specific domain (for example, if separating caching and authoritative name servers is not an option). An ACL can be created specifically for local addresses and bound to the caching zone entry. In fact, BIND has a builtin ACL for local address called localnets. The localnets ACL consists of any address in one of the netblocks bound to the name server interface. For example, if the name server has an address of 10.10.0.10 with a netmask of 255.255.255.0, then addresses 10.10.0.1 through 10.10.0.254 would be able to connect to a localnets ACL.

BIND has three other native ACLS:

1. Any allows all hosts to connect.
2. None denies all hosts.
3. Localhost allows any IP that is bound to an interface on the name server.

There may not be a need to apply ACLs to the name server if they duplicate what is already attached to the router. On the other hand, redundant security is rarely a bad thing.

## A Caching Name Server

Many of the security precautions discussed in this chapter can be applied to a caching-only name server. In particular, very stringent ACLs should be applied to this device. For example, using the localnets ACL described in the previous section, the `options` statement should probably look like similar to this:

```
options {
directory "/var/named";
 // query-source address * port 53;
allow-query { localnets; };
};
```

Add in the hints zone and a zone file for the localhost address:

```
zone "." IN {
   type hint;
   file "named.ca";
};
```

```
zone "0.0.127.in-addr.arpa" {
   type master;
   file "127.0.0.in-addr.arpa";
};
```

More verbose logging can be added to improve security, if desired, but if syslog monitoring is in place, that may not be necessary. As long as standard server security precautions are taken (limited access, strong password policy, etc.), a simple caching name server configuration can be fairly secure.

## An Authoritative DNS Server

An authoritative DNS server can be much more difficult to secure because, like a web server, it has to allow access from anywhere. The best strategy with an authoritative DNS server is to block access to rogue addresses, at the firewall or router level, and to restrict the information that the authoritative DNS server will provide.

Once again, using ACLs can help secure an authoritative name server. A common tool used by attackers to map your network is to perform a zone transfer:

```
[root@nsl root]# dig .example.com example.com axfr

; <>> DiG 9.1.3 <>> .example.com example.com axfr
;; global options: printcmd
example.com.      38400 IN SOAns1.example.com. dns.example.com.
99
5551903 10800 3600 432000 38400
example.com.       38400 IN   A   192.168.0.20
example.com.       38400 IN   MX 10 mail.example.com.
example.com.       38400 IN   MX 50 mail.uu.net.
example.com.       38400 IN   NS   ns1.example.com.
example.com.       38400 IN   NS   auth50.ns.uu.net.
anoncvs.example.com.   38400 IN   A   192.168.0.20
cpanel.example.com.   38400 IN   A   198.93.70.124
cpanel2.example.com.   38400 IN   A   198.93.70.125
dcw.example.com.     38400 IN   A   192.168.0.20
exuunet.example.com.   38400 IN   A   192.168.0.20
ftp.example.com.     38400 IN   A   192.168.0.20
jrun.example.com.     38400 IN   A   192.168.0.9
```

```
mail.example.com.     38400 IN    A    192.168.0.20
test.example.com.     38400 IN    A    192.168.0.40
www.example.com.     38400 IN    A    192.168.0.20
example.com.       38400 IN    SOA  ns1.example.com.
dns.example.com. 99
5551903 10800 3600 432000 38400
;; Query time: 5 msec
;; SERVER: 192.168.0.19#53(ns1.example.com)
;; WHEN: Mon Apr 22 17:58:54 2002
;; XFR size: 18 records
```

Using the supplied information, an attacker has a pretty good idea about the netblocks used on the example.com network, and also has an idea of what services are being run on which machines. This information can be used to build a network map and launch attacks against a particular server.

You can stop unauthorized machines from making zone transfers in this manner using the allow-transfer tag. Some machines, a secondary name server for example, have to be able to perform full zone transfers, others do not; a caching name server only needs to pull information for the host name that is being queried. The allow-transfer tag can be applied on a per-domain basis, or it can be applied to all domains. If you have multiple domains, with multiple secondary servers, you may need to apply this information on a per-domain basis.

In the previous example, the secondary name server is auth50.ns.uu.net, or 198.6.1.161. An entry can be made in the zone entry for example.com allowing this IP to perform transfers:

```
zone "example.com" {
  type master;
  file "example.com.hosts";
  allow-transfer { 198.6.1.161; };
  };
```

Now, when the attacker tries to perform a full zone transfer, there is an error:

```
[root@test root]# dig .example.com example.com axfr

; <<>> DiG 9.1.3 <<>> .example.com example.com axfr
;; global options: printcmd
; Transfer failed.
```

However, normal caching server behavior is not affected:

```
root@test root]# dig .example.com www.example.com A

;; QUESTION SECTION:
;www.example.com.     IN    A

;; ANSWER SECTION:
www.example.com. 38400 IN    A    192.168.0.20

;; AUTHORITY SECTION:
example.com.    38400 IN    NS    ns1.example.com.
example.com.    38400 IN    NS    auth50.ns.uu.net.
```

On the slave server the zone entry can be configured to not allow any transfers:

```
zone "example.com" {
  type slave;
  masters { 192.168.0.19; };
  file "example.com.slave";
  allow-transfer { none; };
};
```

To further enhance security, an administrator can restrict transfers from the master name server to slave name servers that supply a correct key. Combining key security with the allow-transfer limitations provides additional security and ensures that domains will not be transferred to spoofed IP addresses—assuming the spoofed IP address does not also have the key.

Messages secured using encrypted keys are called transaction signatures (TSIG), outlined in RFC 2845. BIND has supported TSIG messages since Version 8.2. Messages are secured using an MD5 algorithm. The master and the slave server both need to have the same secret key. When the slave name server requests information from the master server, it sends the secret key. The master verifies that it is the correct key and sends the information. Most experts recommend at least a 128-bit key, though there are no minimum requirements. BIND 9 supports 64-bit through 512-bit keys.

Versions of BIND that support TSIG messages include a tool for creating the secret key. The tool, called dnssec-keygen, is first used to create the keys:

```
[rootroot]# dnssec-keygen -a HMAC-MD5 -b 512 -n \
HOST auth-ns1.example.com
```

The standard convention is to name the keys after the secondary and primary name servers, in this case auth-ns1.example.com. The -b tag tells BIND that the key should be 512-bits. The dnssec-keygen command creates two files, the .key and the .private file. Both files contain the newly generated key; the key file should be copied into the BIND root directory /var/named/. The key will look something like this:

```
EhCCOHJHYYbcoJWIsN7Sh7tfeA8rBCi7KhesBbm/d \
+uEZwIQA2awWdV7 tY8jVprr1OO3fkXbSjY73yBO731pwA==
```

The key has to be defined on the master name server, in the named.conf file:

```
key auth-ns1.{
 algorithm hmac-md5;
 secret " EhCCOHJHYYbcoJWIsN7Sh7tfeA8rBCi7KhesBbm/d \
+uEZwIQA2awWdV7 tY8jVprr1OO3fkXbSjY73yBO731pwA";
};
```

The key name needs to be included in the zone file entry:

```
zone "example.com" {
type master;
file "example.com.hosts";
allow-transfer { key auth-ns1.; };
};
```

The same key entry needs to be made in the named.conf file on the slave server:

```
key auth-ns1. {
  algorithm hmac-md5;
   secret " EhCCOHJHYYbcoJWIsN7Sh7tfeA8rBCi7KhesBbm/d \
+uEZwIQA2awWdV7 tY8jVprr1OO3fkXbSjY73yBO731pwA";
};
```

BIND has to be told that all messages to the master server should be signed:

```
server 192.168.0.19 {
keys { auth-ns1.; };
};
```

Then create the slave zone file as before:

```
zone "example.com" {
type slave;
masters { 192.168.0.19; };
```

```
file "example.com.slave";
allow-transfer { none; };
};
```

The master and slave authoritative DNS servers have now been secured so that the master only allows zone transfers to the IP address of the slave, and it requires that the requests include the encrypted key. The slave name server will not allow any transfers.

Assuming standard security precautions have been followed on both the master and slave name servers, DNS transactions between the two should now be secure.

## DNS Outsourcing

Managing DNS security can be a headache, especially for large organizations. For companies that do not have the staff to manage and support large zone files, outsourcing may be a better alternative.

Some companies, like UltraDNS, Nominum, and easyDNS, offer managed DNS, while other companies, such as Men & Mice, will set up DNS service in-house. The services can range from having the company's team manage and support some, or all, aspects of an organization's in-house DNS services to a fully managed off-site DNS service.

There are some obvious advantages to this type of service. Outsourcing DNS frees up in-house network administrators so they do not have to worry about the day-to-day maintenance of DNS servers, and an organization can quickly have a scalable DNS solution that is redundant and secure.

DNS outsourcing has been around for a long time. Most organizations that do not have the expertise to manage their own DNS let their ISP, or even their registrar, manage their zone files. While these solutions are adequate for smaller companies, midsize and larger companies should consider a dedicated out-sourced DNS provider. Many ISPs and registrars are not equipped to handle hundreds of thousands of request per day to a single domain. ISPs and registrars are not always equipped to handle frequent updates to zone files as well. If your organization makes several DNS changes each week, or even each day, a DNS outsourcing provider may be the best solution.

As with other outsourcing providers, managed DNS providers should be quizzed thoroughly about their security precautions and the types of guarantees they provide.[2]

2. You are welcome to send them a copy of this book to verify they follow all procedures listed in this chapter.

Managed DNS providers not only provide authoritative DNS services, they can also provide outsourced caching DNS. Again, this may be useful for companies that do not want to manage caching DNS servers in-house. However, for a large organization, switching caching DNS from an internal server to an external server can cause significant traffic changes. The impact of those traffic changes should be carefully weighed against the benefits of outsourcing caching DNS.

## djbdns

BIND can be very secure, with the proper precautions. Unfortunately, as BIND has grown, the number of supported features has grown as well. Consequently, most implementations of BIND ship with very few security precautions in place. If a DNS administrator is not familiar with the steps required to secure a DNS server, BIND can be an easy target for an attacker.

One solution is to use an alternative to BIND. The most commonly used alternative is djbdns. Named for its creator, Dan Bernstein, djbdns is a minimal DNS server. It was designed to be small and secure.

Djbdns improves security in several ways. Most of these security enhancements can also be done with BIND, but they are not enabled by default. One of the primary security enhancements administrators get with djbdns is that by default it runs in its own chrooted jail. This separates djbdns from the rest of the operating system and prevents the djbdns user from being able to access files in other parts of the system. Djbdns also separates caching functions from authoritative functions. If a server is only acting as an authoritative name server, it will not be able to perform any recursive queries. Djbdns also uses various security enhancements to secure zone transfers.

**NOTE:** There are many additional security enhancements to djbdns. For more information about djbdns and its security enhancements, consult the djbdns website: *cr.yp.to/djbdns/*

There are some downsides to djbdns. The primary concern is that it does not handle zone transfers in the same manner other DNS servers do. This means that while it is possible to set up a BIND server and Windows DNS server as primary and secondary servers, it is not as easy to set up a BIND server and djbdns server as primary and secondary servers.

## Summary

DNS is a complex area, with a lot of potential for security breaches. It is also an essential service that organizations have to run, if they are going to communicate with the rest of the Internet.

While securing DNS can be complex, it really boils down to five basic principles:

1. Always run the latest version of BIND.
2. Each DNS server should run on a separate platform, in a different network.
3. Separate authoritative and caching functions.
4. Restrict access to caching name servers.
5. Limit the information provided by authoritative name servers.

Depending on how comfortable an organization is with DNS management, it may consider running an alternative to BIND. While BIND is undoubtedly the leader in terms of domains served and available support, many other DNS daemons exist. These daemons are often smaller and boast much better security than BIND. Programs such as djbdns have gained a lot of fame because of their inherent security. Be careful though; because the following for these programs is small and the development team is also small, they tend to come and go. Dents and MaraDNS are two other alternatives to BIND that have faded away in recent years. Building a large DNS infrastructure around these programs may not be advisable.

CHAPTER 13

# Installing an Apache Server

*Quidquid latine dictum sit, altum viditur.*

Before you start putting up your Web server and filling it with content there are a number of things to consider. However, if you're already running Apache you might want to skip this chapter and move on to the next one because this information might not apply to you.

## Choosing a Web Server

The task of choosing a Web server is not always as simple as choosing the best one available.[1] Other things should be considered, but how important those things are depends entirely on your particular situation.

It is the responsibility of every Web site admin to weigh these considerations, and arrive at the decision that is in the best interests of their Web site, their company, and their customers.

Some of these considerations are discussed here, but there will certainly be others in some situations.

### Compatibility Requirements

Frequently, you will have to make software choices based on the need to be compatible with existing installed software. For example, if there is a software package that you are required to run that only runs on IIS, then there is no further need to consider other servers.

### Existing Knowledge

Although you should never be afraid to learn something new, there is certainly something to be said for sticking to your strengths. If you have

1. If it were, everyone would be running Apache!

people on staff that are already Lotus Domino server experts you might be better off sticking with Domino.

### Executive Edict

Let's face it. In most companies, the software that you run is what your manager tells you to run. And what his manager tells him, and what her manager told her, and so on. The fact is that a lot of technical decisions are made for very non-technical reasons. Although it is your responsibility to present the pros and cons of various solutions, it's not always going to make a difference.

### The Customer

If you're in a service provider role—either at an ISP or in the IS department of a company—you will frequently be faced with customer demands to run particular software to meet their particular needs. The customer is always right, even when the customer is not right.[2]

## Hardware and Software Requirements

Apache has very minimal requirements. If you are running a machine as a server, then it probably already satisfies the minimum requirements for Apache. However, as with any software package, Apache runs better on faster systems with more memory.

Having run Apache on everything from a 486/33 to a Pentium-III 850, and several dual-processor machines along the way, the question of minimal hardware requirements seldom comes up. Apache will run on just about anything.

Apache also runs on just about any operating system that you've ever heard of, and several that you haven't. Anything vaguely Unix-like will almost certainly run Apache, and most Unixes ship with Apache installed in a default configuration.

Apache has been able to run on Microsoft Windows since version 1.3, which was released in 1997. It will run on Windows 9x[3] and Windows NT.[4]

2. Note that the term "customer" is applied generically, and applies as much to people inside your organization as to those billed for your services.

3. "Windows 9x" is a generic term which is used to refer to Microsoft Windows 95, Microsoft Windows 98, and Microsoft Windows ME, which share major architectural features, and behave much the same, as far as Apache is concerned.

4. And "Windows NT" is the generic term used to refer to Windows NT 3.51, Windows NT 4.0, and Windows 2000, which, likewise, share major architectural similarities.

Having said that, the INSTALL documentation that comes with Apache makes the following more specific statements:

- You will need at least 12MB of temporary free disk space for the build process. When the installation is completed, it will take up approximately 5MB of drive space. Of course, this number will vary based on which third-party modules that you add to the installation. Also, you will need to take into account the data that you will actually serve from the Web site, which is, of course, not included in that number.
- You will need an ANSI-C compiler, such as GCC, for the compilation of the source code. Unless you install one of the binary (precompiled) distributions, in which case you don't need a compiler at all.
- A Perl 5 interpreter is recommended, but not required. Several of the utilities that ship with Apache use Perl, but you can make do without these utilities.
- Dynamic Shared Object support is also useful to have, but not required. Most modern operating systems support this in some fashion or other, so this is not a very stringent requirement.

## Connectivity

If you're going to run a Web server, you probably want a connection to the Internet so people can see your Web site. In order for this to work, you'll need the following:

- **Internet connectivity:** A modem connection is a possible configuration, but if you expect to have more than a handful of people look at your Web site you would be well advised to get a higher-speed connection, such as DSL, cable modem, or some variety of leased-line solution. Your connection needs to be running 24 hours a day, all year long, so that your Web site is accessible whenever someone wants to use it.
- **Fixed IP address:** Although it's possible to play fancy games with DNS (domain name system) to make a dynamically allocated IP address appear to be in the same place all the time, the techniques for doing so are beyond the scope of this book. If you're actually going to run a real Web site you need to have a fixed IP address and

a hostname (or more than one) in DNS that resolves to your address. You will need to check with your ISP to find out what your address is, and if you are not running your own DNS server, you will need to arrange to get your name(s) to resolve correctly with whoever is doing so.

## Should I Host Somewhere Else, or Do It Myself?

An important question to consider is whether you want to host your Web site on your own server, in your own facility, or at someone else's facility, either on one of their servers, or at your own collocated server. This will depend on a number of factors, only a few of which are discussed here.

### Connectivity

Can you afford the necessary connectivity? If you put up a Web site that suddenly becomes popular, will you have sufficient bandwidth to service the traffic? If you host it in your own facility, you will be entirely responsible for the cost of that connectivity, and scaling your connectivity to meet the demand can become costly. If you host at an ISP's facility they will likely have more connectivity than you will ever need, and you won't be shouldering the entire cost for all that bandwidth.

### Reliable Connection

Is your connection reliable? If you have a small office, and are considering hosting your Web site on your own Internet connection, you should consider the possibility that your connection might go down occasionally. If this happens, and it stays down for a considerable period of time, you will need to consider alternative ways to provide service to your site's users. On the other hand, if your server is hosted at a remote facility, they will likely have redundant connections to the Internet, so when one goes down, the others will pick up, with no noticeable downtime to the users.

### How Much Access Do You Need?

What level of access to your servers do you need? If you are running a fairly simple site, on a normal day you might only need to put content on the server. However, if you have a site that relies on a large amount of custom software, or even nonstandard hardware, you might need to have physical access to your server on a regular basis.

If you are running your server on a Windows operating system, or any other operating system for which remote management is problematic, you might not want to have that server very far off site in case you need to do something that requires direct access to the console. (You might also need to consider a remote control application, such as VNC or PC Anywhere, which enables you to export your desktop across the network and work on that machine from anywhere. There are, however, security considerations in doing this.)

If you are running a Unix-like operating system, then you need to make sure that you have as much access to your hosted server as required. If you need daily root access, you need to make sure that your ISP permits this. Some ISPs are reluctant to permit this, because they are then unable to guarantee that the system will stay up.

## Questions To Ask Your ISP

If you choose to host your Web site at some other facility, rather than having it in house, you need to make sure that you understand your ISP's policies, and make sure that you're getting what you think that you should be.

The following are some of the things that you should ask your ISP, and things that you need to consider yourself, to make sure that there are no unpleasant surprises.

### Shared Space, Dedicated Server, Colloc?

There are a number of different ways to lease space at an ISP. The two primary categories of service are leasing space on a server owned by the ISP, and putting your own server, completely managed by you, at the ISP facility. The latter is referred to as collocation, or a colloc.

If you are leasing space, you need to know to what extent you have control over that machine. Do you have your own server, or are you sharing it with someone else? This knowledge will affect the manner in which you will need to secure your files. If there are other users that will have login privileges on your server, you will need to be much more cautious about files with group and world permissions on them.

Do you have root access to the machine? Normally, if you are not collocating your own server, you will not have root access to the machine. This is necessary for the ISP to have sufficient control over the machine to guarantee its performance. If you do have root access to the machine, it is typical for the ISP to withdraw guarantees of any kind because they no longer have any control over the things they would be guaranteeing.

## What Happens When Something Goes Wrong?

Is the server monitored by a package such as Watchers (`http://www.cre8tivegroup.com/web/watchers.html`), which will send notification in the event of system outages? If so, to whom do those notifications go? In the event of a catastrophic system failure (such as a kernel panic on Unix, or a blue screen on Windows, will someone at the ISP be willing to reboot the machine? If not, what is the procedure for getting your server back up?

Do you have an emergency contact number? Will a real person answer it? During what hours is there actually someone in the office that will be able to help you with problems?

## Backups?

Are there any backups run, and if so, how often? Are the backup tapes stored on site, or off site in a safe box? What is the procedure for getting a file restored? How long are backups kept before the tapes are cycled?

## Installing Software

If your server is not a dedicated server on which you have root access, then you need to know what the policy is on installing new software. Whether you need the latest Text::Template Perl module installed from CPAN, or you want Majordomo installed, or you want to have the installation of BIND upgraded to fix the latest security alert, you need to know what the procedures are for getting this done, what you can expect for turnaround on installation, and whether they are even willing to do such things. Although some ISPs are very willing to accommodate your whims, others have very strict requirements about what can and cannot be installed.

Small ISPs, such as `cre8tivegroup.com`, where I host my Web site for example, are often willing to install things for you, make small configuration changes, and keep up to date on the latest security alerts. However, much larger shops tend to be less flexible, insisting that every server have identical loads of software, so that they don't have to do any custom maintenance. Consequently, if there is anything fancy you want to do, such as `mod_perl`, mailing-list software, or custom Perl modules, you are probably better off going with a smaller ISP that is likely to be more flexible.

## FTP, Telnet, SCP, SSH: Getting Content To Your Site

After you have your server set up and configured, you'll need a means of providing content to the server. This will ordinarily be done in one of two ways. Either you will log in to the server itself and create content there, or you will create the content somewhere else and copy it to the server machine after it is complete.

Most Web-development professionals agree that it's always a good idea to develop on a machine that is not your production machine, and then copy content to the live server after you have verified that it works. There will, however, frequently be situations where emergency fixes are required, and in those cases, you should work directly on the server.

### Telnet and SSH—Connecting To the Server

If you have any Unix experience, you are probably at least somewhat familiar with telnet. You might be unfamiliar with SSH, however. If your experience is primarily on Microsoft operating systems, you might be unfamiliar with both of them. Although a telnet client is provided with most versions of Windows, neither a telnet server nor an ssh server are widely available for Windows.

Telnet is simply a means of logging in to a remote server (that is, not the machine you're sitting at) and getting a command line, just as you would if you were at that machine. The telnet client is part of most modern operating systems. On either a Windows or Unix machine, you'll find a telnet client. This can ordinarily be accessed directly from any command line by typing `telnet hostname`, where `hostname` is the network name of the machine to which you want to connect. After you have connected to the remote machine, you will get a login prompt, where you will need to provide a valid username and password for an account on that machine. After you have successfully logged in, a command prompt will appear.

### *Advantages of Using Telnet*

There are a several reasons to use telnet.

Because you are working directly on the live server your changes will be immediately available on the Web site.

Also, you are working in exactly the environment where the Web site is running, so there will not be any strange system dependencies between one machine and another. That is, occasionally you'll find that, for some reason, something that works fine on your test server somehow inexplicably does not work on the live server.

### *Disadvantages of Using Telnet*

The main disadvantage of editing content directly on the live Web site via a telnet session is the same as what I listed as the first advantage. Because you are working directly on the live server, your changes will be immediately available on the Web site. Consequently, when you mess something up, it will be immediately evident to your viewing public.

### *SSH—Exactly the Same, Only Different*

SSH (the Secure Shell) is effectively the same thing as telnet, with one important difference. SSH provides you with a connection that is encrypted.

With telnet, your username, password, and all your data, is passed in plain text across the Internet. Anyone with a little bit of knowledge, and the right tools, can intercept this traffic, and either snoop on what you are doing (for example, steal your username and password) or alter the data as it goes past. And, there's very little you can do about this.

With SSH, on the other hand, everything is encrypted, so even if someone does intercept your data, it will be meaningless to them. SSH uses a public/private key system, so that the data can be viewed only by the two endpoints of the conversation. Decrypting this data is extremely difficult and time-consuming.

You can find out more about SSH, and download the free clients and servers for a variety of platforms at `www.openssh.org`.

## FTP and SCP—Getting Content To Your Server

If you develop your content on a test server, and then copy it up to your live Web server—which is really what you ought to do—you will probably use FTP or SCP.

Like telnet and SSH, FTP and SCP, respectively, are the insecure and secure versions of file transfer.

### *Using FTP*

FTP, which stands for File Transfer Protocol, is the most common way to copy files around the Internet. It requires an FTP server, which you will connect to with an FTP client, and transfers files from one machine to another. FTP is fairly easy to use, and there are an enormous number of available FTP clients, from standard console (command line) FTP clients to very sophisticated GUI (graphical user interface) FTP clients that make the remote server look like a part of your local file system.

To connect to a remote FTP server with a console FTP client, you will type

```
ftp remote.host.com
```

You will be prompted for a username and password, and then you will be logged in. You can navigate around on the remote server with the cd (change directory) command. cd directoryname changes into a particular directory, whereas cd .. moves back up one directory. To move around on your local filesystem while you are logged into the remote server, use the lcd (local change directory) in the same manner.

When you are in the place you want to be, use the put and get commands, respectively, to put and get files.

```
put index.html
get otherfile.html
```

### *Disadvantages of FTP*

Two primary disadvantages of using FTP are the clients are insecure, and the servers are insecure.

Due to the nature of FTP, FTP connections are insecure. Like telnet, all data, including your username and password, are passed in the clear across the network, and could be captured as they go across the Internet.

A huge number of the available Unix-security exploits are performed by compromising an FTP server. There are a number of known FTP exploits, and it seems that more of them show up all the time. Although a vigilant system administrator should be able to stay abreast of the latest security exploit, many sysadmins will simply choose to avoid the problem all together.

#### *The Solution—SCP*

SCP, which stands for Secure *CoPy*, can be thought of as an encrypted FTP, although that's not quite accurate. Technically, SCP is file copy *tunneled* over SSH. Exactly what that means is probably not terribly important for our pur-poses here. The important thing is that it enables you to copy files across the Internet in a secure manner. Neither your authentication information, nor the data itself, is passed in the clear, and so it cannot be intercepted in a useful manner.

You can find out more about SCP at `http://www.openssh.org/`, and you'll likely get it when you install SSH.

There are SSH and SCP clients for Windows, the best of them being the ones that come with Cygwin.[5] Cygwin is available from `http://cygwin.com/`.

The decision of which Web server to use must be carefully considered to make sure that you're making the right choice in using Apache.

The decision of whether to host your Web site at your own facility or at an ISP, is also an important one, and there are a variety of considerations that you need to think about.

## Acquiring and Installing Your Apache Server

*Everything that Mr. Smallweed's grandfather ever put away in his mind was a grub at first, and is a grub at last. In all his life he has never bred a single butterfly.*

*Bleak House*—Charles Dickens

Apache is an Open Source product. This means that the source code is freely available for you to download and tinker with. This also means that most people will install Apache by downloading that source and compiling Apache their own particular way.

## Overview for the Impatient

For those of you who want to get something installed immediately, and don't care about all the details, this is for you. This is labeled "Overview for

5. In my humble opinion, anyway

the Impatient" in the INSTALL file that comes with Apache. After you have unpacked the archive file, do the following:

```
./configure —prefix=PREFIX
make
make install
PREFIX/bin/apachectl start
```

There, you're done. Note that PREFIX should be replaced with the base directory under which you want everything else installed. For example, throughout this book we will be making the assumption most of the time that you have installed Apache in the directory /usr/local/apache, so in the above code example you would use the commands:

```
./configure —prefix=/usr/local/apache
make
make install
/usr/local/apache/bin apachectl start
```

OK, now some of the details.

## Where Do I Get It?

The Apache Software Foundation (ASF) Web site is `http://www.apache.org/`. The part of the Web site specific to the Apache Web server is `http://httpd.apache.org/`. The Web site contains comprehensive documentation about the server software, information about the ASF, and, of course, the software itself.

Additionally, there are a number of mirrors around the world, so you can usually find a server that is near to you, particularly if you live outside of the United States. To find the mirror closest to you, go to `http://www.apache.org/dyn/closer.cgi`, which will dynamically figure out your closest mirror and send you there. After you click the Download link, you'll find yourself in the directory of downloadable files, `http://httpd.apache.org/dist/httpd/`, where you can select a file to download. Which file you choose depends on what format you're most comfortable with, and what version you want. Several versions are usually available for download—usually the most recent, and one or two versions back, in each of the various branches that are currently being supported. At the time of this writing, for example, 1.3.19, 1.3.20, and 1.3.22 are available for the 1.3 branch, whereas 2.0.16 and 2.0.18 are available for the 2.0 branch.

For each version there are usually six different files. The software is available in three different compression formats, and a `.asc` file accompanies each format, which is a PGP signature that verifies the authenticity of the file.

The three compression formats are `.tar.Z` (compressed tar archive), `.tar.gz` (gzipped tar archive), and `.zip` (pkzipped or Windows zip). The different compression formats are purely for the convenience of people that like the different formats, or might be more familiar with tools for extracting a particular format. All of the files contain the identical contents.

If you're not sure what you want, you should get the file labeled Current release in whatever compression format you're familiar with.

The `.asc` files enable you to verify that the files you are downloading are actually the same files that the Apache developers put on the site for you to download, and have not been tampered with by a third party. This is particularly important if you are downloading the files from a mirror of the Apache site, rather than the main download site.

You can check the validity of the signature files using PGP, which you can acquire at `http://web.mit.edu/network/pgp.html`. If the signature on the file matches, then you can be certain that the file has not been tampered with.

## Unpacking the Source

The method used to extract the archive will, of course, depend on which compression format you download.

Move the archive to a convenient location for unpacking. `/usr/local/src` is a good place.[6]

To extract a `.tar.Z` file, type the following command:[7]

```
tar ·vZxf httpd-2_0_xx.tar.Z
```

To extract a `.tar.gz` file, type the following command:

```
tar ·vzxf httpd-2_0_xx.tar.gz
```

6. You don't have to move the archive if you don't want to. Just change to the directory where you want to unpack the file, and provide the full path to the file when you type the following commands.

7. In each of these command lines, xx will be replaced with the particular version of the code you have downloaded.

Or, if you are using a version of tar that does not accept the -z argument, try:

```
gunzip < httpd-2_0_xx.tar.gz | tar -zx
```

To extract a `.zip` file, type the following command:

```
unzip httpd-2_0_xx.zip
```

Or, if you are uncompressing this file on a platform other than Unix, there are a variety of decompression utilities available, such as WinZip, which simplify the process of extracting compressed files.

## The Source Tree

After you have unpacked the source code, a directory listing will show you several files in the top-level directory—most of them documentation—and several subdirectories. Although it is not essential that you know everything about the source code to be a good system administrator, it's a good idea to understand something about the code that you're installing on your server.

There are six subdirectories created when you unpack the source archive.

### cgi-bin

The `cgi-bin` directory contains two very simple CGI programs, one in shell, and the other in Perl. They both perform the same function—displaying the contents of your CGI environment. They are not particularly useful, but we'll refer to them again when we get to the chapter on CGI (15). A number of other CGI programs used to be distributed with Apache, but most were removed because of security concerns. If everyone on the planet knows what CGI programs are preinstalled on a default installation of Apache it gives them an upper hand when trying to compromise your server through Apache.

### conf

The `conf` directory contains the default configuration files that will be installed on your server. During the configuration process variables in this file will be filled in with values that you provide to the configure script, or with default values if none are provided. These configuration files enable you to get a default Apache installation up and running in just a few minutes.

### htdocs

`htdocs` contains a default index page for the server, with the Apache logo and some text explaining that this is a new installation of the server, and pro-viding links to the ASF Web site for more information about the Apache server. This page is available in a number of languages and a variety of character sets. Apache's content negotiation ensures that (correctly configured) browsers will get the document in their own language.

The `htdocs` directory also contains the Apache users' manual in a subdirectory called manual, which contains exhaustive documentation on the server, as well as a number of "how to" style tutorials on a variety of topics. You need to be aware that although the documentation contained in this directory was the best thing available when that version of Apache was released, the Apache documentation gets updated almost on a daily basis, and the online docs (at `http://httpd.apache.org/docs-project/`) will be more up-to-date than what you have installed.

### icons

`icons` contains a number of images that are used in directory listings and other automatically generated documents, as well as some you can use for your own documents.

### logs

The logs directory is empty. This is where your log files will be put when you start up your server.

### src

The most fun, of course, is in the `src` directory. `src` contains the source code for the server. This directory is subdivided into a number of subdirectories, but we won't talk about them all right now. If you are going to hack on the Apache server code, it is in this directory that you will be working. However, modifying the Apache server code is beyond the scope of this book.

## Installing Binary Distributions

Before we proceed with what happens next, we need to address binary distributions. If you are using some non-Unix operating system, such as Windows, Mac OS, or OS/2, it is very likely that you don't have a compiler installed, or even available to you. Outside of the Unix world, a compiler is typically a software package that you'll have to pay a good amount of money for, therefore, relatively few people are going to have them.

For these folks, the ASF provides binary distributions, which means that someone else has gone to the trouble of compiling the source code for you, and all you have to do is download the files and install them on your system.

Binaries are provided for an impressive list of platforms. Most of them are there either because compilers for those platforms are expensive or difficult to use. Some are just there for the convenience of people who don't want to spend the time building it themselves. In any case, the user will just need to download the package, and run the installation program, to have a fully functional installation of Apache server.

### Installing on Windows

On Windows, the provided installation file is a familiar InstallShield file, which will ask you for some information such as where you want to install the server. It will then place the various files for you.

If you are installing on an NT operating system[8] you will further want to install Apache as a service, which can be done by selecting "Install as a service" from the Start menu.

### Binary Versus Source Installation

Some folks will wonder why they would want to go to all the trouble to build their own installation when someone has already provided binary installations for their specific operating system. There are a number of reasons that you might want to build it yourself. Some of them are philosophical, but most of them are very pragmatic.

The spirit of the Open Source movement is that you have the source code, and can do whatever you want with it. This necessitates, in many

8. "NT" is used here, and throughout the book, to refer to Microsoft's server operating systems, including NT and Windows 2000. The desktop operating systems are referred to generically as "Win9x", which includes Windows 95, Windows 98, and Windows ME.

cases, a large degree of understanding of what's going on behind the scenes, even to the point of hacking on the source code to get it to work. As more and more Open Source projects spring up, and as the quality of the source code improves, it becomes less and less necessary to work directly with the source code. This is definitely a good thing. But, for the present at least, it has left behind it a strong sentiment that to be a responsible system administrator, you should really understand the code that you are running on your system. Security reasons are hidden somewhere in there—someone could hide something malicious in code that you blindly install on your servers—but most of it is a philosophical belief that as a system admin, you should know as much as possible about what is on your servers.

Although I personally believe these sentiments, it might ring a little hollow to the sysadmin who has about 12 free minutes on a good day, and really doesn't have the time to mess with the source code of everything she installs. If it works, that's sufficient.

However, a number of more practical reasons exist to build Apache from source yourself.

If you install binaries, you trust someone else to make the decisions about what the best configuration is for your server. Although this person has tried to make those decisions in the best interests of the majority of installations, he did not know the particulars of your server—what sort of load it will be under, what sort of content it will be serving, or what expectations your users have about performance. And, necessarily, when trying to make everyone happy, decisions are made that are not the best for everyone.

By building the source yourself, you can make decisions in the configure process that will accurately reflect how you want your servers to work. During the configure process, you can decide where files are put, what modules are installed and which ones are left off, and a variety of other things. This way, Apache is built in such a way that is most fitted to your system, the way that you work, and what you expect the server to do. It won't leave out modules that you will want, and perhaps as importantly, it will not be weighted down by a bunch of modules that you will never use.

## `configure`

The next step in the installation process, if you have chosen to install from source, is to configure the build process. This is done with a script called `configure`, which is in the main directory where you unpacked the source archive file. `configure` enables you to specify a large number of options about how your server will be compiled and installed.[9]

To run the `configure` program, change into the directory where the archive has been unpacked, and type

```
./configure
```

Running `configure` without any arguments at all causes it to get ready for a default installation, taking all the default arguments to all options.

Upon typing this command, you'll see a large number of messages scroll by that will say "checking for," "checking if," and "checking whether" various things are available, installed, or working. You'll then see a lot of messages stating that it is creating various files for your particular configuration. This means that by the time you get around to compiling the code, it already knows all about your system, and it can do the right thing for your particular situation.

However, it will also make a lot of decisions for you that you might want to make for yourself.

By typing `./configure –help`, you can see a complete list of the things that you are able to configure. Most of them you'll just want to leave as the default, and in each case the default is specified in square brackets [].

Rather than wasting two pages reproducing this here, I encourage you to run this command on your own system while you read along, so that you can see what we're talking about.

Configuration options are divided into four main sections: configuration options, directory and filenames, host type, and features and packages.

## Configuration Options

The Configuration options are those that affect the configuration itself, and apart from the `–help` option, it is probable that you will not want any of these options, at least the first few times you build Apache.

These options enable you to do things such as suppress the rather verbose output of the configuration process; run the configuration, but not

9. Please note, going into this section, that there is another way to configure your installation, with the deceptively similar name of Configure (uppercase C, rather than lowercase c), which does much the same thing, in much the same way. This might seems a little silly, but there are some historical reasons that we'll touch on very briefly later.

create any of the resultant files after it is done; and cache the test results (where it is checking for various files and utilities) in a cache file for later use.

## Directory and Filenames

The next set of options deals with directories and filenames. The bulk of this is specifying where particular files are put. In a default installation, all the files are put in `/usr/local/apache`, but you can change this, and you can change where particular parts of the installation are put.

Some people have very strongly held beliefs that certain files should go in certain places, regardless of their origin. For example, these people would hold that configuration files should go in `/etc`, log files in `/var/log`, and man files (documentation) in `/usr/man` or `/var/man`.

Other people feel that one application (such as Apache) should keep all its files in one place, so that they can be e asily located.

This portion of the configuration process is there to keep everyone happy. Although the default is to keep everything together by specifying such arguments as –`prefix` (The directory which, by default, everything else will go under), –`bindir` (where the compiled binary executables will be placed), and –`mandir` (where the man pages will be placed), you can specify where each type of files in the installation will be placed.

## Host Type

You are unlikely to have to change these options in a normal installation. They enable you to specify a few options about the host on which you are building Apache. If you do not specify these options, the configure process will automatically look up your hostname and type, and fill in these values for you.

## Features and Packages

This is where things get really interesting. In this portion of the configuration you can specify which packages get installed, what features are enabled or disabled, and a variety of other options.

The most commonly used aspect of this section is turning various modules on or off, so they are built into the server, or not.

## A Default Installation

Note again that if you don't specify any options, Apache will be built with a sensible default list of modules, or some definition of sensible, and with files in some sensible place, so you can run a normal Web site without too much difficulty. Consequently, the first few times you build Apache, at least until you think you have a good idea of what is happening, it is recommended that you accept the defaults to learn the ropes.

The technique for a default installation is covered at the beginning of the chapter in the "Overview for the Impatient."

## make && make install

The final step of this process is very simple. You type the following command:

```
make && make install
```

And then you wait. This can take a while, but the time will vary depending on your processor, the amount of memory you have, and what you consider to be a long time.

During this time, the C source code that comprises the Apache server will be compiled into executable binary files, which it will then put in the locations that you specified during the configuration process.

These are actually two commands. `make` does the compilation, and `make install` puts the various files in their correct locations. The `&&` between the two commands means that upon the completion of the first command it should proceed immediately to the second. If there is a problem of some kind during the build process, execution will be aborted, and the installation process will not be run.

If you want to see where the installation will put all the various files, type the following:

```
./configure —show-layout
```

This will show you a full listing of the various directories that the installation will create and put things into:

```
root@rhiannon:/usr/src/apache_1.3.17# ./configure —show-layout
Configuring for Apache, Version 1.3.17
 + using installation path layout: Apache (config.layout)

Installation paths:
               prefix: /usr/local/apache
          exec_prefix: /usr/local/apache
```

```
               bindir: /usr/local/apache/bin
              sbindir: /usr/local/apache/bin
           libexecdir: /usr/local/apache/libexec
               mandir: /usr/local/apache/man
           sysconfdir: /usr/local/apache/conf
              datadir: /usr/local/apache
             iconsdir: /usr/local/apache/icons
            htdocsdir: /usr/local/apache/htdocs
               cgidir: /usr/local/apache/cgi-bin
           includedir: /usr/local/apache/include
        localstatedir: /usr/local/apache
           runtimedir: /usr/local/apache/logs
           logfiledir: /usr/local/apache/logs
        proxycachedir: /usr/local/apache/proxy

Compilation paths:
           HTTPD_ROOT: /usr/local/apache
      SHARED_CORE_DIR: /usr/local/apache/libexec
       DEFAULT_PIDLOG: logs/httpd.pid
   DEFAULT_SCOREBOARD: logs/httpd.scoreboard
     DEFAULT_LOCKFILE: logs/httpd.lock
      DEFAULT_XFERLOG: logs/access_log
     DEFAULT_ERRORLOG: logs/error_log
    TYPES_CONFIG_FILE: conf/mime.types
   SERVER_CONFIG_FILE: conf/httpd.conf
   ACCESS_CONFIG_FILE: conf/access.conf
RESOURCE_CONFIG_FILE: conf/srm.conf
```

This option is not available in Apache 2.0 as of this writing.

By this point, you should have Apache successfully installed. It's OK if you have done a default installation the first time through. You can move on with that for a while, and then when you understand things better, you can come back and customize your installation a little more.

## Starting, Stopping, and Restarting

*There are two kinds of fool. One says, "This is old, and therefore good." And one says "This is new, and therefore better."*

*The Shockwave Rider*—John Brunner

Now that your server is installed, you need to get it running. It really is simple. But, there are some additional things that you'll want to know about starting, stopping, and restarting your server.

## apachectl

Most of the time, you want to use `apachectl` to start and stop your server. `apachectl` is a handy little script designed to take the grunt work out of starting, stopping, and restarting Apache.

You'll find `apachectl` in the `bin` directory of wherever you installed Perl. You might want to copy, or symlink, it into `/usr/local/bin`, or somewhere else in your path, because you might need it frequently, at least while you're learning about Apache.

`apachectl` can be run with one of eight different options.

A complete listing of the options can be obtained by running `apachectl` with the `help` option:

```
% apachectl help

usage: /usr/local/bin/apachectl (start|stop|restart|
        fullstatus|status|graceful|configtest|help)

start       - start httpd
stop        - stop httpd
restart     - restart httpd if running by sending a SIGHUP or
              start if
               not running
fullstatus - dump a full status screen; requires lynx and
             mod_status enabled
status      - dump a short status screen; requires lynx and
              mod_status enabled
graceful    - do a graceful restart by sending a SIGUSR1 or
              start if not running
configtest - do a configuration syntax test
help        - this screen
```

These options are, for the most part, self-explanatory.

`configtest` will be discussed in more detail when we discuss configuration directives later in this chapter.

The `start, stop, restart,` and `graceful` options are of particular interest to this section of the book. The first two do exactly what you would expect. `restart` does what you would expect also, but it's important to know that it also rereads the configuration files, so if any changes have been made, those changes go into effect on a restart. `graceful` is useful because any connections to the server that are currently active will be completed before the server is restarted. This is important because it means that nobody's connection will be unceremoniously dropped in the middle of receiving a file, therefore, the perceived downtime of the server will be lessened.

For both `restart` and `graceful`, if there is a syntax error in the configuration file(s), Apache will not successfully restart. However, Apache is smart enough to check the syntax of the configuration files before shutting down, rather than waiting until it is time to start back up. So, if there is a problem with the configuration files, Apache won't even shut down in the first place. This was not true with earlier versions, where a restart would occasionally leave you with your server down, if you did not check your configuration syntax before attempting the restart.

### `httpd`

`httpd` is the server binary—that is, this is the actual executable file that is run when you start up your Apache server. You'll find this file in the `bin` directory of your Apache directory tree. The size of this file will vary depending on what you have built into your server, but it will be around 1MB in size, and will be the largest file in that directory.[10]

`apachectl` is just a wrapper that feeds arguments directly to the httpd binary for common options. There are a number of other things that you can do by passing arguments directly to `httpd`.

## Starting and Stopping with `httpd`

To start the Web server, without any special options, simply invoke `httpd` directly:

```
/usr/local/apache/bin/httpd
```

To stop the Web server, you'll need to know the PID (process ID) of the Apache parent process. You can acquire this PID from the file httpd.pid, which is located in the directory with your log files—usually `/usr/ local/apache/logs`.

```
cat /usr/local/apache/logs/httpd.pid | xargs kill
```

10. Note that if you installed Apache from a binary distribution, or built Apache with a file and directory layout different from the standard, `httpd` might be located elsewhere.

## Command-Line Flags

By passing additional arguments to `httpd`, you can have it behave in ways slightly different from what you have configured in the server configuration files.

For a complete listing of the available command-line options, invoke `httpd` with the -h option:

```
# /usr/local/apache/bin/httpd -h
Usage: /usr/local/apache/bin/httpd
                        [-D name] [-d directory] [-f file]
                        [-C "directive"] [-c "directive"]
                        [-v] [-V] [-h] [-l] [-L] [-S] [-t] [-T]
Options:
  -D name           : define a name for use in <IfDefine name>
                        directives
  -d directory      : specify an alternate initial ServerRoot
  -f file           : specify an alternate ServerConfigFile
  -C "directive"    : process directive before reading config
                        files
  -c "directive"    : process directive after  reading config
                        files
  -v                : show version number
  -V                : show compile settings
  -h                : list available command line options
                        (this page)
  -l                : list compiled-in modules
  -L                : list available configuration directives
  -t -D DUMP_       : show parsed settings (currently only
  VHOSTS                vhost settings)
  -t                : run syntax check for config files (with
                        docroot check)
  -T                : run syntax check for config files (without
                        docroot check)
```

We'll come back to a number of these options as we talk more about the surrounding information necessary to understand what they do, but of particular interest at this time are the following options:

- **`httpd -v`**: Shows you what version of the server you are running. This is a good way Ïto convince yourself, after a new install, that you are in fact running the new version, and not some old version that happened to be laying around in your path somewhere.

- **httpd -V**: Tells you what compile settings were in effect when you built Apache.
- **httpd -l**: Lists the compiled-in modules. This will give you some assurance that what you did in the configuration phase actually paid off, and you got the modules that you wanted.

## Starting on System Startup

If you are going to run Apache on a production system—that is, if you want people to be able to look at your Web site all the time—then you need to make sure that Apache starts up when you reboot your computer.

This is accomplished a variety of ways on different systems, but they are all typically just a small variation on the same theme.

In `/etc/rc.d` you will find a collection of scripts, typically with filenames starting with `rc.` (such as `rc.inet1`, `rc.firewall`, and `rc.local`) which run when your system starts up. The exact layout of this directory varies. Sometimes these scripts are located in subdirectories. Sometimes there are several subdirectories, corresponding to the various runlevels[11], containing the scripts, or symlinks to the scripts, and sometimes the scripts are all directly in `/etc/rc.d`.[12]

When you know how your system does things, you should create a startup script (called `rc.httpd`, for example) which contains a call to either `apachectl` or `httpd`, as you prefer, telling it to start your server. Alternately, many systems have a script called `rc.local`, which is specifically for you to put in your customizations to the startup process; this enables you to keep all your startup alterations in the same place.

So, for example, you can add the following line to either your `rc.local`, or to a separate file called `rc.httpd`:

```
/usr/local/httpd/bin/apachectl start
```

11. A Unix machine can start up in one of several runlevels, or modes of operation, such as single-user mode or multiuser mode. The details of this are not particularly important for this discussion. Consult your OS documentation for further information.

12. And, of course, other systems put it yet other places. Some systems, such as HP/UX, SuSE, Digital Unix, and others, like to put these startup scripts in `/sbin/init.d` or `/sbin/rc[0-6].d`. It can be a little hard to keep up with. Contact your local guru if you don't know how your system does things.

Or, if you want to start Apache with a configuration file other than the one in the default location, you could use the following line instead:

```
/usr/local/httpd/bin/httpd -f /etc/httpd/host2.conf
```

## Microsoft Windows

As should be expected, Microsoft Windows does things a little differently. Apache on Windows offers a few other ways to manage things, more in line with the expected Windows way of doing things. For example, you can install Apache as an NT service, or start and stop it from the Start menu. However, there are also several ways to start and stop Apache from the command line as well.

### Starting from the Command Line

The various command-line options previously listed for `httpd` also work on Windows, except that the executable on Windows is called apache, and is (by default) located in `c:\program files\apache group`

```
cd "\program files\apache group"
apache
```

After doing this, you might need to press `control-C` to regain control of your command prompt. Apache will continue running. Make sure that you can start Apache in this manner and that it is serving pages correctly before you proceed to the next step, to ensure that things are mostly set up OK.

### Installing as a Service

As previously described, if you are running a production server, you'll want to install Apache as a service. This is done with the following commands.

To install Apache as a service with no special options, do the following:

```
apache -k install -n "service name"
```

If the "`service name`" option is omitted, the service name "`Apache`" is used as the default name of the service.

If you want to install the service to use a particular configuration file, different from the default location for configuration files that you specified during the installation process, you can specify a different configuration file when you install the service. This way, you can have multiple Apache services, with different configurations.

```
apache -k install -n "service name" -f "\path\to\alternate\conf"
```

To remove the Apache service after it is installed, you can use the following command:

```
apache -k uninstall -n "service name"
```

## Starting and Stopping Your Apache Service

After you have Apache installed as an NT service, you can start and stop it a number of different ways.

### *apache -n "service name"*

You can call the Apache binary directly from the command line if you like, passing it arguments as we discussed previously with `httpd`. To start, restart, or stop the Apache service, you would use the following three commands, respectively:

```
apache -n "service name" start
apache -n "service name" restart
apache -n "service name" shutdown
```

Where, in each case, "service name" is whatever you called the service when you installed it.

### *NT NET Command*

Alternatively, you can use the NT `NET` command, which can start and stop any NT service:

```
NET START "service name"
NET STOP "service name"
```

### *Services Control Panel*

Finally, there's the NT GUI (graphical user interface) way to do things. NT provides you with a Services dialog, which lists all of the NT services, and enables you to start and stop each one. Additionally, it enables you to set properties on each service, such as whether they start automatically on server boot.

The Services applet is located in the Control Panel.

### Console Application

Under Windows 9x (Windows 95, Windows 98, and Windows ME), Apache does not, by default, run as a service. Windows 9x, not being server operating systems, do not have the concept of a service.[13]

Consequently, under Windows 9x, Apache runs as a console application. Which means, as it sounds, that Apache runs in a console (DOS window), and that console stays open for the entirety of the time that Apache is running. This is a little less than convenient, but then you really should not be using Windows 9x as a server platform, so hopefully this will only inconvenience you during testing.

If you are running Apache as a console application, you will launch it from the Start menu, in the Apache submenu. This will open up a console in which you will see an indication that Apache is running. To shutdown Apache, or restart it, the recommended method is to open another console, and type the commands

```
apache -k shutdown
```

to shutdown the process, and

```
apache -k restart
```

to restart it.

Doing this with the -k option, rather than just pressing control-C in the console window, or just closing the console window, is preferable, because it enables Apache to shutdown cleanly, rather than abruptly disconnecting from any open connections. However, because you are hopefully not running this in a server environment, it probably does not matter much.

Apache provides a variety of ways to start, stop, and restart your server. This makes it easy to automate these processes, and ensure that your server is always running when it needs to be.

## Configuration Directives

*Oh I have slipped the surly bonds of earth*
*And danced the sky on laughter-silvered wings*

*High Flight*—John Gillespie Magee

13. Yes, there are third-party applications that enable you run things as services. They are, however, not part of the base operating system.

Apache's behavior is configured via one or more text configuration files. These files are read on server startup, and contain directives that control everything about the server. Here we'll talk about how these configuration files work, and what you need to do to get your server acting exactly the way that you want it to.

Please note that this is not a comprehensive blow-by-blow, talking about every configuration directive that Apache supports. There are two main reasons for this.

One is that the Apache documentation itself, which is available free online, contains just such a comprehensive listing. There is a copy of this documentation on the CD that accompanies this book, but the version online is guaranteed to be the absolute latest information, including changes and corrections that are made on almost a daily basis by the Apache documentation team. This documentation can always be found at `http://httpd.apache.org/`.

The remainder of this chapter discusses the configuration files themselves—their formats, their syntax, and techniques that can be used to simplify their maintenance.

## Configuration Files

Apache has one main configuration file in which all the parameters controlling the operation of the server are specified. This file, called `httpd.conf`, is located in the conf/ subdirectory of wherever you installed Apache. Ordinarily, this is `/usr/local/apache/conf`.

When you first install Apache, you'll find a number of different files living in that directory. Most of these files, however, are example files, put there as a sort of tutorial by demonstration.

The first files you will see in `conf` are `highperformance-std.conf` and `highperformance.conf`. These files are identical—the idea is that the -std version, you'll keep around as a backup in case you do things to the other one, and want to get it back the way that it was originally. This configuration file is intended to give you a head start in configuring a Web server that is tuned to peak performance in your particular setting.

The next set of files, `httpd-std.conf` and `httpd.conf`, are the main server configuration file. We'll come back to this in a moment.

`magic` is the configuration file for `mod_mime_magic`, which is a module dealing with mime types.

`mime.types` is a configuration file relating file extensions with MIME types.

`httpd.conf` is the main server configuration file, and the file that you will most often be working with. `httpd-std.conf` is there so that you can make changes to the configuration file with impunity, and not be concerned that you won't be able to remember how to get it back to its original state.

It is a very good idea to make backup copies of known-good configuration files, particularly when you are going to try some modifications. In particular, you should keep around the configuration file that is distributed with Apache, as a good example of a well-formed configuration file. This file is usually called `httpd.conf-dist`.

## Configuration File Syntax

`httpd.conf` consists of just a few types of lines.

Directives actually make configuration changes to the server, so these are what you will become the most familiar with. Sections, although technically a form of directive, divide your server into different pieces on which different sets of directives are to act. Comments provide documentation so that you remember why you made particular configuration changes.

### Directives

The basic currency of the Apache configuration file is the directive. A directive is a keyword that is followed by a value, or values, which dictates one particular aspect of the server's behavior.

Here are some examples of directives:

```
KeepAlive On
MaxThreadsPerChild 20
ServerAdmin rbowen@rcbowen.com
Alias /icons/ "/usr/local/apache/icons"
IndexOptions FancyIndexing VersionSort
```

The directives that are available for you to set is determined by what modules you have installed. A number of directives directly affect the Apache core, whereas others are for configuring the behavior of individual modules.

To show a complete listing of all directives that are available to you on your particular server, you can use the `-L` flag with `httpd`, as shown here:

```
/usr/local/apache/bin/httpd -L
```

This will list every module that you are able to set, listing the name of the module that provides the directive, the expected argument or arguments, the contexts[14] that the directive can be used, and what override conditions, if any, must exist in order for the file to be permitted in a `.htaccess` file. (See Chapter 14, for more information on `.htaccess` files.)

## Sections

A section[15] is a method for limiting the scope of one or more directives to a particular directory, a set of files, or a set of URLs. Sections look similar to HTML tags, and enclose one or more directives.

```
<Directory /usr/local/apache/htdocs/private>
    Deny from all
    Allow from 192.168.1.105
</Directory>
```

The directives enclosed in the section apply only to the limited subset of your server's space, which is specified by the section. In the previous example, the Deny and Allow directives will apply only to files located in the `/usr/local/apache/htdocs/private` directory, and any subdirectories thereof, unless overridden by a directive applied to a specific subdirectory.

There are a number of different types of sections, specifying a number of different ways to divide up the content served by your Web server.

### `Directory` and `DirectoryMatch`

A `<Directory>` section, as you would expect, specifies that the enclosed directives apply to the particular directory listed, and all subdirectories

14. This concept will be covered in more detail in the next section on containers, and in the upcoming chapter on .htaccess files.

15. Note that the documentation alternately refers to them as directives, sections, and containers, depending on the context, and the author of that particular part of the documentation.

thereof, unless overridden by another directive applied to a deeper directory. The directory path specified is the full path.

If a `<Directory>` section is used on Microsoft Windows, and if the directory being specified is on the same drive letter as the `ServerRoot` directory, then the drive letter doesn't need to be specified.

In the following example, the ServerRoot is on the `D:` drive, and so the `<Directory>` section is also assumed to be referring to the `D:` drive.

```
ServerRoot d:\apache\

<Directory \apache\docs\private>
    AllowOverride None
</Directory>
```

`Directory` sections are easier to use when your site has been well planned out, and the content in a particular directory is of a particular type.

A `Directory` section is used to indicate that a particular part of your site contains resources that are to be treated somewhat differently from files in the rest of the site. These files are treated differently because they are either a different file type (such as being image files, or CGI programs), or because there are different restrictions on their use (such as a requirement of a certain authorization to get in).

A `<DirectoryMatch>` section behaves much the same way as a Directory section, except that instead of taking an exact directory path as its argument, the argument is a regular expression. The enclosed directives are then applied to any directory that matches the regular expression.

Stated simply, a regular expression is a way of describing a particular pattern of characters. The regular expression engine will compare the pattern to a given directory, and determine whether or not it matches. This allows you to specify more than one directory in a single section, if there are multiple directories that share common traits.

In the example that follows, the `<DirectoryMatch>` section specifies that the enclosed directive (the `AllowOverride` directive) is to be applied to all directories that look like `/users/`, followed by a string beginning with either A or B (uppercase or lowercase):

```
<DirectoryMatch /users/[aAbB].* >
    AllowOverride All
</DirectoryMatch>
```

So, for example, the directory /users/Bowen would have the directive AllowOverride All applied to it, by virtue of matching the specified pattern.

This gives you a lot more control over which directories directives are applied to, and allows you to do in one directive what otherwise could potentially take a large number of individual directives.

### *Files and FilesMatch*

<Files> sections indicate that the enclosed directives should be applied only to the specified files. Wildcard characters can be used. A ? will match a single character, and * will match any sequence of characters.

```
<Files *.gif>
    DefaultType image/gif
</Files>
```

As with <Directory>, <Files> has a sibling <FilesMatch>, which accepts extended regular expressions as arguments.

These directives are particularly useful for restricting access to some files in a particular directory, but not others, as shown in the following examples.

If you have several CGI programs, one of which is intended solely for site admins, you could use a Files directive to restrict access to just that one file:

```
<Files admin.cgi>
    AuthName Admin
    AuthType Basic
    AuthUserFile /usr/local/apache/passwords/admin.passwd
    AuthGroupFile /usr/local/apache/passwords/admin.groups
    Require group siteadmins
</Files>
```

(See Chapter 16, "Apache Authentication and Authorization," for more details on authentication and authorization.)

Alternatively, if you have been a little less consistent in your naming scheme, but your admin files have somewhat similar names, you can still restrict access to them all with one directive.

```
<FilesMatch "admin.(cgi|pl|exe)">
    AuthName Admin
    AuthType Basic
    AuthUserFile /usr/local/apache/passwords/admin.passwd
```

```
    AuthGroupFile /usr/local/apache/passwords/admin.groups
    Require group siteadmins
</Files>
```

Because the `Files` directive accepts wildcard characters, creative use of that directive is often simpler and more intuitive than resorting to the `FilesMatch` directive.

### *IfDefine*

The `<IfDefine>` section will be applied only if a particular parameter is defined. A parameter can be defined when the server is started up, with the `-D` command-line option.

Thus, if your `httpd.conf` were to contain directives as follows:

```
<IfDefine ReferLog>
     LogFormat "%{Referer}i -> %U" referer
     CustomLog logs/referer referer
</IfDefine>
```

And, if you were then to start your Apache server with the command line:

```
/usr/local/apache/bin/httpd -D ReferLog
```

Then the directives enclosed in the `<IfDefine>` section will be applied. In this case, starting your server with the `-D` ReferLog flag would cause the server to maintain a log file listing of the URLs from which people followed links to your site.

An `<IfDefine>` section can also be defined to apply directives when a particular parameter is not set. This is done by prepending a ! to the specified parameter:

```
<IfDefine !ReferLog>
...
```

The directives enclosed in the previous section would be applied to the server if the `ReferLog` variable were *not* defined. That is, if you start your server *without* the `-D ReferLog` flag, these directives would be applied.

### *IfModule*

Placing directives for a particular module inside of a `<IfModule>` section ensures that they are only applied if that particular module is loaded. This is a convenient way to have a standard configuration file, and not have to make per-system configuration changes just because a particular module is not installed. This is also the way that the default Apache configuration file is distributed, so no matter which modules you choose to build into your server, the configuration file will still work.

In the following example, the directives are applied only if the threaded module is loaded.

```
<IfModule threaded.c>
  StartServers  3
  MaxClients  8
  MinSpareThreads 5
  MaxSpareThreads 10
  ThreadsPerChild 25
  MaxRequestsPerChild    0
</IfModule>
```

### `Limit` and `LimitExcept`

`<Limit>` and `<LimitExcept>` sections refer to request methods. The enclosed directives are applied only if the HTTP request was made with one of the specified methods.

A request method is the manner in which the document, or resource, was requested from the Web server. This will usually be `GET`, `POST`, or `HEAD`, but will occasionally be something else. Without going into too much detail `GET` is usually used to get a document or resource. `POST` is usually used to send in the contents of a Web form. `HEAD` is a way to check the status of a document, typically to see if it has changed since the last time you looked at it, or if you can just reuse the copy you already have cached.

The `<Limit>` directive, then, allows you to restrict access to a particular document based on how that document (or resource) is being accessed.

`<LimitExcept>` is the opposite of `<Limit>`, limiting access for methods not listed.

### `Location` and `LocationMatch`

When Apache receives a request for a resource, there is a phase during which Apache maps the URL to either an actual file on the server, or to some resource. A `<Location>` section defines a mapping from a URL to some non-file resource. And, as with the other `Match` directives, `<LocationMatch>` maps from a URL pattern to a resource.

The resource can be just about anything, but generally it will be a handler of some variety. A handler is an action that is to be taken when particular files, types of file, or particular URLs, are called. Some handlers are part of the core server, and others are included in modules.

### *VirtualHost*

When multiple Web sites, with different hostnames, are served from one Web server machine, they are referred to as virtual hosts. Chapter 14 has information on virtual hosts, so we'll just say that directives enclosed in a <VirtualHost> section apply only to documents served from that virtual host.

## Comments

Lines beginning with the hash character (#) are comments, and are completely ignored by Apache when it reads through the configuration file on server restart.

Note that the line must begin with the hash. You can't start a comment mid line.

The default configuration file that comes with Apache is very heavily commented. Many beginning Apache users find that they can configure their server just by looking at the comments in that file and making changes based on the recommendations outlined there. All the basic directives are discussed, with examples and default settings, right in the comments.

As a result of this, the default configuration file is rather large, and nearly half of it is comments. That can be a little frustrating for an experienced user who already knows what he's looking for but has to scroll through dozens of lines of comments.

When you make configuration changes, it's a good idea to add comments explaining what the configuration is for, when it was made, and who made it. This will help you to remember, when you look back at the file several months later, why you were doing it.

It is also a very good idea to put your configuration file into some sort of revision management system, such as CVS, so that you can track changes, and undo them if they have undesirable effects.

## Specifying a Different Configuration File

There are a variety of different circumstances in which you would want to load your configuration from somewhere other than your main server configuration file. If, for example, you are testing a different configuration, but don't want to overwrite your existing configuration file, you might want to maintain multiple config files, and switch among them.

You can do this with the `-f` flag when you start Apache:

```
/usr/local/apache/bin/httpd -f /path/to/alternate/apache.conf
```

Note that the specified configuration file is loaded in place of your regular configuration file, and therefore must specify a complete configuration.

`apachectl` is not aware of what configuration file you have loaded, nor does it allow you to pick an alternate configuration file. So if you `apachectl restart` when you are running with an alternate configuration file, Apache will be restarted with the default configuration file, rather than the one that was specified by `-f`.

## Testing Your Configuration

Apache reads your configuration files only on server startup. This means that when you make changes to your configuration file, they do not take affect right away, but only when you restart the server. This gives you a chance to test your changes before putting them into production.

You can test your new configuration file using the configtest argument to the apachectl command. This is done simply by typing

```
apachectl configtest
```

apachectl will read through your configuration file and ensure that you have used correct syntax in the file. It is important to note that it does not verify that your configuration will work, but merely that it is correct syntax. If, for example, you refer to a DocumentRoot that does not exist, this error will not be caught at this stage, but only when you restart the server with the new file.

If the configuration file has bad syntax, `apachectl` will report this condition to you, and tell you which line the bad syntax appears on, as shown in the following example:

```
% apachectl configtest
Syntax error on line 26 of /usr/local/apache/conf/httpd.conf
Illegal option FollowSumLinks
```

In this example, I had misspelled the option `FollowSymLinks` as `FollowSumLinks`, and this was identified as an invalid configuration directive.

Having corrected this error, and running the command again, I get an indication that the problem has been resolved:

```
% apachectl configtest
Syntax OK
```

Note that if you have bad syntax in your configuration file when you try to start your server, it will not start. If you try to restart your server with a bad configuration file, it will ignore the restart and continue running so that it does not get stuck in a state of not running, and be unable to start up.

We highly recommended you run `apachectl configtest` each time you make any modifications to your configuration file. Apache gives you the option of including a file into your `httpd.conf` configuration file at the time that the server is restarted and the configuration files are loaded. This is accomplished with the Include directive, as shown here:

```
Include conf/modperl.conf
Include /etc/apache.otherconf
```

If the file path does not start with a leading slash (or, on Windows, with a drive designation) then the path is assumed to be relative to the `ServerRoot`. Why would you want to do this?

As your server configuration becomes more and more complex (Which it will, unless you have a very simple site, and are content to leave it that way forever), it becomes increasingly desirable to split it up into smaller, more manageable parts. Although this might, in some way, harken back to the day when there were three configuration files,[16] if handled carefully, this can greatly simplify your server administration. I'll give three examples where this might be a good thing to do, but I expect that your own situation will suggest other possibilities.

First, there's the situation when you have a very large, very complex module, which you have built into your server for some added functionality.

16. srm.conf, httpd.conf, and access.conf, presumably split the directives into sensible categories, but the distinctions were always rather nebulous.

mod_perl, mod_ssl, and mod_rewrite come to mind. These are very useful, very powerful modules, which can double the size of your configuration file.

In Apache 2.0, the default SSL configuration is in a separate file, which is loaded with an Include directive.

By separating the directives for that particular module out into a separate configuration file, you can make both parts of the configuration easier to read.

There is, of course, a slight performance hit on server start, because there is additional file I/O, but this only happens once, and is a very minor consideration.

Second, and perhaps most commonly, included configuration files are very useful when managing a large number of virtual hosts. By putting the configuration for each virtual host into its own file you can very swiftly locate the configuration for a particular host, and modify it without having to paw through dozens of other lines of configuration files looking for a particular host.

However, before you rush out and implement this plan, make sure you read the next section on including directories.

Note also that the performance hit on server start is going to go up as you add additional files. If you have hundreds of virtual hosts, and each one is in a separate file, not only will you have hundreds of include lines, but you'll have to open and read in those hundreds of configuration files. You might want to consider using mod_vhost_alias, which is discussed in Chapter 14. mod_vhost_alias allows you to configure large numbers of virtual hosts with just a few directives, rather than needing directives for each virtual host.

And third, there's the question of multiple people managing different parts of the Web site. By putting these different parts of the configuration into different files, and giving the necessary file permissions so the right people can edit them, you can delegate responsibility for the configuration file without letting everyone in the company have write access to the main server configuration file. This is particularly useful in the case of virtual hosts, where you are very likely to have a different person managing each virtual host.

Note, of course, that you will still have to have someone with root privileges restart the server in order for the configuration changes to take effect.

## Including Directories

Of course, if you really buy into this notion of splitting configuration off into other files, you might end up with an inordinate number of Include directives in your configuration file. This is particularly the case if you are using this scheme for virtual hosts.

Fortunately, there's a really good solution for this. The Include directive also takes a directory, instead of a file, as the value of the argument. When given a directory, the Include directive reads every file in the specified directory and includes it into the configuration.

So, if you have dozens of virtual hosts, you can put all those configuration files in a single directory, and include them all with one directive:

```
Include conf/vhosts
```

When you start (or restart) your Apache server, you'll see something like the following in your error_log:

```
[Sat Jun 30 21:52:58 2001] [notice] SIGHUP received.
Attempting to restart
Processing config directory: /usr/local/apache/conf/vhosts
 Processing config file: /usr/local/apache/conf/vhosts/apache
 Processing config file: /usr/local/apache/conf/vhosts/
                            /boxofclue.com
 Processing config file: /usr/local/apache/conf/vhosts/buglet
 Processing config file: /usr/local/apache/conf/vhosts/cpan
 Processing config file: /usr/local/apache/conf/vhosts/cvs
 Processing config file: /usr/local/apache/conf/vhosts/dates
 Processing config file: /usr/local/apache/conf/vhosts
                            /drbacchus.com
 Processing config file: /usr/local/apache/conf/vhosts/
                            /gaddisphoto.com
 Processing config file: /usr/local/apache/conf/vhosts/
                            /photos.tm3.org
 Processing config file: /usr/local/apache/conf/vhosts/
                            /reefknot.org
 Processing config file: /usr/local/apache/conf/vhosts/rt
 Processing config file: /usr/local/apache/conf/vhosts/tm3
 Processing config file: /usr/local/apache/conf/vhosts/
                            /zzz_last
[Sat Jun 30 21:52:59 2001] [notice] Apache/1.3.19 (Unix)
   mod_perl/1.25
     configured — resuming normal operations
```

Notice that the files are included in alphabetic order. More specifically, they are included in the order that they appear in a directory listing. In the previous example, you'll notice a `zzz_last` file on the end. This is the one containing the virtual host settings for the `_default_` virtual host, and perhaps some other global server configuration directives.

It is also very important to note that every file in the directive will be included, therefore, you should make sure that no stray files end up in the directory, which can cause Apache to fail on startup. Temporary files generated by your editor are a frequent source of problems, for example.

## Options: Turning on Features

The Options directive is one of the main tools for turning features on and off in various parts of the site. Judicious use of this directive will allow you to control very tightly what is allowed, and not allowed, in each content directory. It can be set in your main server configuration, in a VirtualHost section, in a Directory section, or in a .htaccess file. For the scope of the section in which you set it the specified options will be turned on.

Options takes one or more of seven possible values, All of them, or None of them.

### General Syntax

The syntax of the Options directive is as follows:

Options `[+|-]` *option* `[+|-]` *option*Prepending a [ps] to a particular option adds that option to those that are turned on, whereas prepending a ñ turns off that particular option.

```
Options +ExecCGI +Includes -FollowSymLinks
```

In this example, the `ExecCGI` and Includes options are turned on, and the `FollowSymLinks` option is turned off.

Although the [ps] and ñ are optional, omitting them means that you are turning off all other options that might have been set, and turning on only those that you have specified. The following directive, for example, turns on Indexes, but also turns off any other options that might have been turned on. It helps to remember that directives set in a particular directory also apply to any subdirectories of that directory.

```
Options Indexes
```

### ExecCGI

```
Options +ExecCGI
```

The `ExecCGI` option turns on the capability to execute CGI programs inside the specified scope.

---

**CAUTION:** Although this directive allows you to execute CGI programs in a directory which is not marked with a `ScriptAlias` directive—that is, to execute CGI programs in a document directory—this is generally not a good idea for two reasons. First of all, it makes it very difficult to track down all the CGI programs on your site if and when you are having problems. Secondly, it is a potential security problem. Any CGI program is a potential security hole, and permitting them in directories where the file permissions are typically a little more lenient is asking for trouble.

---

### FollowSymLinks

```
Options +FollowSymLinks
```

By default, symbolic links are ignored when they appear in a directory served by Apache, which makes it impossible to escape from the document directory. If, for example, you had a link to `/home` in your document root, following that symbolic link would permit Web users to download arbitrary files from anyone's home directory, which would clearly be a security problem.

However, if you have `Options +FollowSymLinks` turned on, then Apache *will* follow these links.

---

**CAUTION:** Make very sure you are aware of the security implications in turning on this option. Make sure that you do not have any symbolic links to directories that might contain files that should not be available to the general public. Never permit this option for directories that are managed by potentially untrustworthy people. If you absolutely must have symbolic links from your content directories, see the `SymLinksIfOwnerMatch` option as a possible alternative.

---

Because Microsoft Windows does not permit symbolic links, this option does not apply to Apache on Windows.[17]

17. No, shortcuts are not the same as symbolic links, and Apache will not follow shortcuts.

## SymLinksIfOwnerMatch

```
Options +SymLinksIfOwnerMatch
```

This is the same as the previous option, with one important difference. Apache will follow symbolic links only if the target of the directory is owned by the same user as the link itself. That means a user cannot link to a directory that they do not own, and thus get access to the contents of that directory.

As with `FollowSymLinks`, this option is not available on the Windows version of Apache.

## Includes

```
Options +Includes
```

Options Includes turns on the capability to have Server-Side Includes (SSI) in files. SSI gives you the ability to embed a variety of commands in HTML documents, and have them evaluated when the page is served to a client.

---

**CAUTION:** SSI has many of the same security concerns as CGI programs, in that it allows the execution of arbitrary commands on the server. To defang this beast, consider using `IncludesNOEXEC` instead.

---

## IncludesNOEXEC

```
Options +IncludesNOEXEC
```

This directive turns on permission to use SSI, but forbids the use of the #exec command, or using #include to load a CGI program. This removes most of the security risk associated with permitting Server-Side Includes.

## Indexes

```
Options +Indexes
```

This option enables the generation of automatic indexes in directories that do not have an `index.html` file (or whatever file you have indicated with the DirectoryIndex directive.

**CAUTION:** Turning on this option means that files in directories—even if you don't have links to them from anywhere on your site—will be visible to anyone looking at your Web site. However, if you are planning the security of your Web site around the principle of "hoping nobody notices," then you will have larger problems than this. That is to say, if you would not want random strangers to be in possession of certain files, you should never have them available on an unauthenticated Web site.

### `MultiViews`

```
Options +MultiViews
```

The `MultiViews` option turns on a very powerful aspect of content negotiation. `MultiViews` is a feature whereby Apache figures out which document is most likely to be acceptable to the client, and gives them that one.

### `All`

```
Options All
```

As you would expect, Options All turns on all the various Options. Well, almost all of them. `MultiViews` is not turned on with `All`, and must be explicitly asked for.

### `None`

```
Options None
```

And, of course, None turns off all the available options.

## Configuration Security Considerations

Please remember that there are serious security concerns when you start splitting up your configuration file and putting it all over the place; particularly if you start giving out permissions to edit those files.

Being able to edit those subfiles is no different from being able to edit your main server configuration file. Any directive can be put in those included files, and will have every bit as much weight as though it had appeared in the main server configuration file.

Make very sure of two things. First, ensure the files themselves are in secure directories. If the file is world-writeable, so are all the files in it, and even if they can't edit the file itself someone could delete or rename them. For example, if `/usr/local/apache` is world-writeable[18] someone can remove the directory apache, and replace it with his own directory, with anything he wants in it. So it's not enough that the individual files in that directory have the correct permissions on them.

Secondly, make sure that you trust the folks that you're giving file write permission to.[19] If they can edit these files, they can do whatever they want to your server configuration.

Apache configuration files contain three types of things. Sections, specified with HTML-like tags, delineate the scope, or range, of a particular set of directives. Directives, specified as a directive name, followed by a value, configure all the individual settings on the server. And comments, specified with a leading pound sign (#), are ignored by the server, and serve only to annotate the configuration file.

Apache ships with heavily commented default configuration files to get you started quickly.

18. Yes, I know, that's a horrible thought, but I've seen it happen.

19. And, of course, the first law of security is "Don't trust anybody." See Chapter 15, "Apache Security," on Security Considerations.

CHAPTER 14

# APACHE CONFIGURATION UTILITIES AND VIRTUAL HOSTS

*"Software suppliers are trying to make their software packages more user-friendly...Their best approach, so far, has been to take all the old brochures, and stamp the words, 'user-friendly' on the cover."*

Bill Gates

## GUIs and Configuration Files

Apache, in the Unix-server tradition, is configured via text-based files. This has several advantages, including:

- You only need a simple text editor such as vi or emacs to modify the configuration of an Apache server.
- It is possible to access the machine through a remote shell (using telnet or ssh, a secure version of the Unix remote shell command).
- The bandwidth requirements are small and you can administer servers over slow links. You can connect a modem to a serial port and be able to dial-in and administer the machine remotely, even if it is unreachable from the Internet.
- You can put the configuration files under a source control system such as CVS, and keep track of who changed what and when. You can easily maintain different configuration versions and revisions, and you can safely return to the last set of configuration files known to work.
- The Apache configuration file format enables insertion of comments alongside directives. This provides valuable information about the configuration and provides administrators the opportunity to document, in detail, specific settings. This is useful in environments where more than one administrator modifies the same set of Apache server configuration files.

- You can automate the generation and modification of the configuration files using shell commands of scripting languages such as Perl or Tcl. This is useful if the same task has to be repeated over time, for example for different ISP customers. The configuration files are usually generated via template files from customer information stored in relational databases or LDAP directories.

Text-based configuration systems have several disadvantages. The following reasons are why GUI or Web-based installation and configuration tools are useful, especially for new or inexperienced administrators.

- The configuration file formats vary significantly from one program to another. Even if you are familiar with the Apache configuration syntax, other popular server packages such as Sendmail or Samba use different configuration formats. A well-designed GUI will provide you with a centralized, consistant interface to a variety of server programs, thus lowering the learning curve.
- The number of available directives is overwhelming. Setting up a server such as Apache usually involves reading a long set of documentation and manual pages. This is necessary even if you only need a handful of options to configure a typical installation. A well-designed GUI will organize the options in a sensible, task-oriented interface that will guide the user, collect the information needed, and produce the appropriate configuration.

Other advantages of well-designed, GUI-based administration tools are context-sensitive help, delegated administration, and the capability to abstract the specific configuration syntax details.

Poorly designed GUIs have disadvantages. A GUI can be unstructured, offering configuration screens with a myriad of options that confuse the user. Some GUIs can only configure a limited set of functionality, thus being useful only for initial configurations. When users need the advanced functionality, they must access the configuration files directly, defeating the purpose of the GUI. In some cases the GUI does not interact nicely with the underlying configuration files, keeping its own metadata and overwriting the configuration files when needed. Thus, any configuration changes done by editing the file directly will be lost because the GUI will not recognize those changes.

This chapter introduces you to two popular GUI configuration tools for Apache. You will learn how to install and use them to configure your server.

# Webmin

Webmin is a Web-based administration system for Unix-like operating systems. It is Open Source under the GPL license and James Cameron is the main author. It is written in Perl and is extensible, meaning that developers can write modules to configure different programs, including one to configure Apache.

In this section you will learn how to install and configure Webmin and use it to perform basic Apache-administration tasks. These tasks include starting and stoping the server, changing server parameters, creating new virtual servers, protecting directories, and so on.

Before using Webmin or any other configuration utility make sure you backup your Apache configuration files. In particular you need to backup `httpd.conf` and any other files referenced in it via the `<Include>` directive.

## Existing Webmin Installation

You might have Webmin already installed if you are using a recent Linux distribution. You can use package management utility of your distribution to check if Webmin is already installed.

---

**TIP:** If your system is rpm-based (such as the ones from Red Hat, Suse, or Mandrake) you can check if Webmin is already installed by issuing the `rpm -q` webmin at a shell prompt.

---

If you do not have Webmin installed, please proceed to the next section where you can learn the steps necessary to get Webmin up and running.

Webmin is accessed via a Web browser. Before you can do so, you need to start the Webmin Web server. The Webmin application is protected by a password.

To change the Webmin default password issue the following command:

```
/usr/share/webmin/changepass.pl/etc/webmin/admin newpassword
```

Substitute *`newpassword`* with the new password to protect access to Webmin. The command needs to be executed as root.

---

**TIP:** Each distribution places files in a slightly different location. You can check where the files are installed in your system by issuing the following command:

```
# rpm -q -l webmin | more
```

If you want to know where `changepass.pl` was installed in your system, you can issue the following command:

# rpm –q –l webmin | grep changepass.pl

---

## Installation

If you don't have Webmin installed in your system, you can download it from `http://www.webmin.com/webmin/`

Users of any of the BSD-Unix variants such as FreeBSD or OpenBSD have Webmin available via the ports collection.

You can download an rpm package from the Webmin site. If you are using an rpm-based Linux distribution you might want to check if your distribution already includes a Webmin rpm and install that one instead. You can check your vendor's Web site or an rpm repository like `http://rpmfind.net`. In any case, make sure to check the Webmin Web site for the latest version, to make sure your rpm is up to date.

Issue the following command as root to install a new rpm in your system:

```
# rpm -q -i webmin*.rpm
```

## Installing Webmin from Source

Webmin is written in Perl, so you need to have a version of Perl installed in your system. You can verify that you have Perl installed in your system by `typing perl` in the command-line prompt. Executing the command `which perl` will give you the exact path of the program being executed.

If you do not have Perl installed in your system, you can install the package that came with your Unix distribution or visit `http://www.perl.com`. The Webmin Web site also provides precompiled packages for Solaris and HP-UX.

The installation of Webmin is straightforward. The steps need to be performed as root. After you have downloaded the Webmin compressed sources package (tarball) from the Webmin Web site, you need to uncompress it and execute the installation script:

```
# gunzip < webmin-xxx.tar.gz | tar xvf -
# cd webmin-xxx
# ./setup.sh
```

*xxx* needs to be replaced by the version of Webmin you are installing. You will be prompted for the information Webmin needs:

- You need to specify where Webmin will install its configuration and log files: `/etc/webmin, /var/webmin`
- You need to enter the path to the Perl interpreter, which you already learned about earlier in this section.
- You need to provide the specific vendor name and version for your operating system. This is necessary because each operating system distribution places configuration files in a different place.
- Finally, you provide the required values for the Webmin server such as the listening ports and the username and password, to protect the pages.

Webmin usually listens on port 10000 and the Web server might or might not allow for secure access depending on whether the appropriate libraries were installed in the system. You might want to change this port number if you are concerned about people scanning your computer for services at specific ports.

You can access the specific configuration of your Webmin server via the `miniserv.conf` file, located in `/etc/webmin`.

## Starting Webmin

To access Webmin, assuming it is configured with the defaults outlined in the previous sections, you need to type the following URL in your Web browser: `http://127.0.0.1:10000/`

If your Webmin server has SSL support, the URL changes from `http://` to `https://`.

This will take you to the Webmin login page if Webmin is already running. Webmin can be configured to run at startup time. You can start and stop Webmin manually with the following commands:

```
/etc/webmin/start
/etc/webmin/stop
```

## Using Webmin

You need to enter the appropriate username and password to access Webmin (see Figure 14-1). After a successful login you can access the main Webmin page. Here you can configure different aspects of Webmin itself. It even includes support for themes.

You can navigate the different sections by clicking on the different tabs (see Figure 14-2). The System tab enables you to configure the underlying operating system, including users, file systems, and packages. The Hardware section enables for configuration of bootloaders, disk partitions, networking, and printers.

In the Others section you can access Webmin modules that permit the execution of remote commands, a Web-based file manager, and so on.

You can find Apache under the Servers section, together with the configuration options for mail, DNS, and FTP servers.

You can click in the Apache icon to enter the main Apache configuration page.

The first time you enter Apache configuration you might be asked to provide information about available third-party Apache modules. If you are not sure about what modules are installed click OK because Webmin tends to guess right and you can always change that selection afterwards.

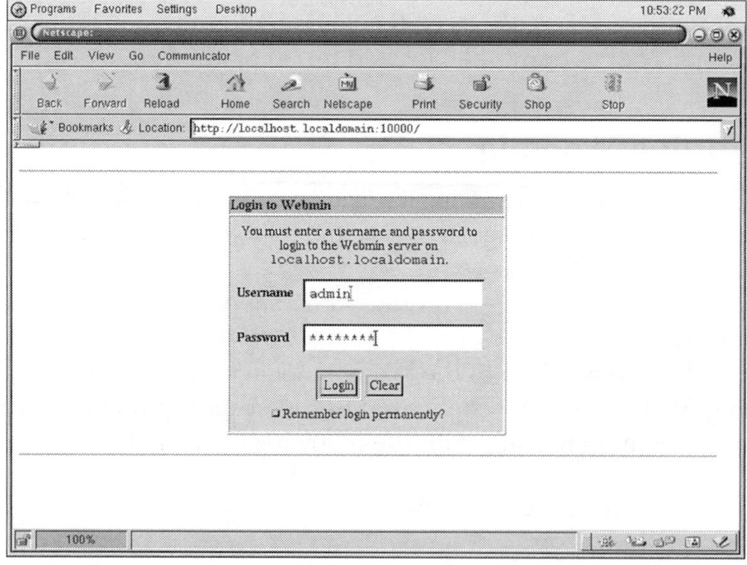


**Figure 14-1** Webmin login screen.

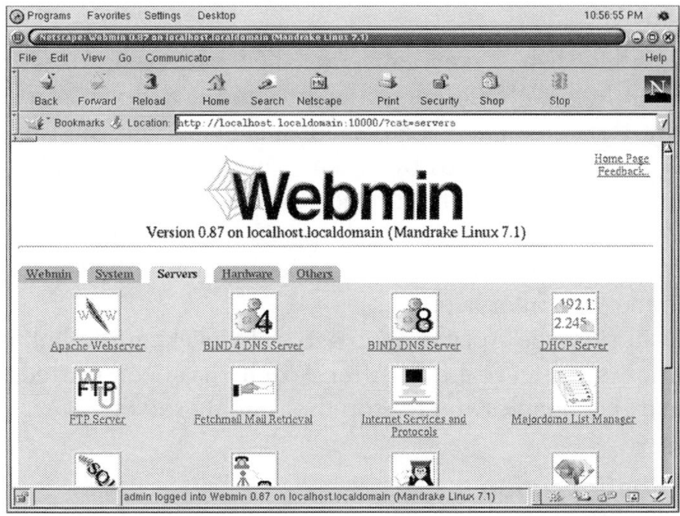


**Figure 14-2** Webmin server screen.

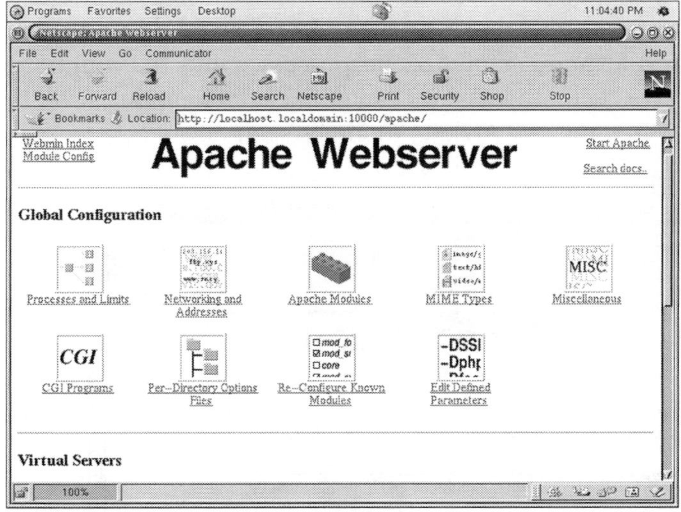


**Figure 14-3** Webmin Apache main configuration screen.

The page is divided in three different areas, as shown in Figure 14-3:

- Top area, where you can find links to configure the Apache instances being managed and links to start the server.
- Global Configuration, with links to configuration options.
- Virtual Servers, which is a list of all the available servers to be configured.

### *Top Area*

If the Apache Web server came installed with your operating system distribution then Webmin knows how to find it and you can configure it right away. If you are using a custom installed Apache you can specify the location of the relevant files by clicking on the module configuration link (see Figure 14-4). You need to provide the commands for starting and stopping the server, the location of the httpd executable, and the root directory of Apache. Other options enable you to specify how virtual hosts will be displayed in the Web interface.

You can start the Apache Web server by clicking the link on the top-right corner (see Figure 14-3). After Apache has been started, a new link will appear that enables you to stop the running server.

### *Global Configuration*

You can configure parameters that affect the server as a whole via the links in this area. Most of the options here are usually required only for advanced configuration scenarios. The default settings are usually appropriate for most situations. Under the Processes and Limits section you can configure the number of Apache processes and the number of requests these servers will process. You can define which modules will be loaded by the Web server at the Apache modules section.

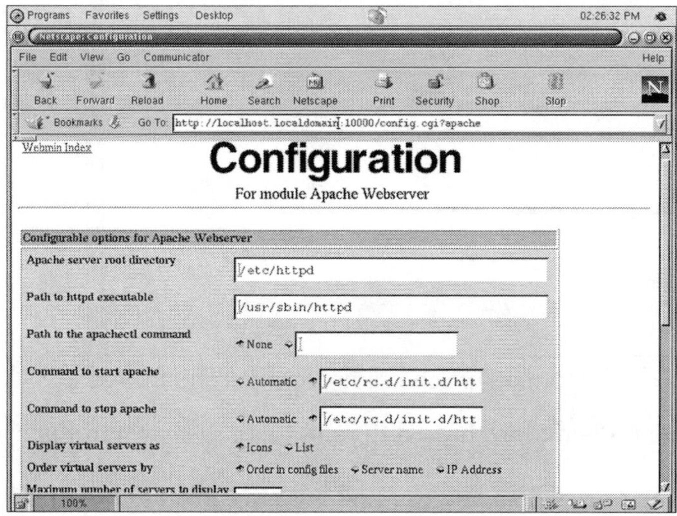


**Figure 14-4** Apache Web server configuration options.

Apache enables you to specify certain configuration options on a per-directory basis, via special files called `.htaccess`. You can configure them in the per-directory options files section.

### *Virtual Servers*

Here you have access to a list of virtual hosts available for your Apache installation. You can configure the default Web server. Other virtual hosts will also inherit the properties specified here.

### *Configuring a Virtual Host*

You can add a new virtual host (see Figure 14-5) by providing the address and port the new server will listen to, the document root where documents will be served, and the server name for the host.

You can delete a virtual server by clicking the virtual server link, server configuration, and then selecting to delete the server.

You can configure the properties of the virtual server via the configuration links. Some of the practical configuration parameters include:

- **Error Handling** You can customize the pages to be displayed in your Web site when an error occurs. For example, when a document

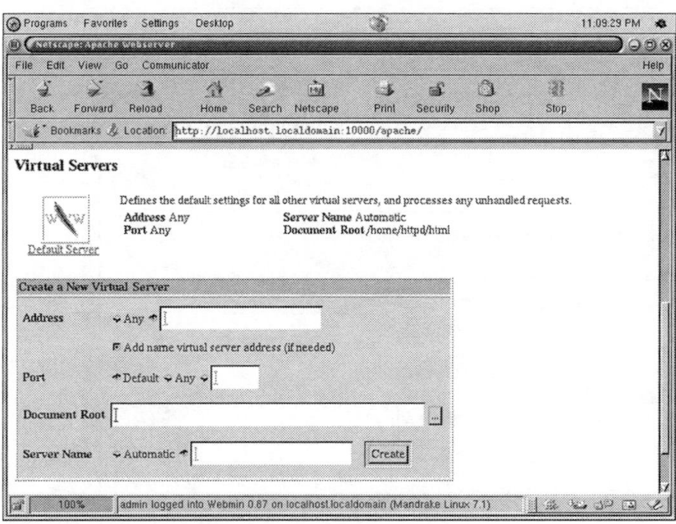


**Figure 14-5** Adding a new virtual server.

is not found you can present the user with a page that explains the error and allows them to search the Web site for similar documents.

- **Log files** You can define the location of the files where Apache will log the Web server accesses, the possible errors encountered, and the format of the information recorded.
- **Aliases and redirects** You can associate directories in the hard disk with specific URLs that are easier to remember and type. You can also specify the permanent or temporary redirection of certain URLs in your Web site. This is useful if the Web site has gone through layout changes. Your users will not encounter "Document not found" errors, they will be redirected to the appropriate page instead.
- **Show directives and Edit directives** These allow you to have a direct look at the underlying configuration directives. You can edit specific directives or even add new directives for custom or not supported modules.
- **CGI** You can mark certain directories as containing and allowing the execution of CGI scripts.

You can configure directory, location, and file sections in each of the virtual servers. As well as define specific portions of the URL space that you can configure separately.

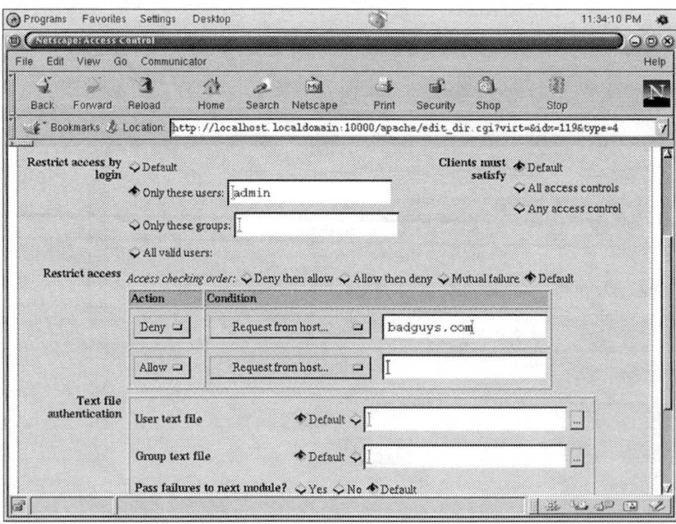


**Figure 14-6** Restrict access screen.

You can configure these sections by clicking them and then selecting one of the links. The Access Control (See Figure 14-6) section enables you to restrict access based on the IP address the user is coming from, its username and password, or the browser he is using.

### *Delegated Administration*

More than one user can administer the Apache installation with Webmin. You can restrict access and configuration rights on a per-user or per-group basis You can accomplish this by following these steps:

- **Create a new Webmin user** Click the Webmin tab, select Webmin users, and then select Create a new Webmin user. Select Apache module as part of the creation process.
- **Restrict configuration** You can now select the created user link and configure the level of configuration access. You can restrict the ability of the user to start or stop the server, change addresses, pipe logs to programs, or manage only a certain virtual Web server (See Figure 14-7).

You can also create Webmin groups and set policies based on them.

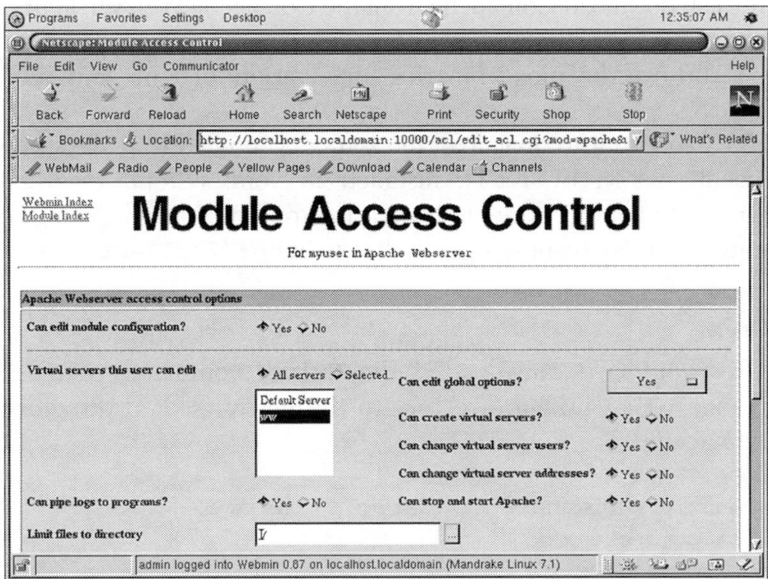


**Figure 14-7** Restricting configuration on a per-user basis.

#### *Related Links*

You can learn more about Webmin by visiting the following Web sites:

- Official Webmin site: `http://www.webmin.com/webmin`
- Joe Cooper's Webmin guide: `http://www.swelltech.com/support/webminguide/index.html`

## Comanche

Comanche stands for Configuration Manager for Apache. It is a standalone GUI (not Web-based) distributed under an Apache-style license, and its primary author is Daniel Lopez. It is written in the Tcl/Tk scripting language and works on Unix and Windows platforms. Although it can be extended to easily configure other servers, its primary focus is Apache.

Before using Comanche or any other configuration utility make sure you backup your Apache configuration files.

### Installation

You can download Comanche from the Comanche Web site at `http://www.comanche.org`.

You can download binaries for a variety of Unix and Windows platforms.

If you want to download the source, you need to make sure you have a recent version of Tcl/Tk installed in your system, together with the `[incr Tcl]` object-oriented extension to the Tcl language. You can get this software at the Tcl developer exchange `http://tcl.activestate.com/`.

#### *Unix*

After you have downloaded the tarball, you need to uncompress it, change your working directory to the newly created directory, and start Comanche:

```
# gunzip < comanche-xxx.tar.gz | tar xvf -
# cd comanche-xxx
# ./comanche-xxx
```

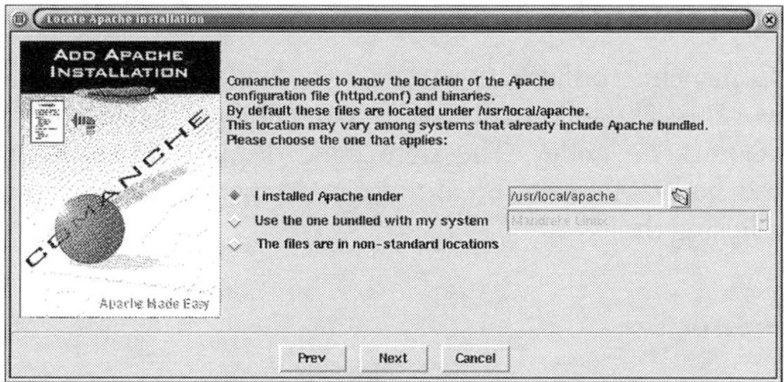


**Figure 14-8** Initial Comanche setup.

Where `xxx` is the Comanche version.

If you downloaded the source distribution `itkwish main.tcl` is the command you need to start Comanche.

The first time you start Comanche no Apache installations will be available. You can press the New Installation link to provide Comanche with the location of the Apache Web server. You can select one of three options—you compiled Apache manually, you are using the Apache bundled with your installation, or you are using a custom Apache installation. After you have provided the data, you are ready to proceed with the configuration of the server.

### *Windows*

You need to have Apache installed in your system prior to installing Comanche in Windows. Comanche supports Windows 95/98/NT/ME/2000, but you should only run production Apache versions on server versions of Windows, such as Windows 2000.

The Windows binary is contained in a zip file. You can use Winzip or any other Windows compression utility to extract the contents of the archive.

You can start Comanche by double-clicking the Comanche.exe icon. Comanche will read the location of Apache installations directly from the registry, so you do not need to perform any extra configuration steps.

## Using Comanche

The Comanche configuration screen is divided in two main areas (see Figure 14-9). The left area is a tree-like structure that enables you to navigate Comanche nodes. The right pane displays information about the selected nodes. You can create, delete or perform actions on nodes by right-clicking them.

### *Node Structure*

The Apache Web server node enables you to add or remove Apache installations.

Each one of the Apache installations contains a node called Server management. Under Server management you can start or stop Apache (only in Unix), as well as create and restore backups of the configuration files.

Under Server management you can find several nodes:

- **Module management** Enables you to select which Apache modules Comanche will configure (See Figure 14-10). Selecting a module

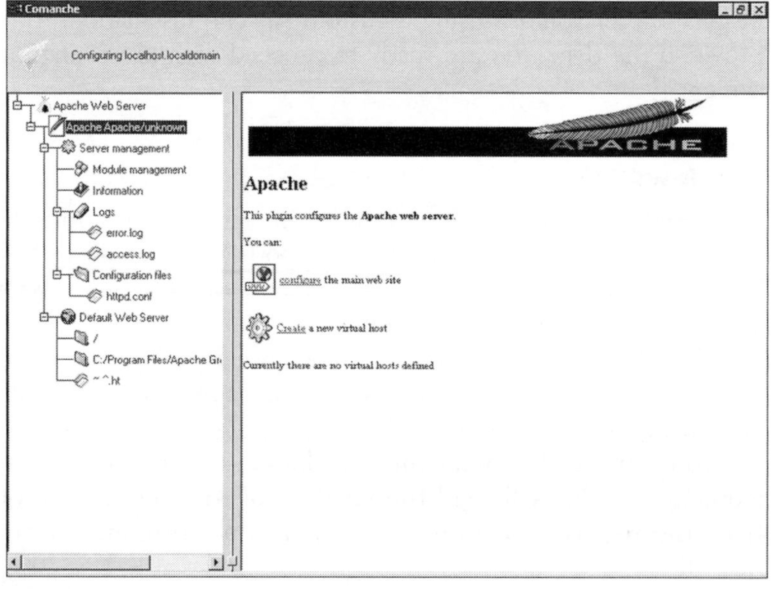


**FIGURE 14-9** Main Comanche screen.

here means that the associated options will appear later when configuring Apache. Deselecting a module means that those options will be preserved in the configuration file, but you will not see them when configuring Apache.

- **Information** Displays information about the Apache instance being configured (only in Unix).
- **Logs** Provides access to the log files being configured.
- **Configuration files** Provides access to the contents of the configuration files.

Each Apache installation contains a Default server node. You can configure the properties of the default Web server in this node. The other virtual hosts will inherit most properties, but some properties, such as number of processes, apply to the server as a whole and you can only configure them here.

You can configure the default server by clicking on the properties link in the right pane or by right-clicking on the node and selecting the properties entry in the pop-up menu. A window containing different property pages will appear. When you are done configuring properties you

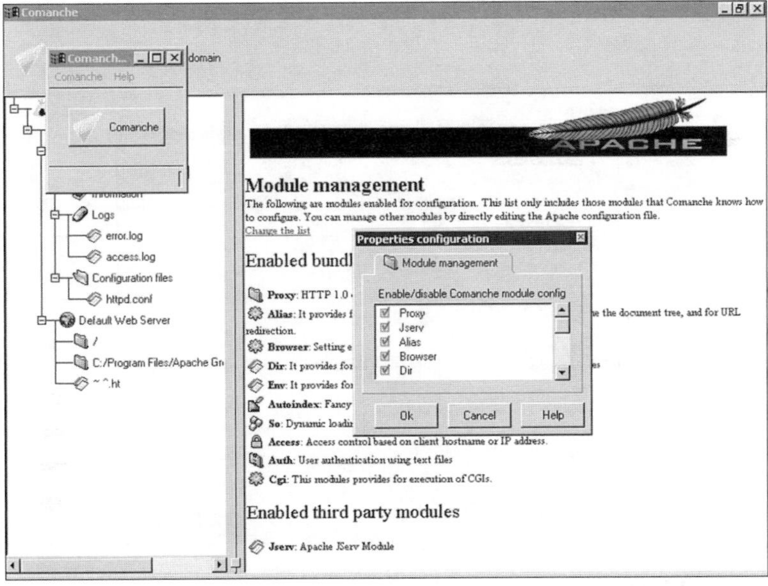


**Figure 14-10** Module management screen.

can press Ok and the changes will be applied to the configuration file. You need to restart the server before the changes affect a running server.

Under basic properties (see Figure 14-11) you can configure the document root for the default server. This is where Apache looks for requested documents. If the document root is `/usr/local/apache/htdocs` then a request for `http://localhost.localdomain/index.html` will return `/user/local/apache/htdocs/index.html`.

You can also define the server hostname and the administrator e-mail address. Under the basic properties node, in the listening properties node, you can configure the addresses and ports you want Apache to listen to.

### *Virtual Hosts*

You can create virtual hosts by right-clicking the Default Server and selecting New virtual host.

You can configure the virtual host properties by right-clicking the virtual host node and selecting properties.

You can define basic and advanced parameters. The changes will be incorporated when you press OK.

Some of the advanced parameters include options for redirecting links, associating files with MIME types and directory listen formatting.

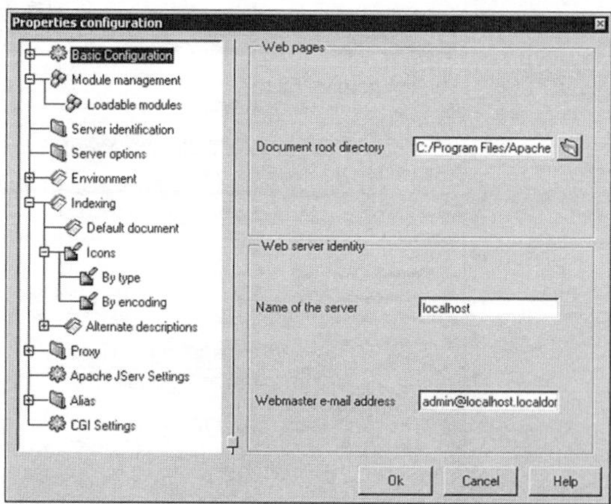


**Figure 14-11** Configuring basic properties.

### *Containers*

You can create location, directory, and file nodes. They relate to the corresponding `<directory>`, `<location>` and `<file>` sections in the Apache configuration file. This enables you to apply specific configuration directives to certain portions of the filesystem or URL space. For example, by clicking on the security node on the directory or location property pages window, you can restrict access based on where the client is coming from (IP-based access is shown in Figure 14-12), or who he claims to be (User auth).

Containers can be created by right-clicking Virtual hosts or other containers and selecting the add option in the pop-up menu.

Comanche provides context-sensitive help. In any of the property pages you can press Help to have access to the Apache directives related to the information present on the screen. In the basic properties screen you will get information about the `ServerRoot`, `ServerAdmin` and `ServerName` directives.

We have described two of the most popular GUI tools for configuring Apache. You can find other tools at Open Source sites such

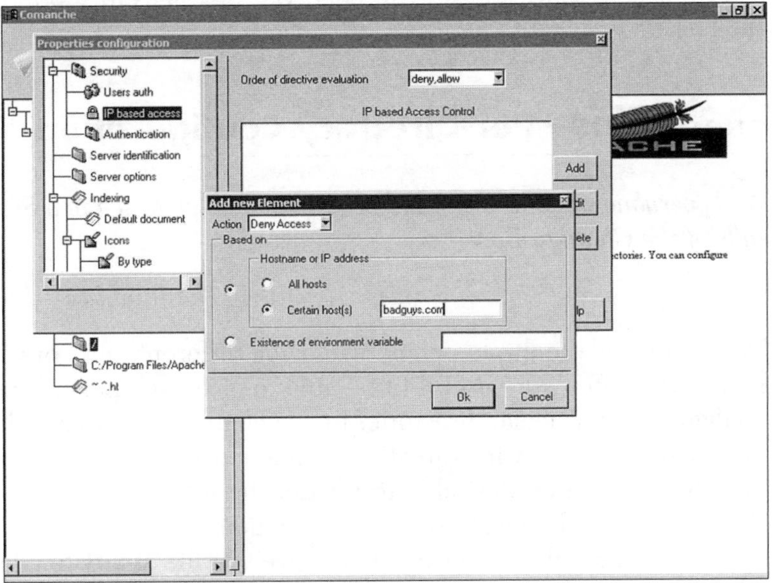


**Figure 14-12** Restricting access.

as `http://freshmeat.net` and `http://sourceforge.net`. We have analyzed the drawbacks and advantages of GUI tools. Whether or not you use them depends a lot on your personal level of comfort with Apache, Unix, and command-line tools. As the tools mature, they become more and more attractive, even for experienced system administrators.

Webmin is a powerful tool for configuring Apache. Its main strength is the capability to remotely configure the server.

Webmin respects the original Apache configuration file structures and contents. It is possible to alternate between the configuration of Apache via Webmin and editing the configuration files directly. Indeed, it is possible to edit those files via Webmin itself.

Webmin only runs on Unix, but it includes support for a wide variety of platforms, providing a consistent, easy-to-use interface for a variety of system configurations and popular Internet servers.

Comanche provides a powerful cross-platform tool for configuring Apache. Its main strengths are structured, user-friendly interface, and context-sensitive help.

You can still edit Apache configuration files with a file editor. Comanche will detect and incorporate those changes.

Comanche can be easily extended via XML files to support additional directives.

## `.htaccess` files—Per-Directory Configuration

*And everyone said, "If we only live, We too will go to sea in a Sieve—To the hills of the Chankly Bore!"*

*The Jumblies—Edward Lear*

When you have multiple people managing different parts of your Apache server, it is often very useful to be able to give each person the ability to configure the particular directories for which they are responsible. This can, of course, be done with directives contained in `<Directory>` sections. However, it is often desirable to restrict the number of people that have direct access to the main server configuration file.

`.htaccess` files, described here, give you the ability to allow this sort of per-directory configuration without giving access to the main server configuration file, and without having to add directives for everyone, each time they want something changed.

A `.htaccess` file can be placed in any directory on the server, and may contain almost any configuration directive. The directives in each file apply to resources served out of that directory, and any subdirectories thereof, unless they are further overridden by directives appearing in other `.htaccess` files within deeper subdirectories.

Finally, directives in `.htaccess` files take effect immediately, as opposed to restarting your server for them to take effect, as is necessary for changes to the main server configuration file(s).

However, there are tradeoffs associated with using `.htaccess` files, and you should make sure that they are actually needed on your site before you put a lot of your configuration into them.

## AccessFileName

Although the filename `.htaccess` will be used throughout this chapter, and in the rest of this book, to indicate the file in which you put per-directory configuration directives, this filename is configurable, using the `AccessFileName` directive. This directive appears in the main server configuration file, and tells Apache what files to look in for per-directory configuration directives.

The default value for this directive is `.htaccess`. However, on Microsoft Windows, where filenames starting with a dot are problematic, the directive should be given the value of `htaccess`, or some other file without a leading dot.

You can set this to whatever value you like, if there is some name that you find to be more intuitive. For example, if you would prefer to call your per-directory configuration files `directory.conf`, the following directive would let you do this:

```
AccessFileName directory.conf
```

You will notice, if you look at the documentation for this directive, that it is possible to set more than one filename to be used for per-directory configuration. Just because it's possible doesn't mean it's a good idea. Setting multiple values for this directive should be avoided for two reasons.

First and most importantly, it's confusing. If there are two (or more) possible files in any given directory where directives can be lurking, it will take longer for you to find that rogue directive that is causing undesired or unexpected results on your server. Likewise, if you are working in one file, but there are conflicting directives in the other file, then you might spend unnecessary time trying to figure out why your configuration is producing unexpected results.

Secondly, as is explained in more detail in the "Performance" section, looking for, and parsing the contents of `.htaccess` files takes time. And doubling the number of possible locations of `.htaccess` files by giving it two names to look for, rather than just one, will cause Apache to spend twice as much time looking for these files than it would with just one, *even* if you are not using any per-directory configuration files.

## AllowOverride

Because this feature allows anyone with write access to any directory served by your Web server to make configuration changes, you will be glad to know that you can limit what you permit these files to override.

The `AllowOverride` directive can have one or more of five possible values, specifying what category of directives will be permitted in the files. In addition to these limitations, the documentation for each directive indicates the contexts it is permitted in, and this will specifically indicate whether that particular directive is permitted in `.htaccess` files.

The syntax for this directive is as follows:

```
AllowOverride All|None|directive-type1 [directive-
type2] [directive-type3] etc
```

The possible directive types are detailed in the following sections.

## AuthConfig (Authentication)

```
AllowOverride AuthConfig
```

The presence of the previous directive will allow use of the authorization directives (`AuthDBMGroupFile`, `AuthDBMUserFile`, `AuthGroupFile`, `AuthName`, `AuthType`, `AuthUserFile`, `Require`, and so on) in `.htaccess` files. These directives are covered in more detail in Chapter 14, "Apache Authentication and Authorization," but an example follows.

To require password authentication in a particular directory, you might add the following to a `.htaccess` file in that directory:

```
AuthType Basic
AuthName admins
AuthUserFile /usr/local/apache/secure/passwords
AuthGroupFile /usr/local/apache/secure/groups
Require group admin
```

If `AuthConfig` is not one of the directive types permitted by your `AllowOverride` directive, directives that fall into this category will be ignored.

## FileInfo

```
AllowOverride FileInfo
```

The presence of the previous directive will allow use of the directives controlling document types (`AddEncoding`, `AddLanguage`, `AddType`, `DefaultType`, `ErrorDocument`, `LanguagePriority`, and so on) in .htaccess files.

An example of how this might be used is shown here.

To specify the error document for a particular directory, you might add the following to a `.htaccess` in that directory:

```
ErrorDocument error.html
```

## Indexes

```
AllowOverride Indexes
```

The presence of the previous directive in your server configuration file will allow the use of the directives controlling directory indexing (`Add-Description`, `AddIcon`, `AddIconByEncoding`, `AddIconByType`, `DefaultIcon`, `DirectoryIndex`, `FancyIndexing`, `HeaderName`, `IndexIgnore`, `IndexOptions`, `ReadmeName`, and so on) in `.htaccess` files.

These directives are primarily used when there is no index file in the directory, and Apache automatically generates a directory listing. The `DirectoryIndex` directive, on the other hand, tells Apache which file to use as the default for a particular directory, when there is no filename specified.

The following example sets the default file for a particular directory to something other than what is configured for the rest of the server.

```
DirectoryIndex menu.shtml
```

Placing the previous directive in a `.htaccess` file in a particular directory will cause that file to be displayed when no other file has been specified.

### Limit

```
AllowOverride Limit
```

The presence of the previous directive in your server configuration file will allow use of the directives controlling host access (`Allow`, `Deny`, and `Order`) to be used in `.htaccess` files.

For example, in a directory containing documents internal to your company, you might want to restrict access to hosts within your own network. This could be accomplished with the following directives, placed in a `.htaccess` file in that directory.

```
Deny from all
Allow from yourcompany.com
Order Deny,Allow
```

See Chapter 14 for more detail about using these types of directives.

### Options

```
AllowOverride Options
```

The presence of the previous directive in your main server configuration file allows use of the directives controlling specific directory features (`Options` and `XBitHack`).

`XBitHack` turns on (or off) the capability for Apache to determine what files to parse for SSI (Server Side Include) directives.

The Options directive is rather powerful, turning on or off a variety of different behaviors such as CGI execution, SSI, directory indexing, and following symbolic links. The directive itself is discussed in Chapter 13, but is mentioned in many other places because of its widespread effects. Consider carefully before permitting this functionality in `.htaccess` files.

### All

```
AllowOverride All
```

The previous directive will enable all the previously listed categories of directives in `.htaccess` files.

### None

```
AllowOverride None
```

The previous directive will cause Apache not to honor any directives placed in `.htaccess` files. In fact, it will cause Apache to not even look for these files. This has performance implications. See the section on Performance for more details.

## Caveats and Limitations

Use of `.htaccess` files has two primary consequences, which you should carefully consider before allowing their use: performance and security.

### Performance

To understand the performance impact of `.htaccess` files, you need to know a little about how they work.

When a client requests a resource from your server, that resource request is mapped to a directory path, or perhaps to some nonfile resource. If the target of the request is a file living in a directory, Apache then has to determine what additional configuration directives, if any, apply to that directory, and perhaps also to that particular file. The main server configuration file has already been parsed, and that configuration information is stored in memory. Therefore, this can be very quickly checked for references to the affected directory and/or file.

However, if the use of `.htaccess` files is enabled, there's another step that must be taken. For each directory along the path to the file, Apache has to check for a `.htaccess` file. Remember that `.htaccess` files apply not only to the directory they are in, but also to all subdirectories thereof. Therefore, to know what has to be applied to a particular directory, you have to check all parent directories, all the way to the root.

For example, if you are serving a file out of `/usr/local/apache/htdocs/products/watchers`, Apache has to check for following files:

```
/.htaccess
/usr/.htaccess
/usr/local/.htaccess
/usr/local/apache/.htaccess
/usr/local/apache/htdocs/.htaccess
/usr/local/apache/htdocs/products/.htaccess
/usr/local/apache/htdocs/products/watchers/.htaccess
```

Apache checks for the existence of each of these files, in that order. If it finds one of these files, it opens it and parses it for directives. If not, it moves on. It does this every time a file is requested out of any directory in which `.htaccess` files are permitted. Note that it does this whether or not there are any `.htaccess` files in any of those directories, so you pay this penalty even if you don't have *any* `.htaccess` files. As you can imagine, this slows things down.

It is therefore preferable, if it's at all possible, to set `AllowOverride` none and put any per-directory configurations inside of the `<Directory>` sections in your main server configuration file.

## Security

When you allow per-directory configuration, you're allowing whoever has write access to directories on your server to affect the behavior of your Apache server. A few security considerations go along with this.

For the most part, the people that have access to make these configuration changes can only make changes that affect things in their own directory. In a sense, they can only screw up their own stuff. However, this is not true for several reasons.

### *Insufficient Directory Security*

First, it is likely that you have directories on your server that are insufficiently secured. This is particularly going to be the case if you have multiple people providing content for your server. File and directory permissions might be a little relaxed so that more than one person can modify the content. Yes, you should use user groups for this, rather than making the files world-writable, but perhaps you were a little sloppy with a directory or two. You've now made a situation where someone can come in and add a `.htaccess` file to change the behavior of files served out of that directory. Whether this is done in malice, as a practical joke, or for some other reason, it can result in a denial of service by making files load with incorrect MIME types, redirecting content to other locations, or other configuration changes.

The solution to this problem, of course, is to be vigilant about security. You need to read Chapter 15, "Apache Security," and you need to make sure that any new directories that are created have reasonable file permissions on them. This can best be accomplished by a nightly cron job that sets the permissions to what they should be.

### *CGI and SSI*

If you allow `AllowOverride Options`, your users have the ability to add `Options ExecCGI` and `Options Includes`. These two abilities—to execute CGI programs and to have Server Side Includes (SSI) in their files, are potentially pretty big security problems. So, be very cautious about allowing `Options` in your `AllowOverride` policy.

CGI programs can contain any code whatsoever, and can potentially do malicious things. You are somewhat saved by the fact that CGI programs are run (usually) as the "nobody" users, or some other unprivileged user, but even that user can do a lot of damage doing a `rm -rf /`[1] because there are always a number of files with world-writable permissions.

Likewise, SSI can execute arbitrary code, with the added benefit that with the #exec `cmd` syntax you can embed arbitrary system commands in the HTML and have them executed.

More importantly, if your users don't really need to be able to do these things, don't enable `AllowOverride Options`. If users really need this functionality, still don't enable it. In your server configuration file, simply enable `Options ExecCGI` for perhaps one directory that only trusted users have access to. You can also enable a tamer version of `Includes` by enabling `Options IncludesNOEXEC` in your configuration file. As the name implies, this enables SSI, but does not enable the use of the #exec directive.

### *Symlinks*

For Windows users, this is not an issue. For most other operating systems, symbolic links are not, by default, followed by Apache. That is, if you have a symbolic link to a directory, within a directory you're serving content out of, Apache will not allow retrieval of content out of that directory. This is for security reasons.

If, for example, you were to create a symbolic link to `/etc`, within your document directory, then anyone could happily download `/etc/passwd` or `/etc/shadow`, and crack your passwords at their leisure. That would not be desirable.

However, with `Options FollowSymlinks` turned on, Apache will follow symlinks quite happily. Although there are cases where this is useful, you don't generally want nonadmin users to add `Options FollowSymlinks` to their `.htaccess` file and be able to then serve your entire hard drive on their Web site.

1. Windows users, think format c: -y -y

As with CGI and SSI, the solution to this is to not allow `Options` to be overridden. If there is some reason that users really do need to follow symlinks in their file space, you can add, in your main server configuration, an `Options SymlinksIfOwnerMatch` directive. This allows Apache to follow symlinks, if and only if the directory or file it is linked to is owned by the same user as the link itself.

`.htaccess` files allow users to set per-directory configurations without modifying the main server configuration file. This is handy on sites where users are running content out of their home directory, or any other situation where you have more than one person providing content on a Web site. They should, however, be avoided if they are not actually necessary, because there are performance and security concerns with using them.

## Virtual Hosts

*"Pilgrim, how you journey on the road you chose*
*To find out where the winds die and where the stories go"*

*Pilgrim—A Day Without Rain—Enya*

Fortunately, you don't need a separate Apache server for each Web site that you want to run. Virtual hosting is the term given to the capability to run multiple Web sites on the same computer and on the same Apache server process[2].

There are a number of different techniques for setting up virtual hosts. This section covers these various techniques and offers some examples for setting up common configurations.

In all the various methods for doing virtual hosting, the concept is basically the same. The user goes to a URL specifying a particular hostname and gets different content for each hostname. Generally, the user is not aware that they are loading content from the same physical computer system. Somehow, Apache determines which Web site you are requesting content from, and gives that to you, even though all the different sites are running on the same Apache daemon.

The two most common ways of accomplishing this are IP-based and name-based virtual hosting.

2. Webster's dictionary defines the word "virtual" as follows: "being such in essence or effect though not formally recognized or admitted." I'm not sure what is "virtual" about a virtual host. It's just as real as the main host is, but in the mid-90s everything was "virtual."

## IP-Based Virtual Hosts

With IP-based virtual hosting, each hostname on the server is given its own IP address.

### Setting Up Multiple IP Addresses

All modern operating systems allow you to have more than one IP address on one physical network card. Earlier operating systems actually required you to add an additional network card for each new IP address. That is no longer the case, however, in any operating system you are likely to encounter.

The specific details of how this is accomplished—the exact procedure for putting multiple IP addresses on your network interface—will vary from OS to OS and you need to consult your documentation.

On the other hand, if you do have multiple network cards in your machine, IP-based virtual hosting will work for that also.

In addition to setting up the IP addresses on your machine, you will also need to set up the DNS records that will direct the hostnames to the IP addresses you have assigned to your server. That, also, is beyond the scope of this book. Contact your DNS administrator to add the hostnames to your DNS zone, or to register a new DNS domain. You can't just make up hostnames and have them magically work.

If you are not able to add records to DNS, or if you just want to test, you can access the IP-based virtual hosts by simply using the IP address in the URL. For example:

```
http://192.168.5.10/
```

### Configuring the Virtual Host

After you have your IP addresses set up and have the DNS records pointing the correct names to the correct IP addresses, you can proceed with configuring your Apache server to answer to these names.

This is done in a `<VirtualHost>` section, as was mentioned in Chapter 13, All the configuration directives for a virtual host are contained in the `<VirtualHost>` section, with one section per virtual host. A `<VirtualHost>` section looks like the following:

```
<VirtualHost 192.168.1.2>
  ServerName vhost1.apacheadmin.com
```

```
  ServerAlias www.vhost1.apacheadmin.com
  DocumentRoot /usr/local/apache/vhosts/vhost1
  ErrorLog logs/vhost1.error
  AccessLog logs/vhost1.access
</VirtualHost>
```

The address in the `<VirtualHost>` directive can be specified as a hostname, rather than as an IP address, but it is highly recommended that you use the IP address instead. The reason for this is simple. If, when the server is rebooting, it cannot immediately contact a DNS server to determine the IP address of the `VirtualHost`, it will simply start up without that particular `VirtualHost` being loaded. Apache needs the IP address, not the name, to answer requests, so if it cannot determine the IP address from the name it is simply unable to load the configuration. Using the IP address avoids this lookup and ensures that the server will start correctly, with all host configurations loaded, even if the network is unavailable at the time the server is coming up.

The server uses the name of the virtual hosts, specified by the `ServerName` directive, when it constructs self-referential URLs, such as for a redirect.

It's a good idea to have a separate log file for each of your virtual hosts, although it is not required. By logging each host separately, you can much more easily determine problems on a per-host basis. If all your hosts log to the same log files it becomes very difficult to isolate problems when they occur because they become buried in with entries from all the other hosts.

You only need to put directives in a `VirtualHost` section when the values are different from those set in the main server configuration. All other values are inherited from the main server.

## Name-Based Virtual Hosts

Name-based virtual hosts are the same as IP-based virtual hosts in almost every way, except you don't need more than one IP address. By having more than one name pointing to the same IP address, you can arbitrarily host many virtual hosts on the same IP address.

**NOTE:** Multiple host names pointing to the same IP address are referred to in DNS lingo as "cnames."

The configuration is almost identical to that of IP-based virtual hosts, except that you need to tell Apache, with the `NameVirtualHost` directive, which IP addresses on your server will be used for name-based virtual hosts.

```
NameVirtualHost 192.168.1.3

<VirtualHost 192.168.1.3>
    ServerName vhost1.apacheadmin.com
    ServerAlias vhost1
    DocumentRoot /usr/local/apache/vhosts/rhiannon/htdocs
</VirtualHost>

<VirtualHost 192.168.1.3>
    ServerName vhost2.apacheadmin.com
    ServerAlias vhost2 www.vhost2.apacheadmin.com
    DocumentRoot /usr/local/apache/vhosts/demo/htdocs
</VirtualHost>
```

The name of the server, specified by the `ServerName` directive, is used to determine which virtual host is displayed. The browser supplies the name of the host that it is trying to connect to in the request headers, and Apache uses this information to map the request to the correct files or other resources.

Older browsers[3] were unable to use name-based virtual hosts because they did not supply this request header.

More specifically, clients or proxies that support only the HTTP 1.0 protocol might fail to get the right virtual host because the `Host` header is not part of the HTTP 1.0 protocol, and is required for name-based virtual hosting.

However, all currently available browsers support the HTTP 1.1 protocol, which contains name-based virtual host support as one of its requirements. And almost all HTTP 1.0 clients and proxies support the `Host` header as an extension to the 1.0 protocol.

The Apache documentation contains instructions for working around this limitation in older browsers, if you think that it is worth the effort. However, the solution is inelegant and might not be necessary for your site. You should watch your server logs to see if you are getting visits from browsers old enough to warrant this sort of work-around. You might want to consider using IP-based vhosts if you feel older browsers are a large enough portion of your visitors.

3. Really older versions you are unlikely to see in any real-world setting.

Note the use of the `ServerAlias` directive in the previous examples. This directive is useful when a particular site can be accessed by more than one name. Two specific examples, illustrated previously, come to mind. In the first example, I have a host that can be accessed from the inside, or from the outside, of my network. Inside the network, or from the machine itself, I don't need to type the entire name of the machine because it will check the local domain first, so the `ServerAlias` allows me to do this. In the second example, I have added a `ServerAlias` of www followed by the original hostname. It has been my experience in recent years that people are so trained to expect Web addresses to start with www that they are incapable of typing a URL without it. Simply adding that to the hostname saves a lot of time on the phone explaining to people that the www is not necessary.

## Port-Based Virtual Hosts

It's not a very common practice, but it is also possible to set up virtual hosts by varying the port number that the server is running on, rather than the host name or IP address. The configuration for such a setup would look like this:

```
<VirtualHost 192.168.1.103:75>
ServerName vhost.apacheadmin.com
ServerAlias vhost
DocumentRoot /usr/local/apache/vhosts/strange
</VirtualHost>
```

You must also add a `Port` directive for each additional port on which you want your server to listen. The `Port` directive would look like this:

```
Port 75
```

If you choose a port below, or equal to, 1024, you will need to be root to start the server. Stated differently, you can run a Web server as an unprivileged user by choosing a port higher than 1024.

This host can be accessed via the URL `http://vhost.apacheadmin.com:75`

Note that SSL, which runs on a different port from unencrypted HTTP, is generally set up in the configuration file as a port-based virtual host. However, browsers know that when a URL is prepended with `https://` rather than `http://`, the connection is to be made on port 443 rather than 80.

SSL is a technology that provides for secure encrypted connections on the Web. You cannot use name-based virtual hosting in conjunction with an SSL site.

The short form is that the negotiation of the connection encryption takes place before the client has a chance to tell the server which named host it wanted to connect to. Consequently, by the time it gets to that stage, it might have already negotiated a secure connection to the wrong site.

So, if you want to put up a secure Web site using SSL, you have to have a unique IP address for each SSL-enabled virtual host.

## Bulk Virtual Hosting

Frequently, when you're running virtual hosts, you'll find that the number of hosts grows faster than your ability to sensibly manage them. A few techniques you might use to simplify the task of managing these hosts' configurations follow.

### `Per-vhost` Configuration Files

As recommended in Chapter 13, when you are configuring your virtual hosts, you might consider putting each virtual host's configuration into its own individual file. Then you could place these files into a subdirectory of your `conf` directory, perhaps called `vhosts`. Then add the following directive to your main configuration file, `httpd.conf`:

```
Include conf/vhosts/
```

Note that the directory path given in the example is relative to the `ServerRoot`, and not an absolute path.

Apache will read all files in the specified directory and parse directives found in those files. Therefore, you cannot have any files in this directory that are not configuration files, such as temporary files, `Readme` files, and so on.

The more virtual hosts you have the longer it is going to take to parse all the `vhost` configurations[4], and, therefore, the longer it is going to take for your server to start up.

4. This will be the case whether the configurations are in external (`Include'`ed files) or in your main configuration file.

## mod_vhost_alias

When you are running more than just a few virtual hosts—when you start getting into the tens, or even hundreds, of virtual hosts, you will notice a substantial time taken to start your Apache server. During this time, your server is not responding to HTTP requests. That is, while your server is starting, or restarting, it is effectively unavailable to the end-users. When you are a service provider—which, as a server admin, you really are—this sort of downtime needs to be avoided whenever possible.

`mod_vhost_alias` is one of the modules available for making bulk virtual hosting more efficient. If each of your virtual hosts has essentially the same configuration, you can configure them all with one set of directives.

`mod_vhost_alias` provides just four directives—two for use with name-based virtual hosts, and two for use with IP-based virtual hosts.

If you are using name-based virtual hosts, the directives that you will be using are `VirtualDocumentRoot` and `VirtualScriptAlias`. These directives mean exactly what their names imply, but the syntax is a little unusual. The value given to the directives will contain one or more variables into which will be substituted all or part of the hostname being requested by the client. If you are familiar with C, or similar programming languages, these variables will remind you of arguments to the sprintf function. The following things can appear in the directive value.

| Template | Meaning |
|---|---|
| `%%` | A literal % character. |
| %p | The port number of the virtual host being requested. |
| %N.M | All or part of the host name, depending on the values of N and M. |

The values N and M are, respectively, the portion of the dot-separated hostname to be inserted, and the number of characters from that portion to be used.

The interpretation of the value of N is as follows:

| | |
|---|---|
| 0 | The whole name |
| 1 | The first part |
| 2 | The second part |
| -1 | The last part |
| -2 | The next-to-last part |
| 2+ | The second and all following parts |
| -2+ | The next-to-last part, and all preceding parts |

1+ and -1+ would mean exactly the same thing as 0.

If the value given results in selecting more of the name than there actually is available to select, then a single underscore is interpolated in place of the given variable.

This will all be made much clearer by several examples.

The trivial example is to use the full hostname in the directive, as follows. In your configuration file, put a directive that looks this:

```
VirtualDocumentRoot /usr/local/apache/vhosts/%0/htdocs
```

Then, any incoming request for a valid virtual host—that is, any hostname that DNS points to your server—will have files served out of a directory named by the hostname. For example, a request for the URL `http://www.boxofclue.com/vhosts.html` will get the file located at `/usr/local/apache/vhosts/www.boxofclue.com/htdocs/vhosts.html`.

This technique has one large problem: Most virtual hosts can be accessed by more than one hostname. For example, if the previous URL was requested instead as `http://boxofclue.com/vhosts.html`, which should give the same resource, Apache will attempt to serve the file `/usr/local/apache/vhosts/boxofclue.com/htdocs/vhosts.html`, which is not the same file path it tried in the other case. It might either be a different file or not exist at all.

This dilemma can be solved in a few different ways. The simplest way around this is to simply create symbolic links from all alternate possible file paths to the "correct" file path, and allow Apache to locate the files in that way. However, one of the major reasons for using this module in the first place is to reduce the amount of administrative tasks required to create a new virtual host, so this is hardly ideal.

The better way to solve this is to use a different combination of variables provided by `mod_vhost_alias` to construct unique filepaths per virtual host.

The following example proposes one such configuration option. Put this directive in your configuration file:

```
VirtualDocumentRoot/usr/local/apache/vhosts/%-1/%-
2/htdocs
```

The variable `%-1` will evaluate as the last part of the hostname—usually com, net, org, or some other top level domain (TLD). So, your virtual hosts will be divided into subdirectories by their TLD.

The second variable, %-2, evaluates as the next-to-last (or, as the documentation refers to it, the penultimate part) of the hostname. For example, for the hostnames www.boxofclue.com and boxofclue.com, %-2 will evaluate to the string boxofclue, and files will be served out of the directory /usr/local/apache/vhosts/com/boxofclue/htdocs, giving you a more manageable subdivision of your virtual host directories.

In the event that you have many hundreds of virtual hosts, as is the case for some large ISPs, you might want to subdivide your directories even further. For example, you might split hosts into subdirectories alphabetically, as follows:

```
VirtualDocumentRoot /usr/local/apache/vhosts/%-1/%-2.1/%-2/htdocs
```

In this configuration, files for the host www.boxofclue.com will be served out of the directory /usr/local/apache/vhosts/com/b/boofclue/htdocs.

This subdivision can continue to any depth you like, as required by the number of virtual hosts you are serving, you could, for example, further subdivide with the following directive:

```
VirtualDocumentRoot /usr/local/apache/vhosts/%-1/%-2.1/%2.1%-
2.2/%-2/htdocs
```

In this case, files for the host www.boxofclue.com will be served out of the directory /usr/local/apache/vhosts/com/b/bo/boxofclue.com. The variable combination %-2.1%-2.2 gets evaluated is the first, followed by the second, letters of the next-to-last part of the hostname; this is what gives the subdirectory bo.

Continue this subdivision until you have sufficiently few hosts per-directory to keep track of them.

Note that you can use this same technique to have each virtual host served out of the home directory of the particular user, if you choose usernames appropriately to map directly to the hostnames of their respective sites.

## Running Multiple Daemons

In very rare cases, you might want to run more than one Apache server process on the same machine to handle different virtual hosts. This might be done, for example, when you need a very different set of modules for different Web sites. You could run one Apache process to serve static HTML pages and images, and a separate Apache process running `mod_perl` to serve your dynamic content.

In these cases, all that is required is that you maintain separate configuration files, and start the Apache server with the `-f` flag to specify a configuration file located somewhere other than the location specified when the server was built.

```
/usr/local/apache/bin/httpd -f/usr/local/
apache/conf/host_two.conf
```

Virtual hosts provide the best way to serve multiple Web sites off of the same physical server machine, and, therefore, make the best use of your available resources.

CHAPTER 15

# APACHE SECURITY

*Probably the last man who knew how it worked had been tortured to death years before. Or as soon as it was installed. Killing the creator was a traditional method of patent protection.*

*Small Gods*—Terry Pratchett

One of the strengths of Apache is that its developers are very security conscious. Open source projects are sometimes criticized for having too many security holes. Amazingly, the opposite appears to be true with Web servers. In September of 2001 the Gartner Group, a research organization, recommended that companies switch from Microsoft's Internet Information Server to Apache, among other Web servers, because there are fewer security risks (`http://www.gartner.com/DisplayDocument?id=340962`).

At times this chapter might seem excessively draconian in its recommendations. To quote Andy Grove, co-founder of Intel, "Just because you are paranoid does not mean they are out to get you." When it comes to security you can never be too paranoid. Implementing many of the suggestions in this chapter might cause riots among your users, and that is fine, you can use that as a divining rod for measuring the success of your security policy. The sweet spot in security is somewhere between several flaming e-mails from users and the users lined up outside of your office door with voodoo dolls and pitchforks. Unfortunately, in this world of script kiddies and hacker wars, a restrictive security policy is necessary.

When discussing Apache security, there are four areas you need to think about:

- The Apache program
- The external security risks
- The internal security risks
- The vendor security issues

The source code is probably the least of your worries. The Apache source code is tested and retested for security holes and potential security holes. As of this writing, the last time a security hole was found in the source code was in 1998.

External security risks are problems that arise from someone attacking your server. These problems can range from a denial of service attack, to someone trying to exploit a security hole in a piece of software you have installed. They are best dealt with as part of a broader security strategy, which will be discussed later in this chapter.

Internal security risks are by far the biggest problem that Apache administrators face. Generally, these are not attacks, as much as misconfigured CGI scripts, poorly written modules, and other issues that can cause a server to crash, or worse, leave your valuable data exposed.

Vendor security issues are another big problem. When you purchase or download an operating system that includes Apache as part of the base installation, you do not know what configuration changes the vendor has made to Apache. You also do not know what type of security bugs might have been introduced during the installation process. Most vendors are good about posting updates, but it is important to stay abreast of any security holes that the vendor reports.

The focus of this chapter is external and internal security problems. These two security problems are the ones you have the greatest control over, and the ones you can most easily prevent from turning into full-fledged crises. They are also the easiest problems to prevent. As with any other security issue, it simply requires careful planning.

A Web server presents a unique security challenge that almost no other networked server faces. A Web server needs to be accessible to anyone on the Internet, yet it needs to be protected from potential damage that can be inflicted by one of these remote users.

To better understand the challenges faced in securing a Web server contrast the security policies needed for a Web server versus a mail server. A mail server is similar to a Web server in that it needs to be publicly accessible; otherwise you will not be able to receive mail. It is also a potential target of attacks because other people can use a mail server to send Unsolicited Commercial E-mail (UCE), more commonly known as spam, to thousands or even millions of people.

So, a mail server administrator is left with this problem—keep the mail server publicly available, but don't allow anyone, except for trusted users, to send mail through it. The solution to this problem is relatively simple.

A mail server administrator can create an access list of hosts that are allowed to send mail, or relay, through the server. The mail server stays public, but only trusted users can actually relay mail.

Unfortunately, the same sort of panacea does not exist for Web servers. As we will discuss in this chapter, the majority of the security problems associated with Web servers are caused by the fact that the servers have to provide access to everyone.

## Developing a Security Strategy

A Web server does not operate in a vacuum. It is an integral part of your business, and your network. Therefore, a security strategy for your Web server has to include discussion of a broader network and server strategy.

The best way to develop a security strategy is from the outside in. The strategy has to include the network, the server, the operating system, Apache itself, and finally the individual Web sites. This is outlined in Figure 15-1.

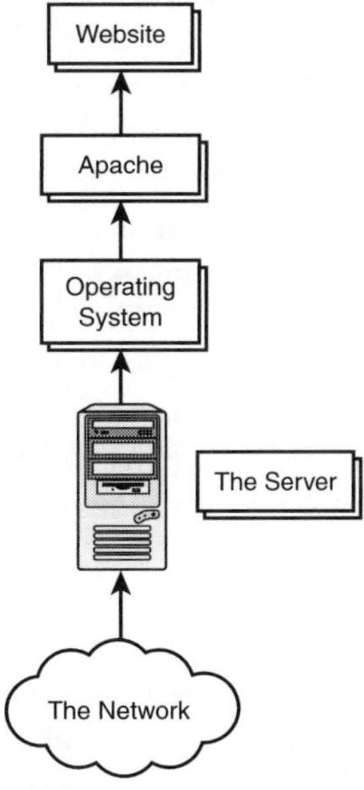


**Figure 15-1** A security strategy has to involve the entire network.

The first security decision you need to make is whether you want to host your server in house, or collocate it with a hosting vendor. From a security perspective hosting a server in house forces you to add a layer of complexity to your network, which we will discuss later in this chapter. However, collocating your server in a remote data center means that you will lose a level of control because you will not be able to administer or monitor the remote data center networking devices. The in house versus collocation debate is discussed in greater detail in Chapter 13.

If you decide to host the site on an internal network you will need to create a Demilitarized Zone (DMZ) for the server. A DMZ is a firewall term used to describe an area between the Internet and the protected portion of your network. The DMZ is still part of your network, but it is more open than the rest of the network, with a less restrictive ruleset, and, therefore, more vulnerable to attacks.

If you have a database driven Web site, especially one with confidential customer information, another layer of complexity is added to your network. Obviously, your database serve: has to have very strict access restrictions, which means it will have to reside the behind firewall, but it still has to be reachable by the Web server. Your firewall will have to be configured to allow the Web server access. It is also a good idea, whenever possible, to encrypt the transactions between the Web server and the database server, providing your customers with the maximum amount of protection.

The next decision you need to make is what services, in addition to HTTPD, you are going to run on that server. The temptation, especially for smaller companies, is to run as many services as possible on a single server. If possible, this is something you should resist. Adding additional services, such as mail, DNS, and NNTP to a server increases the number of open ports, and, therefore, increases the potential for security holes to be found.

You might be asking yourself why it is so important to separate services. After all, if someone were going to break into the server why would it matter if there were one service or many?

The answer is simple. The most common form of external attack is called a root exploit. A root exploit is an attack where a remote user takes advantage of a security hole in a program and uses it to gain root access to a server. If an attacker were to take advantage of a root exploit in Sendmail, a very common mail program, that attacker would then have the ability to deface your Web site, or access your customer database. Conversely, if an attacker were to find a root exploit in Apache she would now be able to read mail stored on the server, modify DNS zone files, and more.

One of the most common internal security problems is poor programming. A runaway CGI script, or a poorly written program, can consume all the memory on a server and render it virtually useless. Obviously, you do not want a poorly written CGI script to knock your mail and DNS servers offline. Nor would you want to have a Sendmail module develop a memory leak and crash your server.

By separating your services you are providing an extra level of protection for your network, if one server, or service, is compromised it does not impact other services.

After deciding on a server, and where to locate it, the next step is to secure the operating system. Although securing an operating system is beyond the scope of this book, there are several excellent resources detailing ways to protect your operating systems. One title that is particularly comprehensive is *Sams Maximum Security, Third Edition.*

There are, however, some general guidelines for securing any Web server. To start, disable any ports that are not in use. In this case, a port is shorthand for port number, which is a numerical value mapped to an application on the server. The server is always listening on open, or active, ports. When it receives a packet with that port number it activates the proper application. By disabling unused ports you will decrease the likelihood that someone performing a port scan against your server will discover a security hole you were not aware existed.

It is also useful to remove any unnecessary user accounts from your server. For instance, many flavors of *nix include a games account. The account is used to record high scores for games on a shared user system. Hopefully you will not be using your Web server to play Unreal Tournament, so it can be deleted.

It is important to be as restrictive as possible with system files. Any file that could cause irreparable damage to the server, or worse someone else's server, should have the tightest security permissions and only the root or Administrator account should have access to it.

Finally, don't use telnet. This was touched on briefly in Chapter 13, but it bears repeating. Sending passwords over the Internet in clear text is a very bad thing, especially if it is your root password. Both telnet and FTP send passwords in clear text, and should be avoided. SSH provides you all the benefits that telnet does, and it encrypts your connection.

This chapter has moved from the general to the specific. Starting with the location of the server and migrating to the server configuration. The rest of the chapter focuses on operating system and Apache security. These are the aspects of your Web server over which you will exert the most control and that deserve the most attention.

## Understanding *nix File Permissions

To fully understand how to secure the Apache server, and individual sites, it is necessary to understand how *nix file permissions work.

The best way to visualize *nix file permissions is as a matrix. Along the side of the matrix are the three levels of access to the file:

- Read—able to view the file
- Write—able to make changes to the file
- Execute—able to run the file as a program

At the top of the matrix are the three users or groups that might want access to the file:

- Owner—the user who owns the file
- Group—the group to which the owner of the file belongs
- World—everyone else

*nix file permissions are set by assigning a value of read, write, or execute to each of the three groups. This is displayed from the command line by requesting a long file list:

```
 [allan@ns1 conf]$ ls -l
-rw-r—r—   1 root   root    348 Oct 18  2000  access.conf
-rw-r—r—   1 root   root 46467 Sep 29 23:56  httpd.conf
-rw-r—r—   1 root   root    357 Oct 18  2000  srm.conf
```

Setting file permissions is a matter of arithmetic. Each permission type is assigned a numerical value. Read permission has a value of 4, write permission is assigned a value of 2, and execute permission has a value of 1. 0 indicates no permission to access the file. To combine permissions add the numbers together. For example, to assign the read and write permissions, for the file owner, to the `access.conf` file you would add 4 and 2 together for a permission value of 6.

Permission settings are set using the chmod command. So, to assign read and write permissions to the file owner, read only permissions to the group, and read only permissions to other users for the `access.conf` file you would type the command

```
[allan@ns1 conf]$ chmod 644 access.conf
```

Similarly, if you wanted to set the permissions so that all users had read, write, and execute permissions (never a good idea) you would use the command

```
[allan@ns1 conf]$ chmod 777 access.conf
```

As an administrator of a Web server you should strive to enforce 644 permission settings for all text, non-CGI, files. There is no reason to have these files with execute permissions. You also do not want to risk having the files overwritten by someone who does not have permission.

The only exception to this rule are files updated by multiple users in the same group (we will discuss groups further in the next section). In cases where multiple users need to update a file, make sure all the users are in the same group and set the permissions to 664.

As with any security concerns, you should always err on the side of caution when setting file permissions. If you need to loosen the file permissions to make the site usable, it is a simple matter to adjust them. It is better to be cautious then to have to recover from an attack that was expedited because of inappropriate file permissions.

## Users and Groups

*nix and Windows both use "users" and "groups" to track file ownership, and limit the capability to access critical operating system files. A user is an individual login, whereas a group is one or several users that have the same level of access to the server.

Let's take a look at the long file list we used earlier:

```
 [allan@ns1 conf]$ ls -l
-rw-r—r— 1 root  root    348 Oct 18  2000 access.conf
-rw-r—r— 1 root  root  46467 Sep 29 23:56 httpd.conf
-rw-r—r— 1 root  root    357 Oct 18  2000 srm.conf
```

The third column is the username that owns the file, and the fourth column is the group to which the user belongs. In the previous listing the access.conf file is owned by the user root and the group root.

For some flavors of *nix the default setting for a new user is to create a group with the same name. This provides some level of protection because it prevents users from one group from editing files owned by someone in another group, assuming good permission settings are practiced. However, if you have multiple users that need to have access to the same set of files, it is better to put those users in the same group. This allows all users in the group to edit the file and upload it to the server.

Another level of user and group security you can enhance is restricting access to which users can become root.

Unless your version of *nix ships with enhanced security settings, any user who finds the root password can become root and make changes.

You can prevent this by only allowing certain users to become root. The settings for the su command are stored in the file /etc/pam.d/su. You can edit the file to only allow users from the "wheel" group to become root. Depending on your operating system, there are several ways to do this. For example, if you were running RedHat 7.1, you would type the following:

```
auth  sufficient /lib/security/pam_wheel.so trust use_uid
auth  required   /lib/security/pam_wheel.so use_uid
```

Wheel is a special *nix group that is designed specifically for the purpose of creating a special group of administrative users.

Superuser do (sudo) is another option for granting limited privileges to certain users. Sudo is maintained by Todd Miller and can be downloaded from the sudo Web site `http://www.courtesan.come/sudo/`.

In a traditional su environment a user who becomes root has the same privileges as root, and all commands are logged as if a single root user performed them. Sudo allows a server administrator to restrict access to certain commands. When a user becomes root, a sudo shell is invoked, as opposed to the normal root shell. The user can only execute the allowed commands, and all information is logged. If something goes wrong, the server administrator can quickly determine what happened, and hopefully, how to fix it.

Sudo also limits the idle time in a session to five minutes before timing out. If the five-minute idle limit is reached, the user is forcibly logged out, and has to restart the session.

## The Apache User

Apache is shipped with fairly tight security measures. However, if you are using a preinstalled binary, it is a good idea to double-check some of the security permissions.

It is especially important to know which user is running the Apache process. There are several ways to do this. You can look in the `httpd.conf` file for the User/Group variables: another way is to run the top command. If the Apache `httpd` executable is running you should see an entry similar to this:

```
PID USER PRI NI SIZE RSS SHARE STAT %CPU %MEM TIME COMMAND
22071 apache 14 0 9680 9680 7812 S 3.5 1.8 0:01 httpd
```

As you can see on this system, Apache is running as the apache user. Apache should always run as an unprivileged user, usually apache or nobody.

If you notice that your server is running Apache as root, you should definitely change to a different user, one that has no other function on the server.

Although the Apache process should be run as an unprivileged user, the configuration files for the Apache should be well protected. As in the previous example, the files should be owned by root, and have as many restrictive permissions as possible.

## User Permissions

Depending on the type of server you are running you will either have multiple users updating files on the same Web site, or multiple Web sites, each with a different user.

There are many levels of access you can assign to users depending on what role they will be playing in terms of updating the Web site. Of course, before determining the role a user has in developing the Web site, the first thing that needs to be determined is the level of access a user has to the server.

In Chapter 13, the four main types of access to a Web server were discussed—Telnet, FTP, SSH, and SCP. Telnet and SSH are redundant as are FTP and SCP. In an ideal world you would not want to use either Telnet or FTP because both programs send passwords in clear text. Unfortunately, using SCP can be confusing to some people. If you do have control over how users access the servers, such as in an enterprise environment, then you should consider permitting primarily SCP access and enabling SSH only when necessary, and never enabling Telnet or FTP access.

You might be wondering how you can grant access to SCP and not SSH because SCP runs over a SSH tunnel. There are a couple of ways to do this, but the most common is to change the login shell for the SCP-only user, so that it will only run the SCP program. The user still makes a connection using SSH, but the only program she can run is SCP.

Limiting a user to a SCP-only connection enables you to limit the number of people who are making shell connections to the server, and making file changes directly on the server. It also limits the number of mistakenly deleted or accidentally overwritten files that you will have to restore from backup. Presumably, if a user is forced to upload files, that user will have local copies of all the files that are being changed.

If you do allow files to be changed and modified directly on the server, you should consider using a version control system, such as resedit. A version control system requires users to check out files, edit them, summarize the changes made, and then check them back in. This type of version control has two advantages. The first is it keeps track of who edited a file, so if a mistake is made you will know who did it. The second advantage is that an archive of the file is kept. If something goes horribly wrong with the file, it can quickly be reverted to an earlier version.

In addition to access and version control, you also have to worry about user permissions. If you are not going to personally monitor all the files on a server, you should be as restrictive as possible with file permissions.

The best permissions for non-CGI files on a Web server are 644. Again, this enables the user to read and write to the file, but no one else to write to it. CGI scripts, which generally have permissions of 755, should all be quartered in a special directory. Although it is useful to be able to have executable files in all directories, it is not very secure.

If you are very paranoid about security permissions, you can create a cron job that will check file permissions nightly and save a list of files in violation of your permissions to a file. You can then either investigate the files or change the permissions yourself.

A cron job is a task that an administrator tells to perform at regularly scheduled intervals, ranging from once a minute to once a month.

The cron job would use the find command to search for permissions in the root directory of the Web site or sites. Assume the content of your Web site is stored in /home/website/httpd/. The find command you ran would look something like this:

```
find /home/website/httpd -type f -perm -ga=wx > /root/bad-
files.txt
```

This command looks for all files that are writable and executable by the group and everyone in the /home/website/httpd directory, as well as its subdirectories. If it finds a match, it will write the filename to a file called badfiles.txt.

You can make your life even easier by making the change automatically, like this:

```
find /home/website/httpd -type f -perm -ga=wx  | xargs
chmod ga-wx
```

This will automatically remove write and execute permissions from the files that are found in violation of your permissions policy. Be warned, this might cause angry users to call you and tell you their site no longer works.

Another solution is to install a program that will monitor these changes for you. Tripwire (http://www.tripwire.com and http:-//www.tripwire.org) is a program that runs on *nix systems and monitors file system integrity. When you initialize Tripwire you tell it what files or directories to watch, and what changes you want to generate alerts. For example, you may want check file permissions for every file in your root web. Feed this information into Tripwire's database, it encrypts it, and checks the specified files. If it notices a problem, it alerts you, so you can take appropriate action.

## Limit Modules

The modular nature of Apache is one of the reasons that it is so popular. You can install a myriad of modules, or even write your own.

From a security perspective each module presents an additional security risk.

This risk is exasperated by precompiled binaries of Apache. Most often these binaries include modules, aside from the standard Apache modules that the developer thinks you will need. Most often these are modules that incorporate Perl, mod_perl, PHP, and MySQL into Apache. That is great if you are going to use these features, but if you are not going to use them they do present a security risk, however slight it might be, to your server.

Before installing Apache, you should consider what Web site enhancements you intend to use right away, as well as enhancements you intend to use within six months, and what you plan to use in a year. If you are unsure, ask your developers what enhancements they would like to add.

Even if you do not intend to add any enhancements you will want to review the standard modules, and decide if you need them. You can view a list of currently installed modules by appending the -l flag to the httpd command, like so:

```
[root@ns1 allan]# /usr/sbin/httpd -l
```

You can also review the installed modules directly in the httpd.conf file.

To remove a module from being compiled when Apache is first started simply comment it out in the httpd.conf file. Make sure that you comment it out both in the Dynamic Shared Object Support section and the AddModule section of the httpd.conf file.

If you are not sure if you need a module, you can review what the module does on the Apache Modules Web site at http://httpd.apache.org/docs/mod/. If, after reading the description, you are still not sure if you need it leave it in rest assured that the standard modules have been repeatedly tested and used by, literally, millions of administrators, so they are fairly secure.

## Do You Really Need FrontPage Extensions?

Chances are, if you run a large Web site with a lot of users, or a Web server with a lot of sites, someone will tell you they need to have FrontPage Extensions installed.

If at all possible, try to avoid doing this. FrontPage is notorious for its security holes, and although each version of the software has gotten more secure, there are still fundamental security problems with it.

The biggest problem, and one that is integral to the way FrontPage works, is that when FrontPage publishes files to your Web site it does so using an HTTP connection. As with telnet and FTP your password is sent as clear text, so it is readable by anyone with a sniffer.

Older versions of the FrontPage software stored the usernames and passwords for the site and the sub webs as plain text files within the main directory. This meant anyone who knew where to look would be able to find the password.

A FrontPage enabled Web site also uses significantly more storage space than a site that does not use FrontPage. FrontPage makes copies of all files that are part of the Web site, and stores them in private subdirectories. It also has executables that enable the file transfer, and the FrontPage bots (CGI programs that are built into FrontPage). These bots sit on the server, even if they are not being used. Again, this means that anyone who knows where the executables are kept might be able to exploit them and break into your server.

There are many other programs, such as Dreamweaver (for more information check out *Sams How to Use Dreamweaver and Fireworks 4*), that provide the same type of functionality as FrontPage without the associated security holes.

## Cautious Server-Side Includes Usage

Server-Side Includes (SSI) are a great way to enhance a Web site. They enable users to embed CGI scripts, other files, and Unix commands into a regular HTML file.

Unfortunately, SSI can also be a nightmare to a server administrator. The same problems inherent in CGI script security are now exacerbated by the fact that the scripts can be called any non-executable document. Which means that even documents that you have secured with 644 permissions can still be used to cause problems on the server.

If you are going to use SSI, there are things you can do to lessen the potential security risks.

One of the best things you can do is only enable SSI on a per-directory basis. If a directory does not need SSI there is no reason to enable this feature. You can do this by disabling SSI for the server and selectively enabling it for certain directories.

When you do enable SSI for a directory, make sure the server-parsed documents end in `shtml`, or some suffix that is not `htm` or `html`, the standard HTML file extensions. SSI forces Apache to parse every file in that directory every time it is requested. If your site is filled mostly with non-SSI enabled files you are placing an unnecessary burden on Apache by forcing it to parse the non-SSI files.

In addition to limiting the location and type of files that can contain SSI executables, it is a good idea to limit what can be executed in the file.

You can limit the types of files that can be executed by adding the `IncludesNOEXEC` flag to the `Includes` directive. So, it would look something like this:

```
<Directory "/home/website/httpd">
    AllowOverride None
    Options IncludesNOEXEC
</Directory>
```

This will disable the `exec` command within SSI documents. You can still execute CGI scripts using the "include virtual" tag. Any scripts referenced by the "include virtual" tag will need to be in a directory defined by the `ScriptAlias` directive.

## Cautious `.htaccess` Usage

There are two different reasons for using `.htaccess` files. The first, and most common is to setup password protection, the second reason is to overwrite the Apache system-wide settings.

Although password protection is, technically, a way of overwriting Apache system-wide settings it is the most popular use of `.htaccess` and deserves special attention.

As with any optional Apache setting, you do not have to enable the use of `.htaccess` files.

If you do decide to enable the use of `.htaccess`, you should do it selectively. Start with a very restrictive level of user control:

```
<Directory />
AllowOverride None
Options None
Allow from all
</Directory>
```

This creates a default setting that is very restrictive; you can then pick individual directories that will have system override enabled.

In addition to selecting which directories will have override capabilities you will need to determine which directives you will allow to be overwritten.

There is a temptation when enabling the use of `.htaccess` to just enable all directives to be overwritten:

```
<Directory />
AllowOverride ALL
Options None
Allow from all
</Directory>
```

For some directives, such as `ErrorDocument`, which enables a user to change the default error document, this is no problem. However, other directives, such as `Includes` can cause problems by enabling them.

For example, if you have disabled SSI for a directory and you leave the `AllowOverride` directive set to all, a user will be able to enable SSI, without letting you know.

Deciding which directives you will enable is a matter of choice. However, it is something you should carefully consider, enable selectively.

## Password Protection

As mentioned earlier, `.htaccess` is most commonly used for password protection. It is a good way of handling password protection, and it is secure.

Unfortunately, there are some fairly common practices, implemented by users, which diminish the effectiveness of this tool.

One common mistake made by users is to put the file that contains the usernames and passwords in the same directory as the `.htaccess` file, or in the root Web directory. This file should not be in a publicly accessible directory. Keep it in the root directory of the user, or some other directory that they have write access to, but is not accessible through the Web site.

Another common request is to use the system password file to handle authentication. This is obviously a bad idea. One of the nice features of `.htaccess` is that it creates virtual users, with no permissions on the server. If you query the system password file, you are taking that advantage away, and by creating more system users, some of which will undoubtedly have very simple passwords; you are increasing the security risk to the server.

Finally, make sure that your `httpd.conf` file has the following lines:

```
<Files ~ "^\.ht">
    Order allow,deny
    Deny from all
</Files>
```

This will prevent site visitors from reading the contents of your `.htaccess` file. It also prevents site visitors from reading `.htpasswd` files, which are commonly used to store the username password combinations (of course you won't have to worry about that because your users will not have their `.htpassword` files in Web accessible directories).

## Using a Staging Server

So far we have discussed ways you can tighten the security of your server, and of Apache in general. Although these suggestions are great in a perfect world controlled by system administrators, they are not always practical in a corporate environment.

One way to combine the security you, as an administrator, desire with the enhancements that your users demand is to setup a staging server.

A staging server is a server that is a mirror of your Web server. It has the same operating system, the same version of Apache, with all the same modules, the same version of PHP, Perl, and so on. New content is published to the staging server, tested, and then published to the live server. The staging server enables users to test code in a near production environment before making it live.

There are several advantages to running a staging server.

At a minimum forcing users to publish to a staging server enables you to close off unnecessary ports on your production server. As an example, although it might not be practical to force users to use SCP versus FTP, you can force all connections from the staging to the production server to be SCP. Which means you can disable FTP on the production server.

A staging server provides you with a testing ground for software upgrades. If you are worried that an upgrade might cause problems on your server, you can perform the upgrade on the staging server, giving yourself some room for error. If the installation is successful, perform it on the live server. Otherwise, determine what went wrong and try the installation on the staging server.

Having a staging server also enables you to lock down your server and tightly control what addresses can connect to the live server. On most variants of the *nix operating system this type of control is done through the `hosts.deny` and `hosts.allow` files. As the names suggest, the `hosts.allow` file determines who to allow access to selected services on the server, although the `hosts.deny` file lists addresses and services that are denied access to the server. The files can contain multiple lines, each one representing a different rule and the `hosts.allow` rules overwrite the rules in the `hosts.deny` file.

The `hosts.allow` and `hosts.deny` files are formatted in the same manner: service, hosts, and command. The service column is the service, or services (a comma-delimited list)—expressed as the services daemon—represented by a given rule. The hosts column is also a comma-delimited list of hosts to which the rule applies. The command column is a special command, executed by a query to the port, to which the rule applies.

In this case, you are trying to create as restrictive an environment as possible, so you would want to create a `hosts.deny` file that looks like this:

```
# /etc/hosts.deny
#
# Disallow all hosts.
ALL: ALL
```

This will block all traffic, on all ports to the server. Very secure, but not very practical. To compliment this restrictive `hosts.deny` file, you can create a `hosts.allow` file that looks something like this:

```
# /etc/hosts.allow
#
# Allow all traffic from the server.
ALL: LOCAL
#
# SSH traffic is allowed from the staging server and the
# local network
sshd: staging.domain.com, 10.10.100.
```

This enables the server to access all services, for sending mail, and other Web interfaces to services on the machine. It also enables all incoming traffic to the Web server, but blocks SSH traffic from all hosts, except the staging server and the local network.

Notice the local network is listed as `10.10.100`. The server interprets this to mean that any address from `10.10.100.1` through `10.10.100.254` is allowed to make a SSH connection. If you wanted to be more restrictive you could specify individual workstations that are allowed SSH access to the server.

Of course, this does not prevent a nefarious user from using a CGI exploit, or another security that can be accessed through the `httpd` server, but it does prevent them from accessing a security exploit on any ports you might have forgotten to close.

An important consideration with a staging server is the level of control you are going to allow the users of the server to have. There are two different models of staging server security. The first model enables users to upload their content to the staging server, test it, and then push it to the live server themselves, using staging tool servers you install. The second method is to have users upload content to the staging server, test it, and then send the server administrator, or group of administrators, an e-mail asking to have the documents published to the live server.

The second obviously provides tighter security control, however it makes a lot more work for the server administrator. It is important to

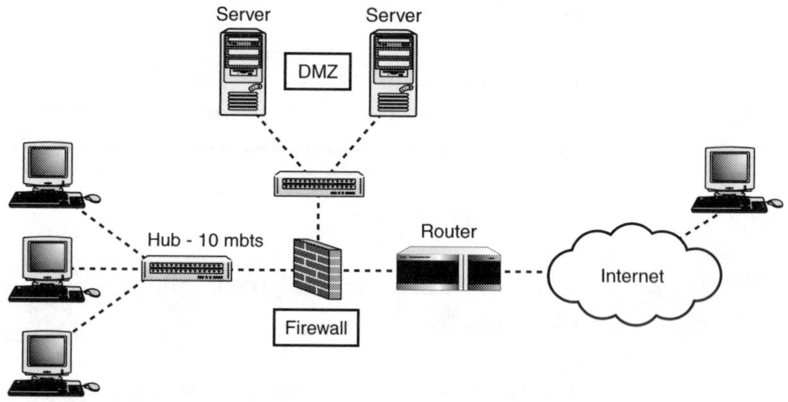


**Figure 15-2** A Web server residing in a firewall DMZ.

determine how much time you are able to devote to managing content before deciding on a staging server strategy.

The placement of the staging server is an important consideration. Because you are, essentially, leaving this server wide open it is a good idea to place it behind a firewall. This will enable users from your network to access it, but no one from the outside. The live server can then be placed in a DMZ, between the firewall and the Internet, as shown in Figure 15-2, or placed in a collocation facility.

## Special Issues for Virtual Hosts

If you administer an Apache Web server for a hosting company, especially a shared server, you might have read this chapter and thought, "There is no way I am going to be able to implement and track these security guidelines for 200 different sites on a server."

The truth is, many of the more restrictive suggestions in this book are difficult to implement across the board for small hosts. Inevitably a customer will demand to have a feature enabled that you know is a bad idea. The quandary then becomes do you risk losing the revenue from that customer to maintain tighter security, or do you make an exception to your security policy?

Generally speaking, the same rules that apply to a multiuser single site also apply to servers with multiple Web sites:

- Restrict shell access to the server.
- Only allow SSI and `.htaccess` when necessary.
- Don't enable modules that you are not going to use.
- Make file permissions as tight as possible.

Fortunately, there are many control panels on the market that aide in maintaining site and system settings, while still giving you full control over Apache.

Control panels come in two varieties: open source, such as Webmin (`http://www.webmin.com`), and commercial, such as Plesk's Server Administrator (`http://www.plesk.com`). These control panels allow you to control more than just Apache. But their Apache control is exceptional, letting you set default directives that are enabled for each account, as well as making exceptions for each individual account.

## Special Issues for Windows and Apache

Repeated security issues with Microsoft's Internet Information Server have caused many Windows-based Web server administrators to abandon it and switch to Apache.

Apache is certainly an excellent choice on any platform, but there are some special security issues to be aware of when running Apache on the Windows platform.

If possible, run Apache on Windows 2000 versus Windows NT. Windows 2000 has more secure default system settings, which means you will be running more secure right out of the box.

As with a *nix installation you should be as restrictive as possible with file and directory permissions. Only providing write and execute capabilities when necessary.

It is also important to maintain a secure "user" and "group" structure so users cannot access the files of other users or groups.

Disabling ports and services that you are not using is also important. Windows 2000 does a good job of not running unnecessary services, or leaving unnecessary ports open, but you might have to manually make these changes in Windows NT.

Unlike a *nix systems, Microsoft recommends putting a Web site's root directory in a separate partition or on a different disk. Segmenting the site from the system files will prevent a user from accessing the system files, by changing directories to the server root.

You might have requests from users to access the Web server through a GUI interface such as PCAnywhere, or Terminal Server. Windows does not have the same type of control that *nix does, so if a user has access to the desktop, she can access all files on the server. In other words, this is not a good idea on a shared server.

If you do have a dedicated server, and don't mind giving users access to it, use Windows Terminal instead of PCAnywhere whenever possible. Windows Terminal connections are secure and encrypted. Everything in PCAnywhere is sent in plain text.

Finally, as with any operating system, it is important to keep up with the latest security patches and service packs. Microsoft does a good job of updating users when a new patch is released, but you also have to review and install the patch.

Hopefully reading through this chapter made you feel more paranoid about the security of your Apache installation.

You should not live in constant panic that your site is being attacked, but you should be aware of security issues, and take reasonable steps to ensure the security of your server.

The basic steps that can be taken to help secure Apache on any server are

1. Limit access to the server.
2. Only allow the root user to access the configuration files.
3. Maintain strict user and group rules.
4. Restrict the Apache features you enable to only those you need.
5. Keep up with operating system and Apache security patches.

If you follow these guidelines, you should have no trouble maintaining a secure Apache installation.

CHAPTER 16

# APACHE AUTHENTICATION AND AUTHORIZATION

*"Mr. Cruncher himself always spoke of the year of our Lord as Anna Dominoes: apparently under the impression that the Christian era dated from the invention of a popular game, by a lady who had bestowed her name upon it."*

*A Tale of Two Cities*—Charles Dickens

Apache has three distinct ways of dealing with the question of whether a particular request for a resource will result in that resource actually being returned. These criteria are called *authorization, authentication,* and *access control*.

Authentication is any process by which you verify that someone is who he claims to be. This usually involves a username and a password, but can include any other method of demonstrating identity, such as a smart card, retina scan, voice recognition, or fingerprints. Authentication is equivalent to showing your driver's license at the ticket counter at the airport.

Authorization is finding out if the person, when identified, is permitted to have the resource. This is usually determined by finding out if that person is a part of a particular group, if that person has paid admission, or has a particular level of security clearance. Authorization is equivalent to checking the guest list at an exclusive party, or checking for your ticket when you go to the opera.

Finally, access control is a much more general way of controlling access to a Web resource. Access can be granted or denied based on a wide variety of criteria, such as the network address of the client, the time of day, the phase of the moon, or which browser the visitor is using. Access control is analogous to locking the gate at closing time, or only letting people onto the ride who are more than 48 inches tall—it's controlling entrance by some arbitrary condition which may or may not have anything to do with the attributes of the particular visitor.

Because these three techniques are so closely related in most real applications, it is difficult to talk about them separate from one another. In particular, authentication and authorization are, in most actual implementations, inextricable.

If you have information on your Web site that is sensitive, or, is intended for only a small group of people, the techniques in this chapter will help you make sure that the only people to see those pages are the people that you want to see them.

## Basic Authentication

As the name implies, basic authentication is the simplest method of authentication, and for a long time was the most common. However, other methods of authentication have recently passed basic in common usage, because of usability issues that will be discussed shortly.

### How Basic Authentication Works

When a particular resource has been protected using basic authentication, Apache sends a 401 Authentication Required header with the response to the request to notify the client that user credentials must be supplied in order for the resource to be returned as requested.

Upon receiving a 401 response header, the client's browser, if it supports basic authentication, will ask the user to supply a username and password to be sent to the server. If you are using a graphical browser, such as Netscape or Internet Explorer, you will see is a box that gives you a place to type your username and password to be sent back to the server. If the username is in the approved list, and if the password supplied is correct, the resource will be returned to the client.

Because the HTTP protocol is stateless, each request will be treated in the same way, even though they are from the same client. That is, every resource requested from the server will have to supply authentication credentials over again to receive the resource.

Fortunately, the browser takes care of the details here, so that you only have to type your username and password one time per browser session. However, you might have to type it again the next time you open up your browser and visit the same Web site.

Along with the 401 response certain other information will be passed back to the client. In particular, it sends a name that is associated with the protected area of the Web site. This is called the *realm,* or just the authentication name. The client browser caches the username and password that you supplied and stores it along with the authentication realm so if other resources are requested from the same realm, the same username and password can be returned to authenticate that request without requiring the user to type them in again. This cacheing is usually just for the current browser session, but some browsers allow you to store them permanently so you never have to type your password again.

The authentication name, or realm, will appear in the pop-up box to identify what the username and password are being requested for.

## Configuration: Protecting Content with Basic Authentication

Two or three configuration steps must be completed to protect a resource using basic authentication, depending on what you are trying to do.

1. Create a password file
2. Set the configuration to use this password file
3. Optionally, create a group file

### *Create a Password File*

To determine whether a particular username/password combination is valid it will need to be compared to some authoritative listing of usernames and passwords. This is the password file, which you will need to create on the server side and populate with valid users and their passwords.

Because this file contains sensitive information it should be stored outside of the document directory. Although, as you will see in a moment, the passwords are encrypted in the file, therefore, if a cracker were to gain access to the file it would be an aid in their attempt to figure out the passwords. And, because people tend to be sloppy with their passwords, for example, using the same password for Web site authentication as for their bank account, this could potentially be a very serious breach of security, even if the content on your Web site is not particularly sensitive.

**WARNING:** Encourage your users to use a different password for your Web site than the use for other more essential things. For example, many people tend to use two passwords—one for all their extremely important things, such as the login to their desktop computer and their bank account, and another for less sensitive things, the compromise of which would be less serious.

To create the password file use the `htpasswd` utility that came with Apache. This will be located in the bin directory of wherever you installed Apache. For example, it will probably be located at `/usr/local/apache/bin/htpasswd` if you installed Apache from source.

To create the file, type:

```
htpasswd -c /usr/local/apache/passwd/password username
```

`htpasswd` will ask you for the password, and then ask you to type it again to confirm it:

```
# htpasswd -c /usr/local/apache/passwd/passwords rbowen
New password: mypassword
Re-type new password: mypassword
Adding password for user rbowen
```

Note that in the example shown, a password file is being created containing a user called `rbowen`, and this password file is being placed in the location `/usr/local/apache/passwd/passwords`. You will substitute the location and the username, which you want to use to start your password file.

If `htpasswd` is not in your path, you will have to type the full path to the file to get it to run. That is, in the previous example, you would replace `htpasswd` with `/usr/local/apache/bin/htpasswd`.

The `-c` flag is used only when you are creating a new file. After the first time, you will omit the `-c` flag, when you are adding new users to an already-existing password file.

```
htpasswd /usr/local/apache/passwd/passwords sungo
```

The example just shown will add a user named sungo to a password file that has already been created earlier. As before, you will be asked for the password at the command line, and then will be asked to confirm the password by typing it again.

---

**WARNING:** Be very careful not to use the `-c` flag by mistake when you add new users to an existing password file. Using the `-c` flag will create a new password file, even if you already have an existing file with that name. That is, it will remove the contents of the file that is there and replace it with a new file containing only the one username that you were adding.

---

The password is stored in encrypted form in the password file, so users on the system will not be able to read the file and immediately determine the passwords of all the users. Nevertheless, you should store the file in as secure a location as possible with whatever minimum permissions on the file so that the Web server itself can read the file. For example, if your server is configured to run as user nobody and group nogroup, then you should set permissions on the file so that only that user can read the file:

```
chown nobody.nogroup /usr/local/apache/passwd/passwords
chmod 640 /usr/local/apache/passwd/passwords
```

On Windows, a similar precaution should be taken, changing the ownership of the password file to the Web server user, so that other users cannot read the file.

### *Set the Configuration to Use This Password File*

When you have created the password file, you need to tell Apache about it, and tell Apache to use this file to require user credentials for admission. This configuration is done with the directives in Table 16-1:

**Table 16-1** Configuring Apache to Use the Password File

| Directive | Meaning |
|---|---|
| `AuthType` | Authentication type being used. In this case, it will be set to Basic. |
| `AuthName` | The authentication realm or name. |
| `AuthUserFile` | The location of the password file. |
| `AuthGroupFile` | The location of the group file, if any. |
| `Require` | The requirement(s) which must be satisfied to grant admission. |

These directives might be placed in an `.htaccess` file in the particular directory being protected, or, perhaps, in the main server configuration file in a `<Directory>` section, or other scope container.

The following example defines an authentication realm called "By Invitation Only." The password file located at `/usr/local/apache/passwd/passwords` will be used to verify the user's identity. Only users named rbowen or sungo will be granted access, and even then only if they provide a password that matches the one stored in the password file.

```
AuthType Basic
AuthName "By Invitation Only"
AuthUserFile /usr/local/apache/passwd/passwords
Require user rbowen sungo
```

The phrase "By Invitation Only" will be displayed in the password pop-up box, where the user will have to type their credentials.

If these directives were put in the main server configuration file, you will need to restart your Apache server for the new configuration to take effect. Directives placed in `.htaccess` files take effect immediately because `.htaccess` files are parsed each time files are served.

The next time you load a file from that directory, you will see the familiar username/password dialog box pop up, requiring that you type the username and password before you are permitted to proceed.

In addition to specifically listing the users to whom you want to grant access, you can specify that any valid user should be let in. This is done with the `valid-user` keyword:

```
Require valid-user
```

### *Optionally, Create a Group File*

Most of the time, you will want more than one, or two, or even a dozen people to have access to a resource. You want to define a group that has access to that resource, and manage that group by adding and removing members without having to edit the server configuration file and restart Apache each time.

This is handled using authentication groups. An authentication group is, as you would expect, a group name associated with a list of members. This list is stored in a group file, which should be stored in the same location as the password file, so that you are able to keep track of these things.

The format of the group file is exceedingly simple. A group name appears first on a line, followed by a colon, and then a list of the members of the group separated by spaces. For example:

```
authors: rich daniel allan
```

When this file has been created, you can Require that someone be in a particular group to get the requested resource. This is done with the `AuthGroupFile` directive, as shown in the following example.

```
AuthType Basic
AuthName "Apache Admin Guide Authors"
AuthUserFile /usr/local/apache/passwd/passwords
AuthGroupFile /usr/local/apache/passwd/groups
Require group authors
```

The authentication process is now one step more involved. When a request is received, and the requested username and password are supplied, the group file is checked first to see if the supplied username is even in the required group. If it is, then the password file will be checked to see if the username there and if the supplied password matches the password stored in that file. If any of these steps fail, access will be forbidden.

## Frequently Asked Questions About Basic Authentication

The following questions tend to get asked very frequently with regard to basic authentication. It should be understood that basic authentication is very basic, and, therefore, is limited to the set of features that has been presented previously. Most of the more interesting things that people tend to want need to be implemented using some alternate authentication scheme.

### *How Do I Log Out?*

Since browsers first started implementing basic authentication, Web site administrators have wanted to know how to enable the user log out. Because the browser caches the username and password with the authentication realm, as described earlier in this chapter, this is not a function of the server configuration. It is, however, a question of getting the browser to forget the credential information so that the next time the resource is requested the username and password must be supplied again. There are numerous situations in which this is desirable, such as when using a browser in a public location, and when you don't want to leave the browser logged in so the next person can get into your bank account.

Despite this perhaps being the most frequently asked question about basic authentication, thus far none of the major browser manufacturers have seen this as being a desirable feature to put into their products.

Consequently, the answer to this question is, you can't. Sorry.

### *How Can I Change What the Password Box Looks Like?*

The dialog that pops up for the user to enter their username and password is ugly. It contains unwanted text, it looks different in Internet Explorer and Netscape, and contains different text. It also asks for fields that the user might not understand—for example, Netscape asks the user to type their "User ID". Or, you might want to provide additional explanatory text so that the user has a better idea what is going on.

Unfortunately, these things are features of the browser and cannot be controlled from the server side. If you want the login to look different, then you will need to implement your own authentication scheme. There is no way to change what this login box looks like if you are using basic authentication.

### *How Do I Make It Not Ask Me for My Password the Next Time?*

Your browser forgets your username and password because most browsers only store your password information for the current browser session. So, when you visit the same Web site again, you will need to re-enter your username and password.

There is nothing that can be done about this on the server side.

However, the most recent versions of the major browsers contain the capability to remember your password forever, so that you never have to log in again. Although it is debatable whether this is a good idea because it effectively overrides the entire point of having security in the first place, but it is certainly convenient for the user, and simplifies the user experience.

**NOTE:** Note that there are alternate authentication methods, such as using cookies, which can make logins persistent, and not require you to log in again the next time you visit the site. But this is not something that you can do on the server side when using Basic authentication.

### *Why Does It Sometimes Ask Me for My Password Twice?*

When entering a password-protected Web site for the first time, you will occasionally notice that you are asked for your password twice. This might happen immediately after you entered the password the first time or it might happen when you click the first link after authenticating the first time.

This happens for a very simple, but nonetheless confusing reason, again having to do with the way that the browser caches the login information.

Browsers store login information based on the authentication realm, specified by the `AuthName` directive and by the server name. This way the browser can distinguish between the `Private` authentication realm on one site and on another. So, if you go to a site using one name for the server, and internal links on the server refer to that server by a different name, the browser has no way to know that they are in fact the same server.

For example, if you were to visit the URL `http://example.com/private/`, which required authentication, your browser would remember the supplied username and password associated with the hostname `example.com`. If, by virtue of an internal redirect or fully qualified HTML links in pages, you are then sent to the URL `http://www.example.com/ private/`. Even though this is really the exact same URL, the browser does not know this for sure and is forced to request the authentication information again because `example.com and www.example.com` are not exactly the same hostname. Your browser has no particular way to know that these are the same Web site.

## Security Caveat

Basic authentication should not be considered secure by any particularly rigorous definition of secure.

Although the password is stored on the server in encrypted format, it is passed from the client to the server in plain text across the network.

Anyone listening with any variety of packet sniffer will be able to read the username and password in the clear as it goes across.

Also, remember that the username and password are passed with every request, not just when the user first types them in. So the packet sniffer doesn't need to be listening at a particularly strategic time, but just long enough to see any request come across the wire.

And, in addition to that, the content itself is also going across the network in the clear. So, if the Web site contains sensitive information the same packet sniffer would have access to that information as it went past, even if the username and password were not used to gain direct access to the Web site.

Don't use basic authentication for anything that requires real security. It is a detriment for most users because very few people will take the trouble, or have the necessary software and/or equipment to find out passwords. However, if someone had a desire to get in, it would take very little for him to do so.

## Digest Authentication

Addressing one of the security caveats of basic authentication, digest authentication provides an alternate method for protecting your Web content. However, it to has a few caveats.

### How Digest Authentication Works

Digest authentication is implemented by the module `mod_auth_digest`. There is an older module, `mod_digest`, which implemented an older version of the digest authentication specification, but probably will not work with newer browsers.

Using digest authentication, your password is never sent across the network in the clear, but is always transmitted as an MD5 digest of the user's password. This way, the password cannot be determined by sniffing network traffic.

The full specification of digest authentication can be seen in the Internet standards document RFC 2617, which you can see at `http://www.ietf.org/rfc/rfc2617.txt`. MD5 itself is described in

RFC 1321, which you can find at `http://www.ietf.org/rfc/rfc1321.txt-from TE`. Additional information and resources about MD5 can be found at `http://userpages.umbc.edu/mabzug1/cs/md5/md5.html`.

## Configuration: Protecting Content with Digest Authentication

The steps for configuring your server for digest authentication are very similar to those for basic authentication.

1. Create the password file
2. Set the configuration to use this password file
3. Optionally, create a group file`

### *Creating a Password File (Digest Authentication)*

As with basic authentication, a simple utility is provided to create and maintain the password file that will be used to determine whether a particular user's name and password are valid. This utility is called htdigest, and will be located in the `bin` directory of wherever you installed Apache. If you installed Apache from some variety of package manager, `htdigest` is likely to have been placed somewhere in your path.

To create a new digest password file, type

```
htdigest -c /usr/local/apache/passwd/digest realm username
```

`htdigest` will ask you for the desired password, and then ask you to type it again to confirm it.

Note that the realm for which the authentication will be required is part of the argument list.

Once again, as with basic authentication, you are encouraged to place the generated file somewhere outside of the document directory.

And, as with the `htpasswd` utility, the `-c` flag creates a new file, or, if a file of that name already exists, deletes the contents of that file and generates a new file in its place. Omit the `-c` flag to add new user information to an existing password file.

### *Set the Configuration to Use This Password File (Digest Authentication)*

When you have created a password file, you need to tell Apache about it to start using it as a source of authenticated user information. This configuration is done with the directives detailed in Table 16-2:

**Table 16-2** Configuration Directives to Use the Password File (Digest).

| Directive | Meaning |
|---|---|
| `AuthType` | Authentication type being used. In this case, it will be set to `Digest`. |
| `AuthName` | The authentication realm or name. |
| `AuthDigestFile` | The location of the password file. |
| `AuthDigestGroupFile` | Location of the group file, if any. |
| `Require` | The requirement(s) that must be satisfied in order to grant permission. |

These directives might be placed in an `.htaccess` file in the particular directory being protected, or they might go in the main server configuration file, in a `<Directory>` section, or another scope container.

The following example defines an authentication realm called "Private." The password file located at `/usr/local/apache/passwd/digest` will be used to verify the user's identity. Only users named drbacchus or dorfl will be granted access if they provide a password that matches the password stored in the password file.

```
AuthType Digest
AuthName "Private"
AuthDigestFile /usr/local/apache/passwd/digest
Require user drbacchus dorfl
```

The phrase "Private" will be displayed in the password pop-up box, where the user will have to type their credentials.

### *Optionally, Create a Group File (Digest Authentication)*

As you have observed, there are not many differences between this configuration process and that required by basic authentication, described in the previous section. This is true also of group functionality. The group file used for digest authentication is exactly the same as that used for basic authentication. That is, lines in the group file consist of the name of the group, a colon, and a list of the members of that group. For example:

```
admins: jim roy ed anne
```

When this file has been created, you can Require that someone be in a particular group to get the requested resource. This is done with the `AuthDigestGroupFile` directive, as shown in the following example.

```
AuthType Digest
AuthName "Private"
AuthDigestFile /usr/local/apache/passwd/digest
AuthDigestGroupFile
/usr/local/apache/passwd/digest.groups
Require group admins
```

The authentication process is the same as that used by basic authentication. It is first verified that the user is in the required group, and, if this is true, then the password is verified.

## Caveats

Before you leap into using digest authentication instead of basic authentication, there are a few things that you should know.

Digest authentication does give you the advantage of not having to send your password across the network in the clear, however, it is not supported by all major browsers in use today. So, you should not use it on a Web site that you cannot control the browsers that people will be using, such as on your intranet site. In particular, Opera 4.0 or later, Microsoft Internet Explorer 5.0 or later, and Amaya support digest authentication, whereas Netscape, Mozilla, and various other browsers do not.

Next, with regard to security considerations, you should understand two things. Although your password is not passed in the clear all your data is, so this is a rather small measure of security. And, although your password is not really sent at all, but a digest form of it, someone very familiar with the workings of HTTP could use that information—just your digested password—and use that to gain access to the content because that digested password is really all the information required to access the Web site.

The moral of this is that if you have content that really needs to be kept secure, use SSL. (See Chapter 17, "SSL," for more details.)

## Database Authentication Modules

Basic authentication and digest authentication both suffer from the same major flaw. They use text files to store the authentication information. The problem with this is that looking something up in a text file is very slow. It's like trying to find something in a book that has no index. You have to start at the beginning and work through it one page at a time until you find what you are looking for. Now imagine that the next time you need to find the same thing, you don't remember where it was, so you have to start at the beginning again and work through one page at a time until you find it again. And the next time. And the time after that.

Because HTTP is stateless authentication has to be verified every time that content is requested. So, every time a document is accessed which is secured with basic or digest authentication, Apache has to open up those text password files and look through them one line at a time until it finds the user that is trying to log in and verifies their password. In the worst case, if the username supplied is not in there at all, every line in the file will need to be checked. On average, half of the file will need to be read before the user is found. This is very slow.

Although this is not a big problem for small sets of users, when you get into larger numbers of users (where "larger" means a few hundred) this becomes prohibitively slow. In many cases, valid username/password combinations will get rejected because the authentication module just had to spend so much time looking for the username in the file that Apache will just get tired of waiting and return a failed authentication.

In these cases you need an alternative, and that alternative is to use some variety of database. Databases are optimized for looking for a particular piece of information in a very large data set. It builds indexes to rapidly locate a particular record, and they have query languages for swiftly locating records that match particular criteria.

There are numerous modules available for Apache to authenticate using a variety of different databases. In this section, we'll just look at two modules that ship with Apache.

## `mod_auth_db` and `mod_auth_dbm`

`mod_auth_db` and `mod_auth_dbm` are modules that enable you to keep your usernames and passwords in DB or DBM files. There are few practical differences between DB files and DBM files. And, on some operating systems, such as various BSDs and Linux, they are exactly the same. You should pick whichever of the two modules makes the most sense on your particular platform of choice. If you do not have DB support on your platform, you might need to install it. You can download an implementation of DB at `http://www.sleepycat.com/`.

## Berkeley DB Files

DB files, also known as Berkeley database files, are the simplest form of database, and are ideally suited for the sort of data that needs to be stored for HTTP authentication. DB files store key/value pairs. That is, the name of a variable and the value of that variable. Although other databases allow the storage of many fields in a given record, a DB file allows only this pairing of key and value. This is ideal for authentication, which requires only the pair of a username and password.

**NOTE:** There are actually a number of implementations that get around this limitation. MLDBM is one of them, for example. However, for the purposes of this discussion, we'll just deal with standard Berkeley DB, which is likely to have shipped with whatever operating system you are already running.

## Installing `mod_auth_db`

For the purposes of this chapter, we'll talk about installing and configuring `mod_auth_db`. However, everything that is said here can be directly applied to `mod_auth_dbm` by simply replacing "db" with "dbm" and "DB" with "DBM" in the various commands, filenames, and directives.

Because `mod_auth_db` is not compiled in by default, you will need to rebuild Apache to get the functionality, unless you built in everything when we started. See Chapter 13 for more information about rebuilding Apache with a particular module enabled. Note that if you installed Apache with shared object support, you might be able to just build the module and load it in to Apache.

To build Apache from scratch with mod_auth_db built in, use the following ./configure line in your apache source code directory.

```
./configure —enable-module=auth_db
```

Or, if you had a more complex configure command line, you can just add the -enable-module=auth_db option to that command line, and you'll get mod_auth_db built into your server.

## Protecting a Directory with mod_auth_db

When you have compiled and loaded the mod_auth_db module into your Web server, you'll find that there's very little difference between using regular authentication and using mod_auth_db authentication. The procedure is the same as that we went through with basic and digest authentication:

1. Create the user file.
2. Configure Apache to use that file for authentication.
3. Optionally, create a group file.

### *Create the User File*

The user file for authentication is, this time, not a flat text file, but a DB file (or, if you are using mod_auth_dbm, a DBM file). Fortunately, once again, Apache provides us with a simple utility for the purpose of managing this user file. This time, the utility is called dbmmanage, and will be located in the bin subdirectory of wherever you installed Apache.

dbmmanage is somewhat more complicated to use than htpasswd or htdigest, but it is still fairly simple. The syntax you will usually use is as follows:

```
dbmmanage passwords.db adduser montressor
```

As with htpasswd, you will at this point be prompted for a password, and then asked to confirm that password by typing it again. The main difference here is that rather than a text file being created, you are creating a binary file containing the information that you have supplied.

Type dbmmanage with no arguments to get the full list of options available with this utility.

### Creating Your User File with Perl

Note that, if you are so inclined, you can manage your user file with Perl, or any other language that has a DB-file module, for interfacing with this type of database. This covers a number of popular programming languages.

The following Perl code, for example, will add a user "rbowen", with password "mypassword", to your password file:

```
use DB_File;
tie %database, 'DB_File', "passwords.dat"
    or die "Can't initialize database: $!\n";

$username = 'rbowen';
$password = 'mypassword';
@chars=(0..9,'a'..'z');
$salt = '', map { $chars[int rand @chars] } (0..1);

$crypt = crypt($password, $salt);
$database{$username} = $crypt;

untie %database;
```

As you can imagine, this makes it very simple to write tools to manage the user and password information stored in these files.

Passwords are stored in Unix `crypt` format, just as they were in the regular password files. The "salt" that is created in the middle is part of the process, generating a random starting point for that encryption. The technique being used is called a "tied hash." The idea is to tie a built-in data structure to the contents of the file, so when the data structure is changed, the file is automatically modified at the same time.

### Configuration Apache to Use This Password File

When you have created the password file, you need to tell Apache about it, and tell Apache to use this file to verify user credentials. This configuration will look almost the same as for basic authentication. This configuration can go in an `.htaccess` file in the directory to be protected, or can go in the main server configuration, in a `<Directory>` section, or other scope container directive.

The configuration will look something like the following:

```
AuthName "Members Only"
AuthType Basic
AuthDBUserFile /usr/local/apache/passwd/passwords.dat
require user rbowen
```

Now, users accessing the directory will be required to authenticate against the list of valid users who are in /usr/local/apache/ passwd/ passwords.dat.

### *Optionally, Create a Group File*

As mentioned earlier, DB files store a key/value pair. In the case of group files, the key is the name of the user and the value is a comma-separated list of the groups to which the user belongs.

Although this is the opposite of the way that group files are stored elsewhere, note that we will primarily be looking up records based on the username, so it is more efficient to index the file by username, rather than by the group name.

Groups can be added to your group file using dbmmanage and the add command:

```
dbmmanage add groupfile rbowen one,two,three
```

In the previous example, groupfile is the literal name of the group file, rbowen is the user being added and one, two, and three are names of the three groups to which this user belongs.

When you have your groups in the file, you can require a group in the regular way:

```
AuthName "Members Only"
AuthType Basic
AuthDBUserFile /usr/local/apache/passwd/passwords.dat
AuthDBGroupFile /usr/local/apache/passwd/groups.dat
require group three
```

Note that if you want to use the same file for both password and group information, you can do so, but this is a little more complicated to manage because you have to encrypt the password yourself before you feed it to the `dbmmanage` utility.

## Access Control

Authentication by username and password is only part of the story. Frequently you want to let people in based on something other than who they are. Something such as where they are coming from. Restricting access based on something other than the identity of the user is generally referred to as *access control.*

### Allow and Deny

The `Allow` and `Deny` directives enable you to allow and deny access based on the host name or host address of the machine requesting a document. The directive that goes hand-in-hand with these is the Order directive, which tells Apache in which order to apply the filters.

The usage of these directives is

```
allow from address
```

where *address* is an IP address (or a partial IP address) or a fully qualified domain name (or a partial domain name).

For example, if you have someone spamming your message board and you want to keep them out, you could do the following:

```
deny from 205.252.46.165
```

Visitors coming from that address will not be able to see the content behind this directive. If, instead, you have a machine name, rather than an IP address, you can use that.

```
deny from dc.numbersusa.com
```

And, if you want to block access from an entire domain, you can specify just part of an address or domain name:

```
deny from 192.101.205
```

```
deny from cyberthugs.com

deny from ke
```

Using `Order` will enable you to be sure that you are actually restricting things to the group that you want to let in by combining a `deny` and an `allow` directive:

```
Order Deny,Allow
Deny from all
Allow from dev.rcbowen.com
```

Listing just the `allow` directive would not do what you want because it will let users from that host in, in addition to letting everyone in. What you want is to let in only users from that host.

### Satisfy

The `Satisfy` directive can be used to specify that several criteria might be considered when trying to decide if a particular user will be granted admission. `Satisfy` can take as an argument one of two options—`all or any`. By default, it is assumed that the value is `all`. This means that if several criteria are specified, then all of them must be met in order for someone to get in. However, if set to any then several criteria might be specified, but if the user satisfies any of these then they will be granted entrance.

A very good example of this is using access control to assure that, although a resource is password protected from outside your network, all hosts inside the network will be given free access to the resource. This would be accomplished by using the `Satisfy` directive, as shown here.

```
<Directory /usr/local/apache/htdocs/sekrit>
  AuthType Basic
  AuthName intranet
  AuthUserFile /www/passwd/users
  AuthGroupFile /www/passwd/groups
  Require group customers
  Allow from internal.com
  Satisfy any
</Directory>
```

In this scenario, users will be let in if they either have a password, or, if they are in the internal network.

The various authentication modules provide a number of ways to restrict access to your host based on the identity of the user. They offer a somewhat standard interface to this functionality, but provide different back-end mechanisms for actually authenticating the user.

And the access control mechanism allows you to restrict access based on criteria unrelated to the identity of the user.

CHAPTER 17

# SSL

*"The only system that is truly secure is one that is switched off and unplugged, locked in a titanium-lined safe, buried in a concrete bunker, and surrounded by nerve gas and very highly-paid armed guards. Even then, I wouldn't stake my life on it."*

Gene Spafford

This chapter presents you with the security technologies involved in conducting secure transactions over the Internet. It explains the installation and configuration of mod_ssl, the SSL protocol module for Apache 2.0. SSL stands for Secure Socket Layers and enables Web browsers and servers to protect their communications. Configuring a secure server is a complex task and requires an understanding of the underlying protocols. The chapter starts with an introduction to several security-related concepts and algorithms. If you are already familiar with this background material you can skim through the initial sections. Later sections explain the steps necessary to get SSL up and running with Apache 2.0. Pointers to useful resources are provided at the end of the chapter.

## Cryptography

As the Internet grows and Web technologies evolve an increasing number of business and individuals use this global network to conduct financial transactions and transmit sensitive information. Hence, the parties need to protect these communications from potential attackers.

The threats are easy to understand, but the solutions can be fairly complex. Consider the typical scenario in which an individual wants to buy a book online. Let's call this person Alice (this is a convention started in one of the original academic cryptographic papers, where Alice and Bob are two figured individuals trying to communicate securely).

**NOTE:** For more information on these papers you can refer to Rivest, R.L., Shamir, A., and Adleman, L.M., "On Digital Signatures and Public Cryptosystems" Technical Report, MIT Laboratory for Computer Science, January 1979. These are the fathers of public key cryptography, and invented the RSA algorithm, named after them.

To buy a book, Alice needs to transmit her credit-card number to the book merchant, but she does not want an attacker to be able to intercept this information. With this information *confidentiality* needs to be protected. Alice wants to make sure the attacker cannot successfully modify or replay her order so she does not end up with a different book or several instances of the same book. The *integrity* of the information needs to be preserved. Finally, Alice wants to make sure that she is communicating with the legitimate merchant Web site, and not a rogue Web site set up by an attacker. She needs to *authenticate* the identity of the remote end. Cryptography studies the algorithms and methods used to securely transmit messages to ensure confidentiality, integrity, and authenticity.

## Confidentiality

Encryption is a common method of guaranteeing the confidentiality of an electronic message transmitted over an insecure network. The original message (*plaintext*) is converted by the sender into a new, encrypted, message (*ciphertext*) using a certain piece of information (*key*). The receiver can then use his own key to convert the ciphertext to the original message. The ciphertext looks like random data to an attacker. Only someone with the appropriate key can decrypt that message and make sense out of it.

## Symmetric Cryptography

If the key used to encrypt and decrypt the message is the same then the process is known as symmetric cryptography. DES, Triple-Des, RC4 and RC2 are algorithms used for symmetric key cryptography. Many of these algorithms can have different key sizes, measured in bits. In general, given an algorithm, the greater the number of bits of the key, the more secure the algorithm is and the slower it will run, because of the increased computational needs of performing the algorithm.

## Public Key Cryptography

Key distribution is the main problem with symmetric cryptography. The encryption/decryption key is a shared secret between sender and receiver and needs to be securely transmitted to both parties. Public key cryptography takes a different approach. Instead of both parties sharing the same key, there is a pair of keys, one public, and the other private. The public key can be widely distributed, whereas the owner keeps the private key secret. These two keys are complementary; a message encrypted with one of the keys can only be decrypted by the other.

Anyone wanting to transmit a secure message to you can encrypt the message using your public key; assured that only the owner of the private key, you, can decrypt it. Even if the attacker has access to the public key, he cannot decrypt the communication. In fact, you want the public key to be as widely available as possible. Public key cryptography can also be used to provide message integrity and authentication. RSA is the most popular public key algorithm.

The assertion that "only the owner of the private key can decrypt it" means that with the current knowledge of cryptography and availability of computing power, an attacker will not be able to break the encryption by brute force alone. If the algorithm or its implementation are found to be flawed, then realistic attacks are possible.

---

**NOTE:** Public key cryptography is similar to giving away many identical lockpads and retaining the key that opens them all. Anybody who wants to send you a message privately can do so by putting it in a safe and locking it with one of those lockpads (*public keys*) before sending it to you. Only you have the appropriate key (*private key*) to open that lockpad (*decrypt the message*).

---

## Integrity

A message digest is a method to create a fixed-length representation of an arbitrary message that uniquely identifies it. You can think of it as the fingerprint of the message. A good message digest algorithm should be irreversible and collision-resistant: Irreversible means that the original message cannot be obtained from the digest and collision-resistant that no two different messages should have the same digest.

Message digests alone, however, do not guarantee the integrity of the message, because an attacker could change the text *and* the message digest. Examples of digest algorithms are MD5 and SHA.

## Message Authentication Codes

Message Authentication Codes, or MACs, are similar to message digests, but incorporate a shared secret key in the process. The result of the algorithm depends both on the message and the key used. Because the attacker has no access to the key, he cannot modify both the message and the digest. HMAC is an example of a message authentication code algorithm.

---

**NOTE:** To help you understand what a digest is, think about the following primitive digest algorithm—take a text and assign a number to each letter in the text. The number corresponds to the place it occupies in the alphabet (a=1, b=2, and so on). Add all the numbers. The resulting number is a digest of that message. If you modify the message the digest changes. This is just a simple example and the algorithm is not practical. Although you cannot reconstruct the original message from that number, it is feasible to carefully modify the original message while keeping the number constant. The algorithms used in practice are much more sophisticated and secure for all practical purposes.

---

## Authentication

Public key cryptography can be used to digitally "sign" messages. In fact, just by encrypting a message with your secret key the receiver can guarantee it came from you. Other digital signature algorithms involve first calculating a digest of the message and then signing the digest.

## Certificates

Thanks to digital signatures, you can tell that the person who created that public and private key pair is the one sending the message. But how can you know that person is the one you think he is? An attacker could impersonate his identity and distribute a different public key, claiming it is the legitimate one. It is necessary to have a mechanism that links an individual or organization with its public key. This is achieved by using digital certificates. Digital certificates are electronic documents that contain a public key and information about its owner (name, address, and so on). To be useful, the certificate needs to be signed by a trusted third party (Certification Authority). There are many different kinds of Certificate Authorities, as described later on the chapter. Some of them are commercial entities, providing certification services to companies conducting business over the Internet. Others are created by companies looking to provide internal certification services.

The Certification Authority guarantees that the information in the certificate is correct and that the key belongs to that individual or organization. Certificates have a period of validity and can expire or be revoked. Finally, certificates can be chained. That means that the certification process can be delegated. For example, a trusted entity can certify companies, which in turn can certify their own employees.

If this whole process is to be effective and trusted, the Certificate Authority must require appropriate proof of identity from individuals and organizations before it issues a certificate.

We have seen how confidentiality can be achieved via encryption, integrity via message authentication codes, and authentication via certificates and digital signatures. These concepts have been incorporated into the SSL protocol to enable secure communications on the Internet. The next section explains in detail the inner workings of SSL.

## Introduction to SSL

In this section you will learn how encryption, digital signatures, and certificates all work together to provide Alice with a secure shopping experience.

---

**NOTE:** TLS stands for Transport Layer Security. SSL and TLS is a family of protocols originally designed for securing communications based on the HTTP protocol, but they can be used to protect a variety of other protocols. Netscape released SSL version 2 in 1994 and SSL version 3 in 1995. TLS is an IETF standard designed to standardize SSL as an Internet protocol. It is mostly just a modification of SSL version 3 with a small number of added features and minor cleanups. The name TLS is the result of some silly politics between Microsoft and Netscape over the naming of the protocol.

---

The requirement for SSL connections is indicated by replacing the http scheme in URLs with https (for HTTP over SSL). Examples of such URLs are https://www.modssl.org, https://www.ibm.com, or https://www.microsoft.com. The default port for HTTPS is 443.

The browser will tell you when a secure connection has been established—Netscape and Microsoft browsers will show a small locked padlock in one of the lower corners. The next section explains the details of the SSL protocol.

## SSL Overview

When Alice's browser wants to send an encrypted request to a secure server, it first establishes a secure channel based on SSL. It then communicates using HTTP over this connection.

An SSL connection is divided into two phases, the handshake and data transfer phases. The handshake enables Alice to authenticate the remote server and agree on a set of keys to be used for encrypting the information in the data transfer phase.

The handshake process is the following:

1. The browser sends an initial request with information about the protocol version and algorithms supported. The request includes a random number—r1.
2. The server answers with information about the algorithms to be used, a server certificate, and a random number r2.
3. The browser makes sure the certificate is valid. It then generates a secret string r3, which is encrypted, using the server public key found in the certificate.
4. Both browser and server use r1, r2, and r3 to compute the symmetric encryption keys and the MAC keys using what is called a key-exchange algorithm.
5. The browser calculates a MAC of all the handshake messages and sends it to the server.
6. The server does the same and transmits it to the browser.

The last two steps are necessary to prevent an attacker from manipulating the handshake phase itself (for example by intercepting the messages and modifying the set of algorithms server and client agree to use). Certificate contents and verification are explained in more detail in later sections of this chapter.

During the data transfer phase, HTTP messages are divided into individual pieces. A MAC is calculated and encrypted together with the fragment that is then transmitted. The message is received at the other end, decrypted, and the MAC is calculated.

By using the SSL protocol, Alice achieves:

- **Confidentiality:** After the handshake phase, sender and receiver have agreed on a secret key that they can use to encrypt the data being transmitted, such as Alice's credit card.
- **Integrity:** SSL messages are transmitted together with MACs that prevent them from being altered or replayed. So Alice does not end up buying ten copies of the same book.
- **Authentication:** The server provides Alice with a certificate that provides information about the company or individual running the remote site. Alice can validate the certificate checking that the certificate has been issued or signed by a Certificate Authority that she trusts. The certificates of several well-known CAs are included by default in Microsoft and Netscape browsers.

---

**NOTE:** If a certificate has expired, does not match the name of the host you are accessing, or otherwise is invalid, the browser will pop up a window asking you if you still want to connect.

---

A properly configured SSL server helps secure the communication between a browser and a server. But security can still be compromised in a variety of other ways. An attacker can gain remote access to the server machine and modify the application logic that handles the credit-card transactions. Those credit-card numbers themselves could be stored in an SQL database connected to the Internet with a default password. The attacker could have physical access to the client machine and install a modified version of the browser or a key-logging program.

SSL is an important component of a secure-Internet infrastructure but by no means is the only one. An attacker will always choose the weakest link in your security infrastructure to try to break in into your systems.

# Installing SSL

SSL support for Apache is provided by mod_ssl, a module included with Apache 2.0. mod_ssl requires the OpenSSL library. OpenSSL is an open source implementation of the SSL/TLS protocols and a variety of other cryptographic algorithms. OpenSSL is based on the SSLeay library developed by Eric A. Young and Tim J. Hudson. You can learn more about mod_ssl and OpenSSL in the Web sites noted in the reference at the end of the chapter.

## OpenSSL

This section explains how to download and install the OpenSSL toolkit for both Windows and Unix variants.

## Windows

The required OpenSSL libraries are included with the Windows installer of Apache 2.0 and no further installation or download is necessary. `openssl.exe` is included in the bin/ directory of the Apache distribution. It is a utility for generating certificates, keys, certificate signing requests, and so on.

## Unix

If you are running a recent Linux or FreeBSD distribution, OpenSSL might already be installed in your system. Use the package management tools bundled with your distribution to determine if that is the case or install it otherwise

### *Installing from Source*

OpenSSL can be downloaded from `http://www.openssl.org`. After you have downloaded the software, you need to uncompress it and change into the created directory:

```
# gunzip < openssl*.tar.gz | tar xvf -
# cd openssl*
```

OpenSSL contains a config script to help you build the software. You need to provide the path to which the software will install. The path we use in this chapter is `/usr/local/ssl/install`, and you probably need to have superuser privileges to install the software there. You can install the software as a regular user, but to do so you will need to change the path. Then you need to build and install the software:

```
# ./config --prefix=/usr/local/ssl/install \
Â--openssldir=/usr/local/ssl/install/openssl
# make
# make install
```

If everything goes well, you have now successfully installed the OpenSSL toolkit. The `openssl` command-line tool will be located in `/usr/local/ssl/install/bin/`.

This tool is used to create and manipulate certificates and keys and its usage is described in a later section on certificates.

## mod_ssl

SSL extensions for Apache 1.3 needed to be distributed separately because of export restrictions. These restrictions no longer exist and mod_ssl is bundled and integrated with Apache 2.0. This section describes the steps necessary to build and install this module. mod_ssl depends on the OpenSSL library, so a valid OpenSSL installation is required.

## Windows

You can download a binary distribution of Apache 2.0 for the Windows platform from `http://www.apache.org` that includes mod_ssl.

## Unix

If you are using the Apache 2.0 server that came installed with your operating system, chances are it already includes mod_ssl. Use the package management tools bundled with your distribution to install mod_ssl if it is not present in the system.

### *Installing from Source*

When you build Apache 2.0 from source you need to pass the following options to enable and build mod_ssl:

```
--enable-ssl -with-ssl=/usr/local/ssl/install/openssl
```

This assumes you installed OpenSSL in the location described in previous sections.

If you compiled mod_ssl statically into Apache you can check if it is present by issuing the following command, which provides a list of compiled in modules:

```
# ./usr/local/apache2/bin/httpd -l
```

The command assumes you installed Apache in the `/usr/local/apache2` directory.

## Certificates

We have seen in previous sections the role certificates play in SSL. In this section we explain in detail the information contained in a certificate and how to create and manage certificates and keys using the `openssl` command-line tool.

The main standard for certificates is X.509, adapted for Internet usage. A certificate contains information about:

- The issuer is the name of the signer of the certificate.
- The subject is the person holding the key being certified.
- The subject public key is the public key of the subject.
- Control information such as the dates in which the certificate is valid.
- Signature is the signature that covers the previous data.

You can check a real-life certificate by connecting to a secure server with your browser. You can click the locked padlock icon to open information on the SSL connection. You can open the property pages by clicking on File, Properties, Certificates. Netscape browsers provide a similar interface.

Open the `https://www.ibm.com` URL in your browser and analyze the certificate, following the steps outlined in the above paragraph. You can see how the issuer of the certificate is the Equifax Secure E-business Certification Authority, which in turn has been certified by the Thawte CA. The page downloaded seamlessly because Thawte is a trusted CA that has its own certificates bundled with Internet Explorer and Netscape Navigator.

To check which are the certificates bundled with your Internet Explorer browser, go to the top menu and select Tools, Internet Options, Content, Certificates, Trusted Root Certification Authorities.

You can see that both issuer and subject are provided as distinguished names (DN), a structured way of providing a unique identifier for every element on the network. In the case of the IBM certificate, the DN is C=US, S=New York, L=Armonk, O=IBM, CN=www.ibm.com.

C stands for Country, S for State, L for Locality, O for organization and CN for Common Name. In the case of a Web site certificate the common name identifies the fully qualified domain name of the Web site (FQDN). This is the server name part of the URL, in this case `www.ibm.com`. If this does not match what you typed in the top bar, the browser will issue an error.

You now need to learn to use the `openssl` command-line tool to create and manage keys and certificates. It assumes OpenSSL was installed in the path described in the OpenSSL installation section. The examples refer to the Unix version. All the steps work the same for Windows you just need to use `openssl.exe` instead.

## Creating a Key Pair

We need to have a public/private key pair before we can create a certificate request. We assume the FQDN for the certificate you want to create is `www.yourdomain.com.` (You will need to substitute this name for the FQDN of the machine you have installed Apache on). You can create the keys by issuing the following command:

```
# ./usr/local/ssl/install/bin/openssl genrsa -des3 -rand
file1:file2:file3 \
      Â-out www.yourdomain.com.key 1024
```

- genrsa indicates to OpenSSL that we want to generate a key pair.
- des3 indicates that the private key should be encrypted and protected by a pass phrase.
- The rand switch is used to provide OpenSSL with random data to assure that the generated keys are unique and unpredictable. Select several large, relatively random files for this purpose (such as compressed log files, kernel image, and so on). This switch is not necessary on Windows, because the random data is automatically generated by some other means.

- The out switch indicates where to store the results.
- 1024 indicates the number of bits of the generated key.

The result of this command looks like

```
625152  semi-random bytes loaded
Generating RSA private key, 1024 bit long modulus
.....++++++
.........................++++++
e is 65537 (0x10001)
Enter PEM pass phrase:
Verifying password - Enter PEM pass phrase:
```

As you can see, you will be asked to provide a pass phrase. Choose a secure one. The pass phrase is necessary to protect the private key and you will be asked for it whenever you want to start the server. You can choose not to protect the key. This is convenient because you will not need to enter the pass phrase during reboots, but it is highly insecure and a compromise of the server means a compromise of the key as well. In any case, you can choose to unprotect the key either by leaving the -des3 switch out in the generation phase or by issuing the following command:

```
# ./usr/local/ssl/install/bin/openssl rsa -in
www.yourdomain.com.key \
       Â-out www.yourdomain.com.key.unsecure
```

It is a good idea to backup the `www.yourdomain.com.key` file. You can learn about the contents of the key file by issuing the following command:

```
# ./usr/local/ssl/bin/openssl rsa -noout -text -in
www.yourdomain.com.key
```

## Creating a Certificate Signing Request

To get a certificate issued by a CA you need to submit what is called a Certificate Signing Request. To create the request, issue the following command:

```
# ./usr/local/ssl/install/bin/openssl req -new -key
www.yourdomain.com.key
 -out www.yourdomain.com.csr
```

You will be prompted for the certificate information:

```
Using configuration from
/usr/local/ssl/install/openssl/openssl.cnf
Enter PEM pass phrase:
You are about to be asked to enter information that will be
incorporated into your certificate request.
What you are about to enter is what is called a Distinguished
Name or a DN.
There are quite a few fields but you can leave some blank
For some fields there will be a default value,
If you enter '.', the field will be left blank.
-----
Country Name (2 letter code) [AU]:US
State or Province Name (full name) [Some-State]:CA
Locality Name (eg, city) []: San Francisco
Organization Name (eg, company) [Internet Widgits Pty Ltd]:.
Organizational Unit Name (eg, section) []:.
Common Name (eg, YOUR name) []:www.yourdomain.com
Email Address []:administrator@yourdomain.com
Please enter the following 'extra' attributes
to be sent with your certificate request
A challenge password []:
An optional company name []:
```

The certificate is now stored in `www.yourdomain.com.csr`. You can learn about the contents of the certificate via the following command:

```
# ./usr/local/ssl/install/bin/openssl req -noout -text \
      Â-in www.yourdomain.com.csr
```

You can submit the certificate signing request file to a CA for processing. Verisign and Thawte are two of those CAs. You can learn more about their particular submission procedures at their Web sites:

```
Verisign: http://digitalid.verisign.com/server/apacheNotice.htm
Thawte: http://www.thawte.com/certs/server/request.html
```

## Creating a Self-Signed Certificate

You can also create a self-signed certificate. That is, you are going to be the issuer and the subject of the certificate. Although this is not very useful for a commercial Web site, it will allow you to test your installation of mod_ssl or to have a secure Web server while you wait for the official certificate from the CA.

```
# ./usr/local/ssl/install/bin/openssl x509 -req -days 30  \
-in www.yourdomain.com.csr -signkey www.yourdomain.com.key \
-out www.yourdomain.com.cert
```

You need to copy your certificate www.yourdomain.com.cert (either the one returned by the CA or your self signed one) to `/usr/local/ssl/install/openssl/certs/` and your key to `/usr/local/ssl/install/openssl/private/`.

You need to protect your key file by issuing the following command:

```
# chmod 400 www.yourdomain.key
```

## SSL Configuration

In the previous sections we have introduced the (not so basic) concepts behind SSL and you have learned how to generate keys and certificates. Now, finally, you can configure Apache to support SSL. mod_ssl needs either to be compiled statically or, if you have compiled as a loadable module, the appropriate `LoadModule` directive needs to be present in the file.

Add the following configuration snippet to your Apache configuration file:

```
Listen 80
Listen 443

<VirtualHost _default_:443>
ServerName www.yourdomain.com
SSLEngine on
SSLCertificateFile \
/usr/local/ssl/install/openssl/certs/www.yourdomain.com.cert
SSLCertificateKeyFile \
/usr/local/ssl/install/openssl/certs/www.yourdomain.com.key
</VirtualHost>
```

With the previous configuration, we setup a new virtual host that will listen in port 443 (the default port for HTTPS) and we enable SSL on that virtual host.

You will need to tell the server the location of the certificate and the file containing the associated key. We do so using `SSLCertificateFile` and `SSLCertificateKeyfile` directives.

Now you can stop the server if it was running, and start it again. If your key is protected by a pass phrase you will be prompted for it. After this, Apache will start and you should be able to connect securely to it via the `https://www.yourdomain.com/` URL.

If you are unable to restart your server, check the Apache error log for clues to what might have gone wrong. For example, if you cannot bind to the port make sure that Apache is not running somewhere else. You need to have administrator privileges to bind to port 443, otherwise change the port to 8443 and access the URL via `https://www.yourdomain.com:443`.

mod_ssl provides a comprehensive technical reference documentation. We are not going to reproduce that information here, but rather explain what is possible and which configuration directives you need to use. You can then refer to the online documentation at `http://www.modssl.org` for the specific syntax or options.

## Algorithms

You can control which ciphers and protocols are used via the `SSLCipherSuite` and `SSLProtocol` commands. For example, you can configure the server to use only strong encryption with the following configuration:

```
SSLProtocol all
SSLCipherSuite HIGH:MEDIUM
```

## Client Certificates

Similar to how clients can verify the identity of servers using server certificates, servers can verify the identity of clients by requiring a client certificate and making sure it is valid.

`SSLCACertificateFile` and `SSLCACertificatePath` are two Apache directives used to specify trusted CAs. We can then use `SSLVerifyClient` to restrict access to clients certified by these CAs.

## Performance

SSL is a protocol that requires intensive calculations. mod_ssl and OpenSSL allow several ways to speed up the protocol by caching some of the information about the connection (this can be configured using the `SSLcache`, `SSLCachetimeout` directives), and by providing support for specialized cryptographic hardware to perform CPU intensive computations.

## Logging

mod_ssl hooks up into Apache's logging system and provides support for logging any SSL-related aspect of the request, ranging from the protocol used to the information contained in specific elements of a client certificate. This information can also be passed to CGI scripts via environment variables. `SSLLog` and `SSLLogLevel` allow you to specify where to store SSL-specific errors and which kind of errors to log.

## SSL Options

Many of these options can be applied in a per-directory or per-location basis. The SSL parameters might be renegotiated for those URLs. This can be controlled via the SSLoptions directive.

## Name-Based Virtual Hosts

A common problem for people is how to make name-based virtual hosts work with SSL. The answer is that you can't. Name-based virtual hosts depend on the Host header of the HTTP request, but the certificate verification happens when the SSL connection is being established and no HTTP request can be sent. There is a protocol for upgrading an existing HTTP connection to TLS, but it is mostly unsupported by current browsers (RFC 2817).

## Further Reading

*The* book on cryptography:

*Applied Cryptography,* Second Edition, by Bruce Schneier ISBN 0471117099

An excellent book on the SSL protocol, especially useful if you are programming with SSL libraries:

*SSL and TLS: Designing and Building Secure Systems,* by Eric Rescorla, ISBN 0201615983

OpenSSL project: `http://www.openssl.org`

ModSSL project: `http://www.openssl.org`

OpenBSD, a free Unix-server operating system with focus on security: `http://www.openbsd.com`

Apache reference, by the author of `mod_ssl`: `http://www.apach-eref.com`

SSLv2 Specification: `http://home.netscape.com/eng/security/SSL_2.html`

SSLv3 Specification: `http://home.netscape.com/eng/ssl3/draft302.txt`

SSL related RFCs. RFCs can be obtained from `http://www.rfc-editor.org/`

- Internet X.509 PKI: 2459
- Transport Layer Security: 2246
- Upgrading to TLS Within HTTP/1.1: 2817

This chapter has introduced you to the SSL protocol and to `mod_ssl`, which allows Apache to support SSL. You have learned basic installation and configuration of `mod_ssl` and certificate generation and management. You can access the `mod_ssl` reference documentation for in-depth syntax explanation and additional configuration information.

# INDEX

## M

## N



## O

## P

## T